THE STUDY OF LITERATURE IN HIGH SCHOOL

A BLAISDELL BOOK IN EDUCATION

CONSULTING EDITOR

John I. Goodlad
University of California at Los Angeles

THE STUDY OF LITERATURE IN HIGH SCHOOL

GERALDINE MURPHY WESLEYAN UNIVERSITY

BLAISDELL PUBLISHING COMPANY

A DIVISION OF GINN AND COMPANY

WALTHAM, MASSACHUSETTS • TORONTO • LONDON

Foreword

The decade of the 1950's was a period of intense soul-searching in American education. Early in the decade, books such as those by Albert Lynd, Arthur Bestor, Robert Hutchins, and Paul Woodring (all in 1953) were sharply critical of progressive education. By the end of the decade, the schools had been poked at and probed from every angle, and constructive reform was underway. James B. Conant had come out in support of the comprehensive high school; millions of dollars were going into updating and restructuring the curriculum of elementary and secondary education. An educational reform movement had begun.

A significant part of this movement remained obscure and is only now coming into focus. Education as a field of solid inquiry is coming of age. Education is being seen as central to the welfare of mankind, the nation, and the individual. The study of education increasingly is being recognized as requiring the attention of our very best minds. To be a philosopher, psychologist, economist, or sociologist *of education* is now, as never before, to be respectable in the academic world. The demand for good educationists far exceeds the supply.

The Blaisdell series in education was initiated at about the time that the present period of constructive reform in education was beginning to replace the critical soul-searching of the 1950's. Those of us who planned the series anticipated rapid advance in educational studies and resulting benefits for educational practice. We wished to accelerate these developments through commissioning and publishing fine manuscripts. The same care that characterizes the well-known Blaisdell books in mathematics and the sciences goes into editing, designing, and binding the handsome new volumes in education. The several books so far published are unsurpassed in format and attractiveness.

But, of course, the proof of a book is in its content. The intent, from the beginning, has been to define the scope of education as a field of study and practice. The volumes published to date fall into two general classifications. One group is designed to advance *insight* into educational phenomena: the school as a social institution, the place of religion in the schools, the making of educational policy, and so on. This approach is well represented by the first book in the series, Lawrence W. Downey's *The Secondary Phase of Education* (1965). The second group is designed to advance the *practice* of education and is exemplified by this volume, Geraldine Murphy's *The Study of Literature in High School*.

The basic assumptions underlying *The Study of Literature in High School* are in keeping with those underlying the curriculum reform movement which began in the 1950's and intensified in the 1960's. This movement has been predicated on the integrity of the separate disciplines: not science, but physics, chemistry, and biology; not social studies, but history, geography, and economics; not English, but literature, composition, and grammar.

Replete with specific examples to clarify her concepts and principles, Professor Murphy never strays far from the basic premise: good teaching requires an intimate, almost loving, acquaintance with the subject. Beginning teachers will find ideas for their first day of teaching; experienced teachers will find much to add to their present repertoires of content and technique.

Professor Murphy brings to her manuscript a balance of experience and academic preparation. Her scholarly background includes a doctorate from Radcliffe; she has intensively studied both literature and its teaching. And she has tested the ideas she espouses in rich and varied association with both apprentice and master teachers. Dr. Murphy's volume is a timely and unique addition to the list of Blaisdell Books in Education.

JOHN I. GOODLAD

Preface

The concerns of this book are, on the one hand, more general than those of the usual methods text and, on the other hand, more particular: the book ranges from a philosophical consideration of basic aesthetic questions to the exact wording of topics for end-of-class papers. This combination of theory and practice is, we believe, indispensable to the classroom teacher who needs to know at all times both his ultimate aims and how he can accomplish them at, say, 9:07 on a Tuesday morning.

All the sections of *The Study of Literature in High School* are interconnected, but each is autonomous. Consequently, the book may be used in several ways. Teachers who want to see how the theoretic position described in the first part, "Practice to Theory," is translated into schemes for classroom teaching may begin "at the beginning." Teachers interested in practice only may bypass the first part of the text altogether and begin at the second part, "The Theory in Practice." Those seeking suggestions for the teaching of some one genre—poems, plays, or works of fiction—may go directly to the relevant section in the second part: there, they will find an outline for a basic course to help students learn to read the genre, sketches for a variety of subsequent studies, lesson plans, list of works (annotated and ranked in order of difficulty), composition assignments, suggested "free-day" activities, indeed, even such teaching devices as study guides and aids. In this book all suggestions about choosing and teaching materials are presented not in discrete chapters but in their "natural habitat"—as they would be used in the classroom teaching of poems, plays, or short stories.

This book is intended for all teachers of English—"old hands," "new hands," and prospective teachers—who are interested in making the values of reading literature available to high school students. Consequently, we have exemplified continually so that all teachers can see "what we mean." Where we have cited works, we have chosen titles that are either familiar or readily available in inexpensive paperback editions. And when we discuss the teaching of works of literature, we deal in fundamentals: we suggest how to ask questions, how to sequence them, how to "go into" "Flower in the Crannied Wall," *Julius Caesar*, or "The Bride Comes to Yellow Sky" in ways that can help students discover the meaning. We demonstrate how to make out a timetable for a block of work, how to write a study guide, how to motivate students to work in class, how to build variety into a fifty-minute period.

We offer various kinds of lesson plans in order to illustrate different types of lessons—the lesson that terminates in a critical paper, the lesson that begins with a brief discussion to prepare the way for a half-period test, the lesson that *is* a test, the lesson that requires the use of aids. In some of our lessons we suggest how long we would spend on this or that activity in order to help new teachers avoid the frustration of lessons they can neither finish nor revive.

Finally, we stress planning—of whole courses, of segments within courses, and of individual lessons—because planning is so essential and so misunderstood (indeed, even maligned). We have tried to show that planning is simply deciding on a strategy for achieving an aim; it uncovers alternate routes, reveals the comparative values of them, and alerts us to potential problems. Having been over the terrain, we are free to move productively. Planning prevents groping, repetitiousness, tangents, and dead ends. Planning need not circumscribe, need not lead to inflexible lessons. In creative hands, it does not.

In this book, we avoid the use of the word "unit": this term has been applied to so many different kinds of organizations that it has lost a precise, generally accepted meaning. So, to designate blocks of work of varying durations and types, we use such words as "course," "part," and "section." We use the word "course" to describe a long sequence of lessons designed to help students achieve an important general skill; for instance, the ability to read a poem. We use the word "part" or the word "section" to describe a series of related lessons within a "course," a series designed to help students learn some constituent skill; for instance, the ability to respond sensitively to tone.

In this book, we distinguish among classes according to the quality of the students' reading skill—"competent readers," "average readers," or "less able readers." In some instances, we qualify these labels by the words "motivated" or "unmotivated." We use these designations because the teacher's true guide to appropriate choices of materials and methods is the level of reading ability of a class—a level not necessarily described by traditional designations. Teachers who assume that "college course" means that students are "competent" or even "average" readers and that "general course" means that they are "less able" are often disconcerted by the facts of classroom life. What the teacher of any class must do first is find out, roughly, the quality of his readers, and, then, "college" or "general" notwithstanding, choose materials and methods that will take his readers from where they are to as far as they can go. We have, therefore, set up teaching schemes, materials, and methods to help the teacher do just that.

No high school is a monolith. All have readers of these three qualities (only the ratios differ from school to school). All have the "less able"—the literalists, the dull, the word-callers, the word-poor, the glib. All have the "competent"—that small percentage who, though not *necessarily* the top-ranking scholars, respond precisely and imaginatively to words. All have the "average"—the great middle who can get the story "straight," remember the characters, identify similes, and recall the subject of a poem.

This book is directed to the teachers of all these kinds of readers.

Many years ago, when I first began to teach literature to high school students, I realized that teaching students about works and using works as parables or as stimuli for controversial discussion were not very fruitful ways of helping them to enjoy the values of literature. What was? I found the answer in Reuben Brower's *The Fields of Light.* That was my "Chapman's Homer." My dependence upon it is obvious.

For various kindnesses I am indebted to Gertrude Reif Hughes, Francis Keppel, Irene Nichols, Israel Scheffler, and Peggy Bowles Smith. For "gifts of faith," I am grateful to "those who heard 'the word' and kept it."

GERALDINE MURPHY

Middletown, Connecticut

Contents

PRACTICE
TO THEORY

THE DECISIONS A LESSON INVOLVES

Teaching involves continual decision-making. To teach a single lesson, we must decide what we shall aim for, what work we shall use, how we shall teach and evaluate. There are always alternate courses open to us. What suggests that we should choose one alternative rather than another? On what grounds should such practical decisions be made? In the following pages, we shall try to suggest ways of finding answers to these questions.

To begin, we shall look at a lesson closely to see exactly what specific decisions it involves and what determines our particular choices.

Let us suppose we are teaching poems to an average tenth- or eleventh-grade class and that at this point, we are trying to help the students learn to respond to the speaker's tones so they will grasp his gradually developing attitude toward a certain event. As our poem for this particular day, we have chosen John Crowe Ransom's "Blue Girls."[1] It is a "natural" for achieving this aim: it has many tone changes; they are clear; they obviously build to an attitude. Furthermore, the theme of the poem is relevant to high school students' concerns; and the language is manageable for the majority of students. With the possible exception of "seminary" and "fillets," the words in "Blue Girls" are familiar; the syntax is conventional; there is only one allusion. For all these reasons, "Blue Girls" is an appropriate choice.

Here is the poem, exactly as we would give it to the students at the opening of class.

BLUE GIRLS

Twirling your blue skirts, traveling the sward
Under the towers of your seminary,
Go listen to your teachers old and contrary
Without believing a word.

Tie the white fillets then about your lustrous hair   5
And think no more of what will come to pass
Than bluebirds that go walking on the grass
And chattering on the air.

Practice your beauty, blue girls, before it fail;
And I will cry with my loud lips and publish   10
Beauty which all our power shall never establish
It is so frail.

For I could tell you a story which is true:
I know a lady with a terrible tongue,
Blear eyes fallen from blue,   15
All her perfections tarnished — and yet it is not long
Since she was lovelier than any of you.*

seminary: an academy, a private secondary school
fillet: band

We would begin the teaching of this poem with an expressive, but
not theatrical, oral reading. We would be trying to take the poem
off the page, make the class hear the voice in the poem, this speaker
talking to the girls. For the duration of the oral reading, we would
be the speaker, making and letting our voice respond to the words at
every point. We would be trying now, as always, to make the students feel the dynamic experience a poem is, an experience they
must go through — not just read about — if they are to understand
the poem. But as we moved progressively through the speaker's little
drama, our reading would also be forcing the students to notice
certain aspects of how the speaker says what he says — the syntax,
the rhythms, the sounds he uses, the images and metaphors — the
kinds of things that define the tones, suggest the shifts in feeling, the
very clues that students would probably overlook in their own silent
readings. So, through our oral reading, many of the uses of language
we would want students to notice in their study of the poem will

already have come to their attention before a word has been spoken about the poem. The poem itself would be making students notice the clues to tone. So the clues would be seen not in semi-isolation, as in analysis, but in their natural habitat, working to suggest this feeling, and this one, and this one. Since these devices exist in poems only to express the speaker's feelings at successive points and since we want students to notice them only so that they will sense his experience, it is not only useful but most fitting that the students' attention should be called to them first by the reading of the poem.

We chose to open with an oral reading of the poem, then, not because this is "standard procedure," not because all can enjoy the reading (if nothing else), not just because poems should be heard, but chiefly because, in the several ways we have suggested, the oral reading is crucial to "making the path straight" for the main study of the poem. To reinforce the effect of the oral reading, we would now ask students to read the poem aloud to themselves.

Then, we would begin questioning: to discover whether students are aware of what ideas and feelings are being expressed at successive points in the poem, to find out what clues are directing their responses, and to call their attention to aspects of the poem that they are overlooking. The questioning on any work would, of course, vary from class to class. No two average classes are quite alike. Our set of questions will suggest what, given our aim, we would want students to notice about "Blue Girls" and what we would be *ready* to ask. How many of the following questions we would actually ask would depend upon the performance of the class on a particular day.

We would want to be sure, early in the lesson, that the students sensed the dramatic situation in the poem: that is, that they knew who was talking to whom about what. They must notice the situation if they are to know how they should "take" the poem. In poems, as in life, remarks seem arrogant, or funny, or pathetic, depending on who is saying them to whom.

In "Blue Girls" the speaker's identity is only implied. If students are not too experienced in identifying a speaker from the clues in a poem, we would probably begin with the easier, though no less necessary, question: Who is spoken to? The blue girls, of course. How do you know? The students will probably point to such items as: the direct address in line 9; "you" in lines 13 and 17; the imperatives in lines 3, 5, and 6 — they *even* might mention that "twirling" modifies "you, understood." All these are clues, syntactic (or, if you will, grammatical) clues. If students seize on the first two lines as identifying those spoken to and want to stop there, we would press them to be more thorough; first, because if students are to become the discriminating readers poems demand, they must not indulge in careless jumping-to-conclusions, and, secondly, because by being thorough in identifying those spoken to, students must again notice other aspects of the poem, for instance, the imperatives, which are important determinants of the tone the speaker is using in this part of the poem.

When the class has identified those addressed, we must then ask the more difficult question: Who is speaking to them? The initial responses may vary widely: "the author?" "a man?" "maybe a man, maybe a woman?" "an old man?" If the teacher insists on specificity and on evidence to support answers, the students, forced back to the poem again and again and again, may gradually see that the speaker is probably a man, and that he is not acquainted with the girls, that he is not speaking directly to them, that he observes them from afar — across a school lawn, across the gap of years: that he is maturity speaking to youth.

In some classes, however, the single question, Who is speaking to them? might never elicit such a full identification of the speaker. So we must be ready to supplement the initial question with others such as: What specifically suggests to you that the speaker is a man? What suggests he is middle-aged or older? Does the speaker know the "blue girls"? And if this last question does not get the students to clarify his relation to the girls, then we would try a question such as, Does the speaker know the "lady"? This question will force students to draw a distinction between the two relationships of the speaker. Then we can go on: Is the speaker speaking to the girls *directly?* Where is he standing? What clues you as to where he is? If students are still slow to see the relationship between the speaker and the girls, we might ask: Why does he address them as "blue girls," rather than by name? Bringing students to understand the relation between the speaker and the girls may not be nearly so difficult as these many "tries" imply, but experience suggests that it is better to be prepared for the worst — and safe.

After the students are clear on the social relationships in the poem, we would ask them to say in a sentence what the speaker is talking about. Then, we would begin to explore the development of the speaker's attitude toward the girls. We would ask roughly the same three questions about each stanza: What kind of advice does the speaker give in this stanza? What tone is the speaker using in giving this advice? (There is more than one tone? What tones then?) What suggests to you what tone is being used? Through the last question, we would be trying to call students' attention not just to the devices that define the speaker's tone — the syntax, the imagery, the diction, the sound, and the rhythm — but to the way several of them work together to render tone. If students answer approximately the same three questions about each stanza, they will gradually see in what ways the attitude initially expressed is altered or clarified or unfolded, as the speaker continues to counsel the girls stanza by stanza. And as the students notice the successive changes in the speaker's attitude, they will be moving stanza by stanza through his experience.

However adequate the three key questions seem to be, alone they will probably not suffice. Live classes are not that cooperative. So, usually, the teacher would need more specific, more directive, questions to "get at" what will help the class answer the key questions. Here are some suggestions of where help may be needed and some samples of particular questions that will supply it.

In order to get an adequate answer to the question on the speaker's tone in stanza one, we might have to ask: In lines 3–4, is the speaker chiding the girls or advising them? No answer. So, more specific still: Is he mimicking in line 4? In these questions, we are suggesting alternative tones in an effort to make the students define the initial tones very precisely, so that they will be alert, from the very start, to more than gross distinctions among tones.

In stanza two, we may have to lead some students to see how the speaker is moving from one tone to another as his experience slowly takes shape. Is the tone of the command in lines 5–6 different from the tone of line 3? What suggests this difference to you? Students' responses to the second question may show that they are very much aware of the role the lovely image plays in suggesting a change in tone, but that they did not notice the supporting effect of the soft elided sounds and the regular rhythm. So we would reread lines 5–6 to show how sound and rhythm reinforce image to reflect the shift in tone.

In stanza two, also, we may have to lead students to see how the tone of lines 6–8 differs from that of line 5. Throughout stanza two, the speaker is defining the attitude that the girls should take; he is condoning their carefreeness. But in lines 6–8, there is a sudden elevation in tone; he reinforces his approval by using biblical diction and reference. Couched in sacred language, his advice takes on a kind of divine sanction. To direct students' attention to this sudden elevation of the speaker's tone in lines 6–8, we might ask: Why does the speaker phrase his advice, "think no more of what will come to pass"? If there is no response, we would probably continue: Does the phrase "come to pass" echo any phrasing you are familiar with? If that question succeeds, then: What does the speaker gain by using biblical language? Or, to phrase it another way, How does his using this language affect the advice he is giving?

If our earlier question on the biblical echo did not succeed, we would try again to help students hear it. This time we might underscore line 6 with the phrase, "And so it came to pass." Much of our identification of tone in ordinary conversation is done by means of comparison, so bringing comparisons to bear on lines of poetry often helps students to hear the tone. If such comparison does not help, then an approach through the image of the birds might. We might reread lines 6–8, then ask: What is the function of the image of the birds? The students would probably reply, "To tell the girls what attitude they should take" or "to tell the girls that they are taking the right attitude." What kind of attitude is that? "Carefree"; "walking around doing nothing but chattering." What is this the right attitude toward? "Life," or "the future," or "what will come to pass." (Some students really stick to the poem!) Why does the speaker use birds, instead of, say, children, to express this "right attitude"? Some students may see only that the "blue girls" on the "sward" remind the speaker of bluebirds. If they see *only* this, then to show them that there are, in the bird image, biblical overtones as well, we might read the passage from Matthew, VI, 26, 28–9, 34:

> Behold the birds of the heaven, that they sow not, neither do they reap, nor gather into barns; and your heavenly Father feedeth them. Are ye not of much more value than they? . . . Consider the lilies of the field, how they grow; they toil not, neither do they spin: yet I say unto you, that even Solomon in all his glory was not arrayed like one of these. . . . Be not therefore anxious for the morrow: for the morrow will be anxious for itself.

Once we had underscored lines 6–8 with the reading of the scriptural text, we may then certainly ask: What effect does the speaker's reference to the Bible have on the advice he is giving to the girls? Or, What does the speaker gain by defining the "right attitude" in biblical terms? And then, How does the biblical reference in lines 6–8 affect the way we take line 9, "Practice your beauty, blue girls, before it fail"?

We have given the teaching of lines 6–8 an extended treatment because we think that we would probably have to be very specific and directive in teaching these lines. Many students are deaf to the echoes of biblical references even when they know the scriptural text, and some are almost wholly unfamiliar with the Scriptures. Yet, students cannot identify the attitude the speaker is taking toward his experience in stanza two, unless they sense the biblical underpinning in lines 6–8. Since this is so, we must make them properly aware of these lines, either by urging them to recall the text, or if they cannot, then by providing the text — with the assignment or in class — and, in either case, forcing them to decide how it functions.

In the study of a work it is always best to make students go through as much as possible of the process the sensitive reader would go through. In this instance, the sensitive reader would hear the echo of the phrase, identify it, draw the necessary information out of his own knowledge of the Scriptures, and figure out how the reference *works here.* And it is this process that our questioning would be making the students go through — insofar as they could.

Up to this point, most of the supplementary questions we have suggested have related to the second and the third of the "key questions." In stanza three, however, we might have difficulty eliciting an adequate answer to the first question: What kind of advice does the speaker give in this stanza? For the character of what the speaker says in stanza three is essentially different from his remarks in the two preceding stanzas.

Only the first half of the first line is his usual type of advice, and even this is a symbolic order, not the particular, concrete command of the first two stanzas. To help students to understand the qualitative difference between the order of line 9 and the preceding orders, we would revert to some very simple question. (Complexity does not elucidate complexity!) So our question would probably be: How does a person "practice beauty"? Then, to refine students' understanding: Why does the speaker say "practice" rather than "enjoy" or "preserve"? What is the effect of saying "before it fail" rather than "lest it fail"? What does the speaker mean by this command?

In the third stanza, for the first time, the speaker supports his order with reasons, and he himself promises to help. Both the girls and he *must*, in their own ways, conquer the transiency of beauty. To point out how lines 10–12 ("And I will cry with my loud lips and publish/ Beauty which all our power shall never establish/ It is so frail") make the "advice" of this stanza fundamentally different from that of the preceding stanzas, we might ask: What does the speaker do in line 10? Why does the speaker turn from advising the girls to pledging his help? What is he promising to do? If necessary: What does he mean by "cry with my loud lips and publish/ Beauty"? And we may have to ask, Who cries with loud lips and publishes things? Does he really mean a town crier? What *does* he mean he will do? What does the speaker hope to achieve by "publishing" beauty? And if this last question does not bring a useful response, then: Can *anything* "establish" beauty? If the students can answer that question, then they have seen that the speaker thinks man can *somewhat* conquer the transiency of beauty in two ways: he can "practice" it while he may, and he can "publish" it.

They will see that it is the speaker's realization of these two truths that accounts not only for the essentially different character of the "advice" in this stanza (which is the question we have just unfolded) but also for the markedly different tones: the intense, insistent pleading of line 9, the personal, emotionally charged vow of line 10, and the quiet pleasure that comes from the ironic recognition of lines 11 and 12. Any adequate discussion of the speaker's tones in this stanza would make clear the many tonal ambiguities ignored in the three gross distinctions we have just cited.

Stanza three seems like a conclusion. So, why stanza four? Probably one of the best means of helping students to realize the function of this stanza is a right oral reading, a reading that will reveal that the emphatic, throbbing intensity of the speaker in stanza three has given way to a quiet, intimate intensity in stanza four. So, to show this related contrast, we would probably reread the entire poem orally before discussing the last stanza — no matter how satisfactory the responses of the class to the poem had been up to stanza four. After such a reading, the questions on the speaker's advice and his tones would probably be adequately answered, but we would be prepared, nonetheless, to ask questions about the syntactic clues in this stanza, about the effect of the unusual diction — "terrible," "blear," "tarnished," about why the details of "tongue," "blue" eyes, and "perfection" work well here — and about what the poem gains by this stanza. The questions on the function of the stanza might be: How does the "story" relate to the "reasons" given in stanza three? How is the "story" different from the "reasons"? Why did the speaker add the "story"? Why did the speaker use the "story" last?"

We would conclude the study of this poem with an oral reading — to fuse the reader's experience of the speaker's experience. After that, time permitting, we would ask students to write a ten-minute answer to a central question, such as: What is the speaker's attitude toward the girls? If the ability of the class required a more directive wording of the topic, we would substitute: Write a two-paragraph paper showing that the poem is a little drama which gradually unfolds an experience. Students' responses to either exercise would reveal the extent to which they achieved the aim, that is, understood the speaker's experience to be a changing, progressive one, every stage of which plays its part in the shaping of his attitude.

In some cases, we might prefer to close the class by having students reread a poem that had been assigned but not discussed and answer a question on the speaker's attitude and the clues to it. If students had only a very short time to work, we would reduce the task: we would pinpoint a certain line or word in the poem and ask a single, significant question about it: What tone does the sound of (a certain line) suggest? In what way does a certain word (or phrase) characterize the speaker's attitude?

The two kinds of exercises we have just briefly described are only two of the many types of conclusions that would be fitting. Any conclusion is satisfactory if it leaves students with a unified poem and provides the teacher with evidence of "where the students are" in relation to achieving the particular and the general aims.

Our teaching of "Blue Girls" reveals the many choices a single lesson entails. And it suggests, either explicitly or implicitly, not only the particular reasons that justify these choices but also the more fundamental grounds that made certain courses of action mandatory for us. Let us look for a moment at two practices for which we have offered quite explicit particular reasons — the oral readings and the auxiliary questions — and see what more general justification those reasons have.

The Reasons for Our Reasons

At the opening and at the close of the study of "Blue Girls," we read the poem. For what reasons? At the opening, so that students could undergo the poem as an experience, for, as we said, they must if they are to understand it. We read the poem at the close to leave students with a unified poem. Why do we want the students to have the poem as an experience? Why as a unified whole? Because a poem *is* an experience; a poem *is* an artistic whole. Consequently, it must be perceived as such. It is *the nature of a poem* that tells us how readers must relate to it. *We* decide *how* this relating is to be effected, by what methods we can bring students to experience a poem, to have it as a whole.

Why, then, did we decide on oral reading as the means for helping them experience the poem? Because from considering the nature of experiencing, we know that we cannot convey an experience to anyone else as we convey information. All we can do is try to make it possible for students to have the experience. We can only ease the access. *One way* to do that is to say the poem as the speaker would, assume a persona, become the speaker, and by following the clues in the language closely, give to the words the speaker's feelings and tones. The oral reading vitalizes the experience the words express; it makes students almost think they are hearing or overhearing — much as they do in life — someone telling "his story," a story they are "going through" with him. That is why the reading must be expressive, but not theatrical. Theatricality spoils the illusion.

Why did we decide on a final reading to unify the poem? Not only because a reading will retire to their proper proportions any details that were overstressed in analysis, but also because only when all parts have been seen in detail, can the poem be experienced as the *complex* whole it really is.

Our opening and closing with readings of the poem is not, then, simply a handy way to "kick off" and "wind up" a lesson. We do both for certain reasons which, in turn, have their reasons.

This is true also of the auxiliary questions which we suggested for almost every main question proposed in our teaching of "Blue Girls." The explicit reason for these questions is that the teacher might need them to help the class work out an answer to the main question. But why should *the students* work out an answer? Because achieving the aim requires it. Students are to learn to respond to the speaker's tones. They are to learn a skill. And that makes a certain course of action mandatory for us. *Students* must go through the process of responding to the speaker's tones: they must discover the clues and, from the clues, ascertain the tone and perceive the effect of it — and they must make this complex response again and again and again in as many particular instances as the poem offers. We help them. How? Not by telling them the answer; telling helps only when they need essential information about some clue — for instances, the "blue-bird" allusion. Our main job is to find ways to get students to make the response themselves. That explains the necessity for the auxiliary questions and the character of them. In each instance, where auxil-iary questions are used, they become increasingly directive; but each successive question prods only as much as it must; the questions make the students do, at all times, as much as they can — on their own. In all instances, the auxiliary questions are phrased so that the particular class — average students — *can* understand them and con-sider them fruitfully.

The aim, then, tells us the kind of knowledge students must learn and, as we have been showing, that suggests certain methods. It also rules out others.

What, for instance, did our aim discourage or prevent us from doing? It kept us from asking many of the customary background questions. They would not have been invalid, just irrelevant. For, knowing that the author is John Crowe Ransom, that the poem was published in 1927, that Ransom is a Southern writer, that he has also written such poems as "Here Lies a Lady," "Piazza Piece," and "Bells for John Whiteside's Daughter" — knowing any or all of this would not develop students' response to tone one jot.

That is why, furthermore, we did not ask students to identify or label literary devices. What would it profit our students to identify the image of line 7 as "visual" and that of line 8 as "auditory"? What they must be able to do is sense the various ways these images func-tion in the poems. They must be able to recognize that together the images illustrate the attitude of carefreeness that the speaker is urging the girls to take; that, furthermore, this whole image (lines 7–8) parallels the image of the girls in stanza one, and that the bib-lical suggestion of this bird image (lines 7–8) gives a kind of scrip-tural sanction to the parallel image of the girls. And students must see in retrospect that the image of the birds compares with that of the girls and contrasts with that of the "lady," and so structures the poem and helps to define its meaning. Labeling images is not invalid in terms of our aim; it is just unnecessary and inadequate.

It simply would not take students very far on their way to achieving the aim we set.

Neither would their suggesting the relevance of the poem nor stating its "meaning." In fact, questions on relevance seem superfluous when a poem is chosen for the relevance of its experience and taught to reveal the experience. And questions on "meaning" would be invalid when we are holding, as our practice shows, that the "meaning" of the poem is the whole experience of it.

There are, then, no traditional questions that, the aim notwithstanding, are always good to ask. The aim is the immediate arbiter of practice. It tells us what should be asked about, how it should be asked about, and in what order. It tells us what, because it is superfluous or irrelevant, can be excluded and what, because it is invalid, should be. And when the aim has done its office, then the intellectual calibre and the temperament of each class will dictate with what sophistication or simplicity, with what straightforwardness or ingenuity, we use the methods the aim recommends or allows.

We have discussed only a few of the many practical decisions connected with our teaching of "Blue Girls." But these are enough to suggest how practice is supported by reasons which are in turn justified by more general reasons. For *any* practical decision of the lesson we could have shown a similar hierarchy of reasons. Had we, for instance, challenged any particular question in the lesson, we could have shown how answering that question could develop some aspect of the skill we were *immediately* aiming to help students learn. And had we, in turn, asked ourselves for the justification for our immediate aim — and we might have done so, for it, too, is a choice — we would have appealed to our general aim: to help students learn to read poems. And we would have shown that a sensitive response to tone, which is the *particular* skill we are aiming to have students learn in the lesson on "Blue Girls," is a constituent of the more general skill: an ability to read a poem. And had we then pressed ourselves for a justification of our general aim — asking how we defend teaching students to read poems, we would have shown that the ability to read a poem is probably the central ability in reading literature and that the ability to read works of literature is the primary end for teaching it. And we would go on, then, to justify the reading of literature in terms of its values.

As we examined the teaching of "Blue Girls," we were trying to show that everything involved in this lesson, from the general aim to the most particular question, was consciously chosen, extrapersonally justifiable, and we trust, internally consistent. We were trying to show that our practice was governed, in turn, by a specific aim, a general aim for teaching poems, a general aim for teaching literature, and a theory of literature. This hierarchy of "grounds," interrelated as it is, is what we keep in mind as we make the many practical decisions that planning and teaching a lesson entails.

Through this discussion we have been trying to suggest that a teacher needs a well-thought-out hierarchy of grounds in terms of which he may — and should — make decisions about classroom practice. If he does not have such a position, his choices may be directed by the moment, by "what works," by "what I've always done," "what I like," "what they like," "what's easiest to do" — in other words, his choices may lack consistency and validity.

Often, the practice resulting from such choices is piecemeal, directionless, contradictory, invalid. So the lessons, however exciting, will not bring students steadily and economically into the subject.

Often, the practice resulting from such choices reveals a gap between aim and method that the teacher does not even recognize. He sincerely says he is aiming for one end; his practice shows he is aiming for another. He says, for instance, he is aiming to teach students to read poems, but he is simply telling them data about poems, anecdotes about poets. He says he is teaching students to "appreciate" stories, but he is simply asking them what the story is about and how they liked it. Carrying out the aim *in practice* is what matters in teaching.

Often, the lack of a position creates great insecurity in a teacher, since he must keep making decisions even though he has no firm grounds for choosing between conflicting claims, even though he is never really sure of where he is going or why. Uncertain about what is valid, he becomes a devotee of the feasible and a prey not only to students' whims, but to every passing teaching fad.

Since a teacher's decisions affect practice so significantly and since his inability to make them adequately often affects him too, it seems desirable — indeed mandatory — for him to develop a position on the crucial questions in the teaching of literature so that he will have grounds for making — validly, consistently, and confidently — the many practical decisions he must make. Each teacher must develop has own position; no one can give him one. He must shape it himself by considering the crucial questions seriously and evolving answers that are valid, consistent, and firm, though correctable through the same process by which they were arrived at. A teacher must work his position out for himself, for if he is to be guided by it, he must believe in it. No matter how many others share his position, it must be essentially his own.

SIX CRUCIAL QUESTIONS FOR THE TEACHER OF LITERATURE

Here, posed in the order in which they should be considered, are the six crucial questions that the teacher of literature interested in developing a position should require himself to answer:

What is a work of literature?

What are the functions of a work of literature?

How do we justify the study of literature in the curriculum?

What are the aims for the study of literature?

What kinds of works will help students achieve our aims?

What kinds of methods will help students achieve our aims?

Now, we shall try to reveal what is "in" each of these questions, and we shall suggest what our answer to each is and, more importantly, how we arrived at it. Our discussion attempts only to open up the questions for consideration, to show what we must take into account when we try to answer them, and to suggest how our answer to the first affects our answer to the second, and so on. The answers *we* give to the six questions are valid ones and, as we show, they constitute a position for us, the position we have already seen at work in the teaching of "Blue Girls." But the answers are our answers; we are not implying that they are *the* answers. We are insisting only on the necessity of having *an* extrapersonally defensible position; we are suggesting only *a way* to develop one.

What Is a Work of Literature?

Like a painting, a piece of music or of sculpture, a work of litera-ture is a work of art. That means, most simply, that all parts of the work have been so organized that it expresses an ordered, harmo-nious, whole experience. Recall, for example, "Blue Girls." In it we saw many parts (uses of words) organized to work together to express each tone; we saw many tones, arranged to work together to express the speaker's attitude toward his experience, which though only fleeting and filled with many shifts of feelings, is a harmonious whole.

All forms of art are alike in expressing an experience of order; all differ in the medium through which they express it. Painting uses color; music, notes; sculpture, stone; literature, words. It is the uniqueness of the medium that makes each art a unique mode of expression. For each medium has its own peculiar qualities, and these define what the particular form of art can express and how it can express it. Literature, for instance, cannot express abstract form, as can music, painting, and sculpture, because words are signs for things. But, because language is discursive, because it has phonemic quality and lexical meaning, literature, like music and painting, can express motion and fragility. Language must, however, be "strained," compressed almost to obscurity, for literature to give anything of the presentational effect of painting and sculpture. Each medium has its advantages and its limitations and, to express his feeling, idea, or vision, each kind of artist exploits both to the fullest.

The writer shares his medium with all who use the language. The words he uses are the same as those used in everyday discourse. He is, in fact, confined to the words and to the meanings of each that native speakers in his time have agreed upon. There is no literary vocabulary; there are no "poetic" words. The writer simply makes ordinary words behave in extraordinary ways. He exploits their several literal meanings, their connotations, their image potential, their symbol values, their sounds, their rhythms. He extends vocabu-lary by creating new words like Hopkins' "unleaving" and "worlds of wanwood leafmeal lie," Keats' "mountain-built town," Herbert's "sigh-blown age," and Frost's "pecker-fretted apple trees." And the writer gives surprising, fresh contexts to familiar words. Recall Ransom's use of "practice" with "Beauty" and "tarnished" and "blear" to describe an aging face. Remember Blake's reference to the "fearful symmetry" of the tiger, Keats' "embalmed darkness," Coleridge's "dismal sheen," Herrick's memorable "liquefaction of her clothes," and Wilbur's "radiant squalor." The writer turns to his account all the dimensions words have to offer.

Furthermore, he exploits the other "givens" of his medium: conventional syntax, capitalization, punctuation, and the rhetorical patterns of the language. He uncovers the meanings of the forms; he makes the purpose infinitive say "purpose" — whatever else it says. He use the patterns — correlatives or parallel structure, say — to call attention to the words, and the words to emphasize the patterns. He utilizes the fixed forms as foils for his deviations. E. E. Cummings' reversals and ellipses are expressive because there is an accepted syntax. Faulkner's long periodic sentences with negatives piled on negatives are effective because of the positive subject-verb-object syntax of most English sentences.

The writer uses various artistic principles — balance, repetition, similarity with diversity — and the discursiveness of language itself to control the reader's responses, to make him develop certain expectations and certain tensions.

Words and language conventions are all a writer has to use to express his ideas, feelings, vision. He can only choose and order words in certain ways. If he so organizes language that his work evokes a perception of pattern, an ordered experience, in those readers who respond to the words as they direct, then his work is a work of literature.

Descriptions and definitions of works of literature sometimes refer to such organization of language as "artistic structure," "the harmonizing of all units," "the interrelation of all parts," "the achieved whole," or "the right words in the right order." But whatever they call it, they all agree that such organization is the essential and distinguishing quality of a work of literature. Judicial critics use degree of organization to determine which pieces of writing *are* works of literature and which works have more artistic and aesthetic value than others.

All verbal communication is, of course, organized to some extent. Imagine for a moment many varied samples of it clustered along a continuum according to relative degree of verbal organization. Even in the *first samples* — say, the order to the grocer, the morning gossip — we would see that words are organized syntactically at least, and perhaps structured in one or more of the following ways: chronologically, logically, or dramatically — even rhetorically or connotatively. In other words, there *may* be quite a number of modes of organization operating simultaneously in the report of the latest gossip. There may be, but usually there are not.

Most likely, only the syntactic organization would be consistently functioning. The prose would be dramatic, but there would be few clues to tone *in the language*, although there would undoubtedly be many in the performance (eyebrows, whisper, inflections.) The tense sequence would probably be faulty; the pattern of connotations sketchy; the causal connections few. Such pieces of prose as the order to the grocer and the morning gossip would be, in other words, far less well organized than they might be. Modes of arrangement other than syntax might appear, but not as structures in the sense that interlinked items are — like sequences of tenses, a connotative framework, or consistent reasoning. Only here and there would a word "count" in more ways than one. And rarely would such words be connected connotatively or tonally with others. No structures would be really exploited with a view to shaping the piece. All this is *generally* true of informal prose.

But as we progressed along this imaginary continuum, listening and reading, we would notice that the linguistic acts in the *second cluster* are organized in more ways and that the structures used are more sustained. These acts might include such writings as news stories, reports to a board, results of experiments, history textbooks, personal letters of a reportorial sort, entries in biographical dictionaries, most annals, some philosophical papers, some critical articles. These writings would be organized syntactically, chronologically, logically. They may occasionally exploit the connotations of a word, they may use a figure to illustrate a particular point. We would, however, notice that these linguistic acts rarely use connotative, or metaphoric, or imagistic structures. Indeed, in these acts language does only what it must to convey to a certain audience certain facts as accurately, clearly, and economically as words can.

Some philosophy papers, some criticism, some letters, and many scientific reports are the kind of prose we have just described. But, as we know, other writings of these sorts go well beyond sustained correct use of the several structures we mentioned. They *exploit* these structures for rhetorical effects; they may make liberal use of the connotative, imagistic, and symbolic values of individual words; they may employ controlling metaphors. In the quality of their verbal organization, these philosophy papers, critical articles, letters, and reports are similar to well-written histories, biographies, speeches, travel accounts, and simple stories and plays. So, they form, with them, a third cluster.

Among the works in this *third cluster,* there is, of course, great variation, work to work, in the number and the kinds of structures used, the extent to which they are sustained, and the kind and the degree of the exploitation of words. Some works may be more organized than those in the second cluster in one respect only; others may be interrelating several structures in a most harmonious organization. And it may well be that one history, say, would be more similar to some critical paper in its degree of organization than it would be to other histories; a biography might be more richly organized than an adventure story.

So, as we read along our imaginary continuum from the first

cluster, to the second, to the third, we would begin to sense some shaping in this work, then a greater degree of ordering in that one. We would begin to feel the effects of various patterns that make us consider the material and respond to it in a particular way. We would be having in varying degrees an ordered – a literary – experience.

This experience of order would increase as we read works in the *fourth cluster* – fine histories, biographies, essays, sermons and speeches, short stories, novels, and plays. In such writings as these, many modes of organization, often richly exploited, are consistently structuring the words. Such a basic pattern as syntax, for instance, would not be just a scaffolding. The normative statement, the declarative question, the purpose infinitive, the periodic sentence, the short, normal-order, simple sentence would be expressing their meanings as patterns. And deviations from the conventional – ellipses, reversals, involutions – would be reinforcing the idea or the feeling of a sentence. In these works, important words would be related to others in several ways at once. Should we withdraw one of these crucial words, we would discover that our substitute would have to be a word that would function in several modes of organization. Consider a passage such as the following:

> Poetry and eloquence are both alike the expression or utterance of feeling: but, if we may be excused the antithesis, we should say that eloquence is *heard;* poetry is overheard. Eloquence supposes an audience. The peculiarity of poetry appears to us to lie in the poet's utter unconsciousness of a listener. Poetry is feeling confessing itself to itself in moments of solitude, and embodying itself in symbols which are the nearest possible representations of the feeling in the exact shape in which it exists in the poet's mind. Eloquence is feeling pouring itself out to other minds, courting their sympathy, or endeavoring to influence their belief, or move them to passion or to action.[2]

Now consider the withdrawal of, for instance, "confessing" or "courting." What organizations have to be considered as you choose a substitute? Why won't "admitting" do? Why not "soliciting" for "courting"? What organizations would these substitutes damage?

Furthermore, in the works of this fourth cluster, as the preceding sample suggests, such artistic principles as balance and repetition and rhythm would be shaping the information, the "message," the view being conveyed, or the insight being rendered. And in the imaginative prose in this cluster there would surely be, in one work or another, juxtapositions of scenes and characters, parallels, recurrent words, patterns of images, or the design of an object becoming symbolic. In drama, we would find the plots variously unified; in fiction, the points of view variously exploited.

Works of imaginative prose differ widely in their density, for the good writer does with language only what he must: the more complex the experience he tries to render, the more modes of organization he needs and the more he needs to exploit each richly. And as the density of the verbal fabric increases — whether the work be imaginative or nonfictional — the more we feel a sense of pattern, wholeness, integrity.

Most of the linguistic acts in the *fifth* and *final cluster* of our imaginary continuum would probably be lyric and dramatic poems. For in them words "count" in many ways at once. Such poems are characteristically, as Lalo puts it, a polyphony of five "voices" that are, each in its own way, saying the same word at once.[3] Each voice — verbal meaning, connotation, syntax, rhythm, timbre — is simultaneously calling attention to a certain dimension of the word. The effect is a rich, complex, single sound in which no voice is lost and none could be omitted or changed without changing the whole. This tight interrelatedness is easily seen if we try to put "preserve" into the place of "practice" in line 9 of "Blue Girls." "Preserve" is syntactically the same as "practice," but it is not a fit substitute for it rhythmically, phonemically, denotatively, connotatively, logically, or tonally. "Preserve" is normally iambic; "practice" is a strong trochee — a trochee is needed here. And this command of commands needs the definitive crack of a hard *c*. "Preserve" does not, furthermore, denote the same thing as "practice," and it does not suggest the schoolroom or echo the old adage "Practice makes perfect" and the trite (here ironic) warning about "failing." These suggestions link this command to the twirling of the schoolgirls in stanza one and their primping in stanza two. Finally, the words of stanzas one and two logically lead to the generalization: "Practice your beauty." In a good poem a word participates in multiple structures.

The *degree* of vertical and horizontal interrelating that is characteristic of fine lyric and dramatic poems is not *characteristic* of prose. All modes of organization considered essential to such poems may, of course, be found, as we have suggested, in both nonfiction and imaginative prose, but the rhythmic and phonemic modes are not required of prose nor are they *characteristic* of it. Furthermore, the modes of organization used in imaginative prose are rarely exploited throughout as advantageously and as consciously as they are in poems. And ordinarily, because of the scope, nature, and intent of prose, the organizations used in it are less rigorously maintained than structures are in poems. This does not mean that we are not sometimes astonished by the artistic organization achieved in certain short stories, plays, essays, and novels. When we read such works, we feel, as Conrad did about *The Secret Sharer*, that the work "is it. Every word fits, and there's not a single uncertain note." We are struck by the number of ways each part "counts"; we admire the structure. *Such* prose works would most certainly be found in the final cluster of our imaginary continuum.

By using this construct we have been trying to suggest that organization in verbal communications is a matter of more or less — not of none or much. Linguistic acts vary in the *degree* of their verbal organization, and this is determined by the number of structures they use, the extent to which they sustain them and exploit them. When linguistic acts — whatever their subject or their intention, whether fiction or nonfiction, whatever their particular form — are ordered sufficiently to give to a certain extent the experience of a harmonious whole, they are, to that extent, literary. The greater the degree of organization, the greater the literary effect and the greater the artistic and aesthetic value. A piece of writing is a work of literature, or a good work, or a great work, depending upon the relative complexity of its organization.

It is *not* the significance of its experience, *not* the universality of its arguments that makes a great work "great." The experience it expresses must, of course, be a complex one or else the organization that makes it great would be precious or burlesque. However, *of itself*, the experience, the argument, does not make the work great. The greatest theme, ineptly rendered, has little or no literary value. But works, already considered great because of the richness of their organizations, are often further ranked by the relative significance of their experiences.

What Are the Functions of a Work of Literature?

As we have already suggested, the common function of all works is to evoke in a reader an experience of order. All writings that are literature can do that to some degree, for, in all, ideas, feelings, events are ordered to express some particular interpretation of them, attitude toward them, value in them. So, the reader, responding to the organization of language that *is* the work, can evoke the patterned ideas, feelings, or events and sense the ordering.

This is true whether the work is nonfictional or imaginative literature. Writers of literary biography and history begin with true, past events, discover an order in them, and organize them — in the many ways we have just mentioned — to express the interpretation they discovered. Writers of imaginative literature begin with a significant insight and create, out of words, a world ordered to render this insight. Whether the reader is reading a biography or a novel, *if* he is responding to the organization of language as it directs him, he is making the work function as literature: he is having an aesthetic experience.

Perception of order is the source of aesthetic pleasure. This is true no matter who the reader is. Mature readers can perceive the organization more fully — and can perceive richer organizations — so they have more enjoyment than inexperienced readers. Some inexperienced readers can delight only in the prose sense, or only in the storyteller's "And then," or only in the plot, or only in the escape into "another country" where everything "fits." Other inexperienced readers may enjoy as well the explicit human dilemma that emerges and resolves or the intellectual stimulation that "solving" a poem offers. In all these cases, the inexperienced readers' pleasure arises from *some* aspects of the organization. Their perception of order is partial; their enjoyment is thereby limited. As they learn to perceive more of the ordering — as they grow up as readers — they will reject "pat" arrangement and contrivance; they will desire orderings of more complexity, orderings that take oppositions and conflicting data into account, orderings that represent the confusing, intricate, many-sided events of the public and the private worlds they know.

Besides this common *function* we have been describing, all works of literature have a common *use:* they serve as one kind of cultural document. They can give us a certain insight into the life of the society that produced them that a study of institutions or of other arts might not afford. From the themes, source stories, and subjects of imaginative literature, from the figures biographers chose, the periods historians selected, from the materials of formal essays, and from what was attacked and argued in satires and speeches and sermons — from all of these, we discover what engaged the people of the period, what they admired, contemplated, feared, learned, desired.

The subject matter of works of literature is culturally revelatory, and so are the styles of language that prevail in a period. What forms were current? Was it an age of prose? of poetry? of drama? of comedy? Were certain rhetorical patterns, certain metaphors, certain figures, certain tones common to the period? The ways a society expressed what it considered worth expressing give us the *feel* of the group. This is something more than knowledge of the group. We can *know* from any annalistic account of the Massachusetts Bay Colony that religion was an absorbing interest of the people, but from the homely images of Edward Taylor's poems, from his gentle diction, from his humble yet intimate relation with his Lord that the dramatic situations in the poems reveal — from all these features of style, we *feel* at least one dimension of this absorbing religious interest.

In summary, then, we can say that all works of literature, whether they are fiction or nonfiction and whatever their particular form, have a common use as well as a common function. All can serve as a special kind of cultural document; all have the potential for evoking to some degree an experience of order, unity, harmony and for giving thereby aesthetic pleasure.

Up to now in our discussion of the nature and the functions of literature, we have not especially distinguished between imaginative literature and nonfiction. There has been no reason to do so. Fictionality is not a criterion for deciding whether or not a work is literature, whether it is "good" or "great," whether it evokes an aesthetic experience, or whether or not it reveals its parent society. But fictional and nonfictional works are different in their intentions and natures, and these differences determine the other functions of each. So now, we shall distinguish between these two kinds of literature.

What Other Functions Do Works of Imaginative Literature Have?

They have both *cognitive* and *moral* functions. When readers evoke the ordered experience of a novel, or poem, or play, their understanding of human conduct is being increased (the work is functioning cognitively) and they are being freed from some of their human limitations (the work is functioning morally). And that statement sounds like just another nebulous gittering generality!

To see what that statement means, we need to recall the nature of a work of imaginative literature, recall that it is a particular, concrete experience that the writer creates out of words to represent *fully* some insight into human experience, some vision of life, some attitude toward an aspect of human behavior. What the poet, playright, or novelist wants to express cannot be said in a statement or maxim. It can only be rendered as a *concrete experience,* which when it is undergone by a reader will evoke the insight, the vision, the attitude it expresses. To create this concrete experience, the writer takes from his personal experience, from an overheard remark, an ancient myth, the Bible, history — from anywhere — some bare "germ" of a situation that he "knows" will *fully* express his insight if he builds it up right. He selects, adds, simplifies, reshapes, distorts it to that end — he does whatever is needed to make a *fully* rendered revelatory situation. When the reader reads the work, he experiences a *total* situation — all necessary facets disclosed to him — he "sees" *all.* As we read "Blue Girls," we go through the whole experience with the speaker. Nothing is withheld: all his feelings from his first remark on the blithe girls through his recognition and his reflection are dramatized before us. We do not get a statement about his experience — we have the experience. We do not have to wonder what he *really* feels — we know.

▪ *The Cognitive Function.* Works of imaginative literature are *fully* rendered concrete experiences. So, they can give that special kind of understanding of human conduct that comes only from *experiencing* complex human situations that are *wholly* and intensely rendered. We often describe this special kind of understanding as "deeper" or "penetrating" because when a reader experiences totally rendered human conduct, he "sees" through the surface of overt behavior to the true complexity of the act, the attitude, or the emotion; he "sees" a piece of human conduct as the moral labyrinth that it is. Only recall how William Carlos Williams' "The Use of Force" lays bare the bestial drama which seethes beneath a doctor's routine examination of a child's infected throat. Only think of how Faulkner's "Barn Burning" makes us see beneath the overt action the irreconcilables that are torturing the boy. If we had only Sarty's outward behavior, we would surmise some inner disturbance. But the story breaks through the surface to reveal the terrible conflict of commitments beneath, so we feel all the torment of the words "grief" and "despair." When seemingly routine events between seemingly ordinary people are revealed *totally*, they are amazing disclosures.

As we all know, if the reader is a socially sensitive human being, he does develop *an* understanding of human conduct through his day-in-day-out life experience. But this understanding is different from what he gets from reading literature because the *quality* of literary experience is different. Everyday experience is part of an ongoing flux. A person cannot separate a particular experience from this mass, stay it, and frame it so he can stand and stare at it. Everyday experience is cluttered with details that he cannot immediately identify as essential or extraneous. Real-life incidents do not reveal situations completely; a human being often does not know the motives, the relevant past histories of the participants, all the circumstances. He usually knows only fragments of overt behavior. (And when is he ever an involved, yet unbiased, contemplator of his everyday experience?) Such transient, unorganized, and incomplete experience cannot give the penetrating insight into human conduct that the totally rendered, unified, and intense experiences of imaginative literature can give. Literary experiences are shaped to make the reader undergo a certain situation in a particular way for a particular reason. So even if it *seems* to the reader that he has had similar experiences in life, they are similar only in subject matter; he has never had them *in this way*. In a work of literature he gets "to the bottom of it" as he so rarely does in life. He sees, with all the pleasure and satisfaction of Frost's boy at the well-curb, "for once, then, something."

Reading works of imaginative literature not only deepens a reader's insight into human experience, it also gives him what we usually call a "broad understanding" of human conduct. A vast panorama of possible human experience is rendered in works of literature, so, a sensitive reader, undergoing these concrete situations, is constantly extending the scope of his own experience. He may be having experiences that in his own life he has never had, may never have, and can never have. And we are referring not only to the erotic, the grotesque, and the exotic, but to the host of situations that each individual, limited by time and by the circumstances of his own life and personality, can never undergo.

Through reading, modern man can realize how a Renaissance subject felt about a king. The skeptic can experience what it is like to be a securely religious man. Those who need to love can know what it is like to need love. Naive men can recognize the ironic injustice in the scheme of things. Women can see the world through the eyes of a man; adults, through the eyes of a child. The normal man can experience the world of an idiot. The irresponsible can feel with the dutiful. And the secure can discover the tightrope they walk.

Those who tend to find the tragic, the painful, and the pathetic unendurable in life can have these experiences in literature. In life, they may flee from such experiences, sentimentalize them, protest the injustice of them, or confront them stoically or heroically — indeed, do everything but undergo them dispassionately. But when these same human situations are represented in literature at the remove of form, they can respond to them with objective detachment; they *can have* these "unbearable" experiences. Indeed, they can find what is tragic and horrifying in life tragic and satisfying in literature; they can find what is overwhelmingly pathetic in life ironically humorous in literature or what seems repulsive in life paradoxically comic in literature. Their response to the situation in literature is, of course, what the rendering forces it to be. In life, the death of a young child often provokes sentimentality or unreasonable regret, but Ransom's "Bells for John Whiteside's Daughter" elicits neither reaction. He has rendered the subject so that the poem evokes arrest, vexation, astonishment. Response to painful events in literature is, then, not merely the real-life response in milder form. Because of the literary rendering, it is often a radically different response from any predictable real-life reaction. And it is through such literary experiences that those who cannot "bear to look" at the tragic, the painful, or the repulsive in everyday human conduct can come to understand them.

Reading works of imaginative literature, then, *broadens* experience in ways life cannot. But reading experiences are not just useful substitutes for real-life experiences. For, as we said earlier, all experiences rendered in imaginative literature are organized to be richly revelatory. So, through works of imaginative literature, readers not only have experiences that, for one reason or another, lie outside the pale of their individual lives, but they have them with more penetration, more clarity, and more intensity than they could have them in everyday life even if they could actually experience all the situations represented.

We may say, then, that works of imaginative literature have the potential for giving a reader a unique *kind* of knowledge: a *kind* of understanding of human conduct that he simply cannot get from life, from any intellectual discipline, or from nonfiction. For it comes from experiencing complex human situations that are fully and intensely rendered. To give this kind of knowledge is the *cognitive* function of imaginative literature.

▪ *The Moral Function.* The deep insights into a panorama of possible human situations that the reader gets from undergoing the fully rendered experiences we have been describing free him from some of his human limitations; from, for instance, a sense of meaninglessness in human events, from obtuseness to the wonder of life, from narrowness and rigidity. To produce these kinds of liberating effects is the *moral* function of imaginative literature.[4]

Now let us see how reading literature frees the reader from the several human limitations we just mentioned.

As we said earlier, people do not find coherence in everyday, real-life events. Being neither omniscient nor omnipresent, they always have only disjointed parts, always more surmises than facts. So they rarely see how the "pieces fit" and how they "add up." They cannot see what the event means, so they either satisfy themselves with oversimplified conclusions or let life creep in its petty pace, full of sound and fury, often signifying next to nothing.

When a reader is responding appropriately to a work of literature, he is discovering all the while an internal coherence in the situation that unfolds before him. He is seeing what is there when someone has cleared the dross, stilled the movement, and fused what is severed in day-in-day-out living. He is seeing the reason, the logic — the meaningfulness of the situation. Reading a work provides what Frost calls "a momentary stay against confusion." The stay *is* momentary, but it has a double force: it gives the reader an island of sense in the free water of daily life and it continues long after to suggest to him the organic ordering that lies unseen beneath the confused surface of events. Works of imaginative literature offer "concrete alternatives to the actual world." And these give the reader a chance to recast in the ideal world a world he has no present means of recasting in reality. Experiencing a work is what Santayana calls "a rehearsal in rational living."

It can also be an entrée to richer living. For reading works of literature can help readers free themselves from obtuseness to the wonder of ordinary life. Literature "throws off the covers that hide the expressiveness of experienced things." It removes ordinary events from their customary contexts; organized as experiences, they are no longer dumb and common; they are new, fresh, and revealing.[5] Think of how Frost's "Dust of Snow" (to be discussed in detail later) makes the "imagination wince." In the frame of a single sentence, the reader is alerted to the ironic significance of a simple, common occurrence. A sinister bird on a sinister tree did a "sinister" act in *such a way* as to make it a "saving grace." The bird of rue saves "some part" of a rued day. It is a black-and-white image of a black-and-white world. The incident is ordinary; it is the details — the *crow*, the *hemlock*, and the *dust* of snow — that are unusual. Works of literature call the reader's attention to the details that make "small wonders" of ordinary events.

And works also make readers aware of the variety of experiences any one common human event affords. Such variety goes unnoticed in life because our tendency to classify experiences destroys all enriching discriminations. But because works of literature interpret the same basic event in many ways, take many different attitudes toward it, they reveal to readers the infinite diversity of ordinary, routine events. Consider how the reading of Tennyson's "Flower in the Crannied Wall," Frost's "Design," Louis MacNeice's "Snow," Daniel Rossetti's "The Woodspurge," Emerson's "The Rhodora" would reveal the many different experiences looking at a flower can evoke.

Works of literature, furthermore, encourage the reader to see in the surface of life more than the surface[6] — to see that the long shadow on the lawn is presentiment, the dragonfly's eye is the mirror of the world, the child's weeping at "Goldengrove unleaving" is man's mourning for the "blight he was born for," the flower in the crannied wall is the microcosm of the mystery of existence, and "That shining moon — watched by that one faint star" is the assurance that "The lovely in life is the familiar/ And only the lovelier for continuing strange."* Reading works of literature makes the reader realize that when he is looking at the simplest item of experience he is probably looking at some universal paradox, some timeless tragedy, some bitter irony, some awful comedy.

By uncovering the uncommon in the ordinary, the variety of experiences in a single event, and the symbolic in the surface, works of literature disabuse readers of the erroneous idea that the great moments of life are few, public, and ostentatious. Readers see that,

---

* Reprinted from "Night," by Walter de la Mare, by permission of the Literary Trustees of Walter de la Mare and The Society of Authors as their representative.

like the miracle of falling snow that Emerson spoke of, the great moments are everyday events experienced with full awareness.

Finally, undergoing the experiences of works of literature frees readers from the narrowness of their own beliefs and values. For in order to experience the various human situations that works of literature render, readers must often assent, for the duration of the reading, to beliefs they do not share. They must feel with characters widely different from themselves and recognize that such difference is not necessarily abnormality. And they must realize that however sordid the human experience represented in a work may be, it is one they, as humans, are capable of. This continual process of seeing through someone else's eyes, empathizing with someone else's feelings, experiencing how it is to hold an unfamiliar view of the world or alien values develops the reader's moral imagination.

And moral imagination *moderates* moral intolerance. The morally imaginative reader does not "tag" characters, prejudge an event, reject a situation before he has a chance to see. He waits patiently while the characters define themselves, while he sees what response they do make to the event, while the moral complexity of the situation unfolds. Experiencing any situation in its full complexity stays a reader's moral judgment. With all the circumstances, overt and hidden, laid bare, the reader sees why the different characters responded to the events as they did. So, it prevents him from seeing in men's actions merely an opportunity for the exercise of moral approval or disapproval. The reader sees all, so he sees why, and this makes him less ready to approve or condemn than to simply *understand*.

When a reader becomes morally imaginative, he can broaden his human experience almost indefinitely. Any work can become part of his experience capital. And every experience that he "understands" facilitates his understanding of the next experience. So, as his moral sensibility increases, there is less and less threat that the circle of his individual life will ever close in on him.

From our consideration of the cognitive and moral functions of imaginative literature, we can see how these functions are related to the aesthetic function. Reading a work increases a reader's understanding of human conduct and produces certain moral effects when and only when the work is being read responsively enough to make it function aesthetically. The cognitive and moral functions are consequent. We point out this relationship among the functions because many statements of aims for the teaching of literature in high school do not make clear that a reader must perceive a work aesthetically if he is to enjoy the cognitive and moral values of reading it. But our discussion repeatedly reveals that it is the undergoing of a *totally rendered experience* that affords the reader the deeper and broader understanding of human conduct and the freedom from human limitations that we have been describing. Our discussion also reveals, by its overlapping, if nothing else, that when a reader *is* evoking the experience of the work, it functions aesthetically, cognitively, and morally — simultaneously.

What Functions Other than the Aesthetic Do Nonfictional Works of Literature Have?

If the nonfictional works are biographies, histories, or philosophical, critical, or scientific essays, they could very well be giving true information, for that is the primary purpose of these kinds of writing — whether they qualify as literature or not. If the nonfictional works are sermons or speeches, they could very well be gaining acceptance for certain beliefs, practices, and values, for that is what all sermons and speeches, literary or not, aim to do. In other words, any nonfictional work of literature could be fulfilling its non-artistic purpose. Whether it is doing so or not — and how well it is doing so — must, of course, be judged by non-artistic criteria. A history of considerable artistic worth may have little value as history. Incomplete data, faulty inference, a detrimental bias may preclude its functioning as history. If it is an older history, the uncovering of new evidence may outmode it. Whether an artistically valuable history is fulfilling its primary purpose or not, only historians can decide. But their negative decision affects in no way the work's value as a work of art.

The non-artistic and artistic functions of nonfictional works are not conditionally related. To all nonfictional writing we may apply a double standard. Of a philosophical essay, we may say: "It has good ideas, but a bad style." We may praise an historian's interpretations and assail his turgid writing. We may, on the other hand, applaud a biographer's sensitive use of language and regret that his research was so incomplete. We cannot, of course, talk about a poem, play, short story, or novel in any such way as this. We cannot comment on the insight of the work as something separate from the rendering. The only evidence we have that the insight is true or significant is the work.

When we are discussing any biography, history, or formal essay, we can, in other words, genuinely separate the content, or argument, from the form, or treatment. When we call a piece of nonfiction a work of literature, we are saying that the treatment of the data or of the argument has aesthetic value. What might have been given in some other way — as a body of facts or as a syllogism, say — has instead been organized into an aesthetic experience. What might have been a textbook has been made an artistic history; what might have become a case study has become a literary biography.

What we have referred to as literary "treatment" should not, however, be thought of as a decoration superimposed on material. The selection, the focus, the emphases, the imagery, the metaphors, the tones all suggest the way the writer has thought about the material, the order he sees in it, the order he wants to make clear to the reader. It is the nonfiction writer's artistic *domination* and *control* of a *given material* that evokes in a qualified reader an aesthetic experience. We refer to this domination and control as "treatment" because his material is given.

If we take away the artistic treatment from a history or a biography, the work of literature is gone. Take away the rhythms, the "voice," the tones from Gibbon's history, and, as a work of art, it would cease to exist. But Gibbon's historical materials would remain: the records he used, the arrangement he gave the data, the argument would remain — valuable as historical fact and historical interpretation. If we take away the artistic rendering from Shakespeare's chronicle play, *Henry IV, Part I*, the work of literature is likewise gone. What remains has, however, no historic value, for the facts are facts deliberately telescoped and reshaped for dramatic ends. The imaginative writer has no given material in the sense the nonfiction writer does. James' "donné" and the biographer's "given" are essentially different.

Unlike works of imaginative literature, then, histories, biographies, and formal essays purport to give verifiable knowledge. And we see at once that this knowledge could very well deepen and broaden readers' understanding of human conduct and increase their moral imagination, but we also see that the cognitive and moral effects would be somewhat different from those imaginative literature produces.

History and biography both give the kind of understanding that comes from knowing that particular individuals or whole societies behaved in certain ways in their publicly recorded lives. These two forms give, in other words, the kind of understanding of conduct that knowing *about* human situations affords. *Some* histories and biographies are, however, written as experiences, which the reader undergoes, much as he does the particular concrete experiences of drama and fiction. Through the reading of such nonfiction, the reader can have the kind of insight into conduct that comes from experiencing situations rather than from knowing about them. Is the knowledge he gets from imaginative literature different from this? We think it is — because the experiences of biographies and histories can be only as revelatory and as total as data will allow.

The imaginative writer can fully reveal the experience he creates because he does not have to remain true to any body of data existing prior to and outside of the work. He can, for instance, give a full, new interpretation of the Fall, for his Satan does not have to "square" with the Bible. He may build into the personality of Prince Hal oppositions that foreshadow a worthy king. The Prince does not have to be the base idler tradition made him. The imaginative writer decides what the characters will be like, what they will say and do, what their motivations are. He can give the reader *everything* needed to show why things are as they are, so the reader enjoys that special kind of understanding that comes from seeing all.

The biographer and the historian do not have the imaginative writer's advantage. They can reveal only as much of an experience as the data allow. Often much is missing, much left unexplained. They are bound, as the portrait artist is, by what is there. Like him, they make only the most aesthetically valuable, humanly significant organization they can — of what they have. The writer of imaginative literature alone can always render morally revealing wholes. When we finish reading Edel's fine biography of James, we still must wonder why James did not marry. But when we finish James' "The Beast in the Jungle," we do not have to wonder about Marcher; we know.

We are not suggesting that having fictional experiences is better than having the experiences of well-organized verifiably true events. We are saying that these two types of experience are different and entail different values.

How Do We Justify the Study of Literature in the Curriculum?

We justify the study of literature on the grounds that the effects it can produce are valuable: that it is good for students to have the kind of ordered experience, the kind of knowledge of human conduct, the kind of moral effects, and the kind of understanding of culture we have described. If we think these effects valuable, then the study of literature must be in the curriculum because, as we have been suggesting, only literature perceived as the sort of work of art it is can produce *these particular kinds* of effects. Why do we emphasize this last phrase?

Because reading literature is not the only way for students to have *an* experience of order. They may have one playing a game or watching an athletic event. But these experiences of order are qualitatively different from what reading a work of literature affords, for they are only contingently experiences of order; order facilitates the end; it is an added pleasure. The experience of a work of art is essentially an experience of order; the experience of order is *the* end; it is *the* pleasure. If we consider such an experience valuable, then the study of literature should be in the curriculum.

Students may also have an experience of order through the study of any genuine subject matter. Is that experience similar to that enjoyed while reading works of literature? It is not. If a student goes about his study of a discipline properly, he is continually discovering the internal structure (the order) of the subject. But what he is discovering is an *intellectual* and *abstract* order, one that helps him understand intellectually some particular area of experience. When, however, a student reads a work of literature properly, he participates — mentally and emotionally — with involved detachment in the experience of a *sensuous* and *concrete* ordering of some particular human situation, which he comes to understand feelingly. If we consider that kind of experience valuable, then the study of literature should be in the curriculum.

Reading literature is not the only way for students to develop an understanding of human conduct or to extend their moral imaginations. Psychology, sociology, and, as we have seen, history also can produce these effects. From the social sciences, students can get the kind of understanding of human conduct and moral situations that comes from knowing true descriptions of human behavior: descriptions arrived at by studying a large number of particular cases to discover what is similar among them. From the data of history, as we pointed out earlier, students can get the kind of understanding that comes from knowing a verifiable reconstruction of that part of the behavior of past societies that records confirm. Both the social sciences and history give information — facts and generalizations from facts — that will provide students with an intellectual understanding of human behavior. But the reader of Faulkner's "Barn Burning" does not come away with a true statement either about a certain kind of psychological conflict or about a social phenomenon. For he has not been learning *about* a situation; he has been undergoing one — not a situation used as an example of something else, but one functioning as a revelation of itself. In undergoing this experience, the reader not only realizes intellectually how it is to hold moral standards opposed to one's father's; he also *feels* the tension of this situation, the ambivalence, the irrational pulling, the false hoping — the entire torture of blood struggling against conviction. The reader understands this particular instance of conduct because he has *been through it* totally. But does this really differ from the effect of reading a psychological case study? It does. Faulkner's story is an aesthetically organized, total rendering, bound by nothing but its own truth. If we consider valuable the kind of understanding of conduct that reading "Barn Burning" gives, then the study of literature should be in the curriculum.

Reading works of literature is not the only way for students to awaken to the wonder of life. Perceiving other representational arts will also help them enjoy the variety and the symbolic quality of commonplace experiences. But we hardly have to argue for the pre-eminence of literature in giving us "the everlasting in the front yard." If we think this moral effect valuable, then the study of literature should be in the curriculum.

Finally, as we said earlier, reading works of literature is not the only way for students to have a knowledge and understanding of earlier periods and of their own. There are social and political institutions, and there are other art works, that can recreate the eras for them. But, as we tried to show, works of literature are *singular* cultural documents. And if we consider them *valuable* ones also, then literature should be in the curriculum.

We have been suggesting that literature has unique functions, that no other subject matter could really be substituted for it. So, if students *are* to have the effects that accrue from these functions, the study of literature must be in the curriculum. But the basic question still remains: should these aesthetic, cognitive, and moral effects be available to students? Are they valuable for them? We cannot *prove* that these effects are valuable. But we feel certain that they are, since high school students, like all other human beings, long to understand human conduct, to overcome the superficiality, paro-chialism, and dullness of their day-in-day-out existence, and to find order and meaning and richness in life.

The effects of the study of literature prepare students, not for college, not for jobs, but for themselves, for their inner worlds. A man's inner world determines to a great extent how he uses and enjoys the world outside himself. A man's inner world is where he most truly lives, where he must find his real fulfillment, and where he must make his final assessment. For these reasons, the study of literature must be in the curriculum — for all students.

Literature, like every other subject, must earn its place in the curriculum by the value of its indisputable functions, not by pious hopes or hackneyed clichés about its powers. That is why we have been prudent in defining the functions of literature and citing what we can justifiably expect the sensitive reading of literature to achieve. We have especially eschewed any exaggerated claims for the moral effects reading literature can produce. We can be sure — for evalua-tions tell us — that a sensitive reader develops a keen insight into human experience expressed *in literature,* an acute perception of how organization reveals the meaning of events *in literature,* and a greatly intensified moral imagination in dealing with characters and events *in literature.*

Continual sensitive reading probably disposes the reader to re-spond to life situations — *on the mental and verbal level* — with insight, with sensitivity to order, with wonder, and with moral imagi-nation.[7] Reading probably cultivates these responses as (what we shall loosely call) "habits of mind" that the reader, thereupon, exercises in undergoing both literary experiences and life experiences. This seems psychologically plausible, and we certainly hope it *is* a consequence of sensitive reading. But since we have no evidence that it is, we may call it only a "probable effect."

And we may call the improvement of actual social behavior only a "possible effect," something that reading literature may bring about. It is often supposed, and sometimes even claimed, that when people become aware, through the reading of literature, of their possibilities for virtue and their capabilities for evil, they behave more sympathetically, they act with more moral imagination, they promote social solidarity, communal sharing, and general good will. Reading works *might* produce some of these admirable social effects, but we have no real evidence that it does. And so we cannot rightly cite such effects as justfication for including the study of literature in the curriculum. If such social behaviors were the necessary consequences of sensitive reading, then, as one critic said, literary critics would be the world's most socially exemplary men. What critic would be so uncritical as to claim they are?

It is very possible for men to reveal a penetrating and sympathetic understanding of human conduct both in their responses to literature and in their mental and verbal responses to life situations and still not exercise such understanding in their actions. Moral philosophers from Plato on have regretted that men can have dispositions to act in certain ways and not comply with them. We should not be shy in admitting that we cannot be sure that reading literature will improve social behavior. Can any intellectual discipline or any other art rightly claim that studying *it* does?

What Are the Aims for the Study of Literature?

We justified the place of literature in the curriculum by holding that when works of literature function, the effects they produce are valuable for readers. So, we are obliged to try to teach students to make works function. And as our definition of a work of literature has already suggested, no one can make a work function unless he can respond sensitively to its organization of language. Consequently, our primary aim for the study of literature is to help students learn to respond sensitively to the literary uses of language so that they can read works as works of literature.[8] The aim would be the same for all students. What course they are enrolled in or "where they are going" does not make any difference. It cannot; for their future plans cannot change either the nature and functions of works or the way readers achieve literary value.[9] These things are.

Now, let us examine our aim to see what is "in it," so that we shall know precisely what students must do to achieve it. First of all, the phrase "literary uses of language" reminds us that students must learn to respond to the words of a work as artistic media. A purely literal response will not do. How could it when the words are also exploited for, say, their metaphoric, rhythmic, tonal, dramatic, probably even phonemic, values? Whoever is to evoke the intended experience of a work must respond *in kind* to the language. Only by doing that will he complete the linguistic act. The crucial thing in a work is not the assertion made, but the *way* it is made; not the series of events represented, but the *way* the series is rendered.

And to experience "the way," readers must respond to the language "sensitively" — with great attention, precision, and imagination: they must see *what* is there, *how* exactly words are being exploited, and *in what ways* they are counting in *this* work. If they read with imagination but without precision, they may be evoking inappropriate connotations, seeing connections that do not exist *in* the work at all, and, at worst, tailoring the work to what they think it ought to be expressing. Readers must consider the language of a work as inviolate as the units in a stained glass window.

If they read with precision but without imagination, they may miss the suggestions that syntax, connotation, metaphor, rhythm, repetitions, parallels, and such are making; they may fail to grasp the interrelations among the structures used. Responding sensitively means reacting attentively, precisely, imaginatively — all three — to "these words in this order." It is only in *that* way that readers can undergo the exact pattern of relationships the work embodies and so feel directly and immediately the total ordering, the artistic structure. A work of literature is a potential work of art. It requires a qualified perceiver to actualize it.

We are not suggesting, of course, that a reader must make some almost exhaustive response to a work if he is to evoke its experience. Most readings leave room for many new readings. A reader's response to the whole organization may be a weak one. It usually is if he is a beginning reader or if the work is a complex one. Or a reader's response to this or that mode of organization may be deficient. It often is on initial readings of a work or if he is somewhat insensitive to a certain device, say, metaphor, or parallels, or repetitions. But if he is to experience a work, he must be making a response *in some degree* to all the structures present in it. If he misses some dimension entirely — if he does not hear tones in a poem, or does not notice who tells the story, or does not realize that the rasping sounds of the words work against their mild denotations — then he cannot really have the experience of the work. He cannot, any more than we can have the experience of what somebody is telling us if we do not realize he is joking. All the structures are working together to express the experience, and the reader must work them all together to recreate it.

Since no two works of literature are alike, "learning to respond sensitively to the literary uses of language" cannot be the learning of a system, a master pattern, or a repertoire of responses. It is, rather, learning to make the unique response demanded by each context, learning to react appropriately to whatever presents itself. Consequently, what students need to develop are *flexible tendencies* to respond properly to the various literary uses of language, however they are functioning.

An excellent athlete *is* excellent because he has a most flexible tendency to respond in widely various, but, in each particular instance, highly appropriate ways. No two of an athlete's plays are exactly alike, and he never knows until he reflects in retrospect *just* how similar the play he has just made was to the one before it or to any past play. At the moment of making a play, he simply sees the conditions in a total way, senses precisely what an apt response would be, and executes most fittingly the response he chooses to make. In a similar way, the sensitive reader is clued by the configurations of words before him as to what mode of response he should make, and he reacts appropriately. The reader's responses to the language of a work are not, like the athlete's plays, discrete events; the reader's reaction to one configuration of words in a work affects his response to the next and colors his memory of what he has read, so that, finally, each response is affecting every other. Like all analogies, our athlete-reader analogy holds only so far, but it suggests that the kind of skill that is needed in any activity where every task is a somewhat different one is a *flexible tendency* to respond appropriately. And that is the kind of skill that we would be trying to help students develop.

The tendencies necessary for sensitive reading — tendencies, for instance, "to hear with the eyes," to image with the exact sharpness the words demand, to think metaphorically, to sense irony in words and situations, to release *only* those connotations the context invites, to catch the tone of the narrator precisely, to understand how parts function in the whole — all such tendencies are developed through students' having a large number of varied, intensive experiences with the different literary uses of language. If, for instance, students are to develop a tendency to respond appropriately to images, they must experience images *in the context* of works to see how they *function*. They must experience *a large number* of images — in poems, essays, fiction, plays — so they will see that even images similar in subject differ in detail, in sharpness, in the senses appealed to; they differ as their functions demand. Students must experience this large number of images *intensively* if they are to sense these differences precisely and imaginatively. Neither a concentrated study of two or three images nor a passing glance at a large number will do.

We have been spelling out the terms of our primary aim so that we can see what our aim means and what it requires us to do. We always need to know whether it is information or a skill or an attitude that we are trying to get students to learn and what precisely is involved in it. Aims — whether general or particular — have only one function: to direct what both the teacher and the students do. If aims are to fulfill this function, they must be stated as accurately as possible and we must understand as fully as possible what every main word entails. From such a general aim as we have just stated and analyzed, we must derive particular aims for large segments of study (for courses) and, from those particular aims, deduce in turn, aims for parts of courses, for sections within those parts, for series of lessons in the sections, and for individual lessons. Through such connection among aims, we can be reasonably sure that as students achieve the immediate aim, they are also achieving the general.

The aim we have been discussing is the *primary* aim for the study of literature, not the only one, but the primary one, the aim that must take precedence over all others and be worked for until students have achieved it in so far as they can. This must be so for three reasons. First, as we have said, the responsive reading of works is the *sine qua non* for enjoying literary values, and those values are what justify including the study of literature in the curriculum at all. Secondly, the ability to read a work is a highly generalizable skill. If a student develops tendencies to respond to the literary uses of language in appropriate ways, he is free to exercise his skill if and whenever he chooses. He can on his own enjoy new readings of familiar works, read new works, and, with sufficient experience with a variety of works, read in an adequate way — perhaps even a highly sensitive way — any work he ever happens to confront. This aim is truly liberating. Thirdly, knowing how to read a work is the central knowledge in the study of literature. We mean that, once a student has this ability, he has *the* ability required for engaging in all other types of literary study: formal criticism, literary theory, literary history, and the evaluation of works. How can a student engage in mature formal critical analysis if he cannot first read sensitively a wide variety of works? And unless he is a formal critic of some sophistication, how can he ever be expected to compare works or evaluate them in even elementary ways? If he is not a responsive reader, what can the contextual study of literature be but a memorization of names, dates, titles, catch phrases, and quotable quotes? And what is the study of even the simplest literary theory but a lifeless body of abstractions unless the student has induced the concepts of, say, metaphor, rhythm, assonance, and such from various concrete instances in works of literature? Skill in reading *is* pre-requisite to all other literary studies.

Once students have achieved the primary aim, we would try to help them engage in whichever of these more advanced modes of literary study their interest suggests and their ability warrants. This is our second general aim for the study of literature in high school.[10]

Our two general aims are not the usual high-sounding "calls to greatness." We say nothing about "development of appreciation" or "improving standards of taste" or "stimulating enjoyment" or "developing worthwhile allegiances." Our aims are noticeably plain and straightforward. But unlike the "great" vague aims, ours *can* direct classroom practice. We know what we have to do. We know quite clearly which general teaching methods can help students achieve these aims. And we can "test" to see to what extent each student has, in fact, achieved them. These aims do not give us a smoke screen of words behind which either we or our students can hide. They are verbally merciless. They sound like plain, hard work — and they are.

And if the elevated language of some commonly cited aims for teaching literature in high school were reduced to the language of common speech, it would also simply say "to teach students how to read a work sensitively." How else can anyone develop appreciation and increase enjoyment of literature? Our appreciation, our enjoyment of literature is determined by the precision and the imagination with which we respond to the literary uses of language. Since, spelled out, these "large" aims just say "to teach students to read works competently," they imply the same obligations and restraints that the plainly stated aim does. These "large" aims are neither greater, nor easier to achieve, nor more permissive; they only sound that way. Their words have become protean terms, to which everyone assigns his own meanings. Couched in such language, the commonly cited aims for teaching literature have become a disastrous babel, worse than Babel, because often teachers do not know that their colleagues speak in different tongues.

What Kinds of Works Will Help Students Achieve Our Aims?

Works that meet three criteria. First, the works read in all classes must have literary value. Students cannot evoke experiences of order from works that do not express them. This does not mean, however, that the works read must be "great" literature — or even "nearly great." As our continuum of verbal organization suggested, works vary widely in degree of organization. In all genres, there are works of relatively simple structure and very rich works and, in between, works of hundreds of levels of complexity. There is always a work to begin on, always one to move to — whether we choose to move by slow steps or giant steps. Our aim restricts us to works of literary value, but that does not confine us to a dozen "great" works.

The works chosen must, then, be valid in terms of our aims. But they must also be feasible in terms of the particular class who will study them to achieve the aims. So, they must meet two further criteria; they must be relevant to the concerns of the students and appropriate to their reading ability. In our choice of works these two standards must be applied simultaneously. That is what makes getting the "right" work so difficult. The experience a work represents — say, Faulkner's "Barn Burning" — may be highly relevant to students in a particular class, but the organization may be much *too* complex for them. If they cannot respond to the language well enough to have the experience of the work, what price its relevance?

However difficult it is to find proper works, we must get them, for achieving our aim is not an end in itself. It is the means to all the aesthetic, cognitive, and moral values we have described. As a work is read, students should be having an experience relevant to their concerns; they should be seeing how the shaped experience clarifies, intensifies, and extends some human situation that engages them. If the language is *too* complex, they may end with only an intellectual triumph over a complex organization of words. If the concern is irrelevant, they will not have "felt along the lines."

From the ways we have just used the word "concern" in our remarks about relevance, two things must be clear. First, that we are not talking about the subject matter of the works, but about the theme, the insight, the universal experience rendered. Secondly, that we are not referring to some superficial object of attention — the sport, or hobby, or "cause" that currently fascinates students — but to fundamental questions of human conduct that high school students wonder about, are baffled by, have inklings of — the questions that will be theirs as human beings for the rest of their lives. By the time students arrive at grade ten, their concerns are rapidly expanding, reaching into the far corners of human experience. Some of these concerns may be more intense than others, some more dominant, some more clearly recognized. But the concerns are there, whether the adult world likes to think so or not. And in our choice of works we should surely take advantage of the live concerns of each group of students.

Occasionally, in our search for "right" works for a particular class, we find a work of imaginative literature that meets our three criteria — it is valid, its language is feasible, its concern is relevant, but we reject it because, knowing the class, we know that there is something about the work that, *at this stage of the students' development as readers,* would conflict with the beliefs and values of quite a number of them. This "something" might be the particular attitude the work takes toward the conduct it represents; it might be the particular diction the characters use; it might be the unflattering "picture" the work gives of some racial, national, or religious group. *When conflicts of beliefs are genuine,*[11] they generally occur in those beginning readers who, though sensitive enough to the literary uses of language to read this work, have yet not developed sufficient aesthetic distance to participate *as readers* in those parts of the work that touch their beliefs, hates, fears, or desires. They pull these parts out of context, give them undue and inappropriate attention, charge them emotionally — as the work does not, and quite distort the function of the part in the experience of the work. Such a reader misreads in a similar way parts of works that support his personal beliefs — we just hear less about what he favors. With our aims, we are concerned about all misreading — its causes and cures, for no one who misreads, whatever the reason, is having the experience of a work.

In such a class we would eschew such disturbing works for *the time being,* much as we would postpone introducing in any context a "touchy" subject that we want rationally considered. In the meantime, we would prepare the students for the eventual reading of such works by teaching the works we do choose so as to develop certain awarenesses, certain habits of mind. We would *casually* and *continually* call to the attention of these students that as readers we do not ask whether or not a character's action is ethically right; we ask only if it is dramatically right. We do not ask, for instance, whether little Sarty (in "Barn Burning") should have moved finally against his father. We do not ask ourselves what moral principle he observed or violated. We ask only if his decision is right in the context of the work. Furthermore, we would suggest to these students that we as readers or as playgoers do not care whether *The Crucible* conflicts with what we know to be historically or sociologically true about Salem in the seventeenth century. We care only that the situation represented is a humanly possible, authentically rendered little world. Whether or not it corresponds to what we believe about Salem is beside the point. We would suggest that whether a work coincides or conflicts with our psychological, sociological, historical, or religious beliefs, or our moral commitments does not make the experience of the work one whit more or less significant, sincere, or authentic.

As we led these students through the study of each work, we would make them enter the world of the work, as Bradley says, "conform to its laws, and ignore for the time the beliefs, aims, and particular conditions, which belong to them in the other world of reality." We would show them that, during the reading, the reader gives the experience of the work his imaginative assent only. We would prove it by calling to their attention that *they* can be reading, currently or successively, three works with diametrically opposed insights and that they can assent imaginatively to all insights with no concern whatever that the insights reject one another. These mutually exclusive insights can be equally and simultaneously "true" for them. This, we would remind them, is not the case with conflicting factual statements or incompatible moral rules. They cannot simultaneously believe: "The Declaration of Independence was signed on July 3" and "The Declaration of Independence was signed on July 4." They cannot hold both that "Thou shalt not bear false witness against thy neighbor" and "Lying is a right action." The facts and the moral rules we hold must be synthesized; but we do not have to reconcile insights in several works of literature either with one another or with our own beliefs.

All the while we were reminding students — in a casual remark or interested query — of these truths, we would be raising again and again and again, in work after work, the only question that can be asked about any detail in any work: How does it function in the world that is unfolding in the work? (What does that remark reveal about the character? Why is *that* image used? What is the effect of that word? Why is that scene demanded by the situation? Is that mode of language typical of the speaker?) If a reader is really trying to have the experience of a work fully, these are the questions he raises about all kinds of details: about four-letter words and the the most sacred, about prurient scenes and pure ones, about both lewd and chaste remarks, about coarse and decorous incidents, about degrading or ennobling portrayals of nationalities, races, and religions, about the derision or the praise of religious and cultural symbols. So, as we studied works, we would be asking, naturally and with equal hand, about the "charged" details and all others — about whatever deserved attention.

When, for instance, we read E. E. Cummings'

Buffalo Bill's
defunct
    who used to
    ride a watersmooth-silver
                stallion
and break onetwothreefourfive pigeonsjustlikethat
                             Jesus

he was a handsome man
                 and what i want to know is
how do you like your blueeyed boy
Mister Death*

---

* Reprinted from *Poems 1923–1954*, by E. E. Cummings, by permission of Harcourt, Brace & World, Inc. Copyright © 1923, 1951, by E. E. Cummings.

we would call students' attention to many details, including the word "Jesus." We would want them to see how perfectly the word helps to define the speaker's attitude toward Buffalo Bill: his profound admiration for the handsome man and for his exploits. What could be a more authentic ejaculation *for the speaker of this poem?* That is the framework in which we would ask about this word.

We would be trying to show students that the work controls their response to profanity, obscenities, and sexual situations just as much as it does their response to parallel scenes, the first-person point of view — or anything else in the work. In every case, the work tells them what to bring from their experience. They must select exactly what the work demands — no more, no less — and take the word, the scene in exactly *the way* the work requires.

We would always be trying to *show* these students by many, many small examples that if details *are functioning in a work* to define characters, set a scene, create a mood, or in any other way that renders the experience fully and authentically, the fact that they are offensive *or gratifying* to the social or ethical sensitivities of certain people is as irrelevant as if there were some detail in a work that did not coincide with our Copernican astronomy (for instance, the sun in Donne's "The Sun Rising") or that did not agree with the Judeo-Christian view of creation, (for instance, the myth in Herbert's "The Pulley"). We would try to impress upon students that the only time a reader can rightly object to *any detail* in a work is when it is superimposed on the work, not demanded by it and not functioning to evoke the insight. The detail is, then, anathema, whether it is a propagandist plea, an inspiring prayer, sentimentality, or erotica. The objection to all of these details is the same.

When readers have had a good chance to acquire the awarenesses and habits we have been describing, we would begin to choose the kinds of readings that we had been postponing. But we would move slowly. From their long preparation, these readers now *understand* distance, the suspension of disbelief, and the kind of treatment that they as readers must give all details, but the fact remains that they are now going to have to do more than understand these matters: they must now entertain, for the duration of the work, beliefs and values they are hostile to. We can have *some* feel for the difficulty of this if we think of trying to listen honestly and without bias to a counter point of view. So, recognizing the difference between a student's knowing what he ought to do and his being able to do it, we would move slowly, asking the very same kinds of questions about function we had been asking, and doing it in the same natural, equal-handed way.

Occasionally, a teacher who senses insularity, priggishness, or bias in a certain class decides to choose a work that will enlighten in one fell swoop, that will shock the students into moral imagination. He is simply unbelievably naive about the holding of beliefs and values and about the development of moral imagination. His act *will* upset, but it will *not* liberate. Students' beliefs and values — wrongheaded, parochial as they may be — are part of the bases upon which they build their worlds. If students feel these bases are being challenged or attacked, they become defensive; they will not even entertain alternatives to their beliefs. The teacher has less and less chance of ever getting them to sympathetically understand others' values. There is little hope of expanding the horizons of students who feel threatened. Moral imagination develops through this little recognition, that small enlightenment — it encroaches, as the tide on the beach, one little wave after another, an almost imperceptible movement forward.

Holding the aims we hold, we may never go militantly, book in hand, to overthrow fixed beliefs, not because such shock therapy may send some sincere, alarmed students to the "office" to protest, but because, since we aim to develop moral imagination, such an act will subvert the achievement of our aim. It will do that whether or not any student raises a voice against us.

What Kinds of Methods Will Help Students Achieve Our Aims?

First of all, methods that bring students to the work, not the work to them. The work is a completed artistic product; it is to be perceived as it is. We cannot accommodate it to the students' abilities to perceive it. The work is a mountain. It cannot be altered to fit the climbers; it can only be assaulted in different ways. Like the leader of the expedition, we study the faces of the mountain — and the skills of our climbers — and decide how we shall approach, how our climbers can best move forward to conquest.

A work says what it says — not what students happen to notice and not what they want it to say. It may not be "airbrushed" or revamped — either by them or by us — to make the themes and situations more relevant or more familiar. We must discourage any student comments that "dissolve" literature into life. And we are referring to the comments not only of those who overtly reduce a work to autobiography, but also of those who reshape works in less drastic but no less detrimental ways: students who read a work in terms of their personal, moral, and social stereotypes and so condemn the family in Frost's "Out, Out . ." for not mourning properly, approve the speaker in "The Road Not Taken" for his noble choice, blame the vain "blue girls" for wasting time, feel that Ole Andreson in Hemingway's "The Killers" "got what was coming to him," and believe that all Mathilda ("The Use of Force") needed was a sound spanking. These students make the work say what they want it to say without changing or omitting a word. They simply "turn a deaf ear" to the tone, suppress the meaning of certain words, overlook the sound patterns, the parallels, and all sorts of organizing devices that define the experience.

When we make a reader come to a work, we force him to disengage himself from the assumptions, beliefs, and moral judgments that have become his because of his own history, we ask him to cast off his personal "blinders." Works cannot expand a reader's experience if he is permitted to continually bring them to terms with his circumscribed life. If he does that, he will have nothing but the pleasure of familiarity, of seeing, as Bradley says, his cousin in one work, his birthplace in the next. If he is to have the experience of the work and the insight into conduct that that affords, he must become what *the work* wants him to be.

But our job is not just to prevent the reader from making his life the context in which the work is read, it is also to show him how to use his experience to understand the work. We do this as we draw on his experience for a comparison that will enlighten some point in the work; for example, to clarify the irony of line 9 in "Blue Girls," we make him compare the line with "Practice makes perfect," an adage he knows. And we reach into what is familiar to him for an analogy that will inform the unfamiliar; for instance, to help him understand how syntax represents an action (as in the barn burning at the end of Faulkner's story), we recall to him how *he* tells an incident when he wants to suggest hurry and confusion.

Each reader's fund of experience probably exists in a kind of freed state, let us say something like particles in suspension. As he reads, he repeatedly draws whatever "particles" the work dictates: the meaning of an allusion, three connotations for a certain word, the tentative significance of a certain symbol, the implication of a certain gesture. He must bring to the work just those bits of his experience the work asks for and he must use each bit the way the work requires to make every detail meaningful in the way it must be, if he is to have the insight.

And we must refrain, *during* explication, from asking any questions that will let the reader's experience intrude more than necessary. If, for instance, we were to ask about the relevance of a work *during* the critical reading of it, we might very well lead students away from the work, each into his own autobiographical reminiscence. The reader of "Blue Girls," for instance, might be reliving in his own private world the memory of playing on a school lawn, or of hearing the sound of birds, or of wearing a particular hairband, or of being scolded by a teacher. Will he then undergo the particular experience of "Blue Girls"? Unlikely. He has travelled far, far away from it. Torn out of the poem, none of the little events listed has much to do with the experience of *this* poem. They function in the poem in relation to one another, and they function as they are in the poem, nothing added, nothing subtracted. For the duration of the study of a work, we must keep the reader within the frame of it, and this entails refraining from asking questions on relevance *until after* the discussion of the work is completed.

Then, once the student has had the experience of the work, we may, if we wish, encourage him to bring the work to his fund of life experience to test the "truth" of its insight or to say how the experience of the work relates to his whole body of experience: to say what the work "means" to him.[12] But we must make clear to all students that until interpretation is finished, the phrase "what the work means to me" has no meaning. We may not for any reason, including encouragement, allow students to develop a distorted idea of interpretation: to think, for instance, that their subjective reactions to a work are interpretations, or that any response that touches the work at some point is interpretation, or that people being as different as they are, the work means "what it means to me." Our teaching must make clear that a work is a completed artistic product. *It* decides which interpretations are valid. And valid interpretations will always be those that take into account the total organization of the work, the interdependence of all its parts.

In certain classes, our teaching must make clear to students that there may be several or many valid interpretations of a work. Certain classes enjoy the security of feeling that their one valid interpretation of the work is what the work "means." We must show such classes that the work bears other interpretations, that theirs is only one justifiable meaning.[13]

Secondly, the methods that will help students achieve our aims will be those that stress the literary organization of words.

This *is* what differentiates literary biography from an encyclopedia entry and a short story from a summary and gives the biography and the story their aesthetic value. Consequently, we may never allow the study of a work to stop at the subject matter. We might *begin* a study by asking what the work is about, simply to be sure that everyone has "gotten the work straight." The students' answers to such a question will assure us that the class is headed in the right direction. But that is all the answers do. They say nothing about the experience of the work. Our study of a work, then, may begin with the data, but it must concentrate on what organizes the data into *this* biography; it may begin with what the story is about, but it must stress *what* makes the subject matter this story. It is only by noticing organization that students can have the unique experience of each work.

Thirdly, the methods that will help students achieve our aims will be those that respect the distinction between the kind of knowledge of human conduct that can be gained from reading imaginative literature and the kinds that can be obtained from studying the social sciences, history, and ethics.

Literature does not give factual knowledge; the facts found in works are serving some *literary* purpose. As Boas points out, a qualified reader of Shakespeare's sonnet, "When in disgrace with fortune," never asks whether love can, *in fact,* initiate elation. It is of no importance; he is not reading the sonnet for psychological information.

Literature does not, furthermore, teach moral principles or represent models of human conduct. Works present all sorts of possible human situations neutrally and impartially. They render each as it is: the good as good, the apparent "good" as evil, the evil as evil, and the evil as attractive. Works try only to make us feel how it feels to enjoy or endure a situation. In literature, as in the other arts, all situations are "right" as long as they are developed so that the reader can experience *how* and *why* it all is as it is. It is the quality of the rendering of a situation, not the propriety or nobility of the conduct represented, that determines whether the work can function aesthetically, cognitively, and morally.

In summary, then, if we encourage or allow students to read short stories, novels, poems, and plays as if they were just more palatable versions of discourses in psychology, sociology, history, or ethics, we lose all around. Using literature in ways that suppress its functions does not change its nature. When works are read as typical case studies, as sociological findings, as history, as moral directives, they cannot exercise their proper functions nor can they really function as anything else.

Fourthly, the methods that will help students achieve our primary aim will be those that will bring them into a reader's relationship with works.

This suggests that questioning, for instance, will be a more useful method than telling, because questioning will help the students to do their own discovering and will apprise them of the *kinds* of questions they should be asking themselves when they read independently.

This suggests, furthermore, that the only teaching aids that will be of value to us are those that motivate students to confront a page and those that help them to improve their critical responses. So, essentially extrinsic devices like films, say, would be useful or not, depending upon whether they *move students to begin to read.* They cannot be used as ends in themselves; they cannot be thought of as substitutes for the critical reading of works.

Finally, this suggests that we should eschew methods that bring students into a literary historian's relationship with works, or a literary theorist's, or a judicial critic's. We should, for instance, give students only that kind of background information that will facilitate their making a richer, more precise response to the words of the work. What information that is would have to be determined carefully.

To tell the reader of "Blue Girls" that Ransom is a classicist would not, *in and of itself,* facilitate or enhance his reading of the poem. It would suggest only that Latin roots are probably present. The reader would, then, have to know Latin well enough to recognize the roots in such words as "seminary," "practice," "establish," and "perfection" and to give the added dimensions of meaning to these words. It is knowing Latin, not knowing about Ransom, that would *enrich* the reader's response to the poem. So if the teacher wants a class to have this extra dimension, his underlining the Latin derivatives with their root meanings will serve the students much better than his informing them about Ransom's classicism. Actually, students can read this poem quite adequately without having or receiving any information on its Latinisms. The poem itself gives the reader the clues needed to determine what meanings of these words are released by Ransom's uses of them. If the reader, for instance, sees the girls "practicing" their beauty, and knows that "practice makes perfect"; and if he hears the echoes of the time-worn threats about "practice" and "failing," then, he grasps the terrible ironic twist the phrase *"before* it fail" gives to the threat here. If the reader senses the metaphor of the town crier, then he knows what meanings are at work in "publish"; if he notices "power," he knows what meaning of "establish" is being suggested. That is not to say that a recognition of the Latin roots would not *enhance* the pleasure of the poem, but rather that that recognition is not *essential* to an adequate reading. It *is* to say, though, that knowing of Ransom's classicism is not very relevant to the reading of this poem.

Similarly, biographical notations on the identity of certain figures in works are generally of little more than intellectual interest to a *reader.* In "Blue Girls," for instance, the identity of the "the lady" is as insignificant to the experience of this poem as the identification of the "blue girls" or the "seminary" would be. There are some poems where *certain types* of biographical data might enlighten the reading — for instance, in Yeats' "No Second Troy":

> Why should I blame her that she filled my days
> With misery, or that she would of late
> Have taught to ignorant men most violent ways,
> Or hurled the little streets upon the great,

Had they but courage equal to desire?
What could have made her peaceful with a mind
That nobleness made simple as a fire,
With beauty like a tightened bow, a kind
That is not natural in an age like this,
Being high and solitary and most stern?
Why, what could she have done, being what she is?
Was there another Troy for her to burn?*

Here, knowing who "she" was might be useful to a reader. But it would not be the knowledge that she was Maud Gonne, the grand passion of the young Yeats, that would help, but rather the knowledge that she was an Irish agitator, a modern "heroic" woman. This concept of her could be gotten from the poem, *if* the reader knew the story of the woman with whom she was being compared. In other words, even in Yeats' poem, it is a *certain* knowledge of the myth of Troy that is really crucial to a reader's experiencing the poem. In no wise, is it a knowledge of Yeats' romantic life that is needed.

Although knowing who wrote "Blue Girls" is of no assistance to the reader of that poem, in some poems knowing who the author is might give the reader useful clues for interpreting the language of the poem. This would be true, if, for instance, the name of the writer reminded the reader of some symbol, some device that the particular writer characteristically used to suggest a certain thing. To know that a poem was by Eliot, for example, would help the reader interpret the images, *if* he knew what meanings Eliot recurrently suggests through certain images. In like manner, knowing the poem before him was by Yeats might help the reader grasp the implications of certain lines, *if* the reader already knew Yeats' view of history and his unique mystical system. Knowing who the author is profits the *reader* little, unless the name recalls some additional information that is pertinent in elucidating the work before him.

Knowing when a poem was written is, likewise, of little value to a reader unless the date suggests to him the current literary tradition or "view of man" or something else that the work might be reflecting or reacting to. Being told that the poem before him was written in England in the seventeenth century might be useful in helping the reader invest certain words with special meanings or in helping him hear rightly the tone of the speaker. But he could not do either of these things unless he already knew, for instance, what attitudes the

---

* Reprinted from *Collected Poems*, by William Butler Yeats, by permission of The Macmillan Company. Copyright © 1912, renewed 1940 by Bertha Georgie Yeats.

seventeenth century had toward God, man, the universe, kings, love, and empires. And if the reader's knowledge of the literary tradition and the world view is to facilitate his reading, it cannot be merely a compilation of factual data. His knowledge must have engendered a kind of *feeling* for the period, a feeling that makes it possible, for example, for him to sense the ground of religious certainty and belief that underpins the overt brashness, familiarity, and this-worldliness of much seventeenth-century religious poetry.

We have been suggesting some ways that our primary aim would control our use of background information in the teaching of literature. If we were aiming to teach students *about* works — the work as it relates to its cultural context or to the history of the literature it belongs to — then biographical and historical information would, of course, be important *in itself*. But, to a reader, such information is significant only if, directly or indirectly, it facilitates his experiencing what the work is expressing.

This is true also of information about literary devices. If we are trying to help students become sensitive readers, we would feel no need to ask them to label and categorize the devices in works. Readers do not have to do these acts. They have to be able, first, to *recognize*, consciously or unconsciously, the presence of the various literary devices; and, secondly, to respond appropriately to them, singly and in concert, as they function in the work they are reading. The same literary devices recur repeatedly. But they are used variously. What *readers* must learn is to respond to the peculiar *use* made of the devices in each new context. So this is what we must ask them about. Once a reader has seen what a certain device is doing as part of the organization of a work, then the name of the device is simply a convenient shorthand, useful when he wants to talk concisely about how the effect he has noticed is being evoked.

If the process of identifying and classifying devices becomes an end in itself, it is not just an unproductive activity for readers: it is a detrimental one. The student who, for instance, pigeonholes the "bluebirds that go walking on the grass" as a visual image is moving away from the *living* work to generalize this particular use of a literary device into a *static* category. This act of classifying makes him, furthermore, lose sight of two important facts; first, that several different means (image, rhythm, sound, and "plain stile" diction) coexist in this one line and function together, affecting one another in a dynamic whole; and, secondly, that *all* these devices are interrelated with others elsewhere in the work.

Classifying always results in a piecemeal, moribund description of what is essentially a vital unity. Sometimes, especially in the case of rhythm, formal description is actually made false by the function of the line in the poem. If, for example, a student formally describes line 12 of "Blue Girls" — "It is so frail" — as iambic dimeter, he would have classified the line correctly, but, of course, this is not the correct description of the rhythm of *this line in this poem*. Read in the context of this poem, the line is spoken with at least three heavy accents. And by design — in order to overstress this crucial line, so that the reader will not miss it, so that he will feel its full impact, word by word. Furthermore, the variation in rhythm is not working alone to produce this effect; it is supported by the marked shortness of the line, a shortness intensified by having the line follow the longest line in the poem. But the student who is just formally tagging devices is insensitive to this interdependence that is so crucial to the reader's experience of the poem.

In the last few pages we have been mentioning *some* of the general methods that would (and would not) be valid in terms of our aims. And in the succeeding sections of this book we shall be detailing and specifying valid methods for classroom practice. The matter of valid methods deserves the attention we give it. For, in the "chain of command" that links the nature of literature, its functions, the aims for teaching, the works to be taught, and the methods for teaching them, the broken link is most commonly that between aim and method: the teacher aims for one end and uses a teaching method that cannot achieve the aim.

Why does he do this? Occasionally, because he has not spelled out his aim so that he knows precisely in terms of behaviors what it involves and what he must do to achieve it. Occasionally, because he decides or assumes that some of his students — the non-academic, usually — are incapable of achieving the aim or because he fears he is incapable of getting them to achieve it. So instead of teaching them to read, for instance, he "plays safe" — he entertains them with films, records, anecdotes, oratory, or projects. Generally, however, the teacher uses invalid methods because, as anyone who has tried knows, it is difficult to adapt valid methods for students who are less able or uninterested. It taxes the imagination to create appropriate reading tasks, phrase simple but not oversimplified questions, and prepare usable writing assignments — all properly spaced and paced to provide variety while reinforcing and deepening and intensifying the skills being learned. To discover feasible ways to teach literature *validly* to these students is our greatest challenge.

There is no danger that a teacher will long use unfeasible methods — public pressure in the classroom will soon dissuade him. But there is a danger that when the demand for ingenuity becomes great, he will choose whatever method "works" — its invalidity notwithstanding. And when he uses an invalid method, his students will be, at the end of that lesson, as far away from achieving the aim as they were before that lesson started — however successful the method may have been in *other* ways.

Aim and method are related as end and means. For every question we write, for every exercise we give, every aid we use, we must *always* be asking: In what way does this help students achieve this aim? And we must answer *most honestly* — not justifying the device as "a good experience for them to have" — most things are that! Exactly how has the device moved *these* students closer to achieving the aim? On that basis and on that alone rests its value as a method of teaching.

The worth of any *method of testing* depends upon the extent to which it reveals students' progress toward achieving the aim. We give written questions, quizzes, short and long papers, and tests because we want to know, at many successive points during the teaching of a unit, "where students are" in terms of their achievement of the aim.

Evaluative devices must, then, be valid; that is, they must measure what they purport to measure. If that is students' skill in some phase of reading works, then the test cannot be one that simply asks them to tell what they have learned about a work studied in class. It must offer them new material similar to what they have practiced on and must ask them to perform similar tasks. If a testing device is not valid, we cannot know at all whether or not the students have achieved the particular aim. So we have no useful guide for the further teaching of the skill.

Evaluative devices must, moreover, be reliable; that is, they must be designed so that they will indicate the precise degrees to which various students achieved the aim. The questions or essay topics must be devised so as to allow answers of many qualities. If the testing device is not reliable, we cannot know accurately whether we should revert or progress, or who needs help and what kind of help he needs. We have a guide for further teaching, but it is a gross one. We are not much better off than if we had made a rough estimate of students' progress on the basis of oral responses.

So we conclude our discussion of the six crucial questions for which a teacher must develop internally consistent answers if he is to have a position to guide his practice. In the remainder of this book we show how the position we have been detailing would be carried out in the teaching of imaginative and nonfictional literature. We show how our two general aims — to help students learn to read works as works of literature and to enable them to engage in advanced modes of literary study — are analyzed into particular aims and how those aims are sequenced for learners. We suggest many works to teach each particular device. We offer plans for the actual classroom teaching of certain uses of language. We show how the same basic question may be phrased for different kinds of learners. But the most important thing we try to do in the pages that follow is to show how the position that our discussion of the six crucial questions has defined affects *all* our practical decisions — from the most general to the most specific.

NOTES

1. To see exactly where the study of this poem would come in the first course in reading poems—and to see what alternate poems we might have chosen to achieve this same aim, see page 151 of this text.

2. From John Stuart Mill, "What Is Poetry?" *The Monthly Repository, 1806–1838,* 7 (Jan. 1833), pp. 60–70.

3. For his full discussion of the organization of a poem, see Charles Lalo, "The Aesthetic Analysis of a Work of Art, An Essay on the Structure and Superstructure of Poetry," *The Journal of Aesthetics and Art Criticism,* 7 (June 1949), pp. 275–283.

4. For somewhat similar views on the cognitive and moral functions of literature, see Robert B. Heilman, "Literature and Growing Up," Dwight L. Burton and John S. Simmons (eds.), *Teaching English in Today's High Schools* (New York: Holt, Rinehart and Winston, Inc., 1965), pp. 37–41.

5. Literature reveals, among other things, the humor in situations—something to which most of our students are *singularly* obtuse. For a delightful exposé on this topic, see Howard Storm, "Shut Up, I Explained," *English Journal (EJ),* 56 (Feb. 1967), pp. 208–210.

6. The references that follow are, in turn, to Emily Dickinson's "Presentiment," Issa's haiku "The Vision," Gerard Manley Hopkins' "Spring and Fall," Alfred, Lord Tennyson's "Flower in the Crannied Wall," and Walter de la Mare's "Night."

7. For an interesting article in which students "testify" that the reading of literature educates their capacity for moral imagination, see Nick Aaron Ford, "What High School Students Say About Good Books," *EJ,* 50 (Nov. 1961), pp. 539–545.

8. For a fine article on sensitive reading as an aim, see Margueritte J. Caldwell, "Who Speaks for Reading?" *EJ,* 56 (Feb. 1967), pp. 245–248. For discussion of a similar aim, see Grace Beam Smith's report on Dr. Powell Stewart's program for improving the teaching of English, "Not *the* Method, But a Method," *EJ,* 54 (May 1965), p. 380.

9. Does this mean that some can never enjoy literary value? It does not. Degrees of literary experience *are* available to everyone; it is the extent and the quality of the experience that vary with the individual reader. See Leonard Wolf, "Teaching a Poem," Kinescripts, Set I, Commission on English (New York: CEEB, 1965), p. 3.

10. In the second part of this text—"The Theory In Practice"—we detail three first courses to show how students might be helped to achieve our primary aim. And we suggest a wide variety of second and later courses to show how we could implement our second aim in all kinds of classes.

11. They often are not. They are pretended by students who, for some reason—perhaps a poor grade, perhaps a squelch—dislike the teacher. They choose this mode of retribution because they know the value of such an issue—what unquestioned support they will get from schoolmen and community alike.

12. The Commission on English believes that no reading or study of a work is complete without such consideration of "possible extrinsic meaning." *Freedom and Discipline in English* (New York: CEEB, 1965), pp. 72–73.

13. For a valid, untechnical article on the question, "If a poem can have many meanings, why not *any* meaning?" see Laurence Perrine, "The Nature of Proof in the Interpretation of Poetry," *EJ, 51* (Sept. 1962), pp. 393–398.

REFERENCES

I. The Nature of Literature

BEARDSLEY, MONROE C. *Aesthetics, Problems in the Philosophy of Criticism.* New York: Harcourt, Brace and Co., 1958. The following chapters are perhaps the most directly relevant: chapters 3—"The Literary Work"; 5—"Form in Literature"; 9—"Literature and Knowledge"; 11—"Aesthetic Value"; and 12—"The Arts in the Life of Man." But the reader who bypasses the chapters on "Aesthetic Objects," "Artistic Form," and "Artistic Truth" misses a great deal. This is not really a difficult book; it can be comfortably read by anyone who is interested and careful and has "cut some teeth" on a book like the following.

DAICHES, DAVID. *A Study of Literature.* New York: W. W. Norton and Co., Inc., 1964. This book is a pleasant, useful introduction to the nature of works of literature and to the varieties and the values of literary experience.

DEWEY, JOHN. *Art As Experience.* New York: Minton, Balch and Co., 1934. (Now published in paper as a Capricorn Book) Though this enlightening book is not for "beginning" readers in aesthetics, one of the crucial chapters, Chapter 3—"Having an Experience," is quite readable.

HOSPERS, JOHN. *Meaning and Truth in the Arts.* Chapel Hill: The University of North Carolina Press, 1948.

KRIEGER, MURRAY, and ELISEO VIVAS. *The Problems of Aesthetics: A Book of Readings.* New York: Rinehart and Co., 1953. It is valuable for a teacher of literature to see the art he teaches set in the context of the other arts. Exploring the problems of creator, art object, and perceiver helps him to be aware of what he can mean when he says he "teaches literature." Both this book and Beardsley's relate the arts so that the teacher can readily understand the similarities and the differences among them.

LANGER, SUZANNE. *Problems of Art: Ten Philosophical Lectures.* New York: Charles Scribner's Sons, 1957. Essays 7–10 are probably the most relevant.

II. The Criticism of Literature

DAICHES, DAVID. *Critical Approaches to Literature.* Englewood Cliffs, N. J.: Prentice-Hall, Inc., 1956. An overview of theories of literature from Plato to the present, of critical methods from the Elizabethans to the moderns, and of the relation of other disciplines to literary criticism.

GOODMAN, PAUL. *The Structure of Literature.* Chicago: The University of Chicago Press, 1954. For those interested in seeing how inductive formal analysis is applied to certain plays and poems.

OLDSEY, BERNARD S., and ARTHUR O. LEWIS, JR. (eds.). *Visions and Revisions in Modern American Literary Criticism.* New York: E. P. Dutton Co., Inc., 1966. This inexpensive paperback offers nineteen essays, each of which represents some "school" that has influenced American criticism since 1911. Some of the essayists are H. L. Mencken, Van Wyck Brooks, T. S. Eliot, Cleanth Brooks, Lionel Trilling, F. O. Matthiessen, R. P. Blackmur, Allen Tate, and Richard Chase.

RICHARDS, I. A . *Practical Criticism: A Study of Literary Judgment.* New York: Harcourt, Brace and Company, 1929. This still valuable book presents students' responses to poems and an analysis of these responses which reveals some basic problems students have in reading literature critically.

SCHORER, MARK, JOSEPHINE MILES, and GORDON MACKENZIE (eds.). *Criticism: The Foundations of Modern Literary Judgment.* New York: Harcourt, Brace and Company, 1948. A collection of fifty-five significant essays in literary criticism from Plato to the present arranged under three headings: (1) Source—where art comes from; the artist's experience, the matter that goes into art (nineteen essays); (2) Form—how art becomes what it is: the structural elements that compose the work, the formal means (twenty essays); and (3) End—what art does: the response of the audience, the functions of art (sixteen essays).

SCOTT, WILBUR. *Five Approaches of Literary Criticism.* New York: Collier Books, 1962. Each of the five current approaches to literary criticism—the moral, the psychological, the sociological, the formalistic, and the archetypal—are discussed briefly and are illustrated by a group of three essays. A fine book for those who would like to see any or all of these five approaches actually applied to the criticism of works.

III. The Teaching of Literature

These are not "how to do it" books. They are, rather, discussions of positions, some of which are illustrated by instances of teaching practice.

FRYE, NORTHROP. *The Educated Imagination.* Bloomington, Ind.: Indiana University Press, 1964.

HOLBROOK, DAVID. *English for Maturity.* Cambridge, Eng.: Cambridge University Press, 1961.

ROSENBLATT, LOUISE. "A Performing Art," *EJ*, 55 (Nov. 1966), pp. 999–1005.

―――. *Literature As Exploration.* New York: D. Appleton-Century Co., Inc., 1938.

Because we have tried to call attention to less well-known sources of theoretical and practical help, we have, so far, bypassed two extensive bodies of research. We are referring, on the one hand, to the large scale curriculum studies being made at such curriculum study centers as Carnegie Tech, Hunter College, and the University of Oregon. We are referring, on the other hand, to the publications of the Commission on English. Descriptive lists of current and completed curriculum research projects are available annually from the National Council of Teachers of English (NCTE): both information about particular projects and materials may be obtained from the project director at the address given on the NCTE list. The publications of the Commission on English—including its "position paper," *Freedom and Discipline in English,* the Kinescripts, and the still very valuable *End-of-Year Examinations in English*—may be obtained from the Executive Director, 475 Commonwealth Avenue, Boston, Massachusetts.

IV. Handbooks of Terms

Handbooks are helps "in a pinch"! Looking up a definition in a handbook is, however, no substitute for building up an understanding of a literary concept by responding to a wide variety of its uses, or by reading an extended analytic treatment of the device. But teachers with five classes a day are often "in a pinch," so we suggest three handbooks any one of which might be used until it is possible to consult the kinds of studies listed in the references of the following three sections of this text.

ABRAMS, M. H. *A Glossary of Literary Terms.* New York: Holt, Rinehart and Winston, 1962. (105 pages)

BARNET, SYLVAN, MORTON BERMAN, and WILLIAM BURTO. *A Dictionary of Literary Terms.* Boston: Little, Brown and Company, 1960. (96 pages)

THRALL, WILLIAM FLINT, and ADDISON HIBBARD. *A Handbook to Literature.* New York: The Odyssey Press, 1960. (598 pages)

THE THEORY
IN PRACTICE

PRELIMINARIES

In order to translate our position into practice, we had to decide, first, on an overall plan to achieve our two general aims. There were many options. We chose to organize in terms of first courses, second courses, and later courses. First courses are basic studies aimed at teaching students to read works sensitively; in other words, they are courses devised to help students achieve our primary aim. There are three first courses: one introduces students to the reading of poems, another to the reading of plays, and the third to the reading of fiction. During each of these courses, we try to help students develop basic reader responses which they will, then, vary and strengthen in their later studies of literature. These three first courses are crucial foundations. So, in these courses, *all students* should have the best teaching the English department can provide.

Second courses and later courses are advanced studies aimed at enhancing and diversifying students' skills as readers and at introducing them to more specialized kinds of literary study: thematic, comparative, and contextual studies, for instance. In other words, these courses, which would follow the introductory courses the same year and/or in later years, are designed to help students achieve our second general aim for the study of literature. Under no circumstances would these second and later courses simply "mark time" or repeat a somewhat disguised first course. Rather, they would continue the work of the first course, progressively increasing students' abilities to read works of many kinds and deepening their knowledge of the nature of literature. So, by the time these readers finished high school, they would be as skilled and as knowledgeable as their capacities allowed.

Once we settled on the overall plan, we had to decide on the character of our first courses. Since, as our plan implies, we had already chosen to organize in discrete courses, rather than in one all-inclusive introduction to literature, we now had only three questions to answer.

First: Should the first courses be organized so that the uses of language involved in reading each genre are studied *simultaneously* or *discretely?* For instance, in the first course in reading poems, should students be learning to respond to diction, syntax, metaphor, and rhythm simultaneously or successively? There are no data to tell us which of the two ways is more effective, and there are no tests to ascertain this kind of information. But much has been said on both sides. Those who support simultaneous study of all relevant devices insist that to distinguish certain literary uses of language for discrete study is to make artificial distinctions. They remind us that a work of literature *is* an artistic unity and, in the responsive reading of it, all of the reader's sensitivities are functioning simultaneously. So to study all uses simultaneously is to come about as close as one can to making the learning correspond to the task the learner must finally perform. Those who use this type of organization generally arrange a goodly number of poems, or plays, or stories in an ordering of increasing complexity and have students read each work as exhaustively as possible.

Those who, on the other hand, hold for successive study of the relevant uses of language agree that a work of literature is an artistic unity and that a sensitive reading is a unified response. But they believe that most beginning readers need to have the various uses of language emphasized successively, that an intensive concentration on each of the relevant uses of language is a better way to ensure the reader's steady movement toward the goal of sensitive reading. They also believe that discrete study of uses makes it easier for the teacher to diagnose learning difficulties and to know, continually and precisely, the strengths and weaknesses of the class.

We agree with this second group. And so, in the three first courses that we propose, the uses of language relevant to the reading of each genre are focussed on *successively.*

Whether or not discrete study unnaturally categorizes language devices and violates the integrity of the works read depends entirely upon how the works are taught. A focus need not be exclusive attention; it can be attention to one thing in terms of others — so that many devices are always being noticed but with degrees of attention that vary according to the main interest at the time. Focus can, in fact, be handled so unobtrusively that students need never be conscious that one device is being emphasized or that they are now concluding the study of one use of language and beginning the study of another. Discrete study does not, furthermore, entail a rigid, formalized treatment of works nor a direct teaching of critical terminology. The teacher may stress critical terminology or not, and he may teach it directly or indirectly, whether he teaches the devices simultaneously or discretely. There is nothing *in the nature* of the discrete study of the uses of language, however systematically carried on, that would cause or occasion invalid use of works, the imposing of "systems," or any other aesthetically deleterious effects.[1]

Second: Can the same kind of first course be taught to different grade levels and different sorts of students? It can — if it is suitably varied in the intensity of the treatment, in the works chosen, and in the methods used to teach the works. The uses of language that a reader of a certain genre must respond to are the same — whatever the grade, whatever the group. The teacher's leeway is only in the materials and the methods, in the pace and the intensity, of the study. The first courses that we suggest in the following sections of this book offer, at every point, a wide variety of works, modes of questioning, and exercises from which a teacher can build many different valid and feasible first courses for high school classes.

Third: Which genre should students learn to read first? Once again, there are no data to direct our decision; only opinions to persuade us that this is the "easy" genre to begin with, or that is the "natural" one. But, works of literature being what they are, there are no simple beginnings — only more or less justifiable ones. To us, it seems most justifiable to begin with poems. For, the reading of poems is the most economical entrée to reading literature.

THE TEACHING OF POEMS

Poetry is the central genre; it is the form in which words are exploited most continually, most variously, and most intensively. Consequently, the precise and imaginative reading of poems will heighten the sensitivity of students' responses to the language of plays, fiction, and nonfiction. Furthermore, a poem is the most *frankly* "made," the most *openly* demanding, and the most *obviously* organized form of literature. Consequently, the reading of poems *forces* students to develop attitudes that are crucial to their experiencing any work of literature.

Because a poem is so frankly "made," it compels the reader to recognize immediately that a work of literature is a composition of selected materials, artificially ordered, framed. The way language is used in poems is always reminding the reader that someone *made* this this way for a reason. So, the reading of poems helps students develop the distance they must have if they are to avoid confusing their experience of plays and of stories with life.

Because a poem is so openly demanding of the reader, it forces him to develop the alert, attentive attitude that perceiving any work of literature requires. If the reader of a poem is unobservant and listless, all he gets is the memory of a phrase or two and frustration. No one need convince him he did not "get" the poem. He cannot emerge, as he often can from the reading of a story, with a plot and a smug conviction that he has all there is. Reading poems helps students become aware, perceptive readers, prepared to see more in plays and stories than narrative lines and more in nonfiction than a mass of facts.

63

Because a poem is obviously organized, it is possible for the reader to see readily how various uses of language structure a work and to notice how these structures function together to render meaning. The reading of such a frankly designed form of literature prepares students for seeing how elements count in the longer, more complicated, less obviously organized forms of literature.

For all these reasons, we begin with poems.[2]

Enticing Resistant Readers

But high school students "hate poetry"!

It is true that in some classes if the teacher announces a forthcoming study of poems, some students will groan. Some do so because this is the expected response — and they do not want to disappoint the teacher! Others groan because, for them, the announcement has in the past signaled the onset of memorizing mystifying lines, identifying allusions, figures, and meters, enduring rhapsodies on beauty, hacking through "great" poems. Students who groan for these reasons are not groaning about reading poems. They may never have read a poem; they probably do not know how one "works." They groan because of what they have been led to think reading poems consists of. Granted that when they do begin to read poems, some may still groan — and others may start! But at least they will then be groaning about the substance, not the shadow. It is the substance we must get them to experience — dislike it then, if they will!

In most classes, we can begin our first course in reading poems without any preliminaries. But in certain sincerely resistant classes a circuitous approach may be advisable. How can we entice the reluctant and obstinate to begin to read poems?

We can start without a word of warning and ease into our reading of poems — beginning during the study of composition, for instance. If students are working on expository writing, we might use, as an early assignment, an exercise in writing two definitions — one denotative, one metaphoric — for the same word. In preparation for this writing task, we would work out with the class pairs of definitions for such words as "hate," "moon," "lightning," "skaters." As models for the metaphoric definitions, we would examine, without identification or telltale marks, such lines from poems as: Hate is "Fear's ugliest child" (Elizabeth Coatsworth); "The moon is the North Wind's cooky" (Vachel Lindsay); the moon "is a child's balloon, forgotten after play" (T. E. Hulme); "The moon is a golden petal" (D. H. Lawrence); "The lightning is a yellow fork [dropped]/From tables in the sky" (Emily Dickinson); the skaters are "black swallows swooping or gliding/In a flurry of entangled loops and curves" (John Gould Fletcher). When the students write their own pairs of definitions, using the preceding words or "new" topics, they will be not only creating a crucial poetic figure but also impressing upon themselves the nature and function of metaphor and the difference between factual and artistic truth. (A large return for an unimposing exercise!)

If the composition "work in progress" includes such common types of assignments as a paragraph description of a person or a paragraph character study, we would prepare students for this writing task by examining, as *one* of the models, a character poem, which we would write out in paragraph form. Such poems as William Carlos Williams' "Lighthearted William," or T. S. Eliot's "Aunt Helen," or Edwin Arlington Robinson's "Aaron Stark," or any of a large number of "portraits" from Edgar Lee Masters' *Spoon River Anthology* would be useful. If, in response to the assignment, any students wrote poem-paragraphs, we would probably discuss the language of these with the class, and possibly divide one of these into lines that emphasize crucial words and effects.

If the composition "work in progress" includes such tasks as a description of a scene or the response of a character to an object or a scene, we would assign, as a topic for a paragraph theme, the central image of some poem, say, Richard Wilbur's "Boy at the Window" (a small child inside laments the snowman's being outside) or Ted Robins' "The Dive" (an observer's slow-motion description of one dive) or Robert Francis' "The Base Stealer" (a sportscaster's view of a ball player stealing a base).[3] After the writing, we would discuss the "poem qualities" in students' papers and then show students how another person — the poet — responded to the same central image. Our discussion of the poem would center on what the poet "made of" the image; that is the students' immediate interest and our long-range interest.

In certain classes, we might use all three of these kinds of assignments in a week-long study of composition that would lead steadily through writing into the reading of poems. But whether we used such a block of writing or just a task or two as an entrée, we would try to make the shift to the study of poems virtually imperceptible. Any overt transition or introduction defeats the whole purpose.

We can also ease into reading poems by another, quite different route. Poems are "verbal contraptions"; so we can exploit the puzzle value of a poem. Without mentioning poems at all, we could engage the class in solving a series of increasingly difficult puzzles, using such short poems as Robert Frost's "One Guess," his "Assurance," his "Lodged," or his "A Question"; or Emily Dickinson's "To Make a Prairie" or her "Surgeons Must be Very Careful." As an easy first exercise, we would ask students to read, say, Frost's "One Guess" and write a sentence telling *how they know* what the object is. In the discussion following their writing, we would make sure students recognized that if they did not notice all of the clues they could not be certain of the object. (We would ask: What else might have "dust in his eyes and a fan for a wing"? and so on.)

We would follow this exercise directly with one on a poem like Frost's "Assurance":

> The danger not an inch outside
> Behind the porthole's slab of glass
> And double ring of fitted brass
> I trust feels properly defied.*

After students had read the poem, we would ask them orally how they knew what the "danger" was; doing this would reinforce what they had learned through the first exercise. Then, we would ask them to write a sentence telling *why* the sea should feel "properly defied." The discussion of their answers would call attention to the irony of the situation, to the triumph of man over nature, and to the implications of personifying the situation.

For our third exercise, we would use a poem like Emily Dickinson's "To Make A Prairie":

> To make a prairie it takes a clover and one bee,
> One clover, and a bee,
> And revery.
> The revery alone will do,
> If bees are few.†

Our question would be: Does the speaker mean that "revery" is the only thing necessary "to make a prairie"? Or what does she mean? And we would continue with still more puzzles, and more challenging ones, as long as they were needed — without much worry about time — because, though we would not have mentioned poems or poetry, we would, of course, have already begun the first course.

The success of the "puzzle-clue-solution" approach depends largely

---

* Reprinted from *Complete Poems of Robert Frost* by permission of Holt, Rinehart and Winston, Inc. Copyright © 1923, 1928, 1939, 1967 by Holt, Rinehart and Winston, Inc. Copyright 1942, 1951, 1956 by Robert Frost.

† Reprinted from *The Complete Poems of Emily Dickinson* by permission of Little, Brown and Company. Copyright © 1960.

on the teacher's attitude and acumen. If he is vitally engaged in the solving of the puzzles and if he is able to ask *the* little question that spotlights the last clue, the question that impels discovery, he can, through this device, do much to avert possible hostility. No one who has every played the game of words with an initially lethargic or reluctant class has ever forgotten that fine moment when, the interpretation of the puzzle quite agreed upon, he called attention to that little word that overturned it. Recognition, delight, consternation — the effect is electric. Who leads students to such exciting discoveries? Teachers who are themselves always discovering because they are always looking on familiar texts with innocent eyes.

There are many other ways of "softening up" pockets of resistance.[4] But, like the two simple approaches we have just described, whatever means we employ not only should avoid what might raise the "ghost of poetry past" but should focus students' attention on the literary uses of language. Any means used to dissipate resistance *must be* an *intrinsic* part of the study of the subject matter. Even during the "softening up," students must be learning, however covertly, to read poems. Enticements should never be synthetic "come-ons." They must not be. For such extrinsic motivations are not only dishonest but ineffective. After the ruse has been used, the teacher is left still trying to find a way to lead students into the subject matter.

So much for our devious routes into the course. Now, to the course itself.

A First Course in Reading Poems

What uses of language should we emphasize? In what order should we focus on them?

Those who have discussed the dimensions of poems[5] and those who have written introductions to the study of poetry[6] all generally agree that a reader of poems must be able to respond sensitively to diction and syntax, sound and rhythm, image, metaphor, and symbol — as these uses of language are exploited in poems and as they are interrelated (in what is variously referred to as a "pattern," "performance," "design," "plot") to render an experience. There is, however, far less agreement on how these uses should be grouped for teaching and on the order in which they should be taught.[7] Some writers have, for instance, grouped all kinds of comparison and substitution under "image," while others have subdivided them into "image," "metaphor," "personification," "metonymy," "symbol," and "allegory." And although all writers seem to agree that the final emphasis should be on the poem as a total structure, some begin with rhythm and sound, some with diction, some with "voice" or tone. Beyond that, the orderings used by the various writers reveal no pattern. And, once again, there are no data to suggest what grouping of uses or what ordering of them "works" best, or better than another.

The variance among the orders the writers use *may* suggest only that different orders worked better for different teachers. But this is assuming that feasibility was the sole criterion for decision. It might not have been. Some teachers might have chosen to begin with diction because that is most central. Some, with sound and rhythm because, to students, those are the hallmarks of poetry; to begin with them is to begin with the familiar. Some teachers might have chosen to start with metaphor because that is the "most distinctively poetic" use of language. Some, with "voice," or tone, or poem as a performance because all these help students perceive poems as wholes immediately and continually.

We belong to the last group, although the order we shall propose differs somewhat from any of those used by other writers. We arrange our course in five sections.

In the first section, the Introduction, we concentrate on two aspects of dramatic organization: dramatic situation and dramatic movement. In the teaching of this section, we would be helping students recognize not only who speaks to whom about what but also how a knowledge of the "situation" affects their response to the poem. And we would be helping them pay attention to how a poem progresses from its opening to its close by a succession of shifts of attitude, changes in feeling, "motion and countermotion."

The body of our course consists of three sections. In the First Part, we emphasize the significance of the connotation, the sound, and the placement of single words and of chains of words and the function of syntactic and rhythmic patterns. In the Second Part, we focus on language that makes the reader think of one thing in terms of another: comparisons, metaphors, symbols. In the Third Part, we emphasize tone and attitude. In the final section, the Conclusion, we help students notice how various kinds of structures — conventional forms, metaphoric patterns, dramatic patterns, and other kinds of organizing devices — work to render the experience of the poem.

How do we justify the order of study we have just suggested? As we said, we favor an organization that focuses on the poem as a whole immediately and continually. Ours does. Attention to dramatic movement demands attention to the whole poem, and since our course would be cumulative, the studies of diction and syntax, metaphor, and tone that follow the Introduction would always be refining, now in this respect, now in that, a whole experience. Each of the emphases in the body of the course would be adjusting the lens to sharpen the initial picture.

This order of study seems "right" not only aesthetically but also psychologically. Every reader wants to know immediately what a poem "means"; he feels the need of a "hand-hold," something understandable to cling to while he explores. So great is this need that a reader will either take a hold or abandon the poem. Our job is to lead him immediately to a productive hold on the whole poem, one that *is usable* for further exploration. We must protect him from the frustrations of grasping abortive "meanings" and from the confusions of having many pieces without a pattern to fit them into.

Teachers have long used two other general ways of helping readers to a productive hold. Some have asked students to "sum up the poem in a sentence," or to say what it is "about," or to express each stanza in a sentence. Others have begun the study of poetry with narrative poems, since such poems ensure the reader's having a story line to cling to.

In what ways is dramatic movement a more productive hold than these two others? It is the progression of the poem *as an experience*. It encompasses all of the poem. It characterizes all poems. "Summary" does not meet these criteria. Neither does "story" — which is, of course, only *part* of the dramatic movement of *one kind* of poem. If, by any chance, the study of any poem were arrested at summary, or a narrative poem at story, consider how far short of the experience of the poem the reader's experience would fall.[8] If, however, the study of a poem ended at dramatic movement, the reader would have at least a partial hold on the whole poem *as a poem*.

Now, why did we choose to refine the reader's initial experience of the poem by concentrating first on diction and syntax, then metaphor, then tone? This series of emphases is, we think, a natural progression from simplicity to complexity in the use of words. Students are asked to notice, first, how the connotation, the sound, and the placement of single words affect the experience of the poem; then, how connotative and sound patterns, syntactic and rhythmic patterns modulate what is being expressed; then, how comparisons and metaphors clarify it; and finally, how words patterned in these several ways (connotatively, syntactically, rhythmically, metaphorically) suggest the speaker's attitude toward the experience he dramatizes.

This order of emphases seems appropriate, furthermore, because of two common problems students "bring." Many are obtuse to the literary uses of diction, of syntax, and of rhythm, and many are unfamiliar with tone *in writing*. To overcome either problem, students need time.

For, when students are habituated to responding to words only referentially, they find it difficult to learn to recognize the nonequivalence of synonyms, to sense associations, and to perceive the function of the sounds of words. They need *immediate* and *continuing* practice "fooling around" with words to free themselves from what they take for granted and to begin to see words anew. When, too, students are accustomed to responding to syntax and rhythm with a "naming of parts," it is hard for them to learn to think of these patterns as suggesting this meaning or that. They are so preoccupied with what construction a line is or what meter it is that they do not think to ask — why that construction? that meter? Slow erosion is the most effective way to dispel such firmly fixed habits of mind, so it is desirable to begin work on diction, syntax, and rhythm early in the course.

So many devices work together to "fix" tone that it takes time to prepare students who are unfamiliar with tone in writing to respond sensitively to it. Therefore, throughout the study of diction and metaphor, we would be covertly readying students for the coming focus on tone. They would be gradually learning to respond to the various uses of language that define tone and, as they listened to oral reading after oral reading, they would be developing some awareness of how a reader ascertains tone from a page. By the time they came to focus on tone, they would be formally studying the familiar. And their attention could rightly center on the function of tone. The only students who can be introduced to a study of tone without such a foreground are the few who have learned, one way or another, to "hear" discriminatingly with their eyes.

This, then, is our justification for the order of study we shall use in our first course. We have discussed the order at this length, not to justify ours as best, though it is both valid and feasible, but rather to show how we arrived at it and to suggest the kinds of considerations involved in making decisions of this sort. All teachers have to make such decisions, either with other department members or by themselves. Curriculum is just the product of many such decisions.

Before we detail our organization, let us see what our aim says about the modes of teaching and the kinds of poems we may — and should — use.

We are trying to help students learn to read poems — all poems. Consequently, our teaching of each poem must help them develop tendencies to respond sensitively to certain uses of language *wherever* and *however* they occur. Moreover, our teaching must always be emphasizing the *function* of these uses of language as *means to meaning*. Furthermore, our teaching of these means must be cumulative. It must not leave the old for the new.[9] In our study of each poem we will probably stress a certain use of language, but concurrently we must be reinforcing all other uses emphasized so far. As we focus on each use of language, we must give it primary formal attention, not to the exclusion of the others, but in relation to them. Our aim, then, requires that our teaching help readers develop a flexible skill, so that they may be able to have a rich response to any poem — as a whole.

Now, what sorts of poems should students read to achieve the aim of the first course? The poems must, of course, be appropriate to students' concerns and to their current ability to respond to literary language.[10] Furthermore, the poems must be a representative sample: lyric, narrative, dramatic, comic, serious, satiric — no poems are "off limits" for the reader we are trying to develop. Beyond these general requirements, four other "rules" regulate our choices.

The poems should be short, for short poems can be given many readings. Each reading leads to new discoveries — and to the recognition of how inadequate initial readings are ("Who would have thought there was all that in it?") and indeed, how partial *all* readings are. Furthermore, if poems are short, students can study many poems, and, as their reading experience increases, so their aptitude for making fitting responses increases, too. Moreover, unless poems are short, beginning readers cannot "hold them together" as they notice various parts: at the least, the poem goes intermittently out of focus; at the worst, the experience of the poem is lost. Finally, the poems chosen must be short, since the study of works in a first course must be intensive. It is a rare beginner who can sustain an intense pitch and postpone reward through the reading of a long poem.

The poems chosen for study should be free of features that make special demands on the reader. They should, for instance, be as free as possible of allusions — classical, biblical, geographical, literary — *even* if students are adequately versed in such information. Beginning readers should learn to respond first to the various ways in which ordinary words work in a poem before they are required to make the complex responses demanded by such references. If we abide by this rule, we must, of course, postpone the reading of all those fine poems that are jeweled with allusions. We must also forego poems that require knowledge of a particular philosophy, of certain literary conventions, or of the intellectual or cultural history of an age. We say "require" because we are referring to only those poems in which such information is a *necessary condition* to giving certain words and modes of expression their relevant meanings. We refer not only to such poems as Milton's "Lycidas," Herbert's "Love," Marvell's "The Garden," Pope's "The Rape of the Lock," Wordsworth's "Ode on the Intimations of Immortality," and Keats' "The Eve of Saint Agnes," but also to such poems as Emerson's "Brahma," much of Whitman's "Song of Myself," and many of the poems of

Yeats, Pound, and Eliot. The reading of many poems which use references is, of course, enhanced by the reader's having such special knowledge, but the poems can be experienced adequately — indeed richly — without it.

The poems chosen should be ones that "naturally" stress the particular use of language being emphasized.[11] Careful readings of such poems will force students to respond more frequently, more variously, and more intensively to that use of language than to any other. The poems chosen for the teaching of any use should exhibit as great a variety of examples of the use as possible, and these examples should include simple and blatant instances, as well as complex and subtle ones. If each natural example is studied *as a poem,* the reader's sensitivity to the particular use of language the poem emphasizes will be greatly stimulated, and, at the same time, his response to all other uses will be intensified, but to a lesser degree. The teacher will be simply helping beginning readers to *let* the poem do what, being what it is, it would naturally do.[12]

Finally, the poems chosen for the first course should be ones that the teacher has found to be such personally satisfying experiences that he is eager to lead students to share them.

In the last several pages, we have been showing how the aim for our first course in reading poems affects the organization of the course, the mode of teaching, and the works chosen for study. The prologue is over. Now we shall suggest *one way* in which the five-part organization we proposed *might* be detailed into a resource plan from which a teacher could create first courses appropriate for helping many different kinds of classes learn to read poems. We stress "one way" and "might" because we are not suggesting that this is the only plan or the best one that could be derived from our organization. And we stress the creating of appropriate courses from the plan, because, like all patterns, it is something to adjust, adapt, depart from as circumstances dictate. Any detailed plan *appears* formidable and lock-step, but those who have used such plans sensibly and selectively know that it is the detailing that makes the plan capable of widely different accommodations. How a thing is used determines whether it serves its purpose or defeats it.

In every section of our plan we offer *lists* of poems[13] that would be especially effective in helping students learn to respond to the particular use of language being studied. Why do we suggest lists of poems rather than one or two poems? If we purport to teach a certain use of language to readers of different qualities, we must have on hand poems of varying literary complexity. And if we purport to teach this use to students of different ages or of different social groups, we must have on hand poems of varying subject matters and concerns. As experienced teachers know, two classes may be similar in their reading ability (both average, let us say) and different in their maturity, social orientation, and immediate concerns. (And, of course, to teach any one use of language we might need more than one poem; perhaps, one to begin on, one to reinforce that learning, and one to "grow on.") So, given these conditions, if we are to have poems (or plays or stories) that are "right" for each class, we must have a large, varied cache for the teaching of *each use* of language. Our lists try to suggest what *kind* of cache might be valuable for a teacher.

The poems in the lists are arranged roughly in order of their literary complexity and are annotated to suggest their concerns and to propose strategies for helping students learn to respond to the particular use of language being studied.

The Introduction: Two Aspects of Dramatic Organization

Through the study of a series of poems, we would be trying to help students to respond to a poem both as something said by a certain sort of person to another and as a little drama that moves — by a series of incidents or attitudes or reactions — from its opening to its close. Specifically, we would want them to hear the voice in the poem saying the words, to be able to decide what kind of person the speaker is and what his relation to the auditor is, to recognize how this sort of speaker conditions the way in which we as readers "take" the poem, and to sense how each part of the poem evolves from what precedes it and leads on to what follows it.

We shall begin with the simplest and most obvious instance of dramatic situation and dramatic movement and proceed by slow steps to the more complex and subtle instances. We are not, of course, suggesting that every class must take every step in order to achieve the goals we just listed. One class may have to; another may be able to leap from the simple beginning to the very subtle; still another may be able to begin with the subtle. The performance of each class is always signaling the teacher when to "inch along" when to "giant step." We offer this sequence of steps to suggest what seems to be an effective progression; whatever "steps" need to be taken by a particular class probably should be taken in this order.

The Simplest Instance

As far as a reader is concerned, the simplest instance of dramatic situation is one in which *both the speaker and the addressee are identified for the reader and in which the voice (or voices) is very obvious* and baldly indicative of certain human qualities. So we begin with poems that have that kind of dramatic situation. Here are six poems arranged, as we said earlier, in rough order of increasing literary complexity and annotated to suggest their dramatic situations and organizations and to propose ways we might bring students to perceive both.

In A. E. Housman's six-stanza, modern ballad, "Farewell to Barn and Stack and Tree," a young man who has just impulsively murdered his brother, Maurice, takes final leave of a friend, Terence. The kind of person the speaker is and his feeling about his act are revealed in his thoughts about his mother's aloneness, in his repeated reference to his hands as "bloody," in the simple pleasures he half-enviously wishes his friend, and in his sad recognition of the permanent loss of the life he knew. From stanza three on, the ballad is pervaded by the speaker's regret, remorse, and sad realization that his unnatural act has deprived his widowed mother of a family, and perhaps of a home, and has lost him the right to the innocent world he knew. He is not fleeing the law; he is suffering the punishment of Cain.

This poem is an easy[14] introduction to both dramatic situation and dramatic movement. For even a very ordinary student can readily discern that the first stanza sets the scene of the poem — a farewell between friends. The second stanza tells us why the scene takes place — the reader will suppose, for a moment, that the speaker is trying to escape legal punishment. And then he will see that it is just that false supposition that is corrected by the speaker's remarks in stanzas three to six. The average reader may need a prodding question or two to help him see *why* the thought of each event (lines 9–24) touches off the next and *why* the eight events are ordered as they are.

In Langston Hughes' three-stanza, free verse lyric, "Mother to Son," a mother who has persevered in her difficult life tries to motivate a discouraged, faltering son.

> Well, son, I'll tell you:
> Life for me ain't been no crystal stair.
> It's had tacks in it,
> And splinters,
> And boards torn up,   5
> And places with no carpet on the floor —
>
> But all the time
> I'se been a-climbin' on,
> And reachin' landin's,
> And turnin' corners   10
> And sometimes goin' in the dark
> When there ain't no light.

So, boy, don't you turn back.
Don't you set down on the steps
'Cause you find it's kinder hard.   15
Don't you fall now —
For I'se still goin', honey,
I'se still climbin'
And life for me ain't been no crystal stair.*

We can highlight the kind of person the mother is and the dramatic movement of the poem if we begin by asking, What do you think was happening just before the opening that the mother should say what she does in the first line? And then, Where does she give her advice to the boy? Why, then, all these preliminaries — three sentences of them? (If that question evokes no answer, or an inadequate one, then: What is the mother's purpose in describing life's stairway in such detail? What is her purpose in expressing the details *item by item?* [Notice how the arrangement of the poem on the page calls your attention to this slow listing.] How do the details in stanza two relate to those in stanza one?)

From the way she says what she says in stanzas one and two, how would you *now* describe the mother? Then, What three pieces of advice does she give her son? Why does she arrange them in this order? She called him "son" at the beginning, why does she call him "boy" now? From the way she says what she says in lines 13–15, how would you *now* describe the mother? And then, What is gained by her adding the last three lines?

The dramatic movement could, of course, be emphasized by pointing out how the stanzas reflect the logic of her persuasion, how her addresses to the boy reflect her changing feelings, how the first sentence and the last line relate. The poem is as available as Housman's and, though there is a pervading metaphor, it is a well-known one.

The five-stanza, old ballad "Lord Randal" — a play of two voices — is familiar fare in first courses. As the poem progresses — mother questioning, son answering — the reader gradually sees how different these two speakers are, how different their interpretations of the poisoning, how different the cause of sorrow is for each. Before the poem opens, the mother has suspected foul play to her noble "son," her "handsome young man." And, from the pent-up anxiety released in her first question ("Where *have* you been?") forward, she simply confirms — by a premeditated, step-by-step interrogation — her terrible suspicion. To her, Lord Randal's responses are only "evidence";

---

* Reprinted from *Selected Poems*, by Langston Hughes, by permission of Alfred A. Knopf, Inc. Copyright © 1926 by Alfred A. Knopf, Inc. and renewed 1954 by Langston Hughes.

she is insensitive to the feeling of betrayal he is suffering, to his wish
to die. Her disregard (lines 5–6) of his response (lines 3–4) initially
suggests a gap between their feeings that widens progressively as
the ballad goes on. By the final stanza, the two speakers are regret-
ting really different things, a breach which is ironically emphasized
by the similarity of the words they use. Because of its archaisms, the
poem might baffle some students, might intrigue (and so distract)
others. But it is a fine reading if the teacher wishes to convince students what a significant effect speakers have on what readers "make"
of a poem. No one who pays attention to the voices in this poem
could possibly reduce it to a murder story.

(The mother-son relationship in "Edward," a longer old ballad
[seven stanzas, fifty-five lines], might be more engaging to certain
classes than that in "Lord Randal." The dramatic movement of the
poem, with its shift of power from mother to son in the middle
stanza, would be a relatively easy and an interesting one for students
to discover.)

Enough of mothers and sons now! Enough, too, of "easy" poems.
Here, as our fourth suggestion, is a somewhat more challenging
poem, though a familiar one in first courses — A. E. Housman's seven-
stanza, "To An Athlete Dying Young." Why does the event in this
poem not affect the reader in the customary way? Partly, of course,
because of the metaphor of the victorious race that the speaker uses
to represent the funeral and the burial. But partly, too, because of
the speaker's restrained, reasonable, philosophic voice. He states
(notice the prevailing sentence form) calmly, simply, and can-
didly the truths of the human condition: death *is* the necessary
end, the "road all runners come"; success is fleeting; death ends the
evils of life. But death is lifeless, strengthless. The speaker's voice
makes the reader quietly recognize the losses not only in transient
life but also in eternal death. The study of this poem readily reveals
to students how a speaker's voice controls the experience they may
have.

Like the preceding poem, Robert Browning's "My Last Duchess"
is commonly included in first courses. It is a standard reading whenever "voice," tone, or poem as drama is being taught. In this dramatic monologue, as the Duke of Ferrara comments to a visiting
emissary on the portrait — and the nature and fate — of his last
duchess, he reveals his own personality quite graphically. Though
the poem is long — fifty-six lines — its narrative line, its clear dramatic
movement, and the conversational language of the Duke, all seem to
make it available, even to average readers. But what students sometimes fail to realize is just how crucial this casual, matter-of-fact
language is in creating the image of the Duke and in determining
how readers "take" the poem. So this is what we would stress.

Does the reader have to know the allusion to Claus of Innsbruck?
No. What he does have to recognize is why the Duke points to that
statue: the unconscious parallel between the two "tamers."

For an able class, Randall Jarrell's "A Sick Child" might be an
appropriate first poem; for an average class, a "right" second reading
or a fitting transition to the next group of poems.

> The postman comes when I am still in bed.
> "Postman, what do you have for me today?"
> I say to him. (But really I'm in bed.)
> Then he says — what shall I have him say?
>
> "This letter says that you are president   5
> Of — this word here; it's a republic."
> Tell them I can't answer right away.
> "It's your duty." No, I'd rather just be sick.
>
> Then he tells me there are letters saying everything
> That I can think of that I want for them to say.   10
> I say, "Well, thank you very much. Good-bye."
> He is ashamed, and turns and walks away.
>
> If I can think of it, it isn't what I want.
> I want . . . I want a ship from some near star
> To land in the yard, and beings to come out   15
> And think to me: "So this is where you are!
>
> Come." Except that they won't do,
> I thought of them . . . And yet somewhere there must be
> Something that's different from everything.
> All that I've never thought of — think of me!*   20

The reader knows that a child is speaking, but to whom? The
reader cannot be fully sure; the child may be talking to himself, or
to a figment of his imagination, or even to someone else. The child
is both bored and self-centered, and the poem renders successive
stages of his increasingly frustrating struggle to imagine always new,
unusual fictions in which he is the center of attention. The poem
moves from the very ordinary make-believe of the first stanza to the
monomaniac prayer of the last line.

A More Difficult Instance

As far as a reader is concerned, a more difficult instance of dramatic situation is one in which *the reader is told who the addressee*

---

* Reprinted from *The Seven-League Crutches* by Randall Jarrell (Harcourt,
Brace and World). Permission granted by Mrs. Randall Jarrell. Copyright ©
1951.

is, but has to find out for himself, from the clues the poem offers, who the speaker is. In some classes, the teacher might want to begin the first course with poems using this kind of dramatic situation; in other classes, he might want to study two or more poems like the preceding six before asking students to read any poems like the six that follow.

Carl Sandburg's little six-line poem, "Plunger," would be an appropriate reading for students who entered poetry through puzzles. Who is the "plunger"? Obviously not the addressee; he is being urged by the speaker to become one. Notice the speaker's pattern of persuasion: the imperatives, the statements (all the "great" are kin to a plunger), then the epithet (you *make* a man what you *call* him), and the imperative. Who is the "plunger"? A man afraid to risk? A man afraid to die? Both. He may be the speaker motivating himself. This is a fine little poem to show students dramatic movement in a "grain of sand."

How can we help students to realize immediately what sort of person the speaker of Alfred, Lord Tennyson's six-line "Flower in the Crannied Wall" is?

> Flower in the crannied wall,
> I pluck you out of the crannies,
> I hold you here, root and all, in my hand,
> Little flower — but if I could understand
> What you are, root and all, and all in all,
> I should know what God and man is.

We would probably begin by asking students: What sort of person would see so much in such a flower? Then, follow with: Tell in a sentence what it is that the speaker recognizes. Students' sentences will probably sag under grand, weighty phrases: "mystery of all being," "least of God's creatures," "defying the laws of nature," and such. Now, what is the difference between your phrases and those the speaker uses? Students will soon see what a simple, homely philosopher this perceptive speaker is.

How can we call students' attention to the movement of this poem? Probably by asking them why the speaker says "but" rather than "and" in line 4.

In Rolfe Humphries' sonnet, "Heresy for a Classroom," an adult speaker urges Jean, a schoolgirl, to "look out" the classroom window and "wonder" about the barrenness-to-bloom that is spring. It will be relatively easy for students to shape, from the clues in the poem, the personality of the speaker and to discern the six stages by which he moves from the statement of the first two lines to the final exclamation. But beware! Some students will so approve of certain statements in the poem that they may miss the poem. And some may come to this sonnet convinced that a Shakespearian sonnet has to have four and only four motions, so they may oversimplify the dramatic movement of this poem.

The speaker of A. E. Housman's four-stanza "Soldier from the Wars Returning" is a gracious innkeeper who is welcoming a returning soldier to the life every weary soldier dreams about — ease and idleness and freedom from all the evils of war. The host's vibrant words ring with flattering salutations, solicitous imperatives, and reassuring promises. It is not until the final line that the reader knows that the speaker is host of the "inn of night." Is it a "cheap" surprise? No; it is, rather, a paradox revealed. Like "To An Athlete Dying Young," this is a good poem to use to show students how the treatment of an event affects the reader's response to it.

We would open the study of Robert Herrick's "To the Virgins, to Make Much of Time" by asking: Whom is the speaker addressing? About what? But the speaker doesn't say a word about "using time well" until the first two lines of the last stanza. Why the delay? What strategy is the speaker employing to persuade the girls to "use their time"? If the response to this question was not precise enough, we would ask: Why does the speaker present them with the "facts of life" *in that order?* Why does the speaker present these as "facts," not counsels? How do the last two lines function in this speaker's strategy of persuasion? Through some such approach as this, students will at once perceive the successive motions of the poem and recognize what sort of person would counsel the young this way. Herrick's sixteen-line poem, which seems an appropriate choice for a class of girls, is a somewhat more challenging reading than the four preceding poems.

When a reader has grasped the dramatic situation in Robert Frost's sixteen-line lyric "Tree at My Window" he is well into the poem. For when he has defined for himself the speaker's relationship to the tree he addresses, the reader will have perceived the relationship between man and nature that the poem suggests. The two dream-heads are similar, indeed intimate, but they are crucially different, quite separate. The speaker's salutations in the first line — "Tree at my window, window tree" — suggest what the tree *is* to the speaker. Like many of Frost's other poems, this lyric seems more overt than it is.

The Most Difficult Instance

As far as a reader is concerned, the most difficult instance of dramatic situation is the one in which *he must discover for himself who is speaking, to whom,* about what, and what the speaker's attitudes toward the addressee and toward the subject are. Sometimes the poem using such a situation offers explicit clues; sometimes, mere hints. Sometimes the speaker is almost an "effaced narrator"; sometimes the poem is addressed to the reader — as a universal man. The seven poems that follow suggest the sorts of readings that would help students to learn to respond to a variety of instances of the kind of dramatic situation we have just described.

In the first three poems the clues to the situation are quite clear. Some classes need the help of such explicitness every time they begin something "new."

With what loving pleasure the speaker in Robert Frost's "The Pasture" anticipates his routine farm tasks! And with what tender indirection he confesses to his beloved how much he needs her: "I shan't be gone long. — You come too." This eight-line poem (p. 87) is, in every detail, a love lyric.

It seems as if the speaker of E. E. Cummings' one-stanza "Portrait" sets out to sardonically chide "Mister Death" for taking his own "blueeyed boy," Buffalo Bill. But when the speaker says "defunct," he realizes suddenly how ironic it is that this vital and handsome hero is lifeless. And the admiring speaker recalls, probably to himself, the prowess, speed, gusto, and theatricalism of the late hero. The poem gives readers a chance not only to experience a speaker switching addressees, but also to see how the poem on the page directs the reader.

The dazed speaker of Wilfred Owen's fourteen-line poem, "Futility," (p. 82) looks unbelievingly at the corpse of a boyhood friend. After he asks a bystander — or perhaps several — to move the corpse into the sun, the speaker first hopefully muses, half to himself, about the power of the sun to wake; then he desperately insists on it. The internal monologue finally explodes into a challenge to the sun, and a questioning of the purpose of life and of the world. The speaker addresses first the bystanders, then himself and possibly the bystanders, and, finally, the powers of the universe. From his first calm request to his last anguished question, the speaker's attitude shifts, rather obviously, about seven times. So, among other things, this is an excellent reading for helping students who are still obtuse to dramatic movement.

The next four readings use dramatic situations that tax the reader's sensitivity to this device.

Who is speaking in Robert Francis' "The Base Stealer"? Is it a sportscaster giving an eyewitness, play-by-play description of a base stealing? Probably. If the reader can identify the voice, he will see at once how the apparent interpolations work because he will recognize the sportscaster's familiar dramatic touches: goading the base stealer in line 5, chiding the team in line 9, and prolonging the suspense in line 10.

What kind of person is the speaker in Edwin Arlington Robinson's "Reuben Bright"?

> Because he was a butcher and thereby
> Did earn an honest living (and did right)
> I would not have you think that Reuben Bright
> Was any more a brute than you or I;
> For when they told him that his wife must die,   5
> He stared at them and shook with grief and fright,
> And cried like a great baby half the night,
> And made the women cry to see him cry.
> And after she was dead, and he had paid
> The singers and the sexton and the rest,   10
> He packed a lot of things that she had made
> Most mournfully away in an old chest
> Of hers, and put some chopped-up cedar boughs
> In with them, and tore down the slaughter-house.*

The speaker's reaction to Reuben Bright reveals the logic of a narrow, opinionated mind, sure of a certain correspondence between outward signs and inner reality: butchers are brutal, men who weep are gentle, and so on. The poem exposes and satirizes this kind of mind. Unless students recognize, from the clues of the first quatrain, what kind of person the speaker is, what her purpose is, and who "you" is, they may not realize how the reader is supposed to respond to the poem. They could find the poem meaningless. So, in some classes, we would probably preface the study of this poem by asking such questions as: Is a butcher necessarily cruel? What kind of person makes such connections? Listen to this sentence: "Just because John Doe is a butcher, I would not have you think that he is any more brutal than you or I." What *does* the speaker think? What does he want you to think? Then, we would read Robinson's sonnet, giving the lines all the self-righteous certainty and the maligning innuendoes the voice in the poem demands.

If it was difficult to get students to recognize what "Reuben Bright" is really about, we would ask them, What would the poem be about if we had only lines 5–14? Or, to pinpoint more, If the poem were only lines 5–14, how would the reader account for Reuben Bright's tearing down the slaughter house? What is the reader supposed to think about that incident in the sonnet as we have it?

An old favorite in first courses is Walter de la Mare's "The Listeners."

---

* Reprinted from *The Children of the Night,* by Edwin Arlington Robinson, by permission of Charles Scribner's Sons.

This thirty-six line poem will introduce students to the speaker as fictional narrator, and will prepare them for more complex variations of this device — say, in Spencer's "The Circus" or in Auden's "O Where Are You Going?" So, in the study of this poem, we would ask students, What is gained by having an omniscient narrator tell this poem? What in the poem suggests to the reader the kind of person the narrator is? and What means does the narrator use to control how the reader "takes" the poem?

Although Theodore Spencer's "The Circus; or One View of It" resounds with the classic ballyhoo of the circus man, he is not the speaker. The speaker *is* quoting the barker for about thirty-four of the thirty-six lines. Nevertheless, the slim framework does exist. Why? Why, for instance, does the poet want to put the reader at a remove from the barker? What, for instance, did the speaker "see" in the circus man's talk that he should quote it verbatim? These are the kinds of considerations we would raise to help students understand the role a speaker might have in such an organization.

Our annotations on the nineteen poems we have just cited have been largely confined to the dramatic situation and dramatic movement of the poems, for these are the emphases of this Introduction. But, as we said earlier, in the actual teaching of the poems, these particular emphases would receive special, but not sole, attention. We would be interested in many other features, and we would be stressing the way all features work together to render the meaning of the poem.

Since an illustration of how this may be done in a lesson is worth a thousand statements that it would be done, we offer now a plan for teaching one of the poems we annotated above, Wilfred Owen's "Futility."

> Move him into the sun —
> Gently its touch awoke him once,
> At home, whispering of fields unsown.
> Always it woke him, even in France,
> Until this morning and this snow.   5
> If anything might rouse him now
> The kind old sun will know.
>
> Think how it wakes the seeds, —
> Woke, once, the clays of a cold star.
> Are limbs, so dear-achieved, are sides,   10
> Full-nerved — still warm — too hard to stir?
> Was it for this the clay grew tall?
> — O what made fatuous sunbeams toil
> To break earth's sleep at all?*

---

* Printed from *The Collected Poems of Wilfred Owen* by permission of New Directions Publishing Corporation. Copyright © 1963 by Chatto & Windus, Ltd.

Most classes who would be reading this poem would have studied two or more poems previously. We would, therefore, expect students to do the "spadework" themselves, most of it as an out-of-class assignment or, in the case of some unmotivated classes, all of it as an in-class exercise on the day before the study of the poem. A crucial part of the "spadework" is, of course, sensitive reading of the poem: looking at print and hearing a voice say the words with certain pauses, speeds, inflections, rhythms, tones. So we would introduce the assignment by asking *the class* to: Read the poem "aloud to yourself," so that you can hear it in your mind's ear. Students would know, from practice, what we meant. For, from the study of the first poem on, we would have stressed hearing the poem.

When the class began the study of the first poem, we would read it orally, the students simultaneously watching the printed words and hearing a voice say the words as their "signals" directed. We would follow this oral reading with such questions as: Why was the fourth line said [repeating the line]? Why couldn't it be read this way [here we would distort the intent of the line by disregarding punctuation or the stress]? When the class studied the second poem, we would read the poem orally, students following, and we would insert a flat or wrong reading of a phrase or line and ask them to detect it — and correct it. By the time we were assigning "Futility," the students would have taken over the initial reading of the poems, reading "aloud to themselves" so that they would feel the words in their throats and hear them in their minds' ears. After such silent reading, we would ask how this phrase, that line, is said — and as the first course progressed, we would be gradually asking the same questions about stanzas, and, finally, during our study of tone, about whole poems.

But that is "getting ahead of our story"! We are still in the early stages. So, after the class finished their initial silent reading of "Futility," we would probably ask them how lines 2–3 are said (to see if they caught the wistful disjointedness of reminiscence), and lines 8–9 (to see if they sensed the excited, blurting insistence), and lines 13–14 (to see if they recognized the prolonged bitter anguish that this massing of accents suggests). Then, we would complete the assignment by reading the poem orally and distributing, to be answered in writing, such guide questions as the following:

1. What has occurred just before the poem opens?
2. What scene do you visualize at the opening of the poem?
3. Who is speaking? What is his relation to "him"?
4. To whom is he speaking in line 1? Why does he want "him" moved into the sun?
5. What reasons does the speaker give for thinking the sun will help? Be thorough and explicit.

6. To whom is he giving these reasons? How do you know? Give
   precise evidence.

We have tried to keep the wording of these questions as free from
clues as possible. The purpose of the questions is to occasion students to read the poem carefully, discover the situation for themselves, and "have it straight," so that we can spend the class time on
the study of the speaker's shifting reactions to his friend's death.
However, for some groups of students, the teacher might choose to
begin the class period asking all or some of the guide questions —
probably 4, 5, and 6 — to refresh students' memories and to provide
a firm base on which to build the lesson.[15]
We would open the in-class study of "Futility" with an oral reading[16] of the poem and a *brief* clarification of any textual problems
students had encountered. The question we really want students to
answer is: What are the speaker's reactions to his friend's death?
But we would not ask a class such a general question unless the class
was the sort that would, then, work carefully through the poem,
pointing out both the obvious and the subtle changes in the speaker's
feelings, indicating how one state of mind relates to the next, and
identifying the pattern the feelings show. It is a *rare* class that can
answer a general question in that fashion — at this point in a course.
In most classes, general questions evoke general answers. So, in the
usual class, we would put our general question on the board and ask
the class *as many* of the following questions *as necessary* to have
students perceive how the speaker moves — motion and countermotion[17] — toward his recognition. As the class gradually revealed
the "motions," we might note them on the board. This helps less able
or inattentive students to see a pattern developing; it helps all students to learn how to answer a general question and to become
capable of handling one competently — orally and in writing.
Here are the questions. Occasionally, we have suggested the
response average students would *probably* make to the question and
the "move" we would *probably* make to call their attention to what
they did not notice. The course of lessons never did run smooth!
What is the speaker's feeling in the first line? (Probably: "confident.") What suggests he is "confident"? (Probably: "giving an
order"; "the decisive way *you* say, 'Move him.'")
Now read through the remainder of the stanza very slowly and
carefully to see whether or not he becomes more confident, less confident, or has some other feelings altogether.
What feeling does he have in lines 2–3? (Probably: "confident,
because he remembers him alive, because he remembers the sun
waking him.") Is there any other feeling fused with his hope?
Why does the speaker include "whispering of fields unsown"?

What feelings are expressed in the remainder of the stanza? (Probably: "very confident in line 4, but he loses confidence; is depressed; hopeless in line 5.")

As evidence for his high confidence, students would probably offer: "Always," "even," possibly, "the decisive way you have to say line 4" and "the order of the sentence." But we *might* have to ask about those features. If so, we would use such a single question as: Would it make a difference if the line read, "It always woke him"? When students discussed line 5, we would probably have to ask: What has "this snow" to do with his feeling? And, unless someone had already pointed out that the speaker of line 4 was too insistent to be confident, then in the discussion of line 5, we would ask: Is there any hint that this loss of confidence is coming?

What are the speaker's feelings in lines 6–7? (Probably: "he's hopeful again"; "he still relies on the sun.") What is the difference between saying, "kind old sun" and "bright, hot sun"? *Is* the speaker entirely confident in these lines? If necessary: What words suggest he is not? What does an "if" clause suggest? How, then, would you describe his state of mind at the end of stanza one? (Probably: "fearful," "getting desperate," "refusing to believe what he sees is true.")

Now, read through stanza two, noticing especially the speaker's feelings in lines 8–11.

How would you describe the speaker's state of mind in these lines? (Probably: "very excited"; "the sentences are broken up the way an excited person talks"; "confident; he thinks of the big things the sun *has* done and he doesn't see why it can't revive just a man.") Then, to get the class to be more precise: What kinds of sentences is he using in these lines? *Whom* is he ordering, questioning so excitedly? After answering all these questions, students would probably be saying by now, "he's desperate;" "really lost hope." If they were not, we would probably ask, Does a confident person talk like this? Then, to call students' attention to the way the state *evolved:* Did stanza one prepare you for this state?

What does line 12 imply the speaker has realized? What is his reaction to it? (If necessary: Why, for instance, does he say "clay grew tall" — why not "man grew up"?) To whom is he speaking now?

What does the final question mean? Why does the speaker choose to put it in the *terms* he does? What is his final attitude? (Here we would want students to mention such clues to his attitude as the dash, the use of the exclamatory question, the words "fatuous" and "sun*beams*" and the rhythm to which we have referred already.) To whom is he speaking in lines 13–14?

The questioning finished, we would reread the poem to "pull it together."

To conclude the lesson, we would assign *one* of the following kinds of topics as a ten-minute written exercise. The first topic seems appropriate for an able class, the second, for less able students, the third, for the average.

1. Why is there a break between the first seven lines and the second seven? [We want to see if students noticed that the poem expands beyond the particular event, that on the basis of the event, the speaker raises a series of fundamental questions of increasingly crucial import. The shift comes at the stanza break. We *mean* to leave the question "'unguided.'"]

2. Show *from the poem* that the speaker never *really* believes that the sun can "wake" the dead man.

3. As we noticed, the speaker changes his addressee during the course of the poem. Point out how these changes suggest changes in his state of mind.

As this lesson on "Futility" suggests, there is no such thing as studying dramatic situation or dramatic organization "in a vacuum." Students have to notice the effects of certain word choices, metaphors, sentence forms, rhythms, stanza organizations, and punctuation, if they are to grasp the speaker's successive responses to the situation and understand the attitudes that constitute the dramatic movement of the poem. The study of any of the nineteen poems we suggested would *entail* students' noticing many uses of language.

They would be continually alerted to the ways words are exploited to achieve the effect needed: to the way, for instance, abstract and concrete words are fused into striking phrases — "fatuous sunbeams," "limbs so dear-achieved" ("Futility"), "ecstatic bird" ("The Base Stealer"), "final clinging heartbeat" ("Plunger"); to the way that placement can call attention to the significance of words — "That's *my*" opening "My Last Duchess" and "for *me*" closing it, "defunct" as a one-word line in "Portrait," "Little flower" opening the fourth line in "Flower in the Crannied Wall," rather than closing the third line. As students read the poems, they would be continually alerted to the various ways repetition works: "and" in "Mother to Son" points up endless hardships; "round" in "The Circus," unrelieved circularity; "delicate" in "The Base Stealer" creates an agony of suspense, and the mother's refrain in "Lord Randal" hints of the speaker's shifting feelings. Students would see how effective the colloquial "all in all" is in "Flower in the Crannied Wall." How shockingly the word "strengthless" shatters the delusion the metaphor creates in "To An Athlete Dying Young." What a load of meaning "sick at the heart" carries in "Lord Randal," "show" in "The Circus," and "sick" in "A Sick Child." Studying any of the poems suggested in our listing would naturally occasion students to notice repeatedly how ordinary words are made to achieve extraordinary feats.

And studying any of the poems would naturally call students'
attention to the ways sentence patterns and other syntactic structures are suggestively exploited. They would see how the strictly
conventional sentence structures of "Reuben Bright" help to define
the speaker and how the sudden interpolations in "Heresy in a Classroom" and the distortions of normal syntax in "A Sick Child" render
the leaps and associations of the speaker's mind-stream. How is
evidence effectively piled up in lines 18–22 in "The Circus"? By
parallel constructions. How is the poignant finality of the last stanza
of "Farewell to Barn and Stack and Tree" intensified? By inversions.
And what contributes to the wonderfully evocative power of the
last line of Frost's "The Pasture"?

> I'm going out to clean the pasture spring;
> I'll only stop to rake the leaves away
> (And wait to watch the water clear, I may):
> I sha'n't be gone long. — You come too.
>
> I'm going out to fetch the little calf   5
> That's standing by the mother. It's so young,
> It totters when she licks it with her tongue.
> I sha'n't be gone long. — You come too*

The meaning and the utter simplicity of the words contribute, of
course, but so do the expressed "You" in the imperative and the
rhythmic pattern of the sentence: the massing of accents that forces
attention on the words and the dash that arrests the reader altogether.

Whenever students try to discover the speaker's feeling or attitude
in a line or a passage in any of the poems, they will be, as we just
were, considering the effect not only of the words and the sentence
form, but also of the rhythmic pattern. They will be noticing how
the sudden regularity of line 7 in "Futility" suggests the reduction
of tension, how the rhythm of "The Circus" helps create the cease-
less, senseless whirl the poem criticizes. They will be seeing how
some metrical substitutions just "make us notice," how some rhythms
enhance our pleasure and some hint that we should not take the
"serious" poem too seriously.

As readers study the dramatic organization of a poem, they become aware, then, of the many effects that patterning certain words
in certain ways can create. So the change from the Introduction to
the First Part of the course will not be another beginning. It will be

---

* Reprinted from *Collected Poems of Robert Frost* by permission of Holt, Rinehart
and Winston, Inc. Copyright © 1923, 1928, 1939, 1967 by Holt, Rinehart and
Winston, Inc. Copyright 1942, 1951, 1956 by Robert Frost.

largely a shift in emphasis: from noticing certain features in a passing way to concentrating on them. As our lesson plan on "Futility" shows, we have noticed words like "snow," "kind old sun," "clay," "fatuous," and "sunbeams"; we have noticed that certain lines are certain kinds of sentences and others are non-sentences; and that certain lines read rapidly, others slowly — but we have noticed all these features only cursorily, as they functioned to render some "motion" in the drama of the poem. Other dimensions of the words, other connections might have "come out," but we did not press for these — nor would we have emphasized them if they had been suggested.

In the study of the poems in the Introduction, we would have paid attention to diction, syntax, and rhythm only as we *had to* to help students grasp the whole outline of the dramatic movement of the poem. Students would have, at the close of any lesson, the entire "framework."

Now, in the body of the course that follows — the First Part, the Second, and the Third — we shall gradually help readers to refine and enrich their perceptions of the "framework." We begin with a concentration on diction, syntax, and rhythm.

The First Part: These Words in This Order

In this part of the course, we would be trying to help students strengthen and diversify their sensitivities to the ways in which the qualities of words and the patterns of syntax are exploited to render meaning and to the ways rhythm works to clarify it. We would be emphasizing, first, diction; then, syntax and rhythm. A teacher might, of course, stress all three aspects at once. It is indeed somewhat false to withhold attention from what is clearly there. But it is also somewhat confusing to certain students to ask them to attend, *at the outset*, to several things at once. So, we have arranged to help them *see* gradually what they are already looking at. In the actual teaching of the poems in this part, one emphasis would blend into the next, as shown by the annotations on the poems that follow.

The previous performance of a particular class will determine which of these three aspects of language a teacher will, *in fact*, emphasize, what facets of the aspect he will stress, how much attention he will give to each aspect, where he will begin and end. Since students have "met" all three aspects of language through the study of poems in the Introduction, the teacher has some grounds for deciding what now needs a "full treatment," what requires a concentrated study of one or two facets, what needs only a glance. So, the schemes for developing sensitivities to diction and to syntax and rhythm that we shall now offer are meant only to suggest what seems to be, in each case, a usable progression. Whatever facets of diction and of syntax and rhythm students in a particular class need to strengthen probably should be stressed in the order we propose.

Diction: Words that Call Attention to Themselves

Some of the words in poems attract a reader's attention because of their connotations; others, because of their departure from the prevailing diction, or their sound, or their placement — or because of several of these reasons. What happens when an experienced reader sees such words? In slow motion, his reaction would probably go something like this: he notices the word; he sees what effect is being achieved by using this word (or these words) rather than some other and by placing it (or them) there rather than elsewhere; he perceives the function of the word — why this effect is desired — and he responds to the word accordingly. Consider, for instance, the reader of Frost's "Dust of Snow."

> The way a crow
> Shook down on me
> The dust of snow
> From a hemlock tree
>
> Has given my heart
> A change of mood
> And saved some part
> Of a day I had rued.*

At the end of stanza one, the reader has somewhat negative expectations. But when he sees the first phrase in stanza two, "Has given," he is pulled up short for he realizes that "give" has positive as well as negative connotations and that this tense means a prolonged action. (So that's why the poem is divided in this odd way!) The reader qualifies his negative expectations. This "dust of snow" *may* be a good thing. And, of course, it is; every phrase that follows furthers the positive element in the experience — and the irony of it.

This little anatomy of the experienced reader's response does not pretend to be a psychologically true description. It tries only to suggest that several acts are involved in the response that we want to help beginning readers learn to make, and it attempts to point out roughly what these acts probably are. It is good to keep such an anatomy in mind as we teach the poems. For we find that it is easy

---

* Reprinted from *Complete Poems of Robert Frost* by permission of Holt, Rinehart and Winston, Inc. Copyright © 1923, 1928, 1939, 1967 by Holt, Rinehart and Winston, Inc. Copyright 1942, 1951, 1956 by Robert Frost.

to get students to *notice* such words — even to name the devices if we want them to — but hard to get them to make the rest of the response: to perceive the effects such words create and to recognize their function in the rendering of meaning. We know that the harder it is to teach something, the easier it is for us to "forget" what the learning really involves. Our anatomy reminds us that "noticing" is only the first step in a reader's response. Words in poems call attention to themselves — but not for their own sakes. And we may not allow the reader's "noticing" to be an end in itself. We must find ways to get him to perceive effect and function.

The study of diction that follows is divided into two parts. In the first half, we emphasize the connotation of words; in the second half, the sound. We say "emphasize" because, while in the first half, we center our attention on the intellectual and affective associations words evoke, we also notice the effects of sound, of placement, and of words that depart from prevailing diction. And while, in the second half, we focus on sound, we also attend to connotation and the other two features just mentioned. In each part, we open with exercises in which we concentrate on single words or small groupings of words that are obvious or simple instances of the ways connotations and sounds function. Then, we move from single words and phrasings to more intricate patterns: to help students begin noticing how connotations and how sounds "chain" to structure a poem. Though the opening exercises *are* "finger exercises," in all of them we have used whole poems, however brief, and we have tried to avoid, especially in the section on sound, selections that are anomalies. We want students' practice to be preparation — for poems "as they are."

■ *Connotation.* It is delightful — and usually fairly easy — to teach students something that they have never thought about before. There are no ill-remembered fragments, no fixed misconceptions to contend with. And there is all the excitement of newness and discovery to stimulate learning. Most students in a first course have not thought about dramatic situation or dramatic movement — nor of the importance of the placement of words, nor the significance of the exotic word. So students bring to the study of these devices only the innocent eye. This, alas, is not true of either the study of connotation or the study of sound.

OPENING EXERCISES. When we begin to teach connotation, we are often confronted with two problems: literalism and license. For some students, words in a poem seem to evoke almost nothing; for others, almost anything. Our opening exercises, then, must simultaneously stimulate and discipline students' imaginations, must at once unfetter them and lead them to see how the context of the poem implies which intellectual and affective associations of the word the reader should release in each instance. An opening exercise like the following would give many classes a "right start."

We would take an obviously connotative word — "fire," for instance — and put it on the board. We would elicit from the class both the literal meanings of the word and the associations it arouses — making on the board a circle of the connotations. Since, at this point, there is as yet no context for the word, all relevant associations stand. Now, we would show students a poem that uses the word "fire" — say, Robert Frost's "Fire and Ice":

> Some say the world will end in fire,
> Some say in ice.
> From what I've tasted of desire
> I hold with those who favor fire.
> But if it had to perish twice,   5
> I think I know enough of hate
> To say that for destruction ice
> Is also great
> And would suffice.*

We would ask students to read the poem carefully to decide which of the associations on the board are relevant *in this poem.* In the discussion that followed, we would try to get the students to see that this context *ruled out* certain associations, *designated* others, and *allowed* a third group.

If additional exercises of this sort seemed desirable, we might use a word like "star" and Frost's six-line "Fireflies in the Garden," or a word like "dust" and his six-line "Dust in the Eyes," or, for the more mature students, a word like "barbaric" and Wallace Stevens' seven-line "Thirteen Ways of Looking at a Blackbird — VI."

We might vary this practice in precise imagining by using either of two other types of tasks. In some classes we might read again poems students read during their study of dramatic organization. For instance, we might return to "Mother to Son" and focus now on the connotations of "crystal," or to "Tree at My Window" and concentrate on "lost," or "To the Virgins, to Make Much of Time" and ask about "rosebuds" and "spent." This kind of task would also help the students see how later readings can enrich their experience of an already familiar poem.

---

* Reprinted from *Complete Poems of Robert Frost* by permission of Holt, Rinehart and Winston, Inc. Copyright © 1923, 1928, 1939, 1967 by Holt, Rinehart and Winston, Inc. Copyright 1942, 1951, 1956 by Robert Frost.

For some classes, however, the new is always more engaging than the familiar. So for them we might design, from new poems, an exercise that will show the same word evoking different connotations, depending upon its context. For example, we might use these three haikus — by the poets, Basho, Sokan, and Fugyoku, respectively — featuring the word "moon":

> Poverty's child —
> he starts to grind the rice,
> and gazes at the moon.

> If to the moon
> One puts a handle — what
> a splendid fan!

> The harvest moon:
> and no dark place to empty
> the ash-tray-spittoon. *

While students were learning, through these little finger exercises, to evoke appropriate connotations, they would also be strengthening their responses to dramatic organization and developing an awareness of arresting word choices, of sound effects, and of the uses of placement. For while they were studying "Fire and Ice," we would probably ask about the contrast of "have tasted" with "think I know enough of" (How does the speaker's experience with "desire" differ from his experience with "hate"?); we would ask about the value of that seemingly unimportant line 8, "Is also great" (Is line 8 necessary? Why not omit it and end the poem, "for destruction ice/Too would suffice"? What meanings are suggested by "great"?) and finally, we would ask about the attitude of the speaker toward what he tells.

During a discussion of "Fireflies in the Garden,"

> Here come real stars to fill the upper skies,
> And here on earth come emulating flies,
> That though they never equal stars in size,
> (And they were never really stars at heart)
> Achieve at times a very star-like start.
> Only, of course, they can't sustain the part.†

---

we would probably ask about the tenderly humorous, condescending speaker and about the dramatic movement that dwindles by concessions. And we would want to know what is gained by the multiple meanings and the multiple uses of "star" (if discussion of connotation has not exhausted that!), by the use of such an odd word as "emulating," by the rhythm of the first line, and by the rhythm and the sound of "a very star-like start." If students in some classes would, at this point, find terms like "rhythm" and "sound" unfamiliar, we would refer to these features simply as "the way we have to say . . ." (What is gained by the way we have to say, "a very star-like start"?)

During our study of "Dust in the Eyes," we would want to ask students: Where in this poem does the speaker change his feeling? What sort of person does he seem to be? Is he *really*? (If necessary, What does the last "if" clause mean? How does it affect the way we take the poem?) How must we say line 4, "Let it be overwhelming, . . ."? What forces us to say it that way? Why use such an awkward word as "overwhelming"? What words in the last line do we especially notice? What makes us notice these ("blind," "me," "standstill," "must")? How are they important to the meaning?

As we discussed connotation in Stevens' poem

> Icicles filled the long window
> With barbaric glass.
> The shadow of the blackbird
> Crossed it, to and fro.
> The mood
> Traced in the shadow
> An undecipherable cause.*

we would also ask about those verbal surprises: "undecipherable" and "mood" (What did you expect would "trace in the shadow/An undecipherable cause"? How does the insertion of "mood" change the meaning?), about the placement of "Crossed" and "Traced," about the superiority of "to and fro" to "back and forth," and about the dramatic movement of this slender poem.

So, while students were learning to react precisely and imaginatively to the connotations of single words, they would also be strengthening and varying their responses to dramatic organization and developing an attention not only to word choice and sound but to syntax and rhythm as well. We would continue these secondary interests, as we moved on to emphasize the ways the connotations of several or many words "chain" in a poem.

---

* Reprinted from *The Collected Poems of Wallace Stevens* by permission of Alfred A. Knopf, Inc. Copyright © 1923 and renewed 1951 by Wallace Stevens.

CHAINING.   A poem like Frost's "Dust of Snow" offers students an easy introduction to chaining. If the class was low average or less able, we would probably begin by showing students — on the board — only the first stanza of the poem and asking them what little scene they see, what colors predominate, what the connotations of "dust" and "snow," "crow" and "hemlock" are — and, finally, what, from all these associations, they think the effect of the crow's act would be. We would then add stanza two and ask: What *is* the speaker's reaction? (And we would want students to define it precisely, not just say "He didn't mind!") As the class answered the question, we would circle the key words in stanza two, discuss their connotations, and ask about their relation to the key words of stanza one. Then we would go on to ask, What difference would it make if he had said, "gave my heart"? If he had said, "a day I rued"? If he had said, "That a crow"? What would be lost if the stanzas were each written as two lines, instead of four? And finally, *Why* does the speaker tell the incident? (If necessary, What did you expect the outcome of the "dust of snow" would be? What was the outcome? What does this suggest about experiences?)

A poem like Edwin Arlington Robinson's four-stanza "Richard Cory" is a somewhat more challenging introduction to the interlinking of connotations. But once students have ascertained the dramatic situation and defined the speaker from cues in his language, certain words will stand out as uncharacteristic of this speaker's diction: "imperially," "admirably," for instance. Why does the speaker use them? What other words develop the "royal" image that the shocked speaker tries to create? A chain of about nine connotatively linked words will appear. Then we would ask, What do "arrayed" and "glittered" suggest? What other words suggest superficiality? *Why* doesn't the speaker realize the superficiality of the description he gives? About whom is the poem?

During the discussion of "Richard Cory," we would question students about what is gained by the repetitions of "And he was. . . . ," by the use of unqualified flat statements, by the shift from soft sounds in stanzas 2 and 3 to the hard sounds in stanza 4, by the placement of "Good-morning," "everything," "light," and "night."

Probably comparable in difficulty to "Richard Cory" — and consequently a good alternate choice — is Eleanor Wylie's six-stanza "The Eagle and the Mole." As in Robinson's poem, once students have listened carefully to all that the rousing, didactic speaker has to say, they have both gotten his "message" and noticed many of his techniques of dissuasion: the series of "orders," the alternation that compares the eagle and the herd in stanzas 1–3, the decisiveness of "all those short words" — and, of course, the repelling connotations of that

chain of words that opens with "reeking" and closes with "spotted."
What students might not notice is the chain of words with desirable
connotations — words that connote independence, courage, integrity,
pristine values. Furthermore, they might not notice how context has
reversed both the usually positive connotations of such words as
"warmth," "folded warm," and "shelter" and the usually negative
connotations of such words as "burrow," "underground," and "disem-
bodied bones." Or even if students noticed these reversals, they
might not see how they support the argument of the poem. So we
would be ready to call their attention to these several uses of connotation and also to the sound effects that emphasize these connotative chains — not only the assonance ("lathered pack," "steaming
sheep"), the alliteration ("Live like," "flocks — folded," and "sails,
storm, stares, sun"), and the rhyme that supports the alternating
comparison in stanza 1–4, but also the cacophonous sounds that arrest
the reader and the shift of vowel quantities ("Begets and fosters
hate") that intensifies the sense. The sounds get the reader to notice
the words; then the connotations persuade him to "shun the herd."

Like the readers of "Richard Cory," those who read Emily Dickinson's "There's A Certain Slant of Light" have to discover the relationships among a chain of abstract words. But Emily Dickinson's
poem is a much more complex, more subtle, and more compressed
work. It is for able readers.

There's a certain slant of light,
On winter afternoons,
That oppresses, like the weight
Of cathedral tunes.

Heavenly hurt it gives us;   5
We can find no scar,
But internal difference
Where the meanings are.

None may teach it anything,
'Tis the seal, despair —   10
An imperial affliction
Sent us of the air.

When it comes, the landscape listens,
Shadows hold their breath;
When it goes, 'tis like the distance   15
On the look of death.*

To bring even able readers to discover the connections among words in a poem like this poses a teaching problem: both because we want to preserve at least some of the mystery, indefiniteness, and ineffable quality of what is being described and because the interrelations are so dense. We would try to overcome the first problem by concentrating, as the speaker does, on the *effects* of "a certain slant of light." And we would attempt to ameliorate the second by conducting our study as simply and directly as possible, letting the complexity reveal itself. We would ask only, What is the speaker's purpose in this poem? Then, What *are* the effects as the speaker cites them? Using the words of the poem, we would list the effects on the board vertically and leave adequate space at one side for the noting of multiple meanings and associations and adequate space between the "effects" so that at the end of the discussion we could "line in" the interconnections among words, if necessary.

We would begin with "oppresses," eliciting two meanings for it — "dispirits" and "tyrannizes" — and the connotations of both. As students worked on stanza two, they would discover that the effects cited in that stanza develop mainly the first meaning of "oppress" ("dispirit"): the "slant of light" gives a "Heavenly hurt," an invisible scar, an "internal difference." But these words qualify "dispirit" both by their own multiple meanings ("Heavenly," for instance, means not only "beautiful," "peaceful," "spiritual," but also "beyond human control," "irresistible") and by their own relevant connotations.

As students went on to stanza three, they would see that the effects cited in the first two lines of that stanza develop the second meaning of "oppress" ("tyrannize"): "None *may* teach it anything" and "'Tis the seal" — and "seal" means both "an irrefutable power" and "something that preserves secrecy." These meanings of "seal" have already been hinted at in "Heavenly" and they are qualified now by all that the word "Heavenly" draws after it.

Finally, students would see that the meanings and connotations of the words in stanzas two and three are drawn together in the last two lines of stanza three: "An imperial affliction/Sent us of the air."

If at this point, it seemed as if our questioning had not uncovered connections clearly enough, we would ask students to suggest the lines we might draw to show the connections among the effects, or to save time, we would draw them — slowly and without comment: a line from "oppresses" to "Heavenly" to "none may" to "seal" to "imperial" to show the "tyranny" connection; a line from "oppresses" to "hurt" to "no scar" to "internal difference" to "affliction" to show the "dispirit" connection. We could then go further, drawing a line from "oppresses" to "Heavenly" to "give" to "meanings" to "seal" to "imperial" to "Sent us" to show the "divine burden" connection. The lines would eventually reveal the many different connections and interconnections of each of the key words. And by taking this way into the poem, we hope we would help students not only to see the interrelating among the words but to perceive, through its effects, the nature of "a certain slant of light."

During this study of the effects, we would also be asking students about the function of such devices as the alliterations, the verbal surprises — ("internal difference," for instance), the syntactic reversal of line 5 ("Heavenly hurt it gives us"), and the partial paralleling in the last stanza. The study of this poem would, in other words, be no less whole than that of the other seven we have discussed. In all eight poems, though our emphasis has been on helping students develop responses to connotations and multiple meanings, we have been paying varying degrees of attention to other features that work with connotation to render meaning. One of these features has been sound; and it is to sound that we now shift our focus.

■ *Sound.* Students are very likely to have one or another well-developed misconception about sound. Some identify the pleasure of poetry with sound; it has never occurred to them how very limited the pleasure of "sensuous surface" *must* be when the medium is the word. Some think *the* function of sound in poetry is pleasure; so they have never questioned what else sound might be doing. Others have had such a surfeit of "bells" and of "hisses" and "buzzes" in their pasts, that now subtleties go unnoticed; variations seem "wrong"; and any word that is not onomatopoeic "isn't sound." Finally, some know sound functions to support sense, but they have developed rigid sound-sense equivalents ("*s* is pleasant"), and they apply them inflexibly to the most various contexts.

Our aim is to expand students' limited views of the function of sound by making them sensitive to the three following ways in which sound supports sense. Through the study of poems, we would try to help them "see for themselves," first, that sound patterns — such as, the euphonious and cacophonous sounds of particular words, the massing of explosive sounds, or of thin or full vowels — reinforce meaning by seeming especially appropriate to it. Secondly, we would help students recognize that configurations of sounds in words control the time and effort it takes to say the words and so control the speed and movement of lines, and that the speed of a line sometimes reflects the sense of the line and sometimes simply makes us notice the line. Finally, we would help students see that similarities in sound — alliteration, assonance, consonance, rhymes, repetitions — are often used just to focus our attention on words that are somehow crucial to meaning.

We would stress just these three uses of sound. We would not claim that the sound of words imitates the sense of them — either directly, as in "hark," "cuckoo," "buzz," or, by mysterious connection, as in "tatter," "spatter," "patter." "Who would surely recognize the sound of a cuckoo on hearing the word if he did not already know that it referred to a cuckoo?"[18] And if the sound of "atter" suggests smallness, how does one account for "matter," "platter," and "squatter"? Is it not probably the visual and sound images evoked by "tatter," "spatter," and "patter" that we are confusing with pronunciation images?[19] We would not, in other words, claim sound-sense connections that are open to valid objections and vulnerable to counter evidence. If we insist on dubious connections, students who are discerning, commonsensical, or just afraid of being "taken" might discount all functions of sound. And that would indeed contravene our intention. For, what we want our study to do is to help students become sensitive to three general uses of sound and, in the process, perceive *how much more* there is to sound in a poem than we try to account for, how many significant effects defy description.

By the time students begin their concentrated study of sound, they will have read five or six poems. And they will be somewhat prepared for the approach to sound they must now take, not only because our questioning on recent poems has taken account of sound but also because our oral reading — and their oral and silent reading — has, from the beginning, been calling attention to the poem as "heard." And we suspect that so far in this course, both we and they will have done some exaggerated reading to make points: overstressing stresses, prolonging pauses, striking *k*'s, and *t*'s, and *d*'s, elongating *a*'s, and emphasizing similarities of sound. If, from these experiences, students have not become aware of sound, *we* at least shall have become aware of their unawareness. So we shall know how much more exaggerated reading we must now do.

As we said earlier, we would begin the study of sound as we began the study of connotation, with exercises which we would use in whatever way necessary to correct and to strengthen the response to sound of a particular class. In some classes, it might be better to work on one or two exercises thoroughly; in others, to read more poems, studying just a few aspects of each. Let the students' usual pattern of attention dictate. The poems chosen for such exercises should offer experience with as many uses of sound as possible; and the teaching of the poems should stress not only sound, but dramatic situation and movement, connotation, the placement of words, and, wherever they are crucial to grasping the passage being examined, syntax and rhythm, too.

OPENING EXERCISES. Here — in rough order of difficulty — are four poems that represent the *kinds* of works that would be appropriate for opening exercises. Our annotations suggest *some* of the features to which we would call students' attention during study of the poems.

In James Stephens' "The Main-Deep," the speaker, looking down on the ocean, describes — in a series of impressionistic remarks — the approach and the breaking of a single wave on the deep. So, we would begin by asking where the speaker is and why the poem is written in a series of short lines; then, we would go on to ask what suggests continuous motion (if necessary, Why would not "slow-slid*es*," "cold-rush*es*," "chill rush*es*" be as good?); then, we would ask why "green glacid" is better than "green wave" or "green glassy," what meanings of "flushing" are *not* working here, what sound dominates the first stanza, the last stanza — and, of course, why.

In the first stanza of Elizabeth Coatsworth's poem, the speaker states "Swift things are beautiful"; in the second stanza, "And slow things are beautiful." In each stanza he follows his statement with seven lines of evidence.

> Swift things are beautiful:
> Swallows and deer,
> And lightning that falls
> Bright veined and clear,
> Rivers and meteors,   5
> Wind in the wheat,
> The strong-withered horse,
> The runner's sure feet.
>
> And slow things are beautiful:
> The closing of day,   10
> The pause of the wave
> That curves downward to spray,
> The ember that crumbles,
> The opening flower,
> And the ox that moves on   15
> In the quiet of power.*

The first stanza moves quickly, mostly because of many short *i*'s, long *e*'s, and one-syllable words with clipped endings — *d*'s and *t*'s. The second stanza moves slowly, mainly because of many long *o*'s, long *a*'s, and *ow*'s, and two-syllable words accented on the first syllable — "closing," "flower," "power." These sound patterns, not the rhythm, control the speed of reading and emphasize the "swiftness" and the "slowness" the details suggest. Our teaching of this poem would stress this relation of sound to sense.

---

* Reprinted from *Collected Poems*, by Elizabeth Coatsworth, by permission of The Macmillan Company. Copyright © 1934 by The Macmillan Company, renewed 1962 by Elizabeth Coatsworth Beston.

But we would also want students to notice how syntax and stanza form cooperate to suggest the meaning of the poem. We would call attention to the fact that each stanza is a sentence, that the parts of these sentences are related in certain ways, and that the two sentences (stanzas) are roughly parallel in form and contrasting in meaning. We would ask students what is probably "meant" by a poem's suggesting that opposites are similar.

In Theodore Roethke's "Big Wind," (thirty-three lines) a worker in an old greenhouse dramatizes the events of a wild, stormy night in the glasshouse in terms of a crew and a ship gallantly riding out bad weather. We would begin by asking students: Who is telling the story? What, in his mind, were the "turning points" in the ship's struggle? And, of course, what *in the telling* suggests these points. What we would want to help students see is that not only the connectives ("so," "but," "finally") and the changes in syntax, but also the sound patterns call the reader's attention to the various stages in the "ship's" struggle — indeed, in some cases, to the character of its changes in fortune. If necessary, we would ask questions directly about the effects of such features as the alliterations in the first three lines of wild questioning, the repetition of *w*'s in line 16 (the pronunciation of which brings the poem to a momentary rest), the pair of approximate rhymes that open lines 17–18, the assonance of long *o*'s in lines 21–23, the intricate rhymings that describe the "wind-waves" in lines 28–29, the vowel changes from long *e* to short *i* in lines 30–31 that recount the petering out of the storm ("Finally veering, wearing themselves out, merely/Whistling thinly under the wind-vents"), and the alliteration and the massing of full vowels in lines 32–33 that report the triumphal sailing of the "ship into port."

And who could leave this poem without asking what is significant about the stale mixture from the "manure-machine" saving the "cargo of roses"?

Alfred, Lord Tennyson's slender little poem "The Oak" is a stimulating reading for both average and more able students.

> Live thy Life,
>   Young and old,
> Like yon oak,
> Bright in spring
>   Living gold;   5
>
> Summer-rich
>   Then; and then
> Autumn-changed,
> Soberer-hued
>   Gold again.   10

> All his leaves
> Fall'n at length,
> Look, he stands,
> Trunk and bough,
> Naked strength. 15

If we were teaching this poem to average students, we would emphasize how sentence units, stanza units, punctuation, alliteration, consonance, assonance, and rhyme all work together to make clear to the reader that it is the "gold" of the oak that the speaker most wants his hearers to resemble. If we were teaching this poem to more able students, we would want to go beyond noticing these basic functions of syntax, stanza form, and sound to help them see also that syntax emphasizes the rhymes that are especially relevant to the "meaning," that the vowels shift gradually from short, light ones to long *o*'s and *u*'s as the seasons change from spring to winter, and that, even in this simple poem, there is a verbal surprise — "Naked." And we would call attention to the surprise in some such way as this: Look at the last lines of the first and second stanzas. On the basis of those, what last line does the reader expect in this stanza? (Students will probably answer: "Golden strength" or "Silver strength.") But, instead, the ending is "Naked strength." How does frustrating the reader's expectation with this word support the speaker's theme?

For such opening exercises in sound as we have been describing, some teachers might prefer to use poems students had read previously rather than new poems. They might, for instance, choose "Lord Randal," to show, among other things, the function of refrain; or "Heresy for a Classroom," to emphasize the use of euphonious sound to complement sense; or "The Listeners," to show how consonant sounds control the speed of reading. Other teachers might prefer to open with quite a different kind of exercise from what we have proposed. They might favor, for instance, a comparison exercise of some sort; let us say, a series of pairs of passages, one of which is a selection as it was written, the other the selection with a word change that affects sound. For example, from Robert Francis' "The Base Stealer," these lines:

> How he teeters, skitters, tingles, teases,
> Taunts them, hovers like an ecstatic bird*

might be changed to:

> How he teeters, skitters, tingles, teases,
> Mocks them, hovers like an ecstatic bird

---

* Reprinted from *The Orb Weaver*, by Robert Francis, by permission of Wesleyan University Press. Copyright © 1948 by Robert Francis.

or, to make the exercise more challenging, "Tempts them" could be used instead of "Mocks them." The question on such an exercise might be, Which passage is better and why? Or it might be: The first is the passage as it was written. What is lost by the change the second passage shows? For this kind of introduction, the teacher might create his own exercises from new passages or passages from poems already studied, or he could use ready-made exercises. Laurence Perrine in *Sound and Sense*, pages 176–177,[20] offers fifteen pairings. The custom-made exercise usually fits better, but creating it takes time.

Kenner, in *The Art of Poetry*, page 114,[21] suggests a variation of this kind of exercise: he offers a four-line passage from Donne and six alternate renderings of it, beginning with a prose version and ending with a passage that varies from the original by a single word. The question is: what is lost by each change?

These are only two of many kinds of discrimination exercises that might be devised to increase students' sensitivity to the ways sound work. And, though they might be used in lieu of the opening exercises we suggested, they might also be used prior to them, or together with them — as certain classes or even certain students required. The revealed needs of each class will suggest the kinds of practice that would be most beneficial, but, in general, exercises that offer experience with *many different* uses of sound and with increasingly subtle uses are the most beneficial for developing flexible and discerning responses.

The comparison exercise is a versatile instrument for developing discrimination in other uses of language also (connotation and rhythm, for instance) and, later, for determining how adequately students perceive the *many ways* a word functions, on how many grounds one word is a more appropriate choice than another.

CHAINING.   Whenever students began to suggest how this or that sound effect functions (and it might be after a single exercise), we would, as we said earlier, move on to study poems with more intricate sound patterns. Our aim would be to help students see how these patterns relate to "meaning" in these poems. In the discussions of the works we would, of course, continue to be interested in dramatic organization, in the choice and the placement of words, and, wherever especially relevant, in syntax and rhythm. The following four poems, which are arranged roughly in order of difficulty, are the *kinds* of poems that would be appropriate readings for achieving our aim.

There is no question as to the general way in which sound supports sense in Edward Arlington Robinson's sonnet, "Aaron Stark." In the process of creating his harsh image of this character, the speaker uses

over thirty words with harsh sounds, some of which end with *d* and
k for extra force and abruptness and many of which are emphasized
by alliterations and repetitions, by the unusual rhyming of the octet,
and by stress. Besides noticing this sound pattern, we would want
students to understand the function of the syntactic pattern — de-
layed subject — that is repeated in six of the seven sentences. We
would ask: What has this syntactic pattern to do with the image
being created? Then, *How* does the speaker try to lead you to think
Aaron can be "reached"? *Why* does the speaker do that? Why does
Aaron laugh? Why can't a reader be sure? Finally, we would ask
students about the first word of the poem, "Withal," an archaism, an
obvious departure from the diction of the poem: Why is that archaic
word used? (If necessary, we would ask: How is the reader supposed to take the character sketch that follows such a word as that?)

In A. E. Housman's two-stanza poem, "Eight O'Clock," the narrator tells of the last moments of a condemned man's life, the moments
during which the clock strikes the four quarters and pauses before
the first stroke of eight.

> He stood, and heard the steeple
>   Sprinkle the quarters on the morning town.
> One, two, three, four, to market-place and people
>   It tossed them down.
>
> Strapped, noosed, nighing his hour,   5
>   He stood and counted them and cursed his luck;
> And then the clock collected in the tower
>   Its strength, and struck.*

The sounds all through this little poem are appropriate to the
sense. In the first stanza, the full vowels and final *d*'s of the one-
syllable words that describe the inaction of the man waiting to be
hanged contrast sharply with the light vowels and feminine endings
of the words that describe the action of the steeple, the man's
adversary:

> He stood, and heard the steeple
>   Sprinkle the quarters on the morning town.

As a transition to the full vowels of stanza two, the last line of stanza
one uses a falling vowel pattern: "It tossed them down" — a suggestive sentence (to say the least). In the second stanza, the pronunciation and the punctuation of "Strapped, noosed" rightly restrain the

---

* Reprinted from *The Collected Poems of A. E. Housman* by permission of Holt,
Rinehart and Winston, Inc. Copyright © 1950 by Barclays Bank Ltd.

reader; the fluid sounds of "nighing his hour" appropriately speed the reader on; the full vowels, the *d*'s and the *k*'s, as well as the syntax of "He stood and counted them and cursed his luck" make the reader labor. And the syntax, line division, and sounds of the last two lines of the poem — especially the prolonged sound of "tower" and the *k* sounds —

> And then the clock collected in the tower
> Its strength, and struck.

make the reader suffer the man's suspense — and his end.

When the structure of sound so completely and obviously reinforces the structure of "meaning," as it does in this poem, expressive oral readings will greatly help even less able readers to make perceptive responses. Wherever oral reading fails, then substitutions of words and of syntactic structures will serve. Students will see quite readily what would be lost if the last two lines read:

> And then the clock collected all its strength
> In the tower, and struck.

And substitutions will, furthermore, show all students — dramatically — how much "these words in this order" matter, how many things are sacrificed by one change.

In the octet the speaker in Robert Frost's sonnet, "Design," tells of a little natural scene in which those things usually associated with loveliness and innocence — "white," "dimpled," and "satin" — are signs of death and blight. In the sestet the speaker asks two "innocent" questions about the cause of this ironic conjunction of horror and gives, in a third question and its afterthought, two terrible answers: "What but design of darkness to appall? —/If design govern in a thing so small."

In the discussion of this sonnet, we would ask about the connotations of "white," "dimpled," and "satin," as well as of "innocent," "heal-all," and "kindred"; about the homonym for "right," and about the multiple meanings of the word "kite" and of the phrase "had to do with." But, more importantly, we would want to call students' attention to the various ways in which sound supports sense; for instance, to the way the repetition of "white" in the first three lines intensifies the shock of reversal in line 4 ("Assorted characters of death and blight"), to the way the repetition of "What" ties the three questions in the sestet together, and to the way alliterations ("snow-drop spider," "flower-like froth," "design of darkness," "so small") and phrasings that are difficult to pronounce focus our attention on ironic elements. But, above all, we would want students to notice how the structure of the sentences emphasizes the rhyme and how the rhyme, in turn, emphasizes the paradox of the poem. For, though the octet is one sentence, the construction is such that each line is a unit; so the rhymes are not blurred by the reader's running-on. And though the sestet is composed of three two-line sentences, they are paralleled questions, each line of which is a syntactic unit. Because of this syntax, the linking of the oppositions suggested by the rhyming of "white" and "right" with "blight" and "kite" and "night" comes through very clearly to the reader. If we needed to call students' attention to this relationship, we would probably ask, at the end of the study of the poem, such a simple, open question as: How does the rhyme scheme function? Or: Now, see if the rhyme scheme supports the "meaning." As soon as students letter the rhyme scheme, they begin to see.

The concern of W. H. Auden's four-stanza poem, "O Where Are You Going?", is highly revelant for high school readers. In this poem, the voices of three who fear confrontation with the world as it is try, in their separate ways, to dissuade the active man, the confident man, the truth-seeker from going out to experience the world. They fail; he goes. Students, competent to read a poem like this, would notice the interlinking effected by the rhymes and approximate rhymes, by the alliterations, by the paralleling of the stanzas, and by the final synthesis. What they might not realize is *the extent* to which the flavor, the characteristic tone, of the argument in each of the first three stanzas is being suggested to the reader by sound devices. So we would be prepared to point out to students how in the first stanza alliteration, assonance, and internal rhyme make us notice that "reader" thinks of the dangers of experience in the terms of medieval romance; how in the second stanza the unusual patterning of alliteration and approximate rhyme ("Your diligent looking discover the lacking") makes us sense the chiding anxiety of "fearer"; and how in the third stanza both the use of three kinds of sentences and the massing of magic details (emphasized by the massing of *s* sounds) suggest to us how desperately "horror" wants to terrify.

To conclude our discussion of the poem, we would want to ask students why all the answers were withheld until the final stanza, and why the narrator says "he" left "them" (Are the rider, the farer, and the hearer just one person? Or, Is the singular "he" contrasted with the plural "they" to suggest how rare the adventurer is in this world and how common the fearer? Or what?). And, finally, to top it off, we would ask: Why does the poem have a narrator?

So far in this discussion of the First Part of our course, we have been stressing diction, emphasizing the function of the *connotations* and the *sounds* of words in rendering the meaning of poems. All the while we have been noticing the effects of the placement of words and of the use of exotic words. Occasionally, too, we have paid attention to the ways that syntax and rhythm work with the other uses of language to determine the reader's experience. But, up to now, our attention to syntax and rhythm has been informal.

Whenever we dealt with syntax, for instance, we "traded on" two things that students, as native speakers, bring: an acceptance of the normal order declarative sentence as the basic English sentence and a consequent assumption that, if the voice in a poem departs from this basic sentence form — that is, gives an order, asks a question, inverts, adds, omits, scrambles, or becomes noticeably organized in some way — then "something is up." What? To help students discover what, we have been asking such questions as: What would the speaker lose if he used the "regular" sentence order? If he had said what he believes in statements rather than questions? What did he gain by putting the ideas in parallel phrases? And so on.

Up to now, our attention to rhythm has been similarly informal. We have noticed it only as oral reading always notices metrical patterns and their variations and only as an occasional question about how a line is "said" calls attention to a mass of stresses that slows a line or to a sudden difference from the "way the rest of the poem is read."

Syntax and Rhythm

Now as we change emphasis from diction to syntax and rhythm, what responses would we try to help students to develop? Our previous informal attention suggests the answer: we would aim now, continually, directly, and quite overtly, to help students perceive how the syntax of a certain poem and how the rhythm of it assist in making the "sense (the idea, the mood, the development of feeling) perfectly plain."[22]

About syntax we would now be asking quite explicitly, What kind of sentence (or what kind of construction) is the speaker using here? (Or, if necessary, What is the difference between saying, "What but design of darkness to appall?" and "It is only design of darkness to appall"? and such substitutions.) What is the speaker gaining by this construction (by using an inverted order, or subordination, instead of coordination, or a colon at this point)? Why is that effect desired? By phrasing the questions simply and by using substitutions, we can discuss syntactic features with classes quite ignorant of syntax in a formal sense — indeed we can teach them syntax this way!

About rhythm, we would now be asking quite explicitly, What is the dominant meter of the poem? Where does the speaker depart from it? How does he say those words? What is the effect (effects) of saying them that way? (If necessary, How does that pattern of stress disclose the meaning of the words? Does it emphasize the words? or de-emphasize them so that you notice something else? Does it make the line move fast or slowly or how? Why should the line move that way?) And, finally, How do the metrical pattern and the "meaning" (dramatic, rhetorical) pattern relate to one another? (If necessary, emphasize one another? restrain one another?)

Although we would be giving our major attention to such questions on syntax and rhythm, we would continue to notice the effects of certain words, their sounds, and their placements — not only because discussions of the effects of and the reasons for rhythmic variations entail noticing features of diction, but also because we would always be trying to impress upon students that, since many uses of language work together to render the meaning of a poem, the reader cannot be "through" with diction when he begins to attend to syntax and rhythm.

In the teaching of syntax and rhythm the teacher is often especially tempted to emphasize the learning and the use of formal terminology. In some classes, the use of terms seems appropriate, for students either know the formal terms already or they could *readily* learn them and use them as convenient labels. It would be just as ridiculous to refrain from using formal terminology in those classes as it would be to insist on its use in others. For in certain classes, the terms would confuse students; or worse, learning them would become an end in itself. And a knowledge of terms is not even a means to the end we have set. For, knowing the established names will not facilitate students' learning to notice syntactic and rhythmic patterns or to recognize how they function. Learning terms would unwarrantedly deter such a class from developing the crucial skills. In all classes, we should talk about syntax and rhythm, and all other uses of language, in whatever words the particular class will understand. And in some classes that means resisting the lure of terminology.

In the teaching of rhythm, as in the teaching of sound, the teacher is especially tempted to emphasize the pure example, the rarely used but more ear-catching, more soul-stirring instance. Too often he chooses poems that are rhythmic anomalies. They are fun, but studying them is not very useful preparation for making sensitive responses to the rhythmic patterns that poems tell us most poems use: iambic meters with variations. So if we aim to prepare students to respond flexibly to the most prevalent rhythmic patterns, we must *feature* poems that use iambic meters. And if we aim to help students with what is, at once, crucial to meaning and difficult for them to learn on their own, we must stress the effect and the function of rhythmic variations. These are *our* aims, and they account for the kinds of poems and the teaching emphases we use in the study that follows. Students *can* get from Ghent to Aix all by themselves. So we let them.

■ *Opening Exercises.* We would open our study of syntax and rhythm in as uncomplicated a way as we could devise. We would probably begin with exercises on short poems that the class had previously read carefully enough to have a sense of "how the poem goes" and of why it goes that way ("He's giving an order"; "He's very upset"; "The speaker *would* emphasize these words, because they're crucial to him"). For, if students already have a rather good idea of the "meaning" (rhetorical, dramatic) pattern of the poem, we have only to reveal the metrical pattern and to show how the two interact, at one time the meaning forcing variations in the prevailing meter and so highlighting it, at another, the meter controlling the words and emphasizing their meaning. To further facilitate the *opening* exercises, we would use poems that have metrically regular first lines so that students can more easily notice the variations that come later in the poem. If students have to wait two lines for a regular line, they are seeing variations before seeing what is being varied — a guarantee of confusion.

For our first exercise we would choose a poem *like* "Dust of Snow" — which admirably meets our two requirements — and we would teach it somewhat as follows. First, as a "refresher," we would ask the students to read the poem silently. We would follow that by an oral reading that clearly recognized the meaning pattern, a reading that registered not only the provoking pauses at "tree" and "heart" but also the variations of line 4, of the phrase "some part," and of line 8. Then, we would ask students to watch the text and listen closely as we read the poem again. This time we would read *as if* the poem had been written throughout in unvaried iambic meter. Then, we would read the poem once again in the same way. But this time, students would mark the beats as we read and check off "places" at which the regular metrical reading "seemed wrong." At the end of that reading, we would turn to the board copy of the poem and have students direct us as to how to mark the rhythm.

We would discuss, first, the variations all agreed upon — probably "Has given" and "some part" — and then others. The discussion would make clear that it is meaning that effects variations of the basic meter. Once this crucial discussion was completed, we would do as much formal work — marking off feet, counting them, naming the dominant foot and the variations — as the class' interest and need at *this* time warranted.

We would immediately reinforce this exercise with another, using a comparable poem, probably the now familiar "Fire and Ice," and, in less able and average groups, a similar procedure. In able groups, however, after our first metrical reading of "Fire and Ice," we would let students work on their own — doing the second reading silently, marking the poem, annotating reasons for the variations — carrying on, in other words, as much of the work as we think they can do fruitfully. In this second exercise, most students in all classes would sense the prevailing meter and identify the variations in lines 3 and 6 ("I've tasted of" and "I know") — phrases we discussed in the earlier connotation exercise. Furthermore, in this second exercise, *some* students would be able to point out that the initial "I" in lines 4 and 6 is also accented and that the initial "Some" in lines 1 and 2 is partially stressed — to contrast the world's view with the speaker's. Some might say that "But" in line 5 is accented (the shift to the contrasting view) and "Is" in line 8 (a stating of fact). Others might say that "for" in line 7 is not. (Why not? What is gained by its being unstressed? What already emphasizes "destruction"? Why should "destruction" receive so much notice?) Once again, we would conclude this discussion of rhythm with as many of the formalities — marking feet, counting, naming — as appropriate, but this time, if the preceding discussion had gone well, we would ask the class to do these formalities individually; we would, then, do them with the class' help on the board copy — as a check. Finally, to pull the poem together, we would ask the class *how* the contrast of this poem is made clear to the reader. The answering of this question would call attention to the balanced sentence, the parallels, the repetitions, the metrical similarities — indeed, even to the reason for the last two lines being written as two lines, instead of one. And, of course, students would be realizing, during such a discussion, that *all* of these devices were functioning together to express the contrast.

Now, most classes would be ready to try working on their own. So we would assign, as an out-of-class exercise (or as in-class work, if students are less able or unmotivated), a poem and a task highly similar to the ones we had just done. The poem would be a familiar one, perhaps, Frost's "The Pasture" (not to stay close to Frost, but to what we have practiced!), and the task: Read the poem twice to hear in your mind's ear how it is said. Now read it metrically. Mark the accents. Now examine places that in ordinary reading seem to depart from the regular meter. Mark them as they would be *said*. Now note in the margins the reasons for these variations. And, if appropriate: When you have done all that, mark the feet, count them, name the dominant foot and the variations.

Our subsequent class discussion of this exercise on "The Pasture" would reveal how important sentence units and pauses (lines 4, 6, 8) are in the rhythm that is heard and felt, how appropriate to the speaker's state of mind the syntax, sound, and rhythm of line 3 are, how crucial to the meaning of lines 4 and 8 the substitution of spondees is, and, of course, how effectively sound and rhythm work together to emphasize meaning in lines 4 and 8 (note, for instance, "gone long. — You come too.") The performance of the class on this exercise will suggest whether or not more "fingering" is needed before students proceed to more demanding study.

Through simple exercises like these, students will begin to realize that "the personal voice [is always] speaking through the formal convention," so they will understand that rhythm "is determined by meaning more than meter, by feeling more than feet."[23] They will see that absolute agreement on the scanning of a line is less important than knowing why we disagree and that distinguishing between stressed and unstressed syllables never really accounts for all the degrees of stress we actually give when we read a poem. In other words, they would begin to understand something about the functions — and the complexities — of rhythm.

■ *The Main Study.*   What would follow such introductory exercises? With less able classes — where the security of the familiar is valued — we might choose to continue the study of syntax and rhythm through the reading of additional familiar poems. If we wished to increase somewhat the difficulty of the work, we could do so either by choosing poems that are longer but not more intricate — say, "Richard Cory" and "The Oak" — or by selecting short poems with more complex rhythmic variations — say, "Eight O'Clock." With competent readers, with the bright but bored, and with other groups who seem ready, we would now begin to study new poems. We mention "ready," because at this point in the course, studying a new poem — whatever the poem and whoever the class — would entail making many responses: not only noticing syntactic and rhythmic patterns, seeing their effects, and determining their functions, but also identifying the dramatic situation and discovering how certain word choices and certain sound patterns worked together with the syntactic and rhythmic patterns to render the dramatic movement of the poem.

Whatever materials the teacher decided to use with a particular class at this point — familiar poems, new ones, or a combination of the two, he might still choose to continue *some* of the procedures used in the opening exercises. He might, for instance, continue to guide the class through its examination of the meaning and metrical patterns of poems. Or he might continue to incorporate formal metrical work at pertinent points in the lesson. Some teachers like to continue such metrical work quite regularly; others, to include it only when the understanding of a certain part of a certain poem requires it. Though we do not mention scanning in our annotations of the poems we suggest below, we assume that it would be done at least whenever necessary, and this varies not only class to class but poem to poem.

Following are six new poems that might be studied profitably by one class or another whenever the particular students were ready. Either of the first two poems would make beginning easy.

The speaker in Thomas Hardy's twenty-line poem, "The Man He Killed," is a soldier reflecting on the irony of having killed — in chance encounter — a man, probably much like himself, a man he would have befriended in an equally chance peaceful meeting.

> Had he and I but met
> By some old ancient inn,
> We should have sat us down to wet
> Right many a nipperkin!
>
> But ranged as infantry,   5
> And staring face to face,
> I shot at him as he at me,
> And killed him in his place.
>
> I shot him dead because —
> Because he was my foe,   10
> Just so: my foe of course he was;
> That's clear enough; although
>
> He thought he'd 'list, perhaps,
> Off-hand like — just as I —
> Was out of work — had sold his traps —   15
> No other reason why.
>
> Yes; quaint and curious war is!
> You shoot a fellow down
> You'd treat if met where any bar is,
> Or help to half-a-crown.*   20

We would begin the study of the poem by asking: What is the speaker contrasting in the first two stanzas? How does the sentence structure point up the contrast? And how do the variations in rhythm emphasize it? (If necessary, How is rhythm varied in line 3? in line 7? How do these variations point up the contrast?) Then, on to what we are most interested in — the change that comes over the speaker in stanza three: What causes the change in stanza three? How does syntax signal the change? How does repetition? Internal rhyming? Why does the reader lose the sound of the end rhymes? How do

---

* Reprinted from *Collected Poems*, by Thomas Hardy, by permission of The Macmillan Company. Copyright © 1925.

variations in rhythm emphasize the soldier's answer? Why is "although" placed at the end of stanza three instead of at the beginning of stanza four? Finally, in our discussion of stanza five, we would want to ask, What does "Yes" mean? What is the effect of calling war "quaint" and "curious"? (What would *you* call what he described?) What is suggested by "you," "you'd" that would be lost with "I" or even "we"? How does the last stanza pull together the contrast suggested at the beginning? And to conclude, Why is the poem called "The Man *He* Killed" when the speaker is first-person?

A. E. Housman's two-stanza "Epitaph on an Army of Mercenaries" expresses the irony of finding virtue where one expects none — in this case, in professional soldiers who died to save a country. We would want students to see how many uses of language work together to reveal this irony to the reader: the pairings of words (lines 1–2, 5–6), the alliterations of these words and others, the placement of words (for instance, the withholding of "are dead" and "for pay"), the syntax (the order of the first sentence, the use of "and's" in compound predicates, the structure of line 6 and of line 7), and the rhythmic variations that emphasize the placement and the syntax. To help students notice the relation of these means to meaning, we would question somewhat like this: For whom are epitaphs usually written? What does "mercenaries" usually connote? What irony is expressed in this title? Now, What irony is expressed in the poem? How do the contrasting pairs of words, syntax (and so on) call our attention to the irony? As the class pointed out how the means worked, many facets of the irony that had thus far gone unnoticed would appear.

Both of the next two poems demand much more of the reader than the two preceding poems; they ask him, for instance, to infer from less obvious cues both syntactic connections and relationships among details. The poems are excellent alternates because they are equally difficult and widely different in tone and concern. The first poem, John Wheelock's eight-line "Silence," suggests that only silence can express deep emotions and truths. The second poem, Phyllis McGinley's three-stanza "Six Nuns in the Snow," reflects on the calm assurance of the spiritually secure. Students understand both of these poems much more readily if they are clear on the dramatic situations in them.

To open the study of Wheelock's poem, we would therefore ask, Who is speaking to whom? How are you sure this is a public utterance, not an internal monologue? (To answer this question, students *must* notice the quality of the diction, the oratorical rhetoric.) What is the speaker's intention? Then, we would ask students to: Point out the succession of "moves" the speaker makes to achieve his purpose. (If necessary, What is the function of lines 7–8? Why is "the

unreturning traveler" an especially relevant example? See line 2.)
Finally, What makes us notice the key points of each stage of the
speaker's argument? If necessary, we could be more directive: How
does syntax, and so forth, make us notice . . . ? or we might use
such substitution questions as, What would be lost if we changed
lines 3–4 from "What word shall hold/The sorrow sitting at the heart
of things" to "What word can speak/The sorrow grieving at the
heart of things"? Or, What would be lost if we changed line 6 from:
"Silence will serve; it is an older tongue" to "Silence, an older tongue,
will serve"? Through examining such substitutions, students would
see that, by changing the sound patterns, the connotative chaining
of words, and the rhetorical effects certain sentence patterns produce, one destroys the dramatic impact of the poem. Substitution
is always a way of *showing* students how much depends upon this
word, upon that construction — how different is the "gist" from the
thing in itself.

What must readers of "Six Nuns in the Snow" recognize about the
speaker?

> Beautifully, now, they walk among these new
> petals the snow shook down —
> identical figures, going two by two,
> each in a black gown.
>
> With what a placid tread, what definite,   5
> calm impulse each proceeds,
> two by two, black on bewildering white,
> swinging her long beads;
>
> an absolute six, taking their candid way
> undazzled by this whiteness,   10
> who have grown used to walking without dismay
> amid incredible brightness.*

Readers must recognize that as the speaker watches the nuns, he
is musing. The poem is his series of impressions — said as they occur
to him. If readers realize that, they will understand features that
might otherwise puzzle them: the "associational" syntax, the uncapi-
talized beginning words, the grammatical disagreements ("they,"
"each," "her," "their"), the muted rhymes, and the rhythm that
almost simulates the nuns' "two by two" "placid tread" and "candid
way." In other words, once the dramatic situation is clarified, readers
can join the speaker and go with him through his reflection to his
final realization.

---

* Reprinted from *Times Three,* by Phyllis McGinley, by permission of The Viking
Press, Inc. Copyright © 1934 by Phyllis McGinley. All rights reserved.

And once the dramatic situation is clarified, the way is open for all the precise questioning on diction and sound, syntax and rhythm, we would want to do to make the students' experience as quietly penetrating as the speaker's. We would want to ask: Why does the speaker say "petals"? How are *they* "identical"? What is being suggested in such a phrase as "definite calm impulse"? What meanings are working in "absolute"? in "candid"? in "incredible"? *How* are these words called to the reader's attention?

We would want, furthermore, not only to help students notice the effects produced when highly varied rhythm works with complex sound patterns but also to help them see how the placement of a single word — "brightness" — can reveal to the reader the significance of the poem: What would be lost if the rhymes of lines 10 and 12 were reversed and the last line read: "amid incredible whiteness"?

Finally, here are two poems that are yet more challenging readings; the first, because of the unusual verse form and the changing quality of the speaker's voice; the second, because of its apparent simplicity and its actual subtlety. Both poems give shape to concerns deeply felt by serious high school students.

Richard Wilbur's "Junk" (thirty lines) suggests that the making of gimcrack and junk destroys the maker, not the materials. The violated material, cleansed by the weather and the fire of the dump and "buried/To the depth of diamonds," is remade by nature, but the maker has "bartered" his pride "like the bought boxer" or "the paid-off jockey." During the study of this poem we would want students to see how the Anglo-Saxon verse form is manipulated to render the successive voices of the speaker as he moves from his first notice of the axe handle, to his exclamation, to his quiet judgment on the makers and his biblical "voice of God" condemnation of the materials — to purging fire and "making dark." At the close of our study of this poem, we would want students to consider: What is the significance of using the Anglo-Saxon verse form to render *this* theme? If necessary, we might precede this question with, How does the poem expand in time and place as it proceeds?

This poem uses references in lines 22–28 and lines 29–30; these would have to be glossed when the poem was assigned, even though only able readers would be studying this poem.

Robert Frost's five-stanza "Come In" dramatizes the tension between man's attraction toward the awesome mystery of the unseen world and his fear of it.

> As I came to the edge of the woods,
> Thrush music — hark!
> Now if it was dusk outside,
> Inside it was dark.

> Too dark in the woods for a bird   5
> By sleight of wing
> To better its perch for the night,
> Though it still could sing.
>
> The last of the light of the sun
> That had died in the west   10
> Still lived for one song more
> In a thrush's breast.
>
> Far in the pillared dark
> Thrush music went —
> Almost like a call to come in   15
> To the dark and lament.
>
> But no, I was out for stars:
> I would not come in.
> I meant not even if asked,
> And I hadn't been. *   20

During the study of this poem we would want students to perceive the successive "acts" in the speaker's little drama: his casual beginning and initial arrest (lines 1–4), his progressive involvement with the "dark" (lines 5–14), the critical moment of near captivation (lines 15–16), his decisive retreat to the world of light (lines 17–18), a withdrawal so fearful that he treats it with casual wit (lines 19–20). Because of the quality of the readers who would be studying such a poem as this, we would prepare for discussion simply by *being ready* to call their attention to whatever we guessed they might overlook. We would *be ready* to ask such questions as:

How does the rhythm of the first stanza give the feeling of sudden arrest? What uses of language transport the reader to the world of the woods? (And we would want comments on repetitions, rhymes, approximate rhymes in parallel structures — at least.)

Why does the speaker use the word "sleight? Why the word "better"? (Why not "improve"?) What meanings of "still" are working here (line 8)? How is stanza two connected with stanza three?

Why is line 11 crucial? What calls the reader's attention to what line 11 is suggesting? (If necessary: Contrast the pace of the line with that of the preceding lines. Notice the sound of "Still lived," the placement of the phrase, and the tension in its meanings. Notice the reversal of "one song more.")

Why does "Far in the pillared dark" give a "haunting feeling"

(students' usual phrase for this)? Why does the speaker say "went"
—not "came"? What is the effect of the dash (line 14)? Of the
placement and rhythm of "Almost" (line 15)? Did "lament" surprise
you?

What do stars *now* suggest? What makes lines 17–18 so definite?
Why should the speaker be so definite — it was only "Almost"? In
the last sentence (lines 19–20), how has his feeling changed? If you
did not know, what would you think the speaker was referring to in
these lines? How does the end of the poem relate to the beginning?

Our comments and our questions on the poems we have suggested
for the teaching of diction and syntax and rhythm should not be
construed as lesson plans. They are, rather, jottings in a teacher's
journal: things we would be interested in and strategies to "get at
them," ways to show the working together of the several means to
meaning the class has studied, little sequences of questions — in other
words, the "raw materials" that, shaped and spelled out, would make
lessons. For examples of developed lesson plans, look back at the
teaching of "Blue Girls" or the teaching of "Futility." Both illustrate
usable plans for day-to-day lessons. The plan we shall now detail,
to conclude this section, is for the *kind* of lesson we would teach to
average readers if we wanted to evaluate how well they had achieved
the aims of the course so far; in other words, if we wanted to find
out how well the individual students in a class could sense dramatic
situation, trace dramatic movement, and suggest the ways certain
words, sounds, syntax, and rhythm function to render the meaning
of a poem.

Our poem is Michael Drayton's sonnet, "Since There's No Help,"
which is a good test vehicle for such a class because it is obvious
enough for all to respond to some extent and challenging enough to
elicit varying qualities of response.

> Since there's no help, come let us kiss and part,
> Nay, I have done; you get no more of me,
> And I am glad, yea glad with all my heart,
> That thus so cleanly I myself can free;
> Shake hands for ever, cancel all our vows,   5
> And when we meet at any time again,
> Be it not seen in either of our brows
> That we one jot of former love retain.
> Now at the last gasp of love's latest breath,
> When, his pulse failing, passion speechless lies,   10
> When faith is kneeling by his bed of death,
> And innocence is closing up his eyes,
> Now if thou wouldst, when all have given him over,
> From death to life, thou mightst him yet recover.

The assignment, to be done the previous day or the previous night, would be as follows:

Read Drayton's "Since There's No Help" aloud to yourself. Decide how the speaker would say each line. Check any line or phrase you are unsure about and jot down what puzzles you. (Who, for instance, does "his" refer to in line 10? line 11? line 12?) Answer the following two questions in *writing:*
1. What is the dramatic situation in this poem? (Who is speaking to whom about what?) What is the speaker's initial attitude?
2. List, in order of occurrence, the points in the poem at which the speaker *modifies* his initial attitude. How, in each case, is it changed?

In class we would spend about twenty minutes clearing up the puzzling lines and answering the two homework questions. The answering of question 2 should *not* be detailed — just a list of a few points. The purpose of this part of the lesson is to make sure that the text and the basic dramatic organization are "straight" for everyone.

Then, for the remaining thirty minutes, the students would answer in writing the following duplicated questions:

1. Lines 9–14 are no surprise to the careful reader. He has never quite believed that the speaker "meant it." Point out three clues in lines 1–8 that would make the reader doubt the speaker; for instance, why kiss before parting?
2. Now point out a chain of words in lines 1–9 that suggest the kind of fellow the speaker is and so prepare the reader for the "grand scene" of lines 9–12.
3. Lines 9–14 are all one sentence. (a) How would you describe the order of the sentence? (b) Why is it ordered as it is?
4. (a) Point out *two* places in these lines where sound and rhythm together attract the reader's attention. (b) *How* do they attract attention? (c) *Why* do they attract attention?

The breakdown of questions 3 and 4 into lettered parts and the overly explicit wording of some questions are necessary in some average classes in order to prevent students' consuming the test time by asking questions on the questions.

During this First Part of our course, students have been learning to respond to the connotations, the sounds, and the rhythms of individual words and to the effects these words create when they are patterned in certain ways. But while students were concentrating on "these words in this order," they were continually "reviewing" what we had stressed in the Introduction. For they were continually seeing how much the choice and the patterning of words are affected by and express the character of the speaker, his state of mind, and his changing attitude. What a difference it would have made to the choice and the patterning of words had a cynic reflected on "The

Man He Killed," had an intimate friend reported Richard Cory's death. Think how a different speaker would have modified the word patterns of "Silence," how a different state of mind would have altered the syntax of "Six Nuns in the Snow." Students cannot talk about the function of diction, syntax, and rhythm without talking about the speaker's experience as it unfolds in the poem.

And they cannot talk much about the speaker's experience in certain poems without considering, to some extent at least, the images, metaphors, and symbols that help to define it. Only think of what would be involved in any discussion of "Dust of Snow," "The Eagle and the Mole," "The Main Deep," "Big Wind," "Design," "Six Nuns in the Snow," or "Come In." So when students move on to the Second Part of the course, they will simply concentrate on what they have noticed in passing when they discussed such poems as those.

The Second Part: Speaking of One Thing in Terms of Another

In this part of the course, we would be trying to help students learn to respond appropriately to images, similes, metaphors, and symbols — wherever they occur in poems and however they are functioning. We phrase our aim this way to emphasize that it is a flexible skill students must develop: an ability to sense the presence of these devices in the poem being read, to recognize how they are working in the poem — in concert with all other devices we have emphasized so far, and to react accordingly. By the wording of our aim, we want to stress that, although noticing an image, discovering in what ways term A and term B in a metaphor are similar, and realizing what "snow" symbolizes are all necessary acts, they are just preliminaries to the real task of recognizing how these devices function in the poem, what effects they have on the meaning — how, for instance, this metaphor said by this speaker in this syntactic construction and in this rhythmic pattern urges us to "take" the poem this way, rather than that. Like dramatic situation, dramatic movement, connotation, sound, syntax, and rhythm — images, similes, metaphors, and symbols are means to meaning, and, works of literature being what they are, readers must learn to respond finally to the simultaneous working together of many such means. To develop such readers is our goal, but we shall once again in this part of the course, as in earlier sections, proceed toward the goal by easy stages. We shall begin with a study of images, move to similes, to metaphors, and finally to symbols.

Because of the nature of these literary devices, this order of study seems most feasible. We would begin with images because an image is usually one of the terms in the other three devices and, in most cases, a reader's response to simile, metaphor, or symbol begins with his evoking precisely the relevant "imagined sensory reaction." Furthermore, an initial familiarity with the functions of images *can* facilitate students' responding appropriately to the other three devices. If a reader has learned to respond to a detailed image that leads to a statement, it is easy for him to read a poem with a detailed image leading to a simile. If he is familiar with images used singly or in related groupings to *illustrate* or *clarify* an idea or feeling, he can easily adapt his response to comparable imagery used in similes and metaphors to *explain* an object, idea, or feeling. If he is able to infer an otherwise inexpressible experience from a detailed image or a coupling of images, then it is easier for him to sense an evolving symbol. The possibility of such transfers as these make the study of images a useful point of departure for our study of similes, metaphors, and symbols.

Studying these four devices in this order seems right, furthermore, because each succeeding device requires the reader to perform an increasingly complex mental process and gives him less direct help in doing it. Generally speaking, to respond appropriately to images, the reader has only to evoke the relevant sensory perception and see how that *illustrates* or *clarifies* a more or less explicitly given idea, feeling, or impression. To respond to similes ("Hope is like a harebell"), he must, of course, evoke the "imagined sense reaction" and see how an object, idea, or feeling is *explained* by being *expressly compared* to an apparently dissimilar "thing" in such a way as to reveal certain similarities between the two. He must see from a literally false comparison a new truth. Metaphor demands the same kind of perception, but to respond rightly to it, the reader must *identify*, in certain respects, apparently dissimilar things. Some metaphors overtly direct the reader ("Hope is the thing with feathers"): A is B. Some merely imply in some way the identification of the apparent dissimilars ("Hope sings"): A B's. Since it is easier for the reader to follow a direction than to infer from a suggestion, we study "equation" (A is B) metaphors first, then the "submerged" (A B's) metaphors. Finally, to respond rightly to a symbol, the reader must evoke the relevant "imagined sense reaction," recognize that the simple object (a bird, say) is more than itself, and discover by accurate and imaginative responses to the clues in the poem what that "more" might be (Hope, say). The reader is given the B term (the bird); he must recognize either from tradition or from the detailing in the poem what complex of ideas and feelings — what A term — that B term denotes. A challenging task for our readers, who, of course, *still* must discover how the symbol functions in the poem!

Studying these four devices in the order we suggest seems not only logically but also psychologically "right." The devices make increasing demands which facility with each device makes the reader increasingly able to meet. By this sequence of study, we hope to bring students slowly but steadily from being satisfactory respondents to the easiest instances of images to being adequate respondents to symbols created within poems.

Now, we shall detail our proposed four-part study into a practically usable sequence, and we shall suggest poems that would be appropriate readings for sensitizing various kinds of students to each of the four literary devices. But, as we said earlier, in actual practice only the particular teacher can decide which devices a certain class needs to study and to what extent it should concentrate on each. And only the teacher can decide which poems would be most apposite for teaching each device. For a certain class, the teacher might decide to eschew new poems, and instead to read again some that the class had read during its study of dramatic situation, or diction, or syntax and rhythm. For another group, he might decide to use poems that he had rejected in an earlier part of the course because then they would have been too difficult or less relevant for the particular class. We are thinking of such poems as "To An Athlete Dying Young," "Heresy for a Classroom," "Tree at My Window," "The Listeners," "There's A Certain Slant of Light," and "Six Nuns in the Snow" — all of which would be appropriate for the study of one or another of the devices now being emphasized. Since the attentive reading of poems facilitates the reading of them, many poems that have to be foregone at one time in a course are feasible later on.

Our annotations on the poems we cite are, in most cases, brief remarks on the poem's particular use of the relevant devices. By now, it would seem excessive to point out in our discussion of each poem what features of its dramatic situation and movement, its diction, its syntax, and its rhythm we would ask about during the study of the poem. Suffice it to say, we would always be especially interested in *all* the means to meaning featured so far in the course.

Image

By "image" we mean a word or group of words that can evoke an "imagined sensory reaction": visual, auditory, olfactory, gustatory, tactile, kinetic, kinesthetic, thermal, as well as combinations of these sensations.[24] The reader's job is to respond to such a word or group of words sensitively enough to, in fact, have the "reaction."

A person's ability to respond to an image depends on the range and the quality of his experience, on the precision of his memory of it, and on his ability to read. In order to evoke the sensory experience being represented, the reader must have undergone a relevant sensation *in some way*, must have *somehow* noticed his experience, and must now be able to recall it accurately and use it selectively, as the words on the page direct. There are, in other words, many points at which a reader's response to an image may "break down."

Some high school students have trouble responding sensitively to images because throughout their lives they have tended to glance at the world and glance at a page. We cannot now give them a rich fund of well-remembered experience, but we can make them "stand and stare": we can repeatedly assign writing tasks that require precise sensory reactions. We mean exercises like Walker Gibson's on "looking,"[25] like many in Hart Leavitt and David Sohn's excellent *Stop, Look, and Write!*[26] and like some suggested later in "Collateral Writing for a First Course in Reading Poems." We cannot now give students a legacy of careful reading, but we can, of course, help them to notice precisely what sensory reaction the words are calling for: we can require them to examine the words closely to see how they state, suggest, or imply certain physical conditions, certain degrees of specificity, certain intensities. This will make it possible for students to evoke precise responses, accurate and undistorted, neither omitting details nor elaborating, neither heightening effects nor lessening them.

It is precise responses, not identical ones, that we are trying to help students make. When they read a certain image, all students must notice, for instance, that it is snowing, that it is evening, that a bell is ringing, and they must hear the bell sound in the atmosphere. One student's bell sound probably will not be another's, but all students who have in their lives listened attentively to "bell through snow" will probably now have a rather similar and at least adequate sensory perception and a similar and at least adequate emotional response. That is enough.

When students can look at a configuration of words, evoke the appropriate sensory reaction, and enjoy the emotional response the image elicits, *then* they are ready to ascertain how the image functions in the poem, how it affects the meaning. To discover *that* is what we are really aiming to help students learn to do because it is what as readers they must be able to do.

What organization of material will we use to help students achieve an adequate response to images? We wish, of course, that there were a truly simple way to begin, that there were poems with images appealing to only a single sense, for instance, or poems that were "pure examples." But poems *are* complex and their words make many concomitant claims upon readers. We could, however, limit the field initially for these beginning readers by first studying poems that have one dominant image. This is what we would do. And when students became somewhat competent at responding to single images and sensing their functions, then we would begin reading poems with two juxtaposed images. Finally, we would study poems that interrelate several images from different areas of experience.

■ *Poems with a Dominant Image.* We would try to make students' initial experience with images as diverse as possible: we would want them to begin immediately building a flexible response to images. So we would read some poems with brief images and some with extended images, some with images appealing mainly to a single sense and some with images appealing to several senses, some with graphic images and some with muted ones, some with particular images and some with general ones. From a list of poems like the following, we could select several different groupings, all of which would provide this kind of variety.

Here, first, are some haiku "finger exercises" that we might use to begin our study. The poems are, we think, in a sequence of difficulty: Buson's "Spring Breeze," Kyoshi's "The Snake," Shiki's muted "Spring Road," Hashin's subtle "Loneliness," and Basho's "Stillness" and his "Lightning at Night."[27] Since in Basho's poems the second line completes the first and opens the third, and so fuses both, we have a fine opportunity, as early as this, to show students slight, simple interrelating.

Some short imagist poems that we might read as "openers" or as sequels to one or more of the haikus are:

William Carlos Williams' "Nantucket." A ten-line visual image.

H. D.'s "Storm." A thirteen-line poem with visual, kinesthetic and kinetic images.

William Carlos Williams' "Dawn." A sixteen-line poem with auditory and kinesthetic images especially, as well as remarkably effective use of abstract words and of line division.

And to conclude the brief poems, F. S. Flint's image-to-impression "Beggar":

> In the gutter
> piping his sadness
> an old man stands,
> bent and shriveled,
> beard draggled,   5
> eyes dead.
>
> Huddled and mean,
> shivering in threadbare clothes —
> winds beat him,
> hunger bites him,   10
> forlorn, a whistle in his hands,
> piping.

> Hark! the strange quality
> of his sorrowful music,
> wind from an empty belly   15
> wrought magically
> into the wind, —

Finally, some poems with less obtrusive images:

John Clare's simple Shakespearian sonnet "Young Lambs." The images illustrate the statement of the first line: "The spring is coming by a many signs."

Theodore Roethke's twenty-seven line "Night Journey." Syntax and line division produce a kaleidoscope of visual, auditory, kinetic, and kinesthetic images.

Wilfred Owen's muted war poem, "The Send-Off." In four five-line stanzas, visual and auditory images (and a simile and two metaphors) create a pervading darkness, a false quiet, so right for the event. The syntax and the line division are beautifully appropriate. And the brief poignant image of a return in the last three lines makes this poem a fine transition to the following, second group of readings.

■ *Poems with Two Juxtaposed Images.*   In John Keats' sonnet "On the Grasshopper and Cricket," the initial statement — "The poetry of earth is never dead" — is "proved" by two largely auditory images, that of the grasshopper's voice and that of the cricket's, which become revealingly identified at the close of the poem.

> The poetry of earth is never dead:
> When all the birds are faint with the hot sun,
> And hide in cooling trees, a voice will run
> From hedge to hedge about the new-mown mead;
> That is the Grasshopper's — he takes the lead   5
> In summer luxury, — he has never done
> With his delights; for when tired out with fun
> He rests at ease beneath some pleasant weed.
> The poetry of earth is ceasing never:
> On a lone winter evening, when the frost   10
> Has wrought a silence, from the stove there shrills
> The Cricket's song, in warmth increasing ever,
> And seems to one in drowsiness half lost,
> The Grasshopper's among some grassy hills.

In Keats' poem, the two images *illustrate* a statement; in each of the following three poems, the pair of juxtaposed images *lead to* a statement.

Images of "Hyla Brook" — then and now — in Robert Frost's fif-
teen-line poem lead to, and create, the ambiguity of the statement
of the final line, "We love the things we love for what they are."

The images in Edwin Denby's modern sonnet, "First Warm Days,"
render the feeling of human community that the final couplet states:
"We are pleased by an air like of loving/Going home quiet in the
subway-shoving." This sonnet's effective use of alliteration and
approximate rhymes provides the class with a good opportunity to
"look backward"; its use of personification gives us a good chance to
"look ahead."

In Richard Blackmur's variation of a sonnet, "Mirage," the initial
image of flat, colorless, moribund calm is "suddenly" replaced by an
image of fertile, colorful, vital activity. Ironically, the world of death
and nothingness is the real world; the world of vigor and promise
is a mirage. But, as the last line says, from the moment of the mirage
on, the speaker simply exists in the first world, he "lives" in the
glimpsed vision of fulfilled desire. The rhythm, the syntax, the
sound, the use of abstract and concrete words — all work with the
images to suggest the ironic death-life contrast and make the
speaker's choice of the imaginary world indisputably "right."

Each of these last three poems leads from two juxtaposed images
to some sort of statement; the next four poems merely *imply* a certain
relationship between the two images they present. This a "giant
step" for the reader. But, if his study of one or more of the preceding image-to-statement poems has been careful, it should now help
him infer appropriate relationships in these unguided poems.

An easy reading is Carl Sandburg's thirteen-line poem, "The
Harbor." The first five lines are an image of a "huddled and ugly"
city slum, a funnel-like hell of human hunger; the last eight, an
image of an open, free, "blue burst of lake" at the city's edge. The
point-for-point contrast is obvious: city—country, enclosed—open,
dark—light, shackled humans—free animals, semi-death—life. And
the structures of sound and of rhythm in each of the two parts underscore the impressions the images evoke. The ironic contrast of images
suggests a meaning which can be further refined if students notice
the relative length of the images, the order of them, the fact that,
though the two form one sentence, the city image is subordinated
syntactically — and, finally, if they notice that the poem is called
"The Harbor," with all that implies.

James Stephens' "The Shell" is not a more difficult poem than
Sandburg's, but it probably has a more limited audience. Why?
Not only because the imagery is often general and always muted,
but also because the chief world evoked by the sound of the shell is
the eerie "other world" of the highly imaginative. The poem juxtaposes for a final revelatory moment the world of "sea sound" and the

world of "cart sound." Indeed, in this poem, these two sounds come to symbolize the two spheres of human experience that relieve one another. This thirty-line poem makes rich use not only of auditory, tactile, visual, and kinetic images, but also of word sounds to support the impressions the images are evoking, of rhythm and line division to suggest ocean movements, and of a clear, conversational voice to render the fascination, the fear, and the relief of the speaker.

In Wilfred Gibson's fourteen-line "Battle: Hit,"[28] the speaker juxtaposes two images of himself: one, lazing on a ledge at the ocean side; the other, sprawling, wounded, in a trench. What is the reader to make of this juxtaposition? The second stanza, read carefully and imaginatively, will illuminate the relationship between the images. But this poem *is* for average-to-able readers.

And so is our final suggestion, William Carlos Williams' "The Yachts." At the end of the eighth stanza, there is a sudden shift of image: the serenely beautiful scene of the yachts preparing for the race changes without warning to the grotesque, nightmare image of the last three stanzas — a collage of frantic, drowning men and "skillful" boats indifferently passing over them. Williams' juxtaposition of images in this poem will provoke able readers to *many* justifiable interpretations. In their search for meaning, students should ask why certain fears are developed in the first four stanzas and ironically reversed in the last three, and they should take into account the effects created by the "prose" style, by the insect comparisons, and by the quiet restraint of the speaking voice that heightens the ominousness of the beginning and intensifies the irony of the outcome.

■ *Poems with Interrelated Images.*   Able readers probably need no special introduction to the reading of poems with interrelated images, but less able and even average readers might. So, to help less able readers make the transition from grasping the relationship between two images to perceiving the interrelatedness among several, we would probably begin with poems like Adelaide Crapsey's "Triad":

> These be
> Three silent things:
> The falling snow . . . the hour
> Before the dawn . . . the mouth of one
> Just dead.*

poems that are "miniatures" and that guide the reader's interpretation.

---

* Reprinted from *Verse*, by Adelaide Crapsey, by permission of Alfred A. Knopf, Inc. Copyright © 1922 by Algernon S. Crapsey and renewed 1950 by The Adelaide Crapsey Foundation.

To introduce average readers to interrelated images, we would study poems in which the several images used complement one another rather clearly and build rather obviously to a total pattern, the meaning of which is clear without statement, interpretation, or overt suggestion of any sort. Winfield Townley Scott's twenty-line "The Child's Morning" and Robert Francis' nine-line "Preparation"[29] are short, generally usable readings of this sort; John Keats' thirty-three line triptych, "Ode to Autumn," is a rich, sustained instance.

After such introductory studies as these, some less able readers and many average readers would be ready to learn to respond to more complex uses of interrelated images. So we would introduce them to two kinds of poems able readers might begin on: poems in which the relationship among the disparate images is much more intricate and multifaceted than the statement in the poem seems to suggest and poems in which the reader has to grasp, without guidance, a subtle relationship among the several images. W. H. Auden's "Musee des Beaux Arts" and Louis MacNeice's "Snow" are instances of the first kind of poem; Robert Frost's "To Earthward," of the second.

In Auden's twenty-one line poem, a reflective narrator defines the "human position of suffering" by means of images of increasing length, concreteness, specificity — and irony. As his successive examples gradually reveal an ever greater incongruity between suffering and the circumstances attending it, the narrator moves from his initial casual attitude to a quiet bitterness. This is a fine poem for showing students how syntactic, rhythmic, and rhyming patterns express the change in attitude that the successive images evoke. For this reason, and because of the special preparation required for reading this poem, we suggest, below, a plan for teaching it to average students. For them it is a good final exercise on images.

In MacNeice's twelve-line poem, "Snow," the initial image of the collateral snow and roses touches off a bevy of insights and associated images which suggest at once the compatibility of incompatibles and the gap between collaterals. The successive images are spurted out by the speaker as "evidence" for the "suddenness," the "craziness," the "variety" of the world. The patterning of images, the range of diction, the complex speaker, the inner drama that the poem plays out, and the importance of the poem on the page to the meaning of the poem — all make "Snow" an excellent closing for a mature class of sensitive readers.

A good alternate reading for them would be Robert Frost's "To Earthward." Through a series of olfactory, visual, and especially tactile images, an aging speaker recalls the gradual change, during his lifetime, of his sense of joy. In this eight-stanza poem, sound and rhythmic and stanzaic patterns call attention to the speaker's shifting "requirements" and help the reader infer the unstated connections.

A TEACHING OF AUDEN'S "MUSEE DES BEAUX ARTS." As we select a certain poem for a certain class, we are always imagining how the students will respond to it. We are trying to discover what necessary information they will lack, what features might confuse them, what negative attitudes they might take. Then we try to prepare so as to obviate these potential obstacles. Teaching some poems requires several sorts of preparation. "Musee des Beaux Arts" is one of these.

When we assess this poem, we realize that most students probably will not be familiar with the phrases "Musee des Beaux Arts" and "Old Masters," with the Icarus myth and with Brueghel's painting. The question is what precisely do they have to know about each of these things to read this poem. (For we should provide that and only that at this time.) They must know only that Musee des Beaux Arts is a museum, a place where art works, including paintings, are displayed; only that "Old Masters" is an epithet for great painters. They must know that, according to Greek myth, the young boy Icarus, escaping from the labyrinth on wax wings, flew too near the sun and drowned in the sea. And they must notice the youth of Icarus and the "necessity" of the sun's act, for these are important in the use Brueghel and Auden make of the myth. All of this preparation is information, and students can be given it orally or from the board or on duplicated sheets.

But what about Brueghel's "Icarus"? Beyond the fact that Brueghel was a sixteenth-century painter, and so an "Old Master," no information *about* the painting will really prepare students to respond adequately to the reference in the poem. Since the poem comments interpretively on the painting, uses it as an "instance," the reader needs an image of the painting. The words, of course, evoke a visual reaction, but seeing a print of the painting helps students markedly. They should be shown one.[30]

When we assess Auden's poem for teaching, we realize that, in addition to these kinds of preparation, students will probably need another sort. For many high school readers might take the same indifferent attitude toward the experience of this poem that the people in the poem take toward suffering — the very attitude the speaker is disapproving. Students' response might be "So? Eh!" — rather than "So. Ah!" Why would they respond in that way? They are not indifferent to suffering; indeed, they are generally shocked by, and explosively irate at, indifference to it. That partially accounts for why they might react to this poem as we suggested. They expect a *certain* response to suffering — an explosively irate one. The speaker's response does not live up to their expectations. So the speaker would evoke their indifference. If readers do not understand the speaker's response, they do not feel its poignancy.

Students must see *how* the speaker's response evolved, so they will understand *why* it is unostentatious. They might, then, even let themselves feel its quiet and deep feeling! We must make sure, therefore, that students understand the dramatic situation and join the speaker in his drama before they get a chance to blindly dismiss his talk as inconsequential.

Now that we see what preparation is needed for the teaching of this poem, we must decide how, in fact, we can provide it effectively and economically.

Preferably we would teach Auden's poem in two thirty-minute blocks of time on two consecutive days. The first half hour would be used for the necessary preparations, the second for the discussion of the images. This division of the lesson would give us a chance to prepare students for the reading and give students a chance to work independently and individually on the imagery. So although the poem could be taught in a single class period, with a concluding assignment to pull it together, the divided lesson has more benefits.

Think of our lesson, then, as beginning during the last half hour of a class period.[31] We would open by telling students we were about to read a poem called "Musee des Beaux Arts" (writing the title on the board).[32] What does the phrase mean? (And, What is a museum?, if it is a class in which some might not know.) We would tell the class, then, that this poem mentions a famous painting by one of the "Old Masters" (writing the phrase on the board). Who are they? The painting is called "Icarus" (writing the word on the board). Who is Icarus? We would give the information if necessary. Now, let's see how Brueghel represented this story in his painting. It will help us understand how the painting *works in the poem.* We stress "works in" because we want to prevent students from going to the reading of the poem with the erroneous assumption that it is about Icarus or about "Icarus."

If a print of Brueghel's "Icarus" is used, it should be projected on a screen since the details of the painting must be seen. They are what Auden interprets. As we showed the print, we would ask successively about the position of the farmer, of the sun, and of the ship and about what is suggested by their respective positions. We would ask about each item separately so that students would feel the details "piling up." We could then ask, What is the whole painting suggesting? These preliminaries would take about fifteen minutes. Then, we would go directly to the poem — and to the second part of our preparation.

It is difficult to read this poem well orally every time. For it is difficult to suggest casualness without flippancy, understated bitterness without sarcasm. So, in some quiet moment, we would make as good a tape as we could of this poem (and of other similarly demanding poems). We would use the tape now, students following the poem in their texts.

When all were poised for the reading, we would ask students to decide during the reading how they would describe the state of mind of the speaker. (We are purposely using a "loose" phrase so that students can do as much as possible on their own.)

Here is Auden's poem:

About suffering they were never wrong,
The Old Masters: how well they understood
Its human position; how it takes place
While someone else is eating or opening a window or just
    walking dully along;
How, when the aged are reverently, passionately waiting   5
For the miraculous birth, there always must be
Children who did not specially want it to happen, skating
On a pond at the edge of the wood:
They never forgot
That even the dreadful martyrdom must run its course   10
Anyhow in a corner, some untidy spot
Where the dogs go on with their doggy life and the torturer's
    horse
Scratches its innocent behind on a tree.

In Brueghel's *Icarus*, for instance: how everything turns away
Quite leisurely from the disaster; the ploughman may   15
Have heard the splash, the forsaken cry,
But for him it was not an important failure; the sun shone
As it had to on the white legs disappearing into the green
Water; and the expensive delicate ship that must have seen
Something amazing, a boy falling out of the sky,   20
Had somewhere to get to and sailed calmly on.*

After the usual questions on dramatic situation, we would spend about fifteen minutes clarifying the speaker's "state of mind." In an average class the quality of responses generally varies more widely than it does in other groups. Some students might simply call the speaker "disorganized" or "reminiscent," while others would say, "He's remembering, so he's saying it as it occurs to him, kind of associating things" or, "He's admiring the insight of the Old Masters; then, he's thinking quietly about the irony of suffering going on that way, sort of meditating." The evidence they would offer in support

---

* Reprinted from *Selected Poetry of W. H. Auden* by permission of Random House, Inc. Copyright © 1940 by W. H. Auden.

of their decisions would vary widely too, but many would notice the reversals of syntax, the long, loose-jointed first sentence, the succession of "or's" in line 4, the indefinite references. We would probably have to ask the class if the rhythm supports their contentions. They probably would not notice that metrical substitutions and punctuation and rhyme scheme conspire to create the irregular "run-stop-run-stop" of thought association. But with a few well-placed "nudges," average readers would grasp the speaker's state of mind well enough at this point to know what *not* to expect of him. So they would be ready to study the function of the images in the poem.

The assignment for tomorrow's class would be:

Read the poem carefully once again, paying particular attention now to the images the speaker uses. Answer the following questions in writing:
1. What is the speaker's purpose in using the images?
2. In what ways are the images similar?
3. In what ways different? [This question would be followed by "leads" if it seemed advisable in the particular class.]
4. Why are the images ordered as they are? We know, of course, that they are in the order in which they occurred to the speaker, but the question is *why* do they occur to him in that order?
5. Today in class, we talked generally about the speaker's "state of mind." Now, you have just examined the images closely and have noticed especially the ways they differ and the way they are ordered. What changes in the speaker's attitude did you notice? What suggested these changes to you?

During the first half hour of class the next day, we would discuss the function of imagery in the poem. How, would depend upon the quality of preparation we felt we could count on. If most of the students were haphazard, mediocre workers, we would have the class discuss the questions one by one. We would need the "pooling" to arrive at adequate answers, and unless the class had adequate answers to the first three questions, they could not have them to questions 4 and 5. Ill-prepared students are not ready to answer "the big question"; they simply do not have the data. But good, thorough workers do. And if most in the class were good workers, then doing the assignment would have given them all the data necessary for handling a broad question productively. So, we would ask one opening question and let them develop an answer. Our question would probably be: "The first two and a half lines tell us what the poem is about. Do we really *need* the images?"

Whenever a class recognizes how images are working, now in this instance, now in that — and this may be after the study of two poems, or after the reading of one from each of the three sections, or after the study of one from the first section and three from the second —

in other words, whenever the students are ready, we would begin the study of similes.

Simile

By "simile," we mean a group of words that expressly compares two apparently dissimilar things — for instance, white moonlight gables and still hands at prayer — so as to reveal some existing similarity and give the reader a new truth.[33] Or, as we would probably put it to a less able class, Simile says, "Now compare this with that: white moonlight gables with still hands at prayer. A and B don't seem to be alike at all, but they are. Let's see how." And after we had seen "how," we would ask, What new truth about the gables does this comparison reveal that comparison with, say, "still tents after a battle" would not?

Since our aim is to help students learn to respond sensitively to similes, let us see what, specifically, such a response consists of. It begins, of course, with the reader's recognizing a simile — not confusing it with a literally true comparison. Then, he must read the terms of the comparison precisely, letting A and B simultaneously modify one another, so he can see in exactly what respects A and B are alike.[34] The reader must, that is, let the gables tell him the color, texture, and position of the hands — they are white, not weathered; smooth, not gnarled; with palms pressed, not fingers folded. He must let the hands suggest the attitude of the gables. When he has done all this, he must perceive the new truth that reveals itself — the contemplative attitude of the gables, say. Finally, the reader must see how this simile said by this speaker works both at the point at which it is said *and* in the whole poem.

This seems like a large order, but our students have been practicing several aspects of this response during their study of diction and imagery. They have been letting context tell them what meanings and suggestions are relevant; they have been seeing how juxtaposed elements affect one another; they have been evoking precise reactions to images; and they have been continually going beyond the recognition of devices to ask about their functions. So, they come to the study of similes prepared in ways that will help them to achieve the specific aims of the study: to learn to discover the exact similarities between the A-term and the B-term and to recognize the function of similes in particular contexts.

As we discussed the interaction between the terms of each simile, we would continually, though unobtrusively, stress the fact that the similarity the simile uncovers is a similarity *in dissimilar things* — a point of likeness in the unlike. Since this is so, the reader must not lose sight of either the similarity or the dissimilarity of A and B. For only by realizing both at once can he have the whole truth of a simile. Perceiving similes offers students a fine chance to extend their own life experience, extend it not by accumulating more or by differentiating what they have, but by discovering unities in their dissimilar experiences.

Many different organizations of material would help students learn to respond to similes. We propose *one* of these: a three-part scheme designed to sensitize readers to several of the common forms of this figure.

We would *begin* this study by reading poems[35] in which *one thing is gradually explained by several related similes.*

Two poems suitable for less able readers are Langston Hughes' "Harlem" and Henry King's "Sic Vita." In Hughes' poem, five similes propose the possible detrimental effects of a "dream deferred." In King's, six comparisons define concretely the transiency of man's life. Here is King's poem:

> Like to the falling of a star;
> Or as the flights of eagles are;
> Or like the fresh spring's gaudy hue;
> Or silver drops of morning dew;
> Or like a wind that chafes the flood;   5
> Or bubbles which on water stood;
> Even such is man, whose borrowed light
> Is straight called in, and paid to night.

In both King's poem and Hughes' the images are graphic, the areas of experience they are drawn from, fairly familiar. In both, the general function of the diverse comparisons is clear, so the reader can give much of his attention to other matters: to the way the comparisons are patterned (in King's poem, leading to a statement; in Hughes', arising from a question), to the effects achieved by the particular pattern, and to the reasons for the way the comparisons are ordered in the poem. (Why, for instance, does King begin with the falling star and end with bubbles?) Because of the subject matter of these two poems, the assistance they give the reader, and the opportunities they leave him, they are fruitful readings for the less able.

An appropriate poem for average-to-good readers is Archibald MacLeish's prescription for a poem, "Ars Poetica." Similes in eight of the twelve couplets explain the characteristics a poem should have. In each simile, the reader is told the basis of the comparison; he has to see how the B-term qualifies the characteristic ("A poem should be palpable and mute/As a globed fruit"). Discussion of the last four stanzas will introduce students early and naturally to the concept of symbol.

We would *continue* this study of the forms of simile by reading poems in which *one thing is explained by comparison with just one other thing which is extensively detailed to bring out many 'points of correspondence between the two things.*

Less able readers might study a poem like John Gould Fletcher's six-line "Irradiations X" ("The trees, like great jade elephants") or a slender poem like

CENTRAL PARK TOURNEY
— *Mildred Weston*

Cars
In the Park
With long spear lights
Ride at each other
Like armored knights;
Rush,
Miss the mark,
Pierce the dark,
Dash by!
Another two
Try

Staged
In the Park
From dusk
To dawn,
The tourney goes on:
Rush,
Miss the mark,
Pierce the dark,
Dash by!
Another two
Try*

This fine extended comparison between cars and tilting knights gives us an opportunity to show students how the rhythm of a poem and its placement on the page work with the simile to dramatize an irony.

Average readers might study poems like Emily Dickinson's two-stanza "Longing Is Like the Seed" and Robert Frost's sonnet, "The

---

* Reprinted by permission of The New Yorker Magazine, Inc., Copyright © 1953.

Silken Tent." In addition to our usual work on the terms and the functions of the similes, we would want to help students see why the seed in Miss Dickinson's poem is defined so abstractly and how the style of Frost's sonnet represents the temperament the simile explains. So, about "The Silken Tent" we would ask: How many sentences are there in Frost's poem? *How* does he include all that in one sentence? As you read the poem, were you aware that it is a highly organized single sentence? What form of poem is it? Were you aware that the poem is in strict Shakespearian sonnet form? *How* does the poem keep you from being aware of its restraints? *Why* is the poem written so that you are kept unaware of its restraints?

Average-to-competent readers might study such poems as Richard Wilbur's three-stanza "Mind" ("Mind in its purest play is like some bat"), his twelve-line "A Simile for Her Smile," and E. E. Cummings' nineteen-line poem "spring is like a perhaps hand." It takes a precise reader to know not only what is being compared with what in "A Simile for Her Smile" but also what kind of "ease" the images in the clauses are defining. It takes a flexible reader to let the line division of Cummings' poem control his experience and to let the participles create in him the feeling of continuous, quiet motion.

We would *conclude* this study of the forms of simile by reading poems in which *various kinds of similes function variously.*

With less able and average readers we would probably read such poems as:

Oscar Wilde's three-stanza "Symphony in Yellow," in which four separate similes reinforce one another and work with many other visual and kinetic images to develop a single dominant impression of artificiality and incipient decay.

Or Robert Graves' "A Pinch of Salt," in which the first stanza only hints a "dream—bird" comparison; the second stanza, in a six-line extended simile, expressly compares "dreams" and "a tantalizing, elusive bird"; and the third stanza identifies the two.

Or Marianne Moore's fourteen-line "Silence," in which a single, casually stated, but thought-provoking, simile that compares "superior" people and cats not only explains the people but also subtly characterizes the man who used the comparison. Average readers might not understand what is gained either by the narrative framework used in this poem or by the long parenthetical in the cat simile. So we would be prepared to ask them about the function of both features.

With able readers, we would study such poems as George Barker's "Sonnet to My Mother" and Richard Wilbur's eight-stanza "A Black November Turkey." In Barker's poem, several separate similes which explain different characteristics of the speaker's mother are linked by the paradoxical overtones common to their B-terms: grossness and grandeur:

> Most near, most dear, most loved and most far,
> Under the window where I often found her
> Sitting as huge as Asia, seismic with laughter,
> Gin and chicken helpless in her Irish hand,
> Irresistible as Rabelais but most tender for 5
> The lame dogs and hurt birds that surround her, —
> She is a procession no one can follow after
> But be like a little dog following a brass band.
> She will not glance up at the bomber or condescend
> To drop her gin and scuttle to a cellar, 10
> But lean on the mahogany table like a mountain
> Whom only faith can move, and so I send
> O all my faith and all my love to tell her
> That she will move from mourning into morning.*

During the study of this poem, we would ask students about the dramatic situation, about the relation of rhythmic and rhyming patterns to the intent of the poem, and especially, about why such ordinary similes — almost cliché — are so effective in this context.

In Wilbur's "A Black November Turkey," the several similes are separate, but all center on incompatibles that are ironically reconciled in the turkey ("darkly auspicious as/The ace of spades," "As a cloud over thrashed branches"). We would want to call students' attention to the way these similes work with the oxymorons and with the ironically contrasted visual images and auditory images to point up the coexistence of opposites — indeed the need for them — and the value of each "side."

So much for our three-part scheme for teaching similes.

Are the three parts ordered according to increasing difficulty? Perhaps not. Our third part *should* come last. It clearly requires an experienced and flexible respondent. But for some students the order of our first two parts should be reversed. Some find it more difficult to recognize the point of similarity in each of several successive similes and to see the interrelationship among the separate B-terms than to follow the many ramifications of a single B-term. In other words, these students become confused by a series of comparisons, but they do not get "lost" in an extended simile. We placed the study of extended simile second because many students *do*

---

* Reprinted from *Selected Poems*, by George Barker, by permission of the author. (The Macmillan Company, 1941.)

"forget what the poem is about" while they are reading the long B-term. For them, the B-term becomes the poem — a long image signifying nothing beyond itself.

Perceiving many related similes and perceiving an extended simile are different kinds of mental acts requiring different kinds of attention. If the class has worked on interrelated and extended images, then when the teacher plans the study of similes, he can know — roughly at least — which order of study would be a "right" one for the particular class.

Whenever students are recognizing rather consistently how similes are working, it is time to begin the study of metaphor.

Metaphor

By "metaphor," we mean a group of words that identifies in some respect(s) two essentially unlike things. The identification may be stated ("Hope is the thing with feathers") or it may be assumed ("Hope sings"). But whether explicit or submerged, metaphor suggests a literally false "new" truth, which affords the reader a new sense of "Hope," say. Or, as we would probably put it to a less able class, Metaphor says, "*See* this as that:[36] see hope as the thing with feathers. A and B do not seem to be the same thing, but they are, in some ways." Which ways? And after the class had seen in which ways, we would ask: What new aspects of "hope" does this metaphor uncover that, for instance, "Hope is a candle" or "Hope is an anchor" would not uncover?

Now, let us see, more specifically, what is in a reader's response to a metaphor. It begins with his recognizing the group of words as a metaphor. Then, he must react precisely to whatever images are involved; he must see in what respects the A-term and the B-term are identified, and he must sense the insight and the feeling that the interaction of these terms suggests. And having perceived the metaphor, he then must recognize how this identification said by this speaker functions both at this point in the dramatic movement and in the whole poem.

We realize, at once, that during their study of images and of similes, our students have been practicing many of the acts that an appropriate response to a metaphor involves. So, by now we could expect them to read images accurately. And we could rely on their having some competence in establishing the points of identification of the A- and B-terms, some competence in relating the ramifications of an extended B-term to the A-term, and some competence in recognizing how several B-terms or several separate metaphors interrelate. (We say "some competence," both because students have had less practice in these last three acts and because these acts are, by nature, complex — demanding many trials to develop a tendency to respond appropriately.) Finally, we could now count on students' stressing the *functions* of the metaphors and on their having some sensitivity to the ways figures work.

But do you *really* think you can safely rely on such past learnings? *Now* — yes. Earlier in the course we would have been more hesitant to assume that what was taught was learned. For, it is often hard to convince some students, initially, that the course is cumulative: that they will need tomorrow what is taught today. Their past experience tells many of them that what is taught today they will write on a test on Friday and forget. But if our teaching *shows* them immediately and continuously that what is studied today is needed tomorrow and the week after and on and on, this "new" experience dictates a new behavior. Most students adjust. And by this point in the course, they expect to use the past in the present; they expect to see similarities to what they have been learning — and differences from it.

Needless to say, we cannot count on the same degree of competence in all classes. Less able students, for instance, learn thoroughly but often inflexibly. They are slow to adapt their learnings to new situations; they are well prepared but only potentially so. Bright but unmotivated students often concentrate only intermittently and so learn one part of a response very well, another part very superficially. We are less sure of how competent they are and less confident about what will carry over. But this does not mean that we, therefore, would abet their inattention — by teaching them as if there had been no yesterday. From the beginning of the course, in an unmotivated class, we would reinforce class study by having the students work individually at various points in each lesson — and then we would *expect* these students to learn the responses precisely and to retain them. They might not always fulfill our expectations but, as the course proceeds, they will come ever closer to doing so — with occasional understandable lapses, naturally!

So we *can* say that most students' earlier work on connotations, images, and similes does prepare them rather well for the study of metaphors, especially for the study of "equation" metaphors. Consequently, we are free to concentrate much of our effort on the study of "submerged" metaphors. This is the form of metaphor that poems most frequently use, the form that average readers most consistently overlook, and the form that most challenges even competent students. Since the average reader does not recognize these "subject-verb," "adjective-noun" metaphors, they rarely function in his experience of poems. The competent reader does notice these metaphors, but, because of the compressed expression of them, he often finds it difficult to clarify the exact basis of the identification of the terms and to ascertain the function of the metaphor without exaggerating or underestimating it. The prevalence of "submerged" metaphor and the problems it gives readers persuade us to give the study of it the lion's share of attention.

And we do. As we said earlier our study of metaphor has two sections: a short introductory section on "equation" metaphors and a longer second section on "submerged" metaphors. By placing the study of "equation" metaphors first, we give students a chance to use immediately what they know and to develop a strong and flexible response to the easier, more accessible form of metaphor. This order of study, furthermore, gives us a chance to familiarize students with "submerged" metaphors — through casual, intermittent contacts — before the regular study begins. We would call their attention to a "submerged" metaphor whenever it seemed natural to do so. For instance, if we were studying the "equation" metaphors in Edna St. Vincent Millay's "Spring" ("Life in itself is nothing/An empty cup, a flight of uncarpeted stairs"), it would be natural to ask, about the final image in the poem, "*Does* April come 'down this hill' every year?" So the study of "equation" metaphors would be valuable in itself and a useful preparation for the longer, second section on "submerged" metaphors.

During the study of "submerged" metaphors, we would be trying mainly to help students learn to recognize this kind of metaphor and respond appropriately to it. But we would also want to help them *grasp* the difference between simile and metaphor: between comparing things and identifying them, between things being alike and things being the same. The uniqueness of metaphor is that it affirms the *sameness*, in certain respects, of two dissimilar things. Responding appropriately to metaphors entails grasping this difference from simile, a difference which the likeness of the two figures seems to obscure.

We would stress metaphor's identification of "things" while we were studying "submerged" metaphors, rather than "equation" metaphors, because the form of "submerged" metaphors ("Hope sings") makes identification clearer, indeed, makes the reader take the identification of the two "things" for granted. A is simply spoken of as if it were the thing that would do B ("yearly, down this hill/ April/Comes"). "Submerged" metaphors do more than make the reader intellectually understand the identification; they make him *feel* it, *assume* it, *experience* A as B, B as A. And it is that kind of response that we mean when we say "grasp."

Whenever we aim to develop a response of this sort — a feeling, rather than, say, a skill or a knowledge of facts — we realize the limits of teaching for such aims and of testing the achievement of them. As we try to help students to "grasp" identification as distinct from comparison, we discover that we can teach them to notice how different the forms of metaphor and simile are, we can teach them to understand intellectually the difference between identification and comparison, we can teach them to describe the difference in the effect evoked by "Hope is like the thing with feathers" from that evoked by "Hope is the thing with feathers" — but we cannot teach them much more. Whenever it is a feeling we are aiming to evoke, whether it is the feeling of sameness, of despair, or of the harmony of all parts of a work of art, we can only lead students to where the meanings are; we can call all things to their attention; we can put them on the most advantageous "stand." We can, so to speak, make way for the feeling. But they must feel for themselves. And we cannot really know whether or not students have experienced — not to say, developed — a feeling. Where feeling is concerned, we have to take some outward sign — the description of the effect, say — as evidence that they have felt the effect. And, as we take such evidence, we know all the time that a "scar" does not necessarily represent "internal difference," and that "internal difference" need not *show* a "scar." Students can explain without having felt and feel without being able to explain.

Now, let us turn to the practical details of the first section of our study of metaphor.

■ *The "Equation" Metaphor.* What kinds of poems would we read to help students develop a strong, flexible response to "equation" metaphors?

In classes that might need some initial help in distinguishing the form of metaphor from that of simile, we might want to preface the main study with the reading of "miniatures" that use metaphors rather obviously: Ezra Pound's two-line "In a Station of the Metro," William Carlos Williams' eight-line "Prelude to Winter," his twenty-line "A Woman in Front of a Bank," and John Gould Fletcher's five-line "The Skaters." The study of these little poems need never deteriorate into a single-focus drill to avoid confusion about what a metaphor "looks like." These miniatures have great potential. If, for instance, Fletcher's "The Skaters" is really read — not just used as preventive medicine — students will strengthen their responses to visual and auditory images and to sound as well. An exercise can always have valuable side effects.

In most classes, there would be no need for such preliminary reading. We could — and would — begin the main study of metaphor directly. It would consist of the reading of a group of poems, say three, chosen both because they used "equation" metaphors unobtrusively and naturally and because, taken together, they would offer students a variety of experiences with this form of metaphor. The group might include, for instance, a poem in which similes and metaphors work together, William Wordsworth's "She Dwelt Among Untrodden Ways" (three quatrains); a poem in which a single metaphor dominates, Ralph Hodgson's "Time, You Old Gypsy Man" (thirty-two lines) or Emily Dickinson's "Hope Is the Thing With Feathers" (twelve lines); and a poem in which several metaphors interrelate, Edna St. Vincent Millay's "Spring" (eighteen lines), Robinson Jeffers' "The Eye" (fourteen lines), Wilfred Owen's "Anthem for Doomed Youth" (sonnet), William Shakespeare's "Sonnet 73,"[37] or his "Tomorrow" speech from *Macbeth* (ten lines).

The poems we have cited as examples vary widely not only in their concerns and their styles, but in their reading difficulty. Wordsworth's poem, for instance, is richly suggestive, but simple. It does not require a highly competent reader, but rather one who has "lived" enough to feel the poignant sense of loss the speaker expresses — so very simply. Hodgson's "Time, You Old Gypsy Man" can be read by less able readers. However, certain aspects of the poem, the metaphor of the gifts in stanza two and the relation between the metaphor and the rhythm of the poem, would challenge average readers. So would certain features of Edna St. Vincent Millay's "Spring" and Jeffers' "The Eye." Owen's sonnet would stimulate good readers; Shakespeare's, better readers, and the soliloquy, the best. From a list like the preceding, we can create groups of poems appropriate for helping readers of very different abilities to develop a strong, flexible response to "equation" metaphors. As in the teaching of all literary uses of language, many roads lead to the same destination. The teacher's problem is to decide what group of poems would be most beneficial for a particular class and what order of teaching, most feasible.

Many of the poems we have just listed use "submerged" metaphors as well as "equation" metaphors. So reading them would provide a useful natural transition to the second section of our study — which we would begin at the earliest practicable moment.

■ *The "Submerged" Metaphor.*   What kinds of materials and methods would we use to help students learn to recognize and respond to the "submerged" metaphor?

Unless students had been consistently able to analyze perceptively the "submerged" metaphors we had asked about during the study of the previous poems, we would begin with many "slow-motion" studies of brief poems that use only one or two metaphors. In our study of the first few of these poems, we would be trying mainly to get readers to recognize the presence of "submerged" metaphors, to cite the terms, and to point out the clues that guided their decisions. Those are the things that many students cannot do. It simply does not strike them that a sea does not "wrinkle" — and it does not occur to them what does!

As soon as it began to, we would ask two further questions about the next brief poems we read. In what respects are the two terms the same? What is the function of the metaphor? It is usually advisable to continue such exercises until *students themselves* are able to carry out on several poems[38] the "four steps" — recognizing the metaphor, citing the terms, mentioning the points of sameness, and telling the function.

Some brief poems that lend thmselves to the kind of study we have been describing are the old standards, Carl Sandburg's "Fog," Alfred, Lord Tennyson's "The Eagle," and H. D.'s "Oread":

> Whirl up, sea —
> whirl your pointed pines,
> splash your great pines
> on our rocks,
> hurl your green over us,
> cover us with your pools of fir.*

Several less familiar, short poems can serve the same purpose — William Carlos Williams' "The Yellow Chimney" or his "The Bitter World of Spring," Richard Wilbur's "Exeunt," and E. E. Cummings' "the moon looked into my window." And, for abler students, or as final exercises for the average, there are such poems as Amy Lowell's "Night Clouds" and Emily Dickinson's "I'll Tell You How the Sun Rose," both of which juxtapose contrasting metaphors.

It might seem as if the specific aims we have for our "slow-motion" reading would preclude our teaching these brief poems as poems. But, of course, the fourth question — the question on the function of the metaphor — allows, indeed requires, us to consider them as poems. In "Night Clouds," for instance,

> The white mares of the moon rush along the sky
> Beating their golden hoofs upon the glass heavens;
> The white mares of the moon are all standing on
>   their hind legs
> Pawing at the green porcelain doors of the remote
>   heavens.
> Fly, mares!   5
> Strain your utmost,
> Scatter the milky dust of stars,
> Or the tiger sun will leap upon you and destroy you
> With one lick of his vermilion tongue.†

---

* Reprinted from *Selected Poems of H.D.* by permission of Grove Press, Inc. Copyright © 1957 by Norman Holmes Pearson.
† Reprinted from *The Complete Poetical Works of Amy Lowell* by permission of Houghton Mifflin Company. Copyright © 1925.

what can students say about the function of the metaphors if they are not aware of the speaker's little drama: first, enjoying the frolic, then, sensing the danger, and finally, ordering the "mares" to flee for their lives? What the reader sees is how the metaphors, the contrasting syntax and line lengths of the two parts of the poem, and the "turn" in the middle ("Fly, Mares!") all work together to render the speaker's experience. In discussing Emily Dickinson's poem, too, if students say that the differing impressions of sunrise and sunset are created by the metaphors, they are telling only half the truth. For the differing sentence forms and the differing shapes of the stanzas are also responsible. Even in the discussion of miniatures like "Oread," students cannot talk about the metaphors without talking about the order of the imperatives, the shift in rhythm—indeed about the juxtaposition of "over us/cover us." These are the features that, working with the metaphors, give the reader a poem rather than a picture.

Whenever the "slow-motion" study of metaphors seemed to be taking effect, and this might be after one day's work or several, we would begin the reading of several poems that would help students refine their responses to "submerged" metaphors and strengthen especially their ability to see how these metaphors work with other devices to render the meaning of a poem. We would want students to see, for instance, the significance of the syntax of a metaphor, of the way it is lined, of the sound effects of its words. We would want them to see how a metaphor characterizes the speaker who uses it, how it counterpoints rhythm to express an irony, how with the help of syntax and sound it creates a comic effect. Learning to be aware of such "workings" as these is a more demanding task than those we have been asking students to do. So, in order to give them the assistance we surmise they would need, we would choose relatively simple structures with rather accessible metaphors. Here are seven such poems, arranged roughly in order of their reading difficulty: Edgar Lee Masters' "George Gray" (sixteen lines), Ralph Waldo Emerson's "The Snow-Storm" (twenty-eight lines), Philip Larkin's "Next, Please" (six quatrains), Andrew Young's "Hard Frost"[39] (three six-line stanzas), Elinor Wylie's "Sea Lullaby" (six quatrains), Emerson's "Days" (eleven lines), and Dylan Thomas' "The Hand That Signed the Paper" (four quatrains).

To conclude the study of metaphors, we would read one or more poems in which the metaphors are less obvious, occurring here and there quite naturally—"invisible to the naked eye." For less able readers we would choose from among such poems as: Robert Frost's "Moon Compasses" (eight lines), Edna St. Vincent Millay's sonnet "Not in a Silver Casket," and Donald Justice's sonnet "The Poet at Seven." For average-to-good readers, we would select a poem like

Emily Dickinson's "After Great Pain" (three quatrains) or one like Elizabeth Bishop's "Little Exercise" (seven three-line stanzas). The mature, competent readers deserve the stimulation of Conrad Aiken's "One Star Fell and Another" (twenty-three lines) or Richard Eberhart's "The Cancer Cells" (twenty-two lines).[40] Both of the last poems have adult themes; both are complex literary structures which might mystify a reader who could not respond simultaneously to many unifying features. In Aiken's poem, for instance, the reader would have to grasp the parabolic form, recognize the reason for the unusual "narrator-speaker" dramatic situation, follow the speaker through his many shifts in attitude, and realize how the dominant metaphor and the gradual convergence of "worlds" and "words" unify the poem. This is a task for the sophisticated only.

Whenever students recognize how metaphors work, now in this context, now in that—and this may require the reading of many poems — we would begin the study of symbols.

Symbol

By "symbol," we mean a word that denotes[41] a literal meaning (the B-denotation) and a symbolic meaning (the A-denotation)— a complex of ideas and feelings either assigned to the word by tradition or accruing to it from its uses within a poem. In John Crowe Ransom's "Piazza Piece," for instance, the "gentleman in a dustcoat" denotes an insistent, unwelcome, elderly suitor (we imagine him dressed in a duster and half-hidden in the porch vines). In the course of the poem, he comes to denote "forces of decay," "the end of youth and beauty," "physical death." In the same poem, "the roses on your trellis dying" denote withering flowers (we image them brown at the edges, drooping on the trellis). But "the rose" traditionally denotes "perfect beauty"—so, in this context, it denotes "the transiency of beauty," "the inevitable death of the fairest."

Now, what does a reader's response to a symbol consist in? Very simply—he must know both the B- and the A-denotations of the word, and he must perceive how this word with these denotations functions in the poem. The reader knows the B-denotations (the literal meanings) from having learned them—from a dictionary or reference book, from reading, or from being told. It is from these same sources that he knows the A-denotation of *conventional* symbols. How else could he know that the rose, not the lily, means "beauty," "fairness," "perfection," with all the attendant feelings. In itself, the lily is also beautiful and fair. But tradition says that *it* means "purity," "chastity," and "virginity," and the reader has learned these meanings.

So, we can say that the reader brings to the reading of a poem the

B-denotations of all symbols and the A-denotations of a conventional symbol. He *discovers* during the reading of a poem the A-denotations of a created symbol.[42] Some word in the poem comes to denote more than its literal meaning. As the reader reads the poem, carefully accepting its objects for what they seem to be, he notices a detail of some sort that suggests, blatantly or subtly, that this fish, or buck, or ship, or gentleman is not only what it seems to be—but more. In Ransom's "Piazza Piece," for instance, the reader gets his clue in the first line—from the word "dustcoat." The reader rightly visualizes, as colorlessly and indefinitely as the word suggests, a gentleman in a duster. But why is it called "dustcoat," he asks himself. So, he is aware already that "the gentleman" is not just the usual suitor. From that point on, the reader notices this detail and that one—the dying roses on *her* trellis, the spectral singing of the moon. Each confirms his initial supposition, corrects it, or broadens his perhaps rather narrow, original A-denotation.

Knowing what a symbol denotes—no matter how the reader comes by the knowledge—is only the first part of his "job of work." A symbol is just a means to meaning. So when the reader knows the A- and B-denotations of the "rose" and of the "gentleman," he still must determine how these symbols work in the poem.

Responding appropriately to a symbol is, then, a rather complex act; the reader must sense the symbol, discover its A-denotation, and recognize how the symbol functions in the poem. As students learn to make this response, they frequently have one or another of several common problems to overcome.

A number of students have difficulty discovering from the clues in a poem the A-denotation of a created symbol. Overanxious, some leap to a premature conclusion and blind themselves to further clues. Others, unimaginative, do not notice hints; the A-denotation never emerges; the object remains its literal self—and odd old man trying to entice a young girl. Still others see the clues, respond to them precisely and imaginatively, but undermine their efforts by wanting —oh, so badly—to get a neat, concise A-denotation, a one-to-one correlation.

When some students discover the A-denotation, they discard the B. To them, the B-denotation is just a booster rocket that has served its turn. These students never enjoy the rich coalescence of meanings that a symbol can evoke and never really perceive its function.

When other students discover the symbol—especially the symbol created within the poem—they assume they "have" the poem. They forget that discovering the denotations is not an end in itself, that the reader wants to know the denotations so that he can then see the function of this symbol in this context. Why, after our stress on the function of devices all through this first course, should readers react this way to symbol? Perhaps because the A-denotation is a universal and, when the reader discovers it, he feels he has "arrived."

Now let us see what mode of study we would use to help students overcome such difficulties as these.

In less able classes and in low average groups, too, we would begin the study of symbol with the reading of poems that will suggest to students not only that objects mean more than they seem to, but also what the "more" is. The following three poems present an object and then guide, in one way or another, the reader's interpretation of it.

In Richard Eberhart's "The Horse Chestnut Tree" (three eight-line stanzas), seeing boys illegally raiding the great tree leads the speaker to realize that "we" are "outlaws on God's property," wishing, as the boys do, for a "tangible good from the unknown" and being prematurely driven "from the scene" by death, as they are driven by evening, with only "a little handful." In this poem, the image evokes a universally relevant direct analogy.

In Paul Engle's "Four Elms" (three six-line stanzas), noticing the hundred-year-old elms shading and endangering the house evokes from the speaker a "home truth" with enormous suggestion: "We take a chance on anything/We want to keep for long."

During the study of poems such as these two, we would ask students to show that what the poet "saw in" the object—the analogy, the philosophical statement—*was* warranted by the image. Then, we would ask them, If the poem did not have the analogy (or the commentary), what would you have "seen" anyway in the object as it was presented? What in the poem makes that object "stand out" as significant? Finally, we would invite the students to evoke another justifiable analogy from Eberhart's image, another comment from Engle's. In some classes, we might withhold the interpretive parts of the poems, showing students, first, only the images and asking them to say what analogy or idea each gives rise to.

In the third poem, Robert Frost's "Departmental" (forty-three lines), the last two lines guide the reader's evaluation of the ant world, but the very image of this world makes the reader aware early that these ants are not just ants. After the reading of the poem, we would ask: What *first* suggests that the poem is not describing *just* ant society? What successive details confirm our "suspicion"? What *kind* of human society is being criticized? How would you know anyway—even if the last two lines were not there?

To reinforce—and test—what students learned through the reading of one or more poems like the preceding, we would give an in-class exercise. We would assign a poem *like* Robert Frost's "Leaves Compared with Flowers" (five quatrains) or Percy Bysshe Shelley's sonnet, "Ozymandias." The students' task would be to discover, on their own, what "leaves" (or the broken statue) comes to mean. Specifically, their assignment would be:

> Your job is to show what "leaves" [or the broken statue] comes to mean in this poem. List on your paper the very first hint you get that "leaves" means *more than* just leaves. Beside the hint, write the meanings that the context suggests "leaves" might have. Then list the next hint and its meanings, and the next, and so on to the end of the poem. Now, what do your data suggest "leaves" means?

Through this assignment, students would be showing themselves how a complex A-denotation builds in the reader's mind. When they finished, we would discuss what was discovered, and then, we would try, as a group, to find out how the symbol works in the poem.

After some such "warm-up" as we have been describing, less able and low average students could go on to the study of poems that do not overtly interpret: Robert Frost's eight-line "Nothing Gold Can Stay" (What does "gold" mean in the first line? What does "gold" mean in the last line? How did it come to mean that?), or Stephen Crane's eleven-line "A Man Saw a Ball of Gold in the Sky," or John Crowe Ransom's sonnet "Piazza Piece," or Richard Wilbur's twenty-six-line "Digging for China."

These poems would also be useful *initial* readings for those average students who would not need the preliminary study we have been describing. After beginning on one or more of these poems, such students could, then, strengthen their response to symbols through the study of one or another of the following poems: Elizabeth Bishop's "The Fish" (seventy-five lines) her "The Imaginary Iceberg" (three eleven-line stanzas), Robert Frost's "The Figure in the Doorway" (twenty-two lines), and his "The Most of It" (twenty lines). Reading any one of these poems would also afford the average reader a most revealing stocktaking at this point in the course. For he would discover that he could not experience much of these little dramas unless he could do many things: hear a speaker sensitively, see the reasons for a parallel construction, feel the irony generated by a tiny image slipped in unobtrusively, sense the effect of rhythmic substitutions, of massed sounds, of the exotic word, and, of course, recognize the difference it makes that this fish, this iceberg, this man, this buck has gathered, during the poem, *this* complex of ideas and feelings.

If competent readers needed an initiation to symbol, we would probably study with them one or both of the Frost poems just mentioned. Most able readers, however, could do without prologues.

They could study the development and the functions of symbols through the reading of such stimulating poems as Gwendolyn Brooks' "The Explorer" (fourteen lines), Archibald MacLeish's "Voyage West" (nineteen lines), and Robert Graves' "Warning to Children" (thirty-seven lines).

During this Second Part of our course in reading poems, students have been learning to respond to those devices which speak of one thing in terms of another: coupled images, similes, metaphors, and symbols. In the process, they have had to continually notice such other features as, diction, syntax, sound, rhythm, and dramatic organization.

They have had to because the effect of any figure depends upon how it is said and who says it. Think what a difference it would make if, for instance, George Barker's "as huge as Asia" were "as large as Asia," or if Wilfred Owen's "each slow dusk a drawing down of blinds" were "each twilight a lowering of blinds," or if Gwendolyn Brooks' "There were no bourns/There were no quiet rooms" were "He found no bourns/Or quiet rooms." If we change an apparently small feature, we still have the figure, but we have lost the effect.

Furthermore, students have had to notice features other than the figures because figures are rarely the poem. They work with much nonfigurative language to render the experience of the poem. And when we teach a poem, it is the experience that all devices subserve that we are trying to help students have—and learn to give themselves. So, whatever the current focus, we ask about all features that will achieve these ends.

Consequently, long before now, we have been asking about tone— though not by name. We have, in fact, been talking about tone continually—however informally—since our first attention to dramatic movement. We have asked about "changing states of mind," about "shifting attitudes," about how the speaker feels toward the person he speaks to and toward his subject. A recall of our questions on such poems as "Futility," "Fireflies in the Garden," "The Eagle and the Mole," "The Man He Killed," and "Come In" will suggest what a long "history" our interest in tone has. And our recent comments on "Mirage," "Snow," Marianne Moore's "Silence," and "Sonnet to My Mother" all suggest that our questions about the ways the images and similes in these poems are expressed[43] would really be calling students' attention to the ways tone is "fixed."

So, through our continuing conversation about the speaker's attitude in this poem and that—how he felt and what "told us," we would by now have done what we hoped[44]—provided the kind of foreground for tone that would allow students to *formally* study the familiar.

The Third Part: Tone

By "tone" we mean the attitude toward the audience and the subject that is implied at various points in a poem by the way the speaker expresses what he says.[45]

Our aim in this part of the course is to help students learn to sense the tone of what is being said and so respond appropriately to it. In order to do that, the reader must be able to infer the speaker's attitude from the clues in printed words—from syntax, punctuation, sound, rhythms, figures, word choices and placements. And the reader must be able to make these inferences whether the clues are blatant as in Cummings' "Portrait" and Robinson's "Aaron Stark" or subtle as in Frost's "The Pasture" and Denby's "First Warm Days."

Furthermore, the reader must be able to make these inferences repeatedly during the reading of a poem: since a poem is an experience, tone changes. Though we often speak of "the tone" of a poem, what we mean is the over-all attitude that the separate tones at this point, and this, and this, taken together, reveal. These changes in tone that the reader must respond to might be a series of shifts from one feeling to another, or they might be an intensification of one feeling.

Sensing tone is, then, a demanding, complex task. It would be so even if the reader had only to sense the speaker's attitude toward his subject *or* toward his audience. But at least in those poems in which there is an expressly addressed audience, the reader must be able to infer the speaker's attitude toward both, and how these attitudes relate. In John Suckling's "Why So Pale and Wan, Fond Lover," for instance, the reader must infer the speaker's attitude toward love, his shifting attitudes toward the lover, and the causal connection between these attitudes. In Wilfred Owen's "Futility", as we saw, the speaker expresses feelings toward several audiences and several feelings toward the same event. The reader must infer all these. Furthermore, the reader must recognize when the speaker is condemning by approving, as in Samuel Johnson's "To a Young Heir," and when the author's attitudes differ from those of the speaker, as in Robert Browning's "My Last Duchess" or W. H. Auden's "The Unknown Citizen." We could continue citing such "special cases"—all of which complicate in some way the reader's basic task of repeatedly inferring tone from the clues of written language.

Now, to see what will help the reader with this task, let us notice what a reader probably does when he is reading the first line of Wordsworth's sonnet, "Composed Upon Westminster Bridge": "Earth has not anything to show more fair." As he hears the line in his mind's ear, he notices that it is a statement—the vehicle for expressing facts—that this statement is blanket, unqualified; that even in *such* a statement the phrase "not anything" is very strong—stronger than "nothing"—and that the whole sentence is much more arrogantly positive than, say, "This is the fairest sight on earth." And how slowly the sentence moves! Every word is a pronouncement. How the voice hangs onto these final words! And now a colon: here comes the "evidence." Who makes so assuredly such an extravagant statement?

In some such way as this, the reader senses the tone of the line.

What is helping this reader infer tone? Both information and skills. His ability to recognize a certain pattern of syntax and a certain mark of punctuation, his knowledge of what these forms are *usually* used for, his ability to recognize what their functions are here. Furthermore, the reader is helped by his ability to sense metrical substitution, a sound effect, an unusual wording, and to grasp how these features function in this sentence. Finally, he is helped by his ability to underscore the sentence with another wording of the same thing that by contrast highlights the tone the speaker chose and reveals his attitude.

Our protracted anatomy belies the unconscious way in which the trained reader uses his knowledge and skills. And one line of poetry does not represent all problems in inferring tone. Still, this analysis *suggests* what kinds of knowledge and skill will help a reader. It reveals, for instance, that beyond the general ability to hear words as spoken and to recognize and see the "meaning" and the function of certain linguistic patterns, the reader needs a knowledge of "how people talk" under certain circumstances. His job of sensing tone is greatly facilitated if he is familiar with the speech patterns of the angry, the reminiscent, the depressed; with patterns used in intimate, informal, and formal relationships; with the language of the braggart, the persuader, the euphemist; with the rhetoric of public oration, of nursery rhyme, of prayer, of incantation; with the forms of speech used by the storyteller and the reporter. If the reader knows such speech patterns as these, then he has a cache of touchstones. When he reads a line that *somehow* uses a familiar pattern, he hears the echo, recognizes the pattern and tries to see how it is being used in this poem—whether it is "imported" without change or adapted, even altered to reverse its usual effect. Ability to make this kind of comparison is a most valuable skill for readers to develop.[46]

Students do not have to be taught the kinds of speech patterns we have been referring to. Most have a fund of such information—some of it is active, some dormant. To make this information operative, we have only to recall these patterns to students by asking, "Who talks like this?" or by underscoring a line with a typical phrasing—as we did in the discussion of "Reuben Bright." The students will remember, and more importantly, begin to use comparison to enlighten their reading when they are on their own.

Now to the practical questions: what kind of organization and what sorts of poems might we use to help students learn to infer tone from written clues? Each class gives us the answer to this question. Because we have been continually preparing for the explicit study of tone, we can know rather accurately how sensitive to tone each class is. We can know which classes must now clear up their uncertainties about tone and develop a precise understanding of what tone is and of how a reader decides on it in particular cases. We can know which classes now need extensive practice to increase their nascent abilities. And we can know which groups of students now need their responses simply strengthened, differentiated, and refined. What needs to be done in each class, then, tells us what kinds of poems we should study in this part of the course and how we should study them.

For a class of less able readers—students who have been uncertain in their discussions of attitude, who perhaps have vacillated between precision and vagueness—we would now choose poems in which the tones and the changes in tone are unequivocal enough to evoke general agreement among the students as to what the tones are. We would forego poems with ambiguous tones—leave the reading of them to the time when they can be, for these students, sources of pleasure, rather than of confusion. Furthermore, we would choose poems that a large number of the students will be able, from the very beginning, to detect the tones of and point out the clues that guided them. If the teacher has to do either job for students like these, many lose confidence in their own ability to sense tone; some feel that the tone the teacher does cite is just his personal opinion. So, in short, we would choose poems that "announce" their tones and changes in tone, and, by oral reading (and rereading of lines), by comparisons, and by relevant questioning, we would try to bring the students themselves to both see the clues and decide on the tones.[47]

Of the poems we have previously cited in other parts of the course, the following would be useful initial readings for the kind of class we have just described: Cummings' "Portrait," Hardy's "The Man He Killed," Frost's "Dust in the Eyes," Millay's "Spring," Owen's "Futility," Hughes' "Mother to Son," Drayton's "Since There's No Help," and Humphries' "Heresy for a Classroom." We have listed the poems roughly (so roughly!) in order of difficulty, but all have tones such students could identify and agree on; all have obvious changes in tone which would show these students how poems move forward tone on tone. None is really difficult reading; all will do their office. So the teacher could really choose among these poems on the basis of the class's interest.

A second reading of a familiar poem *could* be very beneficial for uncertain students. For if, earlier, they have understood the dramatic movement of a poem, they are less likely now to misconstrue the tones of it. But whether or not second readings should, in fact, be used has to be decided class by class. In some uncertain classes, reading a familiar poem is reassuring and motivating. So the teacher might very wisely use, initially or exclusively, poems that had earlier been successful readings or favored ones. In other uncertain classes, however, the familiar should be avoided altogether. Students find it enormously boring. They desire novelty, require it. In these classes second readings, however beneficial they might be to the class's study of tone, must be eschewed. So here are five "new" poems which, because they meet all the tone requirements we have just laid down, could be used as initial readings for such a class: Siegfried Sassoon's "Base Details" (ten lines), John Gillespie Magee, Jr.'s sonnet, "High Flight," John Suckling's "Why So Pale and Wan, Fond Lover?" (fifteen lines), Sassoon's "Does It Matter?" (fifteen lines), and Karl Shapiro's "The Leg" (thirty-five lines).

Now let us consider *a class of average readers*—students who have understood and responded adequately to previous discussions about this or that speaker's attitude, but who now need to develop their sense of tone. For them, we would choose poems *somewhat* more subtle and *somewhat* more complex tonally than those in the preceding groups. We would, for instance, feature poems in which the attitude of the speaker and the author differed—like "My Last Duchess" and "Reuben Bright"; ironic poems of varying intensities—like "Anthem for Doomed Youth," "Mirage," and "Epitaph for an Army of Mercenaries"; poems with more than one voice—like "Ozymandias" and Marianne Moore's "Silence"; restrained poems that detach the reader from the emotion, like "Next, Please" and "Design." Such poems as these, if they have not been studied previously, would give appropriate practice to average readers. (Furthermore, they would be useful advance readings for less able classes, once those classes had succeeded with several introductory poems.)

If the particular average class has already exhausted the preceding list in the earlier parts of the course, here are some other poems equally "right" for helping such students improve their response to tone. In very rough order of difficulty: William Wordsworth's sonnet "Composed Upon Westminster Bridge," Dylan Thomas' "Do Not Go Gentle into That Good Night" (nineteen lines), John Crowe Ransom's "Blue Girls" (seventeen lines),[48] Gerard Manley Hopkins' "Spring and Fall" (fifteen lines), Henry Reed's "The Naming of

Parts" (thirty lines), and Ransom's "Bell's for John Whiteside's Daughter" (five quatrains).

Now, to get down to cases, what kinds of questions might we ask average readers about the pattern of tones in, for instance, Wordsworth's "Composed Upon Westminster Bridge"?

> Earth has not anything to show more fair:
> Dull would he be of soul who could pass by
> A sight so touching in its majesty:
> This City now doth, like a garment, wear
> The beauty of the morning; silent, bare,   5
> Ships, towers, domes, theatres, and temples lie
> Open unto the fields, and to the sky;
> All bright and glittering in the smokeless air.
> Never did sun more beautifully steep
> In his first splendour, valley, rock, or hill;   10
> Ne'er saw I, never felt, a calm so deep!
> The river glideth at his own sweet will:
> Dear God! the very houses seem asleep;
> And all that mighty heart is lying still!

The outline of our lesson would be something like this.

First, *to get the scene clear:* after students had read the poem carefully (there would be no oral reading), we would ask:

What time of day is it?

Where is the speaker?

What has he been doing just before he begins to speak?

What is he doing as he speaks?

Then, *to ascertain the initial dramatic situation:* after students had read the poem again, we would ask:

To whom is he speaking?

In a sentence, what is he speaking about? (We would insist on some mention of the particular *qualities* of beauty he suggests: the clearness, brightness, stillness of the enormous city.)

Now, let us notice how the speaker talks about what he sees, so that we can know how he feels about it. Once again, read the poem through carefully, and this time, note in the margin the attitudes you detect at various points in the poem and jot down what "clues" you in each instance. If you sense a change in feeling, but do not know what it is or why you sense it, put a question mark in the margin. (Our discussion will, of course, clear up these questions, but we would not tell the class that, for that would be a signal to some students to do nothing but write question marks.)

Then, *a discussion of the tones:*

What tone is the speaker using at the beginning? (The answers would probably be: "very positive," "very authoritative"—citing the syntax and the diction of line 1.)

Does this tone continue in lines 2–3? (If necessary, we would supplement with such questions as: How does the speaker's saying "Dull would he be," rather than "He would be dull" reinforce his attitude? Is it *just* the emphatic order? Or does his saying "dull," rather than "slow" or "dead," matter also? Does the pace of lines 1–3 support *or* relieve the "positive" or "authoritative" tone you suggest?)

Now, why is the speaker using this tone—he *is* talking to himself? (Probable answers: "He's overcome by the scene"; "so thrilled"; "surprised"; "carried away by the scene, so he's very extravagant.")

Does this tone continue? (Probable answers: "He's feeling his way"; "he's trying to describe the beauty to himself"—student citing the interpolated comparison; "he's trying to make clear to himself what's affecting him so"; "the tone is quieter in lines 4–5"; "more restrained"; "more meditative." We have cited these answers in the order in which they once actually emerged because they illustrate perfectly the way an average class often responds to a question. Notice that the early responses are answering a "why" question—the *previous* question *was* a "why" question! But, finally, the answers do begin to respond to *this* question and become gradually refined. Suppose after a minute or two they did *not* focus. What then? Without fanfare, we would simply say: The question is, "Does this tone continue?" That would suffice.)

Does the speaker discover "what's affecting him so"? Then: What is "the beauty of the morning"? (Here it is useful to have students list the particular beauties the speaker specifies in lines 6–14—just to make sure that some students will not be discussing the speaker's attitude toward some feature the rest of the students have not even noticed. It can happen. This list of features will prevent confusion and it will serve a second purpose also: it will provide a frame for the discussion of the tones, since, in this poem, the speaker shifts tone as he mentions each feature.)

What tone or tones does the speaker use as he notices these various beauties? (If the students' responses run to generalities—"He becomes more and more excited"; "very delighted"; "enthusiastic"; and so on—we would ask them to reread lines 6–14 to see whether the speaker was "delighted" all through these lines, equally "delighted" in all places—in other words, to discriminate. The responses would then probably suggest that the "delight" in lines 6–8 increases in lines 9–10, intensifies in line 11, subsides in line 12, and rises to a crescendo in lines 13–14.) With the general tone pattern outlined, we would ask particular questions about each "stage."

What in lines 6–8 suggests the speaker is "delighted"? (Probable answers: "the piling up of details, as if he's looking at one thing, then another, and another"; "the syntax of line 7." If necessary: How does line 8 suggest an excited delight that, say, line 3 does not? You say the speaker is greatly excited, delighted, raptured and such. Is it a frenzied excitement? What suggests it is not? How do rhythm and sound "hold back" the excitement?)

What is it about lines 9–10 that suggests increased delight? (Probable answers: "the reversal"; "the word 'never'—so positive, no exceptions." If necessary: Would it make a difference if line 10 read "Valley, rock, or hill in his first splendour"? If it read, "Hill, valley, or rock in his first splendour"? If "his first" were changed to "early"?)

What in line 11 suggests intensified delight? (Probable answers: "the reversed order of the syntax"; "the 'never's'—he means the scene is the ultimate in calm"; "the speaker enters as 'I'—really forgets himself." If necessary: Why wouldn't "Never did I see nor feel a calm so deep" suggest as great excitement? We would urge students to notice the contribution of punctuation and rhythm to the strength of this "second thought.")

Why does the speaker notice the river? *In what tone* does he express his notice of it? *Why* does he use that tone?

What features suggest that the last two lines are a crescendo of delight, amazement, rapture? At this point, we would expect students to "go it alone" on the answer—at least, almost.

In this particular lesson, we have abstained from oral reading of the whole poem or of lines from it in order to force students to use the mental ears that their previous experience in the course has been helping them develop. We would now end with an oral reading of the poem that would *try* to bring to life all the students' comments on the speaker's tones. The assignment:

Answer each of these two questions in a well-written paragraph or two:
1. Now that you have read the poem, what sort of person is the speaker?
2. In lines 4–5, the speaker says, "This City now doth, like a garment, wear / The beauty of the morning." We have noticed the details of the "beauty" the City wears. In what respects is it "like a garment"? (When you have answered this question, you will realize *why* this scene impresses the speaker so deeply.)

Finally, let us consider *a class of competent readers*—students who need their already adequate responses to tone strengthened, differentiated, and refined. For them we would choose poems that would really tax a reader's sense of tone. Among their readings we would include poems that seem, at first, toneless, and those that move from quiet beginnings to great crescendoes, and those that reverse this order, and those that "orchestrate" tones. We would include poems of profound tenderness, of quiet despair, of muted bitterness, of strong emotion restrained by comic elements, by reportorial form, or by the ritual of prayer. We would choose from among such poems as Owen's "The Send-Off," Barker's "Sonnet to My Mother," Denby's "First Warm Days," Frost's "The Pasture," his "The Most of It," MacLeish's "Voyage West," and Shakespeare's "Tomorrow" speech from *Macbeth*—if the class had not already studied all of these poems. If it had, we would select from among these poems: Robert Frost's "Desert Places" (four quatrains), W. H. Auden's "The Unknown Citizen" (twenty-nine lines), T. S. Eliot's "Journey of the Magi" (forty-three lines), Frost's "Neither Out Far Nor in Deep" (four quatrains), George Herbert's "The Pulley" (twenty lines), Gerard Manley Hopkins' sonnet, "In the Valley of the Elwy," Randall Jarrell's "The Death of the Ball Turret Gunner" (five lines), Walter Savage Landor's "Rose Alymer" (eight lines), Richard Selig's "From the Sixteenth Floor" (nine lines), W. D. Snodgrass's "Ten Days Leave" (thirty lines), and William Butler Yeats' "A Deep Sworn Vow" (six lines).

Although we ordered the first group of poems roughly according to difficulty, we listed the "new" poems alphabetically by author, with the exception of "Desert Places." We think this poem is the least demanding of the ten, but the others, being intricate in one respect if not in another, defy our efforts to order them according to difficulty. They are variously demanding, and we would let *special* relevance to the concerns of the particular class be our criterion for choosing among them.[49]

Now, how might a lesson on tone for a competent class differ from the lesson for average readers? Briefly, able readers would be expected to read a more subtle poem more independently and more discriminatingly. We would assign, for instance, Hopkins' "In the Valley of the Elwy."

> I remember a house where all were good
> To me, God knows, deserving no such thing:
> Comforting smell breathed at very entering,
> Fetched fresh, as I suppose, off some sweet wood.
> That cordial air made those kind people a hood   5
> All over, as a bevy of eggs the mothering wing
> Will, or mild nights the new morsels of spring:
> Why, it seemed of course; seemed of right it should.
> Lovely the woods, waters, meadows, combes, vales,
> All the air things wear that build this world of Wales;   10
> Only the inmate does not correspond:
> God, lover of souls, swaying considerate scales,
> Complete thy creature dear O where it fails,
> Being mighty a master, being a father and fond.*

---

* Reprinted from *Poems of Gerard Manley Hopkins*, 3d ed., edited by W. H. Gardner, by permission of Oxford University Press, Inc. Copyright © 1948.

This is a challenging poem. For readers must discern the speaker's attitudes toward his addressees (himself and God) and toward his subject. And they must feel the internal drama well enough to perceive, on somewhat subtle clues, *how* each recognition touches off the next; if readers cannot do this, they will find the poem disjointed.

Competent students would be assigned such a poem as this with *no* preliminary oral reading of the poem, no "clearing up" of the "it's" in line 8 or the meanings of "cordial" or "fond." The only guidance we would provide is a gloss on "Elwy" (so that they would not spend time investigating this unimportant item), an in-class oral questioning on the possible meanings of "inmate" (a perennial source of misreading), and the following study "advisory":

1. Read the poem carefully twice and, on the second reading, notice where the speaker is, to whom he is speaking, and very generally, what sort of person the speaker seems to be.

2. Read the poem again and note the parts of the dramatic movement. Tell yourself, tentatively, how these parts are connected.

3. Concentrate on each of the parts in turn. Study each carefully to discover the attitude or attitudes the speaker is taking toward his addressee and toward the subject he talks about. (If the tone of a phrase or a line eludes you, read the line aloud to yourself. Be the speaker for a minute.) Be as precise as you can be. (Are there places where two tones overlay one another?) Jot down your decisions on the speaker's tones and cite the clues you used.

4. When you have decided on the tones, read the poem once again to ascertain clearly what experience the dramatic movement represents and how the "parts" of the dramatic movement are connected. In a few sentences tell what you discovered.

In class on the following day, we would question briefly about the speaker, the addressees, and the parts of the dramatic movement. Then, with the frame clear, we would ask straightforwardly about the tones in the successive parts of the poem. Our strategy would be to let these students develop, on their own, as complete answers as they could. We would be *ready* to urge wherever necessary, not only with incisive questions on this or that word, or sound, or syntactic pattern, but also with substitutions, comparisons, and oral reading of lines. We would do this urging without comment: just asking the question, just reading the line orally, just stating the substitution.

Where might help be needed? In competent classes, this is difficult to anticipate, unless the particular class has consistently shown some weakness. But we would be especially ready to ask: What is the function of "God knows"? What suggests the speaker's relation to "all" in the first two lines? What is the tone of "as I suppose"? What are the meanings of "cordial"? What suggests the speaker's relation to the "people" in lines 5–6? What evokes line 9–10? (Why

does he speak of "air" as being "worn"? Why is "build" used?)
What does line 9 refer to? What is the speaker's attitude toward
God in line 13? How does "air" unite the poem? We might not have
to ask about any of these features, but we would be ready.

To say, now that we have completed the study of the particular
uses of language, that we have arrived at the study of the poem "as
a whole" is a kind of half-truth. For, from the beginning of this first
course we have always been discussing whole poems. Though we
may have been emphasizing now one device, now another, we have
always had to take into account other uses of language as well.
Furthermore, once we had stressed a certain device, students had to
continue to notice it, even as they shifted their major attention to
other devices. They did not leave the "old for the new"; no one who
reads *poems* can.

From the beginning, students have had to notice, too, how literary
devices organize poems *horizontally* and *vertically*. They have seen,
again and again (and continually in the study of tone), how in a
line or a group of lines syntax, rhythm, sound connotations, and
perhaps a figure, together, make the prose sense mean this, rather
than that. They have seen, again and again, how the dramatic situation "frames" the experience of the poem and the dramatic movement shapes it, how the connotations of words and their sounds
interlink throughout a poem, how images, similes, and metaphors
singly and in patterns structure a poem, how words become symbols
during the course of a poem, and how poems move tone on tone to
an over-all attitude.

So attention to structure in parts of a poem and in the whole poem
is nothing new. And if the teacher has stressed these horizontal and
vertical designs all through the course and if he has just finished
studying tonal patterns in several poems, he may well feel that further attention to structure *in this course* is excessive. Like a sensitive
public speaker, he will rightly drop his conclusion if he feels the
audience has already "gotten the point." Our Conclusion is, then,
for those who sense the need for one.

The Conclusion: The Organizations of Poems

In this final part of the course we would be aiming mainly to help
students become more sensitive both to the important role small
units play in the total poem and to the way many designs work
together in the common cause of rendering meaning.

In the study of poems, then, we would *continue* to make students
aware of the importance, to the whole poem, of this word, that
phrase, this construction, that punctuation, this line division. And
we would do it, as we have been doing it, largely by means of

"substitution" exercises: replacing the true element with another that either violates or does not work as well in one or more of the poem's designs.

Furthermore, in the study of poems, we would *continue* to try to help students see the way various designs—for instance, repetitions of words, rhymings, structures of sounds and of rhythms, dominant figures, tonal patterns, dramatic movement—interrelate in a poem. And we would study poems that would readily show students the need for their responding appropriately to the interrelated designs the poem uses. Such poems as Ben Jonson's "It Is Not Growing Like a Tree" (ten lines), William Carlos Williams' "The Term" (eighteen spare lines), Archibald MacLeish's "You, Andrew Marvell" (thirty-six lines), and Wallace Stevens' "Tea" (eight lines) would be "naturals."

Take Stevens' "Tea," for instance. On a first casual reading, students see what it says, but not what it "says." They want to know, and it is easy to show them that, by responding to the designs working in concert, they can know. Here is a teaching of the poem (for an average class) that suggests one rather covert way to do this.

> When the elephant's-ear in the park
> Shrivelled in frost,
> And the leaves on the paths
> Ran like rats,
> Your lamp-light fell   5
> On shining pillows,
> Of sea-shades and sky-shades,
> Like umbrellas in Java. *

Our questions would be direct, flat, factual. They would be asked in rapid succession to steadily reveal "what is there" in the poem and so build, build, build toward insights into what this juxtaposition of images might suggest.

We would open the study of this poem with an oral reading of it, followed by a silent reading, and then, to set the scene:

What time of year is it?
What time of day is it?
What is "going on" outdoors?
What is "going on" indoors?

By these last two questions, we would hope to elicit all the details of each image, so that students would realize, on one hand, a natural world that is cold (physically cold and lonely), dark, and turbulent, and, on the other hand, a man-made world that is warm (physically

---

* Reprinted from *The Collected Poems of Wallace Stevens* by permission of Alfred A. Knopf, Inc. Copyright © 1923 and renewed 1951 by Wallace Stevens.

and socially), bright, and still. We would *not* encourage interpretive comment; just quick answers that bring "outdoors" and "indoors" into sharp contrast. With that accomplished, we would go on:

How do you *feel* about the outdoors? (Probably: "repelled"; "abhor it"; "want to get out of it")[50]

What causes that feeling? (Probably: "the sounds: r-r-r 'Ran like rats'"; "the image of the frost-bitten plant"; "the sight and sound of the dried leaves—all that motion"; "the simile of the rats.") Why should the frost-bitten plant repel? ("It's being killed; it's withered, disfigured—it was beautiful once.") And the leaves—what's repulsive about them? ("They're dead"; "the sound is scratchy"; "the wind must be blowing very hard"; "the trees are bare.") What's repelling about the simile? It only explains how the leaves roll. ("But the metaphor 'ran' almost identifies the leaves and the rats. Rats come out when places are destroyed—in earthquakes and disasters; dead leaves drop when nature is destroyed in the fall. So you get a connection between dead leaves and those scavengers that take over when disaster comes.") Does it make a difference that all this [a purposely vague phrase] is happening in a "park"? Does any of the unpleasant feeling arise from the rhythm?

What, then, is your general impression of this natural scene? ("violence"; "death"; "destruction"; "devastation"; "desolation"; "motion and great confusion.")

We would now reread the poem, and then proceed:

Now, how do you *feel* about the indoors? ("like it"; "very attractive"; "I would want to hole up in there out of the elements.")

What makes you feel that way? ("those soft, soft sounds"; "somebody's in there—'your'—it's a friend"; "the images of lamplight, shining pillows"; "beautiful blues"; "those touch images, satin smoothness, softness"; "it's so still, so quiet.") If necessary: How would you describe the rhythm? Say the word "pillows," the word "Java," the word "umbrellas." Say, "sea-shades," "sky-shades." Now, how does the rhythm contribute to the quiet, peaceful effect? How are pillows "Like umbrellas in Java"?

What, then, is your general impression of this indoor scene? ("comfort"; "peace"; "security"; "everything in its place"; "yes, great order"; "protection"; "friendship"; "it's a retreat.")

Why is the poem written in a single sentence? What does "When" mean? Why is the poem written in *that kind* of sentence? (To these questions, there is usually a variety of responses: "The two worlds are part of one"; "they exist together; you can get out of the cold, but it's still there"; "you need the two—you'd never appreciate the indoors if there weren't the outdoors"; "it shows that when everything is breaking down, there's something that isn't.")

The two "worlds" coexist, then. Is one wholly undesirable, the other wholly desirable? ("the outside *is* natural; the indoors seems unreal"; "the outdoors is all death, but it's very alive; the indoors is all bright and glowing, but it's very dead, synthetic"; "you lose something bad when you come inside—and something good, too—and the other way around.")

And there *we* would leave Stevens' "Tea" to set up its own reverberations.

In this part of the course we would choose poems like "Tea" for study because they convince students that texture is not an end in itself, that examining designs is not verbal shadow-boxing. The study of poems like "Tea" shows students that these designs function; by means of them we undergo an experience which, if one design were changed, or one were missing, would not be quite the same: the experience of the poem is what it is only because of these designs, interrelated as they are.

"New" Organizing Devices

In the study of poems during this final part of the course, we would certainly be trying to strengthen the sensitivities students had been developing, but the study would not be just a repetitious "more of the same." For we would now call students' attention to certain kinds of organizing devices that we have not mentioned before.

We would introduce them to *the single word or phrase that structures a poem*. As an illustration, consider the structural role played by the phrase, "silent, bare," in Wordsworth's "Composed Upon Westminster Bridge." Coming at the end of the fifth line, these words say, for the first time, what it is that so surprises, so thrills the speaker. They *are* "The beauty of the morning"; they are what all the remainder of the sonnet details concretely. The first five lines lead to these words; the last nine, from them. Furthermore, these words recall their opposites—noisy, confused, smoky—(the "ungarmented" city) and make the reader recognize, accept, and share the speaker's high enthusiasm for the sight.

This discussion of "silent, bare" suggests the kind of relationship between part of a work and the whole that we would now be especially trying to make students aware of. To do it, we need no special poems. All have crucial elements. But in a study like this, it is almost mandatory for the teacher to work on a poem he favors and with an element that has struck him as crucial to the whole experience. He then has a good chance of having the element strike students the same way. Unless the teacher has something he really wants to show, such study can become a cold clarification of connections, rather than an enlightening discovery.

We would enjoy leading others to "discover" the role of the last line in Wordsworth's "Composed Upon Westminster Bridge," of "blight" in Hopkins' "Spring and Fall," of "correspond" in his "In the Valley of the Elwy," "and I—" in line 18 of Robert Frost's "The Road Not Taken," and the sentence "it was (you may say) satisfactory" in line 31 of T. S. Eliot's "Journey of the Magi."

During this final part of the course, we would also want to introduce students to *such organizing devices as archetype, variations of conventional poetic forms, and parody.* And we would try to help them see what particular poems gain by having such devices as these work with the other vertical designs in the poem. What, for instance, does Robert Frost's "Directive" (sixty-two lines) or Eliot's "Journey of the Magi" gain by its use of the quest archetype?[51] What does W. B. Yeats' "The Ballad of Father Gilligan" (twelve stanzas) gain by its adaption of the ballad form, or Frost's "Acquainted With the Night" by its special variation of the sonnet? What effect is achieved in E. E. Cummings' "a man who had fallen among thieves" (twenty-four lines) by the parody of the biblical parable? What is gained in Donald Justice's "Counting the Mad" (eighteen lines) by his use of the "this little pig went to market" nursery rhyme?

When students become aware of organizing devices such as these, they often tend to forget that the myth or the parable is *just one* of many structures ordering the subject matter. Remind them that the question is: what is gained by using this device *too.* The sense of alienation and desolation that Frost's "Acquainted With the Night" dramatizes is surely created partly by his special variation of the sonnet form. But only partly. For the images also create it, and the identical first and last lines, and the syntax, and the verb tenses, and the load of meaning "night" takes on. It is the interrelating of many structures that makes the experience of the poem penetrating, and it is this interrelating that students must see. And we would prevent them from allowing the newly discovered and often more engaging structural device to usurp undue attention.

So we conclude our Conclusion. Our proposal for a first course for helping students learn to read poems is finished. We turn now to suggestions for collateral writing, for holidays, for a timetable for the course, and—for what "comes after."

Collateral Writing for a First Course in Reading Poems

Doing the composition assignments that follow will, in all likelihood, improve students' writing. For these assignments give students a precise context, exact topics, and, most importantly, an obviously good reason for writing. Furthermore, these assignments require students to write continually—"a line a day"—and it is by such constant and careful practice that a skill is learned and perfected. But improved writing is just a welcome by-product of our composition work. The aim is to improve students' reading of poems.

The composition assignments reinforce the oral critical analysis students do. Having to put their responses in writing helps them to clarify their ideas, feelings, and judgments about poems and to overcome looseness, nebulosity, and undocumented effusions. Both critical and creative writing can make students more attentive, more precise, and more imaginative readers of poems, so our suggestions include assignments of both kinds.

Critical Writing

There are at least four kinds of critical writing students can do to improve their reading of any kind of literature: the preparation of study guides, the critical exercise, the in-class test, and the "full-dress" critical paper. Each of the four has its own special office.

■ *The Study Guide.* The study guide is a set of questions, mainly critical, designed to assist students' independent reading of a work and to prepare them for class discussion of it. Answers to the questions should be written. Early in the course, the class period might be devoted largely to a discussion of the answers to the guide questions; this is not so much to "police" as to make sure *everyone* is understanding and responding precisely. Later, the class period might be spent discussing some guide questions and other questions that students' work on the guide has prepared them to answer. For examples of guides and their uses, see the assignments for "Since There's No Help" and for "Musee des Beaux Arts."

Study guides are useful for all students at the beginning of a new course; for the unmotivated, they are mandatory throughout. To accustom such students to working on guides, have them first do the entire guide in class. Then, as they become more habituated to this type of assignment, have them do one half of the work in class; then, one third of it. Finally, have them do the entire guide outside of class. If, after a while, the guides begin to be incomplete or poorly done, revert to beginning the work in class.

When unmotivated students are assigned work to do in class, see that they begin immediately. Their major problem, in large matters and small, is getting underway. They have little interest in beginning anything, little sense of duty or obligation, little desire for the rewards. They need an initial "push," a good push that will send them so far into a job that they will be interested, they will want to finish, they will taste the rewards and desire them. The unmotivated are those who do not move on their own. We must "get them going," not just by telling them to begin the study guide work in class, but by walking up the aisle to be sure they do begin, and by checking or spot-checking the guides the next day to be sure they have finished.

By allowing these unmotivated students to work in class on "homework," aren't we pampering them? No. To achieve the aims of this course, students must read the works responsively. Study guides help them to do this. And beginning in class or working in class ensures that these students will get the guides done. So, we are recognizing on a very practical level what we must do, in this particular instance, to help students achieve the aims, and we are adjusting our teaching procedures accordingly.

▪ *The Critical Exercise.* The second kind of critical writing is the critical exercise, usually a paragraph or so written in about ten minutes' time, at the beginning of class, during class, or at the close. When students no longer need to adhere closely to the study guide during the class period, then a critical exercise can be used *at the opening of a class* to set up the discussion. If we were teaching Hopkins' "In the Valley of the Elwy" to an average class, for instance, we might begin the period with the following exercise:

This poem is not a drama of alienation, but of the speaker's *discovery* of his alienation. In a well-written paragraph or two, *show* that this statement is true.

Working on such a paper will call many facets of a topic to students' attention, will focus their thinking, and of course, make them eager to talk. Most can hardly wait! So an initial paper naturally channels discussion and guarantees involvement. Call on anyone; everyone has thought about the topic and written about it. Such papers as these may be used solely as a springboard for discussion, or they may be collected at the end of the writing and later graded.[52]

When a class is ready, the opening critical exercise might be like the "big question" we proposed for the conscientious class reading Auden's "Musee des Beaux Arts": The first two and a half lines tell us what the poem is about. Do we really *need* the images?

Critical exercises could be used *during a class period* whenever the teacher wanted every individual to make his own considered response to some question. Usually, the work of the class period would lead steadily toward this crucial question, which would then be answered in writing instead of orally. The answers would be discussed in the usual fashion, and the lesson would continue to its close. Generally only a few sentences long, these exercises might be written in students' notebooks or occasionally handed in for grading. If the teacher wishes to focus students' attention or to motivate, he might announce the forthcoming exercise at the beginning of the lesson;[53] otherwise, he might let it emerge unannounced—quite naturally.

When, specifically, might such an exercise seem appropriate or desirable? Whenever we want students to make the leap from details to implication, whenever we want them to draw together into a critical statement the data the class have expressed so far, whenever we want to test their progress and discuss results. To illustrate the last use: when we are doing several "finger exercises" to sensitize students to tone, say, we might use the third poem as a test—in an exercise like the following:

You will now hear a short poem [or a stanza] three times. Try to decide what tone the speaker in the poem is using. As you listen, watch the text to see what *in the words* of the speaker seems to be signaling the reader. After you have heard the tape three times, everyone will write what he thinks the tone of the speaker is and what *in the text* suggests it.

Or when we are trying to show students that tone changes in a poem, we might choose a poem in which the tone of the first stanza (or section) is modified quite markedly by that of the second stanza (or section), as it is in Owen's "Futility," in Housman's "Epitaph for an Army of Mercenaries," and in Blackmur's "Mirage." After studying the tone of the first stanza (or section) with the class, we would ask them to work individually on the second stanza:

Read the next stanza [or section] carefully. Establish the tone of the speaker. Then tell in a paragraph how it relates to the tone of the speaker in the first stanza.

Finally, critical exercises could be used *at the end of class,* or as an assignment, to close the discussion of a work. The "closing paper" is by far the commonest type of written exercise. The topic for such a paper might take up a facet of the work that was purposely not stressed during discussion; it might pose a problem that, if explored by the students, will pull the work together for them, or it might lead readers into the work once again—by a quite different route. If written in class, the closing paper would be collected, usually graded, and commented upon in some way. If written as an assignment, it would be collected, read, and commented upon. The teacher must decide whether or not he will grade work done out-of-class.

We have already suggested topics for closing papers in our lesson plans for "Blue Girls" and "Futility." Here are other kinds of topics that we might use:

At the close of the study of John Gould Fletcher's "The Skaters," we might ask students to point out specifically how the sound of the words reinforces the image.

At the close of a first lesson on some device, say simile, we might check students' understanding of the device by giving a single question on a new poem, a miniature. If the device were simile, we might use D. H. Lawrence's "Nothing To Save" or, say, Herbert Read's "Night." The exercise, which should be dittoed, might be worded:

Read the following poem carefully.

NOTHING TO SAVE

There is nothing to save, now all is lost,
but a tiny core of stillness in the heart
like the eye of a violet.*

NIGHT

The dark steep roofs chisel
The infinity of the sky:

But the white moonlight gables
Resemble
Still hands at prayer.†

Then in a paragraph tell specifically what is being *compared* with what in what respects.

At the close of the study of Emerson's "The Snow-Storm," we might ask:

What makes the reader feel the bold entrance of snow? the ceasing of activity in stanza 1? the mad frenzy of lines 11–22? Write a paragraph that answers these questions.

At the close of the study of the metaphors in Owen's "Anthem for Doomed Youth," or in Shakespeare's "Sonnet 73," or in Frost's "Moon Compasses," we could test achievement of the aim by means of a topic like this:

In not more than two paragraphs *show* how the metaphors define successive stages of the dramatic movement.

■ *The In-Class Test.* The third kind of critical writing is the in-class test, the familiar evaluative device, which would generally be used at the end of one or several of the five parts of the course to reveal the degree to which each student is achieving the aim of the particular part and of the whole course—since it *is* cumulative. Such a test could take various forms.

It might require students to read a new poem and answer a series

---

* Reprinted from *The Complete Poems of D. H. Lawrence*, Vol. 2, Vivian de Sola Pinto and F. Warren Roberts (eds.), by permission of The Viking Press, Inc. Copyright © 1933 by Frieda Lawrence. All rights reserved.
† Reprinted from *Collected Poems*, by Herbert Read, by permission of the American publisher, Horizon Press. Copyright © 1966.

of questions of the type usually asked in class. For examples of such questions, see our lesson plan for "Blue Girls." The new poem chosen for such a test should be a bit less difficult than the last poem the class has read. Another form of in-class test might ask students, as our test on Drayton's "Since There's No Help" does, to work on a poem they have previously read, but have not studied in class. Since the poem is somewhat familiar, the questions on it should be more challenging. Still a third form of test might require both the answering of a series of questions and the writing of a critical paragraph. And yet another form might ask for the writing of a two-paragraph paper only.

Whatever form of test we choose, we must remember that fifty minutes is only fifty minutes, and if, for instance, students have to read a new poem, they will have used thirty to thirty-five minutes on the reading before they begin to write. They can, therefore, answer only about five questions. Tests should be stimulating, but not unreasonable.

■ *The Formal Critical Paper.* The fourth kind of critical writing—too often considered the only kind—is the formal critical paper, which might be written once during the course by less able and average classes and twice or more by competent readers.[54] In a first course, such a paper should be relatively short, one to two pages, depending upon the ability of the class. For each assignment there should be a single, carefully devised topic which relates to a poem not previously studied. The instructions for the paper, preferably duplicated, should be clear and detailed—including the exact topic, length, necessary glosses, hints, page references, and due date. Preparation for the writing of the first paper should include an in-class examination of an assignment previously used in a comparable class and two or three different but equally good responses to it. Students will then know what constitutes a "good" paper and that different responses to an assignment, if they are of equal relevance and quality, are equally "good." If the class is one that does little out-of-class work or one that receives too much outside aid, these papers, normally written as home assignments, may be written in class on two consecutive days, the draft and notes handed in at the close of the period on the first day. This procedure will not prevent all outside help, but it will reduce it enough to let the teacher know approximately what the *students* can do—and that is what he wants to know. Formal critical papers would, of course, be read, graded, discussed in terms of their adequacy as *written* criticism, and followed up with appropriate corrective exercises.

Formal critical papers would probably not be assigned until the Second Part of the course. Consequently, the suggestions for topics that we offer below are limited to what would be appropriate for the last three of the five sections of the course. On first thought some of the topics for the average students and the less able may seem "too easy." But when you consider that students must read the poem without the help of in-class questions and answers, that they must write a well-organized paper, not just discuss a topic orally, and that the paper, for most, is probably a first one, then the topics for the average students and the less able do not seem unchallenging.

Each of the topics is a kind of frame, into which many poems, other than the one cited, might be inserted. Here, first, are *some topics for very competent readers:*

Image

Read Frost's "Design." Notice the images in the octet. When we read them, we have certain expectations about what kind of "philosophizing," what kinds of questions, they could justifiably arouse in anyone seeing the scene.

Now, notice the questions in the sestet. In a paper of *about* two pages, show that the questions do justice to the ideas latent in the images—they neither exceed nor fall short of what the images could provoke.

If the teacher wants to make the topic harder, he need only phrase the second paragraph as a question:

Do the questions exceed or fall short of the ideas latent in the images? Explain in a two-page paper.

Tone (including dramatic situation)

Read Richard Selig's "From the Sixteenth Floor." Notice the various stages in the experience the speaker undergoes. Identify for yourself the tone he uses at each stage.

From *the way* he tells his experience, what sort of person would you say the speaker is? Give your answer in a one- to two-page paper.

Organization of the Poem

As you read Robert Frost's "Moon Compasses,"[55] clarify for yourself how the various parts of the speaker's experience *connect* with one another. (Do not overlook familiar connectives. Notice in line 3, "And a. . . ." Why not just, "A masked moon. . ."? In line 8, why, "So. . ."?)

When you have discovered relationships among the parts, tell in a one- to two-page paper how the last line works in the poem."

Now, *some topics for average-to-good readers:*

Image

Read Robert Frost's "Hyla Brook" carefully. Notice that the poem gives us a final statement. In a one- to two-page paper, point out *to what extent* and *in what way* the images are really necessary.

Metaphor

In all our discussions of metaphors, we have continually discouraged you from saying "What the speaker really means is—" giving then some literal statement of the metaphor. Now read carefully Emerson's "Days." Suppose after reading it you say, "What the speaker really means is that he had good chances, but didn't take them."

In a one- to two-page paper explain *in what ways* that statement does not express what the metaphor expresses.

Tone

In Edgar Lee Masters' "George Gray" the speaker shows by the way he says what he says that his characterization of himself *is* true.

In a one- to two-page paper point out what *features of his manner of speaking* reveal his character.

If the teacher wants to help students more, he need only phrase the final direction:

Point out how the form of sentence he uses, the personifications he chooses, the diction he employs, and the line division typify the kind of person he describes.

The topic for tone that we suggested for competent readers would also be appropriate for an average class *if* the poem used were, say, Hardy's "The Man He Killed," instead of Selig's poem.

Organization of the Poem

In Philip Larkin's "Next, Please," all the details of the poem develop the statement that comes in the first stanza.
1. Read the statement carefully. Then, put it in your own words.
2. Now, see how the details in stanzas 2, 3, 4, and 5 relate to the statement.
3. Then, look at stanza 6. How does that relate to the statement?

When you have worked out all these steps, write a one- to two-page paper that tells how the details in stanzas 2–6 develop the statement of the first stanza.

Finally, *some topics for the less able:*

Image, Simile

Read this little poem carefully:

> Listen. . .
> With faint dry sound,
> Like steps of passing ghosts,
> The leaves, frost-crisp'd, break from the trees
> And fall.*⁵⁶

---

* Reprinted from *Verse*, by Adelaide Crapsey, by permission of Alfred A. Knopf, Inc. Copyright © 1922 by Algernon S. Crapsey and renewed 1950 by The Adelaide Crapsey Foundation.

On *this sheet* jot down answers to the following questions:
1. What is the impression—the experience, the feeling—you get from this poem?
2. If the *sounds* of the words contribute to the impression, which sounds and how do they contribute?
3. If *images* contribute to the impression, what images and how do they contribute?
4. If the *simile* contributes, how?
5. Does the way the lines are divided contribute? If so, how?
6. Does the way the speaker talks contribute to the impression?

Now that you have all this information, write a paper of about a page that tells what impression—experience, feeling—you get from this poem *and* exactly what features of the poem seem to be creating this impression.

When you hand in your finished paper, hand in also both the rough draft of your paper and these notes that you have made.

Tone

Read Siegfried Sassoon's "Base Details."

> If I were fierce, and bald, and short of breath,
>   I'd live with scarlet Majors at the Base,
> And speed glum heroes up the line to death.
>   You'd see me with my puffy petulant face,
> Guzzling and gulping in the best hotel,   5
>   Reading the Roll of Honor. "Poor young chap,"
> I'd say—"I used to know his father well;
>   Yes, we've lost heavily in this last scrap."
> And when the war is done and youth stone dead,
> I'd toddle safely home and die—in bed.*   10

On *this sheet*, jot down answers to the following questions:
1. What is the speaker's attitude?
2. What uses of language suggest this attitude to you?
3. *If* the speaker's attitude changes (to another attitude or becomes more or less what it is), where does this happen?
4. What uses of language give you the clue to the change?
5. What is his new attitude?

Now that you have all your data assembled, describe, in a one-page paper, the speaker's attitude (or his attitudes—if there was a change) and give evidence to defend what you say.

Organization of the Poem

As you read Hughes' "Harlem," you notice that the questions are in a certain order. Look carefully at that order.
1. Why is it an effective order?
2. Why wouldn't another order be as good? Change the order of the questions—and see why.

---

* Reprinted from *Collected Poems*, by Siegfried Sassoon, by permission of The Viking Press, Inc. Copyright © 1918 by E. P. Dutton and Co. and 1946 by Siegfried Sassoon.

Now, in a one-page paper, tell why you think the questions are arranged as they are.

Spelling out these four opportunities for critical writing—the study guide, the critical exercise, the in-class test, and the formal paper—helps remind us that the formal critical paper is only *one kind* of critical writing that a student in a first course can—and should—do. All four kinds of writing should be given due importance. They all exercise the critical responses we are aiming to develop and strengthen. The study guides and the critical exercises prepare students for successful performances on the tests and the long papers. And together the four types of writing give day-in-day-out practice in both reading and writing. And there is no substitute for careful continual practice of skills.[57]

Creative Writing

When the student is doing the kinds of writing we have been describing, he is a perceiver—he is looking at poems as a reader does. But when he writes creatively, he is a maker—he is seeing words as a poet does. And he comes to appreciate what goes into the making of even one "really good" line.[58]

What sorts of creative writing might this first course include?

During the study of diction and of syntax and rhythm, students might occasionally spend some time just "fooling around" with words.[59] They might first write phrases that attract and phrases that repel; then, stark phrases and muted ones; then phrases in which sound supports sense—and works against it; finally, phrases that reconcile seeming opposites, like Wilbur's "radiant squalor." We would draw models from the poems being read and use subjects that anyone can respond to: "downpour," "sunrise," "wealth," "mud," "hangnail," "morning fog." These little exercises which are fun to do as a class, students writing individually and pooling results, keep readers constantly aware—better than sermons on the "right words in the right order" can—that words are chosen and placed to behave in certain ways to achieve certain effects.

This turning of phrases could gradually yield to a turning of sentences—which might continue intermittently from the study of syntax through the study of tone. To begin rather routinely, first take a single imperative—"Listen," for instance—and ask students to write "other ways it could be expressed," then, discuss the sentences they have written ("You should listen," "You must listen," "I want you to listen"—and so on) to see how these sentences vary in meaning.

Continue with exercises on the different effects produced by changing constructions, changing, for instance, a compound sentence to short simple sentences, changing active voice to passive, inverting a normal order. Gradually, begin asking *who* might say the sentence this way rather than that. Such questioning might, then, lead to rewriting a given basic sentence as several different speakers might say it. Eventually, the speakers would get audiences, and the task would become rewriting a given sentence as a certain type of speaker might express this idea or this feeling to a child, to himself, to a man he despises. Finally, the assignment would be to rewrite a basic sentence four times: to produce, the first time, the effect of decisiveness, then, of conversational looseness, then, of hesitancy, and lastly, of disconcerted excitement.

Why have students rewrite one sentence, rather than create different sentences? Because varying a basic sentence really emphasizes the significance of speaker, audience, intention, tone. Students see that all the sentences in each group "say the same thing," but what a difference these other dimensions make—"a complete difference," as they would say.

If this turning of sentences did continue all during the study of syntax, figures, and tone, we would, in all likelihood, incorporate the writing of images, similes, and metaphors into the sentence assignments. Such a procedure is consistent with, indeed supports, the attitude toward devices we would be encouraging students to develop as readers. Here are some samples of such sentence assignments:

1. Write a sentence in which a favorite uncle makes a child visualize (or hear or smell) the circus.
2. Write a sentence in which a baseball fan uses a simile to explain to a "civilian" the rank injustice of an umpire.
3. Write a sentence in which a speaker uses a metaphor to explain to someone who has never seen an ice storm what one is.
4. In a few sentences, have a driver describe to a friend what the tail lights on the car ahead of him on a foggy night *looked like* to him (or *were* to him).

Some teachers might prefer to preface this kind of sentence work, to supplement it, or to replace it with the kinds of writing assignments commonly used to accompany the study of image, simile, metaphor, and symbol. We refer to assignments that ask students to compose various kinds of images, to write *vivid* description, to complete sentences with similes and metaphors ("Loneliness is _____"), to create an extended simile or metaphor, and perhaps, to develop a symbol.

From mid-course on, students probably should have opportunities to go beyond turning phrases and sentences to "turning" poems. In some classes the writing of serious imitations and parodies is an enjoyable way of helping students see something of what goes into the making of a poem. Among the poets we suggested in the reading lists for the first course, several invite imitation and parody: the Imagists, E. E. Cummings, Emily Dickinson, Edwin Arlington Robinson, Robert Frost, Richard Wilbur. Anyone can "play" with the first three; it takes a more subtle facility with words to imitate the last three—recognizably. Part of the fun of writing imitations and parodies is the session that follows when the student-authors read their "works," "the critics" identify the originals, and all criticize one another's efforts.

In some classes, the writing of free verse portraits is a highly favored activity. This kind of assignment is appropriate when students are reading such poems as "Richard Cory," "Reuben Bright," "Portrait," "George Gray." The assignment might encourage each writer to choose his own subject, or it might offer as the subject a person familiar to all or a certain photograph, one, for instance, from *The Family of Man,* from *Stop, Look, and Write,* or from Henri Cartier-Bresson's *The Decisive Moment.*[60] The assignment might ask for any one of a number of things: for a short verse portrait or a poetic prose paragraph; for a portrait that reveals the speaker as well as the subject; for one that satirizes mildly or savagely; for a portrait that reveals the subject by comparison, or by symbol; or for a portrait that creates a symbol to suggest the personality of the subject. To show students how to do this last kind of assignment, we would rewrite with them Edgar Lee Masters' "George Gray," so that the poem would be ostensibly about a boat in the harbor, but, because of the way the boat was defined, the poem would suggest the meaningless life of a fearful personality. All of the other tasks we cited could be introduced by similar in-class rewritings.

In some classes, the writing of haiku, or imagist poems, or Frostian two-line poems, or compressed quatrains—the writing of all kinds of "miniatures"—is clearly "students' choice." The poems that result from these and other kinds of creative writing assignments may be anything but well-turned. They may be trite, infelicitous, mechanical. But student-poets are rarely discouraged by these products that fall so far short of the poems they meant to write. They enjoy being poets and critics of their fellow-poets. They should be encouraged to be both: because being both develops responsive readers—and because, though poems should be read as carefully and criticized as objectively as any other writing assignment, student-poets always find it easier to accept such criticism from their fellow-poets than from their critic-teacher. In this at least, they are one with all poets.

"Producing" the Course

Holidays

This first course is fairly intensive. And even the ablest readers will welcome an occasional change. This might be simply a variation in the lesson format that the teacher tends to use. However successful any format is, it will, if used continually, become monotonous. Too often in well-motivated classes a course in critical reading turns into an unvarying day-after-day reading of a poem and textual discussion of it. To relieve repetitiveness and encourage frequent renewal of interest, class periods might be organized to include several changes in activities. One class might open with questioning which leads to a brief paper that is then used in discussion which in turn introduces the assignment. Another class might begin with a written question (one *from* the out-of-class assignment or one based on it), and some students' responses might be read to establish the critical discussion for the day. Still another class might start with a twenty to twenty-five minute text analysis that leads to a ten-minute critical paper and, then with the poem experienced and the experience written about, might conclude with a fifteen-minute discussion on some moral issue the poem raises. (Our proposed teaching of Stevens' "Tea," could be shaped into just such a lesson.) For variety, the teacher might indulge in a change of command. When the course has reached the halfway mark, he might occasionally ask average and able readers to create half-hour lesson plans on a certain poem and be ready to conduct next day's class. (*They* are supposed to be learning what to ask themselves about a poem, aren't they?) These are just a few variations in class procedure that can pleasantly interrupt the "circle."

In less well-motivated classes a fifty-minute discussion or the unvaried repetition of a single class format is out of the question. These students *must* have changes in activities in just about every class period—if they are to be continually engaged and committed. Consequently, we *daily* plan varied classes for them. Motivated students enjoy variety, too, but since they quietly tolerate over-extended discussions and calcified class patterns as a fact of school life, their desire for change—and need for it—is often overlooked.

In addition to variations in class procedure, all students like an occasional full-period change of pace. The first change might come after eight or nine days of the course. By then, students are far enough into their study to find such a day pleasurable and to use it productively. During this class period, play recordings of several poems the particular class has enjoyed studying. Use author's readings or those of professional readers or of students. (Students like to hear "one of us.") Discuss how this line or that was said, or simply let students listen for the pleasure familiarity gives. If a certain poet has been especially favored by a class, give him a "day." Put his separate volumes of poems around for students' perusal, feature his recorded readings, recall his myths, quips, and eccentricities. His vital statistics? His "place in the world of letters"? No! No!

On one of these "holidays," show students some critic's unsparing damnation of a poem they have greatly enjoyed. See in what terms they "fight back." Show them a critic's interpretation of a poem that differs markedly from the views they arrived at when they discussed the poem.[61] Who is wrong? Show them Theodore Spencer's "How To Criticize A Poem"[62] when they have done enough criticism to enjoy it, or present them with Ogden Nash's spoof, "Very Like A Whale," when they are in the throes of similes and metaphors. Show them William Carlos Williams' "Poem" ("As the cat/climbed over . . ."). Ask them, confidentially, how much of this kind of innovating they really think is necessary. Keep exploring until someone shows by an expressive reading that the line division creates the image of the cat in action with all the attendant suspense. Many of E. E. Cummings' short poems would be good substitutes for Williams' "Poem."

On one of these days, discuss the making of a poem. To most students, the creative process is a fascinating subject. For materials, you might, on one hand, use a poet's discussion of the making of one of his own poems: for instance, I. A. Richards' description of his creating of "Harvard Yard in April" or Stephen Spender's account of his making of "Seascape." You might, on the other hand, use a poet's discussion of the significance of the changes in another poet's worksheets: Karl Shapiro's article on Spender's "The Express," for example.[63] Why not show students the several versions of the particular poem and ask them what, literally, was changed version to version, and what difference each change seems to make. *Then,* go on to tell them what the author (or the poet-critic) has to say about the changes.

On one of these days, have some fun writing exercises. Ask students to be "last-line" authors, for instance. Give them an "all but last line" copy of Ogden Nash's "The Turtle," or his "The Termite," or David McCord's "Cocoon," or Arthur Guiterman's "On the Vanity of Earthly Greatness," or Robert Frost's "The Hardship of Accounting." And bid them "create." They have a guaranteed audience.

On one of these days, "take off" from the poems already read for a discussion of some of the moral and psychological questions they raise. Invite students to suggest in advance what questions they would like to talk about. Some classes can shape engaging questions on their own; some need help initially.[64]

These are just some ways to spend a "holiday." Students will suggest others and will arrange programs with "something for everyone." The activities planned should be enjoyable, engaging, and imaginative—but never invalid. Whatever the day, poems are poems, and the aim of the course still stands.

A Timetable for the Course

How much time will the first course take? Approximately thirty class periods. That is about the time it would take an average class to study twenty-five poems (five for dramatic organization; six for diction, syntax, rhythm; eight for image, simile, metaphor, symbol; three for tone; and three for the organization of the poem). Twenty-five is about the number of poems an average class would study, although the distribution might be quite different from the one we just suggested. One average class might need, for instance, to do "finger exercises" and study three poems in order to learn to respond to "submerged" metaphors alone—yet, it might be able to conclude without a Conclusion.

Thirty class periods is probably a right round figure even for other than average students. For, though the less able may need to study all five parts of the course and to read each poem painstakingly (slow students "get it" slowly), their cut-off point comes early. In all likelihood, their reading would be limited to the "easiest" poems in each part of the course. So the small number of poems studied would offset the time consumed in the study of each. Able students, too, may need to study all five parts of the course, but they work intensively, proceed out-of-class, and practice to improve the skills they are learning; so, in thirty periods, they will probably have read more than twenty-five poems and have written, not moderately as the average will have done in that time, but frequently.

But what would the less well-motivated classes accomplish in thirty periods? They do, indeed, puzzle us, for, though they would usually need to study all five parts of the course, their performance is inconsistent. At times they work like "top" students, at times like the average, at times like the dull. In the study of one device, they rush to the most subtle discriminations; in the study of another, they become arrested at a relatively gross level. And this variation in performance has less relation to the difficulty of the device being learned than to other factors, an important one of which *seems* to be the degree to which these students are engaged by the first lesson on the device. Strong involvement the first day usually foreshadows average, if not better, performance. One "blue-chip" introduction is a lesson that is crystal clear and relevantly illustrated, a lesson that teaches a shrewdly right poem and that includes an exercise that lets students show themselves before they leave the class that they understand the use of language being taught and *can* make the correct responses. Once "dug in," these students will usually sustain this engagement if the poems are well-sequenced, the "next" always *almost* too much for the class. We say "usually," because a good start will not solve all our problems with less well-motivated students. Such little things can break an engagement!—an assembly that replaces a Friday class, a "wrong" poem, two "snow days." Once the spell is broken, further study of *that* use of language sometimes loses its vigor, sometimes becomes a desultory and unproductive marking of time. It is, then, better to move on to a "new" use (say, from image to simile); the teacher does have repeated opportunities to recoup losses at more auspicious moments, since in this course, uses, once emphasized, are continually stressed.

By virtue of "blue-chip" introductions, "good" days, and the cumulative nature of the course, the less well-motivated classes will probably also achieve the aim of the course in about thirty class periods. But how the time will be spent will depend not only on their needs and abilities but on our capacity to commit them and hold them.

Our figure of thirty classes is, in all cases, a rough estimate. Only the teacher can say what the precise timetable would be for a particular class. He knows what uses of language—or aspects of them—his class needs to learn and how many readings and how much writing will be required to teach the students these uses effectively and economically. Only the teacher can know how long it takes a certain class to study a poem, how much work must be done in class (if it is to be done at all), how much class time must go for direction, explanation, oral and silent readings, assignment, and discussion of written exercises. All these factors must be taken into account in establishing an exact or nearly exact schedule. A first course must be custom-made for each class, and that includes the timetable.

Even when the schedule is decided upon, there is still the question of how long the particular class can continue the course without respite. Can the class spend thirty consecutive class periods on poems and remain relatively on "tiptoe"? If the students are both able and well-motivated, they probably can. But such classes are not the rule. For many classes, two three-week sessions or three two-week sessions would be more productive. Given either division, the time intervening between sessions should be long enough for respite, but not so long that significant loss of skills will result. The very students who require respites of this sort are those whose developing skills and sensitivities decline most rapidly, largely because, on their own, these students give them so little exercise. During these respites, the skills already taught should be continually practiced in some way. How, for instance?

If the teacher decides to interrupt the study of poems with an interlude of writing, he can make students remember the language poems use in several ways.[65] He can simply stress precise diction, "voice," appropriate syntax and figures in every writing assignment and in the correction, grading, and discussion of the papers. Or he can make that use of language the class has just studied the focus for several days of writing and draw his examples from the poems just read. Both dramatic organization and diction and syntax would make useful centers for short intervals of writing. Or if the teacher wishes, he can organize a brief block of descriptive writing—focused on scene, or object, or character—a unit with no *apparent* connection with the study of poems but, of course, very central to it. In some classes, the most refreshing respite is one that *seems* to be very divorced from what students have been doing. The teacher can assuredly effect this feeling by making the writing exercises, *not* reinforcement of what has just been done, but preparation for the study of the *next* use of language: descriptive writing might precede the study of images, say.

If the teacher decides to interrupt the study of poems with work that will discharge some of the department requirements—say, with the teaching of a vocabulary list, of certain points in grammar, of particular rhetorical principles, to mention a few of the more common obligations—he should shape these studies so that either they will reinforce the uses of language that have been developed or will prepare for forthcoming studies. It is possible.

The Second Course—and Later

"After such knowledge," what? Preferably, a first course in reading plays; then, a first course in reading short stories and novels; *and, then,* a return to poems. Thus, the students' second look at poems would probably come in the spring of the year, fourteen or fifteen weeks after their first course. Their reading of plays and of works of fiction would profit from their study of poems, strengthen and diversify the sensitivities they were developing, and so prepare them for this second encounter with poems. This would, in turn, make their responses to the literary uses of language stronger and more flexible and would facilitate their second courses in reading plays and novels. And these second courses and the courses that would follow in the next year and after would be helping students engage in advanced modes of literary study—our second aim for the study of literature in high school.

All courses, after the first, should be, we think, relatively short, specialized studies, designed for, say, ten to fifteen class periods. Whatever content is chosen for them, whatever shape they have, these courses should never be disguised repetitions of the first course; they should always be complements and particular extensions of it. Each successive course should so obviously build upon the last and go beyond it that, whatever their quality as readers, the students will be able to recognize the interconnection and the difference among their courses in any genre and will be able to sense a progressive sophistication in the series. Such a sense comes not from reading more works faster, but from reading more complex works and reading them less partially. (No one ever developed a gourmet by simply loading his plate and timing him!)

What shapes might the second and later courses in reading poems take? Here are six suggestions. Think of them as *some* possible forms for the study of poems beyond the first course. Consider them as alternatives from among which you or the class might choose in the spring and in the following year, depending largely upon the interest of the group *at that time*. Each of the six forms could be varied in many ways, and all could be shaped for able, average, and less able students by, as we have been suggesting, choosing poems, teaching methods, and writing assignments appropriate to each group.

Variations on a Theme

Most classes greatly enjoy reading a group of poems that are thematically related. Themes connected with topics like human aspiration, love, injustice, death, frustration, every-day heroism, and war are very appealing to high school students. But, truly, so all-embracing is the interest of students in what they call "psychology," that almost any theme that relates to man's attempts to define himself as a human being, to explain mystery, or to probe beyond act to motive engages them.

Like most of us, a class really appreciates having a choice of theme. But unless you have time to let them reduce their twenty separate choices to one, it seems best to offer the class a limited choice. If your repository of poems includes three or four thematic groups, let the class select from among those. Otherwise, propose some themes a month before the course begins; let the class choose one; then, gather a group of a dozen poems that will be appropriate both for *that* theme and *this* class.[66] Only about ten of these poems can be studied in class during a fifteen-period course that includes discussions, writing, hearing recordings, and perhaps a "holiday" of some sort.

At least some of the poems read in any thematic study should be ones that render insights into the theme that the teacher is fairly sure will be new to students. For this is a fine opportunity to extend students' understanding of some human situation they are already concerned with. To illustrate what we mean by "new" insights: if the theme chosen related to the defining of man's humanity, poems like Edwin Muir's "The Animals," W. B. Yeats' "Death," William Carlos Williams' "The Term," Richard Wilbur's "The Juggler," and Elizabeth Bishop's "The Prodigal" would present insights new to most high school students.

A study of thematically related poems is a most effective way to emphasize the uniqueness of each poem.[67] If many poems have the same general theme, what makes the experience of each poem different? Not just that each poem concentrates on a particular facet of the theme, but that it takes a particular attitude toward that facet, an attitude that implies a particular set of values. The way the theme is rendered expresses that attitude, those values. Thematic organization is, then, a fine means for bringing students to recognize that their only avenue to the unique experience each work offers is a discriminating response to the rendering. We can, of course, *tell* students that art is a "plurality of unique visions," but why hand down a meaningless pronouncement when we can arrange to have students discover this truth through the study of poems? And thematically similar poems offer unusual opportunity for letting this plurality highlight itself.

The Reading of One Poet

The second course or a later one might consist of a concentrated reading of ten to fifteen works of a single poet.

We might have a relatively narrow aim for this study: to help students discover, through the reading of the poems, some of the characteristics of the poet's style. The general questions would be: What kinds of effects does this poet repeatedly achieve? What special kinds of means to meaning does he habitually use? (well-defined speakers? conversational diction? intricate syntax? highly exploited sound? coupling of images? red images? conccits? compressed language, almost cryptic?) For the students, we would probably phrase the general questions this way: Would you "know a Frost [or an Emily Dickinson or a Browning or a Wordsworth] poem anywhere"? How would you? Or why wouldn't you be sure?

These four poets are fruitful subjects for this kind of study. And they would be appropriate for average and better readers. For less able readers we would probably choose E. E. Cummings, William Carlos Williams, Walter de la Mare, H. D., or perhaps A. E. Housman. For the competent only, Richard Wilbur, Gerard Manley Hopkins, W. B. Yeats, and W. H. Auden seem appropriate. We say these poets are "for the competent only" because some of their poems seem stylistically inconsonant with the others. And readers must be very discriminating to see similarities amid such apparent differences.

We could vary this kind of study in many ways. To expand it, we need only arrange the poems of any poet chronologically to help students catch a glimpse of the *evolution* of a style. To limit the study, we need only to restrict it to an intensive look at one or two characteristics. For instance, students might read the poems giving attention *only* to the kinds of metaphors used, the areas of experience they are drawn from, and the typical uses of them. Or we might focus on tone, using the early part of the unit to notice which tones are most characteristic of this poet; then concentrating, in the later part of the study, on his variations on some particular attitude—the ironic, say, a favorite with high school students, since they are just beginning to sense it.

The study of a style is not, as we so often hear, "too difficult for all but the very best." Since it can be complex or simple depending upon how inclusive it is and which poets and which poems are read, all students who have had a first course are prepared for it. Whether or not all would be interested in it is another matter. But they should not be put off by fear of boredom. For the study of style need not be occult nor pedantic. Whatever can be discussed is *there* in the text and whatever is discussed is the product of a mind and a heart that gradually come to life as we examine the poems.

Now to the practical question: where does one find ten to fifteen poems of one poet? Not in a general literature anthology. Even if it included ten to fifteen poems of one writer, they would rarely be the poems we want. But since the number of poems needed is relatively small, we can create our own collection of the poet's work. Furthermore, thanks to paperbinding, there are fine printed collections[68] available of the works of such poets as Blake, Browning, Byron, Chaucer, Coleridge, Donne, Dryden, Emily Dickinson, Herbert, Herrick, Jonson, Keats, Longfellow, Marvell, Milton, Poe, Pope, Shelley, Whitman, Whittier, and Wordsworth.

We might prefer a broader aim than style for the reading of one poet. We might, for instance, try to help students to discover through the reading of his poems what the poet's characteristic concerns are and how he characteristically expresses them. More specifically, the questions would be: Which aspects of human conduct particularly interest this poet? Which does he neglect entirely? By what means does he usually try to make sense of his concerns. If the poems read are chosen from all periods of the poet's career and read chronologically, students can see which concerns have been continuing, which developed and gained importance in certain periods, and how changes in rendering suggest changes in the maturing writer's response to his concerns.

This can be a most engaging kind of study in any class, and all can enjoy it because the study can be simple or very sophisticated, depending upon the poet and the poems we choose and the penetration we require. For appropriate poets, see our preceding discussion. For some useful schemes, models, and suggestions to assist your planning of this kind of course, see, for instance, such professional criticism as Reuben Brower's *The Poetry of Robert Frost: Constellations of Intention*[69] and Norman Friedman's *E. E. Cummings: The Art of His Poetry.*[70]

Finally, we might want a yet broader aim for the reading of one poet. We might try to help students discover the influence of the public cultural milieu on a poet's work. We would use both readings from relevant cultural history[71] and poems. Though this would not be contextual study in the usual sense, it would show students that cultural context is both general and local, that it is geographical, historical, and literary, and that present historical and literary contexts include all the past. Furthermore, this kind of study would alert students to the fact that milieu can affect more than subject matter, more than theme. Such understandings make a good preliminary base for later contextual study. Poets as diverse as Herrick, Wordsworth, Emerson, and Whitman would be fruitful subjects for introducing newcomers to this mode of study because the relation of these poets to their cultural contexts can be rather readily seen without oversimplifying the truth. And it is that kind of poet that we should choose for an initial study of this sort.

Should we want to point up more dramatically the different ways in which the same milieu affects the work of writers and the different degrees to which it does (witness Whitman on one hand, Emily Dickinson on the other), we may choose two poets from the same public cultural context and read a group of poems specially selected to reveal these differences. Some pairs of contemporaries that would make interesting studies are Herbert and Herrick, Milton and Waller, Wordsworth and Landor, Emerson and Longfellow, Tennyson and Browning, Frost and Sandburg, Edgar Lee Masters and E. A. Robinson. Comparative study will, of course, require more materials, more time, and more continuing interest on the part of the students.

The Reading of One Form of Poem

The second course or a later one might concentrate on the reading of one of the traditional forms; for instance, the sonnet or the ballad, both of which are greatly favored by high school readers. Here are two general ways such a study *might* be organized. First, the more structured way.

Through their reading of chronologically arranged representative poems in the chosen form, we could help students slowly arrive at an idea of "what happened" to the fixed form in successive periods or at the hands of successive writers: how it was varied and how it was accommodated to new subject matters and new intentions.

If we chose to study the sonnet in successive periods, students would probably read three sonnets from the sixteenth century (Spenser, Shakespeare, Sidney, Drayton), the same number from the seventeenth century (Donne, Milton), the nineteenth century (Wordsworth, Keats, Shelley, Arnold, Meredith), and the twentieth century (need we mention names?) If we chose to study the sonnet through the work of successive sonneteers, students would probably read three sonnets of Shakespeare, of Donne, of Wordsworth, and of Frost. Both approaches to such a study of the sonnet have advantages and limitations. Reading the sonnets of several writers in each period will give students an adequate understanding of how the period as a whole used the form, but not necessarily a just idea of how each writer used it. Reading three sonnets from one sonneteer in each period will give students a valid idea of how each of the three poets used the form, but not necessarily a just view of how the period used it. We say "necessarily," because shrewd choices of poems can lessen the limitation of either approach.

If we chose to study the ballad, we would probably study the use of the form in various centuries, rather than by various hands.[72] Students might read three old popular ballads (we would choose from among "Sir Patrick Spens," "The Twa Corbies," "Lord Randal," "Barbara Allen," "Edward," "Binnorie," "Lady Isabel and the Elf Knight"), three Wordsworth ballads (we would select appropriately from among "The Fountain," "Strange Fits of Passion," "Expostulation and Reply," "We Are Seven," "Lucy Gray," "The Two April Mornings"), three literary ballads of the nineteenth century (we would choose from among Sir Walter Scott's "Jock O'Hazeldean," John Keats' "La Belle Dame Sans Merci," Coleridge's "The Rime of the Ancient Mariner," and Daniel Gabriel Rossetti's "Troy Town"), and three modern ballads (we would select from among W. H. Auden's "As I Walked Out One Evening," "Let Me Tell You a Little Story," and "O What Is That Sound," John Crowe Ransom's "Captain Carpenter," Ezra Pound's "Ballad of the Goodly Fere," W. B. Yeats' "The Ballad of Father Gilligan," and his "The Cap and Bells," A. E. Housman's "Farewell to Barn and Stack and Tree," and Rosemary and Stephen Vincent Benet's "Johnny Appleseed").

Now to the less structured of our two general ways for studying a traditional form. Through their reading of a group of twelve or so poems in some chosen form, we could help students see what can be achieved within the confines of a conventional form: the infinite variety of poems that have resulted from writers fusing a personal

vision and this fixed form. The teacher must select a truly representative sampling of poems in the form, and then he must teach
the poems so that both their diversity and their similarity will
become clear to the readers.

If the form chosen is the sonnet, a selection from such poems as the
following would be suitable: Percy Bysshe Shelley's "Ozymandias,"
George Herbert's "Redemption," Archibald MacLeish's "The End
of the World," Gerard Manley Hopkins' "Felix Randal," Edmund
Spenser's "One Day I Wrote Her Name," Robert Frost's "Acquainted
With the Night," John Keats' "On First Looking into Chapman's
Homer," William Wordsworth's "Surprised by Joy," John Masefield's
"There on the Darkened Deathbed," John Donne's "Death Be Not
Proud," John Crowe Ransom's "Piazza Piece," George Meredith's
"Lucifer in Starlight," William Shakespeare's "When to the Sessions
of Sweet, Silent Thought," Robert Frost's "The Silken Tent," John
Milton's "On Shakespeare," Edward Arlington Robinson's "Reuben
Bright," John Keats' "Modern Love," Daniel Rossetti's "On Refusal
of Aid Between Nations," William Shakespeare's "Look in Thy
Glass," and Gerard Manley Hopkins' "God's Grandeur." If the chosen
form is the ballad, such poems as we suggested earlier, rearranged
to emphasize diversity, will serve.

In this kind of second course, the term "form" need not be construed to mean only such traditional poetic forms as the sonnet and
the ballad. Some classes need the variety that a more inclusive form
would allow. It would be preferable for some to study the lyric
rather than just the sonnet, the narrative poem rather than just the
ballad. It would be desirable for other classes to study variations
on the elegy, reading such poems as Ben Jonson's "Epitaph for S. P.,"
John Milton's "Lycidas," Thomas Gray's "The Elegy in a Country
Churchyard," selections from Alfred, Lord Tennyson's "In Memoriam," Walt Whitman's "When Lilacs Last in the Dooryard
Bloomed," W. H. Auden's "In Memory of W. B. Yeats," Theodore
Roethke's "Elegy for Jane," Hart Crane's "At Melville's Tomb," and
Dylan Thomas' "A Refusal to Mourn."

In certain classes it might be preferable to construe form still more
comprehensively, and study, say, satire. Students can read satires if
they are alert to "right" diction and acutely sensitive to tone and if
they know and can recognize whatever literary or social conventions
are being referred to. It is reading the older satires that might give
students problems. They do not really have to know about the
persons being satirized—any more than they have to know who the
subject of an elegy is. But, unless they know the relevant conventions of, for instance, an heroic poem, or of royal succession, or of
courtship and marriage in a certain time, they will not know what is
being mocked and that it is being mocked, so they will not get the

point and have the fun. Luckily, students can be briefed on these conventions as part of the preparation for reading the poem. But the requisite reading skills, the alertness to "right" diction and the sensitivity to tone, they must already have.

The following are some of poems appropriate for readers who "qualify" for satire: Shakespeare's "My Mistress Eyes," John Dryden's "Satire Upon the Dutch," his "Mac Flecknoe," Alexander Pope's "Epistle IV, To Richard Boyle, Earl of Burlington" (lines 88– 176, Timon's Villa), William Blake's "London," and such modern poems as Thomas Hardy's "Channel Firing," T. S. Eliot's "The Hippopotamus," W. H. Auden's "In Schrafft's," his "The Unknown Citizen," Henry Reed's "The Naming of Parts," Rupert Brooke's "The Great Lover," C. Day-Lewis' "Consider These, For We Have Condemned Them," Richard Wilbur's "Tywater," and John Betjeman's "In Westminster Abbey."

If the satires are chosen from different eras, then reading them not only will give students an insight into some particular brand of folly deplored by each age, but also will assure them of the unbroken succession of human absurdity.

The "Poem-ness" of a Poem

The second course or a later one might offer students the opportunity to *arrive* at some answers to the question of what constitutes a poem. Several well-known types of study will do this. One is the juxtaposing, for comparison, of a poem (usually lyric) and a prose account of the event to which the poem is in some way related. We can juxtapose, for instance, the salute to Helen from Christopher Marlowe's *Dr. Faustus*, V, i, and the prose account of this episode;[73] John Milton's sonnet "On the Late Massacre in Piedmont" and the historical account of this event; Richard Wilbur's "First Snow in Alsace" and any account of war in winter; Ralph Hodgson's "Eve" and the biblical account; T. S. Eliot's "Journey of the Magi" and the biblical account; Richard Eberhart's "On Shooting Particles Beyond the World" and the United Press headnote; Randall Jarrell's "Losses" and any newspaper account of casualties; and Marianne Moore's "The Swan and the Cook" and Aesop's fable of the swan and the goose. If students examine several such pairings, they will induce the differences in the intention, the significance, the quality of language, the ordering, and the intensity of the two "accounts."

Another type of study that can reveal the "poem-ness" of a poem is the juxtaposing, for comparison, of an historical narrative poem and the historical account on which it is based, or a philosophical poem and the statement of the philosophy. This can be a more demanding exercise than the preceding; for, as the subject matter of the poem and of the prose selection become more similar, the more discriminating the reader must be if he is to see the crucial differences. Such historical poems as these would be useful: Walt Whitman's "The Battle of the Bonhomme Richard and the Serapis," Donald Davidson's "Lee in the Mountains," A. E. Housman's "1887." And such philosophical poems as these: Emerson's "Brahma," Whitman's "Song of Myself," VI and XV, and Wordsworth's "My Heart Leaps Up." In comparing a poem with either an historical account or the statement of a philosophy, we would be trying to show the difference between two modes of expression, not the superiority of one. So our questions would go somewhat like this: If the historical event (or the philosophical truth) in both is relatively the same, why read both? What is there in the poem *other than* the account of an event (the statement of a philosophy)?

A third type of study that would help students discover the "poem-ness" of a poem is really a version of the familiar "taste test." Use a single poem, as I. A. Richards did, and ask: What *flaws* this poem? Or present students with two poems—without title or author —and ask: *How* do you know [the first] is the better poem? Or, for a more difficult exercise, choose poems more nearly alike in quality and ask simply: Which is the better poem?

Here are some pairs of poems of "middling" difficulty which could be used for either of the last two suggested tasks: Shakespeare's "Let Me Not to the Marriage of True Minds" and Elizabeth Barrett Browning's "How Do I Love Thee?" Emerson's "The Snow-storm" and James Russell Lowell's "The First Snowfall," Lord Byron's "Youth and Age" and Robert Frost's "An Old Man's Winter Night," Walter Savage Landor's "Rose Alymer" and Matthew Arnold's "Requiescat." Other materials for such tasks as we have suggested are readily available in Cleanth Brooks and Robert Penn Warren, *Understanding Poetry*, Third Edition, pages 133–35, 170–71, and 299–301. The pairings in some other books—say, Laurence Perrine's *Sound and Sense*, pages 204–214—are too easily distinguished to be useful for sensitive readers. And, of course, this type of exercise is not for obtuse readers, who may still confuse the personally preferred with the valuable.

Through such types of study as the three we have just cited, we would be trying to get students to realize that "poem-ness" has to do with organization of language, not with the value of the theme, and that artistic integrity is a quality that is realized in this poem and that one, only more or less.

Whatever kind of study we devised for helping students see what constitutes a poem,[74] it would in no case consist of poets' definitions or critics' or aestheticians' statements. The study would always be one that led students to induce "poem-ness" from the reading of poems. What better way is there to get a genuine understanding of the nature of a thing than from the study of the thing both by itself and in comparison with other seemingly similar things?

The Poems "People Talk About"

The second course or a later one might simply give students an opportunity to read many poems "people talk about," "famous poems," the "ones everyone reads"—to use students' own phrasings. Students who would like such a course are not necessarily those who can name the poems they are referring to. Nor are they necessarily those who simply want to say they have read them. Many do want to know "what is in" the famous poems, why they have been acclaimed and remembered.

If, by the end of the first course, most of the students in a certain class have become average or better readers, then the class could read many famous poems without any of the halting, agonizing ordeal with the lines that takes place when uninitiated high school readers confront such poems. Average readers have the skill, and interested readers, the will. So, if the students in a certain class are both, then the poems could be read well with all due speed and with only such routine assistance as glossing, study questions, discussion, and writing.

To understand many of these poems, most students would need various kinds of essential information: about the pastoral convention, the "universe" of Donne, the "society" Pope lived in, Wordsworth's "nature," the "trance" poem—and so on. We would provide this kind of information through analogies, anecdotes, and lines from the featured work and from other enlightening poems. There would be no "characteristics of this" or "definition of that."

To understand many of these poems, students would also need another kind of preparation—one aimed solely at helping them respond to these famous poems as living dramatic experiences. Often students set themslves for an austere occasion; they must be brought to realize that famous poems, like famous men, are really quite human. We would try to do this by showing that all the people in these poems "had their humanities."

Now, for an example of how we would provide the kinds of preparation we have been describing. As we readied the class to read "Lycidas," for instance, we would suggest that the pastoral is a kind of literary ritual that, like our religious rituals, restrains emotion by formalizing its expression. And we would re-create, as movingly as we could, the hopes, the plans, and the fears of the young Milton. So, when the speaker finally begins to speak, students would hear his voice charging the pastoral convention with the powerful feelings of the young Milton and all other young men who question the worth of their efforts, the value of devotion to duty. In this way, students might understand feelingly why the speaker responds to King's death as he does, why he digresses so vehemently—what the poem is really "about." And they might remember the poem as one of the most dramatic dramatic movements they had experienced, a torturing doubt bursting again and again through its ritual framework, as the poem moves, motion and countermotion, to its "answer."

In fifteen class periods, students could read only about seven to twelve poems. Which shall they be? We would probably give the class our list of "fifty famous poems" and let them decide on, say, ten—in consultation with us, if they wished. If they delegated their authority to us, we would teach those ten poems *we* understand most feelingly.

Here is our list of celebrities: Shakespeare's sonnets 18, 29, 73, 116; John Donne's "The Sun Rising," "A Valediction: Forbidding Mourning," "The Canonization," "Batter My Heart"; John Milton's "L'Allegro" and "Il Penseroso," "How Soon Hath Time" and "On His Blindness," "Lycidas"; Alexander Pope's "The Rape of the Lock"; William Blake's "Little Lamb," "Tyger," "London," "The Sick Rose"; William Wordsworth's "Composed Upon Westminster Bridge," "I Wandered Lonely As a Cloud," "A Slumber Did My Spirit Seal," "The Solitary Reaper," "Lines Composed a Few Miles Above Tintern Abbey"; Samuel Taylor Coleridge's "The Rime of the Ancient Mariner"; Lord Byron's "Childe Harold's Pilgrimage, Canto IV," stanzas 178–184; Percy Bysshe Shelley's "Ode to the West Wind," "To a Skylark"; John Keats' "On First Looking into Chapman's Homer," "Ode on a Grecian Urn," "Ode to a Nightingale," "To Autumn"; Alfred, Lord Tennyson's "Ulysses," "Crossing the Bar," Songs from "The Princess" ("The Splendor Falls on Castle Walls" and "Tears, Idle Tears"), from "In Memoriam" (part 2, "Calm is the morn," and part 27, "I envy not in any moods"); Robert Browning's "My Last Duchess," "Meeting at Night" and "Parting at Morning," "Soliloquy of the Spanish Cloister"; Matthew Arnold's "Dover Beach"; Walt Whitman's "When Lilacs Last in the Door-Yard Bloomed"; William Butler Yeats' "The Lake Isle of Innisfree," "The Wild Swans of Coole," "The Fisherman," "Why Should Not Old Men Be Mad?"; Gerard Manley Hopkins' "God's Grandeur," "Pied Beauty"; Dylan Thomas' "Fern Hill"; Robert Frost's "The Death of the Hired Man"; T. S. Eliot's "The Hollow Men," "The Love Song of J. Alfred Prufrock"; W. H. Auden's "Look, Stranger," "In Memory of W. B. Yeats."

All of these poems, except perhaps the last two of Yeats are "famous." Fame—not "greatness" in the sense of literary excellence—is our primary criterion. Not all the poems listed are necessarily the best-known these writers have produced. Some of the best-known are not very relevant to the concerns of high school readers—for instance, Yeats' "Sailing to Byzantium" or Eliot's "Gerontion." Some of the best-known are understandable only if abundant background is supplied—for instance, Eliot's "The Wasteland," Yeats' "The Second Coming," or Wordsworth's "Ode on the Intimations of Immortality." Some of the best-known are simply too long and/or rarely available outside the collected works—for instance, Chaucer's "The Pardoner's Tale" and Byron's "Don Juan."

There are other famous poems, of course—but one must choose. Every teacher has his own list, and his own way of sharing them with readers who can read them and who want to.

"On a Certain . . ."

The study of informal essays is a second course that might very well directly follow the first course in reading poems. Such essays are, in a way, prose counterparts to lyrics: brief compositions in which a writer presents—in a manner engaging in its own right—his attitudes toward seemingly unimportant experiences so as to reveal their significance. Reading essays requires sensitive responses to the speaker and his tones, to various qualities of diction, to implied connections, to the relation between statements and passages of narration and description, to the way structure expresses intention—and to the import of the "trivial" experience and the "insignificant" word. These are some of the very responses that both reading the exploited language of poems and "turning" phrases and sentences have helped readers cultivate. Readers and writers of poems are aware of the delight of phrase making and alert to the significance of the paths and byways of essays. So they grasp what the essayist is doing and what "he's gotten at," and they are in position to enjoy both.

If you think for a moment of the character of the informal essay, you realize immediately how important it is to have students come prepared to read it. For, if they cannot, almost by themselves, savor the delights of verbal surprises, of subtle satire, of wit and "preposterous" truth, what does the teacher do? Unravel eight pages of verbal nuances? Explain the jokes? Defend—or declare—in a disquisition longer than the essay, the significance of the experience, the illumination it provides, the writer's right to "waste his time"? Unless you enjoy dessicated plodding, warmed-over, forced enthusiasm and fruitless persuasion—then, for the coming of the personal essay, "provide, provide"! The reading of poems provides admirably.

If we had any questions about a certain class's fitness for enjoying essays, we would begin cautiously—with an in-class study of three or four "miniatures" widely different in style. For instance, three of the following would constitute a useful proving-ground for us: W. H. Auden's "Pride,"[75] John Henry Newman's "A Definition of a Gentleman,"[76] one of Lafcadio Hearn's "Torn Letters,"[77] Thomas Bailey Aldrich's "Writers and Talkers,"[78] E. B. White's "Democracy"[79] or "Ghostwriting," or "Critical Dilemma," or any of the twenty-four "miniatures" in his "Notes of Our Times."[80]

The in-class study, which would last about one period, would be designed to ascertain *gradually* the class's potential for reading essays. *We* would read the *first* passage (which could be any one of the three or four); the students would follow their copies. Then, we would ask them to summarize the essay in a single written sentence. The class would discuss their summaries, and we would ask about one or two particular features of the passage; for instance, a single word that fixes the attitude of the speaker toward the subject or toward his audience or a single phrasing that suggests the significance of the speaker's experience.

The students would read the *second* passage silently, write their summaries, and then as a class discuss the summaries. We would, once again, ask about the function of some revelatory use of syntax and some significant verbal surprise. The students would read the *final* essay silently, summarize it, and write answers to questions on the speaker's attitudes and the significance of the passage. The students' responses to this three-stage exercise would suggest whether we should read essays, and their reactions to the various styles of the "miniatures" would indicate which kinds of essays we should begin with and which we should probably not include at all. After an exploratory class period like this, we would know which way to turn.

If it is to the familiar essay, then unless we are going to "follow the book," we must decide on an organization for the study, which would probably last ten to fifteen class periods. We might choose a certain subject matter as a center; for instance:

"Brute Neighbors": reading, for example,[81] Henry Thoreau's "Brute Neighbors" from *Walden*, John D. Stewart's "Vulture Country," John Burroughs' "A Life of Fear," and Loren Eiseley's "The Judgment of the Birds."

Faraway places: reading, for instance, Truman Capote's "Ischia," and his "A Ride Through Spain," Lafcadio Hearn's "New Orleans," and George Orwell's "Marrakech."

The ugly American: reading, for example, E. M. Forster's "The United States," Cyril Connolly's "Blueprint for a Silver Age: Notes on a Visit to America," Irwin Edman's "On American Leisure," Agnes

Repplier's "On a Certain Condescension in Americans," Dennis Brogan's "Uncle Sam's Guides," H. L. Mencken's "The Sahara of the Bozart," and Robert Littell's "Let There Be Ivy."

Childhood: reading essays like Dylan Thomas' "Holiday Memory," Thomas Wolfe's "Circus at Dawn," Wallace Stegner's "The Town Dump," E. B. White's "Once More to the Lake," and Robert Louis Stevenson's "The Lantern-Bearers."

First-hand experience: reading, for instance, John Steinbeck's "Battle Scene," G. K. Chesterton's "The Twelve Men," and Paul Gallico's "The Feel."

Instead of a certain subject matter as a center, we might prefer some intention; for instance:

The creation of a mood: reading essays like Robert Louis Stevenson's "Night Among the Pines" and Kenneth Grahame's "Loafing."

Social criticism: reading "preposterous parables" like E. B. White's "The Decline of Sport" and "The Hour of Letdown"; essays like G. K. Chesterton's "Science and the Savages," John Galsworthy's "Holiday" and "Comfort," William M. Thackeray's "On Being Found Out," Robert Lynd's "On Not Being a Philosopher," and for able readers, Samuel Johnson's "On Self-Love and Indolence."

Sheer comedy: reading, say, Robert Benchley's "Take the Witness!"

We might choose to center the study of the essay on the work of a pair of modern essayists: for instance, G. K. Chesterton and E. M. Forster, E. B. White and George Orwell, Robert Benchley and James Thurber, Herbert Gold and James Baldwin. Or we might elect to blend several of the approaches we have suggested so far. We might start, say, with two three-essay subject matter groupings. Through the class's reactions to these six essays, we can discover whether the students prefer the satiric, the comic, or the philosophic mode, and we can then continue the study with the reading of three or four essays in the favored mode. We might conclude the work on the essay with the reading of three or four essays by some one writer whom students had shown they particularly enjoyed. In such an organization as this, there is continuity with considerable variety— a variety that the students themselves determined.

Reading essays occasions writing of many kinds. We would assign little in-class critical exercises on various aspects of the essays being discussed. We would require one longer analysis of the writer's attitude toward the subject and the audience in some essay not discussed in class. We would invite short rebuttals addressed by students to authors with whom they disagree on a certain point. And, of course, we would encourage original one-to-two paragraph essays.[82]

Beyond these conventional kinds of writing, there are also wonderful exercises. Assign students a question from a newspaper or magazine column and ask them to answer it satirically—in the mode of E. B. White's "Answers to Hard Questions." Or ask students to account comically for the demise of some late fad in the school. Or give them an announcement of some sort—from the day's "notices," if you will—and let them react to it, however they choose.

NOTES

1. As Cleanth Brooks claims in his introduction to *Modern Poetry and the Tradition* (New York: Oxford University Press, 1965), p. xi, anything *can* be mechanical. He is suggesting that "close reading" is not necessarily mechanical; all other kinds of criticism can also be mechanical.

2. For related views, see also Lawrence V. Ryan, "The Literature Course for Secondary School Teachers of the Commission on English," *EJ*, *51* (May, 1962), p. 318; Dwight Burton, *Literature Study in the High Schools* (New York: Holt, Rinehart and Winston, Inc., 1964), pp. 214–215; and Stephen Dunning, "Why Poetry?" *EJ*, *55* (Feb. 1966), pp. 158 ff.

3. Wilbur's poem is readily available in *The Poems of Richard Wilbur* (New York: Harcourt, Brace and World, Inc., 1963), p. 99; Robins' in Charles Cooper, *Preface to Poetry* (New York: Harcourt, Brace and Company, 1946), p. 155; and Francis' in his *The Orb Weaver* (Middletown, Connecticut: Wesleyan University Press, 1948), p. 7.

4. For other valid ways of "softening up," see certain of the exercises "for the reluctant, the young, (and) the unimaginative" suggested by Charles Rathbone in "Prelude to the Making of a Poem: Finger Exercises," *EJ*, *54* (Dec. 1965) pp. 851–856. With an occasional class, the ploy in Mary-Jo Powell's "War on Poetry-phobia," *EJ*, *55* (Oct. 1966), pp. 887 ff., might be effective.

5. For instance, see the books referred to as "Discussions of the Language Poets Use," part I of the References for this section.

6. For instance, see the books referred to as "Useful 'Teachers,'" part III of the References for this section.

7. Writers preface their courses in a variety of ways, too. Some begin by distinguishing prose from poetry; others, by demonstrating how elements become meaning. Some open with narrative poems—to take advantage of the lure of story; some, with poems that show what a kaleidoscope of experiences poems render. Such preliminaries as the first two attempt to clear up misconceptions about poetry and to develop "right" expectancies. The last two introductions are motivators for "uncommitted," though not reluctant, students. We cite these "starters" as examples of introductions that teachers have found valuable.

8. To get the force of this important point, look at some teaching plans for ballads. Many of them erroneously take "story line" for "poem." Just see what is lost by not attending to who is saying the ballad to whom and

under what circumstances. Look back at the notes on "Lord Randal" in this text.

9. One of the main difficulties of many printed "teachers" and teaching anthologies is that they are *not* cumulative. Examine some by looking at the questions at successive points in the book. Do they reinforce again and again what was taught earlier? Usually not. Each use is taught discretely, taught and forgotten about, so students never perceive the many "voices" (prose sense, rhythm, sound, image) saying the same word at the same moment.

10. We say "of course" because we have already discussed these requirements in "What Kinds of Works Will Help Students Achieve Our Aims."

11. It is not easy to find such poems. On one hand, many poems that make very clear, very graphic, sometimes remarkable use of a certain device are often too complex in their other uses of language to be read by beginning readers. (Many poems of Hopkins, Eliot, Stevens, and Donne are, for instance, fine for dramatic speakers, but are in other respects inappropriate for novice readers.) On the other hand, many poems, simple in most respects, are too subtle in the use we are currently interested in to be fruitful readings for the inexperienced. (Many poems of Wordsworth, Robinson, Yeats, and often, Frost fall in this category.) One of the major flaws in texts that purport to teach students how to read poems is that they include, indeed feature, poems that are, for the preceding reasons, unusable. Look at the order of poems in some of the commonly used high school anthologies to see how little attention has been paid to what the reading of these poems requires of students.

12. As Hugh Kenner points out in *The Art of Poetry* (New York: Holt, Rinehart and Winston, 1959), p. xvii, if we choose poems in which "some fundamental quality or principle is exhibited in action" (markedly), then, "it can be isolated for discussion without serious distortion."

13. Almost all of the poems we cite are readily available in such inexpensive paperback "teachers" and anthologies as those of Ciardi, Drew, Frankenberg, Warren and Erskine, Untermeyer, Oscar Williams, and Pratt —all of which are listed in the References at the end of this section. These paperbacks may be purchased in commercial and college book stores, even in drug stores. Single copies may also be ordered *prepaid* directly from the publisher.

14. When we speak of a reading as "easy" or "challenging," we simply mean that, in our view, the language of the poem (or play or story) is less complex (less richly exploited) or more so. Generally speaking, the more complex the language of a work, the more able the reader must be. Every experienced teacher knows, however, that if average readers are unusually motivated, for instance, by the subject of a work or by some extrinsic reward (or by a bright or a dull day, for that matter), they can often go through a complex work. They simply "play way over their heads." So, it is true that we *cannot* say, with assurance, what a reader of a certain quality can read. But we *can* say what customarily he *does* read ade-

quately and so what quality poem is customarily "right" for him. And, of course, in no case is the literary complexity of a poem affected by who can or cannot read it. A poem does not become an "easy" poem because mediocre readers struggled through it. So we can *suggest* that poems are "easy" and "challenging" on the basis of their literary complexity, and we can suggest that the first are, under ordinary circumstances, more fitting for less able readers, the latter, for competent ones. If the reader of this text wonders about this lengthy footnote on the obvious, let him look at the teachers' manuals for anthologies, and he will see that such labeling is thought "dangerous" and indefensible.

15. Throughout our discussions of the teaching of works, we repeatedly stress the need for "getting the work straight." For a direct article on this matter, see Seymour Chatman, "Reading Literature as Problem-Solving," *EJ*, 52 (May 1963), pp. 346–352.

16. Why do we keep saying "we" would read? Won't the students ever read orally? We would certainly take advantage of any sensitive oral reader in a class (much as we would take advantage of fine recordings) or any other valid aid to the achievement of our aim—in this case, developing students' sensitivity to the voices of the speakers in the poems. We would, accordingly, eschew the use of any device that did not facilitate the achievement of this aim—whether the device be a poor oral reader or a poor tape.

Does this mean that not "everybody" would get a chance to read? It does. But we are *not aiming* to develop sensitive oral readers; our goal is to develop sensitive *silent* readers, readers who can look at print and feel and hear words as spoken. To achieve this aim, students do not have to perform publicly themselves. As Brower says in *The Fields of Light* (New York: Oxford University Press, 1951), p. 62, "Indeed it may be argued that the best readers of poetry try in reading aloud to render the sounds they first 'hear' as images [pronunciation images], that any actual sounds they make are only helpful as reminders of those heard in the inner ear." Discussion of works repeatedly shows that some students who are mediocre or poor oral readers are discriminating silent readers. They simply cannot render what they hear in their inner ear. Whether they can or not is not relevant to their achieving the aim we set.

For an interesting view of the superiority of silent reading of poetry, see linguist Samuel R. Levin's "Suprasegmentals and the Performance of Poetry," *The Quarterly Journal of Speech*, 48 (Dec. 1962), pp. 366–372.

17. The term used by John Ciardi in *How Does a Poem Mean* (Boston: Houghton Mifflin Company, 1959), p. 994, and others to describe the dramatic movement of a poem.

18. Brower, p. 72.

19. See Brower, pp. 71–74.

20. (New York: Harcourt, Brace and Company, 1956.)

21. (New York: Holt, 1959.)

22. Phrase borrowed from Kenner, *Art of Poetry*, p. 71, who uses it to describe the function of rhythm.

23. Elizabeth Drew, *Poetry, A Modern Guide to Its Understanding and Enjoyment* (New York: Dell Publishing Company, 1959), p. 41.

24. For definitions of images, similes, metaphors, and symbols, this text depends upon the fine discussion of Jerome Beaty and William Matchett, *Poetry From Statement to Meaning* (New York: Oxford University Press, 1965), pp. 163–262. We are *not* offering these definitions as *the* definitions; we are simply trying to make the terms we use clear and to show how the nature of each of these means affects what we must do in teaching it.

25. One of the unpublished *Reports and Speeches of the Fourth Yale Conference on The Teaching of English, 1958.* It is Appendix 7 of the Report of the Committee on Writing and Thinking. For this and other Yale *Reports,* write The Master of Arts in Teaching Program, Hall of Graduate Studies, Yale University, New Haven, Connecticut.

26. (New York: Bantam Books, Inc., 1964.)

27. These haikus may be conveniently found in Harold G. Henderson, *An Introduction to Haiku* (New York: Doubleday and Company, Inc., 1958), pp. 108, 181, 173, 185, 40, and 50, respectively.

28. This fine, rarely anthologized poem was found in David Aloian's *Poems and Poets* (New York: Webster Division, McGraw-Hill Book Company, 1965), p. 290.

29. These poems were found in Stephen Dunning, Edward Lueders, and Hugh Smith (eds.), *Reflections on a Gift of Watermelon Pickle* (Glenview, Illinois: Scott, Foresman and Company, 1966), pp. 97 and 131, respectively.

30. A print that would project well is Plate 3, "Landscape with the Fall of Icarus" in F. Grossman (ed.), *Bruegel: The Paintings* (London: Phaidon Press, 1966).

31. But what does the teacher do for the first twenty minutes? One or another of the necessary, though less dramatic, acts of teaching. For instance, he might use the time to discuss adequate and inadequate answers to the critical exercises the class wrote on the previous day; he might have the "authors" of some good creative work read their papers; or he might conduct an exercise analyzing and correcting one or more awkward constructions found on recent student papers. Teachers are always grateful for an occasional part of a period to do this essential "horsework"!

32. The important point here is that these words are written on the board *as* we mention them. In this way, students' attention will be focused on the item being discussed. They cannot be distracted by wondering "what the next one means."

33. See Beaty and Matchett, *Poetry,* pp. 164–165.

34. "Though B gives meaning to A, A simultaneously modifies B; the process is not a simple action but an interaction. . . . Each term exerts a control on the other. . . . In other words the comparison is not a one-way boulevard open to all traffic; while the B-term explains the A-term, the A-term places limits on our response to the B-term." Beaty and Matchett, *Poetry,* p. 167.

35. Poems that are "pure" simile—or pure anything else—probably do not exist (we are happy, and sad, to say). So, in the poems that we list, there will be metaphors and symbols, just as there were similes in those we suggested for teaching images—"Hyla Brook," being a notable example. In our study of the poems, we shall concentrate on similes and on the other means to meaning we have featured so far in the first course, dealing, as need be, with *any* other literary devices that are present.

36. Beaty and Matchett, *Poetry*, p. 166.

37. This is an excellent example of a poem that seems, on first thought, to be irrelevant to high school students' concerns. But when we notice what "This" in line 13 and "that" in line 14 refer to, we see how very appropriate the theme is. Such discoveries make us careful about excluding a poem because of its subject matter—or including it only because of its author.

38. Teachers *might* want competent readers and college-course students of all abilities to distinguish carefully among various types of metaphors, to learn the accepted names for the different types, and to use this terminology in class discussions and on papers. In discussing "Oread," for instance, teachers might want students to distinguish among personification, metaphor, metonymy. See our previous comment on terminology in our discussion of syntax and rhythm.

39. This poem was found in Stanley Peterson (ed.), *Poetry II* (New York: The Macmillan Company, 1962), p. 132.

40. What kind of help would competent readers need to read these poems? A gloss for "Leonardo," for "Saturn," "Limbo," and, perhaps, "lavender." And wouldn't a projected drawing or two of Leonardo's be revelatory preparation for "The Cancer Cells"? When we plan to assign any task to any student, the primary question is: What would he have to know, understand, feel, be able to do if he is to experience, to learn this? The answer tells us how to prepare him for the task and how to design it.

41. This term is Beaty and Matchett's in *Poetry*, p. 238. We borrow it because it seems to so well express the relation of the symbolic meaning to the word.

42. We are not, of course, referring to symbols from a set of symbols that some particular writer has created for his own use. For these can be used in his poems much as a conventional symbol would be used—without extensive "within-the-poem" preparation. The A-denotation of a symbol from a symbology is learned by the reading of many of the poet's works; the reader induces the symbolic meaning from many instances of use. By "created symbol," we mean a word that takes on a certain A-denotation from the way it is detailed within a single poem.

43. Such questions as: Why is the first image in "Mirage" reported in flat statements? Why are the simple similes of "Sonnet to My Mother" phrased in the diction and rhythm of everyday, ordinary speech?

44. See p. 70.

45. We point this out because "tone" is often used to refer solely to

the speaker's attitude toward his audience. His attitude toward his subject is then referred to as "feeling" or "mood." For a clear, informative discussion of tone, see Cleanth Brooks and Robert Penn Warren, *Understanding Poetry* (New York: Holt, Rinehart and Winston, Inc., 1960), pp. 181–187, 191–193, or Reuben Brower, *Fields of Light*, pp. 19–30.

46. Brower, *Fields of Light*, p. 23. See also other uses of comparison in our teaching of, for instance, "Futility," of "Silence," of simile, and of metaphor.

47. For two useful exercises for such readers, see p. 164.

48. Suggested lesson for the poem is on pp. 4–10 of this text.

49. Unlike most of the poems we proposed throughout this scheme for a first course, some in this list would probably require glossing. For, in order to experience Auden's poem, students would have to know about the "unknown soldier"; to experience Eliot's, about the Magi, and how they have been represented in art; to understand Jarrell's, about the position a ball turret gunner takes; and to grasp Selig's, about the dying God's forgiving and redeeming men. These poems are good examples of works in which knowing the references is not just enhancing, *but crucial*.

50. Throughout this lesson, we are citing typical student responses to these questions.

51. How much do students need to know about the archetype in order to do *this* work? Only an outline of the archetype, a short history of it, and a sketch of its repeated adaptation in literature. All this can be summarized briefly either orally or on a duplicated handout.

52. A simple grading system should be used: a plus sign for a superior answer; C for adequate; a minus sign for inadequate. We favor some such system because it allows the teacher to grade papers quickly and because it prevents students from "mistaking" the relative importance of such an exercise. To some, all A's are equal!

53. Saying, perhaps, something like: Now for the next half hour, we shall be shaping materials for answering a question. When we are finished, you will write the answer as an in-class graded exercise.

54. As a general reference on critical papers for both poetry and prose, see Edgar V. Roberts, *Writing Themes About Literature* (Englewood Cliffs, New Jersey: Prentice-Hall, Inc., 1964). This inexpensive paperback offers valid, direct, and explicit discussions of fourteen different kinds of papers with examples of each. Though the book is directed to college freshmen and sophomores, it would be an excellent resource for high school teachers, beginning teachers especially.

55. In the last section on "submerged" metaphor, this poem is listed among the works appropriate for the less able. Here, however, we assign it to the competent. Why? Because here it is being used as the basis for an exercise on *organization,* an exercise moreover that students must carry on *without help*. Such an assignment as this on this poem could be handled only by competent students. *Moral:* when we are deciding whether or not a certain work is usable in a certain class, we have to consider

what we are going to ask students to do with the work and how much help we are going to give them.

56. The title of this poem ("November Night," by Adelaide Crapsey) is purposely omitted from the assignment to prevent students from saying the impression is of a November night. Their job is to shape the impression from the details of the poem, not fit the details to a "received" answer.

57. For an article that justifies the exclusive use of short papers, see Philip Burnham, "A Beginning in Writing," Edward J. Gordon (ed.), *Writing and Literature in the Secondary School* (New York: Holt, Rinehart and Winston, Inc., 1965); for an article that shows how specific topics facilitate grading and that suggests solutions to the problems of "follow-up" work, see Eric W. Johnson, "Avoiding Martyrdom in Teaching Writing: Some Shortcuts," *EJ*, *51* (Sept. 1962), pp. 399 ff.

58. Three articles that assert the values of students' having "a fellow-craftsman's relationship" to creative writers are Robert C. Pooley, "Poetry Is for People," *EJ*, *52* (March 1963), pp. 170–171; Joseph F. Dutton, "The Slow Learner—Give Him Something New," *EJ*, *52* (April 1964), p. 270; and Joseph J. Feeney, S.J., "Teaching Students to Write Poetry," *EJ*, *54* (May 1965), pp. 395–398.

59. For some very simple exercises "for the reluctant, the young, [and] the unimaginative," see Rathbone, "Prelude," *EJ*, *54* (Dec. 1965), pp. 851–856.

60. The photograph chosen should really be projected while the writing is being done. Only Cartier-Bresson's photographs are large enough to simply stand on the desk or chalk rail. Teachers or students could themselves create the needed materials by taking some provocative photographs and then blowing them up for in-class use.

61. Useful criticisms of this sort are available in the usual critical reviews and occasionally in the *English Journal* (see, for instance, John E. Parish, "The Rehabilitation of Eben Flood," *EJ*, *55* [Sept. 1966], pp. 696 ff.). Such criticisms are readily accessible in, say, Randall Jarrell's excellent *Poetry and the Age* (New York: Vintage Books, 1953) or in the various volumes of Prentice-Hall's paperback series, *Twentieth Century Views* (which includes Eliot, Frost, Whitman, Donne, Jonson, Yeats, Dickinson, Blake, Byron, Hopkins, Keats, Poe, Stevens, Wordsworth).

62. *New Republic* (Dec. 6, 1943). This text is also conveniently available on pp. 489–492, Harold C. Martin and Richard M. Ohmann, *Inquiry and Expression* (New York: Rinehart and Co., 1958). If Spencer's essay is not available locally, E. B. White's "Poetry," pp. 103–105, will ably substitute; it may be found in the Perennial paperback edition of *One Man's Meat* (New York: Harper and Row, 1966).

63. All these essays are conveniently available in Walker Gibson, *Poems in the Making* (Boston: Houghton Mifflin Company, 1963). For Richards' description, see "Poetic Process and Literary Analysis," pp. 230–244; for Spender's, "The Making of a Poem," pp. 77–80; for Shapiro's, "The Meaning of the Discarded Poem," pp. 63–72.

In certain classes students might enjoy hearing *as interviews* some of

The Paris Review interviews, (*Writers at Work*, Second Series [New York: The Viking Press, 1963]), say, those of Robert Frost, Marianne Moore, and perhaps even T. S. Eliot.

64. For our comments on the structure of such questions and on this teaching method, see "Holidays" in "A First Course in Reading Fiction."

65. We suggest writing related to dramatic organization, diction and syntax, and images and figures because usually the kind of break we are talking about would occur after the Introduction and the First Part of the course, if the students were on a two-week schedule, and after images and similes in the Second Part of the course, if they were on a three-week schedule.

66. The teacher can get some help in suggesting themes and finding appropriate poems by looking at thematic arrangements in anthologies. Part II, "Poetry and the Human Condition," in Elizabeth Drew's *Poetry* is useful—even if some of the poems might not be appropriate for a particular class. Pages 250–256, "Transience: Seven Poems," in Hugh Kenner's *The Art of Poetry* offer both variations on a theme, usable poems, and fine questions. Pages 277–289 in Alice C. Coleman and John R. Theobald (eds.), *Introducing Poetry* (New York: Holt, Rinehart and Winston, Inc., 1964) are also valuable, as are such sections as "Mutability," "Carpe Diem," and "In Praise of Woman," in Karl Kroeber and John O. Lyons (eds.), *Studying Poetry* (New York: Harper and Row, 1965). Too often what purports to be a thematic grouping in an anthology is merely a subject matter grouping or topical grouping. The subject matter is "snow" or "sleep," but thematically, the poems within the group are worlds apart.

67. For the possible hazards of premature thematic study and for other comments on this mode of organization, see pp. 436, 438–40.

68. For example, The Laurel Poetry Series (Dell Publishing Co.), Richard Wilbur (ed.). The poems in each volume in this series are well-chosen and chronologically arranged. There is no intrusive annotation. The initial essay discusses some crucial critical problem posed by the works of the particular poet—a welcome relief from the usual biographical summary.

69. (New York: Oxford University Press, 1963.)

70. (Baltimore: Johns Hopkins, 1960.)

71. Such books as the following are the *kinds* of works that could supply the necessary cultural materials: Arthur M. Schlesinger, Sr., *The Rise of Modern America* (1865–1940) (New York: The Macmillan Co., 1951), Harvey Wish, *Society and Thought in America* (New York: Longmans, Green Co., 1950–52), Henry Steele Commager, *The American Mind* (New Haven: Yale University Press, 1950), D. S. Somervell, *English Thought in the Nineteenth Century* (London: Methuen and Co., Ltd., 1929), and G. M. Young (ed.), *Early Victorian England 1830–1865* (New York: Oxford University Press, 1951).

72. When you gather ballads for such a study, you will notice that poetry in English is lyric rather than narrative. And you will probably ask yourself—and rightly so—if lyric poetry predominates, how can one

justify the concentration on narrative poetry we see in certain courses of study?

73. The relevant prose passage may be conveniently found in a paperback: William Rose (ed.), *The Historie of the Damnable Life and Deserved Death of Doctor John Faustus*, 1592 (South Bend, Indiana: University of Notre Dame Press, 1963), Chapter 45, pp. 176–177.

74. Hugh Kenner's "Presenting the Subject," pp. 167–181, *The Art of Poetry*, is different enough from our first and second suggestions to warrant consultation—even though many of the illustrative poems may not be appropriate for high school readers.

75. From "Hic et Ille," *The Dyer's Hand* (New York: Random House, 1962).

76. Conveniently available in George N. Shuster (ed.), *Newman Prose and Poetry* (Boston: Allyn and Bacon, 1925).

77. From *An American Miscellany*, 2 (New York: Dodd, Mead and Co.,' Inc., 1924).

78. Seen in Charles B. Shaw (ed.), *American Essays* (New York: The New American Library, 1955).

79. From *The Wild Flag* (Boston: Houghton Mifflin Company, 1946).

80. From *The Second Tree From the Corner*, Perennial Library (New York: Harper and Row, 1965).

81. We regret that we cannot say, as we could about the poems, that all the essays we cite are readily available in inexpensive paperback anthologies. They are not. Most of them do appear, though, in one or another of the collections we listed in the references for this section or cited in the footnotes. Our suggestions for teaching the essay could be carried out, of course, with essays other than the ones we suggest.

82. A teacher could get ideas for devising creative writing assignments for seven or eight different kinds of brief essays by looking carefully at the "miniatures" we have already cited and at the following from E. B. White's *The Second Tree From the Corner:* "Transient," "Sadness of Parting," "In An Elevator," "Twins," "Little Green Shebang." Some of these essays are highly serious treatments, some ironic, some comic; some are blatant, some subtle; some are extended definitions; some images-to-statements; some are narratives without obvious comment. If, in the assigning of creative papers, the appropriate "miniatures" are used as models, they will suggest to students not only the kind of task they are being asked to do, but also the kind of topic that would be fruitful to use on such a paper.

REFERENCES

I. Discussions of the Language Poets Use: General References

BEATY, JEROME, and WILLIAM H. MATCHETT. *Poetry From Statement to Meaning*. New York: Oxford University Press, 1965. A superb "teacher" for teachers who would like to become at once more sensitive in their reading of poems and more informed about the language poets use. The book moves in easy stages from "the world of prose statement" "where most readers . . . feel at home" to form and from form to meaning. The theoretical discussions are clearly written and are copiously and pertinently illustrated with sensitive (and sane) analyses. A book to begin on—and to keep on hand for many years to come.

BROWER, REUBEN A. *The Fields of Light: An Experiment in Critical Reading.* New York: Oxford University Press, 1951. This invaluable book shows how the study of poems prepares for the study of longer works. The writer never forgets that works of literature are *human* experiences shaped by and perceived by *humans*. (Available in paperback.)

HUNGERLAND, ISABEL C. *Poetic Discourse.* University of California Publications in Philosophy, 33. Berkeley: University of California Press, 1958. This is a scholarly and sophisticated treatment of the poetic uses of language. It might be read as a whole or in part, as a sequel to Nowottny, listed below.

NOWOTTNY, WINIFRED. *The Language Poets Use.* New York: Oxford University Press, 1962. This clearly written, knowledgeable inquiry into what makes the language of poems poetic discusses all the "hard questions," but it requires no more of the reader than first-class attention. Although the topics are presented in a certain progression, a reader may enter the book anywhere his interest dictates: at the elements of poetic language (a superb review), at diction, or metaphor, or ambiguity, and he will enjoy a fine treatment of the particular element he is interested in because it will be discussed in terms of all the others.

PERRY, JOHN OLIVER (ed.). *Approaches to the Poem.* San Francisco: Chandler Publishing Co., 1965. This book is a well-chosen collection of twenty essays by leading literary theorists and practical critics. Since the various papers deal with such topics as objective interpretation, archetypal criticism, irony as a principle of structure, tone, voice, syntax, diction, metaphor, sound, and rhythm, the book provides a good overview (or a good review) of ways of analyzing and interpreting poems.

II. Discussions of the Language Poets Use: Specialized References

DAY-LEWIS, CECIL. *The Poetic Image.* London: Jonathan Cape, 1947. As the title suggests, this study concentrates on the nature and the functions of images. Originally given as lectures, the six chapters are scholarly, sensitive, and delightfully written. This book might be read as a sequel to, or in lieu of, MacLeish's, listed below.

FUSSELL, PAUL. *Poetic Meter and Poetic Form.* New York: Random House, 1965. Some teachers might prefer Fussell's treatment to that of Shapiro and Beum.

HEMPHILL, GEORGE (ed.). *Discussions of Poetry: Rhythm and Sound.* Boston: D. C. Heath and Co., 1961. See especially the last fifteen papers, pp. 36–112. The last six of these fifteen papers are those on linguistics and literature that first appeared in *The Kenyon Review,* 1956, pp. 411–477.

KNIGHTS, L. C., and BASIL COTTLE (eds.). *Metaphor and Symbol.* Proceedings of the Twelfth Symposium of the Colston Research Society, March 28–31, 1960. London: Butterworths Scientific Publications, 1960. Especially relevant are the papers of D. G. James and L. C. Knights. These essays are for those who, having read MacLeish, are further interested in these uses of language.

LANGBAUM, ROBERT. *The Poetry of Experience.* New York: W. W. Norton and Co., Inc., 1963. Chapters 2, 4, and 6 will be enjoyable and very enlightening reading for those who have already read, for instance, "The Speaking Voice" in Reuben Brower's *The Fields of Light* or those who are otherwise already conversant with and sensitive to dramatic situation, tone, and a poem as a dramatic organization.

MACLEISH, ARCHIBALD. *Poetry and Experience.* Boston: Houghton Mifflin Company, 1961. By the time a reader has finished this fluent, engaging discussion of images, coupled images, similes, metaphors, and symbols, he understands—not just knows about—the nature and the functions of these uses of language.

MURPHY, FRANCIS (ed.). *Discussions of Poetry: Form and Structure.* Boston: D. C. Heath and Co., 1964. The first seven of these essays explore and exemplify three rhetorical structures poems use—the repetitive, the progressive, and the syllogistic. The last three papers discuss, respectively, three fixed forms—Shakespeare's sonnets, sixteenth and seventeenth century lyrics, and Keats' odes. These discussions will be salutary reading for those who have forgotten the crucial role of rhetoric in expressing the meaning of a poem.

SHAPIRO, KARL, and ROBERT BEUM. *A Prosody Handbook.* New York: Harper and Row, 1965. This clearly written, well-illustrated manual deals quite comprehensively with rhythm, rhyme, and stanza form. More importantly for teachers, the book goes beyond mere description to discuss the functions of these features.

III. Useful "Teachers"

We suggest the following books as valid, reliable, carefully wrought "teachers," free of superficialty, looseness, and contradiction: they do not aim for one thing and ask about another. These books warrant at least a careful review. You may then want to add some of them to your personal collection or your department library. And you may want to order one or another of them now or in the future for your high school classes.

ALOIAN, DAVID. *Poems and Poets.* St. Louis: Webster Division, McGraw-Hill Book Co., 1965. Over two hundred pages of usable poems grouped in such categories as "Free Verse," "Sonnets," "Ballads," "Great

Themes," "Character Poems." Although many of the poems are appropriate for grades 11 and 12, the approach in "A Guide to Reading
Poetry" seems more appropriate for grade 9, or, in some cases, grade 10.

BOYNTON, ROBERT W., and MAYNARD MACK. *Introduction to the Poem.*
New York: Hayden Book Co., Inc., 1965. This fine introduction to the
art of reading poems would be an excellent text for high school classes.
The organization of the study is clear and progressive; the discussions
are lucid; the questions, valid and precisely worded; the poems, numer-
ous and generally appropriate. No meaningless rhapsodies and no
"talking down" to students.

BROOKS, CLEANTH, and ROBERT PENN WARREN. *Understanding Poetry.*
New York: Holt, Rinehart and Winston, Inc., 1960. This book taught
a generation to read well. An excellent "teacher": the introductions are
direct, informative, and, of course, valid; the questions that follow the
poems ask about the *function* of the device being taught. Used selectively, the organization and the materials in this book would be appropriate for grades 10, 11, or 12.

CIARDI, JOHN. *How Does A Poem Mean?* Boston: Houghton Mifflin
Company, 1959. Although most of the poems are not appropriate for
high school students, the discussions of the language of poems, cast as
they are in teaching terms, are very useful reading for the teacher of
poems.

CUSTER, EDWIN C. *Adventures in Poetry: An Introduction and a Collection.* New York: Harcourt, Brace and World, Inc., 1964. Look past
this unfortunate title. This is an excellent text for academic and non-
academic (average or better) students in grades 10, 11, or 12. The 150-
page introduction to the language of poems is a lucid, coherent, simple,
but never oversimplified, discussion; the writer "knows what he is talking about." The 400-page chronologically arranged collection of well-
known British and American poems is a good, basic anthology.

DREW, ELIZABETH. *Poetry: A Modern Guide to Its Understanding and
Enjoyment.* New York: Dell Publishing Company, Inc., 1959. A
most unusual book: one hundred pages of clear, perceptive discussion
of "The Poetic Process" and another hundred of richly illustrated commentary on the enduring concerns of poetry. This book will suggest
to the teacher many usable poems, many "ways into poems," and many
organizations for the study of poems.

KENNER, HUGH. *The Art of Poetry.* New York: Holt, Rinehart and Winston, Inc., 1959. If there are some able twelfth-graders who have never
had a first course in reading poems, this book may be for them. It is,
in any case, a very useful book for teachers because of its illustrated
discussions, fine questions, and unusual organizations.

PETITT, DOROTHY (ed.). *Poetry in the Classroom.* Champaign, Ill.:
NCTE, 1966. Not a "teacher" in the sense the preceding books are,
but together with a volume of the same name that appeared earlier, a
useful collection of discussions of particular poems. Many of the discussions have been written as lessons.

IV. Useful General Anthologies

We suggest the following simply as books that bring together in one convenient volume *a collection of poems* from which a teacher could draw particular poems for first—and later—courses for many different kinds of classes.

COLEMAN, ALICE C., and JOHN R. THEOBALD (eds.). *Introducing Poetry: An Anthology.* New York: Holt, Rinehart and Winston, Inc., 1964.

DUNNING, STEPHEN, EDWARD LUEDERS, and HUGH SMITH (eds.). *Reflections on a Gift of Watermelon Pickle . . .* Glenview, Ill.: Scott, Foresman and Company, 1966. A fine collection of rarely anthologized modern poems.

FRANKENBERG, LLOYD (ed.). *Invitation to Poetry: A Round of Poems from John Skelton to Dylan Thomas.* New York: Doubleday and Co., Inc., 1956. More than two hundred poems from the sixteenth through the twentieth centuries arranged "to explore poetry in its own terms." Part One asks what poetry as defined by poets is; Part Two asks what poets think of poets; and Parts Three to Twelve deal with the various ways poetry intensifies experience.

PERRINE, LAURENCE. *Sound and Sense.* New York: Harcourt, Brace and Company, 1956.

UNTERMEYER, LOUIS (ed.). *A Concise Treasury of Great Poems: English and American.* New York: Pocket Books, Inc., 1953. The annotations in this good inexpensive collection of poems from Chaucer to Dylan Thomas concern the authors, more than they do the works; the comments are not really intrusive.

WARREN, ROBERT PENN, and ALBERT ERSKINE (eds.). *Six Centuries of Great Poetry.* New York: Dell Publishing Co., Inc., 1955. An excellent inexpensive anthology.

WILLIAMS, OSCAR (ed.). *F. T. Palgrave's The Golden Treasury,* Centennial Edition. New York: The New American Library of World Literature, Inc., 1961. This Mentor book offers works from representative poets from Wyatt to Thomas.

———. *Immortal Poems of the English Language.* New York: Washington Square Press, Inc., 1952. This is an unannotated inexpensive collection of poems from Chaucer to Dylan Thomas.

V. Some Special Anthologies

Some of these books might be class texts if the teacher were teaching a special course—modern poetry, for instance. But we think of these books as inexpensive, valuable additions to a personal or department library. Such fine collections make more live the possibility of getting the "right" poem for each class.

HENDERSON, HAROLD G. *An Introduction to Haiku.* New York: Double-day and Company, Inc., 1958.

PERRINE, LAURENCE, and JAMES M. REID (eds.). *100 American Poems of The Twentieth Century.* New York: Harcourt, Brace and World, Inc., 1966.

PRATT, WILLIAM (ed.). *The Imagist Poem.* New York: E. P. Dutton and Co., Inc., 1963.

WALSH, CHAD (ed.). *American and British Poetry Since the 1930's.* New York: Charles Scribner's Sons, 1964.

WILLIAMS, OSCAR (ed.). *The Pocket Book of Modern Verse.* New York: Washington Square Press, Inc., 1958.

VI. Useful Anthologies of Essays

Essay collections appropriate for high school students are hard to come by. These are some that would be useful in teaching the kinds of organizations we suggested.

ANDERSON, CARL L., and GEORGE W. WILLIAMS (compilers). *British and American Essays, 1905–1956.* New York: Henry Holt and Co., Inc., 1959. A fine paperback collection of twenty essays; no introductions, no questions.

DAVIS, ROBERT GORHAM (ed.). *Ten Masters of the Modern Essay.* New York: Harcourt, Brace and World, Inc., 1966. This book which would be most appropriate for an eleventh- or twelfth-grade class offers three essays by each of ten writers and one by each of sixteen others.

HOOPES, NED E., and RICHARD PECK (eds.). *Edge of Awareness.* New York: Dell Publishing Co., Inc., 1966. Twenty-five mature considerations of the human scene.

NYE, RUSSEL (ed.). *Modern Essays.* Chicago: Scott, Foresman and Co., 1963. This book of more than sixty essays is usable for a course in familiar essays and for the study of more formal essays, either for themselves or for expository composition. There is both a chronological and a thematic table of contents.

SHAKESPEARE, EDWARD O., PETER H. REINKE, and ELLIOT N. FENANDER (eds.). *Understanding the Essay.* New York: The Odyssey Press, Inc., 1967. Six essays are analyzed and discussed as artistic arrangements of language. The sixteen that follow are accompanied by questions to help students see how the uses of language just discussed function together in these essays. The final four essays have no annotations of any sort. The selections vary in subject matter, concern, literary style, and length, but they all have sufficient aesthetic quality to warrant students' spending class time on them.

SHAW, CHARLES B. (ed.). *American Essays.* New York: The New American Library of World Literature, Inc., 1955. Over thirty American essays, two-thirds of them modern, in an inexpensive paperback.

SMART, WILLIAM (ed.). *Eight Modern Essayists.* New York: St. Martin's Press, 1965. Four essays by each of the following: Max Beerbohm, E. M. Forster, Virginia Woolf, James Thurber, Edmund Wilson, E. B. White, George Orwell, and three by James Baldwin. This kind of book allows students to develop a fairly valid notion of the concerns and the style of each of these eight essayists, and this makes comparison of the essayists a more significant activity.

VII. Recordings

A reading of a poem is a performance. And we all have our own views on whose is the "best performance" of a certain work. Some of us like a theatrical reading, some a subtle one; others favor the poet's rendering, however halting. So, rather than recommend this recording of a poem or that one, we make two suggestions: (1) that English department libraries include the current catalogues of, for instance, Caedmon Records, NCTE Recordings, Poetry Records, and Spoken Arts—so that teachers can know what is available; and (2) that, to assist them in making wise choices, teachers use the descriptions and evaluations of recordings that appear both in the annual NCTE *Resources for the Teaching of English* and in the monthly column in the *English Journal,* John R. Searles and Nathan S. Blount (eds.), "Teaching Materials."

THE TEACHING OF PLAYS

A play is a work written to be enacted on a stage by actors before an audience. It is not written to be read. The play on the page consists of dialogue and stage direction. It is only a script for a performance. Actors have to intervene to give it life. An audience has to respond to complete its creation.

The end of a play determines the nature of it. Since it is destined for a stage, a play must be economical. Actors can stand, an audience can sit only so long. Everything in a play must count: episodes must be crucially revealing; dialogue must do many offices, and do them simultaneously; gestures must speak; setting, mean. A play must be clear. The crisis it represents must be somewhat overt, not too intricate. An audience has no helpful narrator to explain or imply; it has no book; it cannot "hold the place" and look back. An audience must "get" the play adequately the very first time it hears the words said and sees the gestures and movements made by live actors in a certain setting lighted in a certain way. A play must be forceful. For it must continually arouse and electrify, engage and re-engage the audience. It must constantly make the audience "care."

More than any other work of literature, it has the resources to do so. For in the performance of a play, real people live through a crisis before us. Our minds and emotions are reached and manipulated in a direct and poignant way. The experience of a play is forever immediate, forever vivid.

An Aim for Teaching Plays

If we say, then, that our aim for the teaching of plays is to help students learn to respond sensitively to the kind of work we have been describing, what does that aim mean?

Logically, it means that we shall be trying to help students learn to respond to plays as initiated theatregoers do. To learn that, students must, of course, see a series of plays. So, however logical and valid that aim may be, it is, for the majority of teachers, unrealistic because it is not feasible: the means to achieve it and to test achievement of it are simply not available. In most areas, students cannot see five or six well-performed plays, which is probably the minimum number of experiences they would need to achieve such an aim. And theatre performances *are* the means they must have.

There are no genuine substitutes. For, in all honesty, we know that seeing a series of school productions, or performing scenes in class—however well-rehearsed and executed, or "taking the parts," or listening to recordings of plays, are not alternatives to theatre performances. Useful as these devices may be for helping students to take a play off the page, none of them resembles a well-done live performance in a theatre. So none can supply what is needed to help students learn to be a sensitive audience. Anyone who analyzes this aim, sees what is in it, and takes the findings seriously readily realizes this.

Why would not a series of films suffice as means? Just consider the two media. A play requires, above all, a sensitive ear; a film, a sensitive eye. (That is why plays are the province of the teacher of language; films, of the teacher of visual arts.) Seeing a play consists primarily in responding to dramatic uses of language; seeing a film, in reacting to artificial visual images. For much that transpires in a film there need be no provision in its dialogue at all. Think of how the flashback takes care of exposition, of how the close-up *shows* feelings. Think of how a film can suggest internal states by clouding a face, by montaging, by flashing kaleidoscopically. Think of a film's narrative voice and of its "inner voices." Think of just these things and you see that film simply obviates many problems that the playwright must exploit dialogue to solve. A play is in fact so much the dialogue that, in the teaching of plays, films are useful only as extrinsic devices: to motivate students to read a play or to see one or to help some students realize what enactment is. Unless a teaching device focuses students primarily on the dramatic exploitation of language, it would not have much *intrinsic* value in the teaching of plays.

But, you say, there are films and films. A film of a theatre performance of a play is different. All the dialogue is there. The focus *is* on language. In these films, film is not functioning; it is simply being used to record authentically a performance of the play. Would not such films suffice as means to achieve the aim we suggested? In many ways, yes, but the fact remains that the experience of seeing a film of a theatre production is very different from the experience of seeing a theatre production. A film is an object already made; a play is an object always becoming, being made before us. A film has pictures of people and a superficial realism; a play, live actors and a frankly make-believe surface. Because of such distinctions as these, the experience of each medium and the demand each makes on the audience's sensations and imaginations are very different. So despite their tremendous value in the teaching of plays, films of theatre performances are not *genuine substitutes* for theatre performances.[1]

Practically speaking, then, if theatre performances are not readily available, we cannot really aim to help students become sensitive playgoers. But this does not mean that we must strike plays from the literature curriculum or that we must contravene their nature if we teach them. There is a feasible and valid way to teach students to respond sensitively to plays: we can help them learn to become an *armchair* audience by teaching them how to *read* plays *as plays*. This aim is quite practicable in the circumstances of the ordinary classroom. And it is entirely valid, for it does *not* permit the reader to *use* the play. He may not merely "get out the story" or explore a character or two. He must rather make the work *function as a play*. This means that with just the dialogue and stage directions in hand, the reader must simultaneously produce the play on the stage of his mind and respond to the performance. This is no small task.

The Play Reader as Producer and Audience

But when a play reader has the printed script, he has all he really needs. For when we say plays were written to be performed, we do not mean *simply* that the dialogue and the structure of a play are such that an attentive and perceptive theatre audience can experience the work from a single transient performance. More importantly, we mean that the language of a play is different from the language of a poem, a short story, or a novel. It implies performance: it implies in what tones and at what tempo the dialogue should be spoken; it implies the gestures and the movements that support the speaking. The words are written to be heard and seen. The language of a play is made actable by the dramatist, not by the director, not by the actors—and not by the reader. The dramatist is the writer of "words-acted, of scenes-set, and of players-performing." The language of a play directs the actors, the producer, the lighting specialist, the set designer, and the reader. The play on the page is a "script for a potential performance."[2] The whole theatre company, responding to the script as it directs and allows, produces a performance of the play; the sensitive theatre audience, responding appropriately to the performance, evokes the experience of the play. The initiated play reader needs only the script to be both company and audience.

Now, to illustrate, we shall suggest, slow-motion, a performance that a reader might infer from the script of the opening scene of Shakespeare's *Julius Caesar*. We are not of course saying that the performance suggested by our reading of the script is *the* production of the scene, but rather that ours is *a* valid one because the text implies it. First, the scene.

Act I. Scene i. [*Rome. A street*] *

Enter Flavius, Marullus, *and certain* Commoners
over the stage.

FLAV.   Hence! home, you idle creatures, get you home!
Is this a holiday? What, know you not,
Being mechanical, you ought not walk
Upon a labouring day without the sign
Of your profession? Speak, what trade art thou?   5

CARPENTER.   Why, sir, a carpenter.

MAR.   Where is thy leather apron and thy rule?
What does thou with thy best apparel on?
You, sir, what trade are you?

COBBLER.   Truly sir, in respect of a fine workman I am but, as you
would say, a cobbler.   11

MAR.   But what trade art thou? Answer me directly.

COB.   A trade, sir, that I hope I may use with a safe conscience,
which is indeed, sir, a mender of bad soles.   15

MAR.   What trade, thou knave? Thou naughty knave, what trade?

COB.   Nay, I beseech you, sir, be not out with me. Yet if you be out,
sir, I can mend you.

---

* The numbering of lines in this scene accords with that commonly used in citing
Shakespeare's plays in standard works such as Bartlett's *Concordance*. In prose
passages there is some slight irregularity in computation, but this does not indicate any omission in the text.

MAR.   What mean'st thou by that? Mend me, thou saucy fellow?   21

COB.   Why, sir, cobble you.

FLAV.   Thou art a cobbler, art thou?

COB.   Truly, sir, all that I live by is with the awl. I meddle with
no tradesman's matters nor women's matters, but with all. I am,
indeed, sir, a surgeon to old shoes. When they are in great danger,
I recover them. As proper men as ever trod upon neat's leather
have gone upon my handiwork.   30

FLAV.   But wherefore art not in thy shop to-day?
Why dost thou lead these men about the streets?

COB.   Truly, sir, to wear out their shoes, to get myself into more
work. But indeed, sir, we make holiday to see Caesar and to
rejoice in his triumph.   36

MAR.   Wherefore rejoice? What conquest brings he home?
What tributaries follow him to Rome
To grace in captive bonds his chariot wheels?
You blocks, you stones, you worse than senseless things!   40
O you hard hearts, you cruel men of Rome!
Knew you not Pompey? Many a time and oft
Have you climb'd up to walls and battlements,
To tow'rs and windows, yea, to chimney tops,
Your infants in your arms, and there have sat   45
The livelong day, with patient expectation,
To see great Pompey pass the streets of Rome.
And when you saw his chariot but appear,
Have you not made an universal shout,
That Tiber trembled underneath her banks   50
To hear the replication of your sounds
Made in her concave shores?
And do you now put on your best attire?
And do you now cull out a holiday?
And do you now strew flowers in his way   55
That comes in triumph over Pompey's blood?
Be gone!
Run to your houses, fall upon your knees,
Pray to the gods to intermit the plague
That needs must light on this ingratitude.   60

FLAV.   Go, go, good countrymen, and for this fault
Assemble all the poor men of your sort;
Draw them to Tiber banks, and weep your tears
Into the channel, till the lowest stream

Do kiss the most exalted shores of all.   65
> *Exeunt all the* Commoners.
See, whe'r their basest metal be not mov'd.
They vanish tongue-tied in their guiltiness.
Go you down that way towards the Capitol;
This way will I. Disrobe the images
If you do find them deck'd with ceremonies.   70

MAR.   May we do so?
You know it is the feast of Lupercal.

FLAV.   It is no matter. Let no images
Be hung with Caesar's trophies. I'll about
And drive away the vulgar from the streets.   75
So do you too, where you perceive them thick.
These growing feathers pluck'd from Caesar's wing
Will make him fly an ordinary pitch,
Who else would soar above the view of men
And keep us all in servile fearfulness.   *Exeunt.* 80

In this scene there are only two stage directions, yet the reader
knows in what tones the words are said and what movements the
speakers are probably making as they say the words and the listeners
as they hear them. Indeed the reader knows even what the commoners are wearing! He infers all this from the language.

In the opening speech, Flavius is shouting to the commoners.
Notice the staccato orders and the rhetorical question. He and
Marullus are herding the men across the stage, but, as Flavius shouts
his sarcastic, "Is this a holiday?," the crowd stops and turns. The
reader knows they do as soon as he hears how restrained and reasonable Flavius' next question is. It is what one says to faces, not backs
of heads. And in a moment (line 5), the reader also knows that,
although Flavius is no longer *addressing* the crowd, he is really still
talking to everyone. He and Marullus, in turn, try to scare the
crowd by making "objects" of individuals in it. The questions are
really threats—masked in a "routine investigation." Now (line 10),
the stage picture changes. Three characters claim attention—the two
tribunes and the cobbler, who is the leader of the crowd. They are
grouped downstage; there is perhaps a small "fringe"—enjoying the
"show." Most of the crowd are now probably deployed in casual
attitudes upstage—talking, indulging in horseplay, and such.

The reader notices the cobbler's "stance," lines 11–36. His teasing
circumlocutions are calculated to irritate and ridicule the tribunes,
but without giving them grounds for reprisal. His tone is the calm,
ingratiating one of sly innocence. The exchange is marked by the
increased annoyance of the outraged tribune—notice the questions,

the shouted epithets—and by the sustained rationality and patient explanation of the cobbler—notice the parentheticals ("Truly sir"), the fine distinctions, the tolerant, measured, full-sentence responses. The gestures and movements are in the words: it is a confrontation, Flavius standing by, Marullus raging, the cobbler smiling pleasantly, in baffled surprise, head denying, "Nay," hand protesting—while his tone winks at the audience. The calculated confusion that the cobbler pays out with such precision works: it drives off Marullus (line 22). The shrewder Flavius takes over the questioning, and his calm directness in the face of the cobbler's witticisms elicits "the truth." In lines 35–36, the cobbler's tone becomes serious, his posture erect. He changes to "we." He is the spokesman for the group now. The stage picture is slowly changing. The others are gathering around. The crowd forms a single group again; as a whole they stand before the tribunes.

If the reader had any question about the stage picture at this point, the character of Marullus' long speech (lines 36–60) would give him the answer. The speech is an oration, the first of the play. And the crowd? It is the attentive assembly at an oration, looking at the speaker standing, perhaps on steps, somewhat above them. Marullus delivers his opening remarks (lines 37–41) with all the voice modulation and gestures proper to the various modes of appeal he is using: the three ever-longer rhetorical questions, then the five epithets that begin with the prolonged "you" and the explosive "blocks" and decrease in loudness, pitch, and insult as they increase in intensity. The crowd is arrested. Marullus' bold accusatory gestures (line 40) give way to his measured head-shaking regret (line 41). Then he moves—physically leans forward to ask *each one* to soul search. He speaks in a quiet, controlled chant. The sound patterns and the accents of the words demand this "voice." With his question—"Knew you not Pompey?"—on the air, Marullus attempts to reach the crowd. Bending toward them confidentially, he pleasantly recalls in an intimate tone their past behavior and culminates affectively by remembering a graphic tender image (lines 45–46). The crowd is silent, touched. The reader knows this because Marullus ends his *appeal* at line 47. He has the crowd "in position." Now, he will really evoke their guilt. He changes pitch and bursts into "large" language spoken in a slow, profound organ roll. Notice the sound and the rhythm. Picture the pose of the orator as he asks this grand rhetorical question. There is a long pause after "shores" (line 52). Marullus' arms come down. He straightens, he withdraws, while the aural and emotional reverberations do their work. Then, he uses the parallel questions to force the crowd to realize. And then the great imperative—"Be gone!"—echoing the initial command of Flavius but now with religious overtone. It hangs on the air; the crowd is transfixed. Marullus finishes; but they do not move.

It is Flavius' speech (line 61) that tells the reader the state the
the group is in, and it is his tone of quiet urging that implies why
the crowd is transfixed. It is the tone one uses to stonied spectators
at the scene of a tragedy they have caused. Flavius shepherds the
crowd out, advising them how to atone. They straggle away silently.

Flavius' comment (line 66) is made as he looks after them. It is
made to Marullus and to himself, a half-musing tone. Then he turns
to Marullus and gives the orders, with physical directions: "Go you
down that way . . .;/This way will I." He brusquely dismisses
Marullus' doubt and gives final orders. Flavius' last four lines are not
said facing Marullus, for they are addressed to himself, to Marullus,
and to the audience. They are the justification for the orders he has
given. The orders are particular and seemingly paltry underground
tricks; but the rationale expressed in the falcon metaphor gives significance to the tribunes' action; they, and all like them, are men
against tyranny. The tribunes leave on opposite sides—a suggestive
exit.

Through these comments on the dialogue of this first scene of
Julius Caesar, we have been illustrating how the script of a play
implies a performance: how it suggests to the director, the actors,
and the reader this pitch, that loudness, this rhythm, that pause, this
tone, that attitude; how it proposes gestures that extend the words,
postures that complement them, and how it implies the continually
changing groupings on the stage that fix and emphasize the attitudes
of the characters toward one another.

We have been concentrating on the role of play reader as producer. But producing a valid performance from the text of a play is
just one part of the play reader's task. He must concomitantly be
seeing the play he is producing on the stage in his head. He must be
responding to it as a sensitive audience would. As he watches the
first scene of *Julius Caesar,* for instance, he will be gathering information: finding out what day it is, what the customs are in feasts
and in trades, what the political past has been, what great event the
immediate future holds.

Furthermore, he will be evoking, as an audience does, a sequence
of four or five impressions. His initial impression arises from hearing
and seeing (lines 1–10) the tribunes and the crowd, the party leaders
and the party; he hears the voice of authority trying to break up a
mob, and he observes its effect. No one leaves. The voice evokes
ridicule. The reader's expectations are thwarted, but his interest is
whetted. At line 10 the initial impression gives way to a second
impression (lines 11–36). Through the dialogue between the cobbler and the tribunes the reader comes to understand the three
characters, but, more importantly, he begins to feel the tensions in

the political situation in Rome. He hears the cobbler veil his defiance in humor at the tribunes' expense; he hears Marullus rage against the cobbler's finesses, and Flavius calmly, flatly "feel the cobbler out." The reader sees that it is the cobbler—the mob—who decides there has been fun enough (line 35), and who baldly states the true reason for the gathering. His directness touches off Marullus' oration—and, for the reader, a third impression forms. So, throughout the scene, as impression follows impression, the reader's attitudes take shape and shift, the reader's sympathies modify. And since, as audience, he is a detached observer, the reader sees the situation totally and objectively. Like the interested spectator at a real-life conversation, the play reader as audience hears and sees each character in terms of all the others and each in terms of his whole performance, so he perceives more than the characters themselves do.

Consequently, he does not respond, for instance, to the people's behavior as the tribunes do. He perceives that the crowd may be pro-Caesar, or may be pro-holiday and pro-parade. He sees that since, like children, they react to a barrage of emotion, they are to be feared for their fickleness, their lack of firm conviction. The tribunes do not see this, so they think the crowd "mov'd" in a genuine sense—even though, ironically, they themselves have turned the mob in moments, not by logical argument, but by sentimental and rousing rhetoric. Similarly, the reader sees, as the crowd does not, that the tribunes are fearful conspirators with public and private faces and ambiguous motivations. And, over-all, the reader perceives, as the participants do not, that this is no clear-cut, two-sided conflict in Rome; it is a complex, fluid situation. At the end of the scene, the reader wants to know what manner of man Caesar *really* is and, given the people and the tribunes as he sees them, what will evolve. At the end of Scene i, he, like the people of Rome, awaits Caesar's coming.

The Limitations and the Demands of Play Reading

Through our discussion of the first scene of *Julius Caesar*, we have been showing that it is possible to read a play *as a play* and how this may be done.[3] In the process we have also been revealing the limitations of play reading. We have, for instance, been showing how impossible it is for any reading experience to approximate a theatre experience. The play reader, giving his best efforts, cannot have more than a simulated performance. He cannot really realize the dramatic potentiality of words shaped for a stage. The reader probably can perceive the structuring designs of a play more fully than an audience can, and so he can have an artistic whole of more density. But he cannot raise, in all its seeming reality, the microcosm of the play. He cannot fully feel its emotional rhythm—only the conditions of the theatre can truly evoke that. So a well-executed performance on the mental stage will always fall short of a well-executed theatre performance.

All this is obvious. But to recall it now helps us to be clear about what our aim—*reading* plays as plays—consists of and what it does not, about what using this skill can achieve and what it cannot. If we are aware of the nature and the end of the skill we are aiming to help students develop, we shall not, in our teaching, "settle for less" than what the skill properly exercised can accomplish, and we shall not erroneously think that students are achieving what no exercise of the skill, however competent, can achieve.

Our discussion of the performance of Scene i of *Julius Caesar* has revealed more than the process and the limitations of play reading. It has shown also the demands that play reading makes on the reader. We have seen rather precisely what the skill requires, what a student must learn to do if he is to create a performance and respond to it as a work of dramatic art.

Many texts on reading plays seem to suggest that all the reader needs is aural and visual imagination. They seem to assume that every play offers the reader explicit directions for every move, every speech. But what playwright, however tightly he holds the reins, specifies, at all times, all actions and all tones for all characters? The counsel most anthologies give, "Use your imagination," implies that *all* playwrights do! Few anthologies mention that before play readers begin imagining, *they must know precisely what the text is asking them to imagine.* If the reader has not read the text accurately and sensitively, then his aural and visual imaginings, however vivid, simply will not be very relevant. The bases for his imaginings are the clues in the dialogue. He must be able to recognize what tone, gesture, movement, rhythm, stage picture the clues are suggesting he should imagine. Then, he must be able to imagine it. Two tasks to perform; two skills needed. Even though for the experienced reader the two responses probably occur almost simultaneously, it is good for those who teach plays to recognize that a play reader's hearing, seeing, and feeling a performance depend, first of all, on how acute his responses to the clues in the dialogue are; *then*, on how "good" his mind's ear and his mind's eye are.

In order to know *what to imagine aurally* in any one remark—what tone, what pace, what pauses—the reader has to notice the social role of the speaker and of the auditor, and the diction, syntax, punctuation, and figures the speaker uses; these are the reader's clues. These are what signal him to hear the remark said "slowly and condescendingly" or "in soft reproach" or in some other tone. Now, *in the reading of dramatic dialogue,* as our discussion of *Julius*

Caesar, Scene i, reminded us, the reader is confronted with a series of such dramatic situations—in each situation someone of a certain position and social stature is saying a certain idea or idea-feeling in a certain diction, syntax, and rhythm to someone of the same, similar, or different social position. The reader has to be able to recognize all the relevant clues *in each instance* if he is to have a chance of hearing the remark correctly. We are "spelling out" the play reader's act of "hearing" dialogue not only to suggest how much is "in it," how very complicated this aspect of the play reader's job is, and at what *various points* it could "break down," but also to make clear what a well-developed sense of tone clues, tones, and tone changes the play reader consequently must have. The able reading of plays requires the most discriminating sense of tone in the most complicated tonal situations.

In order to know *what to imagine visually* at any one moment— what gestures, movements, and positions he should be seeing, the reader has to notice the speaker's tone, the attitudes being expressed, and the "feel" of the whole group. These are his clues to appropriate visual images. For, just as in life, gestures support and extend dialogue. From his experiences in life, the reader knows what gestures, movements, and positions usually accompany certain tones, attitudes, and social situations. That is why as soon as students grasp the tones of "men of Rome," of "Get you gone," of "Go, go, good countrymen," they think of very different gestures in each case. That is why as soon as they recognize that the cobbler is "razzing" an officer, they know some of the cobbler's confreres will be standing around as "audience," some drifting away to their own "sports." That is what a mob usually does at such times.

Not all instances of what the play reader must imagine visually are as simple as these. Often the reader must bring to his mental picture of the gesture his whole understanding of the character and of the intention of the play.[4] When, for instance, Brutus walks alone from the stage after his oration, it is no ordinary exit; it is a great dramatic metaphor. Everything that has gone before is telling the reader *what* he should visualize. The able reading of plays requires a discriminating sense of what the appropriate gestures, positions, and movements would be in the most complicated visual situations.

And of course, once the reader knows *what* to imagine aurally and visually, he must then hear the precise tone and see the exact gesture and movement the particular context requires.

So far, our discussion of the demands that play reading makes on the reader has been confined to what the reader must do *to create a performance*. We have been pointing out the complexity of his making the kind of aural and visual responses to dialogue that he must if he is to evoke from print one heard-seen-felt moment after another.

Now, let us see what the reader must do *to respond to the performance* he is creating so that he has, as audience, the experience of
the play.

Our comments on the reader's building impression upon impression in Scene i of *Julius Caesar* have already hinted at what the role
of play reader as perceiver demands. They have suggested that he
must, without the help of a narrator or of guiding comment, piece
together into a dramatic whole all the heard-seen-felt events he is
evoking. To do that, what specifically must the playreader notice
and how must he notice it?

He must notice the incidents of the main action and see *why* they
are selected, arranged, and treated as they are. Why, for instance,
are certain parts of the story rendered as action? others as exposition?
And what is gained by having the incidents unified as "cause-
consequence" (as in Arthur Miller's *The Crucible* or Shakespeare's
Macbeth), rather than, say, as "thesis-proofs" (as in Miller's *After
the Fall* or Ben Jonson's *The Alchemist*), or as "state of affairs-typical
aspects of it" (as in Thornton Wilder's *Our Town* or Chekov's *The
Sea Gull*)?[5] The play reader must see why certain incidents are
prolonged, others abbreviated; why some are played off-stage; why
the "consequences," "proofs," and "typical aspects" are ordered as
they are; why act divisions come where they do.

And while he is responding to the effect of "these incidents in this
order," the play reader must be perceiving how these incidents affect
and are affected by character. How, for instance, do they define
character? How, in turn, do these characters, by their "encounters"
and their choices, shape the action *this* way rather than *that?* To
perceive the relation of character and incident, the play reader must
see, from sensitively piecing together a host of heard-seen-felt
moments, what kind of person each main character is. What do his
acts, his reactions, his silences, his inaction reveal? Is this impression modified by the estimates of others? How is it affected by the
character's external appearance—even his costume? by his style of
language? Why is a certain character defined so simply (or so
complexly)? How does he function in successive incidents? (What
role has he in the progress of the action?) What does he "discover"?
Why does he "discover" it in this way? How does he change? What
in the play accounts for his changing? What makes the change
plausible, consistent? (The reader is, of course, gathering all this
information about the characters from that rejoinder or this pose,
from a character's absence from the stage picture or from his position in it.)

Furthermore, if the play reader is to have the experience of the
play, he must perceive the function of seemingly non-essential features: subplots, parallels, foils, parodies, transitional scenes. He

must see, for instance, that transitional incidents which are facilitating the continuity of the play—getting characters on and off stage, linking incidents, both main and subsidiary—are also functioning to define character, reveal theme, establish mood, and suggest the norm in terms of which we should judge the main incidents.

Finally, the play reader must notice recurrent elements (a repeated phrase, gesture, pose; a reappearing object) and continuing elements (perhaps the set itself, perhaps a single object, perhaps a metaphor) and sequences of related elements (perhaps the key hours of a day, key moments of life, a series of symbolic costumes or settings, a pattern of verbal images), and he must perceive how all such elements *rendered and placed as they are* count in the play. He must recognize what the function of the element is in *each* context in which it appears, what the effect is of its changing (or remaining the same), how it takes on significance during the play, what roughly its significance is, and what difference it would make to the experience of the play if this design were omitted.

We have "spelled out" the challenging and complex role of the play reader as perceiver to show the kinds of responses it entails: to suggest the many features that in one play or another the reader must notice, realize the function of, and respond to sensitively if he is to have the experience the play intends. Our discussion suggests that *just* piecing together either the events of the main plot or the incidents in which the main character functions does not constitute a sensitive response to a play. The play reader begins to perceive a play when he recognizes such things as why the scenes are patterned as they are, how parallel incidents affect one another, how entrances and exits function, why a symbolic gesture recurs with always modified meaning—when, in other words, he starts to discover how various features in the play work *to make his experience of the main plot one kind rather than another.* The able reading of plays requires a most sensitive perception of how the many seemingly separate heard-seen-felt moments of a play function together as a single *dramatic* unit.

Reading plays as plays demands, then, an ability to create a performance—with all our earlier analysis showed that involved—and an ability to react sensitively to the performance as a work of dramatic art. To put it simply, reading plays requires precise and imaginative responses to dramatic dialogue and to dramatic structure. So, when we say that our aim for the first course is to help students learn to read plays, we mean it is to help them learn to make the kinds of responses to dialogue and structure that we have been suggesting play reading demands. Following is an outline of *one kind* of first course that we think will help students achieve this aim.

A First Course in Reading Plays

How we begin any course in a particular class depends, they say, upon "what students bring." To the reading of plays, a class often brings the unconscious conviction that a play is just a novel without the long paragraphs of description. Some students come with the notion that the study of plays consists of just a continual "bumble-and-stumble" reading aloud—day after day. Others think that the "unit on plays" is their yearly chance to build models, dress dolls, and get out sensational newspapers: "Caesar Killed—Conspirators Flee." Still others think that the study of plays is the signal for hoots and horseplay. If students bring some or all of these convictions, memories, or anticipations, any study of plays *as plays* will soon dispel them.

It is what students might not bring that concerns us. If they come to the study of plays without an adequate sense of tone, we would have to help them develop one *before* they began to read plays at all. For, unless students sense tone, their reading of dialogue consists merely of "getting out what it says." And, however much we would not want to inaugurate or reinforce that kind of abstracting, it is what we are likely to "fall to," if we begin a course in reading plays with students obtuse to tone.

Why not start to sensitize students to tone as they begin the study of dialogue? Because it is not feasible. Only think of the fine sense of tone that play reading demands; then, recall what this fine sense involves—and you can see how slow, tedious, and enormously boring it would be for students and teacher alike to use even the shortest play as an initial exercise in sensing tone.

For students who come innocent of tone, we would precede the first course in reading plays with one or more sorts of preparatory exercises. We might begin either with a close study of several dramatic monologues; say, Robert Browning's "My Last Duchess," "The Bishop Orders His Tomb," "Soliloquy in a Spanish Cloister"; or with a critical reading of some of Robert Frost's dialogues—"The Death of the Hired Man," "Home Burial," or "A Hundred Collars," for instance. From either beginning we would proceed to a careful reading of a "play of voices" like Lucille Fletcher's *Sorry, Wrong Number* (seventeen pages) or Dorothy Parker's *Here We Are* (ten pages).[6] Since there is little gesture or staging to attend to in these plays, students may concentrate on the aural: on sensing tones, the interplay of tones, pace, and pause. In *Sorry, Wrong Number* the tones are relatively blatant and there are some directions; in *Here We Are*, the tones are clearly suggested, but there are no annotations. Reading such a pair of plays in that order would put students gradually and gently on their own.

Preparation like this, if accompanied by written critical exercises, would probably take five to seven class periods. It is a "crash program"; and no emergency measure can produce the same effect as that achieved by the "long foreground" and the concentration on tone we suggested in the first course in reading poems. But such "stop-gap" preparation will *initiate* students.

Furthermore, even students already sensitive to tone—if they are duller, less able readers—will find the study of simple radio plays a useful entrée to a first course in reading plays. For the study of radio plays would give these students a natural opportunity to learn to hear dramatic dialogue sensitively and to visualize a few accompanying gestures before they are confronted with the task of producing even the simplest stage play. And, if the teacher wished, he could, in the study of these preliminary plays, first emphasize only the aural; then, voice and gesture; then, voice, gesture, and movement; and finally, voice, gesture, movement, and stage picture. Dull students tend to profit markedly from such a cumulative step-by-step approach to any new kind of work.

Unfortunately, the lack of a developed sense of tone is not the only deficiency readers bring. Some students have never seen a play. We mentioned innocence of tone first only because it is the crucial deficiency. Without a sensitive response to tone, it is *impossible* for students to make dialogue work. But without the experience of at least one theatre performance of a play, it is difficult for them to visualize some features of performance. So, for students innocent of theatre, we would try to provide some sort of experience that they could use as a touchstone for imagining what this action, or this whole "picture" would look like *on a stage*—at once live and artificial, natural and arranged.

The ideal experience for such a class would be to see a well-performed play in a theatre just at the opening of this course. If we prepared the class to notice carefully certain aspects of performance and if we discussed those aspects thoroughly in a "post-mortem," the students would have the point of reference they need. But in most school situations, this perfect opening would not be practicable. So as a second-best preparation, we would substitute the seeing of a film of a theatre performance. The effect of a live production before a massed audience would, of course, be lost. But such a film would serve our purpose. And we would make the same careful preparation for this experience, and we would conduct the same quality "follow-up" as we would for the live theatre experience. As a conclusion, we would have a second showing—with a film we could.

So much for the necessary preparation for the first course. Now to the course itself. In most classes it would consist of a careful study of three or four short plays and of one full-length modern drama. During the study of the first short play (or perhaps the first two), all classes would concentrate on learning to make dialogue "work," learning to produce a precise performance and respond to it. We would try to help students discover for themselves how dialogue is said, how it suggests production so that the reader can see and feel the play as well as hear it, and how it gives information, furthers the plot, reveals character—all by the natural, unobtrusive means of common conversation. But even as early as the second play we would begin to ask students *occasionally* to "raise their eyes" to see how this or that scene, or object, or character had worked in the play "so far." As students became more skilled in their responses to dialogue, we would gradually ask them to give more and more attention to the function of scenes and to the role of other designs that structure the play. So, by the time classes were working on their third and fourth short plays, all would be giving *at least* equal emphasis to dialogue and to structure; abler classes would be virtually concentrating on structure. Before students began their study of a long play, then, most would already be able to decide, for instance, how certain scenes—rendered as they are and placed where they are—contribute to a play and how parallel characters and partially similar scenes function. Certain classes would be able to discuss as well the role of a series of images, a repeated word, a central metaphor, or an object that becomes symbolic.

There would, then, be a shift of main aim—from dialogue to structure—mid-course, but it would be prepared for gradually, take place almost imperceptibly, and really be only a change *in emphasis*. For, as students began, in the study of the long play, to give their major attention to structure, we would continue to ask about the performance of particular scenes and the function of particular parts of the dialogue. The truth is, of course, that continuing our discussion of dramatic dialogue is not really a matter of choice. We must do so. How can a reader discuss the function of a solitary character in the play, for instance, if he has not heard and seen and felt quite precisely, through a sensitive response to dialogue, how the character *performed* in *that* and *that* and *that* scene?

The kind of first course we have just outlined would require roughly twenty-five class periods. With oral reading, discussion, and collateral writing, the study of each short play would take approximately three periods; the long play, ten to twelve. But all the exceptions and qualifications we cited in discussing the duration of the first course in reading poems apply here also. Initial estimates of time often have to be revised upward. If, for any reason, it seemed desirable to teach the course in two parts, it could be divided very conveniently exactly at midpoint. By that time students will have finished their study of short plays and, more importantly, will have developed to some extent, both of the two crucial skills in play reading: the ability to make dramatic dialogue "work" and the ability to perceive dramatic structure.

The Short Plays

We would begin this first course with the study of short plays because they are especially appropriate vehicles for helping beginners learn to read plays. As "miniatures," they offer readers a dramatic field that is at once fully rendered and conveniently confined. Students can have genuine, representative practice, "writ small." They can also study several short plays carefully—with rereadings—in the same time that they would be reading one full-length play. And their reading of several plays will allow them the variety of experiences with dialogue and structure that they need to develop flexible responses to both. Finally, the short play is drama pared, refined, compressed. The dialogue is absolutely economical; the devices, quite requisite; the construction, taut; the unity, obvious. Readers have a chance to see clearly *what* elements count in a play, *how* each counts, and what kinds of designs unify the work. The study of several brief, well-constructed plays seems to be an ideal way for students to develop the sensitivities to dialogue and structure needed for the easy, responsive reading of the long plays to come.

Choosing Appropriate Plays

What *kinds* of short plays would help students begin to achieve the aims of this first course? Plays that offer readers a diversity of dramatic experiences. A class' reading should include tragedy, comedy, perhaps melodrama and satire; at least one of the plays should be, to some extent, non-representational. A class' reading should include the work of several different playwrights and a variety of dramatic treatments. Why should beginning play readers have such diversity? Not so that they will know "all the kinds" and their "main characteristics." Rather, so that they will become flexible respondents, able to read sensitively whatever play is put before them. To become such readers, they must learn to sense *from a play itself* what its intent is, what kind of performance they should produce, what stance they should take before it, in what direction they should turn their thoughts, feelings, and attitudes. Only a diversity of readings can provide the practice necessary to develop such catholic responses.

Not just any varied group of short plays will do. The plays chosen for any class must be appropriate to the reading ability of the students and to their concerns. The oft-repeated requirements! But, with a difference, since the kind of work we are now talking about is, as we have pointed out, different from other works of literature. What does "appropriate to the reading ability of the students" mean, when the work we are talking about is a play? It means appropriate to their ability to look at print and produce a play on a mental stage. Before we begin this first course, we cannot know *exactly* what a certain class' ability to do this is, but we *do* know that, for all beginners, reading plays *as plays* is a complex, demanding task. And we also know that the more students have to concentrate on the page, the more they lose sight of the stage! Consequently, for each quality of reader—the less able, the average, and the able—we would choose plays the diction of which would be on the *literal* level very familiar, plays as free *as possible* from new words or allusions, from uncustomary terms and baffling dialects,[7] plays *some* basic structure of which could be easily perceived by readers of the particular ability. *All* qualities of readers—able, average, and less able—should begin with plays that are not only *available enough* to preclude that halting, "fits and starts" struggle with the text that destroys any sense of a play as a performance, but also *rich enough* so that the students will not find the plays so transparent, so one-dimensional that *study* of them seems absurd.

The plays chosen for the first course must, then, be both dramatically various and appropriate to students' reading ability. Furthermore, they must be relevant to students' concerns. That means, as usual, that the central problem, decision, idea, or emotion of the work must be, in some degree, related to the basic human interests of the readers. But when the work being chosen is a play, a work that readers must hear and see and feel, then the world that the work *represents* must *also* be relevant to them. By "the world," we mean the cultural milieu of the characters. If we really expect beginning readers to look at pages of dialogue—no narrator, no commentary, no "once upon a time"—and re-create the script so that they *hear* and *see* and *feel* the play, then we must give them works that represent worlds that are *to some extent* known to them, worlds they have had *some sort* of contact with.

As with concerns, some worlds are very familiar to most high school students;[8] others are well-known to one class, known to another, and totally foreign to a third. And this is true not only of the more or less unusual worlds of O'Neill, Synge, and Yeats, say, but also of the ordinary worlds of Inge's *Glory in the Flower* and of Rattigan's *The Browning Version*. As with concerns, a few worlds are strange to almost all high school students. It is a rare class that would not find quite foreign the worlds represented in such plays as Noel Coward's *Hands Across the Sea*, Tennessee Williams' *27 Wagons Full of Cotton*, Booth Tarkington's *The Trysting Place*, and Anton Chekov's *The Boor* and *A Marriage Proposal*. Recreating an unfamiliar world *from the materials a play affords* is such an undue and unnecessary burden on beginning readers that no matter how relevant the concern of such a play might be, the reading of it should be *postponed* until students have become skilled producers. For they will then be able to use selectively and imaginatively the kinds of supporting information that will make the unfamiliar world understandable to them.[9]

So much for the criteria for choosing short plays. Now let us look briefly at three lists of plays, one for less able readers, one for average readers, and the last for competent readers. Each list includes plays that are widely diverse in the kinds of dramatic experiences they offer, in the kinds of concerns they render, and in the kinds of worlds they represent. From each list a teacher could select several different groups of readings, each of which would be exactly right in concern and world for some particular class and all of which could equally well help students achieve the aims of the first course.[10]

First, here is a list of twelve short plays[11] that could be studied fruitfully by *less able* students and that might also be appropriate first readings for some average classes:

Lewis Beach's *The Clod* (ten pages), Brainerd Duffield's adaptation of Shirley Jackson's *The Lottery* (seventeen pages), Lord Dunsany's *A Night at an Inn* (nine pages), Susan Glaspell's *Trifles* (seventeen pages), Kenneth Goodman's *Dust of the Road* (thirteen pages), Holworthy Hall and Richard Middlemass' *The Valiant* (twenty-seven pages), Carroll Howe's *The Long Fall* (sixteen pages), William Inge's *Glory in the Flower* (twenty-two pages), William Kozlenko's *Jacob Comes Home* (nine pages), Eugene O'Neill's *In the Zone* (eighteen pages), Louis Parker's dramatization of W. W. Jacobs' *The Monkey's Paw* (nine pages), Ramon Sender's *The Secret* (sixteen pages).

Except for *In the Zone* which uses the dialects of the crew, the diction of these plays poses only the routine problems. These plays *are* feasible for less able students. They can read them, and they want to. For every one of the plays is *clearly* about a deeply serious significant moment, and every one of these moments is rendered powerfully. Each play poses its question immediately and keeps the reader continually anxious for the solution. This is true even of Inge's play. It is the "suspense" (as students call it) of these plays that holds the reader, but the plays are rich enough to take him well beyond "how it comes out." As each play moves to its resolution, the reader has to see the moral dilemma that the event has touched off, the character revelation it has occasioned, the fundamental irony it has uncovered.

Some of the plays—for instance, *The Valiant* and *In the Zone*—are rather patent in their treatments, somewhat contrived, perhaps sentimental. But such plays as these are useful for classes that need an obvious beginning. All of the plays have literary value; some are excellent. If O'Neill's dialogue seems too explicit and excessive, Kozlenko's is marvelously economical and tense. If Howe's irony is forced, Beach's emerges most naturally. If foreshadowing in *The Lottery* is too bald, it is subtle enough in *Glory in the Flower*. This group of plays offers the less able both a place to begin and a place to move on to.

Now, here are thirteen short plays that *average* students could study profitably and that might also be appropriate as first readings for some able classes:

Stephen Vincent Benet's *The Devil and Daniel Webster* (twenty-eight pages), Lord Dunsany's *The Jest of Habalaba* (eight pages), George Kelly's *Finders Keepers* (thirty-four pages), or his *The Flattering Word* (thirty-seven pages), Maurice Maeterlinck's *The Intruder* (sixteen pages), Arthur Miller's *A Memory of Two Mondays* (fifty-three pages), A. A. Milne's *The Ugly Duckling* (twenty-two pages), Josefina Niggli's *The Ring of General Macias* (twenty-one pages), Stanley Richards' *Through a Glass, Darkly* (twenty-seven pages), Joseph Shore and Richard Lincoln's *The Soldier Who Became a Great Dane* (thirteen pages), John Millington Synge's *In the Shadow of the Glen* (fifteen pages), and his *Riders to the Sea* (eight pages). If Sir James Barrie's *The Twelve-Pound Look* (fifteen pages) could somehow be stripped of its intrusive "stage directions," it would be a fine choice for an average class of girls.

What distinguishes these plays from those for the less able students? We still see in this list some of those powerful dramas with the tension-creating questions. The reader of *The Ring of General Macias*, for instance, is anxiously drawn along by his desire to find out what the general's wife will do. The reader of *Through a Glass, Darkly* wants to know what will become of the son and the father. The reader of *In the Shadow of the Glen* wants to see what the "dead" husband plans. But the real questions of these plays are, respectively, questions of honor, irrational prejudice, and life versus living. Furthermore, although the problem of Richards' play is handled quite as blatantly as any in the plays of the first list, it takes an attentive reader to know what is really transpiring in Miss Niggli's play and a perceptive one to realize—all along—the alignments in Synge's *In the Shadow of the Glen* and to sense the inevitability of the outcome. So, despite the seeming similarity of these three plays to those in the first group, these demand more of the reader. And it is through carefully re-creating plays like these so that they perceive the drama "beneath" and "within" that average students come to enjoy more than the surface, more than the suspense of a play and begin gradually to be able to respond well to plays with less spectacular dramatic plots.

Among this second group of plays, there are two such subtle dramas—Arthur Miller's *A Memory of Two Mondays* and Synge's *Riders to the Sea*. These are plays in which, as some readers might put it, "nothing happens." Only somewhat sensitive readers will realize that *that* is indeed part of the "point" of these plays. To all but one of Miller's characters, nothing does happen: it is just the petty repetition of such lives, the cheap thrill, the permanent entrapment, and the momentary escape that Miller is showing. And to Synge's Maurya, nothing further can happen—but recognition and resignation, and these are great but quiet happenings. Such plays as these two require readers who can hear and see and feel in these overtly undramatic experiences the terrible inner dramas of disappointment, frustration, and despair.

Among this second group of plays there are also two comedies of manners: *The Flattering Word* and *The Twelve-Pound Look*. Comedies require good readers, readers who are very sensitive to the ways men hide—and reveal—their human foibles in words and gestures. The reader of *The Flattering Word* must, for instance, be able to recognize that, in his very first speeches, Mr. Rigley—the stuffy clergyman categorically opposed to the theatre—is himself in the process of making one of the most dramatic of exits. Obviously, Mr. Rigley loves being "on stage." As soon as the reader perceives that, he is set up for Rigley's revelatory response to the ruse that follows. Only an average or better reader is alert enough to the crucial clues to have the right anticipations. So only such readers will enjoy this harmless, long-deserved ridicule of this smug, self-righteous "poor dear." To less able readers, plays like these two seem baffling or ridiculous—so overdrawn, far-fetched, impossible. Such comedies, therefore, rightly belong on this second list, not on the first.

Even the less representational plays in this second group place a greater demand on the reader. Only compare the subtlety of *The Intruder* with the blatancy of *Dust of the Road;* compare the irony of *The Ugly Duckling* with that of *The Monkey's Paw*.

To conclude, here are ten short plays that seem especially appropriate for classes who come to the first course as potentially *able* play readers and for classes who become able during their reading of short plays (some average classes always do):

Sir James Barrie's *Shall We Join the Ladies?* (twenty-three pages), Jean Giraudoux' *The Apollo of Bellac* (thirty pages), Lady Gregory's

Spreading the News (nineteen pages), Tad Mosel's *Impromptu* (sixteen pages), Eugene O'Neill's *The Moon of the Caribbees* (twenty pages), Terence Rattigan's *The Browning Version* (fifty pages), William Saroyan's *The Man With the Heart in the Highlands* (eleven pages), Jonathan Tree's *The Fisherman* (fifteen pages), Percival Wilde's *Pawns* (fifteen pages), and William Butler Yeats' *Cathleen ni Houlihan* (eleven pages).

Such plays as these require precise, imaginative readers, readers who—with a bit of help—can pick up crucial clues to meaning from hearing tones and silences in their minds' ears and from seeing glances, sudden starts, and stunned expressions in their minds' eyes. These plays need readers who are able to grasp implied connections, feel the tension in opposed feelings, respond complexly to complex symbols—even hold, alive and tingling, the many threads of a complicated "vaudeville" satire. These plays need readers who—with a bit of help—can infer attitudes from a stance or from the juxtaposition of the faithful and the faithless, readers who do not mistake innocence for stupidity, bluff for presence, or sensitivity for weakness. To realize the greater demands these plays make on readers, only compare O'Neill's rendering of Smithy's feelings in *In the Zone* with his rendering of them in *The Moon of the Caribbees;* only compare the representation of victimized innocence in Beach's *The Clod* with that in Wilde's *Pawns;* only compare the handling of the effect of the flattering word in Kelly's play with that in Giraudoux'.

Finally, there are two short plays that we think would be appropriate readings for students in all three ability groups: William Saroyan's *Hello Out There* (thirteen pages) and Lady Gregory's *The Rising of the Moon* (eight pages). The diction of both plays is relatively simple; the surface story of both, most engaging: readers want to know if the lynchers come; they want to know if the rebel is caught. But in the process of seeing how either play "comes out," readers will have, to varying degrees depending upon their awareness of details, a crucial human insight. Readers of *Hello Out There* will realize what loving somebody really consists in; readers of *The Rising of the Moon* will perceive what being an enemy really is. These beautifully written plays are simple enough for less able readers and complex enough for the competent. Such plays place themselves on all lists.

Let us now "get down to cases" and talk about how we would choose short plays for particular kinds of classes and how we would teach these plays to help students of different abilities to achieve the aims we have set.

Let us suppose we are about to choose a *second* short play for a less able class that has just completed the study of Susan Glaspell's

Trifles. We now want a play that will reinforce the skills the reading of *Trifles* has helped students develop and that will require students to use some of the skills in more complex situations. William Inge's *Glory in the Flower* would be our choice.[12]

In some respects, the reading of *Trifles* is superb preparation for the study of Inge's play. For *Trifles* is virtually a play of significant movements and gestures, most of which the writer directs very explicitly. So the reader's task is simplified: in most instances he does not have to first decide what movements the dialogue demands or suggests: he has only to visualize the characters' making the gestures the stage directions mention. So through a study of *Trifles*, students would have learned to visualize gestures, to *see* how gesture extends, reinforces, and at times, replaces dialogue. And because of all this, they would be better able to imagine appropriate gestures in plays like Inge's where stage direction is not *so* detailed and where, moreover, the stage picture is quite complicated. Just compare Inge's stage picture with Miss Glaspell's. In *Trifles* characters are on stage, in general, two at a time, but in Inge's play nearly all characters are there all the time; so though the reader may be hearing only two speakers at any time, he must be seeing these two against the backdrop of all the others. The reader has to imagine and visualize what the whole stage is doing at all times. He really needs the preparation in visualizing gestures, movements, and staging that reading *Trifles* gave him.

Inge's stage action, then, demands more of the reader than Miss Glaspell's does. And this is true of his dialogue, too. In *Trifles* two characters rather obviously piece together the past and detail the present *for* the reader. He need only listen to Mrs. Hale's and Mrs. Peters' anecdotes and discoveries to learn not only about the absent Wrights, their lives, personalities, and motivations, but also about the sympathy, the guilt, and the moral tensions of the two speakers. The dialogue of Inge's play informs the reader less directly. He must do his own "piecing together." Take the relevant past, for instance. How does the reader come to know it? He must gather it, bit by bit, from the casual insinuations of the teen-age girl, from Jackie's exchanges with Howie, from Howie's answer to the salesman, as well as from those more obviously expository passages: the teen-age memoirs of Bus and Jackie and Jackie's "serious talk." Even the frankness of these latter passages is somewhat deceptive, for while Bus and Jackie's discussion of their past seems only to be giving the reader relevant data, it is also evoking responses from them which are unobtrusively defining both of them. In Inge's play, the reader may never rest.

The dialogue of *Glory in the Flower* is, besides, more exploited than that of *Trifles*. It is written so that each person is characterized not just by what he says but also by the particular quality of his language. It is when the reader hears Bus using his cliché, name-dropping "big talk" in conversation with Jackie that he is really struck with Bus' gross insensitivity, his essential emptiness. It is when the reader notices the kind of images of the old town that the salesman evokes that he recognizes the drummer's incapacity for being realistic. The plain syntax and the reportorial diction that Howie consistently uses help suggest his clear-light realism. And the simple, straightforward language that is habitually Jackie's truly represents her artless sincerity. Inge's play is richer than *Trifles* in this kind of suggestion.

It is also richer in its ironies. The setting of *Glory in the Flower* is ironic; the situations are ironic, and the words are ironic. The reader sees early in the play that it *does* "pay" the salesman to "make the town," that Jackie is *not* "still a kid herself"; he sees not only what Bus means by "we had some great times together" but also that Jackie mistakes his intent. And what the characters gradually find out about each other in this half hour, the reader has suspected from the start.

Glory in the Flower is a good second play, then, because in several respects it demands "just that much" more of the reader than *Trifles* does. Furthermore, it offers the teacher many natural opportunities to introduce students to dramatic structure. Students *themselves* will open up the question of structure. For *they* will want to know what the salesman is doing "in there," why the "story" has to be interrupted by Joker and Bronco, and what the gang is for. And the teacher may follow their lead and ask why certain scenes are placed as they are, how the parallel scenes function, and how the reader knows that the flower is becoming symbolic. The study of *Glory in the Flower* offers students an easy way to begin the passage from dialogue to structure.

Teaching *Glory in the Flower* to Less Able Readers

Now we shall suggest what we would *in fact* do as we taught Inge's play as a second play to less able students.

The study of *Glory in the Flower* would require *about* four fifty-minute class periods. During the first, we would do close work on the first three scenes to get students started on the reading of the play. During the second period, students would discuss the first half of the play (pages 170–180)[13] and, if time permitted, would write a closing critical exercise. During the third period, students would talk about the latter half of the play (pages 180–190) and, for homework, would answer a brief synthesizing question. During the fourth period, students would write an in-class critical paper. This schedule is, of course, tentative. Some classes may need more time for discussion; others, for in-class oral or silent reading or for work on study guides. See note 14 at the end of this section.

■ *The First Day.* We would ask students to read carefully the description of the set. Then we would question: What is before you on the stage as the curtain goes up? We would want a very detailed description, for we would want students' seeing and hearing to be as graphic as possible. We would prod if necessary, asking, for instance: What is the posture of the salesman? *How* can you see the sign? And, when the visual and auditory images were quite precise, we would ask: How do you *feel* about what you see? What is your reaction to the name "Paradise," now that you have an image of the roadhouse?

At this point, we would draw on the board a stage plan, letting students suggest what goes in where. We would *then* distribute "skeleton" duplicated stage plans and let students fill them in according to the board plan. We would require students to keep their stage plans before them as they read and discussed the play.

What is the value of this? Not so much to give students a continual reminder that it *is* a play they are reading; rather to provide a means of having them ascertain what is going on on the stage here and here and here during the play. The stage plan helps students visualize how characters enter and exit, where those who are talking are located, where the others are and what they are doing, what the effect is when our attention is shifted from two or three people to the whole room and back. Using the stage plan can also help students see the dual functions of certain gestures and movements. For instance, if they visualize the stage, they see that Bus and Jackie's dancing is not only a right way to bring back "old times" but also an appropriate way to bring them across the stage so that they can talk intimately and be, as they should be, the natural center of attention. Both the board plan and the individual "stages" would be used again and again in a variety of ways such as these—all through the study of the play.

With the opening stage picture before the class, we would read orally as far as Jackie's entrance. *Just* before beginning, we would ask students to decide during our reading whether we are saying the speeches correctly—tones, pace, and pauses—what gestures the salesman is making while he is speaking, what Howie is probably doing while the salesman is talking, and what the kids are doing all this time. Here is the scene.

SALESMAN (*to* HOWIE, *showing his drinks*).   Nothing ever stays the same. Why *is* that?

HOWIE (*detached but human*).   I couldn't say.

SALESMAN.   It used t' be, when I came into this town, I'd leave it with . . . sometimes ten thousand dollars' worth of orders. Ten thousand!

HOWIE.   I wouldn't doubt it.

SALESMAN.   'Course I did. Know what I do in this town now? I'm doin' good if I make my expenses. That's right. I'm doin' good if I make my expenses.

HOWIE.   Is that a fact?

SALESMAN (*conscious of his repetitions*).   I'm doin' good if I make my expenses. It don't hardly pay me any more to make this town. I might as well cut it outa my territory, cause I hardly make enough commission here to keep goin'.

HOWIE.   Things is pretty bad all over, ain't they?

SALESMAN.   Sure. Things is bad all over. I don't know why I stay on the road, Howie. The road's gone.*

After the reading, we would ask such questions as these: In a sentence, what would you say the scene is about? This is to be sure all "have it straight." What tones does the salesman use in his second and third speeches? What gestures accompany these speeches? We would want students to see him, say, leaning back and forward, looking at and away from Howie, shaking his head. Too often students equate gesture with arm-waving. How do you know what the gestures are? What sort of person is the salesman? What sort of person is Howie? (If necessary: What is his attitude toward the salesman? How does *his language* suggest his attitude? If it were necessary to call students' attention to the cliché quality of Howie's language at this point, we would ask: When do *you* talk like this [repeating Howie's speeches]?) What would you say, *tentatively*, is the function of this scene? Keep that an open question— we shall return to it later.

At this point, we would say to the class: Just as the salesman says, "The road's gone," Jackie enters. Read the description of her and the dialogue that accompanies her entrance. Visualize her *entering*, not just standing there. Look at your stage plan and *see* her come

---

in, hurrying *across* the stage, calling out, "Howie, has Bus Riley been in here?" We would exhort the class as much as we felt we had to to get their minds' eyes going. After students read the passage, we would ask such questions as: What effect does Jackie have on the scene? Who is not involved? What is he doing? How, precisely, are the speeches in this scene said? What sort of person is Jackie? What is telling you this? (We would urge students to refer not only to the description of Jackie but also to the kids' responses to her, to her responses to them, and to Howie's response to her—and we would expect students to give *some* interpretation of these responses.) What was the salesman's first remark? How does that relate to Jackie? (We would not belabor this, just start the "wheels," that's all.)

To "set students up" for reading the next episode themselves, we would say, "Jackie's at the bar now—there with Howie and the salesman. Read the next episode—a very brief episode which moves very fast—and be ready to tell how it is staged and what its function is."

A GIRL (*to* JOKER, *teasing*).   Jackie Bowen's in love with Joker. Jackie Bowen's in love with Joker.

JOKER.   So what? Maybe I'm in love with her, too. (*The others all laugh.*)

BOY 1.   No fool, Joker. I think she's got her eye on you.

JOKER (*embarrassed*).   Cut it out, will you? She's a swell dame. Gives me a can of beer when I deliver the groceries, and we stand and talk sometimes. She always asks me about my school work . . . things like that . . . like she was really interested.

GIRL (*sarcastically*).   I bet!

GIRL 2.   My mother says she doesn't have a very good reputation, something that happened a long time ago.

JOKER.   I don't care about her reputation. I *like* her.

After the reading, we would ask: What is the scene about? How do you visualize it? By what means is our attention drawn to the kids? What would Jackie, Howie, and the salesman be doing meanwhile? *How* does the girl say, "Jackie's in love with Joker"? *Why* does the girl say that, not the reverse? What is the tone of Boy 1's speech? of Joker's reply? What is Joker doing as he says it? *How* does Girl 2 make her "statement"? (If necessary: at what volume? in what tone? with what gesture?) What is the function of this scene? (If necessary: Does Joker refer to every woman he likes as a "swell dame"? How does his phrase help define Jackie?)

Then, as our attention moves from the kids back to Jackie and Howie at the bar, we move to an assignment. We could ask students to complete the reading of the play. Or we could ask them to read only one-half of it (pages 171–180) and answer guide questions on those scenes. Both assignments would require approximately the same amount of time, but the effect of each would be very different. Through doing the first assignment, students would get an *overall* view of the play which the in-class study of the play during the following two days would gradually refine. Through the second assignment, students would have a very *close* look first at one-half of the play, then, the following night, at the other. Such a division would not violate the play because the halves are natural dramatic units. We would prefer to give the first assignment, but we would do so *only* if we were relatively sure that the particular class could read the play adequately without guides and if the students were the sort who retained interest in studying a work after they discovered "how it comes out." We shall describe the second kind of assignment because we think it *is* the one we probably would be using in most less able classes *at this point* in the first course.

Here is *a* study guide for the first half of the play (pages 171–180). See note 14 at the end of this section for suggestions of ways to tailor such a guide for various less able classes.

GLORY IN THE FLOWER
                                                — *William Inge*

Please put your stage plan in front of you. Reread quickly the part of the play we read in class today. Then, continue reading carefully as far as page 180, "BUS. Let's go back to the bar, Doll. What d'ya say?" Read these pages of dialogue (171–180) "aloud to yourself." Invest each speech with the "right" tones. If you are baffled about how a speech is said, try it full voice. As you read each speech, try to visualize the character's position, head, face, eyes, hands, as he says the speech.

When you have read as far as page 180 in this way, then answer the following questions in writing:

1. What tone (tones) is Howie using when he says, "No. I just didn't like him, and I know quite a few other people felt the same way I did"? Tell precisely *how* you know the tone or tones are what you say.

2. The playwright tells you that Jackie is "trying to laugh it off" as she says, "Oh! you just wanta sound cynical, Howie." (a) What attitude is she taking? (b) If the playwright had not suggested it, how would you have known anyway that that was her attitude in this remark? (c) What gesture is she making?

3. (a) What sort of person does this episode (170–171) show the bartender to be? (b) What does it reveal about Jackie? (c) Does this Jackie-Howie dialogue have any other uses?

4. *Four* very brief episodes follow Jackie's remark to Howie. They

begin at Joker's "entrance" (page 171) and end with Jackie's exit (page 172). Identify the episodes (for example, the first is "Joker-Jackie") and see if you can tell *in a few words* what the playwright *gains* by including *each* of them.

5. What is the dialogue between the salesman and Howie on pages 172–173 about? Prepare to read the salesman's reminiscence aloud—with gestures.

6. (a) List what you have found out about Bus Riley before he even appears. (b) Now picture Bus Riley in your mind's eye (page 173) and listen to him talk at the bar (pages 173–174). (c) From what *you* now hear and see of Bus, who seems to be right about him—Jackie or Howie? From Bus' language and gestures gives evidence that will support your answer.

7. The meeting of Jackie and Bus is a long scene: from Jackie's cry, "Bus!" (page 174) to Bus' "Here's my arms, Doll" (page 177). (a) What purpose(s) does all their talk on pages 174–175 have? (b) What is the purpose of the reminiscences (pages 176–177)? What does the quote mean? (c) Visualize the stage picture as Jackie and Bus begin to dance: look at your stage plan and see in your mind's eye what the kids are doing, the bartender, the salesman. (d) From what you have heard and seen during this episode (pages 174–177), have you changed your mind in any way about Jackie? about Bus?

8. *Why* does that conversation about the past of the town (pages 177–178) intervene *at this point*?

9. While Bus and Jackie are dancing and talking by the door (pages 178–180), they are still revealing their inner selves to us. (a) What do Jackie's questions about fighting recall to you? How is *her* inquiry different? (b) What does Bus' cliché "old married woman" reveal about him? (c) Why is Jackie "quick to reassure him"?

■ *The Second Day.* Students would spend *at least* two-thirds of the class period answering the study guide questions and the additional questions we might occasionally interpolate to clear up certain points in the play and to test students' skill in producing a performance. After the first question, for instance, we might ask, What tone does Howie use in saying, "very fine things"? What gestures accompany this whole speech? During the discussion of the answer to the fifth question, we might ask, Who is Howie talking about when he says, "Seems like folks b'lieve pretty much what they *wanta* b'lieve"? (If necessary: Is Howie talking about *just* the townspeople?) Why does Howie say "paradise," rather than "heaven"? While we are talking about the first part of the seventh question, we would probably ask, How does Jackie say, "Tomorrow"? Why does she say it that way? What does Bus' phrase, "silly dame," echo? When we discussed the reminiscences, we would interject questions like, Do *they* know what the quotation means? In your view how does it relate to the play as you know it so far?

If time permitted, we would assign for the last ten or fifteen minutes of this period a critical exercise on *whichever* of the three following topics seems most appropriate for the particular class:

1. When Jackie says, "Maybe you'll be champion someday, huh?" Bus replies, "Naw. I don't go in for championship bouts. I just fight once in a while now, when I feel like it. And I do a little movie work, too. Sure. When I feel like it. Yah, I been in quite a few pictures. Just small parts, of course. I never take parts where I have to speak lines. You have to study to do that, and I don't wanta be a star or anything. I just like to take a few parts once in a while . . . just for the fun of it. It's kind of a hobby with me, when I'm not fightin."
   Decide how Bus says these lines: the tones he uses, the pauses, the pace, the gestures. Then, when you are sure you have heard and seen Bus as he says these lines, tell in *one* good *paragraph specifically how* Bus *performs* his answer.
2. The kids are continuously present on the stage. In one or two paragraphs tell the reason(s) for their being in the play.
3. In this play we notice little episodes, or scenes, that seem similar to others. (Such scenes are often referred to as "parallels.") When we look closely at such pairs of episodes, we see they are both similar and different. Choose a pair of such episodes, and in one or two paragraphs show *how* these two episodes are alike and how they are different; then, tell *if you can* what is gained by paralleling them in this way.

At the close of this second class period, we would distribute copies of a study guide—somewhat like the following—for the last half of the play (pages 180–190). See note 14 for suggestions about tailoring guides.

GLORY IN THE FLOWER
— William Inge

Please put your stage plan in front of you. Begin on page 180 where Bus and Jackie return to the bar and read "aloud to yourself"—hearing and visualizing—the remainder of the play. Then answer the following questions in writing.

1. Back at the bar, Jackie and Bus continue their long conversation (pages 180–184). (a) Why does Jackie object to being called "Doll" *at this point* (She hasn't before)? (b) Prepare to read aloud the four speeches beginning, "Every girl I see" (page 180) and be ready to tell *why* you read each as you do. (c) *Why* does Jackie tell Bus that she loved him? Why does she tell him what happened when he went away (pages 181–182)? *Why* does he respond as he does? (d) Whom does he echo in his statement, "Those guys don't know anything"? What effect does Inge achieve by connecting these two remarks? What is the stage picture during this dialogue (pages 181–182)? (e) What does Jackie mean by a "better life?" What does Bus mean by it? Now that you know their "story," do you see anything ironic in this difference in their views?

(f) Why does Jackie take such a sad posture at the bar (page 184)?

2. (a) Prepare to read aloud—with gestures—the speeches of the salesman ("You know, sometimes") and of Howie ("Take my brother Elmo"), both on page 184. (b) How do their remarks relate to the previous conversation of Jackie and Bus? (c) What is the "work" Howie takes pride in?

3. Notice Bronco's language and his attitude (pages 184–185). What is the function of the Bronco scene? Why does this scene come right here?

4. Prepare to read the following speech aloud: "HOWIE. Kids today *beat* me. Every one of them kids in there knows more'n *I* knew when I was thirty. They throw orgies that'd surprise a Roman emperor, but they go home to their folks and their folks still wanta read 'em bedtime stories. I don't know what's gonna happen to 'em. They're all ambitious but they all wanta be movie stars or bandleaders or disc-jockeys. They're too *good* for plain, ordinary, everyday work. And what's gonna happen to us if everyone becomes a bandleader, I'd like to know."

Mark this copy for pauses (/), intonations (for instance, "ridiculing"), gestures (for instance, "throwing the towel on the bar and tossing a cocky head"). Put your annotations in the margin *legibly*.

5. (a) What is Jackie's attitude toward Bus when he returns from the phone (pages 186–187)? (b) How do you account for her attitude? (c) If you were prepared for her attitude, what prepared you? (d) If you were prepared for Bus' reaction, what prepared you?

6. *Why* is the last Jackie-Joker scene (page 189) included?

7. *Why* should the salesman and Bus be left at the bar together at the end (page 190)?

▪ *The Third Day.* The class would spend the period discussing answers to a *selection* of the guide questions. Certain of these questions (1c, 1e, 2b, 3, 6, 7) left students much more "on their own" than any of the questions on the first guide. This was, of course, intentional: to see whether or not the class had learned to notice the little details which answers to broad questions are "made of." During the discussion of these certain questions, we would be *ready* to ask whatever supporting questions appeared to be necessary. For instance, about question 2b (How do their [the salesman's and Howie's on page 184] remarks relate to the previous conversation of Jackie and Bus?), we might have to ask why "givin' up" and why "better" are mentioned. To help students answer question 3 (What is the function of the Bronco scene?), we might have to call their attention to the way that Jackie's advice to Bus in the previous scene relates to Bronco. About question 6 (Why is the last Jackie-Joker scene included?), we might have to ask what "try again" means, why Jackie tells Joker, *not Bus*, about "growing up," what earlier scene this one reminds us of, how this one is different, and what the difference suggests. If students needed help in answering question 7 (Why should the salesman and Bus be left at the bar together at the end?), we would ask them to look back at page 188. In that scene the same two—Bus and the salesman—are at the bar: we would read aloud that Bus-Howie-salesman dialogue. Then, we would say to students, The salesman's remarks and Bus' *seem* unrelated. But what is the relation between Bus' and the salesman's remarks *at this time* (page 188)? Do they believe in their delusions? How do you know they don't? Why do they persist in them, then? How is Jackie different from the two of them? What does she know that they do not know? At *that* point we would reask question 7.

As an out-of-class writing assignment we would give some topic that would "pull the play together." If the class' discussion of the final scene had covered the kinds of questions we have just suggested, then we would probably ask students to write a two-paragraph essay on either of the following topics:

1. In how far do the various characters agree with what is expressed in the Wordsworth lines:

> Though nothing can bring back the hour
> Of splendour in the grass, glory in the flower,
> We will grieve not, rather find
> Strength in what remains behind?

2. Recall the salesman's opening remark: "Nothing ever stays the same." *How* does the play relate to that statement? In other words, does it prove it? disprove it? show it is true, but —?

On the fourth day, we would want to give as a final in-class assignment a task that would make students notice *some* aspect of structure —since, of course, students are supposed to be moving, play by play, toward an emphasis on structure. During the study of this play we have asked them about the function of this and that episode, about the placement of the Bronco scene, and occasionally about an "echo" or a parallel scene. Now, we might ask either about the reason for the use and placement of some single episode (or a bit of dialogue) *or* about the function of some recurrent or continuing element. Two *examples* of the first sort of "structure" question are:

1. Look at page 177, Jackie's speech: "Oh, I still like to play ragtime . . . stuff was dull." What does this speech suggest about Jackie? Why should the playwright want us to see *this side* of Jackie right at this moment? Write your answer in a single paragraph.

2. Notice Jackie's reply to Howie (page 188): "It's all right, Howie. It didn't mean anything at all." Where is she standing when she says it? What does *she* mean by it? What does her remark mean to *us*? In a paragraph point out *how* this simple remark sums up all that she has come to realize.

The second type of structure question—the function of a recurrent element or a continuing element—is more demanding, since it is necessarily more comprehensive in scope. Here are four *examples* of such topics:

1. Look again at Howie's remark on page 172: "Seems like folks b'lieve pretty much what they *wanta* b'lieve." When he says it, we notice it is true of what he applies it to. And we remember other things that happened earlier in the play that it is also true of. As we continue reading, we keep seeing other things that the remark also applies to. Make a list of *all* the things that this remark applies to. Then, in not more than two paragraphs, tell *what* things in the play Howie's remark applies to and *how* it applies to them.

2. Remember that the teen-age kids are always on the stage. Notice where they participate actively in the play. What is their function in each case? Is there any relation between the teen-age episodes and what happens between Jackie and Bus? Is there any relation between the teen-age episodes and the theme of the play (as expressed in the Wordsworth quote)? In about two paragraphs, tell the function(s) of the teenagers in this play.

3. The salesman is at the bar throughout the play. Look at his various speeches to find out, first, what decision he is trying to make; secondly, what alternative[15] he chooses, and, thirdly, what *his* decision has to do with *Jackie's* decision about Bus. In two paragraphs tell *why* the salesman was included in the play.

4. What does "the road" come to represent in this play? What is the equivalent of "the road" for Bus? for the kids? for Elmo? Does *everyone* in this play have his own equivalent of "the road"? Answer these questions in a two-paragraph paper.

We have described at length the teaching of this simple, short play in order to suggest two things: that, however unpromising a class may be, there are always good plays that are appropriate for it, and that in unpromising classes a teacher can ask the same *kinds* of questions about dialogue and structure that he would ask in more able classes about more complex plays. He can, in other words, achieve the same aim in classes of widely different abilities if he chooses works and uses methods appropriate to each.

What happens in such a less able class *after* the completion of the study of Inge's play would depend, of course, on what happened *during* the study of it. If most students in the class were relatively successful (that is, if their responses were insightful and relevant, even though not as full and penetrating as we would desire), then we would take one of two courses of action: either we would choose as the third play a more challenging work—one from the group for average readers, say—and study it in approximately the same way we studied the Inge play, or we would select another play from the first group—Lord Dunsany's *A Night at an Inn*, say—and put the students on their own. In other words, in a less able class, we would at this point use *either* a more difficult work *or* a more taxing mode of study—not both.

How might we put these students on their own for the study of their third play? Let us assume a three- to four-period study: the first two days for in-class independent reading of the play, the third day (and perhaps a fourth) for discussion of it.

At the opening of the first period, we would introduce the play, assign it—to be read in its entirety before discussion—and distribute copies of a duplicated stage plan and of a study guide that would direct students' reading much as those we have just detailed do. This guide would, however, do three additional things: it would provide students with a timetable for the reading of the play, it would warn them that there would be a ten-minute quiz at the *opening* of the second class period, and it would state the topic for the out-of-class paper which would be designed to pull the play together at the end of the students' independent reading. Before students began their reading on this first day, we would take time to *point out* this important information on the guide. Ten minutes before the close of this class, we would interrupt the reading to invite students to ask any questions about the text of the play or about the guide that had arisen during their work, and we would refer these questions to the class for answers. Through this procedure, difficulties are cleared up, students have a chance to show what they know, and we have a chance to find out how they are doing.

By the reading of this third play, the aim of the course would be shifting from increasing students' sensitivity to dialogue to developing their awareness of structure. And this change in emphasis should be reflected in the study guide questions, in the quiz that opens the second class period, and in the out-of-class paper that follows the two days of independent reading. The quiz, for instance, would probably consist of one question on the performance and the function of some bit of dialogue and one question on some design in the play. Both questions should be recognizably *related* to questions asked on the study guide. (This practice helps reassure less able students—and convince unmotivated ones—that doing the assignments *is* valuable preparation.) The out-of-class paper might have as its topic a question similar to either of those we suggested for pulling together *Glory in the Flower* or to any of the topics on continuities and recurrent elements that close the study of that play.

The class period that follows the two days of independent reading would be spent discussing the play. Usually in a less able class we would begin by drawing on the board the stage plan according to students' direction and would follow with a rapid-fire sequence of questions, the answers to which would recall the whole play for the class. Then, we would ask students to perform—with "right" gestures and intonations—five or six sections of dialogue, all of which they would have worked on as study-guide questions. After each little performance, the class would discuss the function of the passage in its immediate context and in the whole play. We would choose the passages so that this in-class study of them would gradually reveal the conflict and the resolution of the play. If time permitted, we would conclude the class period with a brief discussion of the topic of the out-of-class paper written for the day.

If we had any surmise that a single period might not be quite enough to discuss the play in this way, then we would plan to begin the study on Monday or Tuesday, so that the extra half-period or period we might need could follow directly—not after a weekend when all would have been forgotten. It is probable that the recall of the play and the reading and discussion of the passages would take the full period on this third day. If it did, we would simply collect the papers students had written as an assignment, and we would have the discussion of the topic on the following day. Since by that time we would have seen the papers, we would probably open the discussion by having several complementary papers read by the writers and go on from there.

Teaching *The Browning Version* to Able Readers

So much for what we would *in fact* do during the teaching of the second and third plays to less able students. Let us see now how we would probably teach Terence Rattigan's *The Browning Version* as a first play to an able class. This study would probably require four or five class periods.

▪ *The First Day.* Since this is the *first* play, we would probably begin by apprising students of the approach they would be taking to plays by asking such questions as the following: How does a play differ from, say, a novel? So it's to be performed, not read. What, then, must someone do who is going to *read* a play? But a reader isn't a company of actors; he isn't even *an* actor. How does he know what to hear and see? But there aren't many stage directions on page 68.[16] Look. What tells the reader's imagination that he *should* be hearing this, not that, seeing this gesture, this movement, not those? Some such reminders of what the nature of a play is, of how that nature affects dialogue, and of how, in turn, dialogue directs the reader's hearing and seeing of the play will serve adequately as an *introduction* to the reading of plays.

The Browning Version itself needs no special introduction. But students may need some special preparation for reading it. The teacher should be sure that students know, for instance, what "up" stage and "down" stage mean, what Rattigan's "above" and "below" mean ("He moves *above* the table"), what Himmler's "discipline" was like, what a "public school" is, what "masters," "forms," and "removes" are, and what, in *bare* outline, the story of *The Agamemnon* is. All this is information, so it can either be told briefly or handed out on dittoed sheets. Beyond this preparation, and more important, students may need some initial help in producing a performance from Rattigan's script. For simple as the play seems on first sight, it demands a reader with a well-developed sense of tone. Except for occasional stage directions that describe the physical movements of the characters, the text is virtually unannotated. The reader must, therefore, be able to recognize continually from the clues in the speaker's language not only what tones he is using but also what facial expressions and what gestures. And then, of course, the reader must be able to hear the tones precisely and visualize the movements appropriately. The dialogue of a play suggests a performance, and in *The Browning Version*, the playwright lets the dialogue virtually speak for itself. Consequently, even in an able class, we would devote the first period to helping students evoke from pages 67–70 a reader's enactment of the play.

We would begin by handing out duplicated copies of an empty stage and asking students to read through the description of the set and make a "decorator's" plan of the room. To be sure the class saw a room, not just a floor plan, we would ask what "chintzy" is, what effect light coming through a stained glass door would have on the room, what the "upright" chair suggests, and why a screen would be situated where it is (to prevent students' considering the screen a "cheap" device).

Into this room comes John Taplow, "a plain moon-faced boy of about sixteen, with glasses."

TAPLOW (*off; calling*). Sir! Sir! (*After a pause he comes back into the room, crosses to the garden door up L. and opens it. He calls*). Sir! (*There is no reply.* TAPLOW, *standing in the bright sunshine at the door, emits a plaintive sigh, then closes it firmly and comes down R. of the desk on which he places the book, the notebook and a pen. He sits in the chair R. of the desk. He looks round the room. On the table C. is a small box of chocolates, probably the Crocker-Harris's ration for the month.* TAPLOW *rises, moves above the table and opens the box. He counts the number inside, and removes two. One of these he eats and the other, after a second's struggle, either with his conscience or his judgment of what he might be able to get away with, virtuously replaces in the box. He puts back the box on the table, and moves up R. to the hall-stand. He selects a walking-stick with a crooked handle, comes down C., and makes a couple of golf-swings, with an air of great concentration.* FRANK HUNTER *enters up R. and appears from behind the screen covering the door. He is a rugged young man—not perhaps quite as rugged as his deliberately-cultivated manner of ruthless honesty makes him appear, but wrapped in all the self-confidence of the popular master. He watches* TAPLOW, *whose back is to the door, making his swing.*) *

After students have read the description of Taplow's entrance, we would ask *such questions* as: What features of Taplow does the playwright stress? What *might* these suggest? (We want students to realize that appearance *may* be significant and to develop appropriate expectations, but we also want them to stay open-minded while the characters reveal themselves.) When does a person emit a "plaintive sigh"? Why is the chocolate episode included? What does Taplow's behavior tell about his attitude toward the people whose house this is? What do you know about Taplow before he has said more than "Sir!"? How does Frank Hunter *show* he is "wrapped in self-confidence"? What do you *see* in your mind's eye? What is the social relationship between Frank Hunter and John Taplow?

We would ask the class to keep the two personalities and their relationship in mind as we read orally the dialogue between them as far as Frank's "Evidently" on page 70.

FRANK (*coming down behind* TAPLOW). Roll the wrists away from the ball. Don't break them like that. (*He puts his large hands over the abashed* TAPLOW's). Now swing. (TAPLOW, *guided by* FRANK's *evidently expert hands, succeeds in hitting the carpet with more effect than before. He breaks away R. of* TAPLOW). Too quick. Slow back and stiff left arm. It's no good just whacking the ball as if you were the headmaster and the ball was you. It'll never go more than fifty yards if you do. Get a rhythm. A good golf swing is a matter of aesthetics, not of brute strength. (TAPLOW, *only half listening, is gazing at the carpet.*)

FRANK. What's the matter?

TAPLOW. I think we've made a tear in the carpet, sir. (FRANK *examines the spot perfunctorily.*)

FRANK (*taking the stick from* TAPLOW). Nonsense. That was there already. (*He crosses up R. and puts the stick in the hall-stand*).

---

* Selections from *The Browning Version* reprinted by permission of Harold Freedman, Brandt & Brandt Dramatic Department, Inc. Copyright © 1949 by Terence Rattigan. All rights reserved.

Do I know you? (*He comes down L. of the settee to R. of* TAPLOW.)

TAPLOW. No, sir.

FRANK. What's your name?

TAPLOW. Taplow.

FRANK. Taplow? No, I don't. You're not a scientist, I gather.

TAPLOW. No, sir. I'm still in the lower fifth. I can't specialize until next term—that's to say if I've got my remove all right.

FRANK. Don't you know yet if you've got your remove?

TAPLOW. No, sir. Mr. Crocker-Harris doesn't tell us the results like the other masters.

FRANK. Why not?

TAPLOW. Well, you know what he's like, sir.

FRANK (*moving away to the fireplace*). I believe there *is* a rule that form results should only be announced by the headmaster on the last day of term.

TAPLOW. Yes; but who else pays any attention to it—except Mr. Crocker-Harris?

FRANK. I don't, I admit—but that's no criterion. So you've got to wait until tomorrow to know your fate, have you?

TAPLOW. Yes, sir.

FRANK. Supposing the answer is favourable—what then?

TAPLOW. Oh—science sir, of course.

FRANK (*sadly*). Yes. We get all the slackers.

TAPLOW (*protestingly*). I'm extremely interested in science, sir.

FRANK. Are you? I'm not. Not at least in the science I have to teach.

TAPLOW (*moving above the desk*). Well, anyway, sir, it's a good deal more exciting than this muck. (*He indicates the book he put on the desk.*)

FRANK. What is this muck?

TAPLOW. Aeschylus, sir. *The Agamemnon.*

FRANK (*moving to the L. end of the couch*). And your considered view is that *The Agamemnon* of Aeschylus is muck, is it?

TAPLOW. Well, no, sir. I don't think the play is muck—exactly. I suppose, in a way, it's rather a good plot, really; a wife murdering her husband and having a lover and all that. I only meant the way it's taught to us—just a lot of Greek words strung together and fifty lines if you get them wrong.

FRANK. You sound a little bitter, Taplow.

TAPLOW. I am rather, sir.

FRANK. Kept in, eh?

TAPLOW. No, sir. Extra work.

FRANK. Extra work—on the last day of school?

TAPLOW. Yes, sir—and I might be playing golf. (*He moves into the window, upstage end*). You'd think *he'd* have enough to do anyway himself, considering he's leaving tomorrow for good—but oh no. I missed a day last week when I had 'flu—so here I am—and look at the weather, sir.

FRANK. Bad luck. Still there's one consolation. You're pretty well bound to get your remove tomorrow for being a good boy in taking extra work.

TAPLOW (*crossing to* C.). Well, I'm not so sure, sir. That would be true of the ordinary masters all right. They just wouldn't dare not give a chap a remove after his taking extra work—it would be such a bad advertisement for them. But those sort of rules don't apply to the Crock—Mr. Crocker-Harris. I asked him yesterday outright if he'd given me a remove and do you know what he said, sir?

FRANK. No. What?

TAPLOW (*mimicking a very gentle, rather throaty voice*). "My dear Taplow, I have given you exactly what you deserve. No less; and certainly no more." Do you know, sir, I think he may have marked me down, rather than up, for taking extra work. I mean, the man's barely human. (*He breaks off quickly*). Sorry, sir. Have I gone too far?

FRANK (*sitting on the settee, L. end, and picking up "The Times"*). Yes. Much too far.

TAPLOW. Sorry, sir. I got sort of carried away.

FRANK. Evidently. (*He opens "The Times" and reads.* TAPLOW *moves to the chair* R. *of the desk and sits*). Er—Taplow.

We would perform these two and one-half pages of dialogue—with all the intonations, the pauses, the pacing, the facial expressions, and the gestures the words seem to demand. As we progressed, we would pause to ask students what clues were directing our performance of the dialogue, how the *next* speech would be performed, what the non-speaker is doing, and of course what the functions of various sections of dialogue are. After reading Frank's first speech, we would *probably* ask: *Why* does *he* use that analogy ("It's no good just whacking the ball as if you were the headmaster and the ball was you")? What added meaning do his remaining remarks thereby take on? What does this first speech suggest about him?

Then, *as we read along*, we would ask *such* questions as:

How would you know from the dialogue that Frank looked "perfunctorily"? What is Taplow's facial expression as he says, "Well, you know what he's like, sir" (page 68)? How is his attitude toward Frank changing? *Why* is it changing? *Why* does Frank remind Taplow of the rule (page 68)? Does he really want to check Taplow? Read Frank's "And your considered view is that *The Agamemnon* of Aeschylus is muck, is it?" (page 69) with the tones, facial expressions, and gestures he would use. Why does Frank say this? What facial expressions and gestures is Taplow using in his reply? *How* do you know what Taplow is doing as he regrets losing his chance to golf (page 69)? Why would Frank use a rather matter-of-fact tone in saying Taplow is "bound to get [his] remove"? *How* is Taplow's attitude toward Frank changing (pages 69–70)? What suggests to Taplow that he has "gone too far"? *How*—in what tones, with what expression—does Frank say, "Yes. Much too far"? What position is he putting Taplow in? How are they *now* (page 70) seated on the stage? What does this seating suggest?

And now that students have all the materials for answering the "big questions," we would ask: What sort of person does this dialogue (pages 67–70) reveal Frank Hunter to be? Why does he check Taplow occasionally? What sort of person does this dialogue reveal Taplow to be? *Now*, in what way is the carpet incident revelatory? What else do we learn from this dialogue?

At this point, we would distribute copies of the following assignment:

Read *at least* through Taplow's exit on page 86. Say the dialogue aloud to yourself investing it with the "right tones" and visualizing the facial expressions, gestures, and movements of the characters. (Keep your "decorator's" plan before you.) Your aim is to hear and see all that goes on at each moment: to create, as we said, a performance for yourself on the stage in your head—and, of course, to respond to it.

Pay special attention to each of the following passages in whatever way the questions and annotations suggest:

page 71   How would you perform the dialogue between Frank and Taplow from "Indeed?" to ". . . like being liked?" What is Frank *doing* during Taplow's long speeches?

page 71   To whom is Taplow speaking in "The funny thing . . . more?"

page 73   What is Taplow doing during his dialogue with Millie? What is Frank doing? If Millie wants Taplow out of the room, why does she detain him? What, especially, is the function of her remarks about his mother?

page 74   Work on the *performance* of the dialogue between Millie and Frank—from "Thank you" to "Where have you been all this week?"—until you are re-creating it so you make clear their *exact* relationship to one another. (If students have noticed, as they should have, Frank's relief when he and Taplow are "caught" by *Millie*, they already "know" to some extent what the relationship is. So they would know that her "Thank you for coming round" is neither the impersonal, gracious remark she might make to an acquaintance who comes to say "Goodbye" nor the heartfelt thanks she might give to one of the few who bothered. There is something tense in the situation. Her tone is probably restrained to flatness, perhaps a bit sarcastic; his reply is probably toneless, awkward, meaningless. Her question is hopeful, not just the routine request. His "if I may" might be the mild joking tone of one who knows he is most desired or the tone of one pretending to be contrite for something. Her reply is instantaneous, an exclamation with heavy stress on "may." She has taken him literally. The remark sets her in motion, and opens the way for her to be a bit snide and finally get to the question, "Where have you been all this week?") *How* does Millie's "If you may!" suggest who is pursuer, who pursued?

pages   What is Millie doing during this dialogue? What is Frank doing?
74–75   How do these actions help characterize them?

page 76   How does Frank *perform* his five speeches from "Possibly not" to "I am"? Can he feel sorry for both Andrew and Millie?

pages   Hear and visualize the episode between Frank and Millie from
78–79   "Only for God's sake . . ." to Andrew's entrance. Place the two characters on your stage plan; see where they are and how they are facing. *How* does Frank say, "I'm coming to Bradford," the first time? the second time? What is his attitude toward Millie in *each* instance?

page 80   Visualize Millie during the dialogue that begins "ANDREW. Please don't bother" and ends "A charming old gentleman." What do you see? *What* suggests these images?

page 81   In what tone(s) does Frank say his first three speeches? What is Millie doing during this dialogue?

page 82   In what tone(s) does Andrew make his remarks to Taplow? How did you decide?

page 84   How would you *perform* the episode that begins with "TAPLOW (*greatly daring*). Yes, but still, sir . . ." and ends with his "Shall I go on, sir?"

pages   Why does Andrew tell of his translation? Does Taplow under-
84–85   stand the reason? Why does Andrew make Taplow "Go back and get that last line right"?

■ *The Second Day.* This first assignment intentionally makes students concentrate almost exclusively on the performance aspects of the play. And the class work of the second day of the study would indeed feature the performing of some of these passages and the discussion of the performance of others. But it would also include questions about the function of certain brief passages, of certain episodes, and of whole scenes. For example, when we asked about the performance of Frank's "drawing out" of Taplow, we would surely ask about the function of the imitation episode (page 72): How does this episode climax the dialogue that began at the opening of the play? How does this "play within the play" reveal what has happened to the master-pupil relationship? How does Taplow's treatment of Frank when they are discovered reveal it? What impression do you get of Frank from this entire first scene?

And, after students had performed and discussed some of the passages of the Frank-Millie scene, we would suggest: The whole scene just confirms by particular instances what the first nine little speeches of it make clear to you—and then wait for the class' reaction.

Furthermore, we would ask students about what they know of Andrew before he appears: Whose views of Andrew do you have? Do the views confirm one another? Whose is least sensitive? Whose is most sensitive? How do you know Taplow senses the complexity in Andrew? And, of course, we would want to ask about what Andrew reveals about himself through, for instance, *his* comments on Lord's (as contrasted with Millie's), his handling of the timetable episode—and, most importantly, his responses to Taplow's misconstrued line.

After two days' study of the play as a performance, able students would know how to do the kind of reading that is expected. So the assignment for the third day would be longer and less directed. Something like this:

Complete the reading of *The Browning Version*. Be sure to consider carefully the performance of *such* passages as the Frobisher-Andrew dialogue on page 87, from "Not, of course . . ." to "lower fifth, Headmaster"; Andrew's speech on page 96, from "Did he?" to "lower fifth"; Andrew's speech on page 98, "There's no need . . . lower fifth"; Andrew's last two speeches on page 103 and his first speech on page 104; and the Frank-Andrew dialogue on page 113, from "Forget chivalry" to "long ago." Tomorrow in class, you will be asked to annotate *a* short passage to tell how it might be performed. This brief exercise will be graded.

During most of the class period tomorrow, we shall be discussing the many purposes that certain passages of dialogue fulfill, and we shall be especially interested in those passages that seem at first glance to have no function; for instance, the inter-scenes: the dialogue between Frobisher and Millie at his exit, the dialogue about how the Gilberts met, and Millie's remarks on Gilbert's future.

▪ *The Third Day.* During this class period (and, if necessary, the next) there would be a scene-by-scene discussion of the play from the entrance of Frobisher who has come to deny Andrew his pension (page 85) to Millie's revelation of Taplow's reason for giving Andrew the Browning version (page 106). We would ask, as seemed appropriate, about the performance, explication, interpretation, and function of each scene. For example, about the Frobisher scene, we would ask *such* questions as these: What is the stage picture when Andrew mentions returning the money to Taplow's father? Does Frobisher hear that remark? Why does Frobisher begin his discussion with remarks about Gilbert? Perform [this remark addressed to two boys] the six-speech dialogue between Frobisher and Andrew, beginning "Not of course . . . ," page 87. [When the "actors" finished, they would be asked to explain any "tricky" decisions they had to make about intonations, pauses, pace, gestures, movements. For instance, they might discuss what suggested that "Andrew" emphasize "soul" or perhaps "lower fifth" or both in the last speech.] Why was Andrew denied the pension? (If necessary: How does *the way* Frobisher describes the Buller case reveal his own position?) What *shows* that Andrew perceives the reason(s)? For what reason(s) is Frobisher's inquiry about Andrew's finances included in the play? How do you know how Andrew says, "Naturally, Headmaster, I wouldn't wish to provide an anti-climax" (page 91)? How does Frobisher's rhetoric help define him? Why is the Millie-Frobisher dialogue included? (If necessary: Consider what it is juxtaposed with. What is Andrew doing while Millie and Frobisher "small talk" in the room? In what way(s) does Millie's mentioning the medicine parallel Andrew's mentioning the money owed to Taplow? How does this paralleling help characterize Andrew and Millie for us?)

Questioning like this, we would move the class as rapidly as possible from scene to scene until we came to the episode in which Millie reveals her interpretation of Taplow's gift to Andrew. And, with the *context* of this episode fresh in students' minds, we would distribute duplicated copies of the following fifteen-minute in-class exercise which would close this third period:

Annotate the following dialogue to suggest how it should be performed. Tell what tones the characters would use, where they would pause (use /), how fast their sentences would follow one another, what the characters would be doing while they are talking and when they are not. How, for instance, does Millie "look" at Frank?

The dialogue has been typed to allow space for you to make *clear, brief* notations in the wide left margin.

If you have annotated this dialogue in your own text (page 105), you may transfer the notes to this paper.[17]

> [Millie has just called Taplow an "artful little beast."]
> ANDREW.   Artful?
>   (MILLIE *looks* at FRANK).
>   Why artful?
>   (FRANK *stares meaningly at* MILLIE.
>   MILLIE *looks at* ANDREW.)
>   Why artful, Millie?
>   (MILLIE *laughs again, quite lightly.*)
>
> MILLIE.   My dear, because I came into this room this afternoon to find him giving an imitation of you to Frank here. Obviously he was scared stiff I was going to tell you, and you'd ditch his remove or something. I don't blame him for trying a few bobs' worth of appeasement. (*She gives the book to* ANDREW, *then moves up R. of the table to the sideboard, where she stubs out her cigarette, picks up some cutlery and starts to lay the table.* ANDREW *stands quite still, looking down at the book.*)

The assignment for the next day has to be some task or tasks that will pull the play together and send the students back to look again at the scenes they have discussed and at the three they have not (pages 106–117). Here is the assignment the class would receive:

Almost all the characters in the play at one time or another refer to Andrew Crocker-Harris as a "sick" soul or a "dead" soul. Are these characters correct in their judgments of Andrew? How do you account for the last scene?

When you have thought out answers to these questions, write a paper of not more than two pages showing how the play prepares the audience for the ending.

■ *The Fourth Day.* We would plan to have the class discuss the preceding topic for about half of the class period. Students of this calibre would usually have noticed all conspicuous—and much subtle —preparation. But would they have realized the importance of the difference between a soul being "dead" and one being "sick"? Between something "destroyed" and something "lost"? Would they have noticed the difference between what does hurt Andrew and what does not? Would they have realized that, whatever Taplow's motivation for the gift, Andrew saw by the verse translation and by the quote that he had twice reached Taplow? Would they have seen the significance of Frank's accepting the wine from Andrew? Would they have noticed that Hunter says, "She's out to kill you," not "She's killed you"? Would they have realized *why* he tells Andrew the truth of Taplow? And keeps on telling the truth about Millie and about Andrew—indeed forcing himself on Andrew, Andrew's protests notwithstanding? Even these good readers *might not* have seen some of these crucial instances of preparation. So we would be ready to ask about these—just in case.

On this last day, we would also plan to spend some time on other kinds of general questions that would give students a variety of retrospective views of the play. Why, we would ask, is the book that is used in the play *The Agamemnon?* And why is this line "We marvel at—thy tongue—how bold thou art that thou canst utter such a boastful speech over thy husband" the misconstrued line? Is Millie "really quite as much to be pitied" as Andrew? Has Frank changed during the play? Why, *really*, did Taplow give Andrew the Browning version? Does it matter? Discussion of questions such as these will help students see how parallels hinted at expand the immediate story, how a writer makes us feel "with and against" a character (if we look with an alert and unbiased eye), how character change is prepared for and expressed, and how only the audience— who see each character more fully than any other character does— can know the rich ambiguity of a character's motives.

At the end of this last class, we would quickly review *for* the class the "performance" exercise done the previous day. *We* would offer the acceptable alternatives for each instance of tone, gesture, and movement—both alternatives we had decided on and those other valid ones that students' papers had called to our attention. *After* this review, we would entertain whatever questions on specific items students wished to raise. If such an exercise is reviewed by the teacher in this fashion, much unproductive haggling is obviated. And if the review is done at the close of class, it cannot sap a period.

During the study of *The Browning Version* the students have occasionally had to "raise their eyes" from the dialogue to notice some aspect of structure. During the study of the next play, structure would become, as we said earlier, a more dominant interest. Students would have to attend to larger and more various aspects of it and they would have to do it more frequently. For instance, if *The Browning Version* were the second play, we would ask—just as we did in the preceding plan—about the juxtaposed and parallel scenes, about the function of the seemingly inconsequential inter-scenes, and about preparation, but, in addition, we would ask about what is gained by the order of the scenes (why, for instance, the

Frobisher scene precedes the Gilbert), why the play is virtually a series of two-character scenes, what in each scene creates the tension toward the next, and what the emotional rhythm of the play is.

What precisely the *conduct* of the study of the second play would be in a particular class would depend, as the choice of the play would depend, upon the adequacy of the class' handling of the study of the first play. We would expect, however, that a *competent* class would be able to give the second play at least one satisfactory performance-reading before any in-class study began. Normally no study guide of the usual sort would be necessary. But on the day when the play is introduced and/or assigned, the teacher probably should distribute *either* a duplicated sheet with essential information (calendar, gloss for references, and such) and a list of "passages to especially notice" (for undisclosed reasons) *or* a series of "hints" or incisive questions on the more subtle features of the play.

In classes of this calibre there would really be no need for an in-class examination of the entire second play. Instead, we would probably have students concentrate on the close study of eight to ten scenes of particular interest because of their placement, their office in the dramatic plot, their significance as stage pictures, their challenge to the "producers," or their role in some design. During the class period on each of the three days of the study, students would perform and discuss two of the scenes (or episodes from them); they would, at least once, write a critical exercise on a third. As a daily assignment, they would reread the entire section of the play from which the scenes "for the day" were drawn and answer a more comprehensive question on it. In other words, the study of the second play would consist of an overall initial view of the play, a penetrating study of crucial passages, and a progressive rereading of the play to allow the close study of those passages to enlighten the whole. This mode of studying the second play should make the students' *initial* reading of the third play generally sensitive.

Teaching the Third and the Fourth Plays

Our remarks on teaching short plays have simply assumed that most classes would read three to four such plays. How many a particular class would, in fact, study depends on how rapidly the students developed sensitive responses to dialogue and structure. In-class exercises and discussions tell the teacher whether the class is ready to move to long plays after the reading of two short ones, or whether students need the study of a third play, and even a fourth one. If they do, then, in less well-motivated classes especially, *some* variation in the way the later plays are studied will probably be needed. For as our preceding discussions have shown, the way we would study the first two plays is quite stark. It has to be. As beginning readers of plays, students need to be fully conscious of how they are evoking a performance from dialogue—with and without stage directions. They need to be aware of how they are deciding the functions of sections of dialogue, of certain episodes, and of whole scenes. Their study of the means must be careful, precise, frank, and undisguised. All this is needed. However, such study can become monotonous. Weariness does not usually set in during the study of the first two plays. For both plays would be, as our aim demands, relevant to students' concerns and different in theme, world, and dramatic method. And the study of each play would be planned to move steadily and quickly. Such appropriateness, variety, and briskness will stay the feeling of monotony—for a while. But, if during the study of a third play and a fourth, students must continue the *same* stark kind of study of dialogue and structure—and some less able and average classes might have to do so—then, if the class is not well-motivated, additional ways of relieving monotony must be used.

For diversion, the teacher might, for instance, pair plays that treat related subjects. As third and fourth plays, an average class might enjoy a pair rendering two different kinds of entrapment—Arthur Miller's *A Memory of Two Mondays* and John Millington Synge's *In the Shadow of the Glen*. A less able group might be engaged by two nonrepresentational punishments for greed: Lord Dunsany's horrifying *A Night at an Inn* and his ironic *The Jest of Habalaba*. An average class might like to read a play in which a wife discovers her husband, Josefina Niggli's *The Ring of General Macias*, and a play in which a husband discovers his wife, George Kelly's *Finders Keepers*. In the former, the wife thought her husband brave; in the latter, the husband assumed his wife honest. Both plays are disillusionments. A less able class might be engaged by two treatments of the "enemy of the state." They would be shocked by Kozlenko's *Jacob Comes Home* and delighted by Lady Gregory's *Rising of the Moon*. Finally, an average class might enjoy reading a pair of comedies—one realistic, the other nonrepresentational—that dramatize the rich rewards of inflating "thy neighbor's" ego: George Kelly's *The Flattering Word* and Jean Giraudoux' *The Apollo of Bellac*.

Even if the class' work on a pair of plays *had* to be largely the same rudimentary study of dialogue and structure students did on the first two plays, the present study could still have diverting—and valuable—sidelights. Pairing always invites comparing. The subjects are so similar; the experiences of the works so different. The question of why this is so naturally arises. And so the study of these plays might include discussion of the effects of representational and nonrepresentational treatments of material, or discussion of the serious, ironic, or comic view that shapes the material, or discussion of the worlds represented. All this is novel and engaging. So, reading a pair of plays related in subject is *one* enjoyable and beneficial way of "continuing the treatment."

Another diverting mode of study that the teacher might use for the third or the fourth play is the juxtaposing of a short play and the short story on which it is based. This sort of study will force students to think very particularly about what is usually done to material to make it actable: how it is pared and amplified, how it is reweighted and rearranged, how scenes emerge from narrated material, how narrated details are expressed in dialogue. After a study like this, no one will ever have to convince students that a play is different from a story or tell them how it is different or exhort them to behave differently when they read the two.

The conduct of such a study might go somewhat like this. Students would first read the story, twice perhaps, and answer guide questions that would help them "get the facts straight" and notice those features of the story that would be markedly changed in the dramatizing; for instance, the descriptions of the setting, the narrated events, and the internal characterization. After a brief in-class discussion of those features, students would then read the play and answer some questions that would help them clarify, generally, the differences between the short story and the play. Once these are discussed, we would proceed to a close examination of a series of corresponding parts of the story and the play—to see *just what* the dramatist does. Through this process, the stark study of dialogue and structure would be continued in new surroundings.

For less able students such story-play combinations as the following make feasible and very attractive studies: Shirley Jackson's "The Lottery" and Brainerd Duffield's adaptation of it; Susan Glaspell's "A Jury of Her Peers" and the play she based on it, *Trifles;* W. W. Jacobs' "The Monkey's Paw" and Louis N. Parker's dramatization of it. For average students, too, "The Lottery" would be appropriate as would Stephen Vincent Benet's "The Devil and Daniel Webster" and the play he based on that story.

Diversions like the two we have just described are probably *necessary* for those less well-motivated students who need to continue the study of the rudiments of drama through three or four short plays. But such variations are often enjoyed by students whose steady progress in play reading prevents any feeling of stasis, repetition, or monotony. In an able class, the study of two plays on a single subject could be *genuine* comparative study of dramatic treatments; the juxtaposition of story and play could be an *inductive* study of "play-ness." To begin such a study, the class might take a selected episode from the story "The Lottery"[18] and convert it into a scene for a play, complete with setting and stage directions. Students might then compare their efforts not only with Duffield's adaptation of that episode but also with the various adaptations that classmates and former students have made. As they examined the validity of these different adaptations, they would be questioning various uses of the dramatic means to meaning. They would be asking: "Should she really be standing alone at this time?" "Where would the group have to be to overhear the remark?" "Is that the tone X would use to Y?" They would be saying, "A's speeches shouldn't carry that information; A, being A, never would have said that." In such a story-play study, these readers would be wearing playwright's cap.

Holidays

During such an intensive study of a series of short plays as the first course would require, both the motivated and the unmotivated, the competent and the less able, usually appreciate a holiday or two after the study of each play. The activities of these days should be various, relevant to the aim, and thoroughly enjoyable.

The class period might be given over to a *planned* performance of two or three scenes from the play just completed. The title? Why, "Scenes from *The Browning Version*," say. Or even, "Great Moments in *The Browning Version*"! The enacted scenes might be the class' selections or surprises; they might be scenes that have been studied closely or those that have been dealt with only in a written paper or on a study guide. The performance on the holiday should differ markedly in its polish from the in-class enactment of this or that bit of dialogue that the study guides often ask all students to prepare. On the first or second day of the study of a play, we would invite students to volunteer for such a planned performance. We would then meet with the "actors" to discuss how the chosen scenes would be produced: how the dialogue would be spoken, what gestures would be used, what movements and what positions on stage would be "right," what properties would be needed—just everything. At the end of this session, each participant would have an annotated actor's copy of the scene he would appear in. Since the rehearsal of a scene does not take long, the cast or casts could rehearse twice. Then, on the holiday, the presentation. If the "actors" had decided on interpretations of the characters that differed from our in-class interpretations, we would arrange to follow the performance of the scenes with an actors-audience colloquium—à la experimental theatre!

So much preparation for the performance of a couple of little scenes in one play? Yes. Unless such performances are well-planned, they have no chance of being well-executed and, unless they are that, they are of little benefit to the "actors" or the "audience." If performances of scenes can be only shoddy, gauche distortions, if they can be only bumbling horseplay, they are of no value *in achiev-ing the aim we set* for the first course in reading plays.

Another holiday "between plays" might be spent discussing some of the psychological and moral questions the last play raised. Since the students would already have had their experience of the play, we might move away from it on any tangent that the class would enjoy discussing. After *Glory in the Flower*, for instance, students might like to talk about such questions as: *Why* do "folks b'lieve pretty much what they *wanta* b'lieve"? Or, Wouldn't making your peace with things as they are cause you to lose initiative? Or, Is it really possible for people *not* to know what they are in love with? Or, When do goals and dreams become dangerous?

For a holiday like this, we would want to give students a genuine choice of questions. We would also want to prevent such a dis-cussion from beginning with five minutes of "dead air," from being prefaced by top-of-the-head irrelevancies, and from being dominated by one or two students. One way to accomplish all of these ends is to give a homework assignment like the following on the day preceding the discussion:

Here are four questions that *Glory in the Flower* raises. [We would cite the four preceding questions, for instance.] Choose any *two* of them and write your answer to each question in two good paragraphs.

On the following day as each question was introduced, those stu-dents who had written on it would take the lead in the discussion, both stimulating and controlling the thinking of others who joined in the talk. If a question had not been chosen at all, it would not, of course, be discussed. We would abide by the students' decisions.

Another holiday "between plays" might be spent looking through the playwright's "glasses." Some students might enjoy the following kind of groundwork exercise; no actual playwriting is involved. We would prepare and duplicate two summaries: one, a summary of a rather undramatic scene from a story (for instance, a portion of Pepe's flight from Steinbeck's "Flight" or Eveline's musing from James Joyce's "Eveline"), the other, a summary of a scene from a play (for instance, the first scene from the play the class will read next; *The Ring of General Macias*, say). The homework assignment for the day preceding the holiday would be:

Read these two summaries carefully and answer the following questions about each of them: Would this be good raw material for a scene in a play? If you think it would, what are your *reasons* for thinking so? If you think it would not, what are your reservations about it? Write your answers.

This kind of exercise can be made appropriate for less able students or very sensitive ones simply by giving summaries that are more or less obviously undramatic or dramatic.

In class on the holiday, students would discuss their answers, and this would naturally lead into a second kind of groundwork exercise:[19] Now, let's look at the summary you think *is* dramatic material (the first scene of *The Ring of General Macias*) to see what a playwright would have to do to make this material into a scene for a play. As soon as students began suggesting something that assured us they were "on the right track" (for instance, "He would have to write opening dialogue, with exclamations, short phrases—something that expresses one woman surprising another, the other being caught"), we would ask students to work individually, listing all the problems a playwright would face in dramatizing this summary and how he would probably solve them. Through discussion of their individual findings, the students could arrive at a master list of crucial "jobs" for this playwright.

Then, if the class had been interested in this exercise and relatively competent in handling it, we would assign a final step:

First, reread the summary and the list of things we decided "a playwright would *have* to do" to create a scene from this summary. Then, think of what else a playwright would *probably* do to make this scene dramatically engaging: *What* would he exploit for its theatrical value? *How* would he exploit it? Write your answer in a paragraph or two.

Rather than the kind of groundwork exercise we have been describing, some classes might prefer a task that combines critical and creative writing. For such classes we would select from the play just read some scene not already closely studied that is especially fruitful in defining some character. For instance, from *Glory in the Flower*, we might choose Bus' entrance scene or, from *The Browning Version*, the opening scene (which helps define Frank Hunter).[20] As a homework assignment on the day preceding the holiday, we would refer the students to the particular scene and ask them to write a two-paragraph answer to the following question:

In this scene *how* do we know that [character's name] is a [mentioning his chief quality] man? Cite *concrete* evidence.

Students' responses will offer specific data from the character's appearance, from his style of language, (including the tone he uses to this or that addressee), from his gestures, from other characters' responses to him, and from the choices he makes in the situation (for instance, Frank's choice to lead the innocent Taplow on and on while seeming to discourage him). In class on the following day, as students give their answers, we would repeatedly mention the *means* they are pointing out, and we would continually emphasize how *several* of these means *work together* in this or that speech.

When this analysis is completed, we would move directly to the creative part of the exercise:

Now that you have seen how the playwright uses his means, write a dramatic dialogue of about five exchanges (with appropriate stage directions) that will *render* one of the following situations (or a comparable one): an athlete alibi-ing to his coach, a "Monday-morning quarterback" instructing the man who lost the game, the self-absorbed "clotheshorse" responding to a compliment on her latest outfit, the "cause-happy" student buttonholing a potential disciple.

So that the teacher can assist with the inevitable "bugs," students should begin the writing of these dialogues in class and should finish the work as a home assignment. After we had read the papers, we would *probably* duplicate one good dialogue and two flawed ones and ask students to write a brief *dramatic* criticism of each.

We have suggested *only* three of the many kinds of activities that would be appropriate for the holidays between short plays. But even these three kinds are potentially many: each could be not only varied in several ways but also adapted for classes of different abilities. The kinds of holidays we have suggested will at once relieve the pressure of close study and reinforce and extend the sensitivities to dialogue and structure that students are developing during the *main* part of the course. Such holidays as these will provide respite without discontinuity.

The Long Play

During the study of the short plays our emphasis gradually shifted from dramatic dialogue to dialogue and structure. Now in the study of the long play, dramatic structure will be the center of attention. And, no matter what class or which play, the aim for the study of this play would be to help students perceive how different sorts of structural elements work together to unify it and how all parts—selected, arranged, and treated as they are—function in the experience of the play.[21]

At the end of their work on short plays, different classes would vary in their understanding and awareness of dramatic structure. Able classes—those who could *begin,* for instance, with a study of *The Browning Version*—would, through their reading of the short plays, have already become quite sensitive to structure. We would now try to help such students see the more complex uses that long plays make of the structural elements they are already familiar with. Some less able classes—even after the study of four short plays—may have only a bowing acquaintance with structure; they may have learned only to identify exposition, to grasp successive clues to character change, to understand the uses of nonplot scenes, and to recognize the significance of the selection and ordering of events. We would now introduce these students to the presence and the function of other structural elements; for instance, to certain kinds of plot unity, certain rhythmic patterns, to parallel scenes and characters, and such recurrent elements as motifs and typical styles of language. So, though in the study of the long plays, dramatic structure is the center of attention for all classes, we would begin wherever the particular class is.

Choosing Appropriate Plays

Now, before we offer our illustration of how we would teach a long play to achieve the aim we have set, let us see what plays would be both relevant to high school readers and appropriate to our aim.

For less able readers, we think of such works as Louis Coxe's *Billy Budd*, William Gibson's *The Miracle Worker*, Frances Goodrich's *The Diary of Anne Frank*, Lorraine Hansberry's *A Raisin in the Sun*, John Steinbeck's *Of Mice and Men*, John Van Druten's *I Remember Mama*, and Emlyn Williams' *The Corn is Green*.

For average readers, we might choose from among Sidney Howard's *The Silver Cord*, William Inge's *Dark at the Top of the Stairs*, Arthur Miller's *The Crucible*, his *Death of a Salesman*, Paul Osborn's *On Borrowed Time*, Terence Rattigan's *The Winslow Boy*, Thornton Wilder's *Our Town*, and Emlyn Williams' *Night Must Fall*.

For able students, there are such plays as Robert Bolt's *A Man for All Seasons*, Carson McCuller's *A Member of the Wedding*, Eugene O'Neill's *The Long Day's Journey into Night*, Terence Rattigan's *The Deep Blue Sea*, and Tennessee Williams' *The Glass Menagerie*.

And there are other plays—plays like William Inge's *Come Back, Little Sheba* and Eugene O'Neill's *Desire Under the Elms*—which are appropriate for those average and better readers who have the *emotional maturity* to respond empathetically to the situations represented. It is penetrating human experience rather than unusual reading skill that these plays require. So they—and other plays like them—would be ideal choices for that mature class of undistinguished readers that sits before us every now and then.

Why have we limited our suggestions to plays written in the last forty years? Because we wanted to give all students the advantages of familiar diction and syntax and of a goodly number of set descriptions and stage directions. Since students must now respond to a longer and more complex work and do it more independently, most can use such help. And some still need, in addition, the help of a very familiar world. That is why in each of the three preceding lists we have included plays that are various not only in the concerns they render and the dramatic experience they offer but also in the worlds they represent. Though few of the societies in these plays would be *really* foreign to high school students, some would be much more familiar than others. And for their first venture in reading a long play, it would be requisite for some classes and advantageous for many others to be dealing with a world that they could *readily* hear, see, and feel.

In their first encounter with a long play, less able classes could use advantages other than those we have mentioned. That is why for these readers we have suggested plays, most of which have strong, suspense-evoking plots, relatively few and relatively unambiguous characters, copious stage directions, short speeches, and generally simple dialogue. Less able readers should have what assistance they can get, for reading any play will always pose problems. Even in a simple play, like *The Miracle Worker*, students must cope with long, detailed descriptions of gestures and movements. And since what is being described is crucial in the play, readers *must* be able to evoke from the descriptions precise images of the exact action that is taking place: *what* is being done and *how* it is being done. (They will need duplicated stage sets and miming to help them.) And visualizing the actions is not the only problem this simple work presents to the play reader. There are the memory scenes, and they are crucial, too. Students *must* recognize the shift to memory each time it occurs; and they must not only hear the voices *the way* Annie hears them but also see *her*—her facial expression, gestures, whole posture—as she is hearing them. And, of course, that is only half their task; then, they must decide *why* she hears them at this time, how the scene functions in the play.

None of the plays in the first group is without its special reading problems. The dialogue in *I Remember Mama* is surely simple, available to any reader, but the staging is difficult to visualize. And a reader must visualize it continually (he needs a mimeographed stage plan always before him), or he forgets the play is a series of memoirs, and he fails to construe it as such. Does that make such a difference? It must, since the playwright consciously chose to organize his subject matter in this flashback-memoir shape. In fact, one of the general questions we would want to ask about the play is—*why* did he?

Futhermore, even though the incidents in Van Druten's play are simple enough, they are not organized in the suspense-evoking, cause-consequence pattern that students expect. The unifying principle is descriptive: the incidents are, in one way or another, "typical embodiments of Mama." The audience—theatre and reading —is told immediately in Katrin's opening speech that that *is* the organization to expect, but the audience must notice the speech and adjust its expectations to the play's intention, or else it will be responding erroneously—it will be baffled by the lack "of a story" or it will overlook all but the couple of incidents that do have "little plots." These remarks on Gibson's and Van Druten's plays will suffice to show that the plays in the first group will give less able readers their fair share of challenges, as well as their much needed advantages.

Average readers can tolerate obstacles. Consequently, though each play in our second group will help them, it will do so only in one way or another. One play may have a starkly delineated, cause-consequence plot unity; another, a small cast; a third, well-annotated dialogue. But in all of the plays in the second list the characters are more complex than those in the plays in the first group; the experience rendered is more ambiguous. Only compare the quality of the tensions in Anne Sullivan (*The Miracle Worker*) with the quality of the tensions in Grace Winslow (*The Winslow Boy*). To perceive Grace Winslow, the reader must reconcile apparent contradictions. And to perceive the play, he must entertain opposed feelings all through it—and at the close. He must feel the oversimplified reactions of Violet and of the mob in the courtroom and the richly complex responses of the various major characters. At the close he must perceive the moral gains and the irreversible losses, and he must see the importance and the inconsequence of both. The suspense-evoking plot is there in *The Winslow Boy*, but, if all the reader of this play finally has is the experience of a scheme of events that leads through disappointments to victory, he has only the experience of the skeleton on which the complex experience of the play is fleshed out.

We have used *The Winslow Boy* to illustrate the challenges that the plays in the second group will offer readers because this play is, on first sight, one of the easier plays in this group. It does not require the adjustment of expectations that the dramatic unity of *Our Town* does, nor the suspension of disbelief that *On Borrowed Time* does; its plot is not a slim skein; its diction is not richly exploited. Yet our brief look at *The Winslow Boy* suggests the considerable demands on the reader this seemingly straightforward play makes. For, in order to evoke the complex characters and the ambiguous experience we have mentioned, the reader must respond sensitively to the interrelated functioning of a host of structural elements: partially parallel scenes, foils, objects that become symbolic, and phrases ("Let Right Be Done") that "take on" ironic significance. If the reader cannot respond to such dramatic elements, he will have the plot, but miss the play. All of the plays in the second group will provide similarly stimulating studies for average readers.

Able readers need no advantages. So in the third group of plays we have included those with long, involved, and slow-moving main actions, those with slight plots, those with symbolic staging and markedly exploited dialogue. Plays such as these make fruitful initial studies for skilled, flexible play readers who can respond both to the language and the gesture of the boldest dramatic scene (the confrontation of the brothers in *The Long Day's Journey Into Night*) and to the wordless symbolic action of the most delicate of moments (the finale of *The Glass Menagerie*). The plays in the third group are for readers who, with the assistance of some papers and discussion, could create a performance of a multifaceted play like *A Man for All Seasons* so that they hear, see, and feel how all constituents work together to render not the death of More, but the death of law. Plays in the third group are for those who need only some help in recognizing precisely how all they already see works in the whole play.

Teaching *The Crucible* to Average Readers

So much for our justification of the kinds of long plays we have suggested and of the way we have grouped them. Now, let us see how we *might* teach Arthur Miller's *The Crucible* in order to help average play readers develop their sensitivity to dramatic structure.

We have chosen to discuss this play rather than others partly because, on first consideration, it may seem inappropriate for helping average high school students to achieve our aim. Its world may seem too foreign; its structure, too spare. But neither is true.

Consider its world. Although the play is set in Salem, 1692, readers do not have to bring to the reading of it any knowledge of seventeenth-century Salem or of the witch trials. Indeed, Miller's "Note On The Historical Accuracy" and his "Echoes" are excess lumber; and his interpolations in the dialogue of the first act are unnecessary, annoying, and often irrelevant intrusions. The *text of the play* gives all that is needed. Furthermore, since the play is not a seventeenth-century play, but a product of contemporary society, readers do not have to assume the beliefs and values of the seventeenth century; they do not have to become seventeenth-century men, mentally and morally, in order to have an appropriate norm to understand the behavior in the play. And, of course, they do not even have to suspend their disbelief in "the wonders of the invisible world," as they would, for instance, if they were reading Christopher Marlowe's *Doctor Faustus*, for in Miller's play there are no witches, and the play makes clear that everyone knows it.

What readers of *The Crucible* must believe, in order to understand the behavior in this play, is that societies always and everywhere—cliques, clubs, socio-economic groups, localities, nationalities, religious groups, racial groups, and the little societies of their high school—have irrational fears and hatreds of certain things; that these fears and hates are expressed in inciting terms, "snarl" labels, which, fixed on a person for whatever reason, and even without proof, bring down personal, social, even legal punishment on the victim's head. Readers of *The Crucible* must believe that so great is the fear and hatred these words evoke that even just men will tend to believe the name-caller and suspect the tagged. Readers must believe that, consequently, these names become convenient weapons in the hands of the unscrupulous who want to rid themselves of their enemies, punish those whom they dislike, and cover their own offenses.

Furthermore, readers must believe that some men are vengeful; that others are sincere, but naive; that some are so proud and others so self-interested that they will save face at any cost; and that some are honest and loyal enough to lose life, rather than self. Readers must believe that a good man's failure to tell the truth can give tremendous power to evil men. These are the beliefs that the audience must bring to *The Crucible*. And, of course, high school readers do bring them. They *know* all these things to be true. The study of this play will, as Thornton Wilder says, "let [them] know that [they] know it."

Miller's play dramatically represents the revelatory crucible that witch hunts everywhere always have been and always will be. The crisis simply lays bare what each man involved most truly *is*. It uncovers the essential self. The "objective correlative" that Miller selected to render this theme—the seventeenth-century Salem witch hunt— was a most fruitful choice. For it points up the timelessness of this behavior, its rank irrationality, and its viciousness. It shows that a witch hunt can happen at any time, anywhere—even among neighbors who know one another intimately and supposedly love one another in Christ. Furthermore, since the audience is divorced from this "objective correlative" by three centuries, it can more easily experience this behavior with appropriate *detached* involvement. We need only think of other possible "correlatives"— the German purge, the McCarthy hunt—to see the wisdom of Miller's choice.

We have talked at this length about the demands that *The Crucible* does and does not make on the reader's beliefs in order to suggest what we should consider when we are trying to decide how familiar to students the world of a certain play is and what preparation would help them experience the play. To summarize: we should first ask ourselves, "What beliefs, practices, and values must a reader of this play understand?" And then we should carefully consider the play to get *its* answer. If we do this, we shall save ourselves from either erroneously rejecting a play as foreign or "preparing" students by giving them irrelevant or excess information.

So much for the appropriateness of the world of *The Crucible*. But what of the structure of the play? It, too, is appropriate: it is both plain enough and rich enough to make this play a fine vehicle for achieving our aim. And the following discussion of our teaching of *The Crucible* will prove that assertion.

The Crucible is a very exciting play to read. It "falls like an ocean" on the reader. In order to give every student a chance to enjoy the full emotional effect of the play, we would have the class read it once in its entirety before the in-class study of the play began. Average students *can* read this play independently, because its language is simple enough and its plot structure plain enough.

In most classes no introduction to the first reading would be needed. We would simply assign the play and give the class a duplicated vocabulary gloss and a piece of advice. The gloss would explain those words that, because of unfamiliarity, might attract undue attention: such words as "Goody," "poppet," "Mister," "were" for "was," "aye" for "yes," "covenanted" meaning bona fide church members, "known" (I have "known" her) in the biblical sense of "had sexual intercourse with." And what would the piece of advice be? We would suggest skipping over Miller's "Note," his interpolations in Act I, and his "Echoes." We would point out to students that these are *not* part of the *text of the play* (students think the remarks may be a narrator's) and that this commentary is never part of a performance. And we would further warn students that if they read these extraneous remarks now, they may be confused later as to what is in the play and what is not.

In a *literal-minded* class an introduction to the first reading probably would be advisable. It should be designed to focus students on the *experience* the play is rendering. Since the tendency of the literal-minded is to give exclusive attention to the *subject matter* of works of literature, our preparation would aim to provoke a few "wild surmises." We would simply discuss, without reference to the play at all, some current or classic instances of name-calling and their repercussions. After we had cited several particular instances, we would ask students some general questions: about the bases of "witch hunts," about the reasons such hunts occur at particular times, and about the reasons they succeed. Then, without stating or suggesting connections—without any further comment at all—we would assign the play and give the students the duplicated gloss and the standard advice about Miller's remarks. The literal need the intimations that our introduction would provide, but they should search out the relationships themselves.

In an *unmotivated* class the introduction to the first reading should be in the form of an initial "push" deep into the play. On the day the play is assigned, we would use half or more of the class period reading the play as performance, investing the reading with all the tension and intensity it demands. Once past Miller's intrusions and into the play, even these readers will, we think, be pulled along by the experience of the play itself. But "to make assurance doubly sure," we would provide these unmotivated readers with the interim goals they often need to sustain interest in a long, independent reading assignment. In addition to the gloss, we would distribute duplicated copies of a brief reading schedule which would include questions to be answered in writing at the end of the reading of each act. For this kind of assignment, we need questions that students cannot answer without reading the *whole act* carefully. We think all of the following questions require them to do that. In fact, to answer some of the questions, students will have to look twice at the act—which is all to the good. Here is a sample of such a schedule.

Schedule for the Reading of *The Crucible*

Monday—In-Class:

Read Act I and write answers to the following questions: Where is Abby while the Reverend Mr. Hale is questioning Tituba? What does Hale's questioning teach Abby?

Monday—Assignment:

Read Act II and answer the following question: In Proctor's final speech (page 81),[22] he says to himself—as if he were just realizing it, ". . . we are only what we always were, but naked now." To whom is he referring? Point out specifically what people this remark applies to.

Tuesday—In-Class:

Read Act III and answer the following questions: In his second-to-last speech in the act (see page 120), Proctor says that God especially damns "our kind" . . . "them that quail to bring men out of ignorance." Who in this play has "quailed"? How? Why?

Tuesday—Assignment:

Read Act IV and answer the following questions: Why does Proctor decide to confess? Why does he change his mind? Are *both* actions consistent with his character as the incidents of the play define it?

Wednesday—In-Class:

There will be a brief *written quiz* on the *whole* play.

All average students *can* read *The Crucible* independently, but the unmotivated probably *will* not. So for them we try to make the assignment as irresistible as possible—we provide a schedule, questions, an in-class "send-off," and two in-class reading periods. But those are not entirely an accommodation to their lack of motivation. We would use the same Monday-to-Wednesday reading schedule for students who, though motivated, are slow readers. For average readers, who are motivated, we would use a Thursday-to-Monday schedule, giving Friday for in-class reading. We want students to read this play without interruption, so, in *all* average classes, in-class reading would be necessary. We would not give *any* average class a Friday-to-Monday assignment of one hundred and thirty pages. Such an assignment is simply unrealistic.

The immense impact of the first reading of *The Crucible* does not exhaust students' interest in the play. It seems rather to arouse it. Perhaps the initial contact gives, as Styan says, "a stimulating insight into [the play's] full complexity." Whatever the reason, after a first reading students usually have a great desire to talk about the play, to "go over the whole thing." And, when the independent reading is completed, that is what the class would be doing for the next ten periods.

On the first of the ten days—whether it was a Wednesday or a Monday—we would open the class period with a fifteen-minute written quiz on the whole play—something like this:

Write brief but very specific answers to the following questions:
1. (a) At what point in the play do we feel sure Elizabeth Proctor will be charged with witchcraft? (b) *How* does the charging happen? (c) *What* results from the charging?
2. (a) At what point in the play do we feel sure Abby Williams will be exposed? (b) *Why* doesn't the exposure happen? (c) *What* results from this failure to expose her?

For this kind of reading check, we would want important, comprehensive questions that require precise, factual answers. We think the preceding questions meet these requirements. Students cannot answer the first question without accurate knowledge of Acts I, II, III, nor the second without the exact facts of Acts III and IV. Any set of questions that makes similar demands is equally useful.

During the last half-hour of the first class, we would ask, rapid-fire, a battery of questions to make sure that everyone had the facts of the play "straight" before we proceeded to any discussion of its structure. We would question act by act, pausing at the end of each act to clear up any questions students wanted to raise about that section of the text. At the end of this class period, we would turn to our main business: a study of the structure of *The Crucible*.

We would start with the main plot both because plot is the structure that students are most familiar with, because it is a structure that will give them an immediate and continual hold on the whole play, and because, by seeing its nature more clearly, students will recognize that plot is not play, but one structure in terms of which they can better see how other kinds of structures work to render the experience of the play.

What kind of first assignment, then, would we give? It should be one that will call students' attention to the nature of plot, to the events that constitute the plot of *The Crucible,* to the "cause-consequence" organization that unifies this plot, and to the handling of exposition in this play. Tasks such as the following two will serve our purposes. For, even though to keep the assignment reasonable, we have had to limit the first task to Act I of *The Crucible,* the kind of work students must do will give them a truly representative conception of the nature of plot in a play.

Dramatic Plot as Structure

Do both parts of this assignment for tomorrow's class. The first part refers to Act I; the second, to the whole play.

1. Here is a summary of *the story* from which the plot of Act I of *The Crucible* was selected. (We would insert a one-page summary of the events as they happened chronologically, beginning with the affair of Proctor and Abby, months before the play opens.) Read this summary carefully. Then write answers to the following questions: (a) Which of the incidents in this story are played *on the stage* during the first act of *The Crucible?* (b) *Of the enacted incidents* which are given more prominence in the play than they had in the story? Why? (c) Are any of the events of the story played offstage? (d) Now, look again at the summary. What happened to those parts of the story that are not acted out? Do they appear in the first act in *any* way? If so, how? Be very specific.

2. Answer the following questions briefly and specifically: (a) How would you describe the state of affairs at the opening of the play? (b) What in this state of affairs suggests that change *may* come? (c) What does *cause* change in the state of affairs? (d) What, *in order,* are the consequences of this event? (e) What is the climax? (f) What is the consequence of that? (g) What is the final state of affairs?

Both parts of the assignment make students *notice* certain features of the plot, but neither part probes the reasons for these features, the effects they create. We would do that in class on the following day. We would guide the discussion of the first part of the assignment so as to emphasize that plot is a selection of just certain incidents from a whole story, that these incidents are chosen for certain reasons (For what reasons?), that they are arranged in a certain order (Why?), that they are treated—expanded, contracted, focused —in certain ways (Why?). We would guide the discussion of the second part of the assignment so that students would see that a playwright chooses one unifying principle rather than another so that his material will achieve one effect rather than another (Suppose this play were a series of incidents dramatizing, in turn, the suffering of Rebecca Nurse, of Giles Corey, of Tituba, of the Proctors, of Sarah Good. Think about the kind of experience you would have—how it would differ from the experience you have in *The Crucible*. Now, what does the play gain from Miller's choice of the "cause-consequence" principle?)

This one- or even two-period discussion of the dramatic plot of *The Crucible* will not exhaust the subject. But it will give students a hold on the whole play, and it will show them—no overt statements needed—what dramatic plot is and how a particular selection, shaping, and unifying of a certain set of events affects their experience of the events. When students see this, they will then be *in position* to see how a lot of other things—parallel scenes, foils, "echoes," recurrent elements, rhythms, apparently insignificant moments and characters and positions on the stage—highlight, flesh out, expedite, and enhance the plot in some way. And they will be *ready* to see how *all* these features in their interrelationships affect the "audience's" experience of *The Crucible*. To help students see what they are ready to see would be our aim for the close second reading of the play.

This close study would require *about* eight class periods—two periods for each act. All classes (motivated and otherwise) would be required to prepare detailed study questions on each of the first two acts. Through doing just that much closely directed work, *most* average classes would learn quite adequately what should be noticed and how it should be noticed, so for Acts III and IV, a list of "hints" or a "study advisory" would suffice to insure a careful reading and satisfactory class discussion. For "men of weak will," the usual study questions would be continued throughout the second reading. Normally, all students would write a short in-class paper at the end of the study of Act II and a one-page paper (in class or out, as seemed desirable) at the end of the study of the whole play.

Now, using Act II, we shall illustrate *the kind* of study questions and of in-class critical paper that we would assign an average class. First, here is the *sort* of study guide the class would receive at the end of the second day's discussion of Act I. See note 14 at the end of this section for ways to tailor a guide for a particular class.

Study Questions for Act II

The setting of this act is different from that of Act I, so please fill out a new duplicated stage plan so that you will have an appropriate one for this act. Then, reread Act II and answer at least questions 1–13.[23] These questions and your answers will be the basis of tomorrow's class discussion. For the following day, answer questions 14–18. After the discussion that day, there will be a fifteen-minute in-class written exercise.

1. Watch Proctor carefully as he moves about the room alone. Now, what do these different actions tell you about him?

2. (a) What in the opening dialogue—as far as the pause on page 51—substantiates the character traits Proctor's actions suggest? Pay attention to the prose sense of what he says, to his style of language, to his gestures and his facial expressions. (b) Do the traits Proctor reveals in this episode reinforce, further develop, or reverse any impression of him we got during Act I?

3. What function(s) has Elizabeth's remark about the rabbit?

4. What in this episode (pages 49–51) conveys to us "a sense of their separation"? Consider "separation" not only as "alienation" but also as "fundamental difference."

5. The first scene of Act II takes place eight days after the end of Act I. But in the performance of the play it takes place just a few minutes after the last scene of that act. What effect(s) does the juxtaposition of these scenes have on us? Consider not only the more obvious effects but also your reaction to Proctor's mention of George Jacobs, of harvest, of spring, next Sunday, flowers, the beauty of Massachusetts.

6. Read aloud to yourself the dialogue between Elizabeth and John from, "I think you're sad again. Are you?" to the entrance of Mary Warren. Give the speeches the intonation, the pace, and the pauses they require. Visualize the performance. Where are the speakers as they talk? What are they doing? For instance, when Proctor says (page 51), "I thought better of it since," is his voice loud or soft? is he facing Elizabeth? what does his face register? When Elizabeth says (page 52) the speech beginning, "It is a mouse no more," what tones is she using? what gestures? While you read this dialogue, ask yourself such questions and decide on answers to them. And when you have done this, answer: (a) What in the dialogue makes clear Elizabeth's real reason for wanting Proctor to go to Salem? (Why, for instance, does she say, "Do as you wish then," *after* she hears he was alone with Abigail? Is it because she feels he cannot prove what he was told?) (b) What in the dialogue makes clear Proctor's real reason for not "going to Salem"? (c) How is Proctor's motivation similar to Parris'? When we recognize this similarity, what do we realize?

7. (a) How do *you* explain Mary Warren's initial attitude and remarks? (b) What is the function of her rehearsal of "the proceedings"? Does it relate in any way to Elizabeth's "proceedings" (page 55)? (c) Why does Mary say, "I saved her life today," rather than "I saved her from being accused"? (d) Why does she take the attitude toward John Proctor that she does?

8. (a) What scene does the scene between Elizabeth and John (pages 60–62) recall? Notice specific "echoes" that *make* us recall it. (b) What is gained by having us recall that scene *now*? (For instance, is Elizabeth right in her suspicion? is she right in her solution? What in the earlier

scene tells us *why* she may have been mentioned? Why is John angry?)

9. In each scene in a play feelings move in a certain rhythm. They may move steadily in one direction, continually intensifying. They may move steadily in one direction, and then shift. They may zigzag. You have now studied three scenes in this act. How do feelings move in each of these scenes?

10. (a) In what ways is the Hale scene similar to the Mary Warren scene? (b) Think of the differences that these similarities emphasize. Now, what do these differences make clear to us?

11. Point out specifically what reveals Hale's *real purpose* for questioning the Proctors. (What, *for instance,* is Hale "thinking" [on page 65] before his reply to Proctor? Why does he ask *Proctor* to say the Commandments? Why does he ask about their belief in witches?)

12. (a) In what way are Hale and Proctor alike? (b) Why is it important that we perceive this similarity?

13. We see what Hale says in his "farewell" (page 70), but what *functions* has this speech?

14. The Corey and Nurse arrests are only reported. *Why* include them at all? Why not introduce Cheever without any preliminaries?

15. Read the Cheever scene (pages 72–78) aloud to yourself so that you hear and see it. (a) What features of this scene give it an initially comic atmosphere? (*For instance,* in what role had Cheever been previously mentioned? How do you visualize the Cheever-Herrick "discovery"?) (b) At this point, what kind of ending do you anticipate for this scene? (c) At what point are your anticipations reversed? (d) What is the purpose (what are the purposes) of developing this scene this way?

16. (a) *Why* does Proctor respond to the turn of events as he does? (Anger? An attempt to save Elizabeth? Discovery?) (b) *Why* does Elizabeth react as she does?

17. Three small scenes (pages 78–79) precede the final climactic scene of Mary Warren and Proctor. What is the function of each of these small scenes? (Think of them, for instance, as scenes leading step by step to the final climactic scene.)

18. (a) In the final scene, *why* doesn't Mary's warning, "She'll ruin you," make Proctor "think better of it"? (b) What has Proctor recognized? (c) What does his final position on stage recall? What is the purpose of reminding you here? (d) Why is his recognition counterpointed by Mary Warren's refrain?

In class these study questions may be used variously. If students are apathetic or haphazard, they should probably discuss every question, pooling their responses to arrive at adequate answers. If, however, students are well-motivated, careful workers, they might discuss some of the study questions and certain general questions based on others. For instance, instead of spending class time answering questions 10–13, these students might better discuss why the Hale scene is the center scene of the act. But however the two-day discussion of Act II is conducted, it should include a written critical exercise.

If the class is one of those very sincere but very mediocre groups that sometimes passes for "average," then the topic for this exercise might be one of the study questions from the assignment for the *second day* (14–18). Question 15 (d) or 16 (a) would be an appropriate choice. The paper should, of course, be written at whatever moment the discussion arrives at the chosen question.

If the class is the usual average group, the exercise would probably conclude the period, and the topic for it should be some question that students' reading and discussion of Act II has readied them to work on. Here are five different kinds of topics, all of which, we think, in one way or another, will evaluate students' achievement of the aim.

1. When the Reverend Mr. Hale makes his final speech to Proctor (page 79), he advises him to look for the *underlying* cause. As usual, Hale is suggesting something more than, or other than, he intends. As an observer, you have seen, without being involved in it, everything that has gone on. What do *you* see as the cause of the "confusion" that "strikes upon the world" of Salem?

In not more than two paragraphs give your answer. Be sure it takes *all* you have heard and seen into account.

2. In this act, Proctor, Mary Warren, Cheever, and Hale all use the word "proof." Recall how each uses it, what each applies it to, what each means by "proof."

Then, in a paragraph or two, show that the ways these characters use the word "proof" help to make clear what very different kinds of people they are.

3. We talked about the emotional rhythm of the first three scenes of this act. Does this same pattern continue in the Hale scene? in the Cheever scene? in the final scene?

When you have considered the rhythm in all these scenes, then, in a paragraph or two describe the emotional rhythm of the whole act, point out what the effect on the audience would be, and suggest why that effect is desired in this play.

4. In a tiny dramatic moment near the end of the act, Giles Corey says to Hale, "And yet silent, minister? It is fraud, you know it is fraud! What keeps you, man?" (page 78). What earlier moment does this recall? What is gained by reminding us of that moment at this time?

In a paragraph or two, answer these questions as fully as you can.

5. The sentence "The Devil's loose in Salem . . . " becomes a battle cry for the witch hunters. It also serves other functions. For what purpose does Mary Warren use it on page 59? For what purpose does Hale use it on page 71? What does Hale's wording of it reveal that Mary Warren's does not? In what ways is the remark dramatically ironic?

In about two paragraphs point out the functions of the quoted sentence.

If students move through their second reading of *The Crucible* noticing the *kinds* of things that our study questions and topics for Act II call to their attention, they will, we think, become aware of how many things and what sorts of things make their experience of the play one sort rather than another. They will perceive, for instance, the effects of juxtaposing certain scenes, of interpolating seemingly "unnecessary" ones, of partially paralleling scenes, episodes, characters—even positions on stage. They will realize what is gained by having the comic repeatedly counterpoint the serious—from the caustic remarks of John Proctor and Giles Corey in the first act to the gentle Lear-like "I've had no breakfast" of Rebecca Nurse on her way to the scaffold. They will feel the effect in scenes and in the whole play of a certain emotional patterning: the steady movement from remarkably quiet beginnings to an intense crescendo. They will see, finally, the significant functions that recurrent words and phrases have. As the repetition of the battle cry "The Devil's loose in Salem" piles irony upon irony, it gradually reveals the true course of the "cause." And the continual use of "pretense" and "liar" by those who are themselves dishonest pretenders makes clear why "God be provoked so grandly." During the course of the play, "can" and "cannot" come to distinguish the courageous from the cowardly, and "name" becomes a symbol of all a human being has to keep or give. Life is nothing without it; men do both good and evil to save it. There's *more* to the structure of *The Crucible* than a causally related series of main events, and it is that "more" that, through the close study of this play, we would be trying to get students to recognize and respond to. Having the experience of a play depends upon reacting appropriately to *all* the "things" that inform the experience.

In order to be valid, our final evaluation of the study of *The Crucible* must test students' awareness of some features of structure. Any of the features we have just mentioned would, for instance, be appropriate subjects for the closing paper. We need only decide which features(s) should be tested in each class and then devise a particular topic. The possibilities are legion. Here are three kinds of topics that could be used either for full-period tests or for out-of-class papers.

First, an example of a topic that deals with the definition of character by partial similars and foils:

One of the ways the play reveals to us John Proctor's moral character is by showing us what others do when they are faced with decisions similar to his.

Before you do any writing, answer these questions for yourself: What important decision does Proctor make? What other characters are faced with similar decisions? Are their reactions similar to his? partially similar? different from his? Are they more admirable than his? or less so?

When you have *in mind* answers to such questions as these, write a one- to two-page paper that shows that the reactions of other characters to decisions similar to Proctor's make clear to us the moral value of Proctor's reactions.

Now, one kind of topic for a paper that deals with the function of a character:

Characters appear in a play only as long as they serve some purpose in the whole experience. Thomas Putnam and his wife, for instance, appear in Act I—and are "heard no more." They have served their turn. Near the close of Act II (page 77), John Proctor declares to the Reverend Mr. Hale, "You are a broken minister." The preceding events of the act surely justify Proctor's remark. But Hale continues in the act and in the play—even to the very last moment. The question is: What function(s) does he serve?

Write your answer to this question in not more than two pages.

Finally, an example of a topic that deals with the function *in the play* of an apparently unnecessary unit:

There are some scenes in a play that, though enjoyable, seem on first sight as if they need not have been included and, if included, as if they might have been placed in any one of several parts of the play. In *The Crucible*, the scene that opens Act IV—the Tituba-Herrick-Sarah Good dialogue (pages 121–123)—seems to be one of these scenes.

Your job is to point out in a one- to two-page paper why this scene is *included* in the play and why it is *placed* where it is.

The in-class study of *The Crucible*, as we have outlined it, would *require* at least twelve class periods. Certain average classes, however, may need more time than we have allowed for the preparation of the study guides or for the discussion of their answers. Classes whose sense of "performance" is not adequate would need additional class time for hearing and seeing certain scenes and discussing the significance of particular tones, gestures, stage "pictures." Many classes may want to spend extra time on kinds of discussion and writing other than the type we have described. Our questions and our exercises have been designed specifically to help students achieve the aim for this part of the first course and to evaluate their progress toward that goal. But other equally valid, though less directly relevant exercises, would also be profitable.

At the close of the study of *The Crucible*, for instance, students might enjoy reacting, orally or in writing, to provocative excerpts from professional criticism of the play. We might offer them such a statement as Henry Popkin's in "Arthur Miller: The Strange Encounter": "At the center of each play [*All My Sons, Death of a Salesman, The Crucible,* and *A View from the Bridge*] is the tension between little people and big issues, and each play confirms our belief that little people cannot live up to big standards. . . . If farmer

John Proctor of *The Crucible* seems to be a superior human specimen, he is benefiting from the enchantment lent by a distance of three centuries."* Or we might "see what they'll say" about Eric Bentley's statement in "The American Drama, 1944–1954": "*The Crucible* is a play for people who think that pleading the Fifth Amendment is not only a white badge of purity but also a red badge of courage."† Or we might want to get their response to a statement on the structure of the play, for instance, Popkin's: "[*The Crucible*] takes the form of an investigation, for it begins with the arrival of the great investigator of witches. Our pursuit of the facts takes us over two paths; while the witch-hunters make their efforts to measure the extent of witchcraft in the community, we follow John Proctor's attempt to weigh the guilt in his infidelity to his wife. The question of Proctor's guilt peters out since his guilt is nothing beside the community's."

Students enjoy contending with the critics. And their discussions of such statements would make clear to them that the play—not the student, not the critic—decides what interpretations of it are justifiable. Any exercise that encourages a healthy respect for the text and a healthy wariness of critics could surely be called "profitable."

At the close of the study of *The Crucible*, students might, furthermore, enjoy and profit from oral or written discussions of some of the psychological, social, and moral questions that the play raises. For instance, Does crisis reveal men truly—or does it distort their true natures? Or, Specifically, how does the name-caller destroy himself? Or, Who benefits most by a witch-hunt? Or, What do you think of Hale's statement to Elizabeth Proctor (page 132), "Life, woman, life is God's most precious gift; no principle, however glorious, may justify the taking of it"? Or, Giles Corey will not confess, but he will not deny either. He stands mute for a very *practical* reason. Is such a death a "good act"?

Most students like both of the supplementary activities we have just described. But no activity that *follows* a completed unit of study should last more than a day or two. When the full-period critical paper is finished, "over-ness" sets in. One day spent evaluating the professional critics, one day of having "our say" is usually welcome and stimulating; more becomes anticlimactic. And "a climax is what one must try to work up to on these occasions"!

With the conclusion of the study of the long play, we would have finished the first course in reading plays. What follows? Later in

---

* Quotations from Popkin's article are from *The Sewanee Review*, 68, No. 1 (Winter 1960), p. 35. Copyright © The University of the South.

† E. Bentley, *The Dramatic Event*, Ch. 54 (New York: Horizon Press, 1954), p. 257.

the same school year, perhaps in the spring, a second course in reading plays(approximately twelve to fifteen classes). And, the next year, at least one more unit of play reading. This is one answer to the question, "What follows?" But it is not the most important one. What follows—whenever it takes place—should be a course designed to force students to exercise and to refine and differentiate the responses to dramatic dialogue and dramatic structure they have already learned. The first course, second course, and all later courses should, in other words, form a sequence, each building on the last, demanding what has gone before, preparing for what lies ahead. And this interdependence among the courses should be clear to the students taking them.

The Second Course—and Later

We shall begin with four suggestions for courses that might properly follow the first course we have outlined. All four would be appropriate for the usual average class or for competent readers, and the first two courses would be especially fitting for less able readers and for those average classes who need more practice. After we have discussed these four courses, we shall suggest two kinds of advanced study that, for average and able students, could properly conclude their sequence of play reading. Our six proposals represent only *some* of the *general* modes of study that *could* appropriately follow the first course we have outlined. Our suggestions about the quality of reader each course would best suit are—as they must be—only tentative. As always, what second or later course a particular class should have depends upon both the students' reading skill—in this case, play reading skill—and their special interests at the time the decision is being made. Since only the teacher has this information, only the teacher can make the "right" choice.

Now, to our first suggestion.

The Long Play—Once Again

If a class' study of the long play at the end of the first course had been only moderately successful—because of a halting start, disappointing papers, loss of "the forest," or any other of a number of reasons—then the second course might consist of the in-class study of another long play and the out-of-class reading of a third. The plays might be chosen from the lists in the chapter "A First Course in Reading Plays." But *at this point* which plays would be appropriate? Should less able students, for instance, read two or more plays from the list designated for them? Or should they now move up to plays for average readers? The answer would depend upon the *kind* of problem the students experienced in reading their first long play. If the class' problem was quite a general one—an inability to perceive structure, say—then two more plays of the same difficulty would be needed. If however, the class' problem was quite specific—an inability to recognize parallel scenes or to notice foils, say—then, for in-class study, we would probably choose a play listed for average readers, and, for independent out-of-class study, another play from the group for less able students. The same considerations would, of course, also guide the teacher's choice of works for those average classes who would need to study "the long play—once again."

No matter what plays are chosen for this second course, students' preparation for the in-class study should be less guided than it was in the first course, but the discussion of the play should be just as precise and intensive. The questioning should aim especially at remedying the class' specific difficulty, and the critical exercises should evaluate the effects.

As soon as the in-class study of the second long play is completed, the third play would be assigned; and students would be *on their own* to use without help the skills they have been learning. For this independent study, there would be no guides, no study "advisories," no discussions. But students would receive an assignment sheet telling them, for instance, that they have a week to do the reading— with no other out-of-class assignments, that they should have completed Act III, say, by class time on a Wednesday, that there will be a twenty-minute written in-class critical paper on that day on some phase of Acts I–III, and that there will be a full-period paper on Friday, say, the day when the reading should be completed. In other words, the students would be "on their own," but not abandoned.

Our description of this second course may suggest that we think of it only as a remedy for deficiencies revealed by the first course. But clearly this kind of study could be pleasurable and profitable for classes of all reading abilities whose study of their first long play had been completely successful. Such advanced, independent reading of long modern plays might be the ideal second course for *some* of these classes. For others, however, a quite different second course would be in order. There are various alternatives.

Narrative and Dramatic

The teacher might, for instance, decide on a comparative study of a novel and a play based on it. By the time the students were taking this second course, they probably would have had a first course in reading fiction and so, in this comparative study, would be able to do more than make an elementary "listing" of what had been omitted from the novel and added to it to make the play. They would be able to offer an explanation for these changes and consequently, they would have an insight into the requirements, the advantages, and the limitations of both genres. Unless a particular class is able, with appropriate help, to do *this kind* of comparative study, it should not be given the option of this course, even if the class has done—and enjoyed—the "finger exercises" in comparison suggested in the first course. The criteria for choosing this second course are two: students' interest in it *and* their potential for it. Lacking one or the other, students will find the course unduly painful.

For average students, such pairings as the following would be usable: Truman Capote's novella and play *The Grass Harp;* Edith Wharton's *Ethan Frome* and Owen and Donald Davis' *Ethan Frome;* and Graham Greene's novel and play, *The Power and the Glory.* In addition to these, able students could handle a comparative study of Herman Melville's *Billy Budd* and Louis Coxe's *Billy Budd*[24] or of Henry James' *Washington Square* and Ruth and Augustus Goetz' *The Heiress.*

Modern Tragedy

For some classes, the teacher might decide that an introduction to tragedy would be a profitable second course. He could always be sure it would be an engaging one, because, of themselves, high school students consider the vision of life that tragedy renders very significant. They are just becoming intensely concerned about man struggling against his world, testing his strength against terrible odds, asserting himself. So tragedy is highly relevant.

The aim of such a second course would be to help students *begin* to understand how the tragic view of life is expressed in dramatic literature. We would limit the readings to modern tragedies because, since they present fewer text problems, students can spend all their energies on developing an understanding of the vision and the form of tragedy.

This second course could be conducted in many different ways. It might, for instance, begin with the class doing an independent "performance" reading of a certain tragedy. This reading might be followed by a week's in-class study of the play as a play: the first period might be spent "getting it straight," the next two discussing crucial features of the "performance" of the play, and the last two talking about its dramatic plot and other structures. At that point, the teacher might spend the next few class periods just casually asking, in nontechnical language, the "classic" questions:

Who is the main character? What is he confronted with? What

are his fortunes at the time? Who brings this confrontation about? What is the relationship of this person to the main character? What is the usual expectation of such a relationship?

What is at stake in the confrontation? Can the main character avoid the confrontation? Does he realize the possible consequences? Why, then, does he act in the face of this? What actually are the consequences of his action? (Most students will see no "good" in these consequences, so—)

Does any good come of his action? Does it affect others in any salutary ways? Does it have any far-reaching effects?

Is the main character an excellent man? What is his flaw? How do you feel about him?

After such questions as these are discussed, the teacher might, then, call the play a "tragedy" and ask the class to suggest what, generally speaking, tragedy *seems* to represent. The discussion should be guided not toward a fixed definition of tragedy but toward a flexible understanding of the nature of the tragic hero, of his impulsion to act in a serious crisis, of his "mistake" and the reason for it, and of both the dire consequences and the positive values of his act. When students have arrived at such a flexible, general understanding, they should then go on to read a second modern tragedy—as out-of-class independent work.

When the teacher assigns this second tragedy, he might recall to students that they began their study of the first tragedy with a careful "performance" of the play and a close examination of dialogue and of structure. He might *show* them that they could not have answered the questions on tragedy unless they had first "performed" the play precisely and imaginatively. Once students are familiar with the "classic questions" of tragedy, they are often so engaged by them that they forget that text comes first. They seem to think that startling but textually irrelevant generalizations and hypotheses about heroes and flaws are enlightening answers to these questions; they seem to forget that enlightening answers can be found *only* in the play read as performance. So the teacher's introduction to the independent reading assignment should head off such forgetting.

The writing assignments that accompany this second course should require at once a close examination of the text and a flexible view of tragedy. The topics might relate to *some phase* of tragedy; for instance, to the revelation of the hero's flaw and the cause of it, or to the appropriateness of the consequences to the act, or to the clues that suggest the value of the hero's suffering. Topics like these will discourage undisciplined students from indulging in an "overflow of powerful feelings" and rigid students from engaging in a careful fitting of *this* tragedy *into* the "five characteristics."

Appropriate plays for the kind of second course we have been describing would be such works as *The Crucible,* Terence Rattigan's *The Deep, Blue Sea,* Eugene O'Neill's *Desire Under the Elms,* his *The Emperor Jones,* and such plays in translation as Henrik Ibsen's *Ghosts,* his *The Wild Duck,* and Fredrich Durrenmatt's *The Visit.*

Three Forms of the Drama

For some classes, the teacher might decide that an appropriate second course would be a study of several basic forms drama has taken during its development. For such a course he might select, for instance, an ancient Greek drama (perhaps, Aeschylus' *Prometheus Bound*) a Medieval-Renaissance play (Marlowe's *Doctor Faustus*), and a modern play (Ibsen's *Ghosts,* say)[25] and help the class read each play as an artistic expression of the culture that produced it. What must students know about the unfamiliar worlds of such plays? If they are to grasp the importance of the hero's course of action and the significance of the consequences of it, they must have *some* understanding of *certain* beliefs, practices, and values of the relevant society. If, for instance, students are to grasp the terrible irony of Faustus' paltry use of the gift of magic, if they are to realize the horror of the finale, they must understand what giving one's soul to the Devil meant to a Renaissance man. The teacher's job, then, is to determine *what* cultural beliefs and values *each play* calls upon and help students to a feeling understanding of those. *Faustus,* for instance, does not require knowledge of English history or Marlowe or the Reformation or the history of drama in the Middle Ages. This play calls upon the Elizabethan audience's beliefs in God, the Devil, Heaven, Hell, repentance, forgiveness; it calls upon Elizabethans' attraction to magic, their familiarity with the conventions of morality plays, their readiness to ridicule churchmen and to applaud the fall of overreachers. These are, then, the customs of Renaissance culture students must understand if they are to experience *Faustus.*

And students need vital understandings—*living conceptions*—of the beliefs, practices, and values that are relevant to a play. A mass of "inky" facts will not do. But creating living conceptions of a culture is not an easy assignment. What might the teacher do to fulfill it? He might try something like this. Ask rhetorically: What sort of people saw Marlowe's *Doctor Faustus?* What did they believe in, fear, hope for, value? And then give a seemingly casual (actually well-devised) anecdotal answer—one that *brings to life* the popularity of Dr. Dee, the chiding of the clergy, the warnings to men puffed-up with superhuman desires; an answer that re-creates the scene at a morality play and retells the common versions of the Faustus' legend. The anecdotal answer should *dramatize* the beliefs, practices, and values of the society; it should *breathe life* into that world.[26] The answer must open students' minds to another possible world as vital as their own. That is all it must do, because once students' imaginations are open and alerted, the play can make these readers into the kind of audience its own particular world requires.

Students must, then, have a living conception of the world the play depends upon. Furthermore, they must *see* the theatre the play was shaped for. And they must see it not just once, but continually, all through their "performance" of the play. So, as the study of each of the three plays is about to begin, the class should examine a model or a plan of the relevant theatre—or preferably both. Then, students should be given the usual duplicated stage plan, and they should be called upon repeatedly during the discussion of the play to describe accurately the current stage picture and stage movements. This will keep students continually aware of the focus and fixity of the Greek play in the arena, of the panorama and mobility of the Renaissance drama on the multilevel, uncurtained stage, and of the realism and intimacy of the play in the three-walled "room." Continually visualizing the play on its stage will help students recognize how the stage determines certain features of the play and how the play takes advantage of the stage.

For such a course as this, all the plays chosen should be short; for no part of the course should be so protracted that students would forget that they are seeing, in sequence, *several* important forms of the drama. The plays we cited are of ideal length—in order, approximately thirty-five pages, sixty-five, and fifty-five. Using such choices as these, the whole course, including introductions to the worlds and the stages, discussions, and three in-class papers, would not take more than eighteen class periods. For such a course as this, the plays chosen should all be tragedies, not only because, as we have already mentioned, students themselves consider the tragic vision as highly relevant (inevitably they have to be *shown* that the comic is!), but also because the worlds of comedy are more idiosyncratic, more convention-ridden, hence, more difficult for noncontemporary, inexperienced readers to realize. The kind of second course we have just outlined is challenging enough.

So we would be trying to alleviate rather than increase its difficulty. And this would be reflected not only in our choice of plays but in our teaching methods. We would, for instance, probably supply students with guides and "advisories" for any play that uses language in abstruse or very complex ways; for example, Marlowe's *Doctor Faustus*. We would probably limit the topics for the critical papers to individual plays, reserving contrasts and comparisons among plays for in-class discussions. In other words, for average and able readers who are interested in contextual study in miniature, this course in basic forms of drama, though challenging, is a delightful one, and we would bend every effort to keep it so.

What follows such second courses as the four we have been outlining? If a class has been *moderately successful* in its study of two long plays or its comparative study of a novel and a play, the teacher might choose to go on to a study of modern tragedy. But if a class has performed *very competently*, then the teacher might consider the course in basic forms as a "right" next choice—or even the study of a Shakespearian tragedy. If students have been *successful* in a second course in modern tragedy, they might now study the three forms of drama, or a comedy, or a Shakespearian tragedy. Any one of these studies would be an appropriate successor to modern tragedy. Finally, if a class has done *good-to-excellent* work in a course on basic forms, it would most likely now study either a comedy or a Shakespearian tragedy.

We have belabored these alternatives for later courses in order to emphasize how many options the teacher has. If at the end of their second course, students cannot realistically move forward, they need not repeat. Mediocre readers can be doing something new without necessarily being confronted with something more difficult. Each class should have the kind of later course its play reading competence permits and its interests suggest.

Nothing is more ludicrous than a teacher's "lifting" unskilled play readers through a certain course or a certain play because that "comes next" or because students must be able to say they have "done" it. Shakespeare's plays are sometimes "covered" for no better reason than that students "expect them" or that "they *have* to have them! What's English without Shakespeare?" What's Shakespeare to a reader still insensitive to dramatic uses of language? A name to drop! They enjoy the comic scenes? the soliloquies? this or that character? these or those great lines? Perhaps they do, but parts are not wholes. And reading a play is reading a whole. We accept as one of the facts of life that, even after three courses in play reading, some students will still be unable to read—in any acceptable sense of the term—a Shakespearian play. But who those students are cannot be decided at the beginning of the first course or even at the end of it. Who those students are cannot be decided by a tag like "non-academic" or "unmotivated." The decision as to who may go on to the most advanced reading of plays—or poems or fiction—must be made on the basis of students' *reading competence* at the *close* of the second or even the third course.

We have detailed these alternatives for later courses to suggest, furthermore, that, even if students have the reading ability necessary to move on to advanced study, they need not; they may take another second course. It may be desirable, for instance, for one class to study both modern tragedy *and* the three basic forms of drama before it begins to read Shakespeare. And even if an able class does move on from a second course to an advanced one, it need not take the *same* advanced course that some comparable class is taking. It may be more interesting to one class to proceed through the basic forms to Shakespearian tragedy; to another, to look first at one view of life (in modern tragedy) and then at the complementary view (in dramatic comedy). Classes of equally able readers may differ sharply in their interests and in their working habits. And we can best keep our good readers "going" if we give them courses that are both worthy of them and engaging to them.

Now we turn to a discussion of the two kinds of advanced study we have been casually referring to—courses in comedy and in Shakespeare.

Advanced Play Reading: Comedy

As we have already intimated, comedy comes late in our scheme partly because of the nature of comedy and partly because of the nature of high school students. To people as vitally concerned as high school students are—overtly and covertly—about "man's condition," about their own role in "the group," and about the tension between being independent and belonging, the comic vision is just as relevant the tragic. We know this, but they do not. In fact, most students have serious misconceptions about the comic and mistaken expectations about comedy.

They identify the comic with the farcical, the burlesque, the roundly laughable, the "funny." In other words, their idea of the comic usually takes into account only the grossest level. The witty may be included, but the tense, the painful, the "dark," and the quietly amusing rarely are. High school students do not see the comic and the tragic as complementing, tempering, and enriching one another. They do in fact, like to have things unalloyed: white or black, true or false, good or evil, tragic or comic. They even like to write off the comic scenes in a tragedy as "relief." They resist seeing crucial connections between two things that are, in their minds, "poles apart," mutually exclusive, the valuable and the valueless.

Furthermore, students do not realize that comedy, as a literary mode, represents a certain vision of man: man in society, part of the social whole, belonging, losing himself in the group. And so students do not recognize this vision as complementary to that of tragedy: man isolated, asserting himself, finding himself as an individual. They do not see that these two visions together express man's paradoxical tension. *If* students understood what comedy expresses, they would see its relevance to their vital concerns.

They would also hold more valid expectations about its form. They would not anticipate that it would share the shape and the qualities of tragedy. They would not expect the primacy of plot, the "cause-consequence" unity, the dominating central character. If they understood what comedy expresses, they would anticipate instead a group of characters interacting in a social situation that shows what human beings are—greedy, self-centered, foolish; generous, disinterested, wise. They would expect the situation to be designed to display social qualities, to reveal follies, and to remedy them. They would not be so disappointed in comic plots or so confused by them. If they understood the intent of comedy, they would realize that whatever organization shows a folly most truly *is* a good plot.

Finally, if students understood what comedy expresses, they would realize how necessary it is for them to discover the values of the society being represented, to accept the norm suggested, and to evaluate the behavior in terms of it. They would not be judging the norm in terms of their own norms, or rejecting as absurd the beliefs, practices, and values of another era.

These misconceptions about the comic and about comedy are responsible for many of the negative reactions and some of the teaching difficulties that so often attend the study of comedy in high school. Since these mistaken notions are rather fixed assumptions, it seems best for the teacher to begin dissipating them gradually and unobtrusively during the first and second courses. How? Through directing students' attention to the *use* of comic elements wherever they occur. Through helping students notice the kinds of effects achieved by structures commonly used in comedy; for instance, the kind of unity achieved by a series of juxtaposed "typical instances." And, of course, through assigning a comedy as one of the plays to be read in the first or second course. Do not mistake this last means as the sine qua non. For even if students do not read any comedy during their first or second course, their attention to the other features we have mentioned will be most profitable. Attention to comic elements will make students aware of the staples of the comic: the perception of incongruity it always evokes, the criticism it always intends, and the seriousness it always involves. Attention to the structures commonly used in comedy will make students realize that "cause-consequence" is not the only way to unify incidents and that the mode of unifying a play suggests the intention of it. Attention to structures commonly used in comedy will, furthermore, make students see that seemingly useless and apparently unconnected elements have important functions and that the reader need only to observe the way these elements are structured—paralleled, juxtaposed—to discover what their functions are. Students' attention to such features as we have listed will preclude their selling the comic short and their rejecting unfamiliar plotting and characterization as "ridiculous," "confusing," and "stupid."

Whatever particular shape we gave this advanced course in comedy, we would utilize immediately all that the students' previous play reading had explicitly or implicitly taught them about the comic or comedy. The "advisory" they would receive for their independent reading of the first comedy would, for instance, suggest that they prepare to show how the unifying principle used in the play organizes *all the incidents* of it. The "advisory" would suggest that they determine the function of certain characters ("yardstick" characters and caricatures) and prepare to say why these characters *must* be as they are to achieve their purpose. The "advisory" would ask students to notice two bits of dialogue—one broadly funny, one generously critical, say—and be prepared to point out in what sense both passages could be called "comic." Such an "advisory" would at once reactivate students' previous learnings about comedy and prevent "spontaneous recovery" of their old reactions to it.

Now, what shape might we give such a course?

If the class has read *no* comedy earlier, then perhaps a study of two modern comedies would make a "right" beginning. We might choose two gentle semi-philosophical plays, like Thornton Wilder's *Our Town* and William Saroyan's *The Human Comedy;* or two unusual love stories, like Lorraine Hansberry's *A Raisin in the Sun* and Emlyn Williams' *The Corn Is Green;* or two torrents of wit and rhetoric—George Bernard Shaw's *Pygmalion* and his *The Devil's Disciple.* No marital intrigue comedies? No. In the usual high school class, such plays do not "move." But for that rare group of sophisticated cosmopolites that may one day come in the door, why not Noel Coward's hilarious *Private Lives* and Somerset Maugham's urbane *The Constant Wife?*

Students *beginning* the reading of dramatic comedy should not have the added burden of understanding an alien world and of recognizing the significance of some foible peculiar to a certain time and place. Consequently, all of the comedies we have just cited represent relatively universal follies. And all but *The Devil's Disciple* represent relatively familiar worlds. Beginning readers could fairly easily enter the worlds of these comedies, recognize the norms, and understand how the behaviors of the characters violate or express the norms. These students could, therefore, spend their energies "performing" the plays, perceiving the structures, and developing some initial ideas about the nature and function of comedy.

If the students *have read* a comedy at the end of the first course or during the second, then, given the preparation the world of the play requires, they might now read such an early twentieth-century play as J. M. Synge's *The Playboy of the Western World,* such nineteenth-century comedies as Chekov's *Uncle Vanya* or *The Cherry Orchard,* such eighteenth-century comedies as Oliver Goldsmith's *She Stoops to Conquer* and Richard Sheridan's *The Rivals,* such seventeenth-century comedies as Ben Jonson's *The Alchemist* and *Volpone,* and of course, such Shakespearian comedies as *The Merchant of Venice* and *Twelfth Night.* The teacher might choose to pair "love-and-marriage" comedies of two periods to highlight the constants and the variables in the renderings. He might choose to contrast a romantic with a realistic comedy: a Shakespeare with a Jonson. He might wish to juxtapose the darkly comic endings of two worlds: Chekov's *The Cherry Orchard* and Sean O'Casey's *Juno and the Paycock.*

When the teacher is deciding what noncontemporary comedies he will teach, he must first consider what period and what plays he himself relates to best—which eras he "lives in" (not knows the most facts about), which comedies he as a reader "performs" and responds to most satisfactorily. For he must build the world of the play for students; and he must, when needed, *re-create a moment* to help students evoke its effect. And it is re-creating moments, not questioning about them, that best helps students grasp *comic* effects. When the teacher has decided which comedies he experiences most fully, then he must decide which of those plays his particular class would be most able to hear, see, and feel—without explanation. (*Explanation* is the death blow to comic effects.) To enjoy a comedy, students must be able to respond virtually on their own to the repartee and the double entendres; they must be able to see largely without help the coincidences, the "unmaskings," the revelatory idiosyncracies. If such effects have to be explained, they are indeed "explained away." They must "break over" the play reader with all the shock, surprise, and sudden revelation that the text gives them. A comedy must make at least its initial impact freely, freshly, and directly. Consequently, it is crucial for the teacher to choose the "right" play for each class and to give students the kind of vital, relevant preparation for reading it we described earlier in "Three Forms of the Drama."

Becoming the producer and the audience that a period comedy requires is one of the greatest challenges a reader faces. That is why we place the study of noncontemporary comedy at the close of our sequence of play reading; that is why we reserve this kind of course for the most sensitive student-readers. For even they will need all the play reading skill they have developed to perform the "feats of language" that re-creating such comedies requires.

Advanced Play Reading: Shakespeare

It would seem as if no one should ever have to justify making Shakespeare's plays the capstone of a study in reading plays. The texts so obviously require experienced readers. Consider the demands the plays make on a reader. Usually, they require knowledge not only of the Elizabethans' social, political, and religious mores, but also of their "world picture"—their assumptions about the harmony of God, macrocosm, and microcosm. Usually, they require a knowledge of Elizabethan dramatic conventions; always, they demand an ability to "produce" and perceive many rapidly changing scenes and a large, complex stage picture; always, they demand an ability to imagine *this* play on a panoramic stage. The plays require a reader who can discover and hold *as a whole* a complex structure of many scenes interrelated by many designs, a reader able to respond sensitively to the often richly exploited poetic language of Shakespeare's dialogue, a reader who can perceive, *in the dialogue,* the directions for a performance—for appropriate movements, gestures, tones.

Just this brief assessment of what is required of the reader of Shakespeare suggests why only those students who have already learned to read plays *and* poems adequately should be reading Shakespeare. Only they can. Just witness a class studying Shakespeare *without* those skills! The students are hacking through a tangle of words to eke out the prose sense; or they are having the play translated to them; or they are enjoying the teaching enjoying his reading of the lines; or they are studying the great moments and running a plot line between them. Memories of such classroom scenes as these sober us when we long to overreach. They boldly remind us that there's more than a knowledge of sixteenth-century archaisms between a reader and the experience of a Shakespearian play.[27]

Some students are ready for Shakespeare at the end of their second course in reading plays, some at the end of their third. Where might such students begin? If they have had no previous reading of Elizabethan drama, they probably should begin with a reading of *Julius Caesar.* But if they have studied *Doctor Faustus,* for instance, perhaps in the course like "Three Forms of the Drama," they should probably start with *Romeo and Juliet* or *Macbeth.* If their initial study is successful, the students might go on to read *Antony and Cleopatra, King Lear,* or, of course, *Hamlet*—as their ability, interest, and time permit.

Entrée to Shakespeare: *Julius Caesar*

We realize that suggesting this sequence for the reading of Shakespeare is not saying anything very new. The sequence is customary. But why should it be? If we look closely at the plays, we see that they themselves recommend it. And what we are now going to do is examine the structure, the language, and the world of *Julius Caesar* to show on what grounds this play recommends itself as a "right" introduction to Shakespeare.

All of this play's structural designs are relatively simple. The dramatic plot, for instance, is a clearly defined sequence of events that moves uninterruptedly from opening to logical conclusion. All scenes seem essential; and the functions of all of them are fairly apparent to an attentive reader. He readily sees how such parallels as the Portia-Brutus and the Calpurnia-Caesar scenes move the main action forward crucially. And he can perceive the vital role played by such seemingly nonessential moments as Act II, Scenes iii and iv, Act IV, Scenes i and ii, and Act V, Scenes ii and iv. Nothing impedes the flow of events. There are no elaborate parallel plots as in *King Lear,* no drastic shifts from the dramatic to the lyrical as in *Romeo and Juliet,* no long soliloquies as in *Hamlet.*

Even the *shape* of the dramatic plot is simple, neat, and clear. The sequence of events is divided into two equal parts, with the turning point exactly in the middle of the play. The events of the first half of the play render the rise of the conspiracy; those of the last half, the fall. The moment of triumph is truly a moment—between the last word of Caesar and the first of Antony's servant. And this pyramidal shape of events is supported precisely by the emotional rhythm that structures the audience's feeling-response to the play. The audience's involvement rises—stimulated by increasingly frequent anxieties—to a crescendo and falls—depressed by lessening hopes—to the conclusion. Finally, the designs that highlight the significance of the events of the dramatic plot are unobtrusive, uncomplicated, and relatively few. Recall, for instance, such designs as the incremental recurrence of the populace, the sequence of portents, the "sacrifice-hunt" and the "stand-fall" metaphors, and the chaining of words like "honor" and word groups like "sleeping-waking" and "face, show, appearance." Everything about the structure of *Julius Caesar* impresses us with its distinctness, economy, fusion, completeness.

The language of the play, too, creates the impression of clarity, necessity, spareness. There is, as Charney says, a "deliberate limiting of imaginative resources." We do not need statistics to realize how restricted the vocabulary is, how simple the diction. The words are stark, the imagery limited, the references and the figures few, and the dominant trope is not the expressive metaphor but the well-defined simile with its sharply curtailed suggestiveness. The syntax is equally classical. In *Julius Caesar* there is no verbal or syntactic luxuriance, no piling of metaphor upon metaphor, clause on clause.[28] As Bradley says, there seems to be "a deliberate endeavor after a dignified and unadorned simplicity—a Roman simplicity perhaps."[29]

By now, it may sound as if *Julius Caesar* is an ideal first reading in Shakespeare because its structure and its language offer students no challenges at all. But nothing could be further from the truth. Spare as the structure of *Julius Caesar* is, it is rich in implication. And the reader must discover its oppositions, its ambiguities, and its ironies if he is to have the experience of this play. He must see that the neat, regular, "pointed arch" of the dramatic plot—the Brutus "arch"—implies an opposite "arch"—the Caesar "arch." He must realize that if the first half of the play reveals the triumph of public interest over private, the last half discloses the reverse. He must recognize that the events of the play suggest a movement from disorder to order to disorder—only if they are viewed from the "Brutus" perspective; from the "Caesar" perspective, they suggest the contrary. The reader must notice the paradoxes: sacrifice is slaughter; rising is falling; falling, rising. He must see that things imply their opposites. Public cannot be wrenched from private, private from public. The reader must recognize that all the designs reinforce the duality, ambiguity, and irony of events. In order to respond to *Julius Caesar*, then, the reader must infer what the *simple* elements in the *clear* structure of the play are implying.

Spare as the language of this play is, it is, like the simple structure, richly revelatory. And the reader who would grasp the ambiguity in the characters must be continually alert and responsive to the load of suggestion in ordinary words, to the crucial ironies in plain speeches, and to the literal-figurative dualisms. He must be aware of how characters' patterns of syntax, modes of argument, public and private speech—indeed, how the terms in which *they* see things (Brutus' "adder," Caesar's "northern star," Casca's "wenches," Cassius' "lion in the Capitol")—reveal their intentions, values, fears, conflicts. In any literary work where much is being effected by little, everything counts—heavily.

Finally, in *Julius Caesar* as in other plays where verbal language is spare, the language of gesture is speaking significantly. It is speaking through positions and movements, ritualistic gestures, significant dress, suggestive tableaux. If the reader is to "hear" this language and grasp its meanings, his visualizing must be very particular, very precise. It is not enough that he visualizes a certain action; he must imagine *how* the gesture is done, *how* the posture is taken, given this character in this circumstance. Only to such a reader will the language of gesture prove enlightening.

Since the structure and the language of *Julius Caesar* are at once comparatively simple and richly suggestive, readers of this play can have both an easy access to Shakespeare and an initial experience with the challenges of his work. And since the reading of this play will tax and fruitfully extend the skills students bring, it will prepare them for the more complex structure and richer language of other Shakespeare plays. Because of what *Julius Caesar* as a work of dramatic literature offers beginning readers and because of what it asks of them, it is a good choice for a first reading in Shakespeare.

Its world also recommends it—though a sixteenth-century play about the first century B.C. may, at first, seem doubly unfamiliar. The world of *Julius Caesar* is a world of Roman beliefs, practices, and values. It is a secular world: there is a moral order but no religious sanction; there is evil, but it is not sin; there is justice and retribution, but it is not Christian punishment. The world of *Julius Caesar* is a world of Roman virtue and valor. Murder *may be* justifiable; suicide *is* the honorable alternative to captivity. The world of *Caesar* is a place where, for some, portents and supernatural elements have significance.

Is such a world as this familiar to most high school students? With one exception, yes. A secular world is familiar enough to most of them. So are the various attitudes toward the supernatural. And, in any case, since the supernatural elements *never determine* anything in the play, readers do not have to believe in them as agents. They *may* consider these elements as symbols of the moral events they are related to, but they need not even do that.[30] Caesar's ghost, for instance, *may* be thought of as the unquiet soul, or *may* be considered the external embodiment of Brutus' guilt—a projection seen and heard only by the man haunted all through the scene by his disillusion, by his awareness of the futile consequences of his earlier act.

The only custom that readers must understand and accept is the moral attitude the Romans take toward suicide. And this play makes clear that for these Romans, at least, suicide is not a reflex response; for the men who commit it, life has already lost all value. If students do not understand and accept the play's attitude toward suicide, these deaths might puzzle them, or might strike them as cheap dramatic resolutions, or might simply attract undue attention. But students' failure to accept this or any other unfamiliar element in this play would not crucially affect their experience of the play. For the little in the world of *Julius Caesar* that is unfamiliar is not of the essence. Ironically, the problem in teaching this play is caused not by students' unfamiliarity with its Roman world, but rather by their familiarity with twentieth-century power struggles and their enthusiasm for democratic revolution. Their unwarranted analogies and biased sympathies sometimes lead students to misconstrue the nature of the conflict *this play* renders, to overlook the complexity of the characters, and to miss the ambiguity of the experience. In teaching *Julius Caesar* we must work just a little harder to make the reader let the play control what he brings.

In summary, then, we can say that if *Julius Caesar* were not, customarily, the first Shakespeare play, we would choose it anyway. Our assessment of the structure of the play, of its language, and of its world tells why. Now let us see how we might teach the play so as to capitalize on the advantages and the challenges we have been showing it offers.

A Teaching of *Julius Caesar*

Since students who would be reading *Julius Caesar* (or any other Shakespearian play) would, we are assuming, have the knowledge and skills needed to respond adequately to it *as a play*, this study can rightly have a more specialized focus, one that will be a fruitful center of attention for this play and useful preparation for the reading of other Shakespeare plays. Students might, for instance, study *Julius Caesar* as a Shakespearian tragedy. Or they might uncover the interrelationships among its dualities. Or they might concentrate on the modes and the effects of Shakespeare's characterization. Or they might investigate the reasons for the ambiguity of their experience of the play. The aim we have chosen for our teaching of the play fuses the last two: we would be trying to help students see how the moral complexity of the characters evokes both the audience's ambivalent responses to the events and its ambiguous experience of the play. To achieve this aim, students must learn to respond sensitively to the means of characterization that Shakespeare uses, to the effects he thereby creates, and to the functions of these effects. What better introduction to later, greater Shakespeare could students have?

Here is a scheme for achieving our aim—in the classroom.

The study of the play would probably begin on a Wednesday with a brief conjuring up of images of an Elizabethan audience entering the theatre. For our data we would rely on such materials as the first four chapters of Alfred Harbage's *Shakespeare's Audience*[31] and on Thomas Dekker's "How a Gallant Should Behave Himself in a Playhouse."[32] Our presentation would probably be something like the running commentary of a human-interest reporter "covering" the audience as it moves from the quays to and through the entrance and into place in the theatre. This commentary would lead us very naturally to our initial discussion of the stage and of Elizabethan stage conventions.

We would show students, on a Vu-graph if possible, drawings of the stage—as the audience saw it when it entered the theatre. And using the first Scene of *Julius Caesar*, the Caesar-Antony scene in Act II, Scene i, and the mistake of Pindarus in Act V, Scene iii, we would specifically illustrate the opportunities afforded by the various features of the stage—for instance, by the several levels, the clear upstage and downstage, by the curtains, windows, and, of course, by the shape of the platform and of the theatre. Furthermore, using the public and private scenes of Caesar and Brutus, we would graphically suggest how the stage picture, the costumes, the artifacts, postures, and positions work to signify characters' relationships and roles, and, hence, their precedence, commitments, and obligations. Still further, anticipating questions about the staging of the stormy night in Act I, Scene iii, we would stress that descriptions of weather, seasons, and such were not poor substitutions for the stage properties and the scenery that the Elizabethans did not have. Rather, these descriptions were intended to make the audience just *glimpse* the image and *focus on* its significance. When images are being used in this way, a piece of scenery or even a graphic, concrete picturing of a setting would distract the audience from the main business of perceiving the significance. In this initial discussion, we would be trying to acquaint students with Elizabethan stage conventions—what Shakespeare's audience "took" for what, and we would be trying to suggest how costumes, stances, and stage pictures significantly complement and emphasize what the words of the play say and imply—we would be doing this, of course, to suggest to students how they should produce *Julius Caesar* in those theatres in their heads.

After our running commentary had evoked useful images of the theatergoers and the stage, and useful understandings of the conventions, we would ask *rhetorically* what Shakespeare's audience probably brought to a performance of *Julius Caesar*. We would suggest three things: a Renaissance man's great interest in things classical, a knowledge of the assassination of Caesar and a sense of its significance, a diversity of opinions about the character of Caesar and that of Brutus and about the justification for the assassination.[33]

If we had decided to brief students on the secular society of *Julius Caesar* or on specific customs or moral attitudes of that society, we would do it now as we described the audience's interest in and knowledge about the classical world. We would decide what information about customs *the particular class* needed, and we would simply present that information as some of the "things" that Shakespeare's audience "knew" about the Roman world. A ruse? Perhaps. But this is an unembarrassing way of widening some students' horizons without challenging their religious assumptions. And it is an unobtrusive way of conveying necessary data to others without precipitating irrelevant debate on the morality of suicide.

If we had decided to brief students on Caesar's "story," we would do it now, as we discussed the audience's knowledge of Caesar's assassination. We would interpolate a brief factual account of just that part of Caesar's story that the play deals with. We would limit the account for two reasons. In some classes a detailed account of the history of Caesar—including, say, passages from Plutarch that record events that preceded or followed the events of the play— would invite students to bring to their interpretation of the play information the play does not ask for. For instance, if some students knew the earlier history of Caesar, they would take annoyed exception to Brutus' soliloquy; they would say, "Brutus *does* have evidence of Caesar's public tyranny. He doesn't have to 'may' and 'might.'" And *they* would not answer this exception by asking, as Coleridge did, what kind of man Shakespeare means *his* Brutus to be.

In some classes a detailed account of the history of Rome that followed Brutus' defeat would invite students to interpret Brutus' act, not in terms of what is expressed or implied *within* the play, but in terms of remote consequences that, though historically significant, are irrelevant to this play. The experience of the theatre- or the reading-audience is one of watching public men with particular flaws making unwise choices that adversely affect their own lives and their state. The audience's concern is with enacted events: with the characters of Caesar and Brutus, of Cassius and Antony as *the play* reveals them, with the justice of the assassination, and with the consequences of the act as *the play* discloses them. The audience's concern is with the universality of *the experience of the play* —not with the historical significance of the event represented. Shakespeare's audience came to hear and see *his* rendering of the "Caesar story" — and, in that, our students are one with them, for that is what they come for, too.

This, then, would be the style of our first day on *Julius Caesar*. We would count the day a success only if our running commentary was, throughout, informative, authentic, natural, and engaging. As an assignment, we would ask the class to read carefully Act I, Scene i, and be able to describe in detail a performance of it, including not only the tones, the pace, and the gestures but also the stage picture at various points in the Scene.[34] We would distribute duplicated stage plans (the same drawing that we projected that day) to help students visualize the movements of characters and the configurations of groups.

Class on Thursday would be given over to a discussion of the performing of the first Scene. We would want to be sure that students are able to infer from Shakespeare's dialogue the clues to performance and that all are hearing and seeing the play on Shakespeare's stage. And we would want to remind all that close *play* reading *is* expected throughout. During this discussion, we would ask, as needed, about the functions of this exposition. We would probably have to call students' attention to the way this Scene reveals the apparent fickleness of the people and to the way it shows how emotive persuasion affects them. We would probably have to help students see how the exposition reveals the tribunes' complex attitudes toward Caesar and how it evokes in us an uncertainty about the characters' motives: Are the people pro-Caesar? or just pro-holiday? Close attention to the functions of the exposition will help students to discover at the very outset the ironies and the ambiguities in the affairs before them—and this will preclude their developing a black-white, wrong-right, good-bad mind set. To conclude the discussion of the first Scene, we would question briefly about the exact meaning of the final metaphor. And, with that, we would assign the reading of the remainder of the play to be completed *by* Monday.

To help students with their independent reading of the play, we would provide an "advisory" which would, of course, focus on dialogue and structure but would do so in such a way as to suggest to students the main aim of this study. The annotations and the questions would help them notice, for instance, how the qualities of a character's language—his diction, images, syntax—suggest his moral complexity and how the moral complexity of a character who is falling, or rising, evokes ambivalent responses to the event. So while students are getting a "hold" on the whole play, they will be moving into position for the close study of characterization that will be the main concern of their discussions of the play.

To be concrete, here is the first section (Act I, Scenes ii and iii) of the kind of "advisory" we would distribute.

ADVISORY FOR *Julius Caesar*

The following questions and directives are to help you with your reading of the remainder of the play. But rather than looking at the advisory first, why not read an act and then look. In that way, you can see how well you are doing "on your own" and know whether or not you need to alter your mode of reading.

Do not write formal answers to the questions. You might, however, find it valuable to make notations in response to them. We shall be asking some of the questions during our intensive discussion of the whole play on Monday and Tuesday. We shall be asking others during our close study of each act next week.

In this advisory, we have used the word "Scene" and the word "scene." The first refers to the formal division of the act-structure as the text of the play designates it; the second refers to a part of a play during which an unchanging group of characters occupies the stage—when someone enters or someone exits a new scene begins. That, of course, is the way we have been using "scene" all through our study of plays. A "Scene" is usually made up of many "scenes."

This advisory begins with what Scene i made us anticipate — the entrance of Caesar.

Act I, Scene ii

LINES 1–24 There are two episodes in this first scene. Notice who takes part in each, what each is about, what attitudes are expressed in each *toward* Caesar and *by* Caesar.

Why are these episodes juxtaposed? (For instance, what manner of man does each show Caesar to be? What ironies does the juxtaposition express?)

What are the functions of this entire little scene? (Among other things: What does it cause Caesar to do? allow Caesar to do? Does this scene relate in any way to the previous one [Scene i, 66–80]?)

LINES 25–177 Why does the offering of the coronet take place off-stage?

How would you describe the pattern of "the temptation" (lines 32–161)? (For instance, how does Cassius order his "arguments"? How do his syntax and his diction change? What postures, gestures, pitches is he using in lines 48–51? in lines 58–60? 80–81? 115–116? 135–136? and 153–157?)

For what reasons does "the temptation" take the pattern it does? [We use the phrase "For what reasons" rather than "why" because we do not want students to be satisfied with a single reason. And we shall not be there to urge them on. The wording of out-of-class assignments must always be just that much more precise.]

LINES 178–214 With your stage plan before you, decide how this scene would be staged.

At line 190 we expect a Casca-Cassius-Brutus dialogue. Why does the Caesar-Antony scene occur here? How does it relate to the Cassius-Brutus scene that precedes it? to the scene that follows it (lines 215–298)?

LINES 215–298 For what reasons does Casca tell "what had chanc'd" the *way* he does? (Among other things: What sort of person is Casca? What reveals his attitude toward Cassius? toward Brutus? What impression of Caesar is he trying to give?)

LINES 299–326 Compare lines 307–310 with lines 162–174. Specifically, what accounts for the difference in these responses?

And finally: Compare the last speech in Scene i with the last speech in Scene ii to see the progress of the "underground."

Act I, Scene iii

Casca could have given his report of the "wonders" of the night to Cassius. What, then, is gained by the Casca-Cicero scene? Why not begin this Scene at line 41?

What scene does the Casca-Cassius scene (lines 41–120) recall? In what respects are the scenes alike? Different? What is revealed by the comparison of these two scenes?

In Cassius' speech, lines 121–130, we notice the joining "honourable-dangerous." Think of the contexts these words have been used in. What is the significance of Cassius' joining them in this speech? What is the significance of his applying the word to "consequence," rather than "enterprise"?

What is the function of the Cinna "moment"?

And, finally: Everyone in Scene iii makes some response to the storm. Notice their responses and decide on the functions of the storm.

Throughout Act I

We notice the gradual building up of a certain group of words— "show," "favour," "face," "mirror," "countenance," "looks." How are all these words related in the play? What purpose(s) does this design serve?

Students would begin their reading of the play on Thursday night. The class period on Friday would be given over to independent reading. But during the first *ten minutes*, we would ask some questions on the dialogue and the structure of Act I—probably a few from the advisory and a few others—just to make clear (again) that the play is to be read *closely as a play*.

The class work on Monday and Tuesday would consist of an intensive questioning on dialogue and structure—planned especially to reveal the shape of the dramatic plot, the presence and role of supporting structures, and the emotional rhythm of the play. The division of our discussion would highlight the "pointed arch" of the play. On Monday, we would concentrate on the rise of the conspiracy, ending the discussion at the conclusion of the moment of glory (Act III, Scene i, line 121); on Tuesday, we would focus on the fall. We would probably select our questions from the advisory— about twelve to fifteen for each day—and reword them so that they would fit gracefully into the sequence for the day. (We mention rewording because it is so disappointing to have good questions fare badly only because, taken out of their original contexts, they are so unconnected that students cannot readily follow.)

On Wednesday, we would begin the close study of the play. We would be aiming, as we said earlier, to help students see how the moral complexity of the characters evokes from an audience both an ambivalent response to the events and an ambiguous experience of the whole. We would anticipate spending approximately two class periods on each act. This time schedule would include the writing of two short, in-class, critical papers, one perhaps at the end of the study of Act I, the other, at the close of the discussion of Act IV. On the day prior to the study of each act, we would distribute duplicated copies of some sort of guide to direct students' second reading of the act. We say "some sort" because certain classes might need a set of rather specific questions for Act I, just several general questions for Acts II and III, and only a list of passages to note for the final acts. Other classes might require specific questions for a longer time, or not at all. Each class' performance will suggest what sort of guide is needed at successive points.

Here is the kind of guide that we, being initially cautious, would probably distribute on Tuesday to direct students' second reading of Act I.

THE SECOND READING

From your first reading of *Julius Caesar*, you know that the consequences of Caesar's assassination were bad, both for the conspirators and for Rome. But was the assassination, nonetheless, a morally right act? What manner of man was Caesar—really?

From your first reading of the play, you know that Brutus and Cassius fall and Antony rises. But *why* do they fall? *Why* does he rise? *All things considered*, what kind of person is Brutus? Cassius? Antony? How do their characters affect their fortunes? How do their characters affect *our* responses to their fortunes?

From your first reading of the play, you know that Brutus feared that Caesar would change when he became king. Does anyone in the play *really* change when he comes to power? You know, too, that Brutus feared Caesar would "disjoin remorse from power." Does anyone in the play not "abuse greatness"?

These are the kinds of general questions you will be discovering answers to through your second reading of *Julius Caesar*. Answers to such questions as these will help you decide what kinds of men these are, how you should take their actions, and what you should "make of" the experience of this play.

Act I

Read Act I again. *Then,* make *notes* in answer to the following questions. Tomorrow, and Thursday, we shall be discussing these and other related questions. On Thursday, there will be a graded in-class critical exercise.

SCENE II   1. For what reasons does Caesar stop when he is called? For what reasons does he dismiss the Soothsayer? [Answering these questions will make students aware of many kinds of reasons—obvious and obscure, apparent and real—and of the fact that a person may have several *real* reasons for doing an act, and of these, some may be *real public* reasons; others *real private* reasons. Answering these questions will show students that all kinds of reasons must be taken into account when they are deciding what manner of man a character is.]

2. At what point in the "temptation scene" (lines 25–177) do *you* first suspect Cassius' motives for remaining behind with Brutus? What are your grounds for suspecting? [We would expect students to cite, among other things, the provocative words Cassius chooses to evoke a response in Brutus: not only such inciting words as "stubborn," and "strange," but also such evasive "vagueries" as "thoughts of great value, worthy cogitations."]

What, in Brutus' speeches (lines 28–53) suggests *why he* does not suspect?

How do you know that his response (lines 64–65) and his question (lines 83–84) are sincere?

For what reasons is Cassius opposed to Caesar? Consider both overt and underlying reasons and distinguish between Cassius' own reasons and those he includes in order to appeal to Brutus.

For what reasons—overt and underlying—is Brutus opposed to Caesar? Notice what does not move Brutus, what does move him, and why.

What differences between the two men do their reasons reveal? Do the men recognize these differences?

Now that you see their reasons—and the reasons for their reasons, what is your reaction to their opposition to Caesar?

3. Cassius' portrait of Caesar reveals Cassius. Does it modify your view of Caesar?

How right is Caesar about Cassius (lines 192–214)? What does the Caesar-Antony dialogue reveal about Caesar? about Antony? about Brutus?

4. Do the responses of Brutus and Cassius in the Casca scene reinforce, qualify, or reverse the personalities they revealed in the "temptation scene"? *For instance*, is Cassius' question (line 226) sincere? Is Brutus' (line 228)? Notice the content and the tone of Cassius' "But soft, I pray you. What, did Caesar swound?" (line 253) and of Brutus' " 'Tis very like. He hath the falling sickness." (line 256)

Casca's portrait of Caesar reveals Casca. Does it modify your view of Caesar? Of the people?

Why does Brutus want to know why Caesar looks so "sad"? Why *does* Caesar look "sad"?

5. How would Cassius' final speech in Scene ii be performed?

To what extent does Cassius understand Brutus?

Has Brutus been "seduc'd"? What exactly *has* happened to Brutus in this scene?

What plan of action does Cassius' final metaphor suggest? Are his motives purely personal?

Are we supposed to despise Cassius? approve Brutus? And how should we respond to Caesar?

SCENE III 1. Through your work on the advisory, you have discovered how Cassius' temptation of Casca resembles and differs from his temptation of Brutus. You have seen how Cassius utilizes Casca's reaction to the storm as earlier he utilized Brutus' response to the shout of the offstage crowd. You have seen how Cassius carefully fits the content and the form of his temptation to his immediate victim.

To what in Brutus did Cassius try to appeal? To what in Casca?

In general, Brutus' responses made Cassius' "work" easy. Casca's responses now facilitate, now complicate it. How? Why? What technique finally "conquers" Casca?

This scene surely reveals Casca. Does it modify your view of Cassius in any way? Does Cassius' treatment of Caesar affect your view of Caesar in any way? How do the various aspects of Casca's "temptation"—the content, the method, his response, and his "fall"—emphasize Brutus' perfections and his defects?

2. Lines 153–160 make the transition to Scene iv—Brutus in his orchard. Many sets of lines would have done that admirably. But these lines have other functions as well. What insight into the conspirators do they give us? What insight into *their* real view of the conspiracy? While the conspirators extol Brutus' virtue, what fault in his character do they imply? Has Brutus ever *shown* this fault? In what way is his fault an advantage to the conspirators? Why does he have this fault?

For the in-class critical paper to conclude students' discussion of Act I, we would assign some topic that relates to the way that a character's personality influences his response to events. This, indeed, allows us a broad leeway. The facet of this general area that we would probably choose is how a character's personality—the whole complex of his qualities—affects his *perception* of events. And here is that facet shaped into a specific topic, a topic "just about right" for our beginning readers of Shakespeare:

About various men's responses to the storm, Cicero says: ". . . men may construe things after their fashion/Clean from the purpose of the things themselves."

We recognize that his statement applies to more than men's interpretations of the storm. What other "things" in Act I have men, construing according to their own personalities, misconstrued the truth of—fully or partially?

Choose two misinterpretations that seem crucial to you, and in a short paper, show how you know they *are* misconstructions, how the characters' personalities caused these misconstructions, and why these misinterpretations seem, to you, crucial.

Throughout the study of the remaining four acts, we would continue to call students' attention to Shakespeare's various modes of characterization, especially to the one students repeatedly overlook— his use of a character's comment on another to inadvertently expose the speaker. We would continue, too, to help students see how the successive interactions among characters substantiate and modify the audience's initial impressions of the personalities of the four main characters—and how these interactions gradually disclose four men of qualified virtues and noble flaws, men whose traits are at war. We would continue to help students perceive the mixed motivations men can have, the opposed qualities they can reconcile, the evil a man's self-assured virtue can engender, the good his brave ruthlessness evokes.

If students are urged to see at every point the many facets of a character's personality, they are less likely to develop for each character that "least common denominator" that so determines a reader's expectations that he is bound to oversimplify his interpretations. Who considers Brutus' speech an "appeal to reason"? "poor politics"? Readers who have already "tagged" him. Who is surprised when Brutus salutes Cassius as "last of the Romans"? Readers who have identified Cassius with the inglorious evil of envy. Who mistakes Antony's moderate final appraisal of Brutus for a glowing tribute? Readers who have equated Brutus with unparalleled nobility.

When a reader does not see the complexities in characters, it is easy for him to make a clear-cut response to events. A reader's judgment pauses, his response becomes ambivalent *only* when he knows the characters involved, only when he perceives the apparent and real motives of all concerned—only when, in short, he sees the "much that can be said on both sides." Such a reader does not simplify Cassius to "the assassin" and Caesar to "the assassinated"; he does not think in terms of the envious killing the ambitious. He perceives an assassin who is at once a brilliant observer of human nature, an exemplar of Roman bravery, a shrewd tempter, a devoted friend, a man fired both by envy and a love of personal freedom, an esteemed general. The reader who "sees all" perceives a victim who is at once a devoted ruler, a physically ill man, a pompous figure enamoured of his public image, a prey to flattery and fear, an esteemed friend, a shrewd leader. And this perceptive reader thinks of such an assassin and such a victim not as contending "still-lifes," but as living opponents in a vital political atmosphere. When a reader sees characters totally, his judgment pauses: how should he "take" the events?

Throughout the study of the remaining four acts of *Julius Caesar*, we would continue to help students see characters and events fully and thereby discover how "seeing all" frustrates simple interpretations.

NOTES

1. For a discussion that contrasts the play with the film, see Alan Thompson, *The Anatomy of Drama* (Berkeley: The University of California Press, 1942), pp. 15–40.

2. Throughout this discussion I have depended heavily on J. L. Styan, *The Elements of Drama* (Cambridge, England: Cambridge University Press, 1960), pp. 1–63. For a similar view, see Henri Ghéon, "The Conditions of Dramatic Art," p. 34, in Robert W. Corrigan and James L. Rosenberg, *The Context and Craft of Drama* (San Francisco: Chandler Publishing Company, 1964).

3. Two articles that describe other teachers' approaches to reading plays as plays are John Sweet, "Notes on the Teaching of Drama," *EJ*, 53

(Nov. 1964), pp. 589–591, and Robert C. Lambert, "Pitfalls in Reading Drama," *EJ, 53* (Nov. 1964), pp. 592 ff.

4. As Alan Downer says in *The Art of the Play* (New York: Henry Holt and Co., Inc., 1955), pp. 142, 143: ". . . the dramatic aspect of an action . . . insists not upon the end of the action ('Kills him'), but upon the way it is done." ". . . the actor has frequently to determine for himself how the author visualized the action. His understanding of his character and the intention of the play will be his trustworthy guides. But very often the playwright is most specific about the effect he intends, even though he may not employ explanatory stage directions." He is "specific" by having created a certain character who would act in a certain way. That is what the reader must realize—this character in this situation: how would *he* walk downstairs? how would *he* die?

For pictures that can be projected to help students understand how an actor's pose and his position on the stage define a character's personality, see J. L. Styan, *The Dramatic Experience* (Cambridge, England: Cambridge University Press, 1965), p. 28, and John Gassner, *Producing the Play* (New York: The Dryden Press, 1953), pp. 125, 167, 429. Gassner's omnibus also offers other illustrations that are very useful in helping students visualize plays on the stage. For instance, for pictures that show settings used for multiple levels of action and simultaneous presentation of interior and exterior scenes, see pp. 68–69, 241, 352–353; for sets that suggest relations, see p. 232; and for scene designs that will help students work on their own stage plans, see p. 103.

5. For discussion of different kinds of unifying principles in plots, see Elder Olson, *Tragedy and the Theory of Drama* (Detroit: Wayne State University Press, 1961), pp. 45–47.

6. These two plays, as well as almost all we cite in this section, are readily available, either individually or in anthologies, in inexpensive paperback editions. These two plays are in Bennett Cerf and Van H. Cartmell (eds.), *24 Favorite One-Act Plays*, A Dolphin Paperback (Garden City, N. Y.: Doubleday & Co., Inc., 1963).

7. Remember: students may use a certain dialect themselves, but that does not mean that they can read it easily!

8. Our list of plays does not, however, include any works that represent the *usual* versions of adult-adolescent conflicts or any that feature the teen-age dating syndrome. In bypassing this body of plays, we have lost little of value—most of these plays are obviously sentimental, downright saccharine, and psychologically untrue. In bypassing them, we have avoided inviting irrelevant responses and confusions of literature and life. For when some beginners re-create such a world and find it highly familiar to them, they begin to assume either that the play *should* correspond to their own quotidian reality—or that it does. Such responses make valid perception of a play—or any other work—impossible.

9. For examples of the use of such information, see "The Second Course—And Later" ("Three Forms of Drama" and "Advanced Play Reading: Shakespeare") in this text.

10. In each list, the plays are arranged alphabetically by author; the lengths cited are, of course, only approximate.

11. The plays in these three lists may be conveniently found in one or another of the following inexpensive books: Marjorie W. Barrows (ed.), *Drama I* (New York: The Macmillan Co., 1962); Paul Kozelka (ed.), *15 American One-Act Plays* (New York: Washington Square Press, Inc., 1961); Irwin J. Zachar (ed.), *Plays As Experience* (New York: The Odyssey Press, 1962); Bennett Cerf and Van H. Cartmell (eds.), *Thirty Famous One-Act Plays* (New York: The Modern Library, Random House, Inc., 1943); and Cerf and Cartmell (eds.), *24 Favorite One-Act Plays*.

12. Both plays are conveniently available in *24 Favorite One-Act Plays*.

13. The page references cited in the discussions of *Glory in the Flower* and of *The Browning Version* are to *24 Favorite One-Act Plays*.

14. Less able classes vary. Some who are conscientious enough but superficial would handily complete this guide in less than a fifty-minute study period. Others who plod would take an hour and a half—or more— on these questions. To preclude that, we would *not* change the questions basically; we would either cut certain questions or simply reduce the detailing. In questions 2 and 3, for instance, we would omit (b); in question 4, we would ask the class to choose *one* episode; in question 6, we would make (b) and (c) into one question; in question 7, we would cut (c) and (d); in question 9, we would phrase question (a): How is Jackie's inquiry about Bus' fighting different from Howie's on page 174? and we would use (b) and cut (c). We are only suggesting *general ways* of tailoring such a guide. What we would, in fact, cut or alter would be determined by each class.

When we discuss the study guide questions in class, we would include those omitted from the guide. Does that mean that "the plodders" would need much more class time for discussion than the "superficial workers" would? No. Though the latter students will have done the guide in its entirety, their responses will be partial and surface. Class time will be needed to "go back and look again" and to pool many ideas to get one adequate answer.

If a particular class *could not* handle such an assignment outside of class—or probably *would not*—we would assign the reading of pp. 170–180 for homework and have the study guide done in class next day. (For our earlier comments on this matter see "The Study Guide," in the section "The Teaching of Poems.") If time permitted on this second day, we would begin discussing pp. 170–180 (as described on p. 235); if doing the guide took the whole period, we would collect the guides and discuss the first half of the play on the third day. As we would probably be handling the work on the second half of the play in the same way, the study would take five days at least.

As we have mentioned, some high school students have never done study guides—indeed, some have never consistently brought books to class. When we get such a group, we have to train them. Such training is arduous, but it will succeed—with occasional lapses, of course. Meanwhile, as we inch forward with this "responsibility training," we are wise to collect study guides, stage plans, and other requisite papers at the end of classes, so that they will be on hand in class when they are needed next day. It is often helpful in the training of such a class to provide each student at the outset with a folder into which he puts all papers relevant to English: his course outlines, guides, written papers, and so on. The folders remain in the room in a file (or cardboard box). They would be distributed daily, first by the teacher, later by a student. This procedure is the first step toward keeping a notebook and, in general, toward recognizing that work, not time-passing, is done in *this* room.

15. Would you use words like "alternative" and "equivalent" in less able classes? You can use any words *you have been using*—words that students understand the meaning of. What you cannot do is use a "new word" on a test or a paper topic.

16. All page references are to the text of *The Browning Version* reprinted in *24 Favorite One-Act Plays*.

17. To grade these papers fairly and efficiently, we would first work out an "actor's copy" of this dialogue, noting all valid alternatives of tone, gesture, and so on. This done, we would read the papers — merely checking omissions and errors; comments are unnecessary since the passage will be reviewed in class. We would grade the papers: +, C, and, −, as we suggested previously. Any other kind of correction seems *indefensibly* time-consuming. This is an *exercise;* it will be reviewed in class; there will be further exercises of this sort—this is only the first play. And, later in the first course, there will be a test which will include annotation of a text.

We would never let our correction "system" become so intricate that giving several exercises becomes physically impossible. Students *need* several exercises.

18. Shirley Jackson's "The Lottery" may be conveniently found in Milton Crane (ed.), *50 Great Short Stories* (New York: Bantam Books, Inc., 1952). Brainerd Duffield's *The Lottery* is included in Kozelka (ed.), *15 American One-Act Plays*.

19. For this idea I am indebted to Edward Rosenheim, *What Happens In Literature* (Chicago: The University of Chicago Press, 1960), p. 104.

20. In *our* teaching of this play, we *have* studied the opening scene closely (p. 246), but we propose it here because the script is reprinted on pp. 242–245, and so you can see *concretely* how the exercise we are suggesting would be carried out.

21. An article that might help a teacher make his own assessment of any long play he is preparing to teach as a play is Bruce Sweet's "The Analysis of a Script: An Act of Love," *EJ*, *56* (Jan. 1967), pp. 125–130.

22. The page references cited in this discussion of *The Crucible* are to the Compass Book Edition (New York: The Viking Press, Inc., 1964).

23. The questions in parentheses are just "hints" and "leads" to help students consider the main question more fully and, consequently, make a more insightful answer to it.

24. Coxe's play is "easy," but Melville's novella is not. Since any com-

parison would require an adequate reading of the story, we must label this pairing "for the competent."

25. These three are suggested by Alan Downer, *The Art of the Play*, p. vi.

26. Sources like Elizabeth Drew, *Discovering Drama* (New York: W. W. Norton & Co., Inc., 1937), Chapter 2, "The Greeks," Chapter 3, "The Elizabethans," and Chapter 4, "The Moderns," will readily give the teacher needed information, as will such books as Hiram Haydn (ed.), *The Portable Elizabethan Reader* (New York: The Viking Press, Inc., 1946) and E. M. Tillyard, *The Elizabethan World Picture* (New York: Vintage Books, Random House, Inc., 1941). For an illustration of the focused theater, see Alan Downer, *Art of the Play*, p. 64; Styan, *Dramatic Experience*, p. 16; or Gassner, *Producing the Play*, (the modern "ring theater"), p. 539. For an illustration of the panoramic theater, see Downer, p. 89 and Styan, p. 23.

To create a living conception of Elizabethan culture and of the Elizabethan theater, the teacher might use certain of the Folger Shakespeare Library's Washington Audio-Tapes, especially "Sports, Pastimes and Amusements" and "The Elizabethan Playhouse." These tapes are available through Washington Tapes, Inc., 5540 Connecticut Avenue, Washington, D. C., 20015.

27. For good counsel on this topic, see Gladys Veidemanis, "Shakespeare in the High School Classroom," *EJ*, 53 (April 1964), pp. 240–247.

28. For a full discussion of the quality of language in *Julius Caesar*, see Maurice Charney's "Style in the Roman Plays," pp. 16–29, in Maurice Charney (ed.), *Discussions of Literature: Shakespeare's Roman Plays*, (Boston: D. C. Heath and Co., 1964).

29. *Shakespearian Tragedy* (2d ed.; London: Macmillan and Co., Ltd., 1932), p. 85n.

30. See Harold S. Wilson, "The Order of Nature: *Julius Caesar*" in Charney (ed.), *Discussions of Literature*, p. 56.

31. A Columbia Paperback (New York: Columbia University Press, 1961).

32. In *The Portable Elizabethan Reader*, pp. 402–408.

33. For these, see T. B. J. Spencer, "Shakespeare and the Elizabethan Romans" in Charney (ed.), *Discussions of Literature*, pp. 10–11.

34. Refer to pp. 212–215 of this text.

REFERENCES

I. Discussions of the Principles of Drama: General References

Drew, Elizabeth. *Discovering Drama*. New York: W. W. Norton & Co., Inc., 1937. Pleasantly readable and enlightening, this book deals first with the dramatist as craftsman, then with the dramatist as artist.

Nicoll, Allardyce. *The Theory of Drama*. New York: Thomas Y.

Crowell, Co., n.d. This older book, probably available in almost any library, offers basic information on the meaning of drama, dramatic conventions, and the forms of drama. See especially pp. 24–102.

Olson, Elder. *Tragedy and The Theory of Drama.* Detroit: Wayne State University Press, 1961. The first 170 pages of this book present a delightfully written, careful inquiry into those principles of drama "we talk constantly about" but are usually "hard put to it to say exactly what we mean" by them: dramatic action, plot, incident, character, representation, dialogue, dramatic effect, and dramatic form. The discussion is perceptive, well-organized, and well-exemplified.

Styan, J. L. *The Dramatic Experience: A Guide to the Reading of Plays.* Cambridge, England: Cambridge University Press, 1965. This 150-page book is for the teacher who has neither taught nor read plays as plays, but would like to begin to do both. The book has a simply written, well-exemplified text that deals with such topics as, the distinction between novels, poems, and plays; the relation between stage and audience in successive periods of the drama; questions of the reality of character, of the relation of plot and character, and of the meaning of comic and tragic. Accompanying this fine text are charts, graphs, and drawings to *visually represent* the essential differences in theatres, the pattern of a soliloquy, kinds of characters, and dramatic tempo. These representations could be readily projected for in-class use whenever the teacher wanted to clarify such abstract matters for students. There is, finally, a good basic reading list on pp. 147–150.

————. *The Elements of Drama.* Cambridge, England: Cambridge University Press, 1960. This highly readable, excellent book (now in paperback) proposes a more complete criticism for drama, "one which embraces both its verbal and its visual and aural elements." It is required reading for those who have not read any books on the theory of drama, for those who have read many, and for those who have time to read only one.

Thompson, Alan R. *The Anatomy of Drama.* Berkeley: The University of California Press, 1942. This book offers useful discussions not only of such usual topics as comedy, tragedy, the unities, the sources of dramatic effects, and the distinction between drama and fiction, but also of less commonly analyzed matters: the differences between plays and films and between the identification tragedy evokes and the detachment comedy elicits.

Finally, two useful collections of essays:

Corrigan, Robert W., and James L. Rosenberg (eds.). *The Context and Craft of Drama: Critical Essays on the Nature of Drama and Theatre.* San Francisco: Chandler Publishing Company, 1964. This anthology is for those who would prefer brief (ten-to-fifteen page) theoretical discussions by "various hands." There are two or more essays on each of ten topics which include the nature, the language, and the structure of drama, characterization, the playwright, the designer, and the critic.

YOUNG, STARK. *Theatre Practice.* New York: Charles Scribner's Sons, 1926. Written by one of the most perceptive dramatic critics, this group of essays on plays, on acting, and on theatrical design and production has discussions on all the arts that make up the art of the theatre, including such aspects of that art as illusion, stage movement, tempo, realistic and poetic methods, voice, music, color, and lights.

II. Discussions of Drama: Specialized References

These references do not purport to adequately sample the available literature. If they serve as basic readings in several significant areas and as entrées to further explorations, they will have done their office.

CORRIGAN, ROBERT W. (ed.). *Comedy: Meaning and Form.* San Francisco: Chandler Publishing Co., 1965. This anthology includes twenty essays on the nature and form of comedy, six on the criticism of comedy, and five on satire and farce. All are by well-known, widely recognized critics of comedy. There is, in addition, a fine bibliography organized to assist those who wish to read further in any of the various aspects of comedy the essays deal with.

————. *Tragedy: Vision and Form.* San Francisco: Chandler Publishing Co., 1965. In addition to four essays on melodrama and six on the criticism of tragedy, this anthology includes twenty-two essays on "the nature of the tragic spirit and the elements of tragic form" by such famous hands as Aristotle, Hegel, Richard Sewall, Murray Krieger, Suzanne Langer, Northrop Frye, Elder Olson, Sidney Hook, W. H. Auden, and Arthur Miller.

FERGUSSON, FRANCIS. *The Idea of a Theater.* Garden City: Doubleday & Co., Inc., 1949. Defining drama as the "art of imitation," this book offers detailed studies of certain plays in order to show how this art was realized in various ways in the changing theaters of our tradition. The plays discussed include the four "landmarks" in the drama—*Oedipus Rex* (the tragic rhythm of action), *Berenice* (the theater of reason), *Tristan and Isolde* (the theater of passion), and *Hamlet* (the analogy of action)—as well as *Ghosts* and *The Cherry Orchard* (the theater of modern realism) *Major Barbara* and *Heartbreak House* (the theater of the platform and the drawing room), and *Murder in the Cathedral* (the theological scene in theater-poetry).

GILDER, ROSAMOND, HERMINE RICH ISAACS, ROBERT M. MACGREGOR, and EDWARD REED (eds.). *Theatre Arts Anthology.* New York: Theatre Arts Books: Robert M. MacGregor, 1950. This anthology of the best of the magazine *Theatre Arts* offers readers essays on playwrights, actors, and directors, on the history of theatre and the architecture of it, on scene and costume design—but above all, it offers them an introduction to that excellent repository of the theatre, the magazine itself.

HENN, T. R. *The Harvest of Tragedy.* London: Methuen & Co., Ltd., 1956. A somewhat sophisticated treatment of the nature of tragedy through an examination of similarities and differences among the tragedies of the Greeks, Shakespeare, Ibsen, Shaw, the Irish dramatists, and Eliot. This book would be a good "further reading" for those who were especially interested in the studies of Sewall or Muller.

MULLER, HERBERT J. *The Spirit of Tragedy*. New York: Washington Square Press, Inc., 1965. This clearly written, abundantly exemplified book is concerned primarily with the "vision of life reflected in tragedy, its historical connections, its philosophical issues, its implications for our living as well as our literary purposes." There are chapters on the ritual origins of tragedy, on Greek tragedy, and on Elizabethan, neo-classical, and modern tragedy.

POTTS, L. J. *Comedy*. London: Hutchinson's University Library, 1948. A readable study that arrives by induction from many, well-chosen examples at the "idea of comedy," the subject matter of it, the style, the nature of its characters and its plots, and its "boundaries." A fine introduction to the whole subject for those who have time to read only one book.

SEWALL, RICHARD B. *The Vision of Tragedy*. New Haven: Yale University Press, 1959. "The theme of the book is the unity and vitality of the tragic vision from *Job* to the present. The early chapters assemble the elements and prepare the way; the later ones show the central theme in its latter-day variations. The whole is a continuous essay on tragedy, demonstrating finally, I hope, not only the possibility but the existence of true tragic writing in our time." So goes the author's description of this engaging book, which has chapter-length discussions on *Job, Oedipus Rex, Faustus, Lear, The Scarlet Letter, Moby Dick, The Brothers Karamazov,* and *Absalom, Absalom*.

WHITMAN, ROBERT F. *The Play-Reader's Handbook*. Indianapolis: The Bobbs-Merrill Co., Inc., 1966. The book deals with the assumptions about the nature of reality that underlie the plays of certain periods and of certain playwrights—assumptions that the theatregoer or reader must share if he is to respond sensitively to the plays. The text first discusses such conceptions as "appearance as reality," expressionism, fantasy, "history" plays, poetic dramas, and the play of ideas; then, it turns to the particular conventions of the great periods of drama: the Greek, Elizabethan, French Classical, Restoration, eighteenth century, and modern. This is a useful reference for teachers who need help in anticipating what preparation a play requires and in "setting up" ways for giving this preparation to students.

III.   Useful "Teachers"

We cite only books that teach plays *as plays* and that do so in such a way as to suggest an approach to teaching plays, a pattern for arranging the study of plays, or a group of understandings and skills that the competent play reader has. In other words, we cite only books that might help the classroom teacher teach plays validly and engagingly.

BROOKS, CLEANTH, and ROBERT HEILMAN. *Understanding Drama*. New

York: Henry Holt & Co., Inc., 1945. Like the other "Understanding" books, this one is well worth a teacher's careful study. The theoretical discussions in the first hundred pages are valid, clearly written, and liberally exemplified. The discussions of particular plays that follow show teachers exactly how to apply in classroom practice what they have learned about the nature of plays: how to organize so as to show the structure of a play, how to question so that students will understand *this* play and learn how to read *any* play, and how to make clear to students the similarities and the differences among plays.

COOPER, CHARLES W. *Preface to Drama: An Introduction to Dramatic Literature and Theater Art.* New York: The Ronald Press Company, 1955. The first hundred and twenty-five pages ("The Preface") discuss, in terms readily understandable to high school students, the nature of a play, the elements of the playscript, the features of stage production, and the problems confronting a reader who would re-create a play. The full texts of three short plays are included to illustrate this discussion. The second part of the text ("The Plays") reprints in full *Antigone, Othello, Hedda Gabler, Candida, Life With Father, The Glass Menagerie,* and *The Crucible.* Though there is a brief headnote before each play, there are no intrusive explications. This book could be used as a suggestive reference by the teacher or as a class text in many different kinds of first and second courses.

DOWNER, ALAN S. *The Art of the Play: An Anthology of Nine Plays.* New York: Henry Holt & Company, 1955. The full texts of *Ghosts, Prometheus Bound, Doctor Faustus, Antony and Cleopatra, Tartuffe, The Sea Gull,* and *The Emperor Jones* are provided to illustrate and make concrete a simply written, basic discussion of such topics as the effects of theatres on plays, the language of action (dialogue, movement, gesture), dramatic structure, and point of view. There is, in addition, a useful bibliography on pp. 445–447.

EVANS, BERTRAND. *Teaching Shakespeare in the High School.* New York: The Macmillan Company, 1966. Already well-known and much discussed, this valuable book spends the first eight chapters answering such questions as: Why Shakespeare? which plays and when? what form of presentation? and what activities—during and after? Chapters 9 and 10 offer notes on the teaching of eight plays commonly studied in high school. (If you do not agree with Mr. Evans, at least do not forget how many of your most productive ideas were "irritated" into existence.)

IV. Collections of Short Plays

We have restricted our listings on IV and V to collections that include a high percentage of appropriate plays and that are priced so realistically that all schools *can* afford them.

CERF, BENNETT, and VAN H. CARTMELL (eds.). *24 Favorite One-Act Plays.* New York: Doubleday & Co., Inc., 1963. A Dolphin Book. This is cited first because it is by far the best collection both for the number of plays and the variety of them.

Two other usable collections are:

Barrows, Marjorie W. (ed.). *Drama I*. New York: The Macmillan Co., 1962. Literary Heritage Series. Eleven plays, seven of which we have cited in our list of short plays.

Zachar, Irwin J. (ed.). *Plays As Experience*. New York: The Odyssey Press, 1962. Fourteen plays, six of which we have cited in our list of short plays.

V. Collections of Long Plays

Cubeta, Paul M. (ed.). *Modern Drama for Analysis*. 3rd ed. New York: Holt, Rinehart and Winston, 1962. Ten plays, five of which we have cited, and two more of which—T. S. Eliot's *Murder in the Cathedral* and Jean Anouilh's *Becket*—we might have included.

Redman, Crosby (ed.). *Drama II*. New York: The Macmillan Co., 1962. Literary Heritage Series. Four plays, three of which we have cited in our list of long plays.

VI. Single Plays

Unless the majority of the plays in a collection are appropriate, then it is more economical to invest in inexpensive paperback editions of single plays. These appear as Signet Classics and Mentor Books (The New American Library, New York), Croft Classics (Appleton-Century-Crofts, Inc., New York), Bantam Classics (Bantam Books, Inc., New York), Ribner's Revisions of the Kittredge Shakespeares (Blaisdell Publishing Co., Waltham, Mass.), The Pelicans and The Penguins for Shakespeare and Shaw, respectively (Penguin Books, Baltimore, Md.), Chandler Editions in Drama (Chandler Publishing Co., San Francisco), and Pocket Library (Pocket Books, Inc., New York). Many of these libraries also publish equally inexpensive editions of groups of plays; for instance, collections of great tragedies and great comedies (Mentor), of great plays of certain centuries and of certain countries (Dell), and of certain writers (Bantam and Harper & Row).

Our suggestions are not intended to be exhaustive, but rather to intimate that there are solutions to the problems of procuring the right texts at the right prices. The current edition of *Paperback Books In Print* will readily show how many solutions there are.

VII. Special References: Julius Caesar

As the teacher prepares to teach early plays—or even those of Chekov and Ibsen, he might wish to *follow* his own careful readings of the text with the reading of *some* critical articles. We stress "follow" because if the teacher begins with critical articles he will not have a chance to make his own free responses to the text. And, if he does not do that, how can he judge the validity of the interpretations in the critical articles? Only the teacher who has read *Julius Caesar* carefully knows when a critic is reading backwards. And only he knows that that kind of reading is not "a brilliant insight," however eminent the critic may be. If a teacher is to use criticism judiciously, his own careful, free readings of the text must always come first. Furthermore, the teacher's "undetermined" readings will suggest what kinds of critical articles he should consult. They should always be carefully selected to fill a specific need he has discovered during his readings: perhaps the function of particular scenes puzzle him or the role of certain images. Specific need will limit his reading, will protect him against being enticed into a random sampling of the bounties offered by bibliographies.

Following is a brief list of references, one or another of which would probably fulfill some specific need of the teacher of *Julius Caesar*.

BONJOUR, ADRIEN. *The Structure of Julius Caesar*. Liverpool: Liverpool University Press, 1958. This small book—73 pages—discusses "The General Structure of the Play," "The Structural Role of Motives," and "Structural Imagery."

CHARNEY, MAURICE. *Shakespeare's Roman Plays: The Function of Imagery in the Drama*. Cambridge, Mass.: Harvard University Press, 1961.
———— (ed.). *Discussions of Shakespeare's Roman Plays*. Boston: D. C. Heath & Co., 1964.

MARKELS, JULIAN (ed.). *Shakespeare's Julius Caesar*. A Scribner Research Anthology. New York: Charles Scribner's Sons, 1961.

SCHANZER, ERNEST. *The Problem Plays of Shakespeare*. New York: Schocken Books, Inc., 1963. *Julius Caesar* is discussed on pp. 10–70. This is a useful reading for a teacher trying to discover a way of helping students see the ambiguity of this play.

TRAVERSI, DEREK. *Shakespeare: The Roman Plays*. Stanford, Calif.: Stanford University Press, 1963. On pp. 21–75, Traversi offers a close, often illuminating, reading of the entire play. Indeed, even our disagreements with Traversi further enlighten us.

THE TEACHING OF SHORT
STORIES AND NOVELS

Why teach the reading of fiction? Because short stories and novels, "besides being the pleasantest things imaginable, are powerful forces on the side. Mutual understanding in the world being nearly always, as now, at low ebb, it is comforting to remember that it's through art that one country can nearly always speak reliably to another, if the other can hear at all. Art, though, is never the voice of a country; it is an even more precious thing, the voice of an individual, doing its best to speak, not comfort of any sort, indeed, but truth. And the art that speaks it most unmistakably, most directly, most variously, most fully is fiction. . . ."[1]

Why teach the reading of fiction? Because "man, more than ever it needs emphasizing now, is not merely social man or statistical man. He is an individual, a person, with a soul to be saved and a private life, a person moreover, who, when all the social services have done all they can for him, remains essentially naked and alone . . . the novel is a result of the solitary man communing with himself. Obstinately, relentlessly, the novelist brings back all the problems of life, all the facts of existence, to the one test: how they affect the individual, man as man, not man as a unit in society, a producer or consumer, or cog in a machine."[2]

Why teach the reading of fiction? Because "fiction offers us the opportunity of knowing representations of human beings with a far greater intimacy than we can ever know actual human beings; and so much is this true that there are many characters in the world's fiction which are in a sense more 'real' to us, more comprehensible, than all but one or two of all the living people we know personally."[3].

Why teach the reading of fiction? Because short stories and novels are the most popular forms of literature. Students read them of their own volition and will continue to read them after their formal education is over, though they may never read another poem, never read or see another play. When we teach students how to read fiction, then, we take advantage of our best opportunity to make the values of reading literature as literature available to them for the rest of their lives.

The Liabilities Students Bring

High school students like to read fiction. For years, they have been enjoying it in school and out. Unless a novel is five hundred pages long or markedly immature, it is enthusiastically received by most high school English classes. There is no reluctance to overcome, as there is at times with poetry, no unfamiliarity as there is at times with drama. So favored is fiction that high school teachers often choose to begin the year's course in literature with the reading of short stories or a novel.

But if the teacher's aim for the study of fiction is, as ours is, to enable students to read short stories and novels as works of art, he soon realizes that too often the cordial attitude students have toward fiction is more of a liability than an asset. For the study of literature that many students have enjoyed so much has been less than literary; sometimes it has not been literary at all. The teacher must now extinguish many responses that are not only firmly set, but that have been rewarding for a long time. He must develop responses that are, to the students, strange, "unnecessary," and initially unreinforcing. This situation is the reverse of what the teacher faces in the study of poems: as students' dislike of "poetry past" is an asset to the teacher, so their fondness for "fiction past" is a liability.

Sometimes students' previous study of fiction has consisted largely in a down-the-middle-of-the-page, nouns-and-verbs reading of works —just enough to prepare the class to participate in lively discussions of political, psychological, or moral issues. In certain instances, these discussions had little to do with the particular experience the work represents. In others, they related either to the theme that the work *seems*, on a superficial reading, to express or to some minor aspect of the work that, out of context, had "fine discussion potential." Such a study of fiction merely *uses* short stories and novels to agitate vibrant bull sessions on those "philosophic" questions that students, beginning their "romance with the universe," find so attractive.

Sometimes, students' previous study of fiction has encouraged or allowed them to confuse the world of the work with the everyday world. They have, for instance, been permitted to suppose what a character's childhood was like, assume motivations that the work nowhere implies, prejudge the conduct of characters, and project the characters' futures as they themselves would shape them. In other words, these students have not been required to distinguish among life, a transcript of life, and a representation of life created out of words. So they do not realize that characters are just masses of words, that the work gives, explicitly or implicitly, all the reader needs to know, and that it directs and limits the reader's suppositions, assumptions, and projections. Why are students invited or allowed to montage the world of a work and their own worlds? Usually, to try to show them the relevance of literature to life. But the effect of this sort of reading is to make the two worlds indistinguishable, and, since the authentic world of the work no longer exists, the readers can hardly profit from experiencing its ordering.

Once students have developed either of the invalid ways of reading fiction that we have just described, they are reluctant to change. It seems tedious to read "all the words." And it is, indeed, very difficult for them to extinguish the habit of montaging. The nature of fiction makes this so. For with its precise places, exact times, its nicknamed characters, and its familiar social roles, fiction represents so closely the everyday world we live in that it is not easy for a reader to withhold his preconceptions, his psychological speculations, his developed expectations, and his sentimental responses as he reads a short story or novel. It is hard for him to have a right "conversation" with a work of fiction, for, more than any other genre, short stories and novels betray the reader into bringing from his experience something more than, or something other than, the represented world requires. Yet insofar as a reader fails to listen to a work and contribute appropriately, he impairs his experience of the fictional world.

In some classes, then, the teacher who wants to help students learn to read fiction sensitively will have to find ways *to extinguish* the kind of superficial reading and montaging that we have been describing. In other classes, he will have *to modify* the effects of two other prevalent modes of studying fiction, each of which is only partially literary. We refer to reading that concentrates on the narrative line and to criticism that stops at "what." The first is common practice in less able classes; the second, in average and competent groups.

Less able and less motivated students have very often been habituated to reading and discussion that virtually reduces "story" to narrative line: the kind of study that stresses the suspense, the "and-then-ness" of short stories and novels, the kind of study that focuses on how an obvious chain of events leads to a clear climax and an explicit conclusion. Students have enjoyed this kind of study. But, through it, they have come to think of "action" as overt doing, of conflict, as a clash of externals—and of all that is not narrative line, as impedimenta. Used initially to engage students, this mode of study often succeeds so well that neither teachers nor students want to move on from this important, yet rudimentary, level to consider all those other features that shape the chain of events into a story. When students have enjoyed again and again the raw excitement of being drawn along the narrative line, they have little wish to temper their excitement by considering the function of all those seemingly extraneous things. But, however rewarding this status quo, it must be upset because it limits students' perceptions of the works they are currently reading and it precludes their ever reading those thousands of fine stories in which "nothing happens."

Average and competent students have very often been habituated to a criticism that, if it gets beyond questions about the sequence of events and the creation of suspense, consists mainly in an *identification* of the literary features of the short stories and novels being read. Who is the leading character? Which of the five ways of portraying character does this author use? Illustrate. What is the setting? What point of view is used? What is the theme? What symbol (archetype, motif) is used? Such questions are "easy to answer if you do the assignment"; many average-to-good students like the security of having only to "name parts."

A sensitive reader has to be aware of the answers to most of the questions we have just cited. These questions are useful preliminaries to critical study. In class a teacher may ask many of them to be sure that students "have it straight" so that he can go on confidently to ask how some of *these* features and others *function* in the short story or the novel being discussed—to ask, in other words, why they are used. It is only when the question changes from "what" to "why" that the kind of criticism that sharpens readers' perceptions begins. Readers need to sense the effect that is being produced by what the writer is doing. They must see, for instance, what the writer gains by using this point of view, by including that character, that remark, this bit of description. They must see not only *what* variation of the journey motif is being used but *how* it works with the other unifying elements in the story. Only as students discover how all the various features of the story *function* are they coming ever closer to the experience that all the features of the particular story functioning in harmony render.[4]

As our discussion has implied, it will not be easy for a teacher to change the invalid and partial reading habits we have been describing. Most students have enjoyed these modes of study. They like reading "just enough" to get an idea for a "good" argument or an "interesting" speculation; they enjoy montaging; most are satisfied with getting the plot and with naming the parts. They are not disturbed by invalidity; they do not know they are not learning to read works. It's been great! So, extinguishing their invalid responses and extending their partial ones will be arduous jobs. All habits die hard; enjoyable ones, even harder. Furthermore, students as a whole "take it for granted" that "anyone can read short stories and novels." So they feel that the teacher who tries to increase their perceptions is making the obvious obscure. He is really creating problems, not solving them. And they often become properly resistant. Finally, even those students who are quite willing to "lay the old aside" repeatedly revert to long-established responses in spite of themselves. All things considered, helping students learn to read short stories and novels *as works of literature* is one of the most challenging jobs in the teaching of literature.

And this might be true, even if students did not bring the erroneous and inadequate responses we have been mentioning. For, in general, readers do not seem to perceive the means to meaning in works of fiction as readily as they do in poems and plays. The presence of a narrative line and the intimacy of reader and fictional world seem to make readers less conscious of the "voice" that tells the story, of the over-all shape the story is given, of why certain material is in scene, what the function of setting is, why particular elements are juxtaposed, paralleled, or repeated. Many readers seem to live in the fictional world of a story obtusely and inertly. Left to themselves, they would often be having an experience quite different from the experience the short story or novel is rendering.

Even if readers *are* perceptive, they frequently have difficulty developing and maintaining the sense of a whole throughout the reading of a long work of fiction. They tend to be overly impressed with this character or that scene, so that at the end of their reading,[5] they do not have in retrospect a dynamic whole experience, all parts in their proper proportions and relationships. Many of these same readers are quite sensitive to the continuities that organize a poem, but they simply are not sufficiently responsive to the structures that interrelate and unify the many strands of a long work of fiction to enjoy the complex experience that the work expresses.

A First Course in Reading Fiction

Given the two conditions we have been describing—the impedimenta that many high school students bring to the study of fiction and the difficulty that readers normally have in perceiving fiction as art— what kind of first course should we offer?

To answer, we must ask a second question: Has any critical reading of works—of poems, plays, or other forms—preceded this course?

If it has, then whatever invalid literary responses students had initially will have been dispelled to some extent, and some sensitivity to the literary uses of language will have been developed. The first course in reading fiction could, then, concentrate on helping students respond to the ways that literary devices function in short stories and novels to define their meaning and unify them. If students had had prior critical reading, this aim could be achieved in a shorter time, more stories could be read independently, and one novella or more could be included in the course. But most important, the teaching of the stories, from the outset, could be more wholistic—the many unifying devices that students were already familiar with from their study of poems or plays could be considered simultaneously. These are at least some differences that a "usable past" would make in the planning of a first course.

During such a course, the teacher could continue to dissipate whatever misconceptions or invalid responses the particular class seemed to cling to—or revert to as soon as a work of fiction is set before them. Such regression is very common even among able students who have become quite sensitive readers of poems and plays. This regression is often so disheartening to new teachers that, fearing their work on poems and plays has accomplished nothing, they are tempted to "begin all over again." They do not realize that students tend to revert to the familiar whenever the strange "threatens." The teacher should hold to the aim for the course, quietly eroding the invalid responses by this small question, that little paper. The understandings and the skills learned in the earlier study of poems and of plays *will* reassert themselves—if the teacher is unobtrusively persistent.

Now, if a class has not had any previous critical reading, what kind of first course should we offer? Something like the one we are now going to discuss. We decided to discuss in detail the course that assumes no prior preparation because some teachers may have to begin with fiction, curricula and book circulation being "fixed" as they so often are. Other teachers may want to begin with it anyway, impedimenta notwithstanding. So here is one way to begin at the very beginning.

The aim for this first course is to help students replace their erroneous or inadequate responses to fiction with appropriate ones. In the First Part of the course, we concentrate on developing "right" responses to mode of narration; in the Second Part, to story, and in the Third Part, to the purpose of a story. In other words, we concentrate, in turn, on developing appropriate responses to *who* tells the story, to *what* he tells, and to *why* it is told. As the wording of the aim suggests, the extinguishing of improper responses and the development of useful ones would go on contemporaneously. The choice of works, the planning of lessons, the character of the exercises—even the ordering of the three emphases of the course—are all designed to dissipate one response while encouraging another.

We begin the course with the study of mode of narration for several reasons. First of all, it makes students realize immediately that a story is *told* by someone. So students automatically know that as readers they can be only cooperative listeners. It is somebody else's story; the narrator shapes the story and controls the range of reactions the reader can rightly have. Furthermore, this stress on the narrator alerts students to the "made" quality of a story: the narrator foreshortens and reorders the past incident; sometimes he makes no mention of what would in life naturally be included. So initial stress on the narrator will begin immediately to correct some of the faulty responses we mentioned.

The study of mode of narration leads very naturally to a concentrated look at what the narrator tells. So, in the Second Part of the course we emphasize that what he tells is a *story*: an event organized so that the reader can experience characters working out in action a conflict that is morally, psychologically, or socially significant.[6] And we stress that a story is a structure, a unified organization of many substructures, *one* of which is a sequence of events, a narrative line. We repeatedly call students' attention to *all those other features* that organize this sequence of events into this story—features like setting; description; half-scenes that heighten the effects the writer is creating; episodes that prepare us to accept what the characters do; motifs and myths that qualify the meaning of the events; and of course, the shape of the story; its objectivity or subjectivity; the character of its diction—not to mention its peculiar mode of narration. What the narrator tells is not just a sequence of events; it is a plot that is so "built and piled high" by means of such features as we have just mentioned that it becomes the fully rendered experience of a particular conflict. That is what a *story* is. The same sequence of events might have been shaped in many other ways— into many other stories.

As we clarify the nature of story in this first course, we would, we hope, be convincing students that a story cannot be described in a one-sentence résumé. And we would, we hope, be persuading them that conflict cannot be equated with physical or overt opposition and that it cannot be oversimplified to comfortable "black-and-white" terms. For all through this course we would be trying to show students that there are various kinds of conflicts and various shapes that conflict can take. What is "worked out in action" may be an overt conflict or an internal one; it may be simple or complex. It may have a clear "complication-climax-resolution" shape; it may be just a moral awakening; and it may be any one of a number of modifications of either. But whatever its nature or its shape in a story, the conflict will be resolved or reconciled so as to effect—or predict—a change of some sort.

The study of *what* the narrator tells naturally leads to an emphasis on *why* it is told. So in the Third Part of our first course we stress the fact that a story has a more than literal meaning: since it objectifies an insight, it has, at once, an immediate literal meaning and a general human significance that becomes clear *only* to the reader who responds to all that is in the story in the way it is there. Through stressing the "two meanings" of a story, we would be trying to stimulate the symbolic sense of those students who tend to become arrested at the literal meaning. Through our emphasis on the necessity of experiencing the *whole* story in order to have the insight, we would be trying to curb other students who scorn the literal meaning and fix upon this or that isolated statement as the expression of the significance of the story.

These, then, are the three parts of our first course, ordered, we think, to facilitate students' replacing their faulty responses to fiction with appropriate ones. Each of the parts has a particular focus, but, as the outline suggests, each new emphasis demands sensitivity to what has gone before. The course is cumulative. Furthermore, students are always reading whole works and discussing whatever is necessary to "open up" the experience of the particular work for them. Works are, however, chosen, as they were in the other first courses, for their "natural" potential for developing and exercising the responses being emphasized at the time, as well as for their relevance to the concerns of high school students.

All of the works we suggest in this first course are short stories; most of them are less than a dozen pages long. Students can, therefore, feasibly read each story more than once during their study of it. And a second reading is highly desirable. For it is then that narrative line takes its place in the scheme of things; it is then that all those other features of the story begin to be noticed. Furthermore, since the stories are only a few pages long, students can feasibly read more of them, and, from experience with a wide variety of uses of the same fictional devices, they can develop very flexible tendencies to respond appropriately to these means. Finally, since stories are brief, students can more easily sense artistic unity.

All these are good reasons for beginning the study of fiction with short stories. But there is yet a more compelling reason. We have chosen to concentrate on the short story because it is *the* form of prose fiction that exhibits the most highly perfected fictional technique. So by repeated close study of this form of fiction, our aim will be most surely and most economically achieved. Furthermore, through the careful study of short stories, students will have a chance to develop a high quality of attention and a catholic sensitivity to the ways fictional devices define meaning and unify a work. They will, therefore, be better able to respond perceptively to the looser, longer forms in their later studies of fiction.

In all three parts of the first course, we have suggested writing assignments. Three of these assignments are the familiar, formal critical papers of two-to-three pages, but all of the others are exercises for in- and out-of-class use. Such exercises are essential to reinforce and refine the responses students are developing, to measure the reading progress of individual students, and to prepare for the longer, "full-fledged" critical papers . Some of the exercises are critical writing, some creative. The critical exercises force students to contemplate closely some moment in the finished product; the creative compel them to render a moment fictionally. Creative writing is just as useful as critical writing for increasing readers' sensitivities to the fictional uses of language. For, when we ask students to write a paragraph changing the point of view, we want them to discover what difference a different point of view would make in the meaning of the story. When we have them write dialogue, we hope they recognize how dialogue reveals the speakers, advances the plot, and vitalizes the story. The creative exercises complement the critical analysis of stories.

Though many of our creative writing tasks may be similar to those in a creative writing course, we are not at all aiming to have the students proceed in an orderly fashion toward the ultimate writing of a story. None of our assignments ask them to outline a plot or to "flesh out" a plot plan into an action or to write an episode or indeed create any of the unifying structures of fiction. It is in the *critical* exercises and papers that students work both on the function of parts of works and on those "continuities" that unite all parts into a whole.

We are not discounting the feasibility, indeed the possible effectiveness, of fusing a course in the writing of fiction with a course in the critical reading of it. We are simply saying that we have not done this because we can achieve our aim without doing it.

Our suggested exercises and papers should be construed as *types* of writing assignments that would be useful in developing readers' responses to various fictional techniques or concepts. These *types* can be adapted in many ways for particular classes. What kinds of writing and how much writing a teacher chooses to do with a certain class would depend on what types of writing students have done previously, on what other composition programs they are currently engaged in, and, of course, on what sensitivities need exercise. It is probably desirable to have all classes do some critical and some creative writing exercises, not just for variety, but because the two types reinforce one another. Indeed, the assigning of the exercises should be patterned to do that. An out-of-class *critical* exercise on point of view might, for instance, be followed by an out-of-class *creative* exercise on changing point of view, and these tasks might be capped by an in-class evaluative *critical* exercise that asks students to tell what is gained, in a certain part of a story, by the point of view the writer chose.[7]

Since the purpose of both the exercises and the papers is to facilitate the reading, the assignments should be made as appropriate as possible to the particular class and, in all instances, the preparation for doing the assignment should be designed to virtually ensure that almost all the students will achieve the aim of the exercise or paper. If these assignments fail, it is not just writing that will suffer.

The First Part: The Mode of Narration

The aim for this part of the course is to help students sense how the mode of narration affects the view of the events the reader is getting and so controls the response he may make. By "mode of narration," we mean not only the technical point of view from which the story is told, but also the character of the narrator, *his* relationship to the event he tells, *his* attitude toward it and toward his "listener," and the attitudes of the author, whenever they are different from the narrator's. The central question of this part of the course is: What difference does it make to the way we take this story that *this* sort of fellow is telling *this* event in *this* way?

Some classes may need an introduction to the study of mode of narration, an introduction that will help them understand *what it is* before they are asked to work with it in stories. For certain groups— especially the less well-motivated—such a composition assignment as the following might be an effective way of helping students recognize the force of a narrator. Hand out to the class duplicated copies of two paragraphs you have written: the first, an incident in "camera" objectivity; the second, the same incident rewritten as a certain narrator would tell it. Ask students to point out, first generally, then very specifically, the differences between the first and the second paragraphs. Then, offer them alternative narrators and ask them to rewrite the first paragraph as either one or the other of these narrators would tell it. Be sure both narrators are types familiar to the class. If students' paragraphs are narrated appropriately throughout, the exercise has succeeded, no matter what grammatical indiscretions appear!

For other groups—especially the less able—the force of a narrator might be more easily understood if it is introduced by an analogy from everyday life. Without any mention of reading, call the students' attention to the fact that when anyone is telling us a story, we are always noticing not just *what* is being told, but *who* is telling it, and *how* he is telling it. Why else do we remark, "Oh, that's his story!" or "He has an 'axe to grind'" or "He's holding something back"? (Here we might ask: What else do we say to ourselves at such times?) By a battery of questions such as these, we could help *students show themselves* that all of us always pay attention to what sort of person the teller is, how perceptive he is, how reliable, how he comes to know what he is telling, and what his purpose is in telling it—both the purpose he expresses and the one he conceals (these we know *may* be different!). And what gives us clues to his *secret* purposes? Not only the facts of his story but his manner of telling them—his hesitation, his exaggerations, his repetitions, his bravado. This kind of class exercise would help students realize that as listeners we are always making all these judgments as *any* teller relates his story or as we reflect on it afterwards, for we are always trying to decide how we should take a story, what we should "make" of it.

Once students have recalled all these familiar facts about a listener's response to a teller and to his story, they will probably be ready to listen critically to some little stories. So we would write a one- to two-paragraph incident in three versions: the first, the incident as told in the first person by the main character (and we would make him a "character"); the second, the incident as told in the first person by an observer of the incident (and we would create an observer similar to the narrator of the first paragraph in order to stress the difference in point of view); and the third, the incident as told in the third person by an observer outside the story. In each version, the clues to the character of the narrator, to his intentions, and to his reliability would be bald. We would, if it were possible, tape or record these three versions; this prevents students from confusing the narrator with the teacher or with the student reading or telling the incident; an unseen, unknown narrator simulates the reading situation more closely.

Then, in class, before students listen to the first version, we would give them (on the board or on dittos) a few simple questions to keep in mind: What sort of person is the narrator? What is his intention? Does he understand what he tells? On whose authority is he telling it? After students had heard the first version a few times, we would ask them to write answers to those questions. Then, we would have the class discuss the answers, conveniently ending with the question on "authority." This is a useful transition to point of view, and it gives us a good chance to have the students assess carefully the advantages and the disadvantages of the technical relationship the teller of this paragraph has to his little story.

We would conduct a similar exercise on the second version, and finally on the third. Each version would be examined with painstaking care; if there were time to analyze only two thoroughly, then either of the first two versions and the third would suffice.

The purpose of these exercises is to impress upon students that the response they *may* and do make to a story is significantly affected by the character of the narrator and his technical relationship to the story. Consequently, for our exercises we would always choose (as we did) three points of view that would shape *obviously* different versions of one incident, and we would use *strongly indicated* narrators for each version. In any opening exercise, we would want such blatancy, so that students could easily recognize—and remember —the differences in effect. For, after such exercises, students must move on to printed stories—move, in other words, from narrators heard "live" to those heard only in the mind's ear. So we would want any introductory exercises to make students as aware as possible of what those printed words will have to offer.

Introductions are for classes that need introductions. In most high school classes, the kinds of preliminaries we have been describing would probably be unnecessary. The students could achieve the aim we set for this First Part of the course by beginning directly with stories. But introduction or no introduction, the content of this First Part of the course would be *roughly* the same for all classes: all would study a group of four or more stories with diverse modes of narration, stories with different points of view and with narrators of different temperaments, capacities, and attitudes; narrators who voice the author's view and those who are at various "distances" from it.

The Stories

Following is a list of stories[8] varied not only in their modes of narration, but also in their concerns and in their levels of difficulty. From a list *such as this*, a teacher could choose groups of stories appropriate for many different sorts of classes. All of the stories we cite here—and in the remainder of this course—are suggested *as examples* of the *kinds* of stories that would be useful in helping students develop the particular response being studied. Any work that is truly comparable in its literary structure will do just as well as the one we cite.

The stories we list are grouped according to certain commonly used points of view (which are arranged, we think, in order of increasing difficulty). Each story is annotated to suggest its concern, the kind of narrator it has, and its approximate length. Since, in this part of the course we are stressing the effect of the narrator—as well as of the technical point of view—on the response a reader makes to a story, we have listed only stories in which the narrator's voice is, if not readily noticeable, at least discernible to a beginning reader. When students have had a chance to become sensitive to the import of the narrator, we shall introduce stories with less obvious narrators. That will be in the Second Part of this course.

To begin, six stories using the point of view that poses fewest problems for high school readers:

■ *First-Person Narration: By the Main Character.* George Milburn, "The Apostate" (five pages). The narrator, a small-town ex-Rotarian, patronizingly accounts to a former brother for his defection. The character of the narrator is easily discernible. How that cliché language reveals his superficiality and obtuseness! Students can readily recognize the difference between the intent of the speaker and that of the story.

Truman Capote, "A Christmas Memory" (thirteen pages). Now grown up, the narrator remembers with tenderness and pathos a relationship he had as a small boy with an old, eccentric, childlike relative—a relationship so loving that her death was the loss of an "irreplacable part" of himself. The narrator's use of "we" and "our" expresses their oneness, and his present tense verbs suggest the permanent immediacy of the events. Though the narrator's language is generally that of a perceptive adult, the details are those of a child's world. The dramatic setting of scene at the beginning transforms the reader into an audience of one.

Marjorie Kinnan Rawlings, "Mother in Mannville" (eight pages). As the narrator recalls an orphan boy's "integrity" and his fantasy, she reveals her obtuseness to the meaning of the boy's responses to her. Though the character of the narrator is not as easy to discern as it is in some of the other stories listed, it does become clear if the reader attends to such things as the narrator's "I-ness," her continual emphasis on her own wants and plans, her acceptance of objective appearance as reality, her tendency to think rather than feel—and her expression of most of her responses in matter-of-fact statements. This story is at once an *easy* introduction to irony and a *challenging* exercise of students' skill in determining the narrator's attitude toward the event she tells.

John Bell Clayton, "The White Circle" (six pages). Now an adult, the narrator tells of his calculated attempt, when he was a young boy—thirteen perhaps—to kill the impulsive bully who had trespassed on his "property," an apple tree. Because this well-wrought, aesthetically interesting story is also viscerally appealing, it is an ideal vehicle for bringing the less academic readers to see how a narrator's tone repeatedly discloses his attitude toward the event he tells.

Ernest Hemingway, "My Old Man" (twenty-two pages). The narrator, the adolescent son of a "funny" jockey, recalls in his own language certain public and private events of the last few years of his father's life. He is trying to "know" what he thinks and feels about his "old man." And that accounts for his conscious recall, his half-musing, his justifications, and his reservations—as he goes along reconstructing. The narrator's character becomes apparent from his direct comments on his feelings about his father, from his sensitivity to natural scenes, to horses, to the excitement of races, and from his ignorance of the significance of some of the things he tells. The difference between the narrator's intent and the story's is not difficult to discern. (Five or six expressions of race-track jargon would have to be glossed for some classes.)

Frank O'Connor, "Guests of the Nation" (ten pages). A former soldier in the Irish Army, the narrator recalls the terrible ordeal of cooperating in the killing of two hostages who had become close friends of his. The buoyant, intimate tone of the narrator at the opening suggests the quality of comradeship they all enjoyed. How disconcerting the experience was, and even now is, for the narrator is conveyed by his explicit requests to a listener to understand, by his telling Belcher's death in the present tense, and by his sense of the world's retreating and leaving him alone.

This is a good story for helping students learn to piece together the character of a narrator and to trace shifts in tone.

Now, four stories using a point of view less familiar to high school students.

■ *First-Person Narration: By a Character Other than the Main Character.* Ring Lardner, "Haircut" (twelve pages). An insensitive village barber tells a customer, a stranger in town, about the great moments in the life of the village "card." The narrator who took no part in these moments has gotten his information from the "card" himself and from various other townsfolk. The long foreground in which the narrator reveals himself as a sympathetic audience to the cruel jokes *clearly* alerts the reader to the distance between the author's and the narrator's attitudes toward the event.

Ring Lardner, "Liberty Hall" (twelve pages). The wife of a musical comedy song writer tells of her husband's ordeals "by home visiting" and his uses of the "emergency exit." She is a participant-observer; she is within all but a small part of the situation. She is noticeably present in the narration of the first few pages, but she submerges during her "story" of the "visit that ended visits." This reading allows students to readily see how a certain narrator makes a certain story: they have only to imagine what the story would have been like had the events been told by the intolerant genius-husband rather than by the good-humored, nonidiosyncratic wife. Furthermore, this reading allows students to readily see how the narrator's intent differs from the author's: though she claims she is "terrible at plots," this narrator innocently tells a plot story complete with a double surprise ending!

D. H. Lawrence, "Wintry Peacock" (eleven pages). The narrator, probably the ideal Laurentian man, is a most casual acquaintance of the "wintry" Mrs. Goyte. He tells, mostly in scene, of a marital crisis that has come about between Mrs. Goyte and her husband because of the rivals both of them have set up. The reader can grasp the character of the perceptive, forthright narrator much more easily than he can ascertain the narrator's attitude toward what he tells. This is a rich story, but one that nevertheless allows mature students of many abilities to enjoy an engaging and satisfying first reading. (Some of the Welsh vernacular might have to be glossed.)

Henry James, "Brooksmith" (sixteen pages). This story of the butler who was so educated by the world of one employer that he had "lost his place" both professionally and socially is told by a member of the employer's "salon," which the butler had for years directed with great artistry. Not so complex as most of James, the story introduces students to the urbane narrator whose under- and overstatements chide the follies, the insensitivities, and the injustices of all levels of society. The story permits students not only to trace rather easily the development of the narrator's attitude toward the event he tells but also to realize how a narrator affects the response a reader makes. What, for instance, is the effect of the narrator's referring to suicide as "getting out of the way altogether"? and referring to the butler's afterlife as "changing the plates of the immortal gods"? How different the butler's story would be had it been told by a narrator with a different temperament and different values. Finally, this story very naturally raises questions about whether the narrator's attitude reflects the author's and about what attitude the reader should take.

Now, four stories using "the storyteller's point of view," a point of view so accepted by high school students that its offices are overlooked.

■ *Third-Person Narration: Omniscient Narrator.* Jack London, "To Build a Fire" (fourteen pages). A one-character story about a lumberman who freezes to death in the Yukon might have been told from the anonymous man's point of view. What, then, is gained by the narrator's comments, by his going into the dog's "mind," by his conclusion, and by his frequent use of language seemingly inappropriate to the subject matter of this story? In other words, what is gained by an omniscient narration?

Thomas Hardy, "The Three Strangers" (twenty pages). The narrator tells an old tale of a rural community to which he is an outsider: the tale of a wondrous escape of a convicted murderer through the hospitality, the naiveté, and the empathy of the people. The presence of the narrator is emphasized by the frame of the story, and his attitude toward the tale is made clear by the sardonic tone he uses and the overdrawing he indulges in. Though a useful story for making students aware of the presence of a third-person narrator, it has two possible drawbacks: it uses nineteenth-century vocabulary, and it demands the suspension of disbelief that a tale requires and that some classes may not *yet* be ready to give.

Stephen Crane, "The Bride Comes to Yellow Sky" (twelve pages). Sensitive to the gentle comic ironies of life, the narrator shows how disarming the "foreign condition" of marriage can be to a swashbuckling "child of the plains." Although Crane's narrator is less obvious than Hardy's, his diction does reveal how he feels about what he tells.

Willa Cather, "Paul's Case" (twenty-three pages). This is the story of a teen-age boy whose hatred of the pedestrian monotony of his home life and whose attraction to the "world-shine" of the music hall, the theatre, and the hotel lead him to crime and suicide. This story is told by a narrator whose commentary and "dazzle" vocabulary expose, if not condemn, Paul's unrealistic approach to living. The narrator limits his omniscience fairly early in the story.

Finally, four stories using the point of view students find most challenging to them as readers.

■ *Third-Person Narration: Limited Omniscience.* F. Scott Fitzgerald, "Winter Dreams" (twenty-four pages). Dexter is denied the "glittering thing"—Judy Jones and the forever-fair world she symbolizes—by the fickleness of the "thing." Though the sympathetic narrator generally maintains Dexter's point of view, he is obviously there in the story. He occasionally looks ahead, and he intermittently intrudes to remind the reader of the purpose of the story. Long, but not difficult, this story is a good vehicle for introducing students to the ways such deviations and intrusions work.

Graham Greene, "The Basement Room" (twenty-eight pages). The child Philip's terrifying and stultifying initiation into the private lives of adults is told mainly as he sees it. But the narrator occasionally assumes a wider omniscience, usually to register more than Philip could understand or to look ahead to the effect of the experience on Philip's adult life.

Somerset Maugham, "The Treasure" (twelve pages). The tongue-in-cheek narrator makes readers immediately and continually aware of his attitude toward the "hero," the smug adherent to the golden mean whose "tragic flaw" the story exposes. Since the narrator expresses his attitude both overtly in commentary and covertly through understatement, through rhetorical effects like the piling up of declarative pronouncements, and through dramatic ironies, this is an excellent story for showing readers the effect that the whole narrative treatment—not just the point of view—has on a subject.

Wallace Stegner, "The Blue-Winged Teal" (fourteen pages). Told from the point of view of the twenty-year-old "alien" son, the story represents his coming to understand and resolve his ambivalence about leaving his father. The story will help readers see that a certain kind of conflict demands a certain point of view, and it will help them detect the presence of a seemingly effaced narrator. For the telling suggests not only the son's attitude toward his experience but the narrator's attitude toward the son's attitude. The narrator quietly scores the son's self-righteousness when he refers to him as "the hunter" and when he says, "He had shut himself off" and ". . . he concluded with some surprise that even Schmeckebier and Edwards and the rest might have found him a difficult companion." For most students, this story is a most revelatory reading.

Teaching the Stories

As we said earlier, in order to achieve the aim for this part of the course, students should read *at least* four stories chosen to give them experience with four points of view and four different narrators. From the list of stories we have just suggested, we could readily select a variety of "quartets"—one of which would be potentially "right" for each class we were teaching. For, the stories in our list vary both in their literary complexity and in the "worlds" they represent.

■ *Some Possible Organizations.* For a class of able non-academic readers, for instance, we would probably choose "The White Circle," "Haircut," "The Bride Comes to Yellow Sky," and "The Blue-Winged Teal." For that "urbane" class of average or able readers, we would select "The Apostate," "Brooksmith," "Paul's Case," and "Winter Dreams." For that class of "all girls," "A Christmas Memory," "Wintry Peacock," "Paul's Case," and "The Basement Room." For less able non-academics, "The White Circle," "Haircut," "To Build a Fire," and "The Basement Room."

The concerns of a particular class and their reading abilities would suggest which four stories would be "right" for them. And their special needs and peculiar habits as readers would suggest in what order the stories within the group should be taught. Some beginning readers are so insecure that, when they see broad similarities among works, they respond as if the works were identical. If, for instance, they read two first-person narrations in succession, the broad similarity of the second story to the first would block their perceiving the differences in the function of the same technical point of view in these two stories. To force these students to confront each story free of such fixed expectations, the teacher might order the stories so as to prevent students reading, consecutively, stories that have similar points of view, similar narrators, even similar subject matters. Should our able non-academics, for instance, have such a tendency, an order such as this would frustrate it: "The White Circle," "The Bride Comes to Yellow Sky," "Haircut," and "The Blue-Winged Teal."

Such a diversified ordering of points of view would be absolutely needed in some classes and would be greatly enjoyed in others. But one man's meat is another's poison. For slow students such continual newness would prove disconcerting. Less able readers need concentration. They will achieve the aim more easily if they begin with stories told by first-person narrators with obvious characteristics, for instance, "Haircut" or "My Old Man"; then move to stories told by more subtly rendered first-person narrators, for example, "The White Circle" or "Guests of the Nation"; and conclude with third-person narrations, at first the "easy," "To Build a Fire," then, the more demanding, "The Bride Comes to Yellow Sky," and, finally, "The Basement Room." An order such as this would give the less able both the initial obviousness they seem to need and the slow progress forward which continually fixes what they have learned and moves toward the new, ever so gradually.

Still other arrangements of stories might be made for those able classes who need the challenge of discovering differences and inducing generalizations. Such students might read two clusters of stories: a group of first-person narrations (perhaps "My Old Man," "A Christmas Memory," and "Brooksmith") and a group of third-person narrations (perhaps "The Basement Room," "The Blue-Winged Teal," and, in lieu of "Winter Dreams," Fitzgerald's "Babylon Revisited"). From reading and discussing each cluster, the students would discover what advantages and what limitations the choice of each of these points of view always entails. Further, they would see how the same technical point of view can be exploited in different stories to gain very different effects. And finally they would realize how the character of the narrator in each story, his intention, and his attitudes contribute to that difference.

If the teacher wishes a certain able class to make even more subtle discriminations than the preceding scheme requires, he might assign two clusters like these: first-person narrations, the narrator not the main character—"Haircut," "Brooksmith," "Wintry Peacock"; and third-person narrations, omniscience limited to the main character—"Winter Dreams," "The Basement Room," "The Blue-Winged Teal."

We have mentioned only a few of the possible organizations of stories that we might use in this or that class to help students learn to respond to mode of narration. But whatever organizations we chose to use in particular classes, *in the study* of the stories we would be stressing many of the same features. *In all classes* we would be asking such questions as:

How does the narrator's *point of view* limit what he *can* know and, hence, what he *can* tell of the incident he narrates?

What kind of fellow is the narrator? How does he reveal his characteristics to the reader? (How do other characters suggest the first-person narrator's personality? How do commentaries, parentheticals, and diction suggest the third-person narrator's character?)

How does the nature of the narrator (his temperament, his capability) affect what he does tell?

How is his intention revealed to the reader? Why does he withhold what he might tell? Why is his telling of the incident ordered the way it is? How do his diction and his figurative language suggest his attitude toward the incident he tells? (And if such hypothesis is needed: How would the story differ were it told from another point of view? by another kind of narrator?)

■ *Some Common Problems.* If we assign the stories with precise direction and if students read them carefully, *most* classes will be able to deal adequately with *most* of these questions. But certain features of mode of narration seem to pose difficulties for certain kinds of students rather consistently.

Some students have trouble sensing the presence of the third-person narrator. As they read, they are not aware of a person selecting, withholding, and commenting on the event explicitly or indirectly, a person who, though seemingly absent, is quite influential on the reader's response to the event. An expressive—indeed, insinuating—oral reading, with or without interspersed close questioning, will help these students discover the narrator and notice how he functions. Excerpts from a story like "Winter Dreams" might be used first and then the opening pages of "The Bride Comes to Yellow Sky."

Some students who discover narrators "without incident" have difficulty determining what the narrator's attitude is towards the story he tells. They are obtuse to tone. As we said earlier in the chapter on teaching poems, two good ways to *begin* to develop students' sense of tone are reading passages orally, the students following in their texts, and underlining certain tonally important phrasings of the narrator with rewordings that the students will readily associate with particular attitudes. Choose passages from any story in the grouping being used and go through the passages in class glossing certain phrases and letting the class suggest the attitude each phrase expresses. This procedure will not only help students sense tone but will impress upon them that a reader's decision on what the narrator's attitude toward his story is has to arise from what the reader discovers the narrator's tone to be here, and here, and here, and here in the story—not from a single instance nor a final instance, nor from some statement of the narrator's about his attitude.

Oral reading and glossing phrases are useful "ground-breakers" for developing a sense of tone. But these teaching devices need to be supplemented or supplanted by a more formal kind of study, a study that will call students' attention to the language clues to tone. For this study the teacher might use another kind of comparison: underlining the narrator's expression of an idea or a feeling with a tonally different expression of it. Using a story the class is currently reading, the teacher might begin by underlining the early passages with expressions that are *obviously different in tone* from the narrator's. Students would be asked what the differences are and what is causing the differences. When students were succeeding on these passages, the teacher might underline the next passages with expressions *more tonally similar* to the narrator's—asking always how the expressions differ in effect and what accounts for the difference. And so on—the next passages further taxing students' ability to discriminate among tones.

Some students who are adequately sensitive to tone still have difficulty pointing out *how* they know what the intention of the narrator is and what the intention of the work is. To help them, assign a story like "The Apostate" or "My Old Man" with a study guide that asks them to list, in the order in which they appear in the story, all the clues they can find to both of these intentions. In class, pool the findings on the board, in two columns, the students offering the clues in the exact order in which the story offers them. Not only will this kind of exercise reveal what both intentions are and whether or not they coincide but, more important, such an exercise will make students simulate in a conscious, slow-motion, public way the experience an attentive reader goes through when he is discovering intentions.

Finally, some students have a still different kind of problem, one that is often more resistant to cure. They can sense the attitude the narrator or the author takes toward the event, but in certain instances, these readers resist taking the attitude that the story suggests the reader should take. Why? The causes vary. Some students feel so strongly about *the event* that they are blind to the treatment of it. Others feel compelled to comb subtle stories to locate some explicit comment that "says" what the reader's attitude should be. Still others have difficulty with certain stories because ambiguity makes them restive; they feel the need of taking a clear-cut attitude. Since the causes for students' inability to take the attitude the story suggests are diverse, the treatment must be.

The first group of students might profit by doing some hypothesizing. Take a story like Frank O'Connor's "The Drunkard."[9] The event is reprehensible, to be sure. But what is the effect? Why? What, then, should the reader's attitude be? At this point, ask the class to point out as precisely as possible what difference it would make *if* the event were told, not by the boy, but by one of the neighbor women. Work out with students the answers to such questions as: What part of the incident would she know about? How does her relation to the incident differ from the boy's? What *would* she tell? What withhold? What would her attitude be? If the author's attitude were the same as hers, what should ours be? Such an exercise would impress upon the class that it is not the basic event, but the shape the event is given, that determines our attitude. It is the shape that precludes one effect and creates another.

For an alternative exercise that will make the same point, the teacher might come closer to home. He might call the class' attention to the personal attitude a certain student insists upon taking toward *the event* of the story the class is reading. He might then ask the class to hypothesize fully how the story would have to have been told in order to evoke *that* attitude in a reader.

As a third sort of antidote for the first group, the teacher might use a reinforcing double dose. He might have the class study consecutively such stories as "Haircut" and "Winter Dreams," both of which express attitudes quite different from what the students' personal attitudes toward *the events* would probably be and both of which suggest rather explicitly what the readers' attitudes should be. Throughout the study of each story, these students should be kept as close as possible to the text, so that when in each case, the question about the reader's attitude is finally raised, it can be so phrased that the answer must be a conclusion from the story (pulling together all preceding parts of the study): If *this* kind of person tells *this* event in *this* way, how are we supposed to "take" it?

The three treatments we have suggested will help the first group to recognize that they ought to respond to a story, not just to its event. But, as moral philosophers have long known, it is one thing for men to know how to do what they ought, another for them to recognize that they ought to do it, and yet another for them to do it. So it may take the whole study of fiction—and more—to habituate these sometimes "painful cases" to *doing* what they know they should.

The second group of students—those who hunt through a story for a directive to tell them what attitude they should take—are frequently just victims of their own lack of confidence. Often promising readers, they have no faith in their own sensitive responses. They are afraid of being "wrong." Reassure them by making them show you what they took into account in the story in order to arrive at the attitude they are—oh, so insecurely—taking. They are right; show them how they can be sure they are.

The third group is, of course, prey to that longing for unqualified truth that plagues us all. One of the moral effects of reading literature is, however, the recognition that, when many situations are fully experienced (as they are in literature), the only possible attitude to take toward them is an ambivalent one. The third group is "tiptoe" on the threshold of this recognition.

These are some of the kinds of difficulties that might arise as we help certain students learn to respond to modes of narration. Like all corrective measures, the "treatments" we have proposed must be reinforced by repeated practice which, for as long as necessary, should be "built into" lessons in the form of a direct question, a short paper, or a "devil's advocate" argument. It is only by many trials that old habits are eroded, that confidence is developed, that thresholds are crossed.

■ *Some Collateral Writing Exercises.* It is only by repeated exercise that new concepts and new skills are learned and strengthened. Appropriate writing activities will help provide this exercise and will test its results. Here are some sample tasks.

First, *some exercises on point of view.* If the teacher wants to help students understand how a certain technical point of view (say, third-person point of view of the main character) limits what is told, he might ask students to state briefly in an in-class paper what episodes *could not have been included* in, say, "The Bride Comes to Yellow Sky,"[10] had the story been told from the sheriff's point of view. Or, for a more challenging assignment, the teacher might have the preceding question answered orally by the class, and then ask students to write a short response to: What difference would the loss of these scenes have made to the final scene?

And now an even more demanding assignment on point of view. Here is the particular topic, which might be used for an in-class or out-of-class critical exercise:

In "The Blue-Winged Teal," [told from the son's point of view], how

would our attitude toward the situation have been different *if* we had
known what was in the father's mind when he first held up the teal?
Answer this question in not more than two paragraphs.

Students' responses to this assignment will show to what extent they
recognize how an author uses the advantages of a certain technical
point of view (in this case, third, limited omniscience) to control
the reader's attitude toward an event.

Critical exercises like the three we have just described might be
complemented by some exercises in creative writing. Students might
realize more fully what the choice of a point of view entails, for
instance, if they take an excerpt from one of the stories being read
and rewrite it, using a different point of view. Such a writing assignment should be preceded by a preparatory in-class exercise: this
might consist of a close comparative study of a passage written
from two points of view, or it might consist of a real rehearsal—the
students first rewriting a familiar passage, using a different point of
view, and then discussing the changes they had to make and the
effects of these changes. The assignment which follows such in-class
preparation should be *in all cases* tightly controlled, the teacher
specifying the exact passage to be rewritten and the point of view
to be used. Left to themselves, students often fail to choose useful
passages, and some spend all their assignment time just choosing.
Choose *for* them so that the assignment will do its intended office.
Both the passage the teacher chooses and the two points of view
involved in the assignment should be familiar to the students; the
changes required should be ones that the students *can* make and
that will produce *noticeable* effects.

Here is an example of such an assignment (and this particular
topic would be appropriate for students of many different abilities):

Tell the first paragraph of Willa Cather's "Paul's Case" in the first
person, as Paul would have told it.

The average student would abide by the limitations of the point of
view; the able would reflect the character of the narrator as well.
Another assignment of the same type—one usable as a first task in
able classes or as a second task in other groups—would be:

Tell the second and third paragraphs of Crane's "The Bride Comes to
Yellow Sky" from the point of view of the sheriff.

Now, *some exercises on the nature of the narrator* and *on his
intentions*. If the teacher wants to help students improve their perceptions of these matters, he might, as a first exercise, choose an
unfamiliar opening passage that has a relatively simple narrator
(say, the first ten sentences of "The Apostate") and ask students to:

Read the passage several times, asking yourself all the while what sort of person the narrator *seems* to be. When you have decided, write a paragraph that points out *the evidence* you have for your decision.

Later, a second, similar exercise can measure students' progress. The passage chosen for this exercise should present a more complex narrator; the second and third paragraphs of "The Bride Comes to Yellow Sky" or the first two paragraphs of "The White Circle" are the kinds of passages that would be useful.

To complement discussions on the narrator, the teacher might wish to assign brief, in-class papers to be written during the final fifteen minutes of the period on the story just discussed. To close the study of "Haircut," for instance, he might ask students to answer:

> How do the two following paragraphs *confirm our view* of the narrator's attitude toward the events he tells?

> They was a time when she would go to whoever he was workin' for and ask them to give her his wages, but after she done this once or twice, he beat her to it by borrowin' most of his pay in advance. He told it all round town, how he had outfoxed his Missus. He certainly was a caution!

> But he wasn't satisfied with just outwittin' her. He was sore the way she had acted, tryin' to grab off his pay. And he made up his mind he'd get even. ["She" is the "caution's" hardworking wife to whom he gave two or three dollars a week to run the house.]

Or, for a more challenging task of the same sort, the teacher might ask the class to:

> Read the two paragraphs beginning "They was a time when she would go . . ."; then point out in a brief paragraph *why* such a phrase as "being so pitiless to" would not work as well as the phrase "just outwittin' " does.

A task like this last one allows all students to respond to some extent and the most able to show that they recognize that the change is inconsistent both with the narrator's vocabulary and with his attitude. Such an exercise as this can be made more difficult simply by substituting for the first phrase one that is closer to "just outwittin.' "

Creative writing exercises on the effect of the narrator can be designed to at once reinforce and extend the understandings that students' critical reading and writing are developing. Such an exercise as the following would do both. Choose some passage from a story that the class has studied carefully, say, the paragraph beginning, "My old man sat there and sort of smiled at me . . ." or the one beginning, "Well, my old man got his license all right . . . .", both from "My Old Man." Then, assign a topic like the following:

> Read this passage several times, imagining what would change if this material were told by *another kind* of narrator, say, the same person when a man—who *does know* now what he thinks. [The teacher might choose,

instead, a long-time acquaintance who despised the father or some other more demanding narrator, if the ability of the class warrants it.] List what would change and how it would change. Now, tell the paragraph as the new narrator would tell it.

In this assignment as we have outlined it, students would be changing narrators, but not point of view. This assignment *could* demand both a change in narrator and in point of view, first to third, let us say. But such an assignment should be given only to those able *and interested* in doing it. And it may be desirable to have a preparatory "dry-run" on such an assignment, an in-class exercise similar to what we suggested for the first creative assignment on point of view.

As a final evaluation of the progress that individual students have made toward achieving the aim of the First Part of the course, the teacher might use an in-class, open-book, critical paper of a page or so. The paper might concern the mode of narration of some story that the class has not studied, or it might deal with some important aspect of narration that was not included in the discussion of some story *recently* studied. Either is a valid way of testing. But if the teacher elects to use a new story, unless it is very brief, he must either allow students to read the story the night before or ask them to work during the exam on only the first three or four pages of the story.

When students are asked to read a new story just before an exam, they know that it is the test story. They can, of course, hold a pre-exam tutorial, asking and answering all the questions that have been repeatedly asked about stories in class. To forestall such artificial "boning," the teacher can tell students that he does not care whether or not they discuss the story beforehand—and then justify his attitude by giving a test question such as this: (Let us say the new story is Somerset Maugham's "The Treasure.")

"The Treasure" is told from Robert Harengay's point of view, but the narrator deviates on one or two occasions. In a one- to two-page paper show what is gained by these deviations.

The teacher can make the topic easier if he cites the deviations. Or easier still, if he offers also some questions:

How do these deviations *contribute* to our understanding of the situation of the story? Why would a glimpse into Pritchard's mind *spoil* the experience of the story? Write a one- to two-page paper that answers these questions.

If, for such a test, the students are asked to work on a story that they have *not previously read*, then not only should their work be confined to the first three or four pages of the story, but the test question might well be highly similar to the questions that they have been repeatedly asked in class about other stories. Let us say the test story is "Mother in Mannville." Here is an appropriate question:

Read carefully the first three pages of this story, as far as, "He became intimate, of course, with my pointer Pat." Notice the point of view and the clues to the narrator's character. Then, in a page or so, point out how *this* point of view keeps us from being sure what *this* narrator is like. Remember you are writing about this point of view and this narrator.

If for such a test, students are asked to work on a story *previously studied* in class, then the question should be on some aspect of the mode of narration *not* featured in class. Let us say that the story is "The White Circle" and that in class, Tucker, the narrator, was stressed. Here is a question on a new aspect:

In a one- to two-page paper show how the character of the narrator and the point of view used in the story prevent us, *all through the story,* from condemning Anvil.

With minor modifications—with, for instance, directions that "lead" more—any of the sample writing topics we have suggested can be adjusted "downward."

For additional writing assignments, see "Holidays," pp. 430–432, under "Producing the Course."

■ *A Sample Lesson: "The Basement Room."* To complete our discussion of mode of narration, here is a teaching plan that shows how the kinds of questions and of writing assignments we have been suggesting are fused in a classroom lesson. This plan, furthermore, documents our claim than an emphasis on mode of narration does not preclude helping students notice other features of the story. "The Basement Room"[11] should be studied at or near the close of this First Part of the first course. Because of its length and double plot and because of the narrator's intermittent deviations from the prevailing point of view, the story requires a somewhat initiated reader. And these very deviations make the story an excellent finale. For they give us a last chance to impress upon students the fact that point of view, like all other literary devices, is only a means. Point of view is determined by the effect the writer wants to achieve. *If the effect requires a shift in point of view, then there is a shift.*

Now, to the lesson.

Students would need approximately two-nights' assignment time[12] to prepare for the discussion of this story. So we would assign the story accordingly and, at that time, distribute duplicated copies of a study guide which would provide the class with useful annotations of unfamiliar terms ("Old Coasters," "Meccano" set, "mackintosh," Pimlico, Belgravia, ginger beer) and with the following three exercises to work out in writing before the first class discussion:

1. Read the opening of the story as far as the entrance of Mrs. Baines. Reread these pages. Then answer the following questions very briefly: (a) What details in the first paragraph make the social world we are entering clear to us? (b) What does the basement room mean to Philip? What does it mean to Baines? Does Philip understand what it means to Baines? Does Philip think he does? Point out *phrases* that support what you say.

Now, as you read the remainder of the story, notice how this first episode has shown the "state of affairs" that makes possible what happens in the story.

2. (a) This story is in five parts. After you have finished reading each part, write *one* good sentence that summarizes that part. (b) This story really fuses *two* plots into one. Name the two plots. Tell, if you can, what fuses these two plots so that one story results.

3. Through whose eyes are we seeing the events of the story? [This question is purposely "open" so that it will not clue students to the narrator's occasional movement from Philip's point of view to Baines' and to omniscience. If students have considered 1(b) carefully, they will have noticed the first shift in point of view. Their responses to this question will indicate how sensitive to mode of narration they have become.]

Since students would, by this time, have already discussed several stories, an average or better class could very well talk about the first two questions on this guide within the first fifteen or twenty minutes of the class period. This would leave a half-hour for the third question, and *if* the discussion was brisk, even some time for a final writing exercise.

Let us see now how discussion of the *third question* might go in an *average* class. When we ask, Through whose eyes are we seeing the events of the story? (or, Whose version of the situation are we getting?), the answer might simply be "Philip's" or "the narrator's seeing and hearing and feeling what the boy does." There may be no mention of any deviations. So, we would then ask again, What does the basement room mean to Baines? Does Philip know that? Do you? Then, if necessary, Why does the narrator go into Baines' mind? (Or, What does the narrator gain by going into Baines' mind for a moment?)

Then, we would refer students to the fourth paragraph in Part II: Precisely what is the narrator telling us here that Philip could not know? Why does the narrator want us to know this and know it now? Look now at the final paragraph in Part II. Does this deviation from Philip's point of view affect our understanding of the situation in any *new* way?

In Part III, we would point out rapidly to the class the narrator's excursions into Baines' mind and his interpretation of Baines' experience. Then, What image of Baines do we get from this information?

Why does the narrator at this point want us to see Baines as this sort of fellow? What image in Part IV contrasts sharply with it?

We would let the students find the deviations in Part IV. Then, Which parts of the description of Mrs. Baines would have been unknown to Philip? Why did the narrator want us to know that Mrs. Baines had "nothing to hope for" and that cruelty raised her above the pitiable?

And, to summarize, If we had only Philip's view of the Baines' conflict, with whom would we sympathize? In the light of the information that the narrator adds, with whom do we sympathize? The answers to these questions will synthesize the various effects we have noticed that the narrator achieved by going beyond Philip's point of view.

We would be ready to ask all of the preceding questions, but, in most classes, we would need only some of them. And if we wanted to reduce the class time and effort spent on the third question, we would simply word the study guide more directively.

If time permitted, (and it might in an able class), we would conclude this class period with a writing exercise that would give the students a chance to show what they had learned during the discussion. A task like the following would do:

Read the second to the last paragraph of the story. Here the narrator lets us see how Baines accounts for Philip's action. Is Baines correct? Why does the narrator want us to know what Baines thinks?

Now, the assignment. For an *able* class, the duplicated assignment sheet would say simply:

Look carefully at any *four* of the following descriptions of Philip's impressions:
1. "Philip Lane went downstairs . . . ."
2. "He heard Mrs. Baines' voice . . . ; it was . . . exposed."
3. "She took him by the arm . . . ."
4. "Baines passed . . . struggle."
5. "It shrivelled . . . to laugh about."
6. "It wasn't right . . . life."
7. "He said, 'She won't be coming back . . . far away."
8. "There had been . . . involved."

In each of the four you choose, point out *the part* of the description that is not expressed the way Philip would think about it. For instance, in the description of Mrs. Baines, "meticulous and loveless" are not words that Philip would have thought in. Tell what is gained by the narrator's using such words instead of Philip's.

This assignment would call students' attention to the subtler ways in which point of view is extended in this story. They would see that sometimes the language the narrator uses to express the boy's impressions accurately reports a child's reactions in a child's words; other times, it is a language that makes the implications of the impressions clear to the reader, implications that are unknown to the boy.

For *less able* classes the duplicated assignment sheet would say:

Today when we talked about the very first episode of this story, we noticed that there was a gap between what Philip thought was "the case" with Baines and what actually was "the case." Go through the story and list in order other episodes in which Philip half understands what the truth is. Then tell how Philip's attitude toward these episodes changes. (And, *if you can,* say what later episode ironically reverses the first episode.)

On the following day in *less able* classes, we would spend most of the period using the responses from their homework papers to show students *one way* in which the story is structured. By this exercise, we would not only be pulling the story together for the class but also making the transition to the Second Part of the course: "The Story."

In *able* classes, we would use about half of the class period on a discussion of various passages from their assignment. At mid-class, we would hand out duplicated copies of the following questions and ask students to then and there make notes in answer to the first question:

1. Reread the last three paragraphs of the first episode ("Did you ever shoot a nigger?" . . . "anything we could understand.") Point out how this apparently irrelevant experience that Baines recalls represents *in a way* the experience Philip is to have in this story. Why would Graham Greene want to relate these apparently unrelated experiences? What would he gain by it?

2. Philip has a waking world and a dream world. Point out how these two worlds are related *throughout* the story.

3. Several words are repeatedly used throughout the story: "responsible," "life," "dust," for instance. Point out how the mentions of the word "responsible" mark stages of Philip's moral change. [This would be an appropriate task if students had not worked on a continuity like this before. If they had had *some* practice, then we would give a task like the following.] Show that the mentions of "live" and "life" in the story mark off Philip's gradual move from attraction to life to fear of it. [If students had had previous successful experiences with such tasks, then the following would be a useful assignment.] Notice the uses of the word "dust" at successive points in the story. Notice what it is associated with in Philip's mind, and in the narrator's. What force in the conflict does it come to stand for?

After students had made notes in answer to the first question, we would work out on the board a "master" answer, the class giving us

the data. Then, we would assign for out-of-class work whichever of
the two remaining questions seemed more appropriate for the group.
Answering either of the questions will lead students to discover another way in which this story is organized. Either topic will, therefore, be a fruitful bridge to the Second Part of the course.

The lesson we have just outlined on mode of narration in "The
Basement Room" began with questions on the "world of the work"
and the fusing of plots, focused on the effects of deviations from a
point of view, and ended with questions on some of the many other
unifying elements in the story. The study of every story in this First
Part of the course would similarly be both concentrating on mode
of narration and preparing students in one way or another for what
follows in the next part of the course. The study of every story
would be making students aware not only of the function of such
fundamentals as selection of material and arrangement of it but also
of the fact that knowing what the plot is does not, in and of itself,
take them very far into the "meaning" of a story. After seeing repeatedly how the narrative voice significantly qualifies, sometimes
reverses, the "face" meaning of an event, after seeing how point of
view slips a special lens before a reader's eyes, these students would
come to the study of "The Story" already knowing that a story is
more than a sequence of events—and knowing to some extent *at least*
one device that makes this so.

The Second Part: The Story

So one of the aims for this Second Part of the first course is to
help students learn to respond to *other* literary features that shape
event into story. The other aim is to help them liberalize their notion
of conflict. Our job, then, is really to help high school students
broaden what they bring. They tend to respond to only the events
of a story; they tend to think of conflict as an overt clash, often
physical. The teacher must expand their awareness of and their
response to the fictional means to meaning; and he must extend their
idea of conflict to include internal tensions of many sorts and many
degrees of intensity.

"Broaden" is the key idea in both aims. But what needs broadening is different in each case. When the teacher is helping students
to take into account *all* that is in a story, he is trying to get them to
see what, because of the modes of study we described earlier, they
have previously overlooked *in their reading of fiction,* and he is
trying to help them respond to what they now see. When, however,
he is helping students to enlarge their idea of conflict, he is trying
to get them to see in literature what they have previously overlooked

in life. Their unperceptive living and unexamined personal experiences have bred a rather gross idea of conflict. Therefore, they cannot now bring to bear on certain stories the quality of life experience that the reading of the stories demands. Since the teacher cannot directly extend students' life experience, he will begin by extending their experience of conflict in literature—an artificial priming of the pump that will eventually make such students more aware of the subtler conflicts in life. When that happens, for them literature and life will have begun to reciprocally enhance one another. (And now that we see the distinction between what the two aims entail, we see how much more difficult it may be to get students to achieve the second aim.)

"Broaden," not "replace," is the key word in both aims. And in this Second Part of the first course, the teacher has to guard continually against the tendency of some students—especially able ones —when they are once "enlightened" about story and conflict, to cast off as naive their earlier interest in event. Instead of expanding and qualifying with their new understandings and skills the knowledge and sensitivity they already have, they want to replace the old with the new. Indeed, they "decide" that the kind of story in which the conflict is internal, the event slim, and the conclusion a recognition is, *in itself*, better than other forms of the short story. Left to themselves, these students would emerge from this part of the course with a new, though just as partial, response to stories. To prevent such substituting from defeating our purpose, the study of each story in this part of the course would emphasize seeing *all* that is in the story. At the outset, the stress would be on seeing that there is *more than* event, *more than* external conflict; and at the end of this part, the emphasis would be on seeing that there *is* event where nothing seems to happen, that there *is* external conflict involved in the internal tension represented.

This Second Part of the course is organized in four sections to encourage a *gradual* broadening of the understandings and skills the readers bring. *In the first section*, students would read the kind of story they are familiar with: the story in which plot is conspicuous and circumstances seem to govern characters, in which conflict seems to be a matter of external events, and in which the conventional "complication-climax-resolution" scheme makes clear what happened; why; what each gained and lost; and what the future will be.

As we teach these stories, we would always be "inching outward": trying to get students to realize that, like so many people they take for granted because they know them so well, there is much they have not noticed about this kind of story they are so accustomed to.

We would use the "innocent" question, But *why* does the author
_____? to make students discover the many things beyond the
external event that count in the effect such a story has on them.

As we teach these stories, we would be asking students not only
the usual questions about the mode of narration, the causal connections among the events, about the climax, and the ways the central
character is revealed to us, but also other questions—about the
design (or shape) in which the plot is told, about the reasons certain
parts of the story are minimized, certain parts are presented in
scenes, about the function of the weather or of an object or of a
repeated word, about the value of some "unimportant" episode or
character. And when in the class discussion of these stories students
showed that they had begun to ask *themselves* about *some* of these
matters, they would be ready to move on to the second section.

The stories students would read *in the second section* would have
all the outward signs of the "familiar" story—the easily discernible
plot and the apparently external conflict. But they would be stories
that would make students realize that the external situation is just
the event that *occasions* a crisis within a character, and that it is
that conflict that is important to a reader.

As we teach these stories, we would be asking students what is in
the situation and in *that* character that accounts for his response to
it; we would be asking them to determine precisely how the character is affected and to seek their clues to the nature of his tension
not only in what he does and says or even in his attitude, but also
in the response of his foils to the situation, in the implications of
setting, and in omnipresent objects. When in class discussion students reveal that they have *begun* to ask *themselves* some of the
questions we have been asking them, when they begin to suggest
how the character's solution to his external problem reveals also his
resolution of his inner crisis, they are ready for the readings in the
next section.

The stories students would study *in the third section* would have
little of the "familiar" form about them. They would be those stories
in which what happens in the external world simply "triggers," as
O'Faolain says, a crucial internal event: a crisis through which the
main character often achieves an insight. As we teach these stories,
we would be trying to help students see how small, often unobtrusive, details both reveal what kind of person the main character is
and show how the crisis affects him and why it moves him as it does.
Furthermore, we would be trying to help students distinguish between what the character recognizes and what the reader perceives.
And, finally, we would want students to realize that what matters
in these stories is the complication, climax, and resolution of the

internal drama. When class discussion shows that students are beginning to be able to perceive these matters on their own, they are ready to read the stories *in the fourth and last section.*

The stories students would read in this section would be those that represent in unusual renderings the ordinary conflicts, the undramatic heartaches, the usual ironies of everyday life. These are the stories that, because of their simple revelations and complex renderings, can be experienced only by perceptive readers who can make sensitive inferences from small details, who can leap to appropriate relationships among parts, who can, in other words, play a large role in the imaginative re-creation of a story. As we teach these stories, we would be trying to help students become just such perceptive readers.

Through the·readings in these four sections, students would move from plot-centered stories to those focused on character, from stress on the external event to stress on the internal, from explicit telling to implicit suggestion. And they would move so gradually that they would see that the differences among the several groups of stories are really differences in emphases: nothing is lost; the relative importance of plot and character alters. As the emphasis on character increases, both the interest in the internal and the use of implication and suggestion naturally increase. But, in stories, as in the Hegelian synthesis, everything remains, varied in prominence and in treatment.

Now that we have described our aims and sketched our teaching organization for this Second Part of our course, we shall develop each of the four sections, listing some examples of the *kinds* of stories that would be appropriate readings in each. We have annotated every story to suggest its length, the kinds of readers which, because of its literary complexity and its concern, it might be suitable for, and some of the literary features students might become sensitive to through the careful reading of the story.

The First Section: Plot-Centered Stories

Through their readings in this section we want students to *begin* to see how much more than a sequence of events a story is. So, we center on the obvious: on how the bare causally related sequence of events is affected by the design (or shape) that organizes them. And we would be calling students' attention to how the events are ordered, what emphasis they are given, whether they are rendered in scene or narrated, what alternations, parallels, or cycles pattern them. We would be noticing all such features as these in order to show students how these features determine their experience of the events. In the First Part of the course, we tried to help students see how mode of narration controls their experience; now we want to help them realize how the design of the events does.

The final reading or readings of the First Part of this course might very well double as the initial reading of this section. In fact, even the plan we suggested for teaching "The Basement Room" would be directly usable for a transitional lesson if it included some questions that *explicitly* called attention to the design of the events: to that series of alternating incidents through which the lines of the plot slowly converge to confrontation. This design is merely touched on in question 2(b) of the assignment.

The story has a double plot: the Baines' complication affects Philip's life and Philip's affects the Baines'. The design makes the reader progress through a series of incidents: now Philip and Baines, now Philip and Mrs. Baines, now Philip and Baines, and so on, to the inevitable confrontation of the three characters on the staircase. Through this ordering of the double plot, the reader experiences not only a growing sense of inevitability but also the continuing tension between the "fear of life" and the "attraction to it" that both Baines and Philip—in their separate and shared worlds—feel.

Other stories—for instance, "The Bride Comes to Yellow Sky," "Paul's Case," or even "The Three Strangers"—would be fruitful transitional readings. In "The Bride Comes to Yellow Sky," the reader's response is *obviously* affected both by the narrator's attitude and by the design of the story. Our teaching could show students how both features are important. We might begin with the narrator's attitude. What suggests it to the reader? Mostly the narrator's gentle ridicule (in the first part of the story) of the devoted, dutiful, naive Potters and their new estate. Notice, for instance, the joshing diction he uses to describe their appearance ("a direct result of his new black clothes was that his brick-coloured hands were constantly performing," "small reservations of velvet," "steel buttons abounding"). Notice the inflated words by which he expresses their feeling about marriage ("glory," "beamed with elation"). Notice his ironic comment on their stereotyped dialogue ("They were evidently very happy"). And notice his discussion of the "extraordinary crime" of "the traitor to the feelings of Yellow Sky." The narrator's attitude toward the Potters is also defined by the way his tone condemns the snobbish reactions and sardonic winks of the porter and some of the passengers. Finally, at the close of the first part of the story, the narrator is gently amused by the awkward, childlike Potter anticipating discovery of his "shame." Did the Potters "make it" home undiscovered? From the narrator's attitude we suspect they did not. The gesturing agent at the railroad station is only "the first effect" of their "extraordinary crime."

The Potters' fear of discovery and the readers' expectations of it are fulfilled—in a comically ironic way. But only the reader sees this coming to pass. For the story is designed in simultaneous scenes, one showing the shy Potters, hurrying home, another showing the town battened down against its "bad buy," and yet another showing the rampaging Scratchy out to get the sheriff Potter. The design of the story keeps Potter and Scratchy ignorant of the collision course they are on from the last twenty minutes of the first part of the story until their "rounding-the-corner" confrontation in the fourth part. Only the reader follows from beginning to end the inevitable convergence.

And, because the story is a parody of the classic western, the reader knows how to anticipate the imminent clash. The flamboyant theatricality of the swaggering Scratchy in the maroon-colored shirt and the boots with gilded imprints has readied the reader for the "big" scene in which the bridegroom armed only with his bride disarms the town's "bad guy" who, in amazement and frustration, funnels ("Aw-shucks!") away. So, the dramatic resolution of the Potters' problem—and the town's.

This is a good initial reading for this first section on "The Story." For it is easy for students to see how important the design of the events is in the effect the story achieves. And it is easy to call students' attention, if necessary, to the specific function of other features that render the events; for instance, it is easy to help students see what is gained by treating certain happenings scenically and by summarizing others. To do this, the teacher need only ask such simple questions as: Why is most of the first part a narrated scene? Why are the bits of dialogue included? Why not have Potter's musings in his own words? What is the function of dialogue in the second part? Why is the whole of the third part a narrated scene? Why does the narrator explain Scratchy's motivation for calling off the fight? Do we need the explanation? How do the physical details that the narrator gives relate to this summary statement?

This is a good initial reading, furthermore, for it gives the teacher an opportunity to call students' attention to the nonplot features that help to unify this story: the chain of situational ironies, the continuous sense of "comes" that pervades the whole story, the constant emphasis on people's real and anticipated reactions to the Potters' marriage, and the realistic detail with theatrical connotation that repeatedly affects the reader's response.

This is a good initial reading, finally, for yet another reason. To students, this story may seem at first to be just a fight averted by chance: circumstances have put these two men on the streets of Yellow Sky; inevitably, they will meet; fight. Only an event—the marriage—prevents the inevitable. Since this is probably what students will think, the story is a "natural" for showing them that the events were determined by personalities. This is a story of the "sharp impulse" versus the "social hedges"—the "impulse" ruled Potter; the "social hedges," Scratchy. Neither really wins; both suffer as the "hangdog" glance and the "funnel-shaped tracks," and much more objective detail, show.

Either a reading like "The Three Strangers" or one like "Paul's Case" would be as good an "opener" as Crane's story for this first section of "The Story." And a work like Hardy's is probably more available to less able readers than Crane's. In "The Three Strangers" the narrator's attitude toward both the characters and the "outside world" is easily discernible. Furthermore, the plot of the tale he recounts is simple: a rural christening party, joined by two strangers, is interrupted by an official call to search for an escaped criminal, who, the guests believe, is the man that moments before came to the door for an instant. The party finds "its man," but, surprise, the real criminal was one of the strangers, now disappeared. He is never found. The story has the familiar introduction, complication, climax, resolution, conclusion.

Because the story is relatively easy in all these respects, little time need be spent "getting it straight" and much can be given to seeing what makes it more than its simple sequence of events. Students should discuss the function of the frame, for instance. How do the first four paragraphs relate to the rest of the story? How do the last three? What is gained by using them? And the class should be helped to see not only that the episode is told as a tale but why it is: Why is the characterization so spare? What details *are* specified? Why those? What is the function of the shepherd and his guests in the story? Why is their pursuit of the criminal rendered comically? Their protection of him is not. Why not? Why has this episode been related for half a century? What is the point? And, after such a battery of questions, students will have the answer to: Why is this episode told as a tale?

While students are discussing these questions, they will come to realize, among other things, that, although external circumstance *seems* to govern the course of events in this tale, actually it is the watchmaker who does; he reverses the course of events in his own favor. And he does it by exploiting the blind belief of the shepherd and his guests that a man's outward appearance must reflect his character. The narrator takes great pains to build up for the shepherd folks' awakening. He reinforces the belief that men are what they look like by giving details of the hangman's clothes, the hedge-carpenter's fingers, the constable's staff, the shepherd's crooks, the grog blossoms, the terrified surprise on the third stranger's face. So, when the shepherd folk finally discover the truth, no wonder they admire the watchmaker—he is the man who stepped *out of character* —the mild man who stole a sheep before the owner's eyes, the escaped criminal who chorused his hangman's song.

A story like Willa Cather's "Paul's Case" probably requires able readers. It is a long story but, more important, it tempts readers to make personal value judgments on the rightness or wrongness of Paul's actions. (The less detached readers will fall.) Furthermore, the narrative voice in "Paul's Case" is more subtly indicated than the voice in "The Three Strangers" or in "The Bride Comes to Yellow Sky," so it would probably be more difficult for readers to determine the narrator's attitude toward what he tells. Students will readily notice his direct *statements* about the quality of Paul's sensuousness and the superficiality of his values, but they must also observe the objective detail that supports these statements and the metaphors and the chains of words that *suggest* to us again and again the narrator's attitude toward what Paul regards as "living." Only able readers observe such features, and even some of them may need help. If they do, we can incisively show them how the narrator's language suggests his attitude toward Paul's "case" by referring them to the following passage in the story:

> It was at the theatre and at Carnegie Hall that Paul really lived; the rest was but a sleep and a forgetting. This was Paul's fairy tale, and it had for him all the allurement of a secret love. The moment he inhaled the gassy, painty, dusty odor behind the scenes, he breathed like a prisoner set free, and felt within him the possibility of doing or saying splendid, brilliant things. The moment the cracked orchestra beat out the overture from *Martha*, or jerked at the serenade from *Rigoletto*, all stupid and ugly things slid from him, and his senses were deliciously, yet delicately fired.

When students finish reading the passage, we would ask them direct, simple questions such as these: If *Paul* were to describe the theatre and Carnegie Hall, which of the words in this passage would he change? Why? Why does the narrator use these words, then?

Beyond being able to ascertain the narrator's attitude, students who read "Paul's Case" must also be able to make several other sensitive responses to various aspects of the narration. They must be able to determine whether or not the reader is supposed to concur with the narrator's attitude. They must be able to decide why the narrator includes the teachers' reactions to Paul, why the teachers' reactions to their own reactions are mentioned, and, finally, why the reader is told about the actresses' "vastly amused" attitudes toward Paul.

If students *can* respond adequately to the narration, then "Paul's Case" will help them see how the handling (the design, the patterning) of a rather simple plot suggests the theme of a story. The first of the two parts of the story is composed of a series of scenes that alternately depict the two worlds of Paul: "Cordelia Street" (school and home) and the "secret temple" (the concert hall and the theatre). The patterning of the scenes makes the reader perceive that, for Paul, unrealistic and romantically blind, these two worlds cannot coexist. So, when at the close of the first part of the story "Cordelia Street" triumphs, the reader is ready for the results: ". . . when they had taken away his bone, the whole thing was virtually determined."

In the second part of the story, the "secret temple" triumphs for eight *golden* days. Here there are four narrated scenes: Paul's entrance, his first day, his last day, his exit. Why does the narrator parallel the entrance and the exit? What is the relationship of the first and the last days? In what way is the Yale man a foil? (Or, Why cannot Paul "pull himself together" and "make the train" as the Yale man does? Notice the only way Paul can do this.) Finally, a synthesizing question on the relation of design to theme in the whole story: How do these formal features suggest Paul's "either-or" world?

If students have been able to perceive how this design of scenes functions, then they will be able to see how such other features as the rain and the snow, the symbolic carnation, and the ironic initiation-journey motif work with the pattern of scenes we have just noticed to suggest how readers should "take" Paul's case.

The four stories that we have been discussing as transitions to the study of "The Story"[13] have all been readings that would be, as we mentioned, most appropriate for average or better students. Now let us see what kinds of stories we would use to introduce less able readers to the study of "The Story"—readers who could not begin even on a story like "The Three Strangers." Here are four new stories, all of which would make beginning easy for less mature, less competent readers: Jessamyn West's "Shivaree Before Breakfast," John Steinbeck's "The Leader of the People," Richard Connell's "The Most Dangerous Game," and Steinbeck's "Flight."

In "Shivaree Before Breakfast" (nine pages), the joke two brothers play on an elderly neighbor results in an inadvertent cruelty to which each of the boys reacts differently. Readers naturally want to know *why* brothers would make such different responses to the same event. So this simple story proves to be an excellent vehicle for helping students see that the story tells the reader why; he need only look carefully and he will see that the reaction of each boy is truly consonant with his character *as developed in the story*.

"Shivaree," furthermore, gives us an excellent chance to reinforce what students have learned about the narrator's attitude and to introduce them to the use of such structuring devices as the initiation motif and situational irony (The boys cruelty results from the celebration of a folk custom!).

John Steinbeck's "The Leader of the People" (twenty pages) is also straightforward reading. The general structure of the story is familiar: introduction, inciting incident, complication, climax, resolution. The narrator's attitude is relatively easy to ascertain. This simple story does, however, admit of a somewhat more intensive study than Miss West's. Take characterization, for example. Students notice that some characters seem inconsistent, first one sort of person, then another. For instance, in the opening paragraphs, Jody seems to be a destructive boy. But his responses later in the story are not destructive. What, *precisely,* changes him? How is the change made known to us? Is the change a reversal? What makes it psychologically acceptable? Why does he see his Grandfather as "small, thin, and black"?

This is, furthermore, a fine story for showing students *why* scenes are used, *how* feelings are objectified, *how* events can suggest empathy between people, and *how* a phrase like "leader of the people" takes on rich implications (What, for instance, is significant in the fact that leadership is transferred from the oldest to the youngest? What is the difference between the meaning of this phrase and, say "our leader"?).

Though Richard Connell's "The Most Dangerous Game" (seventeen pages) is probably a more challenging reading than the two preceding stories, its mystery captures readers, its sudden shock engages them, and its continuing suspense "pulls them along." The story is, then, a relatively easy, quite pleasurable, and very fruitful reading. Since it is the way the events are told that captivates readers, it is easy to get them to recognize the value of extra-plot features; they see how different the story would be if these features were lost. In discussion of the story, we would probably stress the way the frame of the story, the setting, and the diction create mystery; the way the characterization of Zaroff effects shock at his proposal, and the way that the arrangement of the events in the hunt and the economy of the narrator evoke suspense.

John Steinbeck's "Flight" (twenty-four pages) might be a good initial reading for the slow, persistent, less able reader. It would be a "right" *second* reading for most less competent students—the kind of story we would use to reinforce what has been learned from the first reading. "Flight" would also be an appropriate alternative for those average readers who *could* read Crane's story—but probably would not enjoy it.

"Flight" is openhanded about many things. The story is frankly about "becoming a man"; this phrase is a refrain in the first section of the story. The plot is obvious and commonplace: after an impulsive murder, the murderer flees; he is pursued by the law and finally killed. The conflict between the fleeing boy and the pursuers is clearly indicated. But all these things that "Flight" is so candid about do not take the reader very far into the experience of *this* story; they do not, for instance, suggest what becoming a man—and being one—entails. The reader discovers that by responding appropriately to the dramatic point of view from which the episodes of the journey are told and by paying close attention to the symbolic detailing in the several partially similar "draw and hill" episodes of the flight. So these are the features of the story we would want to help students notice.

By means of the dramatic point of view, the reader *witnesses* the boy's experiences in the draws and on the hills. He witnesses his successive losses of the synthetic trappings of manhood, his gradual physical decline, and his symbolic reduction to an animal befriended finally by animals. The reader witnesses the worsening of the land and the lessening of hope. He observes that, ironically, in these experiences the boy's every material loss is a moral gain; his physical decline is accompanied by moral development. The boy is ever more persevering, ever more courageous. Though a crawling animal, he is never more a man. Because of the point of view in this story, all the reader knows is how the boy *acts* at successive stages. And from what the reader witnesses, he comes to know that a boy is a man when he *acts* like one—and the details of the episodes tell the reader what kind of action is manly action.

As we taught "Flight," we would, then, be helping students discover how the use of a particular narrative method and of certain symbolic detail reveals the significance of the story. And, in the course of our discussion, we would also be calling students' attention to the function of such formal features as the arrangement of episodes in the story, the narrator's tones in the second part of it, and the story's adaptation of the quest archetype. Like the heroes of the past, the "hero" of this story is dressed and leaves his people with full ritual farewell, goes into the "winter world," surmounts his ordeals, and achieves his quest.

As we taught "Flight," we might have to convince some students that the long foreground of the story is necessary. We would do this by helping them see how *certain* details work, so we would be ready to ask such questions as, What precisely is gained by the opening description? by the presence of Emilio and Rosie in the story? Why is the father's death referred to? Why does the reader remain at the farm while Pepe goes to Monterey? What is meant by Mama's saying that Pepe became a man *last night* in Monterey? What is the "gift" Mrs. Rodriquez gives Pepe? What is the function of the final

Emilio-Rosie scene? These questions are nontechnical ways of asking about the function of setting, about modes of characterization, and about the use of minor characters. (And they are unobtrusive ways of stressing the importance of listening to the story, not to any one character.) "Flight" has the answers to all these questions, and when the reader has them, he sees the reason for the seemingly overlong first part of the story.

So much for our description of four different *types* of stories that we might use to introduce less able students to the study of "The Story." Whatever kind of story we chose and whatever particular teaching of it we decided on, we would spend some class time making the distinction between plot and story as *graphic* as possible. For instance, near the close of the study of the chosen story, we might pull the discussion together by listing on the board (the students offering the data), first, the events of the plot; then, in a second column, the certain events that are (one way or another) emphasized; and, in a third column, the certain events that are minimized. We would note *how* the events are emphasized or minimized and *why* they are. Finally, we would list certain things that are in the story that are not plot at all, and we would note why they are there. We would do this exercise so that less able students could *see*—on the board before them—that *the way* the plot is told suggests what we should pay attention to, how we should attend to it, and why we should.

The Second Section: Toward Internal Drama

As we said earlier in the outline of our organization for teaching "The Story," in this second section we would leave stories of the customary "complication-crisis-resolution" sort and begin the reading of those that have the outward signs of the familiar form, but have their center of interest in a crisis within a character. In these stories the external situation is important only in terms of the inner drama it occasions and the outcome it expresses.

All of the following five stories would help students begin their gradual move away from the familiar plot story. The group includes stories of different lengths, modes, and reading difficulties. This is one of the points in the course where the teacher *especially* needs a variety of stories to choose from, for what is a good vehicle for introducing one class to this new kind of story may be quite inappropriate for another. Furthermore, in certain classes the teacher might decide to read two stories—"just to make sure"—perhaps a comic story and a serious one, a long story and a short one, an easy one and a more challenging one. If the teacher has a variety of stories available, he can reinforce a learning without "marking time."

Here are the five stories, arranged roughly in order of reading difficulty and annotated to suggest the ways that certain familiar fictional features are modified to produce new effects.

Irwin Shaw's "Act of Faith" (nineteen pages) has a slim but definite plot with a clearly recognizable complication, crisis, and resolution: three G. I. buddies need money for a trip to Paris; no one really has any to loan them, so two of them ask the third to sell his hard-won souvenir gun; he decides to do it; so their problem is solved. "Act of Faith" is a fine choice for students who might mistake plot for story; for the structure of this story will not let any reader do that. It makes clear that the real concern of the story is the main character's reconciling the two "worlds" he lives in: the Gentile world and the Jewish world.

The story is in three parts: the first part dramatizes Seeger's relationships in the Gentile world of his G. I. buddies; the second, equally long, part represents Seeger's responses to the Jewish world of his father; and the brief, final section of the story renders his reconciliation, his "act of faith" in the postwar world. Coincident events in both of Seeger's worlds—the request of his buddies and his father's letter—give him reasons for finally "thinking about it," that is, for confronting his twilight existence and arriving at the stance he will take as a Jew in a Gentile world. His decision to sell the gun—important practically in the first world, symbolically in the other—is the outward manifestation of his "act of faith."

We can, I think, help students see how the three-part structure makes clear the concern of the story by asking about the way readers are prepared—in the first part of the story, in the second part, and in the final part—for Seeger's decision to sell the gun.

About the first part we might ask: What is the function of the first scene of the story? What is Taney's attitude toward Seeger in the second scene? Seeger's attitude toward Taney? Why don't Olson and Welch know what the Luger means to Seeger? What *does* it mean to him at *this point* in the story? The *dialogue* in the first part of the story both stresses the social communion that exists among these temperamentally diverse soldiers and emphasizes their confidence in, and affection for, Seeger for what he has been and done. But the *narrated* sections remind the reader that people are not always what they seem and that attitudes do change. Since those who would understand the tension in Seeger's decision must notice these disquieting hints, we would call students' attention to them by asking: Why does the narrator remind us that a man's appearance (Olson, Welch) may belie him? Why does the narrator mention the differences that have appeared in Taney and Olson "now that the war is over"?

In the G. I. world of the first part of the story, the fact that Seeger is a Jew is immaterial. It never occurs to anyone, not even to Seeger or the reader. How wonderfully the story renders this irrelevance! The second part of the story represents Seeger's other world, the Jewish world that is alien to Taney, Olson, and Welch and hidden from them. This second world is communicated to the reader largely by events that are not part of the plot: those told in Seeger's father's letter and those in Seeger's narrated thoughts about the letter. How does this second part of the story prepare the reader for Seeger's decision? We would try to help students see how by asking such questions as: What state is the writer of the letter in? For what does Seeger weep? Why does Seeger now recall his pre-war school experience? How does Seeger regard the stories Jews "collect"? In the first part of the story, did he remember the "little extra flavor" of the Luger incident? What does the gun mean to him *now*? Considering both the first part of the story and the second part, what do you think is the real decision before Seeger?

About the third part of the story, we would ask, Why do Olson and Welch withdraw all pressures? How do the narrated sections of this last part suggest what *finally* determines Seeger? How will Olson and Welch take his last question? What does it mean to Seeger? to the reader? In what ways are the first and the last images in the story similar? What do the similarities (and the differences) imply?

During the study of "Act of Faith" the teacher has a natural opportunity to ask students about the ways the feelings of characters are objectified and about the use of certain narrative techniques (Why does the story open with a dialogue scene? Why is the narrated description of the characters withheld until after the first scene is over? Why is Seeger's reflection handled as it is?). The teacher has a chance to ask also about the value of certain word choices, say, "grazing" and "use" and about the functions of setting (How does the weather relate to the events? Why is the situation laid in the peculiar social milieu of an army camp? What is gained by having the event happen in the interim between Army and civilian life?).

James Thurber's "The Catbird Seat" (ten pages) is, like Shaw's story, for average or better readers. It would be a good alternative to "Act of Faith" and a fine choice for those students who enjoyed "The Bride Comes to Yellow Sky."

The question we would raise is: What makes us interested in Thurber's bizarre plot? Students would discover that we are engaged partly by the narrative voice, partly by the design of the situation. The narrative voice that recounts, from Mr. Martin's point of view, the offense and the planned retribution, that rechecks the scheme, and that recalls the justification is at once congruous and incongruous. Precise, calm, rational, understated, virtually reportorial, the voice creates the perfect tension; it makes us entertain simultaneously Mr. Martin's view of the affair and our own recognition of what "rubbing out" actually is!

The situation itself is designed so that the long narrated foreground makes us anxious for the "scene": we are kept wondering how the carefully calculated plan will come off. The scene itself is organized to zigzag: events assist Martin's plot, then frustrate his well-devised plan, then generate another plot that carried out, with flawless consistency, does "rub her out." The "big" scene begets a second scene. But the situation does not call for this second scene. What is its function, then?

Thurber's story gives the teacher a chance to introduce students to comedy in fiction—to make them aware of the tentative expectations about plot, character, language, and intention—that are aroused in a sensitive reader as soon as he recognizes that a story is told in the comic mode. Students commonly condemn comic characters as unreal and comic plots as nonsensical because they come to comedy with alien expectations. They must sometime learn how comic conventions *limit* and *suggest* the responses that readers may make. Thurber's story would be a pleasant initiation.

A. E. Coppard's "Fifty Pounds" (fourteen pages) is for students who would enjoy a darker comic irony than that of "The Catbird Seat," and who can read a *somewhat* more complex work. The chain of events in this story is obvious enough: a girl about to leave her lover in order to go to work to relieve their poverty receives, in the nick of time, a surprise legacy; two-thirds of it she sends to her lover anonymously so as not to offend his pride; he never admits receiving it; instead, he gives her quite a send-off. By fairly-tale formula the legacy "dropping out of the sky" should solve their problem and let them live happily ever after. It does not. The girl was leaving for Glasgow before the arrival of the check—and she leaves. Why does not the check change things? It cannot. And the reader must look at the personalities of the characters—not at the events—to see why the check cannot effect a fairy-tale ending. The first part of the story implies what kinds of people Repton and Lally are. The check simply evokes characteristic responses from each of them. The check does what it can: it reveals them unmistakably; it cannot change them.

In the study of "Fifty Pounds" we would try to help students see that the function of the event of the check is to lay bare what the reader already infers about Lally and Repton. We would ask such questions as: What prepares us for Lally's response to the check? Why does she decide to withhold thirty pounds? Are we prepared for that? What prepares *her* for her lover's response to receiving the check? (We would begin at the first paragraph of the story but deal *only* with data relevant to this question.) Now, what prepares *us*? (Noting especially passages that suggest the narrator's attitude toward P. Stick Repton!) Whose response to the check do *we* learn most about? What are the *successive stages* of the girl's response? (What, for instance, is the function of the various events she notices on her day alone?) Show how these successive stages are authentic for the character *as defined earlier in this story*. What is her final attitude toward the event? (Or, How does the image of the elephants suggest her final attitude?)

"Fifty Pounds" is an excellent story not only for showing students the difference between event that determines and event that reveals, but also for giving them a reprise on narrative voice. A careful examination of the first five pages of this story will exercise the sensitivities to mode of narration that they have been developing. We would ask such questions as, How does the narrator's use of language reveal his attitude toward Repton? toward Lally? toward their situation? How is the narrator's attitude toward Repton distinguished from Lally's attitude toward him? How is the narrator's attitude toward Lally distinguished from Repton's attitude toward her?

Through the reading of "Fifty Pounds" students can also be introduced to the darker comedy in which stock comic devices of plot and of character render some of life's more serious inhumanities. As in much of Joyce ("The Boarding House," for instance) and some of Faulkner (the longer version of "Spotted Horses," for example), the way the situation in "Fifty Pounds" is told evokes at once laughter and pity and fear. Of themselves, high school students rarely tend to have such complex reactions. They must, however, develop such a tendency if they are ever to respond richly to literature—and to life. Studying a story like "Fifty Pounds" allows them to make a small beginning.

To casual readers, Kay Boyle's six-page "Effigy of War" seems so easy. The strong "and-then-ness" and the feel of a steady and inevitable closing-in make readers think the story a quite conventional suspense story of the "underground"—until they realize that they cannot say, to their satisfaction, what the plot is, or whose story it is, or why it is set on the Riviera, or why certain details are included: like the "dressed-up dwarf" image of the director or the "monkey" aspects of the barman. Indeed, students finally realize that it is difficult for them to say offhand what the story is about.

As they read the story more closely, they see that it is not, as they initially thought it was, just a new version of the routine story of the horrifying extremes to which wartime patriotism drives men. For students notice, suddenly, that it is a *Greek* who is trying to arouse the French against the "*sale étranger*," and they see that his efforts are futile. More importantly, they gradually see that both the design of the story and the attitude of the narrator toward what he tells suggest what the reader is "to make of" the experience. The story is organized in two equally long, parallel episodes, both of which present one expatriate "persuading" another to get out of France. In the first episode, a suave German hotel director "persuades" a nervous Italian barman; in the second, an enraged Greek waiter "persuades" a stolid Danish swimming teacher. In both episodes, expatriates persecute expatriates; the director, from fear and a sense of injustice; the waiter, from anger and envy. The director's quiet "suggestion" moves the barman; the waiter's noisy taunting fails to intimidate the Dane. Anger and envy explode in physical violence which ends in the waiter's murder of the Dane and the barman.

At first it may seem that the story is indicting only physical violence. The reader may get that impression because physical violence is given such a drastic outcome and because the narrator seems to take such a bland attitude toward the director's nonviolent purge of the barman. The narrator says, "It might have passed off quietly enough like that if the Dane hadn't come into it," and later, if the barman had not talked so long, "nothing would have happened." But the impression that only violence is being indicted is shown to be false: both the *tone* of the narrator *and* the many parallel features of the violent and nonviolent episodes suggest that the reader should regard them similarly.

Whether "*it* passed off quietly" at the hands of the director or violently at the hands of the waiter, the old barman was, in either case, destroyed. The refined violence of the director is as terrible in its unostentatious gentility and its quiet rightness as the "wild holy passion" of the waiter. The narrator's bitter understatements and his way of telling the final episode make it clear that that is indeed his attitude. He describes the waiter's brutality on the beach at night with the same restraint that he describes the director's brutality in the lounge bar at eleven o'clock in the morning. To the narrator, both events are equally terrible. When the reader responds to the design of "Effigy of War" and to the narrator's tone, he experiences neither an exposure of the excesses of wartime patriotism nor a condemnation of physical violence. Rather he perceives something more universal and more terrifying. He perceives how patriotism is used by two very different personalities to justify the inhumane acts of violence that their private fears and hates have led them to perform.

This little story is a good choice for those able and alert readers who cannot give "top" attention to a long work. It is useful, too, as a second short reading for classes whose study of the teacher's first choice was not so successful as expected.

Faulkner's "Barn Burning" is appropriate for any readers who can at this point respond to a complex mode of narration and a rich exploitation of words—and who can sustain a vital attention for twenty pages.

Students who meet these requirements—and others who are steadily improving readers—are probably ready by now to study a story by concentrating on a single major aspect of it and, through answering questions on that, to notice, in a less discrete way than in the study of earlier stories, such crucial literary features as mode of narration, means of characterization, design of the story, and uses of setting. So here we depart from the kind of annotations we have offered for the other four stories in this group, and offer instead an illustrative plan for a lesson on "Barn Burning"[14] that uses Sarty's conflict as its focus.

■ *A Teaching Plan for "Barn Burning."* When assigning the story, take fifteen to twenty minutes to read aloud (students following the text) *at least* the first two pages of the story as far as "Case dismissed." If time permits, read the first three pages, as far as "His mother's hand touched his shoulder." To make students aware of the kinds of connections Faulkner expects readers to make, interrupt your reading intermittently to question briefly on the text, perhaps somewhat as follows: What did the boy actually smell? What did his intestines believe he smelled? What is the other constant smell? What does "pull of blood" mean? What is suggested about "blood" if it also can be smelled? What makes Harris the boy's enemy? Does the boy want to lie? What suggests that he does not want to? Then, why will he "have to"? What adjectives would accurately describe the blood tie? Are the boy and his father alike? Yet the boy is bound to him. (Probably not all of these questions would be needed in any one class, but it is well to be *ready* to ask them.)

Then, assign the story and hand out duplicated copies of the following study guide:

Read the story carefully, being sure to notice especially three paragraphs in it, the two on the washing of the rug and the one on the boy's running from DeSpains' house. Clear up any confusion you have about what happened during the washing by asking yourself: What does the father do with "the flattish fragment of fieldstone"? Clear up any uncertainty about where the boy is running by noticing the glare in the sky.

Then, after you have read the story and solved any text problems:

1. Write *a* sentence that describes the conflict that is represented in the story. [If the teacher's reading and questioning during the last twenty minutes of today's class has succeeded, students should have little trouble deciding what the conflict is and what the effects of it are.]

2. List the features of the story that make the character of the conflict clear to the reader.

3. List in the order of their occurrence the possibilities for resolving the conflict.

4. Point out how the conflict is resolved.

This is really a double assignment, so it would be reasonable to introduce the story on Thursday and discuss it on Monday, say.

On the day the story is to be discussed, clear up briefly and rapidly any remaining text difficulties before the class work on the story begins. Then, during the next thirty to forty minutes of the class period, work for *full* answers to the four topics on the written assignment by asking such questions as these:

1. What conflict is represented in the story?

2. What features of the story make the *character* of this conflict clear to the reader? The in-class introduction will have given students a start on the answers to both of these first two questions. So, in reply to this second question, they will probably suggest the visceral details that define the "pull of blood," the internal monologues that reveal the boy's helplessness and despair, the grapevine simile, and everything that the boy fails to see and feel—all of which implies his blindness and his fear. In addition to these features that one student or another undoubtedly would cite, there are others that no student *may* have noticed. So, the teacher may have to prod, this way:

Brother, father, and boy are all present when the voice calls, "Barn burner." But only the boy responds. What does the syntax of that paragraph suggest about his response? *Why* is he so furious? (p. 164)

Why can't he say, "barn burner" aloud, even to himself? (p. 165)

How does the boy represent the conflict in his internal monologue in the field? What, then, is the effect of this conflict on him? (pp. 174–5)

Where are there other images of "pulling" in the story? (pp. 179–80)

3. From what point of view is the story told? What is gained by this handling of point of view? (Or, Which features that define the conflict would have to be foregone if the story were told entirely from the boy's point of view?)

4. (a) What does the boy continually think is the best possibility for resolving his conflict? Students' lists, chronologically arranged, will have shown them that it is the possibility of *something* making Abner change his behavior. (b) What, in the order of occurrence, are the "things" that Sarty thinks "maybe" will affect Abner? Students will mention that Sarty thinks it possible that Abner will be "satisfied" now (that he has been so luckily acquitted?); that Abner will be unable to harm the DeSpains; that Abner will be changed by

the mansion. But students may not notice that at the time of the fine of twenty bushels, Sarty thinks it possible to restrain his father by his own "collusion" and encouragement. (So the teacher should be prepared to ask them, Why does the boy react to the fine with ,"You done the best you could" and such? Is he conscious of his motive?) Students will, of course, mention the hope suggested in Sarty's internal monologue in the field, but they may not notice the confidence implied in his "partisan defiance" in the second court scene. (c) Why does the boy continually change from one avenue of hope to another? Students should be able to show from the story that no sooner has the boy entertained a certain possibility than it is thwarted by some act of his father's. (d) Why does the boy not *know* beforehand that this will be the case? Beware of blanket responses, such as, "because he is only ten" or "because he is unrealistic" or "optimistic." A careful look at the text will show several more precise reasons: one is that as the story progresses, the father *is* worsening (". . . never before had he paused afterwards to explain why" and never before had he sued an employer!); another reason is that the experience of the mansion is new to the boy, and the boy tends to think his father's reactions will be similar to his own; a third reason is that hard work and the richness of nature in the field create in the boy's mind a reassuring dream. There *are* always *grounds* for the boy's hope. (e) How many days elapse during the story? Is the boy any nearer to resolving his conflict on Saturday than he was on Monday?

5. Why does the boy never consider trying to reform his father's behavior? (If necessary: From whose point of view is Abner seen? By what images? What do they suggest?) The boy says his age bars him from changing the situation or fleeing. Is he telling the truth?

6. (a) When he realizes that Abner is to burn DeSpain's barn, what possibilities of resolving his conflict does the boy then entertain? (b) Why does he not then flee? (c) What is his intention when he breaks from his mother?

7. Does *he* resolve the conflict? How is it resolved?

We would develop the answers to questions 2 and 4(b) on the board. The answer to question 2 would *show* students how the way the story is told—the literary means—function in defining the conflict for the reader. The answer to question 4(b) would help students *discover* that the story is shaped in a series of hope-frustration episodes which occupy the boy's days from the first trial to the advent of the final burning. These hope-frustration episodes represent a gradual loss of alternatives rather than a gradual solving of his conflict. Days succeed days, events move forward, and these changes emphasize his lack of progress.

As the class develops answers to some or all of the questions we have suggested, many literary features of the story will receive attention. But the teacher may wish to give special notice to some particular fictional device which, in the discussion of previous stories, these students have shown they are insensitive to. It seems most *natural* to emphasize the presence and the function of such a device when it is especially pertinent to the question being discussed. For instance, if the class needs to be more responsive to the function of point of view, when discussing question 3, ask, What is gained by the narrator's deviating to tell us what the boy would think as an adult? If the class is obtuse to the function of narrative voice, when discussing the "mansion" in question 4, ask, Why are several voices used in telling of the first sight of the mansion? If students have difficulty seeing how features not demanded by the plot work in stories, then, when part (e) of question 4 is being discussed, ask about the function of the long description of Saturday's activities, or, more particularly, about the function of the boy's moment before the circus posters; or, when discussing the boy's hopelessness and despair, ask about the symbolic use of the sisters in the story, of the mother, or even of smaller details like the stopped clock. It students have been insensitive to devices that objectify qualities of character, point out how a few details "fix" the exact character of the brother or of the sisters, or while the class is discussing question 5, call students' attention to what renders the paradox of a physically and spiritually small man with immense power (the absurd step; the wasp with ravening ferocity; the ill-fitting, tarnished ceremonial dress; the heatless violence). If the teacher feels that incorporating such special emphases into the questions on conflict will unduly delay the discussion or obscure the "main business," then the kind of special questions we have just suggested may become, instead, the assignment.

If such a remedial task is *not* necessary, then we would devise an assignment that would make students rethink (reread, we hope) the entire story, focusing on the meaning of personal integrity. Here is one such assignment:

> Because of his dual allegiances, Sarty lacks integrity, and we have noticed the effect of this on his inner life and on his actions. Does Sarty ever achieve integrity? Write a paper of one- to two-pages that answers this question with, of course, appropriate evidence.

The mode of study that we have been illustrating through the preceding plan can be used with any of the five stories in this section. Our annotations on each story do, in fact, suggest a usable focus. Whether or not such a single focus *should* be used depends upon how precisely and how fully the class has responded to the more explicit questioning on earlier stories. A more mature form of study belongs only to those who have shown they are ready to profit from it.

The Third Section: "Recognition" Stories

Although there is a clearly discernible series of external events in all of the stories in the previous section, the reader's interest is focused not on those events but on the internal drama they evoke. So as we taught these stories, we would help students discover what the events in the internal drama are, how the external and the internal events are related, and how the design of the story centers the reader's interest on the internal conflict and its outcome.

Through the study of the stories in the *previous section,* then, students would have begun the transition from the story in which an external situation is resolved to the story in which an internal situation is revealed. Through the readings in this *present section,* students would complete that transition. For, what the narrator tells in these stories is, as Sean O'Faolain puts it, "an adventure of the mind." All the familiar fictional devices are used, but with a fundamental difference. "There is suspense, but it is . . . an emotional or intellectual suspense. There is surprise [but it is] . . . the surprise of a man who opens a cupboard and finds that a skeleton falls out. There is climax . . . the climax of the woman who discovers her lost happiness in a memory. There is contrivance . . . but of the citizen who deceives his friend." The stock scene of the stories in this section is the author unmasking the hero—or the hero unmasking himself. Incident "is merely a trigger—a tiny piece of mechanism which explodes a projectile that smashes some facade or explodes some concentration of laughter, fancy, tragedy, or delight. . . ."* In these stories something does happen in the external world, but either it is just the *occasion* for a crucial internal event—the making of a decision, the revelation of an irony, the recognition of one's incapacities —or it is the relatively unimportant *outcome* of one.

It is just this kind of story that many beginning readers fail to respond to appropriately. Their reading of the story evokes no experience but bafflement ("I don't understand it") or indifference ("So what?") These responses result from readers' bringing to these stories unsuitable expectations. As we said earlier, some readers unconsciously look only for plot in the usual sense, so they do not even notice the insight the situation reveals or the implications that extend the significance of the event. Consequently, they are mystified.

---

* Quotations are from *The Short Story* (New York: Devin-Adair, 1951), p. 184.

Other readers expect more explicitness, for they feel insecure without the "guidance" of a definite "complication-climax-resolution." ("How can I be *sure* what this situation has revealed?") Still other readers expect such gross and melodramatic conflicts that the quieter forms of frustration, heartache, and irony represented in these stories seem unimportant. Unperceptive in life, these students do not have, as most of us do, some half-perceived modest experience of yesterday or six months or several years ago that this kind of story can now give shape to and get its relevance from.

Anticipating these potential problems, we have been stressing, during the earlier sections of "The Story," some of the subtler forms of human tension and some fictional means other than plot. Our long foreground should help considerably now. But to ensure even further against readers' being either baffled by these "situation-revealed" stories or indifferent to them, we have limited the readings we are suggesting in this third section to two types of stories: those in which the "revelation" is made explicit and those in which the internal conflict is such as will seem to high school students, in and of itself, important—for one of several reasons: because of the crucial nature of what is at stake, or because of the equal value of the options in the decision, or because of the intense, torturing nature of the conflict for the character concerned. Stories with explicitly stated revelations will not only help the less able students to see what the "answer" is and how *they* can arrive at it, but will also give confidence to able, but insecure readers, by confirming what they have already discovered. Stories with "important" conflicts will prevent indifference now and lessen the possibility of it later, when students read more subtle, less overtly arresting stories.

Unfortunately, choosing the "right" types of stories will not preclude *all* potential problems. For certain students respond indifferently even to stories which reveal situations that high school students in general would consider "very important." There are, we think, two causes for this. One is that some students tend—even after much preliminary reading—to unconsciously assume that the main character in stories of this sort is similar—temperamentally and morally—to themselves. Even students who have long since distanced themselves from other types of stories seem to have a "spontaneous recovery" of their old habit of "one-to-one" identifying when they read this "intimate" kind of story. Consequently, they do not really shape up the character that *is* having the experience, and so they tend to judge the probability and the significance of the experience in terms of themselves. When we are teaching the "revelation" story, then, we would try to make sure that readers take into account *all the clues* that define the character and that they have, in so far as possible, an "undiluted" impression. For unless readers grasp the character and suspend their selves, they cannot understand what the experience *can* signify to the character. (And, indeed, if they cannot think and feel in terms of someone else, they will lose one of the important moral effects of reading literature.)

The other cause for certain students' indifference even to "important" stories is their tendency—when no obvious plot is restraining them—to leap to their own expectations of what *must be* at stake: if there is a man and a girl, it must be the *usual* love story. Students do not let the details of the work correct their initial impression. Consequently, they do not have the precise situation. And if they do not have the situation, they cannot very well understand the awareness the character achieves—and they cannot very well achieve any awareness themselves. So when we are teaching the stories in this third section, we must bother such students as these into clarity, much as we do when we are teaching modern poems. All of the stories we suggest in this section *do have* "important" conflicts, but they are stories that careless readers or those with fixed expectations may misconstrue. But if students do read these potentially "important" stories carefully, they *will* experience a conflict that they will consider very significant—one well worth their careful reading.

To summarize, then: as we teach the stories in this third section, we will aim to help students discover precisely what kind of person the main character is and help them undergo as adequately as possible the experience by which he achieves his insight. As we teach these stories, we will *intensify* the stress on accurate response to the text that we have maintained since the very beginning of the course. For so well-wrought are the little moments in these stories and in those that follow in the fourth section, and later, that the demand for precise reading is greater than ever; yet so intimate are these moments that the tendency toward precise reading is less than ever. Any time we are tempted to forego precision, we need only remember that if, at the end of the earlier readings in the course, students failed to grasp the story, they had at least the plot, but if, at the close of these readings, students have not perceived the "revelations," what have they had?

The two groups of stories we suggest below are, as usual, cited only as examples of the sorts of readings that would be fruitful in achieving the aims of this section. All of the stories are very brief, six or seven pages. Since we are asking students to read a new kind of story, we feel we should not complicate their task by assigning unnecessarily long stories. In each of the two groups, there is an example of a story appropriate for the less able, for the average, and for the able. Teachers might choose to read one story from each of the two groups, using the second story to remedy, intensify, or extend what was learned from the reading of the first.

Our annotations on each of the six stories are virtually confined to series of questions that will help students discover the kind of person the main character is and help them undergo the experience by which he achieves his insight or "recognition." In no case should any of these sequences be construed as a *full* lesson plan for the teaching of the story. The questions are, we think, usable, but a plan for the actual study of any of these stories would be much "rounder" than the series of questions we propose. It would include, for instance, questions about the function of a variety of other details. We would undoubtedly be asking: Why does the doctor in "The Use of Force" bother to remark that the patients are "new" to him? What is the significance of the title of Williams' story? What does Sherwood Anderson gain by his handling of time in "Adventure"? By his unrelieved narration? How do the hats of the men, the "scarecrow" boys, and the "pelican-leg" girls function in "Theft"? Why is the main character of that story never named? Why is her face left undescribed? Why do the janitress' eyes "flicker" with "red fire"? When we discussed John O'Hara's little story, "Do You Like It Here?" we would surely ask about the necessity for using that particular point of view. When we talked about Joyce's "Eveline," we would want to know what was gained by the use of the half-scenes, why the narrator speaks in the character's own language, how the design of the story *embodies* the alternation of decision, and what prepares us for the last sentence. About Virginia Woolf's "The New Dress," we would want to ask, for instance, how the syntax and the rhythms of the sentences suggest Mabel's emotional state, why the exposition is withheld so long and why it is given at that particular point in the story, and what the circular design of "encounters" suggests. All of the features we have just cited are simply illustrations of the *kinds* of "other things" that we might be asking about in the actual teaching of these six stories.

Lesson plans for classroom use would be, then, much more fully "true" to the particularity of each story than are the brief series of questions we offer below. Furthermore, the plans would be much more cognizant of the special abilities and insensitivities of each class. The quality of the particular readers would determine the kinds of questions we would actually ask, the wording of them, and the general approach to the story.

Now to the stories.

■ *Stories with Explicit Recognitions.* First, three examples of the kind of story in which the main character's recognition is made explicit.

William Carlos Williams' brief, four-page story, "The Use of Force," is told in the first person by the main character, a doctor who has discovered that, when resisted by a little patient, he is capable of reducing an ordinary throat examination to an animal struggle. He confesses: "I could have torn the child apart in my fury and enjoyed it. It was a pleasure to attack her. My face was burning with it." He explicitly recognizes the nature of his feelings. But what he is less sure of is the true reason for his action. "The damned little brat must be protected against her own idiocy, one says to one's self at such times. Others must be protected against her. It is a social necessity. And all these things are true. But a blind fury, a feeling of adult shame, bred of a longing for muscular release are the operatives." The doctor's comment suggests that both reasons are true, but which really motivated him?

These explicit statements of his recognition and his uncertainty are the narrator's concluding summary reflection on the scene the reader has been experiencing. The reader is not being told anything he has not already seen. He can know, from very early in the story, what is happening to the narrator. And we would teach this story in a way that would *show* the reader that he can. We would, first, briefly call students' attention to the doctor's explicit recognition and his uncertainty, and then we would spend the majority of the class time helping students see how *they* can realize both—*before* the narrator states them.

We might begin the in-class discussion of the story by asking: What does the narrator *explicitly state* he has discovered about his own behavior? If students' replies show they have not noticed the doctor's uncertainty about his motives, that they simply assume he does what he does just for the pleasure of fury, we would refer them to the first four sentences in the paragraph beginning "The damned little brat . . . ," and then ask, Are these just rationalizations? Is it possible for him to be sure of his real reasons? Now, what would you say he has discovered about motives? (And, if the teacher wishes, Why does he change to the present tense in this paragraph? Why does he change to "one"? If necessary, What is he suggesting about all of us always?)

Once the doctor's discovery is clear to students, we would say: But *we* are already aware of what he discovers *before* he states it. What *in his own telling of the experience* lets us know? And we would spend the remainder of the period working out the answer with the class. We would begin at the beginning of the story so that students would undergo the discovery about the doctor in the same way that a sensitive reader does. The following questions suggest the *kinds* of things we would want students to notice about the doctor's revelatory "telling of his experience." (We would actually ask *only* about what students failed to notice on their own).

How does the *diction* that the doctor uses in describing the family group, as he first sees them, suggest a hostile contest? What is his tone? What impresses him about the child? How would most people interpret her expression? How does he register disgust? How do you know he *is* disturbed, when *he* claims not to be? For instance, how does the syntax tell you?

When does the doctor first suggest that he questions his own motives? *How* does he suggest his uncertainty? (If necessary, Why does anyone say, "I had to do it"? What kind of justification does he offer? Is it true? What is it about *the way* he gives his explanation that makes us suspect him?)

How does he evidence his savage delight in the "battle"? What makes *us* lose sight of what the real purpose is? By the language he uses to re-create the scene, what would you *think* he was describing? (If necessary, Notice: ". . . she surely rose to magnificent heights . . . terror of me," and "in an agony of apprehension.") What is his attitude toward the parents? What is our attitude toward them? What function does their behavior serve at this point?

When does the doctor begin to realize his own fury? What is his reaction to it? (If necessary: his full reaction?—meaning his appal, his inability to control his fury, *and his justification.*) Why does he not desist? (Or, Why is it impossible for him to know whether he is motivated by duty or by animal pleasure?) And *if* the teacher wishes to point up the "rightness" of the incident to express the insight, he could ask, Why is *this incident* a good vehicle to reveal man's uncertainty about his motivations?

Now, you see that readers are aware of all the doctor recognizes in his summary *before* he states it. But readers are also aware that the doctor's *narration* suggests attitudes toward the child that his *summary* does not include. What are they? Where are they suggested, exactly?

The kind of study of "The Use of Force" that we have been outlining is helpful to both less able students and to insecure ones. For it shows both groups that *they* can discover for themselves what the character's recognition is (and what the reader's is). This kind of study prepares them for reading stories where they must *infer* the recognition—without confirmation.

Two other stories, longer and more challenging than "The Use of Force," but with recognitions as explicitly stated, are Sherwood Anderson's "Adventure" and Katherine Anne Porter's "Theft." Anderson's story is the better choice for fair-to-average readers.

In "Adventure" (seven pages), the narrator reports, with elucidating comment and suggestive repetitions, certain revealing events of Alice Hindman's life from sixteen to twenty-seven. At the close of these eleven years, she recognizes that she must begin "trying to force herself to face bravely the fact that many people must live and die alone, even in Winesburg." In the study of the story, we would stress that this is a *certain* kind of person undergoing *certain* events and coming to a *certain* kind of awareness.

We would focus first on the kind of person Alice is: How does the narrator let us know in the opening paragraphs the kind of person Alice is at twenty-seven? the kind she was at sixteen? If she had a "placid outer crust" and an "inner ferment" at both ages, what can you infer about her personality during the intervening eleven years? What is the narrator suggesting about her personality by remarking, "Her head was large and overshadowed her body"? Through answering such questions as these, students will understand the important tensions in Alice's personality—the tension between the serene exterior and the inner tumult, the tension between the rational and the emotional. And, throughout the discussion of the story, students will be continually noticing how these tensions are revealed in, and affect, her responses to the events of these eleven years.

Following the design of the story, we would organize our discussion of these events around Alice's three "adventures"— the first, at sixteen with Ned Currie; the second, at twenty alone in the wood; and the last, at twenty-seven, with the old man. We would ask, for instance: At sixteen, what does Alice think she wants? What does she really want? How do we know? (If necessary: from what the narrator tells us? from what Alice says to Ned? from Alice's reaction to Ned's, "Now we will have to stick together"?)

At twenty, Alice has her second "adventure." What does she recognize? What does "happiness" mean to her now? What "side" of Alice's personality is ruling her in this incident? After this incident, did Alice stop "telling herself lies"? At twenty-two, what is her reaction to her fear? At twenty-five? Now, notice carefully *the way the narrator tells what he tells* of her life from twenty-two to twenty-seven. From this, how do *we* know that these "cheats" will never satisfy her?

How does her final adventure make clear to her what she really wants? that she will never have it? (If necessary, What is suggested by the man's being old and deaf?) Why does she turn "her face to the wall"? What *exactly* does she finally realize? [See our first paragraph for the exact wording.] (If necessary, What does "bravely" mean? What is the force of the word "fact"?) Why is the "fact" stated "many people" rather than "she"? How is this realization different from that of the second adventure? How is the tension in her personality revealed in this final adventure? Does the wording of her realization suggest her future?

We opened the study of this story by stressing Alice's personality in order to preclude students' judging her "adventures" or her recognition in terms of themselves. "Adventure" is the kind of experience that invites such a response, so we used a strategy of prevention.

Though the main character's recognition is overtly expressed in Katherine Anne Porter's "Theft" (seven pages), what the recognition means can be grasped only by readers who understand what the events which evoked it signify to the main character. If readers cannot perceive the meaning of the events, then, the expressed recognition will be only an arresting platitude, esoteric—thus impressive. Consequently, a story like this is for readers who are sensitive to language and personally mature. And with such students, we would plan to ask three broad questions—something like these:

What is the function of the flashback? If students' initial responses show that they need the help of more explicit questions, then: What insight does the reader get into the character of the woman through each of the events recalled in the flashback? Is her response to the theft of the purse "in character"?

What does she realize *in the moment* that she is walking away from the janitress? If, in response to this question, students do not point out that the woman recognizes the irony of her "open-door" policy and realizes the character of her losses, the relative value of them, and the cause of them, then such auxiliary questions as these might help: What words or phrases indicate that *she* has robbed herself? Is the order in which she thinks of her losses significant? Which incidents of the preceding evening illustrate some of the kinds of losses she enumerates? What was her rationale for her "unlocked door"? How was this "principle," this "faith," responsible—ironically—for her self-inflicted losses?

After that moment of recognition, what is the function of her final episode with the janitress? If students need help in answering this third broad question, then: Why does she care about the loss of *this* purse? Then, why, having recovered it, does she decide she doesn't really want it? What in the janitress' remarks affects her? (If necessary, Who gave her the purse? *Will* he give another? Why not? What, then, is the value of the purse? Why does the pretty purse *really* belong to the pretty girl? Yet the pretty girl does not really need it. Why not? What is the janitress actually saying about the value of a material thing?) Now, how does this episode lead to the confirmation of the final line of the story?

■ *Stories with "Very Significant" Conflicts.*   Now let us look at three examples of the second kind of story, the story in which the conflict is one that of itself will seem significant to high school readers

John O'Hara's "Do You Like It Here?" (six pages) is a simple story, readily available to less able readers. We would begin the study of it with a summary (by the class or us) of what happens in the story: A new student (Roberts) is called to the office of his housemaster (Van Ness) and is accused unjustly of stealing a watch. We would be sure that the words "new" and "unjustly" were in the summary. Such a summary will ascertain that everyone "has it straight," but it will also emphasize the presence in this story of what students find very significant: a teacher's injustice. In the study of the story we would be trying to call students' attention to those evidences of the teacher's injustice which suggest *why* he is unjust. We would, in other words, be trying to help students see not only the results of injustice but also the causes of it.

Once the summary of the story was before the class, we would ask: How do *we* know that the boy did not steal the watch? Then why should the housemaster think that he did? ("Because Hughes said so.") But why should the housemaster believe Hughes? Let's look closely at the housemaster to see what sort of person he is. As Roberts enters the master's office, what is Roberts' impression? How do we know it is *Roberts'* impression? What is our impression? What is Van Ness' tone in his questioning of Roberts? Where does the tone change? What clues you to the change? Does Roberts' attitude give the housemaster grounds for *his* attitude? Does Van Ness really need this information? How do *you* know he does not? Why, then, is he having Roberts rehearse it? What *might* the data suggest about Roberts? What *have* they suggested to Van Ness? *Why* would they suggest that to *Van Ness?* What sort of life has Van Ness had? What two symbolic details, given earlier, help to round out this picture of him? What effects has this life had on Van Ness? (Positive effects as well as negative.) Is there anything in the account Van Ness gives of the watch that would suggest Roberts is the thief? Is there anything in Roberts' response to Van Ness' inquisition that would suggest guilt? Yet Van Ness is convinced that Roberts is guilty. Why?

Who is Roberts referring to as "the dirty bastard"? Why does he say it "violently, then weakly"? Roberts sees himself as an innocent victim. Is Van Ness an innocent victim too?

Does the "open door" have any significance in this story?

For average-to-good readers who need to be convinced of the significance of internal conflict, a story like James Joyce's "Eveline" (five pages) would be appropriate. The conflict in this story would seem important to students for several reasons. First, the reader sees that both of Eveline's alternatives—staying at home and going away from home—are of mixed value: staying is certainty—certain unhappiness, certain "living death," but the security of the known and the familiar; going is possibility—possible happiness, a chance for "life," but the uncertainty of the unknown and the new. Secondly, the reader realizes—perhaps Eveline does, too—that given such alternatives, Eveline is incapable of choosing. And, lastly, the reader feels that what eventuates is final. However much Eveline desires escape from a "life of commonplace sacrifices," she cannot really choose escape now or ever. The experience of the story shows the reader *why*.

"Eveline" is the kind of story that must be studied carefully not only because readers must elicit from Joyce's seemingly simple, straightforward narration the complex tension expressed, but also because high school readers must be prevented from thinking of "Eveline" as another version of the patent "love story"—a nineteen-year-old girl choosing between her family and her husband-elect. High school readers will consider the internal conflict in this story important *only* if they see what it *really* is.

Some questions that might help them do this are:

What is the setting? (If necessary, What time of day is it? What is suggested by "invade" in the phrase "watching evening invade the avenue"? What image of Eveline do you get at the opening of the story?)

What has Eveline already decided before the story opens? What is she *now* trying to decide?

Why does she consider the life she is leaving "not a wholly undesirable life," as the narrator puts it? (If necessary, What does detail show she values greatly? And if even more particular questions are needed, then, What is the function of her initial memory? The phrase "Everything changes" summarizes what she has just been remembering, but what other purpose might she have in saying it? Why is "leave *her* home" used, rather than "leave" or even "leave home"? What is the function of "leave her home" the second time it is said? What feelings about her new home are implied? How does the recital of her hardships confirm her *value* for the "familiar"?)

Now, if Eveline considers her present life "not wholly undesirable," why is she leaving it? At this point the reader expects her to justify her choice of "another life." What *does* she do? (If necessary, What do details suggest she values? What previous indication of these values has she given? What reason is noticeably missing? What, in the story, indicates how her father views "exploring another life"? or, What, for instance, is symbolized by her father's cold reaction to the photograph of his friend in Melbourne?)

Unless in the class discussion of these questions, it has come out clearly what "her home" and "her new home" represent to Eveline, then the class must at this point be asked explicitly about the "plusses and minuses" (or "positive and negative values") of the alternatives.

Then to go on: Why does she linger? Why does she move from the window? (If necessary, What image does the music evoke?

How does this image make the real nature of the alternatives dramatically clear? What is really moving her? What does she think of Frank as?)

Why does she not go? (If necessary, What details suggest how the station affects her? What *now* does she think of Frank as? Why this reversal? Does she really *choose* not to go? Why is going "impossible"?)

What details have made us realize *all through the story* that leaving would probably be "impossible" for Eveline? (For instance, What is the significance of evening "invading," "deepening" into night? of her inhaling the dusty cretonne? of her exact image of the living room? of the clichés that describe the appeal of "her lover" —as the narrator calls him!)

If readers are sensitive to the narrator's voice and to the function of seemingly unimportant detail, then answering the eight main questions we have suggested will, we think, clarify Eveline's experience for them. If difficulties arise, the subsidiary questions will help. But the most effective assistance will come from oral reading; hearing the narrator's voice will call students' attention to many features of language that will greatly clarify Eveline's conceptions and her attitudes.

Certain internal conflicts seem important to high school students because they are familiar agonies. Virginia Woolf's "The New Dress" (seven pages) renders one of these: it is the story of the torturing misgivings of an insecure person. "The New Dress" is for able readers but, even those students, left to themselves, might think this story is just a very perceptive revelation of the terrors of an "inferiority complex." That, in itself, would be very interesting to them, and they would probably be quite willing to leave the story there without ever grasping the exact quality of *Mabel Waring's* insecurity and without ever realizing that her disconcerting doubt about values both results from and, ironically, causes her insecurity. Furthermore, even these able readers might not recognize that Mabel's inner probing is *not* a static experience, but a dramatic one: through a series of related responses, she moves eventually to the projection of a personal utopia—and to her exit. Since these are the things we think students would not notice, these would be what we would aim to get them to see through our teaching of the story.

One potential obstacle to our succeeding is the mode of narration of "The New Dress." Though students like stream-of-consciousness narration, they often fail to give themselves up sufficiently to this state of mind to comprehend the associations among things and the transformations of them that the nonlogical mind may make. In this story, for instance, students might not grasp the associations among such seemingly dissimilar things as the fly in the saucer, the weevils in the biscuit, the tadpoles in the mirror, the yellow dot in the blue pool, the lamb in the hand of the Goddess, the miner telling of life in the pit. If students do not notice these associations and transformations, they miss the clues that most surely indicate that the introspection is moving in a certain direction.

To some extent, we can overcome the potential difficulty of this mode of narration by one of several kinds of preparation. We can, for instance, give special attention in earlier readings, say, "Fifty Pounds," to states of mind and to nonlogical connections among things. We can even go farther and prepare for the study of "The New Dress" by reading first a similar, though less complex, story, one like James Thurber's "The Secret Life of Walter Mitty." In a series of daydreams, Walter Mitty becomes a variety of "heroes," all of whom are daring, debonair, and brilliant and each of whom is a *recognizable* response to some external event Walter undergoes during the Mittys' weekly trip to Waterbury. To understand this story, the reader must perceive how Walter's many dream experiences are similar to one another and how they are interconnected, both by the recurrence of the same items in successive contexts and by the arrangement of the experiences in an order of increasing personal risk and resulting gratification.

Thurber's story has, then, some things in common with Virginia Woolf's: there is the conflict between what the main character wishes to be and what he is, there is the subconscious creation that the character shapes from passing events to ease his tension, there is the suggestive paralleling and ordering of episodes. But in "The New Dress" Mabel Waring is expressing not only her desires but her fears, and she expresses both not through "heroes" but through objects—"tags from Shakespeare and lines from books she had read ages ago"—which, by the way they are transformed within her imagination, continually reflect the current state of her security. She has her memories and she has her daydream at the close, but her stream-of-consciousness throughout the story is quite a different thing in conception, organization, and intention from Walter Mitty's little compensatory dramas, so it requires a different and more sophisticated response. But reading a story like "The Secret Life of Walter Mitty" is a useful preparation for reading Mrs. Woolf's story and many other modern stories less challenging than "The New Dress."

There are still other ways to prepare students to make a sensitive response to the narrative mode of this story. We can, for instance, precede the reading with some relevant discussion and writing. We might begin by talking about how certain images—the fly in the spider's web, a face over a candle, an empty rubber raft in the ocean, a bird returning to a destroyed nest—*represent* certain human fears.

Out of such discussion would evolve a theme assignment that asks students to:

Write a paragraph that describes an object or a group of objects so that it *represents* some human fear.

Finally, we can help readers make the kinds of associations and transformations "The New Dress" requires by having them work out a study guide prior to the class discussion of the story. The questions on the guide might be the dozen main questions we plan to ask in class (see pp. 374–375). Wouldn't doing that take the edge off class discussion? Not with a story as complex as "The New Dress." It would simply ready students to deal so satisfactorily with the general questions in class that the series of encounters that structures the story and the gradual transformation of objects that symbolizes the inner transformation of Mabel would stand out clearly. In other words, such preparation would preserve the experience of the story—and the interest of the class.

The kinds of preparation we have been suggesting will also help students cope with the other possible obstacle to their experiencing the internal drama of "The New Dress": that is, the quality of Mrs. Woolf's prose. Students *must* give this story a poetry-reader's attention. How can they grasp the character of Mabel's feeling of insecurity as she enters, for instance, if they do not notice what is implied in the word "serious"? If they do not notice the unsettling fear suggested in the indefinite "something" and "it"? And the "twilight existence" first expressed in "not *quite* right?" How can they grasp the quality of her insecurity if they do not notice the way she turns remote possibility into positive fact (Mrs. Barnet's "drawing her attention *perhaps rather* markedly" "confirms" her suspicion)? And if they do not notice the way her suspicion then becomes a predatory animal and "springs" at her—as she greets Mrs. Dalloway? Students cannot "have" the experience of this story without continual perceptive attention; yet, since it *is* a story, since it *is* prose—and since they can indulge their psychological interest without such attention, students are often less willing to give it.

Because of our aims for the study of this story and because of the obstacles we anticipate, our strategy for teaching it—even to a class interested in such a story and able to read it—would be conservative. We would use a series of large—and, whenever necessary, small—questions to "get straight" the experience of Mabel Waring's inner drama. The story does invite us to ask the "big, interesting" question —(Could we say that Mabel's tensions are expressed in water images, rather than in rooms?)—but we would postpone asking that kind of question to another day, to a day when students' consistently sensitive performance had assured us that such a question would evoke full, precise, imaginative responses.

In our less interesting approach, we would probably ask such questions as:

What is the setting of the story? But where does the story really take place? How, then, does the physical setting, the milieu, function?

What point of view is used? Why, in *this* story, *must* the narrator be limited to what Mabel sees, hears, thinks, feels? (Or, in a more "leading" wording, How does the intention of the story require that the point of view be limited omniscience? If necessary, Why must we *not* know, for sure, what Mrs. Dalloway, Rose Shaw, and the others really think of Mabel?)

How does Mabel react as she enters? What, *in the rendering* of her entrance, lets the reader know the exact character of Mabel's feeling of insecurity?

What, in general, is Mabel trying to do throughout the story? What, in the first scene, suggests the ways Mabel usually deals with her insecurity?

Now, let us look more specifically at Mabel's various attempts to deal with her insecurity during her stay at the party.

How, for instance, does she try to relieve it when Rose Shaw speaks to her? (If necessary, How does she attempt to use the fly?)

What suggests that she has not succeeded in relieving her insecurity? What "truth" does her encounter with Robert Haydon make her see? (Or, in a more "leading" wording, What ironic contrast does her encounter with Robert Haydon make her realize? If yet another try is necessary, How is her image in Miss Milan's mirror different from that in Mrs. Dalloway's? What does the "truth" she has discovered suggest about the two images?)

Does she *really* accept the "truth"? (Or, in a more "leading" wording, How do her thoughts about the "rooms" now differ from her thoughts about them at her entrance? What suggests that she really does not accept the "reality" of Mrs. Dalloway's?) Why should she want to express her independence in such phrases as "There's Shakespeare! There's death! We're all weevils in a captain's biscuit"? (Or, in a more "leading" wording, What phrases do these phrases recall?) What *connections* have they with her earlier thoughts? What attitude does she take as she starts across the room? What earlier image does the spear image recall? What does this contrast of images suggest?

How do we know she has regressed? Are Charles Burt's remarks *really* malicious? How do *you* know that a compliment from him would not have "changed her life"? (If necessary, How did she respond to Robert Haydon's polite remark? *Can* the guests say the *right* thing to her?)

What "truth" does her encounter with Charles Burt make her see? Compare this with the "truth" her encounter with Robert Haydon evoked.

How does her encounter with Mrs. Holman differ markedly from her previous encounters? (Or, in a more "leading" wording, How is this encounter a reversal of the previous ones? What does her remark to Mrs. Holman remind us of? What is the tone used in discussing Mrs. Holman?)

What "truth" does her encounter with Mrs. Holman evoke? (If necessary, What has the round mirror become? And the people? What previous images does this one recall? What, then, is Mabel *now* able to do? What image of *herself* does she now see in the mirror? What does seeing the "dot" evoke? Compare this with previous mirror images and her responses to them. What, then, does her present response suggest about her mental perspective? What is the tone of her introspection here?) Why is she "left like this in a backwater"? What did the mirror previously suggest the reason was? What has the dress become now? How does that suggest a change in her values? *But* what does the diction imply she still considers herself? Why does she?

What characterizes her "delicious moments"? Why will the activities of her tomorrow "transform" her?

She projects a "quite right" utopia. What does her exit suggest? What is *she* finally aware of? What do *we* recognize?

If the preparation for the discussion of this story has been adequate, only the dozen main questions would have to be asked in class. However, even in able groups, occasionally, one or more of the main questions will not elicit as full a response as needs to be given; that is why we have suggested the "if necessary" questions and the more "leading" wordings. They are offered as "insurance," as other ways to get at the same point. But preparation should be such that the dozen general questions will consistently evoke full, relevant answers. In this way, students will not lose, in a welter of details, the experience of Mabel's successive encounters.

The Fourth Section: "Recognition" Stories—Again

The readings in the preceding section introduced students to internal conflicts and unconventional story forms. The readings in this section will extend their conceptions of and responses to both. In the stories students will now read, the *situations* are so *usual* that the stories might, on first sight, seem insignificant, and the *renderings* are so *unusual* that the stories might to some students, even at this date, seem pointless.

Because of the nature of these stories, students must now take a larger, and somewhat different, part in re-creating the experience of them. Little in these stories is gratuitous, much is merely suggested, and the burden of inferring rightly is squarely on the reader. The necessary exposition, for instance, is either woven into the story unobtrusively or, like the resolution, merely implied. Character and the effects of events on character are suggested by small details of dress, stance, gesture, by objects associated with the characters, by seasons, weather, locales. The burden is on the reader to sensitively piece together such "hieroglyphics." In these stories there is little commentary; actions are selected to speak for themselves; dialogue is written without annotation. Plot is still an important unifier, but other structural devices—parallel images, myth, the narrator's tone, the natural unities of "day" and "year," the motifs of "journey" and "season"—are also crucial organizing elements. The burden is on the reader to perceive how these many features render the insight of the story.

Students have had a long, gradual preparation for reading such stories as these. They should be ready to respond sensitively to them. Nevertheless, we would still anticipate that some classes may have difficulty. On one hand, these stories *are* more compressed, less explicit, more unusual in structure. And on the other hand, because of students' tendency to read into, rather than out of, texts, all through this course they have been restrained from leaping and intuiting. Although we have encouraged them to bring to works the particular bits of relevant experience that the works demanded, we have curbed students' attempts to "fill in" (a character's past, for instance), to project (what he must have been thinking), or to extend (the story into a sequel). We have been stressing close adherence to what the text says and caution in making inferences from it. Now, we must begin inviting students to develop a *still disciplined yet bolder* imagination so that they can infer the additions and the connections these stories imply. The necessary clues are in the text—nowhere else, but they are only tiny "bright, clear centers" from which the reader must infer the whole aura, they are mere points which the reader must link together into a meaningful chain. In our teaching of these stories, then, we shall continue to insist on precise response to the text, but we shall be spurring as well as reining the readers' imaginations.

In this section we offer three groups of stories rather than two. The first group are "buffer" readings, that will provide any class needing it a gentle transition from the stories of the previous section to those of this one. The second group represent undramatic "day-in-day-out" revelations; and the third group feature unusual renderings.

■ *The Buffer Stories.* The five stories in this group will make students exercise the responses they have just begun to develop through the readings of the previous section and will introduce them to stories in which the tension is less directly engaging and the need for inference greater. So these buffer stories will prepare them for the lower-keyed conflict of the second group of stories and the more demanding forms of the third. The class' performance during their study of the stories in the previous section will suggest whether they need such preparation or not. *Only some* classes do.

Each of the following five stories is annotated to suggest its length, its relative difficulty, the situation the story seems to reveal, some sources of possible misreading, and some of the new re-creative responsibilities the reader has to assume.

Although J. D. Salinger's "For Esmé—With Love and Squalor" (eighteen pages) is appropriate for students who read O'Hara's story well or Anderson's adequately, this story does have some unusual features, so it seems advisable to "get things straight" by a few preliminary questions before beginning a class discussion of it. We might ask, for instance, who is telling the story, in order to call students' attention to the frame that is being used and to the two-part story within the frame. We might ask what the time relation among the three parts is, who "X" is (just in case), and why the point of view *has* to change in the third part. In other words, we would ask just those questions that would clear up confusions that might prevent or hinder discussion of the main character and his "recognition."

Most readers of this story can see that, in general, what the narrator comes to recognize is the curative power of love. But what they sometimes do not notice is that this narrator is a certain sort of person and the love that heals (*in this story*) is a certain kind of love. So we would try to help them discover from the clues in the story both the nature of the narrator and the character of this salutary love.

To understand the narrator, students must infer what is implied by such details as those in paragraphs three through eight of the story (details about the narrator in the camp, in the town, at the choir practice, and in the tea room). It is *that* kind of person who, having undergone certain experiences, comes to recognize the curative power of love. To understand what kind of love it is that heals him, students must notice the instances in the story of its presence and of its absence and the narrator's reactions to both.

The love that cures is present when a little girl senses a man's loneliness and comes over to talk ("I purely came over because I thought you looked extremely lonely"), when she attempts again and again to please him, when she offers to write him, when she waves goodbye, when she insists on Charles' reconciling, and of course, when she gives him the watch she values so highly. Why does Esmé react to the narrator this way? To answer this question precisely, students must notice, of course, her preoccupation with her hair and looks, her aligned feet and such, but they must also infer the connections among her remarks. They can *know* what she is thinking and feeling *only* by figuring out what must be "going on" within her to cause her to move from this remark to that. Students may at first need help in making these inferences from dialogue. We would probably work with them on such a passage as the one beginning, " 'Possibly,' said my guest. . ." and ending, " 'Do you find me terribly cold?' " We would be asking what a reader can infer from such a conjunction of remarks as:

> "I have quite wavy hair when it's dry."
> "I can see that, I can see you have."
> "Not actually curly, but quite wavy," she said.
> "Are you married?"

When students have pieced together from several such passages the reasons for Esmé's response to the narrator, we would go on to ask about the narrator's response to her and the possible reasons for its passivity.

The love that cures is present in the simple empathies of a little girl. It is absent from the "uncomradely scratching" of pens in the Quonset hut, from the self-centered "stale letters" soldiers receive, from the narrator's own mean act of "stealing little Charles' thunder," from the unfilial letter from Albany, and of course from the unbelievably obtuse behavior of the well-named Clay. Why do all these people act as they do? What is the significance of the narrator's including himself among them? What is the significance of X's looking at Goebels' book? How does Sergeant X respond to Clay?

The love that cures, the reader sees, is human communion: that is what relieved the narrator's loneliness, corrected the little boy's limp, and released X's emotional paralysis. For those who feel life deeply, a sense of humor "is not of any use in a real pinch"; but *this* love is. Once students notice the episodes that define the presence and the absence of this love, they *may* notice the irony: such communion does not occur where "by right it should." The two main episodes boldly emphasize this irony: on one hand, there is Esmé, a child, the "perfect stranger," who feels the loneliness of the healthy soldier; on the other, there is Clay, X's peer, "X's jeep partner and constant companion from D Day straight through five campaigns of the war," who views his shattered buddy "with spectator's enthusiasm."

A useful way to pull the study of this story together is to ask about the frame and its relation to the story within: What sort of person is the narrator in the first two paragraphs? Why is it good if the story cause the *groom* "an uneasy moment"? Who is to be "edified" by the story? What is the narrator's tone at the transition between the two parts of the story? What does he mean by linking "squalid" and "moving"? What is the function of the frame?

And here is the kind of writing assignment with which we would climax our study of the story:

> The narrator tells Esmé he has never written a story "exclusively" for anyone. We know he still has not. What is the meaning of the title, then? Consider not only the dedicatory form, but also the combining of the words "love" and "squalor."

To read John Steinbeck's "The Chrysanthemums" (nine pages), students must be not only more skillful at inferring meanings than the readers of Salinger's story, but also more mature; in fact, they must be as mature as high school students *think* they are. Some, of course, are: this story is a good choice for them. They will understand this woman whose well-ordered, secure, homely life with Henry in the quiet, encircled valley is "too small and easy." Elissa is "strong," "eager," vital, a creative Laurentian lover of nature. Only growing the chrysanthemums fulfills her. They are at once lover and child: the natural extension of her self and the testament of her creative power.

The first two images in the story must be studied carefully, so that students will understand the two worlds of Elissa and realize immediately the tension between them. These two images juxtapose the passive, waiting world of December in the closed valley and the vital, energetic world of Elissa-and-the-chrysanthemums, the world which defies death, ushering in spring in the winter. Only if students understand *this* woman in *that* environment will they understand her reaction to the itinerant pot mender. If they do not grasp the intensity of her need for human response, they will probably consider her gullible, "stupid."

They must notice that the pot mender comes from the world outside the valley; he comes out of the "glowing." At first, she sees him in all his dirty, dishevelled detail—a stark contrast to the compulsive order of her own home life. His response to the chrysanthemums leads her to believe she has found emotional kin, a potential satisfier. (Practical Henry had never understood what growing the chrysanthemums meant to her; he wished her "gift" were used in the orchards.) But here is one who does understand. That this repulsive pot mender could appeal to her and that she did not notice the reason for his interest in the chrysanthemums suggest how grave her hunger is. It takes only his imaginative simile, his "brooding" eyes, his half "Maybe I know,"—together with *her* self-generated passion as she describes her liaison with the flowers and the stars—to convince her that he *does* "know," that he has felt as she, and that, at this moment, he is one with her. She is so carried away that she does not realize the reason for his lack of response to her outstretched hand, the comic irony of his next remark, his change of manner, his forgetting the sand. These and many other small details suggest the ecstacy she has to "shake herself free" from.

How does she feel about her "experience"? What is implied by the details of her scrubbing, her ritualistic dressing, her laying out of Henry's clothes, her prim, stiff pose, her boast about being "strong"? What does she think happened?

The sand on the road lets her know what did happen. What does she recognize? This is *the* question; but students can know the answer only by examining Elissa's sequence of reactions at the end of the story and seeing what each implies. For instance, Why does she explain to herself about the plants on the road? Why does she remark about the dinner *in the way* she does? Why does she ask for wine? Why does she question Henry about the prize fight? Why does she decide wine is "enough"—enough for what? Why is she crying? Why does the narrator say she was crying "like an old woman"?

The careful study of this story would help students develop the ability to sense the tone of dialogue *without* the guidance of a narrator's comment, to infer the function of a word ("strong") that is repeated throughout a story, and to recognize the symbolic value of locales, weather, characters, and objects.

In general the experience of Ernest Hemingway's eight-page "Soldier's Home" will be more familiar to students than that of "The Chrysanthemums," but such familiarity *may* hinder them from seeing the particular experience that is Krebs' and the general relevance of *that*. For Krebs is not, as students might assume, an older adolescent rebelling against parental strictures and mores. Krebs rejects his peers, too, both those in the Army and those outside of it. For he discovers that life in society, whether in his family or with his contemporaries, requires that a man violate the truth. He must lie to be thought a hero, to court a girl, to seem exciting, to reassure his mother, to fit the acceptable pattern of success. Krebs discovers that the truth evokes from others only some unfavorable response: indifference, rejection, disappointment, heartache. The cost of telling the truth is high, but Krebs has learned from his experience as "returning hero" that for him the cost of lying is much higher; it is no less than the loss of integrity, and that to Krebs is "everything." Since such a loss is the consequence of involvement, Krebs decides to live as an observer of life, without any demanding human relationships.

If students seemed to be misconstruing Krebs' experience, his decision, and his course of action, we would call their attention to the kind of world—pre-war, war, and post-war—that Krebs lives in, the kind of temperament he has, *how* he realizes what he values most, how he *moves* to a decision about social commitments, how his temperament affects his way of carrying out his decision, what future is implied, and what the narrator's attitudes toward Krebs' situation and his solution are. Since the story is Hemingway's, calling students' attention to these matters would consist in making them notice objective details and urging them to infer the significance of each detail and grasp the connections among them. To help students understand Krebs' world, for instance, we would call their attention to such details as the fraternity picture, the picture on the Rhine, the townspeople's addiction to horror stories, the family car, the "devoted" mother who asks him to talk and then does not listen, the mother who protests her love in clichés, the noncommittal father who cannot read his paper if it is "mussed," the girls across the street and at the Greek's, and his "best" sister whose love entails nothing more than Krebs' going to see her "play indoor." From these details readers construct a superficial and insincere world in which the genuine and candid Krebs is necessarily an alien.

"Soldier's Home" is for average-to-good readers who are already somewhat alert to the significance of seemingly unimportant parts of a story and to the reasons for these parts being placed where they are. For, the reader of this story misses much if he cannot see why, for instance, the paragraph about the family car is placed where it is, why the material about the war histories comes just before the dialogue scenes, why the first dialogue opens with such commonplace material, why the scene with Helen is included, and why it is juxtaposed with the "mother" scene.

"Soldier's Home" is, furthermore, for readers who are sensitive to tone. For, unless students can infer from various uses of language both in the dialogue and in the narrated parts of the story what Krebs' attitudes are and what the narrator's are, they might misunderstand the intention of this story.

Unless readers of Katherine Anne Porter's "He" (twelve pages) understand the sort of person Mrs. Whipple is, they will not recognize her tension. So they will condemn her. The story does not.

Mrs. Whipple is a proud woman who "couldn't stand to be pitied," yet her "simple-minded" son makes her a permanent object of community pity. So, in public, she defends Him and asserts His normality; in private, she rages at His senseless actions, unsympathetically neglects Him, and inhumanely exploits Him. The average-to-good readers who would be reading "He" would notice all the more explicit vestiges of her attitude toward Him, but they might not catch the less obtrusive elements that define her feeling. For instance, they might not notice the narrator's ridicule of Mrs. Whipple's clichés about love and concern (especially, say, in the direct reporting in paragraph seven of the story), or they might not realize the implications of those "unimportant" details the narrator so casually mentions; for example, that Mrs. Whipple sent Him "limping" "three miles" on a "hot day" to get a bull—and worried only about what "people would say" if the bull "came down on Him." We would probably have to call students' attention to *such* telling features as these. But, in general, average readers would recognize quite adequately that Mrs. Whipple neither pities nor loves Him; indeed, that she cannot *accept* Him.

We think, though, that *on their own* these readers might not realize that her attitude tortures her: she feels that she *should* love Him. So we would be ready to help them notice how continually and how variously her tension is expressed. We would be ready to call their attention to her protests of love, "natural for a mother," to her need "to talk about Him first," her continual pretended concern for Him, her justifications for her inhumane use of Him, her upset about the "skinned pig," her "feeling badly about all sorts of things," her wish to be dead, and, at the end, her utopian dream of another chance, and her unwillingness to face what He *is* "accusing her of."

Mrs. Whipple recognizes finally that He *did* mind His life without love. But are her last thoughts just ironically true rationalizations? Or does *she* realize also, as the reader does, the truth of these thoughts? Realize that "she *had* loved Him as much as *she* possibly could"; "there *was* nothing *she* could do to make up to Him for His life."[15] It was indeed for both "a mortal pity He was ever born."

This beautiful story stands for that all-too-familiar human experience in which two people, being what they are, cannot but hurt one another, cannot but suffer from it, cannot be blamed for it. Fully revealed as it is in "He," this disconcerting experience evokes not sentimentality, not indictments of material poverty, not pity for Him and scorn for her—nor any other one-sided or oversimplified response; it evokes understanding.

Because we would want every student to have as fully as possible *on the first reading* this crucial human insight that "He" renders, when we assigned the story, we would give the class some form of "be-sure-to-notice" memo, calling their attention to what we anticipate they might otherwise overlook.

If it seems desirable to have able students read a "buffer" story, a work like James Joyce's "A Little Cloud" (fifteen pages) is a good choice. Such a story will exercise students' alertness to details, their responses to the implications of them, and their sensitivities to the ways attitudes are expressed. In this story an immature man, Little Chandler, enjoys his childish phantasms and suffers the real consequences of them. To understand this story, readers must notice more than such obvious features as the physical and psychological details that suggest the characters of Chandler, his friend Gallaher, and his wife Annie. They must notice more than the three-part design of the story that renders Chandler's emotional descent from exhilaration and buoyant hope to the despair and the shame of his final "epiphany." To understand this story, readers must respond as well to the less obtrusive means that define Little Chandler's unheroic "flaw" and the inconsequence it entails.

In the first part of the story the "little mannie" is revealed (and judged) mainly by the way the narrator expresses Chandler's responses. Consider the *language* he uses to render Chandler's definition of "getting on," or his anticipation of the hero from the "great city," his adolescent pleasure in melancholy and futility, his romanticizing of Corless's and of his night prowls, his admiration for the bravado of the young Gallaher, and, of course, his pathetically unrealistic view of writing and of his own talents. The narrator's language is always exposing and gently ridiculing poor, naive, silly little Chandler, "the great baby" inflated by his childish dreams, deflated by realities—even by the reality of Corless's door, for instance.

In the second part of the story, the narrator's kindly chiding of Chandler yields, in the scene at Corless's, to Gallaher's blatant ridicule of him. Notice Gallaher's salutations ("Tommy," "old hero"), his responses to Chandler's narrowness ("You haven't changed an atom"), his reaction to Chandler's having a son ("I wouldn't doubt you, Tommy")—all these remarks openly deride Little Chandler's immaturity and his insignificance. Furthermore, Gallaher's braggadocio, his recital of the "astonishing" facts of life, his demeaning small talk about Chandler's world not only devalue him, but reveal his contempt for his naive listener. And the "little mannie's" responses to Gallaher suggest he deserves the contempt being heaped on him. For Chandler dislikes *only* Gallaher's vulgar language. He actually envies the "hero," plays an admirable straight man to him, and surely indicts himself by the stupid way he elects to "assert his manhood." No wonder there is no reply to Gallaher's crushing rejoinder.

The whole scene at Corless's testifies to Chandler's insignificance, to the immaturity of his judgment. To re-create the scene sensitively, the reader has to notice all the details we have mentioned: besides, he has to continually decide for himself how the dialogue is said and what the gestures mean. The narrator's help is spare.

In the final part of the story, it is once again the narrator's language that suggests Chandler's immaturity. The narrator's "holding *a child*" implies the incongruity of Chandler's being a father; his phrase "*a young woman*" suggests the inappropriateness of Chandler's being a husband; and the narrator's "*of course, she was in bad humor*" hints at the impossibility of this "little man's" ever being master in the family. Even Chandler's tension between his romantic desires (for a passionate wife, a "brave" life, a career as an "Irish Byron") and his realistic obligations (to a prim and pretty wife, a wailing child, and unpaid-for furniture) is reduced to the ludicrously pathetic by the narrator's attitude toward it.

If the reader does not notice the presence and the effect of the less obtrusive literary means we have been mentioning, he will remain until the moment of recognition as innocent of the *cause* of Chandler's "noon to night" experience as Chandler is. For it is all features of the story working together that let the reader know from the first paragraph on that Little Chandler, like all the immature in "dirty Dublin" and elsewhere, is his own jailor. His external restraints are the consequences, not the causes, of his entrapment. The story renders Chandler's "downward path to this widsom." Able readers watch Chandler discover the truth.

■ *Unspectacular Revelations.* The recognitions in the five preceding stories will, we think, strike high school readers as less dramatic than, say, those of "Eveline," "The Use of Force," or "Do You Like It Here?" Nevertheless, students may find the recognitions both moving and poignant since the concerns of the five stories—the desire for love and empathy, the cost of belonging, the inability to love those "we should," and the penalty for immaturity—*are* the live concerns of high school students. And at the very least, reading the stories in the preceding group will give students the pleasure of surprising discoveries in the supposedly familiar, because high school readers have, as they say, "never before thought about these things *in this way.*"

In the following stories the revelations are unspectacular indeed. The crucial moments in the lives of the characters are not births, deaths, marriages, graduations, festivals or national crises. They are, rather, day-to-day "miracles," "vest-pocket" tragedies, moral choices between two "goods," moral conflicts that end in "draws," the discovery that one is despised, inconsequential, or just doomed to grow old. These are stories which reveal the significance hidden in the most pedestrian events of life. Reading such stories as these will further develop students' sensitivity to the importance of the "day-in-day-out" situations represented in literature and will offer all students a chance to train their "eye" to perceive more richly the unspectacular events of their own lives.

Instead of the usual five or six stories, in this group we list nine—

partly to recall the variety of such stories appropriate for high school students, and partly to suggest the necessity for the teacher's having a large repository of works to choose from whenever what is being taught *demands* that he have the "right" works for each group of students.[16] This is surely one of those occasions. When a teacher is trying to expand students' conceptions of what is significant, he must have stories so "right" for the group that reading them *will* evoke keen realizations about matters that these students have always taken for granted. Then, once they recognize that they have long been looking at familiar things without *really* perceiving them, they are usually more amenable to trying to discover what they have been missing in less familiar experiences.

Several of the stories we list are "old standards," but, at the risk of belaboring the obvious, we have annotated all stories, giving the approximate length and suggesting some of the literary means readers must respond to if they are to grasp the significance of the situation rendered. We have arranged the stories in what we think is, roughly, an order of increasing reading difficulty. Some of these stories are, from a literary standpoint, less complex than those that we suggested for the same quality of reader earlier in this course. This "regression" is intentional. The story of simple truth has to make its impact virtually on its own. The reader has to *feel* the significance of the simple experience as he reads. If he does not, it is, as we know, very difficult to get him to feel it afterwards. So we would give an "easier" story to enhance the possibility of students' having a valid and poignant experience during their own first reading. If we thought a class would still need help in order to have this kind of first reading of a certain story, we would offer an introduction, an advisory, or just a hint or two to highlight something elucidating. We would, in other words, give students whatever kind of assistance they needed so that their first reading would be an insightful experience and their in-class study of the story just a refining of their experience, not a correcting of it.

An average class would probably study two stories in such a grouping as the following, an early story and a late one. But all such practical decisions about how many stories should be read and which stories should be chosen depend entirely upon the ability, progress, and interest of each particular class.

Caroline Gordon's nine-page "The Last Day in the Field" is a good reading for less able students and a useful "opener" for classes that might require several readings. The fact that it is the "last day" for the old man would constitute for many high school students *the* significance of the story. But a careful reading will show them that the greater significance comes from the way in which the old man sees his "last day"—and makes the reader see it.

Aleck sees this day as one day in the continuum of "history"—a day made possible by many preceding days during which he learned from men and birds long since gone, a day making possible many succeeding days during which Joe will enjoy what he is learning from him. Each thing comes to fruition in something else; the trainer's life is extended in his dogs; Uncle James', in Aleck; Aleck's, in Joe. The story implies that nothing really ends; there are many autumns, "many such dogs," eternal springs, and always there is reliably predictable nature; all kinds of details are constantly reminding the reader of this.

Furthermore, the story suggests that no part of life is best: "It's a wonderful thing to be twenty years old"; "Afternoon is different from morning, more exciting." And "evening" may be marvelously vital: witness such symbolic details as the "greened-up" September, the top clusters of the elderberry bushes, that dog that will not be done, the bird that zooms up and whirrs down, wings spread, and old Aleck "who had to hunt it, leg or no leg." Just because the frost will "get you yet," there is no reason to surrender early.

The reader will see the meaning of the last day, if he infers the thematic relationship among such details as these. The connections are quite obvious, but, because of the reportorial style in which the story is (rightly) told, some readers think that the many details of nature and time we have just been connecting are simply devices for particularizing the setting. But if readers perceive the relationship among these details (and this would probably be *our* hint to them), they will grasp the significance of this day. And they will realize why the tension between Aleck's need to give up and his reluctance to do so is never expressed in maudlin nostalgia—or even in intimate personal feelings. The tension has extrapersonal significance, and the old man's view of his "last day" makes this clear to the reader.

During the discussion of this story, some teachers might want to notice *explicitly* the way in which certain details *become* symbolic in the story and the way more conventional symbols release their traditional "meanings."

The experience of "The Last Day in the Field" is not significant just because it is a "last." The experience of Katherine Mansfield's "Her First Ball" (six pages) is not important just because it is a "first." At the ball as Leila is initiated into the wondrous world of parties, she is also made aware of the transiency of this lovely life. When her middle-aged partner imagines her as one of the chaperones she has noticed earlier, he makes her realize that her first ball is "only the beginning of her last ball."

From the outset of the story the reader is being given the impression of transiency. Exactly when things begin is hard to tell, but they rush on unceasingly. Participial verbs of action keep everything in motion: leaping, flying, tossing, spinning, streaming by. The syntax piles activities one upon the other. There is never time enough. Initially, Leila notices nothing but the excitement of this perpetual motion, but the reader's attention is called to its repetitive patterns; the music stopping and starting, stopping and starting; the "round" of parties—the "Bell's last week," "Neaves' on Tuesday," here tonight; the succession of similar partners, all saying similar things. The reader notices the ennui of the habitués and the sameness of the memories of the middle-aged fat man: to him Leila's is just one more "bright little face." Time goes, at once, on and round; life is just so many turns between the first dance and the last chaperoning.

The reader is well-prepared for Leila's discovery of this truth—and for her response to her new knowledge. And it is *her response*, expressed in her reaction to the fat man, that gives her discovery its significance. Readers must attend carefully to the words and gestures of her little drama with the fat man at the close of the story if they are to infer what is implied in her reaction. (Our *hint* would probably link her response with the perpetual motion.)

This is a fine story for showing students how theme is implied by many literary devices and for pointing out, once again, how internal feelings are objectified.

We could say that in Eudora Welty's "The Worn Path" (eight pages) an old Negro woman makes her customary trip on foot from the back hills to Natchez for medicine for her chronically ill grandson. That *is* what happens in the story. But what the reader perceives is a heroine in battle array on a perilous journey through a winter world—like any quester of the mythic past "bound to go. . . . The time come around." The reader perceives this heroine overcoming each obstacle, being assisted by the kindly agents, and arriving at last at the castle: "'Here I be,' she said." So absorbing had the journey itself been, that momentarily the quester cannot recall the object of her mission. Upbraiding herself, she promises "never to forget him again, no, the whole enduring time." The quest achieved, like the Wise Men of old and the knights of romance and the Grail, she "marches herself back" with the elixir of life in one hand and the token of her promise in the other.

The significance of this ordinary old woman is further extended by details which link her to maternal, mythic, and natural symbols. She is the mother bird bringing life to the baby peeping out of the nest; she is the phoenix rejuvenated by its own fire; she is the June bug. In a world of winter and death (of fallow land, deserted houses, the thorn bush, the silver grey trees, the buzzard, the scarecrow), she is vitality, endurance, laughter. The details of this story at once describe an ordinary woman and symbolize her rare quality.

So while the reader *sees* an ancient Negress with a red rag on her head making her way to the city, he *perceives* an extraordinary person, unaware of her courage, her generosity, vibrance, humor, imagination, and nobility. The literary treatment—the images, the symbols, the variation of the quest archetype, and a certain mode of narration —endows an ordinary woman doing a routine errand of mercy with extraordinary significance. (Our hint for the readers? A five-line summary of the quest archetype.)

If a story like "The Worn Path" is not especially suited to the interests or to the reading needs of a particular class, then the "old standard," Ernest Hemingway's "The Killers" (ten pages), might be a good alternative. This initiation story dramatizes four attitudes toward the impending killing of an old prize fighter by two "fingers": the attitudes of the counterman, the cook, the young Nick, and the old prize fighter himself. Nick cannot share the others' passive acceptance of the inevitable. He decides to get out of "this town." He does not yet know that Summit is every town. So he is naively and unconsciously beginning what Ole is just getting through with: "all that running around." (Our hint? This ironic reversal.)

Everything counts in this economical story. So the study of it gives a natural opportunity for asking about the function of seemingly unnecessary details: If this is Nick's story, what is the function of the dialogue of the first two pages? What is gained by the images of the arc lights and the bare branches? What is the role of Mrs. Bell? The story will also exercise students' abilities to invest dialogue with appropriate tones and to recognize what the *structure* of sentences and of paragraphs expresses.

Because the reader of Elizabeth Bowen's "A Queer Heart" (eight pages) sees the events from Hilda Cadman's point of view, *he* can be sure she means no harm. The reader sees not only that she is immature, sensuous, and self-indulged, but also that she *really* does not believe she is irresponsible, inconsiderate, or unkind, as her daughter implies. Hilda does not realize that *she* is incapable of the ordinary deep human allegiances. In fact, she feels that she is unfairly resented, intimidated, censured, "put wrong" in her own home by the "complicity" of her daughter Lucille and her own "dankly virginal" sister Rosa who has "taken" Lucille from her. Hilda truly does not know what she has done to evoke all this. The point of view allows the reader to be sure of what Hilda is and what Hilda thinks she is. So the reader neither excuses nor blames her.

But he does not blame anyone else either. The design of the story and the way the narration is patterned prevent him from doing so. Up to and through the deathbed confrontation of the two sisters, these literary features keep the reader seeing the situation "steadily and whole." They do not allow him to unqualifiedly approve or censure any of the three characters.

In the opening scene, the reader favors the jolly, plump Hilda, but he is checked by what is implied in, "The solid house was not large, and Mrs. Cadman's daughter, Lucille, could look after it with a daily help." The next detail turns the reader's sympathy back to Mrs. Cadman; then as Hilda's self-centeredness slowly emerges from among her thoughts about living and dying, the reader's sympathy turns from her again. Only when this alternation has compelled the reader to feel ambivalent about Hilda is Lucille introduced into the story.

The "seesaw" continues. The reader sees how unfit Hilda is for her present situation; he sees why she considers the house depressing and Lucille disappointing. But he *also* sees that Lucille is dutiful, reasonable, justified in her censure of Hilda, who *is* difficult to cope with, as irresponsible and unfeeling as a child. Only when the reader has felt, through this alternation, "how it is" for both Hilda and Lucille does interest center on Rosa. Though the reader comes to know the "dankly virginal" sister mainly through Hilda's reflections, by this time in the story, he knows how to interpret the reflections; he recognizes the drastic differences between the two sisters; he sees them almost as caricatures of gratification and of denial; so he withholds condemnation of Rosa.

Just before the final scene—the confrontation of these two sisters at Rosa's deathbed—Hilda's memory of their childhood and of the "triumphal march" of her own youth offers the reader one explanation for the sisters being as they are. During the scene, Rosa's memory of their childhood offers another. The two memories complement each other. The reader understands. During the scene, Hilda, too, realizes that she, all unwittingly, has by her silly heart helped to create the "queer" heart of Rosa; and she wonders what she has "done" to Lucille, who is represented in the story as a youthful counterpart of Rosa.

How much is Hilda suggesting in her final remarks? Perhaps she realizes, as the reader does, that both the shallow heart and the "poor queer one," in their separate ways, have unintentionally destroyed what they got. The shallow heart neglects its "fairy doll" and wonders when it is all bedraggled where it could have come from; the queer heart takes its "little present" and "does right by it" till it is something "no one can bear the sight of." Hilda *seems* to realize finally what the reader has gradually seen from the whole story: that neither the overly gratified heart nor the "starved, disappointed one" values what it gets; Lucille, the "fairy doll," is the victim of both.

The point of view, the design of the story, and the way the narration is patterned work together to restrain the reader from judging. He knows that "There were things that couldn't be otherwise," that, indeed, the sisters *may* not "judge each other," and that any partial heart is "a queer one." (Our hint would be a question: Who is to blame?)

The story offers a fine opportunity not only for noticing once again the function of point of view and narrative method, but also for showing students that plot, though slight, is there.

An appropriate alternative to "A Queer Heart" for *certain* classes of boys and for somewhat less sensitive readers is J. F. Powers' "The Forks." This story represents more than a young person's disillusionment with the hiatus he discovers between the ideal and the real. It dramatizes one of our subtler moral experiences: the disconcerting moment when we recognize that, though we may prefer our own behavior to that of others, we are not certain it is "better."

In this fourteen-page story that is what the young Father Eudex comes to realize, with great discomposure. He finds his interpretation of what constitutes priestly behavior challenged not only by his pastor's convictions but also by the views implied by the behavior of many other clergymen and, most importantly, by the responses of different types of parishioners. In a series of eight "panels," the reader watches Father Eudex move from security to disquietude.

The story is told from his point of view, and the tone of the narrator at succeeding points reflects the young priest's changing attitude. At first, the narration gently ridicules Monsignor's pretentiousness, parodies his set speeches, and derides his hopeless ambitions and pre-adolescent "affair" with his car. Then comes the check sent as a gift to all local clergymen by a nearby industrial firm. In Father Eudex the check "triggers" a moral dilemma; he becomes seriously concerned about the whole question of appropriate priestly behavior. Now, humor is no longer a fitting response to Monsignor's actions. Now, Father Eudex' ridicule of Monsignor's grandiose ideas is fused with annoyance at his treatment of the janitor. Then, criticism turns inward: the young priest chides his own docility. His sarcasm about Monsignor's "seasoning" of him becomes increasingly bitter. It is climaxed in the symbolic scene where Father Eudex "breaking bread" with the "Master" compares vitriolically what he thought "following the Master" would be and what it is: not teaching and healing but "knowing the forks." This disillusioning irony makes Father Eudex bold; he condemns the check as "hush money." But, in the final scene, the young priest is uncertain about the rightness of his own position: he neither uses the check nor returns it. He is unable to judge the value of other priests' uses of the checks. He concludes that only the Master can judge the value of a stewardship; he himself is just another steward.

The reader is well prepared for this final recognition. Through all the scenes Father Eudex is continually aware that he can consider Monsignor's behavior pretentious, comic, arrogant, politic, but he cannot condemn the behavior as "wrong" or Monsignor as "bad." None of Monsignor's behavior violates any moral or church law. The deaths of Monsignor's "intercessors," not Monsignor's views, are barring him from a bishopric. By the same token, Monsignor can condemn Father Eudex's behavior as unwise, imprudent, tasteless, unseasoned—but not as "evil." And, though Father Eudex can justify his own behavior as "good," he cannot adjudge it "better" than Monsignor's. In fact, as Father Eudex knows, Monsignor's concept of priesthood is quite popular among the clergy, and, furthermore, it quite fulfills the expectations of some parishioners. The janitor may favor Father Eudex, but Mrs. Klein thinks he "ain't much of a priest." It is his attempt to "teach" Mrs. Klein that makes it clear to him that it would have been better had he "known the forks." Perhaps that is what evangelical Christianity means. Perhaps that is what is of most worth. Father Eudex cannot finally decide.

"The Forks" is a relatively easy story: the tones are obvious; the symbols that define the differences between the two men are blatant; the ironies, clear; the recognition, explicit. Why should such a story be placed midpoint on this list? For two reasons. Significant as the moral experience is, for high school students it will be both unusual and subtle. Most students will readily see the satire on Monsignor's Christianity; many will realize Father Eudex's disillusion, but only fairly able readers will on their own perceive the reason for the curate's final dilemma and the universal meaning of it. Furthermore, the story is a group of episodes. The causal connections among some of these are only implied. The reader has to infer the relationships. He has to decide, for example, why the garden episode is included, why Father Eudex gains courage as he rearranges his silver, why the Mrs. Klein episode is included and is placed where it is. Readers have to relate many things sensitively if they are to experience the young priest's dilemma.

If, for a certain class, stories like "A Queer Heart" and "The Forks" seem too elementary, then either Joyce's "Araby" or his "Clay" will be challenging substitutes. Both of these seven-page stories present, in more complex form, reading problems similar to those of "The Forks."

The recognition in "Araby" *seems* explicit and self-sufficient: "Gazing up into the darkness I saw myself as a creature driven and derided by vanity; and my eyes burned with anguish and anger."

This recognition is, however, only a sentimental ejaculation unless the reader can invest the words "vanity," "driven," and "anguish" with appropriate meanings and the entire sentence with proper tone. And he cannot do these things unless he has undergone the whole of the narrator's rendering of the experience of this boy in his actual and imaginary worlds. The entire story prepares us for the recognition which is, of course, relevant to all of the boy's preceding experience.

From the very outset the reader has to realize that the boy exists in one world, lives in another. He *exists* in a world of musty houses, of boys playing and being called in for tea, of street hawkers at the Saturday market, of a broken window pane, of "small talk" with "the girl next door." He exists in the world of a parochial aunt, of Mrs. Mercer, and of a tiresome, unsympathetic uncle. But he *lives* in an imaginary world, a romanticized version of his actual world. In this world, the old garden with the "relic" in it takes on an exciting wildness. The sights and sounds and smells of the alleys are sensually gratifying; the dark and light is an enchanting chiaroscuro. The boy in the marketplace becomes the priest-knight; the walk to school, a romantic "chase." The sound of rain in the back drawing room evokes a mystical experience; the dark house, a "vision." To *this* boy, doing the "serious work of life" is "ugly monotonous child's play"; but going to Araby is "knight's work," the carrying out of a lady's boon.

The mode of narration is always preparing the reader for the boy's disenchantment. The older retrospective narrator is continually evaluating the boy's imaginary world by phrases like "foolish blood," "confused adoration," "What innumerable follies laid waste my waking and sleeping thoughts." Furthermore, the narrator is always letting the reader experience objectively the various situations the boy is romanticizing. The half-scene, for instance, allows the reader to hear what the conversation with Mangan's sister *actually* consisted in; then, the reader hears what the boy "makes" of this routine talk.

Because of the design of the story—the gradual shift from the panorama of repeated situations to close-ups of singular, highly personal experiences—the reader is made increasingly aware of how much the boy needs this imaginary world and how devastating the inevitable disenchantment will be. And, as the detailed rendering of the day of the romantic pilgrimage to Araby reveals, so strong is the dream that neither the early frustration of the day nor the misgivings nor the grim actualities of the journey can quell the quester. He has to be surrounded by the empty "church" ringing with sounds of the money changers before the "Eastern enchantment" dissolves. All the details in this last scene are imaginatively connected with details of his previous romantic experiences. So, in the one moment all his delusions are exposed. And the reader knows what the recognition at Araby implies for all of the boy's imaginary world.

"Clay" is virtually a report of the events of Maria's Halloween told in the third person from her point of view and largely in her language. It is from this seemingly innocent, yet subtly suggestive report that the reader must infer how the world feels about Maria, how she really interprets its response, and how she responds to the world.

The reader perceives that she is patronized by the matron, the cook, and Ginger Mooney, gently ridiculed by Lizzie Fleming, harshly mocked by the cake store clerk, noticed only by the drunkard, pitied condescendingly by the Donnellys, cruelly derided by the girls, and praised in clichés by the mellowed Joe. This is the kind of attention that this "very, very small person indeed" gets from the world she must live in. Maria remembers these "compliments," greatly values Joe's paltry present, is flattered by the gentleman "with a drop taken" and by the ostentatious considerations of the Donnellys. Doesn't she sense the attitudes of all these people? Doesn't she realize her own alienation? She does.

But, in one way or another, she is continually reassuring herself that she *is* significant, that she *is* satisfied, that she *is* loved: she is the peace-maker where others fail, she is the "proper mother," she finds her body "a nice tidy little body," and her independence a "better lot," she deems herself superior to Mooney—Maria is a genteel lady with a conservatory, with appeal for "colonel-looking" gentlemen—and so on. Occasionally, she explicitly recognizes the fact of her loveless life: she "would have felt herself in the way" at Joe's; she shows a "disappointed shyness" when she is joked about the ring; she realizes that the children are "made" to say "Thanks"; she does not want to know *what* was "wrong" in the game; "She *said* they were all very good to her." And, in the final song, Maria, perhaps unconsciously, summarizes all the unfulfilled desires of her conscious life, the desires that the reader has already perceived. *She* has made no "mistake"; a world in which she would be the hope, the pride, and, most of all, the constantly beloved *is* her dream. But it is only a dream.

To the disappointing, uncompassionate world, Maria responds with delusions, rationalizations, realistic recognition, but mostly with love. That the insignificant, rejected, and ridiculed "clay" still responds with love is the affirming irony that saves this experience— and life in general—from being "too dark altogether."

Hemingway's little five-page story is for students who read well enough to see that "A Clean, Well-Lighted Place" is not "about emptiness," but about a *certain* kind of emptiness—the lack of "confidence"—and about a *certain* response to this emptiness—"dignity." In this story, two waiters conflict over closing a café and sending the last patron—an old man—home. Through this simple, routine disagreement, the older waiter recognizes that he is different from the young waiter not just in age, but in his sympathies, and in his lack of "confidence." He realizes the value of the "pleasant café" for those who lack confidence, those who, in other words, have no trustful, intimate relationship with another, human or divine. The older waiter recognizes the emptiness of his own life, and he chooses to endure it with dignity. A disagreement over closing a café has "triggered" an extraordinary spiritual crisis.

The reader sees that the older waiter and the old customer are parallel characters: both have only financial security; both "need a light for the night," both postpone going to bed; for, there, the potential for intimacy being greatest, the sense of alienation is most acute. A kindred soul, the older waiter not only understands why the old man wants to commit suicide and why he needs the social ritual of sitting in a pleasant café, but he actually emulates the dignity—the serene, noble demeanor—with which the old man "confronts" the bed, when he must.

Reading this story will exercise many skills students have been learning; they must for instance, keep the speakers in the dialogue "straight" without a narrator's help; they must sense the tone of the narrator and of the older waiter in his introspection; they must realize how the meaning of "nothing" expands, what "light" and "the bed" come to symbolize, and how the substitutions of "nada" in the Lord's Prayer and the Ave Maria suggest, together, an embracing desperation. Reading this story will, furthermore, make students notice once again how the design of a story helps to render the meaning: while the dramatization narrows from the three characters to the two waiters and, finally, to the older one, the significance of the dramatization broadens: the plight of the old man is revealed to be the plight of the older waiter, and, finally, the plight of many. Initially, the reader thinks of the waiters as similar to one another, different from the old man, but the dialogue about the soldier begins to distinguish them, and they are steadily contrasted in sympathies, both by their dialogue and by the narrator's occasional qualifying comment ("young," "unhurried," and so on). The older waiter is first distinguished, then, from the young waiter, later from the barman, and finally from all those who "lived in it and never felt it." He becomes one with the old man and with that large society to whom "nada" is all.

Hemingway's story is a good transition to the study of the next group of stories: those in which the rendering is so unusual that, to careless or unimaginative readers, the stories might seem "pointless."

In "A Clean, Well-Lighted Place," plot is slight, the characters are unnamed and described only by symbolic qualities, the relevance of the episodes of the soldier and the barman is only implied, and the waiter's reaction to his recognition is suggested by a physical posture. In other words, the responses readers must make to experience this story are the kinds of things they have usually failed to do when they complain that a story is "pointless."

■ *Unusual Renderings.* Reading the following kinds of stories will introduce students to a variety of unusual renderings and will help them to develop tendencies to respond appropriately to whatever a narrator tells, however uncommon its organization may be, however demanding its mode of expression. When students call such stories as these "pointless," they are usually confessing that either they have resisted giving themselves up to the story, holding perhaps unconsciously to some notion of what the story should be, or they have (as we have just said) failed to make the implied connections because of careless or unimaginative reading. So our study of the stories in this final group would concentrate on helping readers join the narrator and make the kind of inferences *each particular* structure requires.

If the class had to read more than one story, we would try to select works that use very different structural devices and represent very different states of mind. For we would want our choices to frustrate the abiding hope that inattentive and unimaginative readers have of discovering an "all-purpose" key to these seemingly elusive stories. A group like the following seven stories would provide us with a goodly variety to choose from. And since all of these stories offer penetrating insights into *ordinary* experience, reading any of them would also reinforce and extend the sensitivities students began to develop through the study of the stories in the previous group.

We have arranged the stories in rough order of their reading difficulty and have annotated them briefly to suggest approximately how long each story is, what might make each seem "pointless," and what kinds of responses students must be ready to make if they are to experience the story. As always, the abilities and the interests of each class must determine how many stories and which stories should be read.

Allan Seager's "This Town and Salamanca" (eleven pages) is a good introduction to stories that, because of their unusual structure, baffle certain readers. For, on one hand, this story makes readers aware immediately and quite bluntly that the structure *is* unconventional and that they must discover what it is if they are to make sense out of this story, not to say, get the point of it. On the other hand, the structure of the story is not subtle; there are, for instance, clearly indicated "parts," each of which represents some significant episode; there is, furthermore, the thematically suggestive title, the obvious flashback, the scheme of a teller of tales (John) and three listeners (Klug, Gordon, and the narrator), *and* a first-person point of view. *Cooperative* readers can rather easily grasp all this.

If, however, they do not notice how chatty, loose, and conversational the voice of the first-person narrator is (he even opens his story in the middle of a sentence), they will be baffled. For they will not be ready to cope with the sudden interpolations that break up the thought of a sentence and with those seemingly unconnected comments that invade the narration (for example, "Mrs. Gira got well though and it is a fine new railroad station"). If readers are not alert to the narrative voice, they will be unprepared to respond even to the shifts in time the narrator makes and to those reactions of his that evolve quite naturally from the events he tells (for instance, "I remember how bright the gold piece was in his hand"). If, however, readers attune at once to the mode of narration, they will then be able to concentrate on seeing what the functions are of these seemingly rude interruptions, these diversions, loose associations, and "leaps."

Some readers may, furthermore, be baffled about what they are to make of this story—unless they notice not only which episodes of John's life the narrator chooses to tell and why he orders them as he does, but also what parts of the episodes evoke responses from the narrator, what kind of reaction this is in each case, how his responses differ from those of Klug and Gordon, and what this difference suggests.

When readers have noticed *such* aspects of the story as the preceding, they will perceive that the narrator is attracted both toward "Salamanca" (the distant, the romantic, the eerie, the unorthodox) and toward "this town" (work, professional achievement, peace without brilliance). His tension toward one is always counterbalanced in the story by his tension toward the other. Furthermore, readers will realize that John understands his role in the lives of his listeners (indeed, they will see he outdoes himself to gratify vicariously the narrator's desires for "Salamanca"). And students will recognize *how* the narrator rationalizes his own behavior, *how* his attitude toward John changes, and *why* his final response is vindictive and bitter.

A. E. Coppard's "The Third Prize" (nine pages) is another "easy" story, available to average readers and useful for other students who need to be introduced gently to the way that seemingly unimportant parts of a story function. Most students would not think of this story as "pointless"—because they would readily grasp the comic irony of George Robins' unwittingly giving his ill-gotten sovereign to the "second thief," Jerry Chambers. The story would make sense, and students would probably mistake this irony for "the point."

Many would have missed the larger intention of the story mainly because the literary features that work with this main episode to render the intention would have seemed to these readers unimportant, "decorative," even irrelevant. Students would probably fail to see, for instance, the function of the description of the town. They would think of it only as setting an appropriately busy scene or, better, of creating a thronged confusion where George's swindle could plausibly take place. We doubt that most students would notice that every detail in the description shows someone getting whatever he can—and that includes even the neighboring borough and the cathedral. These details suggest that the main episode represents, in a way, the *potential* behavior of the people as a whole.

Many of the other seemingly unnecessary features of the story confirm this. What function have the girls, for instance? Among other things, they are the "hunters" who "attach themselves," having "what they can get"; they are the chorus that approve George's impersonation, his swindle, and his "sacrifice." Personally very different, they represent the crowd; morally similar, they suggest how universal their pragmatic standards are. And the trite, cliché flirtations—"you're as bad as the rest of 'em"; "You're as good as they make 'em"; "I'm as good as I can be"—confirm an ethical unanimity. All are, in varying degrees, men of Jerry Chambers' "own fraternity."

In the world of this story men are not what they seem to be—from those "upstanding" amateur runners of the first paragraph, George Robins and Naboth Bird, to the "kindly" Jerry of the final scene. Details throughout the story suggest this hiatus between appearance and reality. And students would surely notice the more explicit ones, but would they see that the applause is "factitious"? that the countess *looks* like a publican's wife? that the "very gentlemanly steward" is really a fishmonger? and that these two "presumably" go their separate ways? Would students notice such details? Perhaps not. Yet it is just those details that give the reader the *experience* of the almost unrelieved chicanery of this world.

Readers would hear the satiric narrative voice, but would they set themselves for a comic tale? Would they notice how the narrator implies, by his conventional descriptions, the universality of what is going on? Would they see how, by his change from comically inflated language to the dignified, straightforward language of the beggar scene, he leads the reader to believe that there is indeed "one just man"—Jerry? And then with what quiet, controlled language he disabuses the reader of that impression?

These, then, are some of the details that certain students might not perceive the relevance of. Yet it is just such features that suggest the larger intention of this tale: they create a world where the end justifies the means, a world where social virtue and vice, truth and falsity, are fused in dark comedy, a "beautiful Zion," where exploiting a blind man evokes "sincere pleasure."

Both J. D. Salinger's "Uncle Wiggily in Connecticut" and William Faulkner's "That Evening Sun" are, for different reasons, more likely to disconcert readers than the two previous stories are. It is the final "act" of Salinger's sixteen-page story that may perplex them; they may not understand the reasons for Eloise's actions or the connections among them. They will be left wondering: What is it that makes her suggest to Lew that he and the men "march" home? What is it about the maid's request that impels her to respond so sardonically? Why does she pull Ramona into the *middle* of the bed? What evokes "Poor Uncle Wiggily"? What has happened during Eloise's "journey" upstairs that prompts her last question to Mary Jane?

Because Salinger's story is presented as a three-act "play," the narrator does little more than set scenes and report speeches and gestures. From these external clues the reader must infer the main character's motivations, the connections among her actions, and her internal drama. If he *has* been inferring these things from what he has seen and heard in the first two "acts," then he will understand how Eloise's behaviors in the final "act" interrelate and how they consummate the drama.

While reading the first two "acts," students should notice that the three-o'clock flip, "hard-as-nails" Eloise, the showman with the audience of one, gives way to the five-o'clock Eloise, at once bitter and mellow, the girl who exists in one world but lives in another. She *exists* in the present world of her husband Lew and little daughter Ramona, about both of whom she knows virtually nothing; she *lives* in the past, the simple, tender, unpretentious world of her love affair with Walt which she can still recall in precise and affectionate detail. If students have noticed these two different attitudes, they will understand how natural it is for the touching memory of Walt to evoke in the seven-o'clock Eloise her vindictive punishment not only of Lew but also of her happily married maid.

But unless students have *also* noticed in the second "act" the parallel between the love of Eloise and Walt and that of Ramona and her imaginary Jimmy, they may not know how to interpret Eloise's behavior toward Ramona in "act three." Eloise first violently pulls Ramona into the middle of the bed to impress upon her that she cannot substitute a new imaginary love—Mickey—for her now-dead Jimmy. Then, in sudden reversal, Eloise enters into tender communion with the loveless little girl. In this episode with Ramona, Eloise seems to recognize what her *existence* has made her. She craves to be reassured that she "*was* a nice girl." The language of her last speech, so different from the snide, artificial clichés of "act one," suggests that her past innocence has not been entirely lost.

If readers are sensitive to the gradual shift in Eloise's style of language from the first "act" to the last, they will realize the unmasking she is undergoing, they will notice what it concerns, and they will have the "right" expectations for understanding the final scene. And, if they are sensitive to the implications of styles of language, they will recognize the superficiality that Mary Jane's responses reveal and the suffering that Eloise's flip facade seeks to cover.

We suspect that some student-readers of Faulkner's "That Evening Sun" (twenty pages) would say: "Why did he include all that material that interrupts Nancy's story? It spoils the story; it's distracting." They would be referring, not to the narrator's opening comparison of Monday in Jefferson then and now, but to the children's remarks that intersect the dialogue, to the interpolations of much seemingly unnecessary data, to the "leaps" in time, and to all the other exhaustive detail the narrator includes as he reports what he overheard, heard by hearsay, said, and saw of this ordeal of Nancy, his family's wash woman. Calling students' attention to the fact that the narrator, for all but the first four paragraphs, is a nine-year-old boy does not help much. This fact accounts only for the presence of all this detail. This "total" report is what a sensitive, personally reticent, young participant-observer would give. What the students are asking is why have such an account; what is gained by choosing a narrator who will tell the story this way.

We would try to show students how to answer their own question. We would call their attention to several of the key episodes of the story. We would ask them to read each carefully, listening in their mind's ear to the episode exactly as it happened, and, when they finished such a "play reading" of it, to state precisely what the episode *consists of* and what, as a whole, it is really about. By doing such an assignment, students usually discover that, in each of the episodes, while Nancy is undergoing some moment of great terror, seven-year-old Caddy is teasing little Jason about being "scared," or Jason is boasting about not "being a nigger," or out of morbid curiosity Caddy is questioning her father about Nancy, or the father is making futile suggestions to Nancy, or the mother is self-centeredly whining, or Dilsey is offering well-meant, but irrelevant, kindnesses. In each of the episodes, only the narrator seems to realize the quality of Nancy's terror; *his* awareness of it is suggested by his comparisons, his silences, and most importantly, by his perceptive observations of her eyes, her hands, her lips, and her sweat. Through this young boy's full and guileless reporting of several key incidents, the reader experiences the attitudes of a *variety* of persons toward Nancy's

growing fear, her panic, her numbing, and, finally, her hopeless resignation. Nancy's world responds to her abandoned and hopeless
condition with lack of sympathy, ineffectual solicitude, selfish interest, and indifference. Even the narrator who realizes Nancy's fate is
concerned finally only with "who will do our washing now."

By cooperating with all that is in the story the way it is there, the
reader sees that "That Evening Sun" is not the story of Nancy's fear,
but of the attitudes of a "society" toward it. To reveal the true character of these attitudes, the narrator's stark, simple, "total" report of
what was said and done by all is the perfect mode of narration. To
see the point of the story, the reader *has* to see the point of all that
material that interrupts Nancy's story.

And he has to recognize the function of the frame, too. As the
reader begins the story, the opening four paragraphs seem to be just
a twenty-four-year-old man's remembrance of things past, in particular his memory of a curious wash woman who carried hatted
laundry on her head. During the story, the reader realizes how
special that woman was and is in the narrator's eyes, how precisely
the narrator recalls the episodes, how poignantly he remembers. And
when the reader notices Quentin's final remark, "Who will do our
washing now, Father?" he realizes suddenly what the function of the
opening frame is.

If the reader of Eudora Welty's "Death of a Travelling Salesman"
(sixteen pages) responds sensitively to the story's rendering of Bowman's mental states, he will have the beautiful experience this story
creates. If he misinterprets the salesman's states, at the least he may
discount the significance of Bowman's epiphany; at worst he may
even emerge from reading the story with nothing more than a number of disjointed sentences, paragraphs, and episodes. So, in the
study of this story, we would help students to analyze Bowman's
mental states carefully so that they would see their significance.

The title suggests to the reader a general orientation. And, in the
first several paragraphs, certain details make clear that Bowman is
a very ill man, a dying man. There is his feeling of stopped time, of
nature's cruel trickery, of uncertainty about "the way"; there is his
frustration at loss of control, his fleeting, recurrent memory of his
grandmother, and his sensation of "going back, far back." The reader
must recognize these hallucinations and anxieties as typical of the
mind of the dying, and he must ready himself to respond rightly to
the vacillations among mental states that characterize such a mind.

At times Bowman experiences the world about him only as a
physical blur, a mental confusion, a montage of memories; at other
times, however, he responds to it with the customary lucidity of a
normally healthy man; and, at *certain* times, he perceives it with
exaggerated clarity, with new appreciation, and indeed with tor-

turingly true recognitions. These different mental states may occur in rapid succession, the mind emerging from distortions into varying degrees of clarity and retreating again into the unreal and the remote. These changing states may be related in one instance through objective phenomena, in another, by subjective association. Furthermore, any remark, any action might reflect both the response of the healthy Bowman and the reaction of the dying man. Even his innocent questions ("Where am I?" "Why didn't I do something?"), even the narrator's straightforward report (". . . he had never seen this hill or this petering-out path before . . .") have both literal and symbolic value. Like the lamp in the story, Bowman's is a half-clear, half-clouded world of "dulled brightness," "silent blows," and careful dreamy attention.

Unless the reader recognizes and responds appropriately to the mental states that the story represents, he might dismiss all of Bowman's responses as the unreliable, insignificant maunderings of a dying man. He might not see, on one hand, that from Bowman's physical illness come the heightened perceptions that allow him to evaluate with unremitting frankness his fourteen years' "progress." The reader might not realize, on the other hand, that many of Bowman's responses arise from the *spiritual* poverty of his past life as much as they do from his present physical condition. His mistaking the age and the intelligence of the farmer's wife who befriended him after his accident, for instance, is due not only to the visual blur of his semi-delirium but also to his lifelong habit of typing people by clothes, facial masks, and small talk. His responses to the world of the rural couple—his "absurd humble motion," his sense of "a mysterious, quiet, cool danger," his uncustomary questions, his bafflement about how he should act, and the "curious and strong emotion" he feels—result from and reveal *both* his physical illness *and* his spiritual sickness. In this "strange" world the responses he knows do not work. He has lived for many years in a world of appearances, of verbal "lines," of "sunlight," of motion, of independence, of paying your way. The couple's world is one of simple realities, of silence and wordless communication, of darkness and golden light, of rest and contemplation, of mutual dependence, of gratuitous kindness. It is Bowman's spiritual illness, as much as his physical condition, that causes him to regard "something private," "the ancient communication between two people" as something "remote," "mysterious," and dangerous.

Bowman's physical illness gives him a chance to see the world he missed, to recognize how lonely he was all his life, how empty. That he feels deeply his human alienation is implied by his reminiscence of his grandmother, his numb recall of the meaningless liaisons in "the nest of Chinese paper boxes," and by his sense of being stared at, but not being seen, by the farmers along the road. Bowman's delirium brings him to the couple's world, and, for a moment, the realities of that world regenerate his spirit: make him strip away his facade, make him "follow," "depend," and feel "hopefully secure," make him image the river of love and *almost* try to communicate "by simple words and embraces." Bowman realizes that, in the terms of his drummer's ethic of shrewdness, he has indeed been "tricked," "cheated" by life.

If the reader does not respond appropriately to the story's rendering of Bowman's states of mind, he may find much detail excessive, irrelevant, disjointed; he may discount the crucial revelations the images and metaphors offer, considering them merely vestiges of incoherent madness. He may not see how such continuities as the imagery of light and shadow and the repeated references to trickery, practical jokes, and cheating work to express the recognition Bowman arrives at and the pathetic terms in which he grasps it. In other words, the reader may not understand the moral experience that Bowman undergoes from the evaluation of his life at the story's opening to his final "hurrying away"—"to where he had been before."

Bowman journeys to loss of self through a devastated and grotesque world with only the "pillar of cloud" to guide him to the "Castle Perilous" with the green of summer on the roof. There, symbolically posed with his hat in hand, he has at least "for once, then, something."

Two final stories—Katherine Anne Porter's "The Grave" and Ernest Hemingway's "In Another Country"—represent the kind of story that the reader cannot experience unless he discovers the often inconspicuous cues that suggest the relationship among the seemingly discrete episodes of the story. Reading this sort of story, then, really tests students' ability to re-create a work sensitively.

For high school readers Miss Porter's "The Grave" (seven pages) is the more available story for two reasons. First, these readers are especially alert to, and greatly interested in, the situation the story renders: the immediate and the long-range effects of a particularly traumatic experience in the life of a little girl. Secondly, they readily grasp the last third of the story: they *understand* how the original "rabbit" episode affects Miranda and why, therefore, twenty years later, the image can be roused, fraught with its original horror, by a conjunction of relevant circumstances. They realize, too, why she has submerged the episode in a "vague" memory of the entire day and why she buries it again by evoking that particular image of her brother. In other words, high school readers usually do grasp the impact of the "rabbit" experience on the child and generally recognize the result of that impact. The relationships between the episodes in the last third of the story are clear enough.

But what these readers might not realize is how the first two-thirds of the story relates to this last third. Some students might not see any *important* connection between these parts. They might consider the first two-thirds of the story just a foreground of some sort; say, the quiet casual introduction to a traumatic experience. They might recognize that all the episodes of the "burning day" were "hunts" of sorts with "treasures" of sorts, but, at this point in this course, students would not consider that a very adequate way of accounting for two-thirds of a story.

To help them to a more satisfying explanation, we would ask them very simply: *Why* did the "rabbit" episode have such an impact on Miranda? *Why* was it never fruitfully integrated into her total experience? Probing these questions will show them that the first two-thirds of the story suggests the reasons.

For it makes the reader aware of the kind of person Miranda is and the kind of initiation into life she is receiving because of the kind of world she lives in. The narrator stresses her *sensuous* sensitivity. Notice his report of her responses to the intricacies of the dove and the ring, her pleasure in the movements and sounds of hunting, her reaction to her clothes, her admiration of the "pretty" rabbits. Furthermore, the narrator stresses Miranda's *social* sensitivity: her response to trespassing, to the criticism she feels, and to the inappropriateness of her dress. Miranda is represented as deeply impressionable. Though she shares her brother Paul's "thrill of wonder," she is different from Paul.

This sensitive child is being initiated into the fundamentals of life, happenstance. In this and that remark the narrator repeatedly implies it: Miranda fears that "one of the niggers will see us and tell *somebody*," "The motherless family is running down," the Grandmother is "no longer there to hold it together," old crones criticize the father's laxness, Miranda feels a tension between shame and "faith in her father's judgment," "no one had ever told her anything outright." Furthermore, the haphazard character of Miranda's initiation is implied by the travesty on the hunt. Her twelve-year-old brother who has no understanding of the spiritual values of the hunt effects her rites of passage. And, finally, the story shows that those undisputed "truths" which Miranda *has* been taught have little relevance to "the facts of life" that her abandonment confronts her with. She was learning, on her own, what she "had to know."

The first two-thirds of the story, then, defines for the reader a certain kind of child in a certain kind of environment and shows him what happens when that child has certain kinds of experiences. He sees that hunting treasure in empty graves evokes in this child only two feelings: the excitement of doing something new and disappointment in its result. There is nothing in this experience to evoke any intuitions from the recesses of the mind ". . . when the coffin was gone, a grave is just a hole in the ground." There is no confrontation with death. And, though the wedding ring she found in the grave, "turned her feelings against her overalls" and created "vague stirrings" of her imagination, she has no awareness of its significance, no realizations about marriage. But these "stirrings" prepare the reader for what happens when the treasure found in the full grave of the rabbit's womb is recognized for what it is. Seeing these embryos gave shape to the "formless intuition" about generation Miranda had in the recesses of her mind: she recognized at once what the rabbits were and she realized in lightning succession their connection with kittens, with babies—with the generation and birth of all life.

For this sensitive child such a bald confrontation with this crucial fact of life evokes "confused unhappiness." The experience of that "burning day" was never integrated, just buried alive. So, twenty years later on the other side of the globe, in response to some candy rabbits and the smell of meat, this experience leaps from the grave of Miranda's mind "plain and clear in its true colors," not "changed since the moment it happened." An ironic reversal of her grandmother, Miranda has unwillingly carried her buried "treasure" with her across the world, a living "worrisome affair" that returns her "to the places she had left," and that, as the last image suggests, will probably be laid to rest only when she is.

Many features unify the parts of Miss Porter's story. We have stressed only the psychological connections. But, as we were bringing students to recognize these, we would necessarily be calling their attention to such other unifying features as the contrasting episodes that frame the "burning day," the incongruities that chain throughout the story, and the many partial parallels of "treasures" found in "graves." In a dense story, noticing any one unity will reveal others.

At first glance, the episodes of Hemingway's "In Another Country" (six pages) may seem quite discrete. But if the reader notices certain things about the narrator and the mode of narration, he will not be puzzled about the connections among the episodes, about the function of a particular episode, or about the point of the whole story. So we would open our study of this story with such questions as: What sort of a person is the narrator? What do the details in the first paragraph suggest about him? What else in the story helps to define his personality? What is his relation to the event he tells? How is his distance from the event likely to affect his perception of it? his manner of telling it?

As students develop their description of the narrator, they will discover that he is a man in tension—attracted, on one hand, to light, warmth, closeness, and life, and drawn, on the other hand, toward exposing himself voluntarily to all the opposites. The details all through the story confirm this tension. They show that the narrator needs both to belong to the group and to believe in himself. They reveal that he fears death and needs to confront it; that he doubts his own bravery and insists on testing it; that he cannot confront the "blank wall" alone and unafraid yet desires to do so.

As students answer the questions on the mode of narration, they will see that the narrator's account of himself and the five Italian officers, all invalided out of the war, is a reminiscence, many years after the events. The musing quality of the narration is suggested in the structure of the first paragraph, in the piece-by-piece recall of the "ways" in the second paragraph, and in the "thinking-to-clarity" that recurs in the story—the attempts of one reminiscing to "get it straight." So students are aware, long before they are told at mid-story, that "this was a long time ago." Once they grasp that, they are prepared not only to make the "leaps" and associations that reminiscence requires but also to infer the relative significance to the narrator of the various episodes he tells. For, like all others reminiscing, the narrator tells those experiences that for him have had some lasting significance, and he remembers graphically—and places emphatically—what impressed him deeply. So, in order to help students discover what is of most worth to this narrator, we would focus on the selection, the treatment, and the ordering of what he tells.

The narrator remembers only generally and tells largely narratively his experiences with the cowardly "untried" man, with the boldly brave three young "hunting hawks," and with his own dubiously courageous self. What he remembers in precise detail is the two episodes of the stoic bravery of the major. These he tells as dialogue scenes and places first and last in his story.

The narrator's revelation of himself, his treatment of the episodes he tells, and his design of them let the reader know not only that the story is really about kinds of "bravery," but that it is the bravery of the major that is most impressive to the narrator—most improbable for him. The major, with nothing to sustain him—neither a belief in bravery, nor confidence in the machines, nor faith that man can, in any instance, "win"—can lose all and still carry on. The major "cannot resign" himself. It is the the major's invincible courage that is most significant to the narrator. Once students have noticed the graphic quality of the narrator's memories of the major and the emphatic position he gives these scenes, they will see how all the other features of the story work to refine their perception.

Some Collateral Writing Assignments

The primary aim of all the assignments that follow is to help students become more responsive *readers* of fiction. Both critical and creative writing will do that, so both types are included. But, as we said earlier, we have eschewed certain creative tasks—like the writing of a narrative exposition—tasks that would seem artificial to students who are not preparing to write or in the process of writing a story. To increase students' understanding of such narrative features as exposition and plotting, we would rely on appropriate critical tasks.

We have limited our assignments in another way. Because we wanted to offer suggestions for writing that would be generally usable in many sorts of classes and with many kinds of teaching schemes, we selected just four features common to all stories—concrete details, setting, characterization, and scene—and developed a sequence of assignments for sensitizing students to each of these features.

The assignments *may* be used in the exact order in which we have cited them, but to preclude any notions that any exercise demands any other or must be assigned at any particular time during the study of "The Story," we have purposely exemplified the assignments by stories from all sections of this part of the course. Any of the critical or creative tasks we are suggesting may be used whenever the need for that certain sort of paper becomes apparent. As always, too, the assignments we suggest should be construed as "models" to be adapted and varied as the needs of particular readers at a certain time may dictate.

In each of the four groups of assignments, we have included brief, simple tasks, as well as longer, more complex ones. These simple tasks can steadily prepare average and better students to handle more comprehensive critical questions and can greatly improve the reading and writing of other students who may never be able to do the more complex papers. Frequently, discouraged teachers feel that, if certain students cannot do "everything" that good students do, they cannot do "anything." The kinds of simple exercises we suggest are the "something" that even the less able can do profitably.

These exercises, which we refer to as "in-class," could be done in or out of class to reinforce what is being learned, or to test it. Most tasks are brief enough and simple enough to become a functional *part* of a day's lesson or a night's assignment. Some exercises can be answered in a word, a phrase, a sentence. Others require fifteen-to-twenty minutes' working time. The answers to all the critical exercises should be limited to about one side of a page and, to all creative tasks, to not more than one to two paragraphs.

The same type of exercise *may* be done more than once. And indeed if students fail to do some task adequately, another comparable exercise should be assigned. But this should be done only after students have examined duplicated copies of several inadequate papers, pinpointed the problems, and worked on "repairs."

Only when they seem to understand what made the papers inadequate and how the faults might have been avoided should they undertake a second similar task.

Now with the preliminaries over, let us turn to the four groups of writing assignments.

■ *I: Concrete Details.* If students are to read stories responsively, they must learn to notice concrete details and to recognize how they function first in simple instances and finally in more complex uses. The following are three kinds of in-class writing exercises that can help them. These "finger exercises" that combine critical analysis with creative work really begin at the beginning.

1. From the stories students are reading select phrases, sentences, and paragraphs that use details significantly. Examine these passages closely with the class. Help them notice particularly how these details specify and discriminate objects and feelings. Then give the students duplicated copies of phrases, sentences, and a paragraph that you have taken from stories and reduced to abstract language. Ask them to transform these materials so that a reader can *visualize* the details. Discuss their "products," and show them the originals.

2. As a supplementary exercise, ask students to rewrite a "reduced" paragraph so that a reader can *see* and *hear* and *feel* the details quite graphically. Warn them against replacing one abstract word with another.

3. For a more demanding exercise, ask students to concretize a "reduced" paragraph by means of comparison. Before they write, examine with them comparisons in stories they are reading, so they will see *how* comparisons concretize and how they work together in a paragraph. Without this analysis, their concrete paragraphs might turn out to be unintentionally bizarre.

If students have succeeded with these rewrites, they might enjoy doing a "really original" piece of writing, one that gives them an opportunity to use more freely their skill with concrete details. Without saying so, the "finger exercises" have been suggesting to students what the paragraph they will now write should be like, not only in concreteness and length, but in subject matter. The passages from stories that we have used as examples have been calling students' attention to how ordinary the things are that writers write about— nothing exotic or sensational. These examples should have tempered students' usual desire to make their own objects, settings, and characters racy. But it might still be wise to point out to students the ordinariness of the subjects used and to counsel them to stay close to what they know well.

Here is one possible in-class assignment:

Choose some object you have noticed in detail. Think of some angle from which it might be seen. Think of the impression it would create if viewed that way. Now write a paragraph that so describes that object from that angle of vision that a reader will experience the relevant impression.

In this assignment the teacher is setting the aim and the length. He may decide to limit the subject, too, to a certain type of object (static, for instance) or a certain object (a doorway, a bridge, a steeple, a half-demolished building, a photograph by Cartier-Bresson). Even with so tight a rein, the students still have much freedom, enough for many classes to handle on a first assignment.

■ *II: The Function of Setting.* The following in-class *critical* exercise is an appropriate successor to the preceding creative paper. For here students are asked to decide *on the functions* of a detailed description:

Read the following passage, noticing carefully the concrete details that define this setting. Consider the setting first in its immediate context in the story, then in the total context of the story. Write one to two paragraphs that make clear the function(s) of the setting. [The passage designated should preferably be from a story being studied currently. There should be a character in the setting, but not one consciously responding to it.]

Some usable passages for this exercise are the rainy night in "The Three Strangers," the misty exit in "Flight," the room in "Fifty Pounds," the room in "Eveline," the bus stop in "A Queer Heart," and the town in "The Third Prize."

After such an exercise as that, a related in-class *creative* paper can move the writers from attention to setting to attention to character. In preparing for the assignment, we would point out to students that in the passage they just worked on, one or more characters were present in the setting, but none was consciously responding to it. We would then ask them to:

Create in one to two paragraphs a focused, selectively detailed setting with a character either in it or introduced into it. The character *should not be responding* consciously to his surroundings. He *may*, however, be doing something, and he *must*, in some way, suggest his relation to the setting.

Such an exercise as this will once again call students' attention to the reason setting is called "setting" and to the ways setting functions in fiction. Furthermore, when students begin to make clear their character's relationship to the setting, they will discover that only certain features of a character's appearance and certain traits of his personality will serve their purpose. Through such an exercise as this, then, students will come to see how important selection is to achieving certain effects—in both setting and character.

■ *III: The Rendering of Character.* The critical and creative writing exercises that follow are aimed at making students sensitive to ways of characterizing. For every critical exercise we suggest, there is an obvious creative writing counterpart. Consequently, to avoid belaboring the obvious, we have detailed only the critical exercises and commented on the creative tasks whenever it seemed necessary or useful. These parallel critical and creative exercises can be used separately or paired, as the particular occasion suggests.

If students are to do *any* of the creative papers in this group, then, outside of class, each student should work up a character of his own to use in these exercises. Ask them to create a vita for a character. Make clear to them why they are creating the character and that the character may be an imaginary person, or a composite of several persons in their acquaintance (not necessarily an ideal at all), or a real person. The vita should have the usual data, but should also include the significant personality traits of the character. (For less able classes—or less willing—the teacher could facilitate matters by devising a vita form for the students.) Once students have detailed their "characters" in this way, they would be prepared to work *realistically* on the creative papers, using their own creations.

To begin, here are *three types of in-class critical exercises on characterizing by descriptive details.*

1. What does (a certain detail) suggest about (a certain character)? This can be an *easy* exercise if details such as the following are inserted in the blanks: the red carnation about Paul ("Paul's Case"), the fancy boots about Scratchy ("The Bride Comes to Yellow Sky"), the Phi Beta Kappa key about the housemaster ("Do You Like It Here?"), Gallaher's stance about him ("A Little Cloud"). This can be a *more challenging* exercise, if we insert such details as: the monkey resemblance about the bartender ("Effigy of War"), "bovine interest" about the sisters ("Barn Burning"), "cut from tin" about the father ("Barn Burning"), "weightless" about Sarty ("Barn Burning"), the "deep red fire" in her eyes about the janitress ("Theft"), the hats about the respective men ("Theft"), her coat about Mabel Waring ("The New Dress"), her house-counting eyes about Esmé ("For Esmé—With Love and Squalor"), the ill-fitting uniforms about Krebs ("Soldier's Home"), the wrapped quilt about the little boy ("The Worn Path"), her size about Maria ("Clay"), and her hands about Nancy ("That Evening Sun"). Many such

exercises might be used during the study of "The Story." As the examples above suggest, at least some exercises should ask about figurative details and some about details that suggest the conflict within a character.

2. Why do we never *see* (a certain character)? Insert such characters as "she" in "Theft," Eveline in "Eveline," Krebs in "Soldier's Home," Nick in "The Killers," the older waiter in "A Clean, Well-Lighted Place." Instead of the preceding question, we might ask a variation: Why do we see only what we do of (a certain character)? A more leading wording of this same question would be: What is *gained* by showing us what we see of (a certain character)? Why do we need *only* that? What *harm* might a fuller description do? In either wording of this topic, we could insert: the mother in "Flight," Seeger in "Act of Faith," the housemaster in "Do You Like It Here?," Mabel Waring in "The New Dress," and the young priest in "The Forks."

3. *Why* does (a certain character's) description of (another character) make us doubtful about the truth of the description, make us, in other words, want "to see for ourselves"? We might insert the young priest's early views of the Monsignor in "The Forks" or Little Chandler's initial description of Gallaher in "A Little Cloud." As they answer this question, students will come to see that a character's description of another character often reveals something about the describer that puts the reader "on guard."

Many kinds of *creative* writing exercises could be devised to make students sensitive to the three preceding techniques of characterization. Especially fruitful for helping average and better students— or any who want to try—to grasp the *first two techniques* are such exercises as the following:

Describe your character by a figurative detail.

Select some tension your character has and then write a word or phrase that *suggests* it.

Decide what personality trait of your character you want your reader to be aware of. List descriptive details that will precisely and economically *suggest* that trait to the reader. Now, write a paragraph that *renders* those details in such a way as to make your reader know your character "for what he is."

This last kind of exercise will, once again, impress upon students the importance of selection. And, together with the critical exercises or the analysis of passages that would necessarily precede such an assignment, doing this creative task *may* disabuse students of the idea that all description begins with a visual record of a face.

Especially fruitful for helping able writers become sensitive to the *third technique* of characterization is such a creative assignment as the following:

Write a paragraph description of your character that makes the reader justifiably dubious about its truth.

Average and less able students could do a related exercise that is a good "notch" easier:

Write a paragraph description of your character that reveals him *and* the person describing him.

Now, here are *five in-class critical exercises that will help students understand the ways a character can reveal himself through action, reaction, and interaction.*

1. How does a (certain action) suggest what sort of person (a certain character) is? Some insertions might be: the director's dabbing his mouth ("Effigy of War"), Abner's striking the mules ("Barn Burning"), Alice's turning to the wall ("Adventure"), the housemaster's exposing the watch ("Do You Like It Here?"), Esmé's crossing her feet ("For Esmé—With Love and Squalor").

2. How does (a certain character's) *reaction* to (a certain setting) characterize him/her? Before students wrote their responses, they would have to answer for themselves the two questions we have been asking in class: How do we know (what clues tell us) what the character's reaction is? What does *this* reaction suggest about *this* character? Reactions that might be inserted into such a question are: the narrator's response to the room in "Brooksmith," Sarty's response to the courtroom, the mansion, or even the aisle in "Barn Burning," Mabel Waring's initial response to Mrs. Dalloway's drawing room in "The New Dress," Mary Jane's response to the living room in "Uncle Wiggily in Connecticut," Little Chandler's response to Corless' door, or to the scenes from his office window, or on the street, or from the Grattan Bridge in "A Little Cloud," Hilda Cadman's response to her house or to her sister's room in "A Queer Heart," or the priest's response to the projected garden in "The Forks."

3. A topic like the following: How does Lucille's retreat into the kitchen ("A Queer Heart") suggest to us what kind of person her mother is? asks students to determine how the *reaction of a lesser character to the main character* defines the main character. Other possible passages for such an exercise would be the animal's response to Pepe in the second draw ("Flight"), the commanding officer's reaction to Seeger's request ("Act of Faith"), the bank man's reaction to Eulalia ("Fifty Pounds"), the laundresses' treatment of Maria at tea time ("Clay").

4. A topic like the following: How does Sarty's response to his father's delay in town on the last day characterize Sarty ("Barn

Burning")? asks students to determine how *the reaction of the main character to a lesser character* defines the main character. Other usable passages would be Philip's response to the policewoman ("The Basement Room"), Big Britches' response to his grandfather on the porch ("The Leader of the People"), Eveline's response to Frank's stories ("Eveline"), the narrator's response to John's tale of the ship ("This Town and Salamanca").

5. Finally, a topic like the following: How does the *interaction* between the old customer and the young waiter characterize both ("A Clean, Well-Lighted Place")? asks students to determine what attitudes the actions of each express and what, on each hand, one can say about the personality of a man who takes such attitudes to that sort of person.

Creative exercises to parallel the five kinds of critical tasks we have just suggested can be devised so as to give students repeated opportunities to use the "characters" they have created and to reinforce and extend the skills they have learned through doing the creative assignments in I and II. For instance, if the teacher now asks students to write a paragraph showing a character reacting to a setting in a revelatory way, he *could* invite them to simply rewrite their earlier exercise, the one in which they created a setting and put a character into it. The present assignment, which should recall the earlier one and suggest the difference between the two, might read something like this:

Your job is to write a paragraph that shows your character *responding* to a certain setting. Earlier you created a setting and had a character *appear* in it. Meanwhile, you have become aware of how actions characterize. So, in the paragraph you are now to write, your character must *respond to* the setting he is in in a way that somehow *reveals* him. His reaction must be in "character," consistent with the person you created. You may revise your earlier exercise or begin afresh, as you wish.

Creative exercises should not be reserved for able students or competent writers. Tasks on any mode of rendering character can vary widely in difficulty. For instance, an assignment to show how characters' reactions to one another define them can be as *easy* as this:

Write a paragraph that shows your character responding to another in such a way as to reveal some *one* aspect of *your character's* personality.

It can be as *demanding* as this:

Write one to two paragraphs in which your character *interacts* with another in such a way that both characters reveal themselves.

Between these two extremes are several types of potential assignments that would challenge average-to-good students. All of the five modes of characterization we have referred to would allow an equally wide variety of creative assignments.

Whatever kind of creative task the teacher decides on for a particular class, he should, as we said earlier, precede the actual assignment by relevant analysis of appropriate paragraphs from stories the class has read. "Relevant analysis" for the three creative exercises we have just cited would include, for instance, ascertaining what, *precisely,* the character's response is, what *exactly* clues the reader to it, and how we can say the response is at once revelatory and "in character." Such analysis will help the class understand exactly what are they supposed to be creating and how they *might* go about it. Furthermore, whatever kind of creative exercise the teacher assigns a particular class, his grading of the papers should be guided *by the terms of the assignment.* This is always so, but we mention it here, because very often if certain students' *creative* papers exceed what the assignment required (for instance, show an interaction when only a one-sided response was required), these papers are upgraded—to the great detriment of students whose papers *have* satisfied the assignment. When assignments of varying difficulty are possible, the teacher makes his choice; then he must be wary of upgrading papers that do the task that he *would like* to have assigned—or that he sees now he should have.

Although the last three of the five critical exercises we suggested and the last two of the creative exercises have concerned characterizing through the reaction of characters to one another, they have not involved dialogue. The responses have been narrated. Now, we shall offer *a pair of out-of-class exercises to help make students aware of how dialogue characterizes:* how, for instance, the diction, syntax, and figures a speaker *characteristically* uses define him and how the responses he makes to a *certain* person in a *certain* situation at once confirm and extend our insight into him. In fiction, the reader is, of course, often directed as to how a thing is said and/or he is told what the character is thinking and doing, before, after, and during the speech. All these features assist the reader. But in the two exercises that follow we emphasize what the *speeches themselves* reveal, because much of the dialogue in modern short stories (see those of the third and fourth sections) has virtually no authorial commentary. And we would want our writing exercises to help readers learn to respond sensitively to the dialogue in such stories as those.

The *critical* exercise might concern a small segment of dialogue—a group of five or so exchanges—that is in itself a complete revelatory unit. Useful passages are the brief exchanges between Sarty and his father after the Major accuses Abner of ruining the rug ("Barn Burning"), or the conversation between the three soldiers at the opening of "Act of Faith," or that between Elisa and the pot mender about the "lady" who "has got the nicest garden you ever seen" ("The Chrysanthemums"), or between Little Chandler and Gallaher about Chandler's invitation to "spend an evening with us" ("A Little Cloud"). The topic for the paper probably would be broad:

How does the *dialogue* let you know what sorts of persons the participants are?

But the critical discussions of dialogue that would precede such an assignment as this (as well as the study of dramatic dialogue, if reading plays preceded reading fiction) would have made clear to students that their answers to such a question should concentrate on what is revealed about this person *by his saying this thing in this manner to that person.* The critical discussions would, furthermore, have made clear that "this manner" includes the speaker's attitude toward the material as well as his attitude toward his listener, and that attitude is defined not only by diction, syntax, and such, but also by the directness or the obliqueness of the rejoinders and by the pattern of the dialogue (is it addition? alternation? how does it go?) If we suspected that a certain class would not recognize all that is involved in answering our broad question, we would simply give a more detailed assignment.

The *creative* exercise that would complement the preceding task is, of course, the writing of an original dialogue. This is a demanding assignment. Students must, first, decide on what their character is going to talk about and to whom he is to say it. Then, they must imagine what attitude he would probably take toward the subject when he was talking to that person about it. Then, of course, they have the problem of rendering his attitude so that it reveals him. A goodly task! It can be facilitated if the length of the dialogue is limited to a little unit of five exchanges or so and if the preparation not only includes careful examination in class of several illustrations but also requires students to do such a series of tasks as the following *before* they begin to write:

Tell *in a sentence* what your dialogue will concern; suggest in notes the sort of person the listener is; suggest what your character's attitude toward the subject would be if he were discussing it with this listener; trace the course of the dialogue; say *in a sentence* what the dialogue is to reveal.

Only when such preliminary tasks are completed should students begin the assignment:

Write a short dialogue (about five exchanges) between your character and your listener that reveals some aspect of personality that your vita claims your character has. When you have finished, ask yourself: Is the language "in character"? Does the dialogue fulfill its intention? Check any places that you think are ineffective and note in the margin your reasons. Hand in your answers to the preliminary tasks with your finished dialogue.

The following *critical* exercise is an extra: a supplementary, specialized task on dialogue that might be needed in some classes. For, although students have been encouraged continually to listen discriminatingly to narrators, some students do not transfer this attitude to the reading of dialogue. So this exercise, which recalls the earlier one on the "truth" of a character's description of another, aims at alerting students to the speaker's bias and more importantly to the reader's need to be circumspect. Here is the question:

What alerts us to "keep an open mind" about what (the character) says to (the character) in this dialogue?

Or a different phrasing of the same question:

How do we know in *how far* we should believe what (the character) say to (the character) in this dialogue?

This exercise can be relatively easy or very demanding, depending upon the dialogue used. Following are several kinds of usable passages, arranged roughly in order of difficulty: what Taney says to Seeger about the money ("Act of Faith"), what the pot mender says to Elisa about the "lady" who "has the nicest garden" ("The Chrysanthemums"), what Gallaher tells Little Chandler about the "immorality" of France and London ("A Little Cloud"), what the major says to the narrator about marriage ("In Another Country").

Finally, here are *two types of topics for out-of-class critical papers on character.* Both types could be assigned independently of any of the exercises we have suggested; both, nonetheless, would be appropriate conclusions to the preceding series of assignments on character. For both concern character development throughout a story, so they require the intensive study of a sequence of particular instances in order to detect change. Students who are already skillful in perceiving character in particular instances would be especially ready to show the development and make the generalizations that these two topics require.

First, the *easier* of the two topics:

Development of character is shown by a character's successive reactions to the situation of a story. In a one- to two-page paper point out how (the main character's) reactions to the sequence of events in this story refine and expand our first impression of him/her.

Now the *more demanding* topic:

The kind of person (the main character) is becomes clear in the story.

By what means is this achieved? Write a two-page paper that answers that question.

If the teacher wanted a class to do a "means" paper but did not think the group could successfully unfold such a topic as the preceding without some "leading," he might put such guides as the following on the assignment sheet:

Before you write:
Ascertain what sort of person (he) seems to be at the beginning of the story and specify precisely what *means* suggest this personality; make notes on your findings.
List the major episodes in which he participates and note down his response to each.
Ascertain what sort of person his response to each episode shows him to be and pinpoint what *means* are used to suggest these character qualities to you; make notes on your findings.
When you have done this "spadework," draft your paper *on the means* that let you know what sort of person (the main character) is. Revise your draft, and write a final copy. Hand in your "spadework notes," your draft, and your final copy.

In writing on either of these topics—and all others—students should reflect what they are learning from their class discussions of stories as well as from their critical and creative exercises. There are many features that characterize—repeated phrases, juxtapositions, foils, for instance—that students' writing assignments *may* never have touched upon. But their class discussion of their reading will have; the teacher should, therefore, expect that such features will be referred to wherever relevant in students' written papers.

The stories chosen for these two out-of-class papers should be less than twenty pages in length, new to students, and similar in difficulty to what they have been reading. Many stories in our third section of "The Story" would be appropriate: "The Use of Force," "Do You Like It Here?" "Eveline," and "The Secret Life of Walter Mitty," are "naturals."

Either of the two preceding topics could be used as a full-period, in-class evaluation, if the story were assigned two days ahead to be "read very carefully several times in preparation for an open-book test on it."

■ *IV: Scene.* Because the two preceding topics for the out-of-class critical papers require students to begin to think in terms of the entire story, they are useful transitions to this final group of *critical* writing tasks, most of which oblige students to consider how a particular scene functions as part of a whole story.

We might begin these exercises with a *general topic* on the use of scene:

Why should this material (a certain scene) receive "close-up" treatment? In other words, what is gained by our witnessing this part of the story?

We might follow such a paper with an exercise that would call students' attention to the *many* offices a passage of dialogue fulfills in a story. A straightforward, leading topic like the following would be widely usable for an in-class *critical* paper:

Point out specifically on what grounds one could say that (a certain dialogue) simultaneously helps to give *needed* information, to *reveal* character, to *advance* the situation (and, if applicable, to express the metaphoric or symbolic design of the story).

Some useful passages of dialogue for such an exercise are: Baines and Philip talking of the Coast ("The Basement Room"), Krebs and his mother discussing what he is "going to do" ("Soldier's Home"), Ramona describing her "beau" ("Uncle Wiggily in Connecticut").

After two such general exercises as those, we would begin to narrow our focus. We would ask specifically about the function of each type of scene: why certain material is rendered as a *dialogue* scene, other material as a *narrated* one. Here are *three kinds of topics* for in-class *critical* exercises of this sort:

1. Why is the material of the first page of "Act of Faith" rendered as a *dialogue* scene? In other words, what is gained by our receiving this conversation "live"? Other dialogues that might be substituted are the close of "Uncle Wiggily in Connecticut" or the tea scene in "The Third Prize."

This kind of question could be asked not only about first scenes, final scenes, and "showdown" scenes, but also about that very large number of dialogue scenes that let us hear for ourselves (the narrator supposedly recording verbatim) such things as: a tender relationship (the proposal of the mouse hunt in "The Leader of the People"), a superficial affection (Helen and Hare in "Soldier's Home"), a bizarre world before showdown develops (the first scene of "The Killers"), an emotional hiatus (Hilda and Lucille in the dining room in "A Queer Heart").

2. Why is a bit of dialogue (*a half-scene*) used in "The Bride Comes to Yellow Sky" to let us hear the exchanges of the bride and groom about the Pullman? Or, in "Theft" to let us hear the woman's resignation to the loss of the purse? Or, in "Eveline" to let us hear the father's remark? Or, What is gained in "Araby" by our receiving "live" the conversation between Mangan's sister and the boy? between

the uncle and the boy? between the girl and the fellows at the bazaar?

3. Why is the last scene in "Effigy of War" *narrated?* Or, the scene with the school administration in "Paul's Case"? Or, Maria's discovery of her loss of the plumcake in "Clay"?

An out-of-class *critical* paper might be assigned independently of the preceding exercises or after some of them have been completed. In either case a topic like the following will be fruitful, for it requires students to examine the nature of scene and the function of a scene as one unit in a larger whole:

> Because a scene moves dramatically to some sort of resolution, it gives a reader the feeling of having experienced a complete episode. But this little unit is significant only because of the part it plays in a larger unit, the story. In a one- to two-page paper point out *why* (a certain scene) gives the reader the sense of experiencing a complete episode and *how* this unit functions in the story as a whole.

Obvious choices for this task are scenes like the last one between the sheriff and Scratchy in "The Bride Comes to Yellow Sky," the final scene of Seeger and his buddies in "Act of Faith," the first scene between the bartender and the director in "Effigy of War."

In this series of writing tasks on scene, we could have included the *creative* writing of half-scenes, scenes, and narrative-to-scene passages. But we have refrained from doing this because, as we said earlier, these are often very artificial exercises, if students are not doing them as preliminary sketches for a story in process. *If* a teacher really wants to include such writing in a meaningful context, he could assign the kind of critical-creative exercise often used in the study of poems. Give the students all of the text of a story except the final scene or except the narrative-to-scene transitions. Ask them to create a scene (or transitions) appropriate to the story. This task tests two skills; students must *understand* the story in order to imagine what belongs in it, and then they must be able to *create* the missing part.

In this series of writing tasks on scene, we might, furthermore, have suggested *critical* exercises related to scene and summary: exercises, for instance, on the use of narration to summarize the events of many years or to generalize on a scene, before or after it, exercises on the use of narration to change pace by alternating with scene or to force the reader to give certain kinds of attention to certain parts of a work, narration used, in other words, as a kind of broad indicator of what is significant. But these functions of narration are so readily recognized by most readers that it seems uneconomical to assign critical exercises on them.

It also seemed excessive to detail critical exercises on plot, the design of stories, and various other fictional devices that we treated so continually in our annotations of the stories we listed in the Second Part of our course. Our discussions of the stories suggested how these features might be asked about. Many of those questions could, obviously, be used "as is" for written in-class exercises.

■ *Final Critical Papers on The Story.* Class discussions and the in-class and out-of-class papers are continually evaluating students' ability to respond to this or that feature of a story and to stories as wholes. But the teacher might still want to evaluate more formally and fully students' ability to read a story. A test might be given at the end of each or any of the sections of "The Story" or at the close of the Second Part of the course. In any case, the stories used for testing should be either new or approached from some new angle. They should be short and a bit less difficult than what the best students in the class have been able to read well with preparation. The test topic or questions should be capable of evaluating each student's achievement of the relevant aim; in other words, the test should be valid and reliable. Many different kinds of tests can be both. To illustrate, here are two different kinds of final evaluations that might be used in class (or out of class, if you believe in this practice) at the close of the study of "The Story."

The opening of a story puts certain information before the reader. Here, for instance, is the opening of (title). [Cite several paragraphs of the opening.] Notice the information it conveys. Now look at the following paragraph. [Cite a rewrite of the original opening.] This conveys the same information as the preceding paragraphs. The same information might have been conveyed in many different ways. But the writer chose to render it as the preceding paragraphs show. In a one- to two-page paper tell the expectations you have about this story because of *the way* the opening paragraphs *were* written.

The story used must, of course, be new to the students and available enough for all to make *some* relevant response. The teacher may help students to varying extents by defining "the way"—suggesting one or more of the features of language they should be considering. He might insert, "for instance, the tone," or he might offer more suggestions more specifically stated: "for instance, the narrator's tone, the nameless characters, the images, and such." The teacher might, if he wished, "lead" completely by listing all the features the students should consider. The ability of the class would suggest how much help should be given. But the possibility of offering varying degrees of help makes it feasible to give classes of different abilities the same general type of test question. The *kinds* of story openings that would be useful for this task are those of "Fifty Pounds," "The New Dress,"

"The Catbird Seat," "A Little Cloud," "Her First Ball," or "A Clean, Well-Lighted Place."

For the second kind of test either a new story or one that has been studied quite carefully can be used. In fact, if a new story is to be used, students must be warned to read and reread it *most* closely beforehand. For the test, the teacher would choose from the story some short paragraph, or even a sentence, and rewrite it so as to violate the narrative point of view, the narrator's tone, the consistency of some character, and perhaps other unifying elements of the story— but *not* the situation of the story. The test question would direct students to:

Read carefully paragraph _____ on page _____, beginning _____ and ending _____. Consider the ways in which this paragraph is "right" for this story. In a one- to two-page paper tell specifically why the following paragraph [the rewrite the teacher has prepared] could not be substituted for it.

Once again, the teacher may supply as many "hints" as he wishes. If the story has been carefully studied in class, then the teacher's rewrite should be that much more subtle and the "hints" few, if any.

For further writing assignments,[17] see "Holidays," below, under "Producing the Course."

The Third Part: The Purpose of a Story

In this course in reading fiction, we asked, first, about the narrator of a story—what sort of person is he? what is his point of view? what attitude does he assume? Then, we asked about the story itself—how is it more than plot? what does conflict include? Now, we ask about the purpose of a story.

Why is a story told? Because it is a symbol, a concrete, particular experience rendered in such a way as to reveal *at once* its face value and its universal value. The materials are selected and arranged so that "in itself" the concrete situation "points beyond itself." As the sensitive reader experiences the immediate, unique situation, he recognizes its significance, its relevance, and its truth to countless other experiences. The story is told to evoke in a reader an experience that is symbolic.

Some stories seem to actually call their two-dimensional nature to the reader's attention. Certain objects, settings, characters, events, important in the experience of the story, *clearly* come to have, during the course of the story, both literal and extra-literal significance. In "Barn Burning," for instance, the barn and the fire, the courtroom and the mansion, the sisters and the moving, are defined in such ways and work in such ways that "in themselves" they clearly "point beyond themselves." The reader is continually alerted to the symbolic character not only of the individual elements, but also of the experience of the story as a whole.

This is not true of all stories. In some, the details are so real that the only symbolism that is apparent is a kind of "natural symbolism."[18] The characters, events, and objects simply typify, as they do in life. Recall in "The Bride Comes to Yellow Sky," for instance, such natural symbols as the dress of the bride, the boots of Scratchy, and the funnel-shaped tracks. These objects do not cue readers to the extra-literal significance of the experience of the story. That *occurs* to the reader—seemingly "without warning"—near the end of his reading or in retrospect. These stories, then, seem to call only their concrete dimension to the readers' attention.

Other stories seem to emphasize only the universal. Their details appear to be so unreal that the familiar concrete surface expected of stories seems, in varying degrees, to have disappeared. The over-drawn, one-dimensional characters in these stories; the contrived, disjointed action; the bizarre and shadowy settings seem to have little relation to the mundane world. Only the reader who remembers that there is a real world of exaggeration, dreams, nightmares, and whimsy recognizes the concrete dimension in such stories.

Why do many beginning readers have difficulty responding to these several different kinds of stories as symbols? Mainly because they lack either the precision or the flexible "double vision" that is needed. When readers *lack precision,* they forfeit their chance to perceive the story as symbol because they simply do not see all that is in the story in the way it is there. Some misconstrue the concrete dimension of the story to begin with. They do not notice some details at all, or, more often, they do not notice the selection, development, and use of details that would suggest to them what, in the story, is *itself* and nothing more, what in itself is *something more,* what that "something more" probably is, and what effect that "overplus" has on the experience of the whole story.

Other imprecise readers fail to see all that is in the story (and so forfeit their chance to perceive it as symbol) because they fix on some small unit of the story that has Freudian overtones, or mythic suggestion, or a conventional symbolic significance, and they construe the whole story in terms of this one unit. Once these readers have been blinded this way, the context does not have a chance to correct their error. Their imaginations generate symbolic interpretations that "fly in the face of" the text considered as a whole. These readers are writing their own stories just as much as those who dissolve works into their own life experience. Because imprecise readers of whatever kind do not see all that is literally in the story, they block themselves from taking even the first step toward experiencing a story as symbol.

Other beginning readers take the first step successfully; nevertheless, they still have difficulty because they *lack the flexible "double vision"* that a sensitive response to symbol requires. Some of these readers become arrested at the concrete, literal dimension of the story. To them, all soda crackers are only soda crackers. Some of these readers become exclusively engaged by the extra-literal dimension. To them, all soda crackers are nothing but hosts. The first group of readers have not allowed their imaginations to stretch from the concrete situations to the "ranges of meaning" that the renderings of the situations suggest; the second group have become so captivated by the extra-literal dimension that they "give up" the concrete situation as soon as it has done its office. When they read a story, the literalists have only the experience of a concrete world; the others, only a message, a moral, or a statement, for that is what the extra-literal experience becomes when the concrete dimension is given up. To experience a symbol, the reader must experience both the literal and extra-literal dimensions *at once*.

When a sensitive reader reads a story, he remains tied to a concrete center—an object, character, scene, episode, whole story—as he senses the aura that gathers around it. He sees, for instance, that the chrysanthemums *are* flowers. And because of the kind of flowers they are and the way they are introduced into Steinbeck's story ("The Chrysanthemums"), this reader connects them with Elissa. Then, because of the way they work there and there and there in the story, he grasps how they express this woman's spirit, how they define the other characters and account for her reactions to them, and how they help to reveal the emotional conflict she endures. It is by perceiving similarities and by making connections that the reader *comes* to see what the object *comes* to mean and how it functions in the narrative to reveal the immediate crisis the story represents. Similarly, a responsive reader comes to see the *whole* concrete representation—the story—as the bright clear center which "in itself points beyond itself" to a host of life experiences which, though accidentally different, enlighten and are enlightened by the story.

The aim for this Third Part of the course is to help imprecise, inflexible, one-dimensional readers learn to respond appropriately to symbols within stories and to stories as symbols.

After such a concentrated study of stories as any class will have had thus far in this course, a teacher can be fairly sure as to what approach and what sequence of readings would be most productive now for each of his classes. The final part of any course, even more than the earlier sections, should be "tailored" for each class, who by that time will have made its strengths and its weaknesses quite clear to its teacher. So, rather than propose, at this point, any single scheme for achieving the aim we cited, we shall sketch out four alternatives—all dealing with stories as symbols or symbols in stories —just to suggest, as we did in the final part of the first course in reading poems, some directions that planning might take.

The First Alternative

The aim of this first scheme is to help students see that apparently "non-literal" stories *are* "grounded" in a concrete reality and whether that reality is the everyday waking world or not, it is entirely recognizable and familiar. The readings should be stories that will *strike* students as "non-literal." The teacher might so arrange the stories that, with the reading of each, students move a bit closer to the apparently purely "non-literal." The readers' ability to respond to these stories *as symbols* would, thereby, be increasingly taxed. Here is a usable series of readings for an able group that exemplifies such an arrangement: D. H. Lawrence's "Wintry Peacock," Eudora Welty's "Old Mr. Marblehall," J. D. Salinger's "A Perfect Day for Bananafish," Truman Capote's "A Tree of Night," Nathaniel Hawthorne's "My Kinsman, Major Molineux," and Sylvia Townsend Warner's "The Phoenix."

The Second Alternative

The aim of this second scheme is to help students develop a sense of the presence and the function of symbols *within* seemingly "literal" works. To try to gradually heighten students' awareness of the extra-literal dimension of details, we would have them study a series of stories arranged according to the increasing subtlety of their symbolic elements. During the study of the stories we would be continually bringing students to see that the extra-literal import of an element is suggested to a reader by the way the element is functioning in the story. After close study of about three stories, we would test the students' ability to sense the symbolic by assigning the reading of an apparently "literal" story.

In an average class, the first story for close study might be one in which details are blatantly symbolic, Shirley Jackson's "The Lottery," for instance. The idyllic scene, the ominous black box, the superstitious maxim—many such details baldly warn the reader to activate his non-literal sense. The second story might be more subtle, but there should still be some elements in it that obviously have extraliteral import. Here, in order of difficulty, are four Katherine Mansfield stories that would be appropriate: "Mr. and Mrs. Dove," "The Doll's House," "The Garden Party," "Bliss." In each of these stories several elements are clearly more than literal: days are too bright, trees are too perfect; socks and hats, dresses and animals, fathers and carters—all frankly suggest their extra-literal function in the story. If Katherine Mansfield's world is inappropriate for the class, then John Steinbeck's "The Snake" or even D. H. Lawrence's "The Rocking Horse Winner" could be read as a second story. The third reading might be a story like Conrad Aiken's "Silent Snow, Secret Snow" or Peter Taylor's "A Spinster's Tale." In both of these stories, the reader's attention is especially focused on one object that *takes on* a precise symbolic character and brings about a specific effect. In Aiken's story, the object is snow; the effect, psychological death; in Taylor's story, the object is Mr. Speed; the effect, abhorrence of sex. For less able readers, J. F. Powers' "Blue Island" would be an appropriate third story.

Whenever students' awareness of the symbolic value of concrete details seems sufficiently intensified, we would assign the test reading, a story in which the details *seem* purely literal, since the "cues" are somewhat submerged; say, Ernest Hemingway's "Ten Indians," Faulkner's "Wash," or even Wallace Stegner's "In the Twilight," if a less demanding story is desired.

In a more able class, the first reading for close study might be Maupassant's "Love: Three Pages from a Hunter's Notebook," the second, Erskine Caldwell's "Daughter," the third, Bernard Malamud's "Take Pity," and, if a fourth were needed, Carson McCuller's "A Tree. A Rock. A Cloud." Then, to test the readers' "double vision," we might assign such a story as Eudora Welty's "Livvie," Carson McCuller's "The Sojourner," or Hortense Calisher's "In Greenwich There Are Many Gravelled Walks."

The Third Alternative

The aim of this third plan is to help students see how a myth or a conventional symbol is adapted to further the purposes of a story. In preparation for the study of each story we would work out with the class the usual meanings of the relevant symbol or we would assign them the reading of the apposite myth (duplicated, if necessary). In the discussion of each story we would concentrate on how the myth or the conventional meaning of the symbol has been adapted and what has been gained by this adaptation. Usable stories include Erskine Caldwell's "Man and Wife" (the biblical journey to Bethlehem); Maupassant's "Love: Three Pages from a Hunter's Notebook" (the heart symbol); Conrad Aiken's "Silent

Snow, Secret Snow" (the snow symbol); Eudora Welty's "The Worn Path" (the Arthurian quest); and her "Shower of Gold" (the Zeus-Danae myth).

The Fourth Alternative

The aim of this last scheme is to help students see what is gained by a story's being told in a certain conventional form; for instance, as a tale, as a fantasy, or as a comedy. We want students to realize that the writer does not have to use such forms; he chooses to do so. His choice of any of these three forms commits him to a certain kind of reality; his use of a tale or a comedy binds him to certain conventions as well. But in such restraints he finds advantage.

Students would read each of several stories closely in order to discover what the intention of each story is, how the relevant conventional form is adapted in each, and how its limitations and advantages are used. Through such study, students will come to realize that the use of such forms as tale, fantasy, and comedy is not an eccentricity, an affectation, or a gimmick, but, like all other writer's choices, a necessity. They will also realize that, though quotidian reality may be distorted in these forms, the truth of the experience is recognizable and familiar; in fact, the distortions so distance us that the symbolic character of the situation is unmistakable.

Here are three groups of stories that will suggest the variety of usable readings. The stories within each group are arranged in rough order of difficulty. *Tales:* Edgar Allan Poe's "A Cask of Amontillado," Sherwood Anderson's "Death in the Woods," Nathaniel Hawthorne's "Wakefield," or his "Roger Malvin's Burial," James Agee's "A Mother's Tale." *Fantasies:* Saki's "The Open Window," John Cheever's "Thus I Refute Bealzey," Walter van Tilburg Clark's "Why Don't You Look Where You're Going?" A. E. Coppard's "The Fair Young Willowy Tree," Conrad Aiken's "Mr. Arcularis." *Comedies:* Somerset Maugham's "The Verger," Elizabeth Taylor's "I Live in a World of Make Believe," James Thurber's "The Greatest Man in the World," Saki's "Dusk," John Cheever's "Witch's Money."

This alternative admits of many variations. Students may read "three of a kind" or any combination appropriate for them. The teacher may supply information about the various conventions or elicit it from the class; no prior preparation is required of the students. If the stories are chosen according to students' reading ability, this kind of plan may be used with able, average, or less able readers.

In order to read such stories as these, students must allow each story to remake them into the reader it requires. They must suspend their disbelief, join the teller, "go along with it." Such detached involvement is, of course, necessary in the reading of all imaginative literature, but it is crucial to the understanding and enjoyment of forms like these. Nothing will happen until the reader gives himself up to the story. Since many high school readers find it difficult to surrender and cooperate when they read fiction, a study like the one we have just described has important "hidden" values for them.

The four "directions for planning" that we have been describing are only a sampling of the many possible approaches that would help students become aware of the symbolic quality of stories. But, as our four discussions suggested, whatever approach the teacher takes and whatever stories he chooses, he must, in his teaching of symbol, necessarily teach the whole story. When he is teaching the function of *symbols within stories,* he must always be trying to get students to see how the symbolic value of elements is made clear by their function in the story, that is, by their interaction with all other features to render the experience. When he is teaching *story as symbol,* he must always be trying to get students to respond to the whole organization—because that *is* the story—and only by experiencing that wholly can readers perceive the significance of the insight that informs it.

Some Collateral Writing Assignments

There are four patent *critical* questions that could be used for in-class exercises with any of the preceding approaches or with other schemes for teaching symbols within stories: How do you know that (a certain element) is a symbol? How does (a certain symbolic element) function in this story? How does (some other literary device) affect our response to (some symbolic element)? What kind(s) of fictional element(s) symbolizes the central tension (conflict, paradox) in this story?

These questions may be ordinary and obvious, but the critical exercises based on them need not be routine or insipid. Such questions can be easy or difficult, narrow or broad, depending upon what is inserted into the "slots." For instance, if in the second question the teacher inserted "the soldier and girl" from "A Clean, Well-Lighted Place," the exercise would, we think, be easier than if he inserted "the pear tree" from "Bliss" and that would be easier than if he inserted "the glass house" from "Love: Three Pages from a Hunter's Notebook." If the teacher really wanted to challenge students, he could insert "the refrain" from "Daughter." The more subtle and complex *the function of the inserted element,* the more difficult the question. The difficulty does not depend upon the complexity of the story itself.

Since this is so, the teacher may devise "hard" exercises on relatively "easy" stories, and the reverse. If, for instance, into the first question, he inserted "the little lamp" from "The Doll's House," he would have created a more difficult exercise than if he had inserted "the man with the faded orange hair" from "A Tree. A Rock. A Cloud."—even though the latter is a more difficult story than Katherine Mansfield's. So, on those occasions when a teacher wants to stretch a less able class or reassure a competent one, he need not choose a more challenging or less taxing story; he need only vary the difficulty of the exercise he gives.

The four questions we have cited seem ordinary and obvious, but they are devices of great potential. If, for instance, we completed the third question as follows: How does the simile of the cross in the sky affect the reader's response to the final incident of the pair of birds? ("Love: Three Pages from a Hunter's Notebook") we would have a very limited exercise, but a very enriching one. For, *before* the student can answer the question, he must know the allusion and understand the conventional symbol of the cross in *that* context, and he must work out the terms of the simile. He must do all this, before he can begin to decide how the comparison affects the reader's response to the birds.

The fourth question has no less potential. If, for instance, we asked it in succession of "Bliss," of "Love: Three Pages from a Hunter's Notebook," of "A Tree. A Rock. A Cloud.," and of "Daughter," the answer in each case would be very different. Imagine what students could learn if they did answer this "routine" question on each of these stories.

Now let us turn to some suggestions for longer *critical* papers suitable for full-period, in-class evaluations or for out-of-class writing. To begin, we shall mention the kinds of papers implied by each of the four alternative schemes we have described.

The first plan clearly suggests *such* a topic as:

What kind of reality is represented in the final incident of "A Tree of Night"? Write a one- to two-page paper that tells specifically how you arrived at your answer.

The second plan implies that the test story should be the subject of the paper. The topic might be one *like* this:

From Stegner's "In the Twilight" choose *one* element that becomes symbolic in the story. In a one- to two-page paper point out how the extra-literal meanings the element takes on affect the significance of the story.

This topic is a challenging one, for it does *not* ask students to do what they probably could do easily: tell what the extra-literal meanings of the element are. It *assumes* that they can do that. It asks them, rather, to point out how the extra-literal meanings that they have perceived enhance the story.

The third plan suggests *such* a topic as:

In a one- to two-page paper show what "The Worn Path" gains by its particular adaptation of the quest myth.

Whatever specific topic is used for this plan, the myth in question should be one familiar to students. And the paper should *not* focus on the adaptation, but on "what is gained" by the adaptation. Recognizing how the myth is adapted is merely a preliminary.

The fourth plan suggests *such* a topic as:

Consider what changes would have to be made in "Where Do You Think You're Going?" if it were to be told as a realistic story. Now, in a one- to two-page paper show what the story would lose by such changes.

In addition to these four types of longer papers, there is another kind of out-of-class *critical* paper that *most* students should be writing at this point in the course. That is the paper to be written on a story *prior to the in-class discussion* of it, the paper that supersedes study guides. The topic for such a paper should be some kind of problem that will make students see the story centrally, that is, see it in a way that enlightens *at once* the function of many crucial elements. Although the topic will probably focus on some one feature of the story, it should be such as to insure that the student cannot write the paper unless he has had, on his own, at least an adequate experience of the story. The worth of this kind of paper rests entirely on the potential of the topic to make the student perceive the story as a whole and write about a part of it in terms of the whole.

Here is one topic that we think has that potential:

Read Malamud's "Take Pity" carefully. In a one-page paper show how two meanings of the title [or the ambiguity of the title, if you prefer that wording] suggest the central irony of the story.

At this point in the course many students will be coming to class with the kind of understanding of the assigned story that, earlier, they left with. In class, therefore, discussion could very well radiate from the topic of the paper to the whole story. When we annotated "The New Dress," we looked forward to "another day" when the lesson could profitably center on the "big question." In *most* classes, at this point in the course, we would have arrived at "that day."

Since the kind of assignment we have just suggested involves both reading a story carefully and writing an acceptable one-page paper, it is more time-consuming than the usual assignment. But even average and low average students can do such a piece of work comfortably if it is assigned Thursday to Monday or if students are given a full class period for working, as well as the regular homework time. This kind of assignment seems well worth such an allocation of time.

Finally, here are a few *creative* exercises, to accompany the study of the *fourth alternative* which, more than the others, lends itself to original collateral writing.

After study of a fantasy or a tale, most students cannot wait to create one of their own. Encourage them to look for subjects "at arm's length"; suggest a few. Assign only a page or so. When the papers are written, have the well-executed *and* the highly original read aloud by their authors; ditto some good papers for analysis and some *almost* good ones for group "repairs."

If students have shown some sensitivity to human follies and if they are average-to-good creative writers, offer them a chance to write a comic satire. Prime the topic pump by having some informal exchanges about local "worthies" and familiar foibles. Recall the value of dialogue for rendering the braggart, the evader, and the gossip. Assign a story of a page, but expect only a sketch.

In certain classes, especially less able ones, the teacher might choose to read yarns or fables as conventional forms, rather than tales, fantasies, or comedies. Students delight in writing yarns and fables. And such writing gives them a real reason for reading these forms closely; they have to see how it's done.

For further writing assignments, see "Holidays," p. 430.

"Producing" the Course

A Timetable for the Course

How much time will the first course take? If the students are able and if writing is moderate, the course would probably require twenty class periods. We are assuming the class would read about fourteen stories: three in the First Part, three in the Third Part, and eight in the Second Part (one in the first section, two in the second, two in the third, and three in the fourth). If a study of poems or of plays or both precedes the study of fiction, less than twenty periods would probably suffice for the course, and most of that time could be devoted to "The Story," especially to sections three and four. If the number of writing assignments is large, then more than twenty periods would be required. The extra time would be needed not only for writing the in-class exercises, but also for assigning topics and for discussing the resulting papers. Only papers that are carefully assigned, carefully read, and carefully discussed are really beneficial to developing readers and writers.

If students are low average or less able—whatever curriculum they are enrolled in—much more time would be required for this course, perhaps even thirty class periods. Such students usually have to study more stories. (And they can, because their "cut-off" point is later in fiction than in poetry.) Such students, furthermore, have to spend more time on the study of each story. Discussion would be more protracted and individual in-class work, including in-class reading and the testing of students' progress by quiz and exercises, would have to be frequent. Furthermore, there would be "hidden charges" on time: the teacher would have to spend more time reading orally, more time exemplifying and counselling, and more time assigning the in-class exercises, the longer papers—even tomorrow's homework.

If students are bright but unmotivated, they may read only the same number of stories—even the same distribution—as the able students, but they will probably need more time. For much of the work will have to be done, or at least started, in class. Furthermore, such students profit greatly from many written in-class activities, much variation, and frequent, engaging "breathers." All this takes time; how much time is hard to predict, the day-to-day performance of these classes varies so much. But we shall hazard a guess of twenty-five to thirty classes.

The teacher of either the less able or the bright-but-unmotivated students may decide, as we suggested on earlier timetables, that it is not feasible for his class to concentrate on the short story for twenty-five to thirty consecutive periods. He might decide, instead, on two three-week or three two-week blocks of work or some other practicable division. But whatever schedule is chosen, during the first block of work, every class should complete "Mode of Narration" and the first section of "The Story" and begin the second section. In this way, students will have developed, before the first "break," an adequate sense of narrator and at least "rough" responses to the chief fictional elements. These basic responses can, then, be progressively refined in the block or blocks of work that follow. When the course is taught in such separated units, each new unit should begin where the preceding one ended. The students should resume by reading carefully at least one story from the last section studied in order to get their skill "in condition" and to give the teacher some idea of what they have lost during the interim.

Holidays

Not all classes will *need* to have their study of the short story divided. And not all will *require* "breathers" during their study. But all will *enjoy* "a day off" now and then. Here are some suggestions for spending those necessary—or gratuitous—days validly, pertinently, and pleasurably.

On a holiday during the study of "Mode of Narration," read orally a story with a marked narrative voice; Frank O'Connor's "My Oedipus Complex," for instance.

On an early free day during the study of "The Story," read the class a shocking "conventional" story: Richard Connell's "The Most Dangerous Game," or Guy de Maupassant's "La Mère Sauvage," or James Warner Bellah's "Attack," or Frank O'Connor's "Guests of the Nation." Or, if the class has studied "Barn Burning," read aloud Ratliff's version of the story as he tells it to Jody Varner in Faulkner's *The Hamlet,* pages 14–20,[19] to show students the crucial importance of treatment in the effect a story creates. On a late free day, read a touching story: Katherine Mansfield's "The Doll's House," or Morley Callaghan's "The Snob," even Ernest Hemingway's "The Battler." You may wish to discuss the stories, invite comments on them, or simply let them work for themselves.

Any time during the study of "The Story," give the class a critic's commentary (or the crucial parts of it) on some story the students have read that week. It should be a commentary that will provoke a lively reaction; for instance, Marvin Magalaner's on Joyce's "Clay."[20]

On a holiday at the close of "The Story" or during the Third Part of the course, use an "intention" exercise. Show students the author's commentary on some story they have read; for instance, John Steinbeck's on "The Snake" or Sherwood Anderson's on "Death in the Woods." After they have read the author's view, ask them what they now think of their class discussion of the story. This kind of activity is both engaging and instructive. Nothing makes the primacy of the work more clear to students than such assessment of a critic's or the author's commentary on it.[21]

On a late holiday use the following diversion. Ask students to read a story that is an artistic failure; for instance, O. Henry's "The Furnished Room." Say to them, "This is a very famous story. Is it really any good?" Such an exercise as this stimulates students' discrimination and precludes their assuming that "well-known" necessarily means "good." Many magazine stories, many anthologized teen-age stories, and many of the lesser stories of good writers would be usable for such an exercise.

Finally, a generally useful and highly favored activity is the discussion of some aspect of human behavior dramatized in one or more of the stories read during the past week. The aspect to be discussed should either be selected by the students or be one that they have clearly evinced interest in. Furthermore, since students know as well as we do that nothing is worth *discussing* if a "pat answer" suffices, the question for discussion should ask about some conflict or complexity related to the behavior being considered. A discussion occasioned by "Theft," for instance, might turn on such a question as, Why should anyone be *uncomfortable* in the *ownership* of things? A discussion provoked by "Paul's Case" might ask, Who is to blame in a tragic life like Paul's? One evoked by "Eveline" might center on, Why is it hard to decide what one's duty is? Or: When two alternatives seem equally "good," how does one decide which to choose? For "Act of Faith," the question might be: Does putting one's confidence in a person always cause a dilemma? For "Araby," Are illusions desirable? Or, Does loss always involve gain? Or, How can one lose in gaining? Answering such questions will allow students glimpses into the baffling nature of moral questions which, in real life and in good literature, most often involve either a choice between two "good's" or a confounding fusion of opposites. As soon as students *can* themselves propose fruitful discussion questions, invite them to submit some and let the class decide what will be talked about.

The kind of discussion we have been describing might begin as a written paper, or it might be exclusively a written exercise—done in class on the holiday. Some of the questions we cited are "naturals" for argument papers; others, for expository papers. The writing assignments might specify the kind of reader to whom the paper is to be directed and even the mode of paragraph development to be used (contrast or examples, say). In other words, the teacher may make answering the question as much of a composition exercise as he wishes. If students are not already familiar with "argument" and "expository" papers, then models should be examined before such an assignment is made.

The discussions we have been describing are not, of course, discussions of the stories. In each case they "take off" from the story, sometimes testing the validity of its insight, sometimes exploring various aspects of its theme or of the behavior that dramatizes the theme. Whether oral or written, such discussions should never take place until *after* the critical study of the particular story (or stories) is completed. Both discussions *of* the work and discussions *tangential to* it are profitable for students to engage in. But these two types of discussions differ in purpose and in value. Our teaching should help students to recognize the difference.

Alternative Schemes for the Study of the Short Story

So far, we have been detailing our own proposal for a three-part first course in reading fiction. Now we shall describe briefly some alternative proposals,[22] any one of which could be used either as formulated or as a suggestive starting point for a teacher who wants to devise his own scheme. To use our scheme or any of these alternatives, a teacher needs only an anthology of good short stories. In the references at the close of this section, we have listed many collections of stories suitable in quality and in kind for the teaching of a great variety of first courses.

Perhaps the oldest, and surely among the best detailed, of the plans for teaching students to read fiction critically and interpretively is Brooks and Warren's course of study in *Understanding Fiction.* It aims to help students recognize the intention of a work "by understanding the functions of the various elements which go to make up fiction and by understanding their relationship to each other in the whole construct."[23] In order to reveal without delay the distinction between the nature and structure of fiction and the intentions and organizations of other kinds of prose, the course begins with a comparative analysis of two types of historical episodes, a character sketch, and three short stories. Four sections follow this introduction: the first *examines stories* to show "how plot reveals," the second, to show "what character reveals," the third, to show "what theme reveals," and the last, to show "how literary devices—for example, indirection and irony, symbolism, and suggestion—function in stories."

Many of the printed "teachers" that have appeared since the Brooks and Warren volume have been, consciously or unconsciously, variations of it. They differ from it mainly in the order they propose for teaching both the elements of fiction and the literary devices. Edward Bloom, in *The Order of Fiction,*[24] for instance, organizes in four sections: "The Nature of Fiction," "The Materials of Fiction" (character, plot, setting), "The Ordering of Fiction" (selection and arrangement, mood and tone, style, point of view), and "The Meaning of Fiction" (theme and intention, symbolism and allegory). Laurence Perrine, in *Story and Structure,*[25] opens with a distinction between escape fiction and interpretive fiction. And then he treats, in turn, plot, character, theme, point of view, symbol and irony, emotion and humor, and fantasy. Joseph Satin, in *Reading Prose Fiction,*[26] stresses consecutively "Action, Character, Setting," then moves to conventional forms, "Allegory and Fable," and, finally, to features of language, "Satire and Irony," and "Symbolism and Ambiguity." Robert Welker and Herschel Gower in *The Sense of Fiction*[27] open with a study of "Unity of Effect," and after sections on "Action and Plot," "Theme and Character," "Symbol, Theme, and Epiphany," "Allusion, Allegory, and Myth," "Fantasy, Ambiguity, and Credibility," "Humor and Pathos," they conclude with "A Novella." Jessie Rehder in *The Story at Work*[28] begins with "What It Says" (concentrating on theme in many different kinds of stories), moves to "How It Works" (stressing character, time and place, plot,

point of view, symbolism, style), and concludes with "What It Does"
(emphasizing the story as an experience that evokes a new reality
that becomes part of the reader's experience.) Throughout the study
of the five pairs of stories in *Adventures in Fiction,*[29] John T. Frederick focuses on both rendering of character and the unified functioning of all parts of a story. In addition to these two continuing
emphases, he stresses in turn point of view, setting, the story of effect
(horror, humor), plot, and the use of framework. Throughout their
little "teacher" for young, beginning readers, *The Narrative Impulse,*[30] Mary Purcell and Robert Wylder insist on close attention
to the words the writers choose. And, in addition to this constant
emphasis, they stress action and conflict, plot, foreshadowing, and
character.

This juxtaposition of these eight schemes reveals several things:
most obviously, that many "teachers" favor stressing the elements of
fiction—plot, character, setting, theme—before they emphasize other
features of language; secondly, that the same basic scheme can be
developed into a complex organization or reduced to a very simple
one; and finally, that some "teachers" open with what *should* engage students first (the intentions of fiction, the nature of it, the
value and pleasure of interpreting fiction); others open with what
does engage students first (the plot, the theme).

In the last fifteen years, *Understanding Fiction* has, then, had
considerable influence on books designed to teach students how to
read short stories and novels. During this time, there have, however,
been other useful proposals. Among the older ones, two stand out:
Mark Schorer's in *The Story*[31] (to which my own course is indebted)
and Robert Heilman's in *Modern Short Stories.*[32] As its framework,
Schorer's scheme uses the four "motives of fiction": to tell a story
("The Story Base"), to tell a story about "individual human relationships dramatized through events within a social context" ("Character
and Action"), to give the surface of life and to penetrate it ("Surface
and Symbol"), and to express the writer's vision ("Style and Meaning"). Schorer's scheme concludes by distinguishing, once again,
according to motive, the short story from longer fiction ("Toward
the Novel"). Heilman's scheme aims to show the variety of kinds
of experience stories render. It is arranged to help students see why
a story is one kind of story rather than another and what specific
methods each story uses to achieve its effect. After an opening
section in which the selection of stories impresses the reader immediately with the potential richness of this form of fiction ("Different
Kinds of Stories"), there follow sections on "Different Points of
View," "Contrasts in Method and Theme," "Fantasy," "Methods of
Character Study," and "Symbolism."

Among the more recently published schemes, those of Arthur

Mizener (*Modern Short Stories: The Uses of Imagination*)[33] and of Robert Gordon (*The Expanded Moment*)[34] deserve special notice. Mizener organizes by differences in "mode"; that is, "in the attitudes toward life which govern an author's sense of reality and the techniques of expression these attitudes dictate."[35] The four-part scheme, ordered to lead from the familiar to the less familiar, begins with stories that represent the real world accurately but suggest that significance lies in what men feel *about* events; next come stories that are uninterpreted dramatic renderings of manners; then, stories that represent the subjective or "passional" life; and, finally, stories that express the Southern sense of experience. Mizener's thesis is that only if the reader recognizes the "mode" of a story does he know what he must notice if he is to grasp the story's implications. Accordingly, the teacher's job is to make beginning readers sensitive to these four different "modes."

As the title *The Expanded Moment* suggests, Gordon stresses the concentration of the short story, the story as a vehicle for the revelatory rendering of a brief significant moment. His five groups of stories show not only *how* such concentration is achieved (specifically, by irony, understatement, and symbolism) but also that such concentration characterizes even fantasies, parables, and stories of political and social crisis. If the teacher used concentration (intension) as the organizing principle for a study of the short story, he could use extension as the organizing principle for a study of the novel. Through such studies, students could come to understand much about the similarities and the differences—in the purpose, the treatment of materials, and the achievement of unity—of these two forms of fiction.

The twelve schemes we have just described—and our own—all assume that the study of short stories should be organized to emphasize, *in sequence*, the various elements and devices of fiction. Other "teachers" assume that, from the beginning of a study of the short story, students can notice all features *in concert* without special emphasis, *if* stories are arranged in an order of increasing literary complexity. Raymond Short and Richard Sewall's *Short Stories for Study*,[36] Robert Stanton's *The Short Story and the Reader*,[37] and Frank Jennings and Charles Calitri's *Stories*[38] are different kinds of examples of such organization. Both Rehder and Purcell and Wylder also exemplify this kind of sequence, for they arrange stories according to difficulty, *as well as* according to their appropriateness for teaching particular features.

Since we are trying to suggest alternative proposals or schemes for helping students learn to read stories, we have not mentioned any collection which does not present an aesthetically relevant "program." And there are many anthologies of fine stories, various in their concerns and methods, which offer only an introduction, questions, and occasional analyses. These collections are organized chronologically, alphabetically according to author, or thematically. Neither a chronological arrangement nor an alphabetical one will naturally produce any ordering of stories that will help beginners learn to read fiction.

Neither will a thematic arrangement. In thematic anthologies, the demands on a reader vary markedly, story to story. Indeed, the anthology may begin with a really difficult story—a Katherine Anne Porter, for instance—and follow that with, say, Frank O'Connor's "My Oedipus Complex," and that with William Carlos Williams' "The Use of Force," and so on. The criterion for including a story at a certain point in a thematic anthology is the story's consonance with a particular theme, not its literary "availability." So most thematic anthologies are really appropriate for the reader who has *already* learned to respond sensitively to many kinds of stories. Only such a reader can read well enough to compare several treatments of a similar theme. *At the end* of a first course in reading fiction, a student *is* ready to read responsively and so discuss fruitfully the thematic clusters in most such anthologies. Thematic study invites unskilled readers to reduce stories to their least common denominators and to dissolve the discussion of the stories into an exchange of interesting views about the particular theme—but we need no stories to provoke that.

Thematic study engages students so easily and continually that we sometimes tend to overlook its hazards. We can, of course, avoid some of them by gathering a group of thematically similar stories and arranging them in an order of increasing literary difficulty. But this is not easy to do, because, the more criteria we apply simultaneously in the choosing of stories, the harder it is to find stories that qualify. Consequently, the tendency is to compromise in one of several ways: for instance, by choosing stories of almost uniform difficulty, by ignoring the literary complexity of one or another story, by broadening the themes so that they are merely general topics, or by construing the themes of stories with questionable liberalism. Unless a teacher has time to work out a scheme that takes both theme and increasing literary complexity into account, then it is perhaps better to substitute the criterion of relevance for thematic similarity.

We have been reviewing representative organizations for helping students learn to read short stories. We have not been recommending certain books, only designating them as examples of certain schemes, as books to which a teacher interested in this or that particular scheme may go to see how it may be worked out for classroom teaching. If he does go to any of the twelve "teachers" we mentioned, he will find few of the limitations that mar other "teachers": mediocre stories, often the "thistles" of good writers; an excess of artistically simple stories; and undue stress (in the study questions) on facts, moral values, and the identification of devices. In other words, the materials and the methods the authors used in working out the twelve schemes we have described are valuable and valid, as well as feasible.

The Second Course—and Later

The kind of study of fiction that would logically follow the first course we have just outlined would be some kind of special study of the short story, or a study of novellas, or of novels. What *actually* would follow the first course in any particular class would be determined by available time, available books, and the interest and the ability of the class. Let us grant time, a book of short stories, and a few novels, and pay attention instead to the way in which the character of a particular class would affect the choice of a second course.

By the end of the first course, the teacher does know "where" the class as a whole—as well as each student—is. He knows this from discussions, critical and creative exercises, longer papers, and from a final evaluation of the sort we suggested at the end of "The Story."

If students have shown themselves to be able readers, the teacher has "carte blanche": he may without delay begin the study of novellas, or novels, or a combination of both; or he may offer these students a chance to do some kind of further study of the short story or of relevant kinds of nonfiction. If, however, students have shown themselves to be only fair-to-average readers—if, especially, they have had trouble perceiving how stories are organized—then, they need further, though different, study of the short story. Now, if these students are motivated, however slow they may be, then the teacher may give them what they need. They will not mind another "go" at short stories through a new approach. Indeed, dull students enjoy "inch" progress and the security of sameness.

If, however, these fair-to-average readers are unmotivated, however bright they may be, then the teacher cannot decide on a second course by need alone. At least two other factors must be considered: how soon must the second course follow the first? and how much variety does *this particular* group seem to require? If, for instance, because of circumstances (the availability of books and such), the second course must follow within a week or two, and, if from dealing with these particular students you know that, without a respite adequate to revive their waning interest, more short stories would be just more short stories, however different the organization, then it would seem best to move on to novellas or a novel, reading ability notwithstanding. If you do this and if you choose novellas or a novel appropriate for these students in both concern and literary complexity, you will have, working with you, all the motivational values that newness and the feeling of progress can give. In certain classes, these are necessary conditions for keeping the will to improve operating.

So we are saying that many factors affect what kind of second course any particular class should have and that only the teacher can decide. And when he has decided, he simply tries to come as close as time and books allow to what he thinks ideal.

On the following pages, we outline six *types* of courses that could logically follow the first course we have detailed. The first four of these are different kinds of advanced study of the short story; the fifth concentrates on the study of the nonfictional "stories"—history and biography; and the last, on novellas and novels. All six courses may be varied, by the use of different works, to suit the reading abilities and the interests of many kinds of students. All could be modified to a twelve-period unit or expanded to as many as twenty classes.

Four Types of Advanced Study of the Short Story

Thematic Study

Even less able and average readers *should* now be adequately ready for the demands that reading a thematic scheme makes. But *will* they perceive the particularity of each experience? Or will some still fall before the temptation to coalesce several thematically similar stories into "the ones about hate" or "about loneliness"? Some *might* do just that. So we would take three precautions. We would tell the class that the readings center on a theme, but we would discourage any mention of a particular theme until all the readings had been discussed. Secondly, we would teach the stories so as to unobtrusively stress the particularity of the experience of each. As story after story was discussed, students would perceive—without any overt encouragement—similarities and differences among the experiences they are having. Finally, we would choose themes that would be not only fresh but also resistant to reduction to mere topics.

Here are two examples of such themes. The first—relating to problems between individuals—may be stated somewhat as follows: Even between intimates, communication is imperfect; there is always some "dead air." Apposite readings are such stories as: V. S. Pritchett's "The Sniff," Sean O'Faolain's "The Fur Coat," and Sherwood Anderson's "Unlighted Lamps." The second theme—relating to problems of individuals in a wider society—may be stated as: The liberal loves the "outsider"—but often not "as himself." Relevant readings are such stories as: Robert Penn Warren's "Her Own People," Flannery O'Connor's "The Displaced Person," and Muriel Sparks' "The Black Madonna."

High school readers will find these themes true, but also new. For, most students tend to think of communication as either entirely perfect or entirely lacking ("My parents don't understand me"—unqualified!). Many tend to think of the outsider as rejected by the avowed biased, accepted by the avowed liberal; they do not, of themselves, realize the truth in the frankly prejudiced and the falsity in the protesting liberal. The concrete experiences of such stories as we have cited can give reality to that irony, paradox, and grayness in human relations which most high school students are just beginning to have intimations of. And experiencing a variety of manifestations of some particular human behavior will help them realize both how prevalent the behavior is and what surprisingly different human relationships it appears in.

Near the close of this ten-class thematic unit—which would concern at most two themes, we would test what we had been teaching with a two-stage evaluation somewhat like the following. The first stage would be an out-of-class (or, if necessary, in-class) written exercise such as this:

> In a paragraph or two state what you think might be considered the theme of [naming the stories in *the second* thematic grouping] and show briefly that your theme takes all these stories into account.

In class on the following day, the students would discuss the themes they have stated and the defenses they have offered. We would let *the class* select the most adequate themes and rule out any unjustifiable ones. Students will have found this assignment hard to do, because during their study of these stories, they will have discussed each story as a discrete experience. To arrive at a "least common denominator," "you have to sacrifice so much! too much!" And that is just what we want them to recognize. That sets the class up for the second stage of the assignment—a full-period, in-class paper to be written the following day.

Here is the topic:

> Use either the theme you decided upon or one of those now on the board. [These will be themes considered "valid" during yesterday's discussion.] In a one- to two-page paper, point out ways in which this theme does not *really* represent the "meaning" of one or two of the stories

concerned. We are limiting your answer to one or two stories, so that you will be able to write concretely and specifically in this amount of time.

In a thematic unit, after the formal study is over and such papers as the preceding are written, students might enjoy a "free" paper. Some might choose to write an "argument," a paper in which they "talk back" ("An Open Letter to Mr. Warren") denouncing or supporting the experiences of one or more of the stories. Some students might prefer a creative paper, the writing of either a brief dialogue that dramatizes the "dead air" between loved ones or a narrative paragraph that represents the attitude of a liberal toward an outsider. "Free" papers deserve adequate preparation, and the teacher should refer students to appropriate models and call their attention to their own previous work on the effects created by ordering and tone.

The Study of One Writer

Another alternative for a second course is the study of seven or eight stories of some one writer that the students have especially enjoyed. As we said earlier when we discussed the study of one poet, such a course might be organized to reveal the writer's themes, his style, his evolution, or any two of these, or all three. Whatever the focus and whoever the class, this kind of study is most valuable if *students* gradually *discover,* through the reading of stories, the writer's characteristic themes, the typical features of his style, and the changes in his work. The study is less valuable—for both teacher and students—if the stories are used largely to exemplify generalizations the teacher has made in an initial lecture.

If the study has been inductive, then the teacher could use a topic like the following for a final paper to evaluate students' achievement:

Read [a "new" story by the author being considered]. In a one- to two-page paper point out *in what respects* this story is typically [the writer] in its [theme or style or both]. Refer to stories we have studied only where such reference is *needed* to *support* your argument.

If the study has been evolutionary, then such phrases as "*early* Hemingway" or "*late* Steinbeck" should be inserted in the second blank. The final sentence in the statement of the topic is included to prevent the "grinds" in all curriculums from regurgitating indiscriminately their notes from class discussions.

Beyond being interesting in itself, the study of one writer is useful preparation for the contextual study of literature that will probably come in later high school years. For, however this present study is organized, not only will it have the concentration and the depth that characterizes good contextual study, but it will also *naturally* provoke questions about why the writer had the concerns he did and about what affected the shifts in his interests—questions that can be answered only by biographical, historical, and cultural data. The study of one writer may actually turn into a "pilot study" in contextual criticism. And that is most desirable.

There are two possible impediments to using this type of second course. One is the lack of appropriate books. For English department bookrooms often do not have class sets of the collected stories of individual authors, although there are now available many excellent paperbound editions. The other possible impediment is the teacher's unfamiliarity with the writer students choose to pursue—probably Hemingway, Salinger, Anderson, Faulkner, Thurber, Steinbeck, Eudora Welty. To do a genuine study of one writer, the teacher must know the canon well enough to select pertinent stories, and he must be conversant enough with the "life and times" not only to answer questions but also to prepare relevant collateral materials. Unfortunately, some teachers who are very familiar with the work of many modern poets are singularly unversed in that of short story writers. This is an area equally well worth a teacher's concentrated study.

Historical Study of the Short Story

This third alternative for further study of the short story would consist of the reading of, say, ten stories that represent successive "milestones" in the brief history of the form. There are several kinds of "ready-made" collections of stories for teachers who are interested in this kind of second course. For those who wish to feature significant short stories whether written originally in English or not, there is Herbert Barrows (ed.), *Reading the Short Story*, Boston: Houghton, Mifflin Company, 1959. And for those who wish to limit the study to the short story in America, there is Wallace and Mary Stegner (eds.), *Great American Short Stories*, New York: Dell Publishing Company, Inc., 1957, or Ray B. West, Jr. (ed.), *American Short Stories*, New York: Thomas Y. Crowell Company, 1959. For teachers who want to restrict themselves to the short story in England, there is Christopher Isherwood (ed.), *Great English Short Stories*, New York: Dell Publishing Company, Inc., 1957. And we have named only a few of the useful chronologically arranged collections.

If a teacher wishes his class to do an historical study "some time," then this seems like the appropriate time. *Now*, having completed the first course, students will be able to read responsively many early stories that previously would have been too difficult for them. *Now* students will know what stance to take before an Irving tale, a Hawthorne moral romance, a Mark Twain yarn, and they will be ready to become the readers which such stories as these demand. And only now will readers be sufficiently skilled to complete an historical study rapidly enough to perceive strongly and clearly "the figure the history makes."

As a second course, this kind of study is in itself valuable. Furthermore, it is, as the study of one writer is, useful preparation for later contextual criticism.

The Evolution of Story

The teacher who decides against an historical survey of the short story but who still does want students to have some sense of its historical development might prefer to offer them as a second course a study in the evolution of certain old forms of story; for instance, the character sketch, the tale, the yarn, or the fable.[39] The main aim of such a study would be to see *how* old forms are modified in later use and *why* they are. The study would, therefore, be both generic and contextual. So, this course would not be a mere repetition of the study of conventional forms we proposed in the Third Part of the first course. In fact, the kind of understanding of the conventional forms and the ability to read them that students would gain through *that* study would make it possible for them now to concentrate on the *changes* that took place in the shape and the use of this or that conventional form.

In most classes this kind of study is stimulating, but not for very long. So, it seems best to choose two forms that promise to be engaging to the particular class and to study each—reading, writing, discussion, oral reading, included—for not more than a week, "quitting while you are still ahead!" Students should probably read about four examples of each form chosen: the first three should be chronologically arranged to illustrate the form at various points in its development, the fourth should be a short story that uses the form for its own "larger purposes." The following four lists suggest the kinds of works that would be useful.

■ *The Character Sketch.* For the *character sketch,* the teacher could select from such readings as the following.
Seventeenth Century:
John Earle's "A Young Man," or his "A Coward"
Joseph Hall's "The Busybody"
Eighteenth and Nineteenth Centuries:

Addison and Steele's "Will Wimble," *The Spectator,* no. 108, or
   "Sir Roger at Church," *The Spectator,* no. 112.
   Samuel Johnson's "Ned Druggett"
   Washington Irving's "The Stout Gentleman"
   Nathaniel Hawthorne's "Endicott and the Red Cross"
Twentieth Century:
   Eudora Welty's "Ida M'Toy"
   Katherine Anne Porter's "The Witness"
Finally, the short story that is "like" a character sketch, but
clearly more than one:
   James Joyce's "Eveline"
   John O'Hara's "Graven Image"
   Robert Penn Warren's "When the Light Gets Green"

■ *The Tale.*   For the *tale,* the teacher might select from such read-
ings as the following.
   Early:
   Chaucer's "The Pardoner's Tale"
Nineteenth Century:
   Sir Walter Scott's "A Highland Anecdote"
   Washington Irving's "The Legend of Sleepy Hollow" or his
      brief "A Contented Man"
   Edgar Allen Poe's "The Cask of Amontillado"
   Nathaniel Hawthorne's "Ethan Brand"
Twentieth Century:
   Leo Tolstoi's "God Sees The Truth But Waits"
   John Collier's "The Chaser"
Finally, the tale-like story:
   Joseph Conrad's "The Tale"
   Robert Louis Stevenson's "Sire de Maletroit's Door"
   Eudora Welty's "Shower of Gold"
   Ivan Bunin's "The Gentleman from San Francisco" and any of
      the stories cited under tale in the Third Part of the first course.

■ *The Yarn.*   For the *yarn,* the teacher might select from such read-
ings as the following.
   Early Nineteenth Century:
   George W. Harris' "Mrs. Yardley's Quilting" (a "Sut Lovingood"
      yarn)
   Augustus B. Longstreet's "The Shooting-Match," or "The Horse-
      Swap (in *Georgia Scenes*)
   "Mike Fink Beats Davy Crockett at a Shooting Match" (an
      anonymous yarn reprinted in Walter Blair, *Native American
      Humor, 1800–1900*)

T. B. Thorpe's "The Big Bear of Arkansaw"
Late Nineteenth Century:
    Joel Chandler Harris' "Miss Cow Falls a Victim to Mr. Rabbit"
    (an Uncle Remus yarn)
    Alfred Henry Lewis' "The Man from Yellowhouse"
    Mark Twain's "Jim Baker's Bluejay Yarn" (in *A Tramp Abroad*), his "A Mississippi Pilot" (the somnambulist Mr. X), or his "Huck's Visit to the Raft" (both in *Life on the Mississippi*)
Twentieth Century:
    James F. Stevens' *Paul Bunyan*, or the stories as told to children in Glen Rounds' *Ol' Paul, the Mighty Logger*
Finally, the yarn-like story:
    William Faulkner's "Was," his short version of "Spotted Horses," or little Ike's brief memory of that episode in part 3 of *The Bear*
    Mark Twain's "The Celebrated Jumping Frog of Calaveras County"

■ *The Fable.* For the *fable,* the teacher might select from such readings as the following.
Early:
    Aesop's "The Eagle and the Beetle," or his "The Bull and the Gnat"
    La Fontaine's "The Dog With the Cropped Ears," or his "The Treasure and the Two Men"
    Benjamin Franklin's "The Ephemera"
Nineteenth Century:
    Leo Tolstoi's "The Peasant and the Horse," or his "The Blind Men and the Elephants," or his "Why There Is Evil in the World"
    Ambrose Bierce's "The Rebellious Ant"
    Robert Louis Stevenson's "The Devil and the Innkeeper"
Twentieth Century:
    James Thurber's "The Bear Who Let It Alone," or his "The Rabbits Who Caused All the Trouble"
    William March's "The Farmer and the Mink"
Finally, the fable-like story:
    James Agee's "A Mother's Tale"

This kind of study can easily deteriorate into a mechanical "checking off" in each reading of the characteristics of the relevant form. So the teacher must preclude this by keeping before the class at all times the three-fold purpose of this study: to discover how each work modifies the conventional form; to see what effects are produced by the particular use each work makes of the form; and finally, to ascertain what, in the social-cultural milieu, accounts for the significance of such an effect.

The Nonfictional Stories

So much for our four proposals for further study of the short story. Now, let us look briefly at a course that concentrates on the nonfictional "stories"—biography and history. This course might follow the first course directly or somewhat later. The important point is that biography and history should not be *studied* until students are average or better readers, until they know that a story—fictional or nonfictional—interprets an event so as to reveal at once its particular and universal meanings, and until they know that the interpretation directs and is revealed by the arrangement of details, the attitude of the narrator—all the uses of language. Only when students know all this will they be ready to respond to history and biography *as literature*. And only when they know what kind of imaginative organization a work of fiction is will they be ready to understand the special kind of work of literature the nonfictional story is. Through their reading and writing during the first course, most students are now ready to respond to history and biography as literature and to distinguish between the fictional and the nonfictional story.

From their readings and exercises in the first course, most students know that a work of fiction is an objective correlative that the writer constructs out of words to express an insight into human experience. They know that this structure must represent life, but need not correspond to it, must be credible and authentic, but not verifiably true, and must be consistent, but only internally so. Students might not *express* their understanding of the fictional story in these terms. But, as long as they have grasped the nature of fiction, they do have a valid basis for understanding the nonfictional story as a different kind of story, the product of a different kind of imaginative act.

From their readings and exercises in *this* course students will come to know that the nonfictional story *begins,* not as an insight, but as a group of facts, which have been *discovered* by the biographer or the historian, followed up exhaustively by him, examined for relevance, tested for truth. Students will see that the facts rule the biographer or the historian. He must allow them to correct one another and to suggest their relationships and relative importance. All the historian or the biographer may do is *discover* an interpretation that the facts do suggest. All he may do is *discover* the conflict, the motivation, and the resolution in the data. He may not enhance the drama of the interpretation by inventing or omitting or minimizing or overemphasizing. All he may do is perceive the significance of the "given" and render the data so as to express what he perceives. Out of the raw material of verified facts, the nonfictional writer shapes a story that must correspond with things as they were.

This course in the nonfictional story is, then, for those students who are ready now to perceive both the similarities and the differences between fictional and nonfictional stories and to respond appropriately to the imaginative organizations that historians and biographers use to render defensible and engaging interpretations of their true data. Our general aim for this study of biography and history would be, then, to help "ready" students *develop* these perceptions and responses.

There are many possible ways to achieve this aim. What we shall describe might be called a *creative-critical approach*. Students would first become makers of history and biography and then readers of these forms. The actual study would go somewhat like this. We would give students dittoed copies of the source materials used for a section or for a chapter of a history or a biography. Each student would study these materials carefully and would propose a focus for them, sort and order them for relevance, and suggest an interpretation of them. In certain classes, we would ask students to take the final step: Write up the data so that your interpretation of them will be implied. Whenever students completed the initial creative phase of this study, we would begin the critical part. We would show them the section or the chapter that the professional biographer or historian had shaped out of the materials they had just worked on. Each student would examine the passage to see how the writer focused the facts, how he arranged them and expressed them. After these matters are discussed in class, we would assign a close reading of the selection to help students notice *what* interpretation is being expressed, *what* suggests the interpretation to the reader, and *how* the passage achieves the effect of a good narration. This kind of creative-critical exercise would help students understand to some extent both the interpretive and the imaginative acts that historians and biographers perform. In any course on the nonfictional story we would expect that students would study four biographical accounts and four historical selections; we would normally ask them to do the preceding kind of exercise twice in the study of each form. Their work on the remaining nonfictional selections would be restricted to the critical phase.

The main obstacle to carrying out the kind of creative-critical approach that we have been describing is that the source material needed for it is not *readily* available. But we can achieve a comparable end by using "second-best" materials; for instance, bodies of "raw" facts found in history texts, in encyclopedia entries, or biographical dictionaries, in the accounts of reliable newspapers, in official records of some sort, and in published letters and journals. We could, for instance, use such published materials as newspaper accounts of the bombing of Hiroshima as "raw" materials for the creative phase and John Hersey's "A Noiseless Flash" or "The Fire" from *Hiroshima* for the critical part. Or we could use such published materials as *Boswell's London Journal, 1762–1763*, edited by Frederick A. Pottle,[40] as source materials for the creative phase and relevant passages of Boswell's *Life of Johnson* for the critical work. Not all the kinds of "second-best" materials that we listed above would be as genuine source material as the Boswell *Journal*, but all would serve adequately to accomplish the purpose of our proposed study.

The readings for the critical phase of this study of biography and history must meet three criteria. First, they must be relatively short pieces that *are units:* chapters, sections, profiles, sketches. Such pieces are not only valid and feasible microcosms for the study of these kinds of writing but also proper vehicles for suggesting the differences between the fictional and the nonfictional story. Secondly, the readings must be selections worth *studying* in class. (The sentimental, ennobling biography so often presented to students rarely needs study of the kind we outlined.) And, finally, the readings must be a representative sample of biographical and historical writing. We think the following suggested readings meet these criteria. Furthermore, they include both "easy" readings and more demanding ones, because the type of study we are suggesting could be carried on in rather ordinary classes as well as in able ones, and even there, the teacher might choose to *begin* with a "soft tread."

First, some appropriate readings in history:

Henry Adams, "The Inauguration" (as far as the Address), in Book I and "The Louisiana Treaty" in Book II, *History of the United States of America During the Administration of Thomas Jefferson,* Volume 1; Hanson Baldwin, "R. M. S. Titanic" in *Sea Fights and Shipwrecks;* Thomas Carlyle, "The Death of the King" in *The French Revolution;* Bruce Catton, "Gettysburg" in *This Hallowed Ground;* Winston Churchill, "Dunkirk" in *The Finest Hour;* Alistair Cooke, "Farewell on P Street—and Mr. Truman Slips Away," reprinted in Wallace Douglas (ed.), *The Character of Prose;* Edward Gibbon, "General Observations on the Fall of the Roman Empire in the West" in *The Decline and Fall of the Roman Empire;* John Hersey, "A Noiseless Flash" or "The Fire" in *Hiroshima;* W. H. Lewis, "The Death of Louis XIV" in *The Sunset of the Splendid Century;* Thomas B. Macaulay, "The Scottish Highlands in the Seventeenth Century," in *The History of England from The Accession of James II;* Francis Parkman, "The Discovery of the Mouth of the Mississippi" in *The Discovery of the Great West: La Salle* and "The Death of Pontiac" in *The Conspiracy of Pontiac.*

Now, some usable biographies:

James Boswell, "The Wilkes Episode" in *Life of Johnson;* Catherine Drinker Bowen, "The Death of Holmes" in *Yankee from Olympus;* Truman Capote, "The Duke in His Dukedom" (Marlon Brando) in *The Selected Writings of Truman Capote;* Anthony Cooper, Earl of Shaftesbury, "Portrait of Henry Hastings," quoted in Brooks and Warren, *Understanding Fiction;* Esther Forbes, "The Alarum," "A Voice in the Dark," and "John Hancock's Trunk" in *Paul Revere and the World He Lived In;* E. M. Forster, "Captain Edward Gibbon" in *Abinger Harvest;* Thomas B. Macaulay, "Boswell," from his review of Boswell's *Life of Johnson;* John Dos Passos, "Fighting Bob" (LaFollette) in *The 42nd Parallel;* Lytton Strachey, "Gibbon" in *Portraits in Miniature;* Deems Taylor, "The Monster" (Wagner) in *Of Men and Music.*

To evaluate the kind of study we have been describing, we could use either of the following two *types* of longer papers. The first type of paper would test the students' ability to recognize the ways in which many features of the imaginative organization of a history or a biography imply the writer's interpretation. Here is the topic:

Read [insert the title of a "new" selection of biography or history comparable to what the class has been reading]. In a one- to two-page paper point out specifically *what* suggests to the reader the biographer's [or historian's] interpretation.

The second type of paper would test students' ability to comment critically on a given statement using the works they studied as evidence:

Read the following statement critically. [Insert statement.] To what extent is it true? In a one- to two-page paper defend your judgment with appropriate evidence from the works we have read.

The statement inserted might be a bland, relatively easy one, like Leon Edel's: "Interpretation need not become . . . moral approval or disapproval of the life itself."[41] Or the statement might be a controversial one, like Philip Toynbee's:

It is true that we react differently to a character in a book if we believe that some equivalent to him had once breathed and talked and suffered, but there is no real difference in kind between the subject of a biography and the hero of a novel. Both, by their artificial constriction, differ violently from the living people we know.[42]

The study of biography and history we have just described would require about twelve class periods. Although students would probably read only eight selections—four biographical and four historical essays, they would need the extra time to work on and discuss the exercises on source materials and to write occasional in-class papers. Now, even though this course would probably take two and one-half weeks of time, it is still only a basic introduction. It could very well be varied and extended either by deepening or by broadening.

Here are three of the many possible ways to *deepen* it.

The *first* is a *study of bias*. We would select a certain biography or history, preferably a work the class has already read from. We would ask students to ascertain the relationship the biographer or the historian had to the subject he wrote about, both his relationship as an individual and as a man of a certain age, society, milieu. After these matters were discussed and understood, the class would then examine portions of the biography or the history to discover how these relationships affected the work.

A *second* way to deepen this course is by the *comparative study of two treatments of history (or biography)*: the narrative and the critical. The selections in our previous lists are nearly all narrative treatments, for this *is* the kind of history and biography that excites beginning readers. But some students might now enjoy comparing a chapter or a section of a narrative history or biography with a critical treatment of the same era or person. They might compare, for instance, Henry Adams' chapter "The Inauguration" in Book I of his *History* with the paragraphs on Jefferson as the new president on pages 271–272, Volume 7, of Justin Winsor's *Narrative and Critical History of America*. Or they might compare those portions of chapters 2, 5, and 6 that discuss the Louisiana negotiations, in Book II of Adams' *History* with the paragraphs about the same issue on pages 272–273, Volume 7, of Winsor's *History*. The excerpts from Winsor's *History* should, of course, include the footnotes and the relevant parts of his critical essay on page 296 and following, Volume 7. Through such comparative study, students will see that the differences in these two types of history are not differences in the historian's writing ability or in his competence in research—as many students initially suppose. They will see that the differences are caused by the differences in the intentions of the two writers and in what each intention entails.

The two types of deepening we have just described would be especially appropriate for competent students. Either kind of study might be done by a whole class or by a few able students within a class. The following—*third*—alternative would be appropriate for either able or average students. It would simply allow them a greater insight into a biographer's sources and into how he takes full advantage of what they allow. The students would first examine a biographer's account of the writing of a certain biography and then read the biography that resulted. Class discussions would focus on the biographer's freedom and discipline in the use of sources. Appropriate materials for such a study would be, for instance, Catherine Drinker Bowen's twenty-eight page account of the writing of the life of John Adams, *The Writing of Biography,* and the finished biography, *John Adams and the American Revolution.*

So much for ways of deepening our basic study of biography and history. Now we shall describe two general ways of *broadening* it that would be appropriate for both average and able students.

We could follow the main study with *the reading of biographies that have no "public sources,"* sketches that interpret the lives of unimportant, unheroic people. We think of such profiles as: Donald Hall's "A Hundred Thousand Straightened Nails" in *String Too Short to be Saved;* Stephen Leacock's "My Remarkable Uncle" in *My Remarkable Uncle;* and James Thurber's "Snapshot of a Dog" in *The Middle-Aged Man on the Flying Trapeze.* Students might concentrate on the ways the interpretations in these sketches are rendered. Or they might compare these biographies with modern short stories, which in subject and in treatment these profiles seem to parallel closely. If students were interested in such comparison, they could consider, broadly, the similarities and the differences between these two forms, or they might focus, instead, on the effects produced on the forms by some one difference between them: for instance, the effect produced on the biography by the demand for truth, on the short story by the demand for credibility. If this were the focus, we might have as our general question something like this:

> What details of ["My Remarkable Uncle"] would be meaningless if the sketch were not "true"? What details of [naming a short story] would be unacceptable if it were "true"? What details do we accept in the true account that we would dismiss as "incredible" in fiction?

If this mode of broadening did not seem appropriate for a particular class, we could follow the main course in history and biography with *the reading of a diverse sample of autobiographical sketches or excerpts.* We refer to such personal records as the following:

Richard Henry Dana's "A Flogging at Sea" in *Two Years Before the Mast;* Loren Eiseley's "The Judgment of the Birds" in *The Immense Journey;* Paul Engle's "Iowa Christmas" in *Prairie Christmas;* Hamlin Garland's "The Homestead on the Knoll" and "Boy Life on the Prairie" (as far as "lords of the soil") in *A Son of the*

Middle Border; Maurice Herzog's "The Third of June" and "The Crevasse" in *Annapurna;* Harold Nicholson's "The Man Who Knew Everybody" and "Christmas Trees" in *Small Talk;* George Orwell's "A Hanging" and "Shooting an Elephant" in *Shooting an Elephant and Other Essays;* "The Quarles Episode" in Mark Twain's *The Autobiography;* E. B. White's "Once More to the Lake" in *One Man's Meat* and his "A Weekend With the Angels" and "Afternoon of an American Boy" in *The Second Tree from the Corner.*

These readings may be studied in various ways. For instance, a selection like Herzog's "The Third of June" might be paired with a good factual news account of the event or an historical record of it in order to emphasize how the author's telling his own story has affected not only the organization and the expression of the facts, but the facts themselves. A sketch like Engle's "Iowa Christmas" might be paired with a fictional first-person narration that has a similar central situation; for instance, Truman Capote's "A Christmas Memory" or Frank O'Connor's "Christmas Morning." Students will be struck by the similarities of the autobiography and the story. The question for them then is: What differentiates the story from the autobiography? If the works chosen for this exercise *are* as similar as the Engle-Capote (or O'Connor) readings, answering this question will really tax students' discrimination. This rather simple kind of task will be demanding enough for the best readers.

If we used either of the forms of broadening we have just described, then we would probably invite students to try their hands at writing biography or autobiography. For after a week's in-class study of the kinds of biographies or autobiographies we have cited, students would know that such writers do not "chronicle little episodes and encounters piecemeal, as mere anecdotes." They would know that these writers select, arrange, and express facts in a certain tone with a certain intention. So, by postponing the students' writing of biography or autobiography until now when they have read the form critically and understand what such a writer's "job of work" is, the teacher will have saved himself those birth-till-last-night chronicles that uninitiated writers mistake for biography and autobiography. The assignment for writing either form should ask students for a one- to two-page paper and should remind them that the art of biography consists in writing *imaginatively* about facts.

The five preceding proposals are, then, *some ways* to deepen and broaden the basic study of biography and history that we suggested as a second course. If the teacher chose not to give the extra *class* time that such "extensions" would require, then he might use *some* of the proposals as reading and writing assignments for certain individuals or *parts* of them as special exercises for certain classes. The actual assignments that the teacher devises from these proposals can be of varying difficulty and of any length, from brief tasks to papers of a few pages.

Novellas and Novels

And now, our last suggestion for the further study of fiction: the course that will introduce students to the reading of longer fiction. For some students a study of novellas and novels might follow the first course directly, but for others it might be preceded by one or more of the courses we have just described. Some classes *need* such interim courses; some would *enjoy* them as enriching interludes. But whether the course in the reading of the novel immediately follows the study of the short story, comes later the same year, or is postponed until the following year, it is a course that all students must *at some time* take.

The moral experience the novel expresses is more complex than that expressed by the short story. Consequently, in the novel there is a more complicated plot; there are more characters and more fully developed characters; setting is more detailed and more variously significant. In short, the work of fiction that renders a complex moral experience has to be more comprehensive, multi-faceted—and longer.

Reading a novel, then, means having a *unified* experience of a *long, involved* experience. The reader must be able to *perceive* each incident[43] and recognize how it functions in that chapter, in that part of the novel, and in the whole organization so far developed, and he must have this "vertical-horizontal" perception simultaneously and continually during the entire time he is reading the novel. Through his study of short stories, the reader has learned to perceive particular incidents, to recognize their function in a whole story, and to be aware of how various literary means work together to unify stories. Now, he must adapt these sensitivities, so that he can hold together in proper relationships the parts of a long, complicated, and often less apparently structured experience, as it gradually unfolds before him. And that is what, in *this* second course, we would try to help students learn to do.

From Short Fiction to Long: Three Proposals

Given this general aim for teaching novels, any one of three kinds of organizations seems usable. Students might make the transition from the short story to the "big" novel by easy stages,[44] beginning with the study of novellas and moving to the reading of novels of increasing lengths. Novellas like the following, which are both relevant to adolescent concerns and readable for students who have performed adequately in the first course, would be appropriate first readings: Stephen Crane's *The Open Boat* (thirty pages); Ernest Hemingway's *The Short Happy Life of Francis Macomber* (thirty-four pages); Joseph Conrad's *Youth* (thirty-five pages); Antoine de Saint-Exupéry's *Night Flight* (forty-four pages); Joseph Conrad's *The Secret Sharer* (forty-four pages); Katherine Anne Porter's *Noon Wine* (fifty-seven pages); Joseph Conrad's *Typhoon* (sixty pages); Henry James' *Daisy Miller* (seventy pages); Edith Wharton's *The Old Maid* (seventy-four pages); and Truman Capote's *The Grass Harp* (ninety-nine pages).

After the study of at least two such novellas, students would read a novel of fewer than two hundred pages. There is a fine variety to choose from: Walter Van Tilburg Clark's *The Ox-Bow Incident*, Stephen Crane's *The Red Badge of Courage*, Joseph Conrad's *Heart of Darkness* or his *The Nigger of the Narcissus*, William Faulkner's long version of *Spotted Horses*, F. Scott Fitzgerald's *The Great Gatsby*, Ernest Hemingway's *The Old Man and the Sea*, Henry James' *The Turn of the Screw*, Herman Melville's *Billy Budd, Fore-topman*, John Steinbeck's *The Pearl* or his *Cannery Row*, Thornton Wilder's *The Bridge of San Luis Rey*.

Following the reading of one or two novels of this length, the class would move on to the final stage: the reading of a long novel. Depending upon students' interest, they might read such classics as Emily Bronte's *Wuthering Heights*, Joseph Conrad's *Lord Jim*, Charles Dickens' *A Tale of Two Cities*, Thomas Hardy's *The Mayor of Casterbridge*, Nathaniel Hawthorne's *The Scarlet Letter*, Mark Twain's *Huckleberry Finn;* or they might read such long novels as John Knowles' *A Separate Peace*, Somerset Maugham's *The Razor's Edge*, Alan Paton's *Cry, the Beloved Country*.

For each of the three stages in the organization we have been outlining, we have suggested works that differ widely in literary complexity in order to emphasize that students *can* move to the reading of longer and longer works without *necessarily* being confronted at the same time with, say, more difficult patterns of narration. They may move, for instance, from the familiar chronological ordering of *The Open Boat* to the familiar chronological ordering of *The Nigger of the Narcissus;* students *need* not go from Crane's story to *The Great Gatsby* or to *The Bridge of San Luis Rey*. The teacher *may*, in other words, increase the reader's burdens one at a time. And with average and less able students this is probably what he would choose to do.

An organization such as the one we have been describing would *not*, in all likelihood, be taught as a single block of work. The study of each novella requires two to four classes; short novels, approximately eight to twelve classes; novels, probably twelve to fifteen classes. So such a scheme would most feasibly be taught over a period of a school year (or more) as two (or even three) separated but sequential units.

Now to the second of our proposals: a two-stage introduction to the reading of novels. Students would begin with the study of a short novel that is structured conventionally and narrated chronologically. But they would quickly move to the reading of two longer novels, works that have less apparent structures and less usual kinds of narration. We would choose from among episodic novels, dominantly scenic novels, stream-of-consciousness or digressive narrations —and novels that fuse two or more of these modes. This second scheme is appropriate for competent readers who need no transition from the short story to the novel and who can respond at once to increased length and less customary and more subtle formal features.

Either of the two schemes we have just outlined *may* follow directly after the first course or after one or more of the second courses we described earlier. This third scheme is designed to let the study of the novel grow "naturally" out of some one of the second courses in the short story. Thematic study, the study of one writer, and genetic study especially lend themselves to an unobtrusive transition to the reading of *longer* fiction. For example, in genetic study, the reading of fables might end with a reading of George Orwell's *Animal Farm* or John Steinbeck's *The Pearl;* the study of the tale, with Joseph Conrad's *The Nigger of the Narcissus* or W. H. Hudson's *Green Mansions;* the reading of character sketches, with Edith Wharton's *Ethan Frome,* and the yarn, with the *long* version of Faulkner's *Spotted Horses.*

All of the three organizations[45] we have just proposed will help students achieve the aim of this second course. They are feasible schemes, and they are also flexible ones. They are patterns to use, adapt, depart from—to vary in whatever way is necessary to help each class learn to read novels sensitively.

A Teaching of Conrad's *The Nigger of the Narcissus*

Now, we shall "get down to cases" and illustrate concretely and specifically how *we* would try to help students achieve this aim through the study of Conrad's *The Nigger of the Narcissus.*

We chose to use this novel as the illustration for several reasons; because it may be taught in any one of the three organizations we proposed; because it may be studied profitably by both average readers and able ones and, therefore, affords us an opportunity of showing how the same novel may be taught for the same aim **to** readers of different competence; and because we hope to add this fine, highly relevant novel to the high school "canon."

Like the teaching of a play, the teaching of a novel is the work of many class periods. It must go well. Consequently, before the teacher begins planning, he should read and reread the novel to discover what his *current* experience of it is, to see how the book is organized, to determine how long it takes *him* to read the work (a count of pages does not always tell that), and to identify potential sources of difficulty. If the teacher does this kind of assessment, he can arrive at a valid—and vital—specific aim; he can plan reading assignments that emphasize the organization of the novel, he can estimate realistically what this or that class *could* read carefully in a certain amount of time, and he can prepare so as to avert problems arising from students' lack of knowledge, from their disbelief, and from the intrusions of the irrelevant they so often allow.

Through such an assessment of Conrad's novel, we came to the following four decisions. First, we decided that the specific aim for the teaching of *The Nigger of the Narcissus* would be to help students see how the structure of the novel—the structure of particular incidents, of chapters, and of the book as a whole—defines the theme (which, to us, stated roughly is: the human character *is* paradoxical; men—"my brothers"—*are* at once fearful and courageous, honest and dissembling, fickle and faithful, and, out of egotism, both compassionate and arrogant. "Poor beggars!" Vanity is their "sin"; self-effacement, their redemption.) This specific aim *is* justifiable in terms of the general aim for the teaching of novels which we stated earlier, and it is usable for any class and in any of the three organizations we cited.

Secondly, we decided that, to achieve our specific aim, the reading assignments would have to be by chapters, and that, *preferably*, Chapters 2, 3, 4, and 5 as far as page 147 would be read within one school week. Each chapter is structured to suggest the theme, and the pattern of Chapters 2, 3, 4, and 5 taken together imply the theme "in large letters."

Thirdly, we recognized that an average or less able class would need about thirteen days to study the novel; an able class, about eight.

Finally, we decided that the reading of *Night Flight* and *The Secret Sharer* should probably precede the reading of *The Nigger of the Narcissus*. The Saint-Exupéry novella would prepare students to believe Captain Allistoun and understand his relation to the ship and the men. *The Secret Sharer* would ready them for Conrad's prose. Together, the study of these two books would take about six or seven days in the average class, about four or five in the able group. In addition to that kind of preparation, both classes would need maps, section drawings of a sailing ship like the Narcissus, and vocabulary glosses, all of which are explained briefly below.

Once these preliminary decisions were made, we developed the two teaching plans which follow.[46] All page references are to Joseph Conrad, *The Nigger of the Narcissus*, New York: Collier Books, 1962.

The Teaching Plan for Average and Less Able Students

■ *Wednesday: Preparation for Reading The Nigger of the Narcissus.* About fifteen to twenty minutes before the close of class, we would distribute duplicated copies of a sample map of the Bombay to London passage with a line showing the approximate course of the ship and copies of a section drawing of a ship the type of the Narcissus, with the parts labeled with the terms Conrad uses in the novel. As students examined the drawing, we would point out to them where the officers live, where the crew lives, where the captain spends his time, where the galley is—just the locations continually referred to in the book. And at this time we would recall to the students that ships sometimes list, why they do, and what happens when they do—how the ship looks, where the men rush (describing the scene very briefly using the data from the novel). All of our commentary would be confined to whatever will preclude confusion about, or undue attention to, certain events when they occur in the novel. Then, we would distribute duplicated copies of a list of terms that might distract or baffle readers. The list, which would be as brief as possible, would serve *as a gloss for the text*: words would be listed by pages (for instance, page 23: chief mate, boatswain, hands, muster, bight; page 24: annas, rupee, pice, toff, hooker; page 26: lanyard knot), and relevant definitions would be given. The copy would explain how the list should be used.

Finally, we would distribute copies of the Calendar that follows:

Wednesday	Plan of the ship, map, vocabulary lists distributed at the close of class. Assignment: Look carefully at these papers and check anything that needs clarifying.
First Day: Thursday	A study of Chapter 1, pp. 23–31. Study Guides for Chapter 1 distributed. Assignment: Complete the reading of Chapter 1 and the answering of the questions on the Study Guide.
Second Day: Friday	Discussion of Chapter 1. A study of Chapter 2, pp. 43–45. Study Guides for Chapter 2 distributed. Continue reading of Chapter 2.

	Assignment: Complete the reading of Chapter 2 and the answering of the questions on the Study Guide.
Third Day: Monday	Discussion of Chapter 2. A short in-class written exercise: papers will be graded. Study Guides for Chapter 3 distributed. Assignment: Read Chapter 3 and answer the questions on the Study Guide. Complete at least pp. 59–68, through "on a bough," before class tomorrow. Refer to plan of ship wherever necessary.
Fourth Day: Tuesday	Discussion of Chapter 3, pp. 59–68. Continue reading of Chapter 3. Assignment: Complete the reading of Chapter 3 and the answering of the questions on the Study Guide.
Fifth Day: Wednesday	Discussion of Chapter 3. Assignment: Out-of-class written exercise: papers *may* be graded. This is a short assignment because Chapter 4 is a long reading. So as soon as you finish your paper, begin reading Chapter 4. Try to finish fifteen pages of it.
Sixth Day: Thursday	Discussion of your answers to the homework question. A study of the opening of Chapter 4. Study Guides for Chapter 4 distributed. Continue reading of Chapter 4. Assignment: Complete the reading of Chapter 4 and the answering of the questions on the Study Guide.
Seventh Day: Friday	Discussion of Chapter 4. Assignment: Out-of-class written exercise; papers *may* be graded.
Eighth Day: Monday	Discussion of your answers to the homework question. A study of Chapter 5, pp. 129–130. Study Guides for Chapter 5 distributed. Continue reading of Chapter 5. Assignment: Complete the reading of Chapter 5 and the answering of the questions on the Study Guide.
Ninth Day: Tuesday	Discussion of Chapter 5. Assignment: Out-of-class written exercise: papers *may* be graded.

Tenth Day: Wednesday	Discussion of your answers to the homework question.
	Preparation of answers to questions chosen by class.
	Assignment: Complete the preparation for discussion tomorrow.
Eleventh Day: Thursday	Discussion of three or four of the questions prepared for today.
	Assignment: Full-period test tomorrow: three questions, two of which are essay type.
	Bring your book; you may want to refer to it. As usual, *no sharing of books allowed.*
Twelfth Day: Friday	Test.
	Assignment: One-page paper that evaluates some insight the novel expressed or implied. The paper *will* be graded.
Thirteenth Day: Monday	Reading and discussion of your papers.
	Return of tests.

This Calendar takes into account, we think, both the character of the aim and the character of the students. Because of the aim—to help students see how structure defines theme—we did not want the study of Chapters 2, 3, and 4 to be interrupted by a weekend. Discontinuous study of these chapters lessens the chances of *students' discovering* that the events are patterned to express the repeated alternation of the crew's responses. We would really have liked to have the class study Chapter 5 within the same week. But, because the students are average and less able (many of whom will also be unmotivated), we did not think it feasible. It would have meant increasing the size of the outside reading assignments, reducing in-class discussion, and omitting in-class reading. Such changes would bring losses. At worst, we might have to settle for a "plot" reading of the book. At best, we would be faced with unfinished assignments, carelessly done study guides, inattention in class. We may have some of these problems anyway, but at least we shall not be inviting them. We think that the Calendar we are proposing is "right" for average and less able students who need variety, instruction, confidence, "things to do," and in-school time to do them. We think that this schedule will allow these students to achieve the aim as economically as possible.

Before we begin to discuss particular lessons, it seems worthwhile to comment on certain teaching procedures mentioned on the Calendar, procedures necessitated by the character of the students that this plan is prepared for.

We notice, for instance, that students receive the study guides chapter by chapter. So although they may "read ahead" if they wish, they cannot complete the study guides days ahead. If average and less able students work out guides days in advance, *they* will not "refresh" the night before discussion. Work done is work done! By withholding the guides, we ensure that they will be worked on the day before discussion. This will give discussion *a chance* to be precise, vital, and meaningful.

Furthermore, we notice that the study guides are distributed *after* the teacher has completed any introductory work he thinks necessary (see the First, Second, Sixth, and Eighth Days, for instance). No procedure can ensure that students *will* be concentrating on what they should be, but this procedure will at least prevent them from being distracted by the next day's study guide.

Finally, we notice that the Calendar is very detailed. That is to preclude spending class time on such questions as: "Is it a test?" "How many questions?" "What kinds of questions?" "Is it going to be graded?" Not only does the Calendar tell students all this information, but it allows them to know it from the first day of the study of the novel. That obviates, "But I didn't know it might be marked" or "I didn't know the test was today." In classes like these where attention is likely to be intermittent and the sense of injustice is strong, it is best to have explicit, written directions. In classes like these where absence might be a common occurrence, a detailed Calendar saves the teacher from having to tell again and again during the study "what we did yesterday" or "what we handed out."

These procedures that we have been calling attention to may seem like trivial matters, but many an imaginative and feasible lesson has foundered because just such details were not taken into account and planned for. What irony! It is like drowning in a teacup.

Now, let us look at the lessons for the thirteen days' study of Conrad's novel. We assume class periods of fifty minutes' duration.

■ *First Day: Thursday.* We would read aloud, pages 23–31 as far as the muster, the students following in their texts. We would stop occasionally to ask questions. For instance, *after the first two pages:* What is going on as the story opens? What has gone on all day? What colors predominate? Who is saying all those remarks (page 24, paragraph 1)? And, *at the bottom of page 27* (at "ferocity"): How would you describe the scene in the forecastle? What sorts of men are introduced to you? What two are juxtaposed? What characteristics of Singleton are stressed? Do you usually associate those characteristics? How does the narrator explain the popularity of *Pelham?* How do we know how we should "take" Belfast? And then *on page 29* (at "Donkin"): Donkin says no more than Belfast. Why does the crew react so differently to Donkin? What is the narrator's tone as he describes Donkin as: "The pet of philanthropists and self-seeking landlubbers. The sympathetic and deserving creature that knows all about his rights . . ."? And then *on page 31* (at the muster): Why do the seamen help Donkin? What sentence tells the reader the reason? Whom are the seamen now behaving like? Who is not "conquered" by Donkin? Why does Donkin challenge the Finn?

At this point, we would assign the reading of the remainder of the chapter and hand out duplicated copies of the following study questions to be answered in writing.[47]

1. What color predominates in the image of the bay? What color is it relieved by? What color predominates in the forecastle? What is it relieved by? What connotations does each color have? What is suggested by using them together?

2. The roll-call is only a check-in for the crew. But what is suggested by the way the narrator describes it on page 32?

3. Why do the crew *now* react as they do to Donkin?

4. What things make James Wait dramatic? What uses does he make of his voice? What does "misapprehend" mean?

5. What image comes out of the dark to Mr. Creighton? How does this image characterize him? Notice the color of the image. In what senses does it relieve the darkness?

6. Notice Wait's response to Donkin (page 38). In what ways does it differ from the response of the rest of the crew to Donkin (pages 28–30)? Can you surmise *any reason* for this difference?

7. Wait's outstanding characteristic is his voice. What is Singleton's chief characteristic? What *might* these characteristics suggest? What is suggested by Singleton's position in the doorway? by Wait's on the chest?

8. What is the function of this chapter?

9. When Wait asks Singleton about the "kind of ship this is," Singleton replies, "Ship! . . . Ships are all right. It is the men in them!" (page 39) From the way they reveal themselves *in this chapter,* how would you characterize the men in *this* ship?

On this first day, the questioning both in class and on the guide aims to help students become acclimated to the mode of narration and attentive to the nature of the crew and to the function of the black-and-white imagery. The questioning is close because we want students to have a firm foothold.

▪ *Second Day: Friday.* Students would spend *approximately* the first twenty minutes of class answering three questions, the first two of which would be questions 8 and 9 from the study guide. (These are "right" questions to start with. For, many of the questions students have answered both in class on Thursday and on the homework guide prepare them for answering these. Furthermore, since questions 8 and 9 are general questions, we can tell quickly from the quality of students' responses to them which specific questions, if any, we need to return to.)

During the answering of question 9, it may be advisable to use the board to help students see how the characters group and what the nature of each group is. As we jot down students' comments on the crew, the board will show the class the different *kinds* of "wise men" the crew includes; and it will reveal the vacillating, egotistical, jovial, naive nature of the largest group and the "tale-hero" quality of James Wait. With these notes before the students, we would then ask: Do you see any relation between the black-and-white imagery and the character of the crew?

Once students have had this good view of the men in the ship, we would turn, as the novel does, to the ship. And we would spend the next ten to fifteen minutes reading aloud pages 43–45 as far as "fleeting dream" (stressing rather dramatically paragraph 1, page 45) and questioning crisply to make sure that the students understand how they are to think of the Narcissus and of the action they are about to experience:

Now at last you see the ship. What image does the word "Narcissus" suggest to you? What is happening when you get the first glimpse of the ship? Why do you suppose you are shown the ship *at that moment?* What are we to think of the ship *as?* Now that you know this, what added meaning does Singleton's comment on ships and men have? What is a "passage"? How does it differ from a "journey"?

For the last ten to fifteen minutes of the class period, students would continue the reading of the chapter, pages 45–58, to be completed for Monday. These are the study questions they would answer in writing.

1. Notice the details that describe the captain. What two or three qualities would you, therefore, say he had?

2. The men are relaxing when Wait appears. How does his entrance affect them? Why do they respond to him that way? How does Donkin respond to him? What lets you know how the narrator feels about Wait?

3. What metaphors does the narrator use to define Wait's relationship to the crew? (See, for instance, page 49.) How did Chapter 1 prepare you for this relationship?

4. What specific incidents does the narrator use to show the uncertainty of the men about Wait? Who is not uncertain? Why not?

5. What two incidents startle James Wait? Why?

6. Why does the narrator bother to tell you how the "weird servitude" to Wait began?

7. Why does Donkin abuse Wait as he does? (Refer if necessary to pages 53–54.)

8. Why does Wait respond to Donkin's abuse as he does?

9. In what *many* ways has Wait "knocked discipline in the head"?

10. How does the *way the narrator* tells of the crew's uncertainty make you *experience* their believing now this, now that?

■ *Third Day: Monday.* The class would spend *about* a half hour discussing the response the men and the officers make to Wait's behavior. Depending upon how the class has been performing, we would conduct this discussion in one of two ways. If performance has been mediocre, we would simply have the class answer study guide questions 2, 3, 4, 6, 9, and then 7 and 8. If performance has been adequate-to-good, we would ask the class a general question that their work on the guide would have prepared them to answer: What response to Wait's behavior do the men and the officers make? As the class gradually shaped their answer, we would be both organizing their findings on the board and *probably* asking such questions as: Why can Donkin and Singleton act with certainty in this instance? What do they *know?* Then, What, in James Wait's reactions to them, make *us* sure that they are *both* right (he is a malingerer and he is dying)? Then, Why cannot the crew, of themselves, perceive either what Donkin knows *or* what Singleton knows? (And probably, What in this chapter or earlier suggests why?)

Whether we used the seven study guide questions or the one general question to discuss the reaction of the men to Wait's behavior, we would have the students spend the last ten to fifteen minutes of the period on a brief in-class exercise. It would be designed to show students that, in the crew's first "test," they revealed not only a character fault but some virtue too. We would introduce this exercise by reading with the class a passage from the last paragraph of the chapter (page 58): "He [Wait] overshadowed the ship. Invulnerable in his promise of speedy corruption he trampled on our self-respect, he demonstrated to us daily our want of moral courage; he tainted our lives." Then we would say to the students, In other words, the crew has not done very well with its first problem. The question you will answer is: Has Wait really *destroyed* the men? Defend your answer with evidence from the text.

For tomorrow, students must read Chapter 3, pages 59–68 through "bough" and write answers to study questions 1–7. For Wednesday, they must have completed the reading of Chapter 3 and the answering of questions 8–22. Following is the entire study guide for Chapter 3.

Note: Check the map to see where the ship is at this point. Have the section drawing of the ship on hand, so that you can refer to it if necessary during your reading of Chapter 3.

1. Who was the main character in Chapter 2? Who seems to be the main character in pages 59–66?

2. You know how most of the crew feel toward James Wait. What is their feeling toward the Narcissus? (Jot down phrases from the text.) Why are you told where she was "born"? Whose fault is her "only fault"?

3. Think of the men at the end of Chapter 2. Now, what effect has the plight of the Narcissus had on them?

4. Why *wouldn't* the captain notice the ship was "losing heart"?

5. How does the narrator make you *feel* the anxiety of the men during the stormy night (pages 63–64)?

6. What exactly happens during the "untrustworthy lull"?

7. What does the crew's echoing the captain's "No! No!" signify?

8. How would you describe the crew's behavior, pages 68–71?

9. Why do they, just then, think of Jimmy? What is significant about *those* five men going to get him?

10. What features make the rescue a kind of comedy? How, for instance, do the men think of their work at the carpenter's shop? Why would the men treat this incident comically? (Notice, for instance, the comic ironies in it.)

11. Why does Wait behave as he does? Under the circumstances of his rescue, why does he *have to* say what he does on pages 77–78?

12. Why *do* the men go to rescue Wait?

13. What reason does the narrator give for their taking such care of him? Would their hate of Wait be a reason for their special care? They hate Donkin. They saved him, but pummelled him. Why do they treat the hated Wait tenderly?

14. What are their *real* reasons for their treatment of Wait?

15. How long are the men lashed to the deck?

16. How does their state of mind change during that time?

17. What incidents boost morale during the long vigil? Why do they?

18. What incident *seems* to lower morale?

19. How do the forces of nature seem to mock this "little world" and its "people" during the long vigil?

20. What keeps the men alive? What sustains the captain?

21. How can these weary men rouse themselves to such vigorous action (pages 87–90)?

22. In the preface to this novel, Conrad says, "My task which I am trying to achieve . . . see" (page 19). Cite one passage from this chapter that makes you "hear and feel and see." How (*not* why) does the passage produce that effect?

■ *Fourth Day: Tuesday.* For the first ten minutes (not much more), we would read (or have the appropriate students read) the "best" answers to the exercise done at the close of class yesterday. This review can be done quickly because, of course, students' reading of pages 59–68 has already confirmed concretely that the men were not "destroyed" by Wait, only "overshadowed" and "tainted" as the quote we cited earlier *and* the men's behavior at the end of Chapter 2 suggest.

We would spend the next ten minutes making sure that everyone is clear about what happened on the ship, pages 59–68. We *might* begin, for instance, with question 1 from the guide; then ask in succession, What signals the coming of dangerous weather? What is the ship's "fault"? What happens on the thirty-second day out of Bombay? What are the men so anxious about all night? and conclude with questions 6 and 7 from the guide.

During the last half-hour of the period, the class would continue the reading of Chapter 3 and the answering of the guide questions. Both must be completed for tomorrow.

■ *Fifth Day: Wednesday.* The class would spend most of the period discussing how the men responded to their ordeal with the ship, how their present behavior differs from their behavior in Chapter 2, and whether the apparent change in behavior is real. If the performance of the class has been adequate up to now, we would probably ask only three questions: How would you describe the men's behavior during their ordeal with the ship? In what ways is this behavior different from their behavior in Chapter 2? Have they now changed into self-possessed, resolute, unwavering men? If students' performance has been only mediocre, we would begin by having the class answer questions 1, 2, 3, 4, 7, 8, 16, 17, 18, 20, and 21 from the study guide. These answers would reveal, in short, that in this ordeal the men—with the exception of Donkin—had shown themselves to be manly, courageous, resolute, enduring, good-humored, self-effacing, self-possessed, and loyal to their duty. Then, we would ask: In what ways is this behavior different from their behavior in Chapter 2? And then, Have they now changed into resolute, self-possessed, unwavering men? To answer that, the students might need to return to the study guide to review their answers to questions 12, 13, 14, and 18.

As soon as the third general question *is* answered, we would hand out the following duplicated assignment to be done for tomorrow, Thursday:

Conrad thinks that the same men can be both resolute and wavering, fearful and brave, wise and foolish, self-respecting and subservient. He suggests this by the way he orders the incidents in Chapter 3. (Notice, for instance, how the men behave, pages 59–70; then, 71–78; then 79–82; and 83; and 84–90). *How* does his ordering of incidents suggest that men can have at once contradictory qualities?

A class that had been performing adequately would get the same written assignment, except for the parenthetical material. No class should be given more help than it manifestly needs.

At the close of class we would remind the students to begin the reading of Chapter 4, a long chapter, and advise them to finish fifteen pages at least—in their own best interests.

■ *Sixth Day: Thursday. After* students have handed in their homework papers, we would have the class discuss the answer to the question. At this point, the relevance of the answer to the discussion of the novel is greatest; and students' interest in the answer is highest. But a brief ten-minute discussion will suffice and satisfy.

The remainder of the class period belongs to Chapter 4. Because average and less able students might find paragraph 1 of the chapter baffling, we would read it aloud, the students following, and we would try to elucidate the meaning by stressing certain elements in the reading, by clarifying the syntax as we go, and by re-creating the tone. When we finished the reading, we would ask quickly: What does "reprieve" mean? What must men reprieved by the sea do? How is this hard, unceasing work to be thought of? How does the narrator feel about those who demand an easy, restful life? Has this view been voiced before? *Has* hard work been "good" for the men? Keep the paragraph in mind. We shall return to it later.

Now we would hand out the guides for Chapter 4, assign the chapter for tomorrow, and speed the readers on their way. It is a long chapter, but it is the *only* long reading students have been asked to do. We warned them about it on the Calendar; we reiterated our warning yesterday. And now they *do* have twenty-five minutes to continue—or begin. Despite all warning some *will* be just beginning.

These are the study guide questions.

1. Is there any gap in time between the end of Chapter 3 and the beginning of Chapter 4?
2. For what reasons does the captain want Mr. Baker to keep the men "on the move"?
3. The men are exhausted. Why do they keep working?
4. How does the Narcissus respond to their efforts? Earlier, how did they respond to her efforts?
5. In this story Donkin and Singleton have frequently been juxtaposed. Why are they juxtaposed here (pages 95–97)?
Note: Check your map to see where the ship is now.
6. Why does Donkin "fascinate" the men? What is the effect of his influence?
7. What earlier "fascination" does this recall? In what ways are the two similar? In what ways are they different?
8. Read pages 99–101 as far as the word "skippers." What attitude is the narrator expressing?
9. What "use" does Donkin try to make of Jimmy? What two things hinder his succeeding?

10. Why does Jimmy *at this point* tell his secret to Donkin? Does he trust Donkin?

11. Notice the description of Jimmy in the dark (page 102) that precedes his disclosure to Donkin. Now notice the moment of delirium (page 108) that follows his disclosure. *How* do these two moments suggest the *reason* for his disclosure?

12. What is the narrator's attitude toward the missionary cook?

13. Why does the cook's "sermon" upset Jimmy so much? What remarks earlier in the book upset him in a lesser, but similar, way? Why do such remarks upset him more now?

14. How do you know, despite the captain's remarks about "shamming," that *he* knows the truth about James Wait?

15. How can James Wait be "the fit emblem" of *all* their aspirations? What two things check the uprising on deck?

16. You have read the scene of Singleton and the crew and that of the captain and the crew. In what ways are these scenes *parallel*?

■ *Seventh Day: Friday.* Students would spend about a half-hour of the class period discussing the response of the men to Donkin's behavior. As in previous instances, the recent performance of the class would determine whether we conducted this discussion by staying close to the questions and answers of the study guide or by asking general questions that the work on the guide prepared students to answer. The general questions would probably be: Donkin has been preaching his doctrines intermittently all through the trip. How have they been received? (If it seemed more economical of time, we probably would cite the occasions and let students recall the crew's responses.) Why, then, *at this point* in the trip, is he listened to? In what instances does it seem that he might prevail? How does James Wait figure in these instances? Why, in each instance, does Donkin not prevail? Is James Wait in any way involved? (If necessary, we would be more direct: Let us consider four instances in which Donkin is checked and see why: pages 104–106, 116–117, 120–121, 124–126.)

In the discussion it will become clear that Donkin is abetted by such things as the men's conceit, their leisure, their folly, their human love of ease, their self-seeking, their lack of realism, and their uncertainty about James Wait. And it will also become clear that Donkin is undermined not only by the sea, the Narcissus, the men's sense of duty to the ship, and their certainty about Wait, but also by such qualities as their common sense and their humor (Knowles) and their fairness (Archie), by their respect for the wisdom of experience, for practicality and for disinterested concern (as shown by their response to Singleton), and by their admiration for keen insight and utter fearlessness (as shown by their response to the captain).

If the class is not "up to" answering general questions, we can evoke substantially the same understanding of the men's response to Donkin as we have just outlined by having students answer study guide questions 6, 9, 14, 15, and 16.

However we had conducted the discussion of the men's response to Donkin's behavior, at the conclusion we would hand out the assignment for Monday:

Write a well-considered answer to this question: How do the incidents in this chapter suggest that conflicting character qualities coexist in the same men?

This assignment would *not* be further detailed or explained.

During the last fifteen minutes of the period, we would concentrate on the *apparent* contradiction of the truths about James Wait. We would ask quickly: What has Donkin's opinion of Wait always been? What has Singleton's been? Are they both right? *Is* he *at the same time* both "shamming" and dying? Was he earlier both "shamming" and dying? Such questioning leads us directly into Chapter 5.

■ *Eighth Day: Monday.* The class period would begin with about a fifteen-minute discussion of students' answers to the assignment question.

Then, we would turn to Chapter 5, reading pages 129–130 aloud, stressing the oppositions that are reconciled and asking: Why are the men "disenchanted philosophers?" In what sense had "Falsehood triumphed"? Who was the first to cooperate in Jimmy's cowardly pretension? Why did he?

Then, we would continue reading, asking *rhetorically* questions that will be on the study guide for tomorrow:

1. What are the reasons for the men's cooperating in Jimmy's pretension? What are the results?

2. What is the meaning of the sentence, "Through him . . . meaning of life" (page 130)?

3. What lets you know the narrator's attitude toward their cooperation, its reasons, and its results?

4. Singleton and Donkin do not cooperate in Wait's self-deception. What are their reasons? What courses of action do they take?

5. The narrator uses several means to let the reader see the true character of Donkin's visit to Jimmy. For instance, he shapes the incident so that it is partially parallel with previous incidents. What previous incidents? How does this incident differ from the others? How do the contrasts make us see this incident in its true light?

6. What are the results of Donkin's course of action? Think in terms of Jimmy, of Donkin, of the men, of the ship. Are the results good or bad? Compare them with the results of the earlier actions of the captain and the other crewmen.

7. Why is the burial treated with comic irony?

8. What function does the conversation among the boatswain, the carpenter, and the sailmaker serve? If necessary, look at page 48.

9. Look carefully at the images of the Narcissus and the metaphors used on pages 147–150. What impression of the Narcissus' homecoming do the images and metaphors evoke? Why do we hear nothing of the men during this period?

10. What earlier incident does the homecoming recall? If necessary, look at pages 43–44. What incident does the docking recall? And what incident does the assembly of the crew at the pay table recall? If necessary, look at pages 24–33. What does this partial similarity suggest? Except for time and place, *is* everything "right back where it started from"?

■ *Ninth Day: Tuesday.* The first half of the discussion would center on three questions: What were the responses to Wait's deception? What were the reasons for these responses? What were the results of the responses? (In general, these are questions 1, 2, 4, and 6 from the guide.) We would scheme the three answers on the board so that the interrelation of good and evil can be graphically seen— so that, for instance, students can see that the captain's support of Wait's deception was given on a moment's impulse out of human pity, and it touched off both the mates' admiration of the Captain's humanity and a near mutiny, which, in turn, elicited just and courageous action.

With the data on the board, we would ask: What is suggested by the ways good and evil are interrelated? How does the narrator make us feel that some of these "tainted" actions are more redeeming than others? some more ruthless than others? some more foolish? (We would refer students, if necessary, to page 119 and to their answers to questions 5 and 7 on the guide.) In what other instances in the book has evil come from good? good from evil? At what other time has the men's latent egotism been the motivation for compassion?

As an assignment for Wednesday, we would ask students to do an out-of-class written exercise that would pull the book together in some *one way*. We could use *one* of the following tasks. The first is for a less imaginative, hard-working class.

In their passage from Bombay to London, the men of the Narcissus are faced with various "tests."

1. Lists the tests in the order of their occurrence.

2. In what way or ways are these tests related to one another? For instance, are they all tests of courage? Are they in an order of difficulty?

3. List the responses that the men make to the tests.

4. In what way or ways are these responses related to one another? For instance, are the men strong in some ordeals, weak in others? Do the men change? learn from experience?

From doing this work, you now can see a pattern of tests and a pattern of responses. What do these patterns reveal to you about the men on the Narcissus? Answer this question in a one- to two-page paper. Hand in the preliminary work with your paper.

Here is a harder task—a topic for a class that has done well.

Conrad says that art tries to render, as perfectly as possible, the world we know by revealing "the truth, manifold and one," underlying every aspect. In what ways does this book reveal *"the truth, manifold and one"*?

Consider the organization of various incidents, of chapters, and of the whole book. Consider the way characters are "built up." Consider the sea images, the description of the landship (page 148). Then, when you have organized your position, write a one- to two-page paper that answers the question. [In our statement of this topic, we would offer students only as many hints on what to consider as we felt would be needed by the particular class.]

Here is another challenging topic.

Many times in the novel we see the "dark seamen" moving in light. They are "lurching" out of it (page 31) and passing through it—from shadows into shadows (page 32); they are "vanishing out of the light" (page 106), "swinging across the light" (page 114), and, finally, at the close (page 155), "The dark knot of seamen drifted in sunshine." That is our last glimpse of them before they "drift" out of sight.

Write a paper of a page or two that points out what these images symbolize. [If we wanted to make the exercise much easier, we would word it: Write a paper of a page or two that points out how these images symbolize the experiences of the crew during their passage on the Narcissus. The particular kind of act the verb expresses is part of the image, remember.]

Here is another easy exercise.

In this novel, men are assaulted by two general kinds of evil, human and natural. Men seem to be able to overcome natural evil, but not human evil. Think over the novel and decide in how far you think this statement is true. Write a paper of a page or two that first tells in *one* or *two* sentences what your reaction to the statement is and then defends your view with concrete evidence.

■ *Tenth Day: Wednesday.* We would spend a half-hour or so discussing the answers to whatever exercise the class had done.

Then, we would distribute the list of questions which follows, give the class time to read the questions over, to talk them over, and to agree on *five* for discussion on Thursday. During the last ten minutes, students would begin preparing answers to the questions chosen.

This is not a review for the test. But the preparation and the discussion of answers to any of the following questions, excepting question 8, will revitalize much that the class has considered during its study of the novel and will, furthermore, call attention to significant elements that might have been overlooked. We have tried to devise questions that will force students not only to think about the novel as a whole again and again but also to concentrate on unifying designs *other than* the one we have stressed in our study. This will, we hope, correct any narrow notions about what unifies a novel that our stress on one unifying feature might have engendered.

These are the questions:

1. What relationship is there between the weather and the men's behavior?

2. (a) Does the narrator's attitude remain the same all through the novel? Explain. (b) Why is it important for us to think of the narrator as a member of the crew?

3. One of the unifying features of this novel is the natural unity of "the passage." In what ways is this an appropriate unity for the human experience that the novel renders? (More appropriate, say, than a "journey" or a "quest"?)

4. Which characters in this novel are incorrupt? Which are purely corrupt? Which characters are *almost* purely evil? Which of all these characters seem(s) almost unreal? Why does Conrad make this (these) characters(s) seem almost unreal?

5. *By what means* is the opposition between James Wait and the Narcissus made clear to the reader? [We chose the word "means" because, since it may be construed as a singular or as a plural, it does not give the readers any clue. They must see for themselves that Conrad suggests this opposition in many different ways.]

6. James Wait is obviously more than James Wait. From the time he enters, we know that he symbolizes something. Show how various features of the story—for instance, events, foils, images, metaphors—suggest to us gradually what he does symbolize.

7. Why is it appropriate for the book to be titled *The Nigger of the Narcissus*, instead of *James Wait?*

8. *How* does Conrad make the reader "see" in the following passages:

> the arrival of James Wait, pages 34–35
> the forecastle on the stormy night, pages 63–64
> the righting of the ship, pages 89–90
> Allistoun quelling the mutiny, pages 124–125
> the death of Wait, page 139
> the Narcissus entering the chops, page 147

Choose *one or two* of the preceding passages or propose others you prefer to examine.

9. Conrad distinguishes the "the children of the sea" from those of the land (pages 46, 152–156). How do these differences account for the downfalls of the crew? Do "simple hearts" always succumb?

10. You recall the "recognitions" we noticed when we read [naming short stories the particular class has read]. Are there any important "recognitions" in this novel?

■ *Eleventh Day: Thursday.* The class would discuss three or four of the five questions chosen.

At the close of class, we would warn students to bring books tomorrow. "The test is open-book; no sharing of books permitted."

■ *Twelfth Day: Friday.* Full-period test on the novel. This is, of course, only one of several evaluations. There have been the marked exercises, as well as the many discussions.

The following test has three questions rather than one. Average and less able students need variety *and* three chances to succeed. They also need an opening question that will allow everyone an opportunity to get underway immediately and successfully. The opening question that follows, with its multiple parts, its choice, and its relatively easy items, will, we think, answer their need.

FINAL TEST ON CONRAD's *The Nigger of the Narcissus*

I. (*10 minutes*)

Choose *three* of the following items. *On this paper* point out *in brief notes* in what *way* each of the items you choose expresses the view of human nature the novel suggests.
1. With Belfast, "it was a tear and a blow."
2. Singleton was reading *Pelham.*
3. The white hail was "round and gleaming in the murky turmoil like a shower of pearls."
4. "As long as she swims, I will cook!"
5. Wait stuck to his "unmanly lie" manfully.

II. (*25 minutes*)

Chapter 3 in the novel renders life during the storm.

When we begin to read Chapter 4, we find that the first seven and one-half pages (pages 91–96) *still* render life during the storm. But the remainder of Chapter 4 concerns other events.

Point out as fully and specifically as you can what is gained by this organization of the chapters. [This question is *not* a repetition of the topic of the paper assigned on the Seventh Day. Rather, students' work on that paper would, with other things, prepare them for doing this question.]

III. (*15 minutes*)

[The question that would appear here would be *the* question that was *not* discussed in class on Thursday, the fifth one that students chose from the list. Since the class was supposed to have worked on answers to all five on Wednesday night, the question could now be answered in fifteen minutes' time. We would not allow the using of *notes*.

If only three of the five questions had been discussed on Thursday, we would offer a choice of the remaining two. Of course, *if* question 8 had been chosen by a class, we would have answered that on Thursday.]

As students turned in their exam papers, we would hand out the assignment for Monday: the writing of a one-page paper in which students may evaluate *one* of the insights of the novel. We withheld this assignment until now because, of course, we did not want students to confuse experiencing a novel with evaluating its insights.

This is the assignment as the students would receive it.

Evaluating an Insight

During the reading of *The Nigger of the Narcissus,* you undoubtedly noticed insights into human behavior—either stated or implied—that you agreed with only partially, or that you disagreed with entirely, or that you felt to be deeply true.

For instance, when you read page 53, you probably asked yourself: Is it true that when men are extremely provoked, they will be just? And when you read page 30, you may have wondered: Are people charitable because they are egotistical? Is this really so?

Choose some one insight into human behavior that *for some reason* you reacted to strongly and, in a *one-page* paper, discuss its truth, its partial truth, or its falsity.

[We offer the sample questions mainly to help *dull* students.]

■ *Thirteenth Day: Monday.* Students would read and discuss their papers for about thirty to thirty-five minutes. To get things going in a productive direction, we would plan to open the period with the paper of some student we were fairly sure had written a careful and productive essay. And then, we "could go on from there."

During the last fifteen minutes of the period, we would answer the test questions, offering for questions II and III several very good answers from students' papers. Or if there were no answers of that quality (there usually are), we would offer as definitive answers as we thought, after such a study, any really good student *could* have given. We would jot on the board the key points of both answers; show why any *prevalent* mistakes were erroneous; solicit questions on the answers we detailed, and announce the value of each answer —probably 20%, 50%, 30%. *Then,* we would return the papers. This order of procedure keeps students' attention on the answers to the questions. A test review should be a learning experience, not a haggle over grades.

As we returned the papers, we would ask students to go over them carefully, in the light of our review, and if they have any generally relevant questions on the answers, to introduce them at the opening of class tomorrow. (Other particular, personal questions on tests would be discussed on makeup night or at some other mutually convenient time.)

If we decided not to spare class time for the review of a test, we would duplicate answers to the questions (as suggested in the preceding comments), show the values of each answer, and hand out these sheets with the graded test papers at the close of class. The students could go over the papers themselves, and raise generally relevant questions on the following day. (An overnight "cooling-off" greatly improves any discussion of tests!)

The Teaching Plan for Competent Readers

We have been describing one way of teaching Conrad's *The Nigger of the Narcissus* to average and less able students. Now, we shall suggest one way of teaching it to competent readers.

We would give an able class the same "hand-outs"—the map, the plan of the ship, the specialized vocabulary lists—and the same preliminary readings, but we would spend only two days on the study of *Night Flight* and three on *The Secret Sharer*. Able readers could study the novel itself more rapidly too, so our Calendar for such a class would be as follows:

Last Twenty Minutes: Friday	Distribute the "hand-outs" and the Calendar. Assignment: Read Chapters 1 and 2.
First Day: Monday	Class study of Chapters 1 and 2. Distribute Continuing Questions. Assignment: Read Chapter 3.
Second Day: Tuesday	Class study of Chapter 3. In-class marked exercise. Assignment: Read Chapter 4.
Third Day: Wednesday	Class study of Chapter 4. Assignment: Read Chapter 5.
Fourth Day: Thursday	Class study of Chapter 5. In-class marked exercise. Assignment: Complete Continuing Questions 1, 2, and 3 for discussion.
Fifth Day: Friday	Discuss Questions 1, 2, and 3. Assignment: Complete Continuing Questions 4 and 5 for discussion.
Sixth Day: Monday	Discuss Questions 4 and 5. Assignment: In-class full-period test (open book).
Seventh Day: Tuesday	Test. Assignment: Free paper.

Eighth Day: Wednesday   Discuss free papers [if the class cares to
                             do so].

We would be prepared to spend an extra day both on the class
study of the text and on the discussion of the Continuing Questions.
The extra days may be necessary, for, though competent students do
work quickly and intensively in class, they also treat questions more
thoroughly and often more imaginatively.

For an able class, the aim for the study of this novel would be
different from the one we used for the average and less able readers.
It would be more inclusive. In the less competent class, we emphasized only *one* of the designs of the novel, and we looked back
briefly at other unities *after* the reading was over. In an able class,
the study of the novel would emphasize *throughout* how *many*
different unifying designs—the structure of events, the setting, the
"passage" motif, the character unities, the tone of the narrator—work
together to render the theme.

And able students would be expected to discover, virtually on
their own, the presence of these designs and their interrelationships.
For in such a class, *we* would call students' attention to these features only during the class study of the first two chapters. As the
Calendar shows, when the in-class study of those chapters was completed, we would distribute the following Continuing Questions
which the students would then work on independently all through
the study of the novel.

These are the Continuing Questions as the students would receive
them:

CONTINUING QUESTIONS

Keep these questions in mind throughout your reading of the novel.
As you read each chapter, make notations on any material that seems
relevant to answering the questions. After you finish reading the novel,
organize your materials into well-written answers to the questions. Have
the answers ready on the days the Calendar indicates.

1. How does structure help to define theme in this novel? (For instance, How does the over-all structure define it? How does the structure
of Chapter 4 define it? How does the structure of the incident recounted
in Chapter 4, pages 114–118 define it? These are just examples of the
kinds of things your answer should take into account.)

2. Why is "passage" a more appropriate natural unity for the experience this novel renders than, say, "journey" or "quest"?

3. How does setting function in rendering theme? [We would expect
such students to deal with weather, seasons, times of day, and the kind
of "society."]

4. Clarify as specifically and definitively as you can the function(s)
of James Wait.

5. Why doesn't the change in point of view disunify this novel? What are the thematic advantages in the use of the participant-narrator?

During the in-class study of the novel, we would ask many of the questions listed on the guides we detailed earlier, amplifying and deepening as it seemed appropriate. For example, *during the in-class study of Chapters 1 and 2* we would be preparing students to work precisely and imaginatively on the Continuing Questions, which they will soon receive. So, when we discussed the crew's responses to Donkin, for instance, we would question to bring out graphically the conflict in the crew's reactions to him (their perceptiveness and the egotism that blinds them, their indifference to his radical remarks and their applause of his defiance). This would alert students to the tensions among the crew and within the crewmen themselves—tensions that the structure of the novel reflects (Continuing Question 1). When we discussed the ship as "world," we would highlight the literal and figurative meaning of "passage" (Continuing Question 2). And when we discussed "light and dark" imagery, we would call attention to such features as light Singleton and dark Wait, to the dark night of the opening and the bright day of the sailing (Continuing Question 3). We would ask about the social expectations of a ship's community (what "shipmate" means and what the unspoken agreements of such a unit are) so that students would have a context in which to understand not only the character of Wait's behavior but also some of the reasons for the crew's kindness and for their annoyance (Continuing Question 3). In addition to the study guide questions on Wait, (see First and Second Days of the preceding plan) we would probably ask: What is suggested by his entering "aft"? by the fact that he enters late? and alone? by the shadows and the lights of his face? by his tremendous height? by his style of language? by the meanings of "Wait"? We would probably stress, more than the guide questions do, both Wait's isolating himself immediately and continually from the social community of the crew and the difference between his isolation and, say, Donkin's or Allistoun's or Singleton's (Continuing Question 4). Finally, our questions would call attention to the two narrative points of view, to what is usually gained by each, and to the narrator's tone at various points in Chapters 1 and 2 (Continuing Question 5). This is enough to indicate the ways we would prepare an able class for productive independent work on this novel.

Our in-class study of Chapters 3, 4, and 5 would be, in general, a rapid-fire questioning aimed at clearing up difficulties, noticing elements that apparently are being overlooked, and elucidating functions and relationships. This kind of class study might obliquely or even directly at times enlighten the students' work on the Continuing

Questions, but there would be *no* discussion of the Questions until after students had completed their work on them.

Here are samples of the kinds of papers we would assign to a competent class:

In-Class Marked Exercises (ten to fifteen minutes)

FOR TUESDAY   Why do the men rescue Wait? [We could expect these students to offer reasons that take into account when the rescue takes place, who goes for Wait, how the event is rendered—in other words, we would expect these students to offer all the "reasons" and the *real* reasons.] FOR THURSDAY   In what ways is the epilogue paralleled with the prologue? Why is it paralleled?

Open-Book In-Class Test for the Second Tuesday (fifty minutes)

Do *one* of the following questions:

1. In many of Conrad's novels characters undergo an experience that evokes a "recognition." What are the "recognitions" in this novel? Do they induce a *change* of any kind? In a well-integrated paper tell how the handling of "recognition" in this novel helps to define the theme.

2. At the opening of Chapter 4 (page 91), the narrator suspends his storytelling to comment. This paragraph of commentary is almost in the middle of the novel. Is the paragraph a statement of theme? Defend your answer.

Final Paper on the Novel—Due on the Second Wednesday

[This assignment would be given to these students as soon as the class study of the text is over, Thursday, or possibly Friday.]

This is an "open paper." It may be your evaluation of the truth of some expressed or implied insight in the novel. Or it may be a critical paper of some kind; for instance, an interpretation of some part of the text we did not deal with specifically or of some part that you can show we did not read adequately. It may be an evaluation of a criticism (see page 158 for some studies of this novel) or an analysis of a passage to show *how* Conrad makes us "see." Finally, the paper may be a creative one. Writer's choice!

The paper should not be more than two pages long.

NOTES

1. Eudora Welty, *Three Papers on Fiction* (Northampton, Mass.: Smith College Pamphlets, 1962), p. 2.

2. Walter Allen, *Reading a Novel* (London: Phoenix House, Ltd., 1963), pp. 21–22.

3. Allen, *Reading a Novel,* p. 12.

4. Three useful discussions on this point are Phyllis Miletich's "An Ariadne's Thread to Theme and Its Interpretation," *EJ,* 55 (March 1966),

pp. 324 ff.; Bernard Peltzie's "Teaching Meaning Through Structure in the Short Story," *EJ*, 55 (Sept. 1966), pp. 703 ff.; and Sarah Youngblood's "Teaching a Short Story: Faulkner's 'Barn Burning,'" Kinescripts, Set I, Commission on English (New York: CEEB, 1965).

5. In *The Craft of Fiction*, pp. 14–19, (New York: The Viking Press, 1957), Percy Lubbock describes the usual experience of the reader of a novel at the end of the book: ". . . again and again, at this point, I make the same discovery; I have been watching the story, that is to say, forgetful of the fact that there was more for me to do than to watch receptively and passively, forgetful of the novel that I should have been fashioning out of the march of experience as it passed . . ." He goes on to describe the job of the *creative* reader.

6. Here I am generally following Mark Schorer (ed.), *The Story* (Englewood Cliffs, N. J.: Prentice-Hall, Inc., 1950), pp. 111–113.

7. For examples of such exercises, see "Some Collateral Writing Exercises."

8. Most of these stories have been reprinted in inexpensive paperback collections, many of which are now used in high schools and all of which are readily available in book stores and drug stores. In many instances, we cited the story we did rather than another equally useful one, because the one we suggested would be more readily available to a large number of teachers. The collections we drew from frequently are Crane's *Fifty Great Short Stories*, Speare's *A Pocket Book of Short Stories*, Warren and Erskine's *Short Story Masterpieces*, Stegner's *Great American Short Stories*. Complete references for all of these inexpensive paperbounds may be found at the end of this section.

We *have* included some new stories—hoping that these fine "newcomers" might find their way into the flood of paperbound short story anthologies constantly coming off the presses. Stegner's "The Blue-Winged Teal" has done just that; it has now been reprinted in Crane's *Fifty Great American Short Stories*. And we look forward to seeing soon in convenient, inexpensive paperback such good stories as: John Clayton Bell's "The White Circle" (the O. Henry First-Prize Story for 1947), Katherine Anne Porter's "The Grave," Katherine Mansfield's "Her First Ball," Eudora Welty's "A Worn Path" (all three in Mizener's *Modern Short Stories*), Hardy's "The Three Strangers," Seager's "This Town and Salamanca," and Erskine Caldwell's "Daughter" (all three readily found in Short and Sewall's hardbound *Short Stories for Study*).

9. The "event" might be summarized this way: A small boy accompanies his father to a funeral to act as a "brake" on his father's drinking. After the burial, they stop at a pub to "refresh." The father orders his porter and falls to talking. The small boy slips the porter off the bar, tries it, tries more, gets drunk. Reeling with stupor and nausea, he is taken home between his father and his father's friend. All the neighbor women witness the homecoming of the singing, bawling, cursing child.

As Frank O'Connor shapes the event, the effect is comic, ending with a comic irony.

10. All of the writing topics we suggest in this chapter, as in the preceding chapters, should be thought of as "frames" into which many other comparable stories might be inserted. We are suggesting *kinds* of topics, ways of asking about stories, that will, we think, help students to develop skills that will make it possible for them to read all stories more perceptively. So when you examine any topic, notice the *frame* (what it is asking students to do). Your not knowing the particular story we cite or the particular passage we refer to will not hinder your grasping the import of the topic.

11. This story may be conveniently found in Graham Greene, *21 Stories* (New York: The Viking Press, 1962). A Compass Book. It also appears in Ralph Singleton (ed.), *Two and Twenty* (New York: St. Martin's Press, 1962).

12. We phrase the time this way, because in less able and in some average classes the actual time given students may be one in-class period to begin the reading and to do at least the first question on the guide, that night's assignment time to finish the reading, and the next day's class period to complete the guide. In most average classes and in all able ones, the time would *actually* be two nights.

13. In each instance, we have spent a good deal of space analyzing the demands each of the stories we cite would make on a reader. We do this to suggest what *kinds of things* a teacher has to consider when he is deciding whether a particular story is a "right" reading for a particular class. Even if you are not familiar with the particular story being described (or cannot readily refer to it), reading the discussion will suggest the *kinds of things* that help students, the kinds of things that *may* give them trouble, *why* such things may be troublesome, and *how* we may prepare to "head off" such blocks. This discussion will give you a "frame" for assessing the stories in *any anthology* you are using so that you can order and teach them more effectively.

14. We selected this story for the lesson because it is now widely known and widely used in high school classes. It appears in two popular texts—Frank G. Jennings and Charles J. Calitri (eds.), *Stories* (New York: Harcourt, Brace & World, Inc., 1957), and Robert Penn Warren and Albert Erskine (eds.), *Short Story Masterpieces* (New York: Dell Publishing Co., Inc., 1954). It also gained country-wide prominence through Sarah Youngblood's discussion of it on the Commission On English Kinescope. All page references are to the reprinting of the story in *Short Story Masterpieces*.

15. The italics are mine.

16. That is why the best thing an English department bookroom can have is class sets of various paperback anthologies of short stories. See, for instance, those listed in the References at the end of this section under "Collections of Stories." Too costly? Compare the cost of several sets of such anthologies with the cost of the hardbound general anthologies commonly used. About three sets of collections could be purchased for a third of the cost of the general anthologies.

17. See R. V. Cassill, *Writing Fiction* (New York: Pocket Books, Inc., 1962) and Edgar V. Roberts, *Writing Themes About Literature* (Englewood Cliffs, N. J.: Prentice-Hall, Inc., 1964). Both books are inexpensive paperbacks. For some of the suggestions made in this section, I am indebted directly or tangentially to Cassill. I have already briefly described the contents of Roberts' book in note 54 in the section on teaching poems.

18. I am borrowing this term from Mary McCarthy, "Settling the Colonel's Hash," *Harper's* (Feb. 1954), and I am using it as she did: ". . . the great body of fiction contains only what I have called natural symbolism, in which selected events represent or typify a problem, a kind of society or psychology, a philosophical theory, in the same way they do in real life."

19. (New York: Random House, Inc., 1940.)

20. "The Other Side of James Joyce," *Arizona Quarterly*, 9 (Spring, 1953), pages 5–16, reprinted in Maurice Beebe, *Literary Symbolism* (San Francisco: 1960), pages 119–125.

21. For a similar exercise on poems, see "Holidays" under "Producing the Course"; for a related exercise on plays, see "Teaching *The Crucible* to Average Readers" under "A First Course in Reading Plays."

22. Because we are describing alternative proposals to suggest possible organizations, not to recommend specific texts, we have not distinguished between texts prepared for college and those prepared for high school. Neither have we distinguished among books that are primarily expositions of a critical approach to fiction, those that are primarily anthologies, and those that are both. Such distinctions do not seem relevant. If the scheme is fruitful, what matter the source.

23. "Letter to the Teacher" (New York: Appleton-Century-Crofts, 1943), p. x.

24. (New York: The Odyssey Press, 1964)

25. (New York: Harcourt, Brace and World, Inc., 1965)

26. (Boston: Houghton Mifflin Co., 1964)

27. (Englewood Cliffs, N. J.: Prentice-Hall, Inc., 1966)

28. (New York: The Odyssey Press, 1963)

29. (New York: Harcourt, Brace and World, Inc., 1964)

30. (New York: The Odyssey Press, 1963)

31. (Englewood Cliffs, N. J.: Prentice-Hall, Inc., 1950)

32. (New York: Harcourt, Brace and Co., 1950)

33. (New York: W. W. Norton and Co., Inc., 1962)

34. (Boston: D. C. Heath and Co., 1963)

35. *Modern Short Stories*, p. ix.

36. (New York: Henry Holt and Co., 1941)

37. (New York: Henry Holt and Co., 1960)

38. (New York: Harcourt, Brace and World, Inc., 1957)

39. I am indebted for this data to John Gardner and Lennis Dunlap, *The Forms of Fiction* (New York: Random House, Inc., 1962), pp. 23–37.

40. (New York: McGraw-Hill Book Co., Inc., 1950) Boswell's *Life* has little obvious organization—but much organization.

41. *Literary Biography* (Toronto: University of Toronto Press, 1957), p. 89.

42. "Novel and Memoir," *Nimbus, 2* (Autumn 1954), pp. 21–22.

43. "Incident" here means a small artistic unit—a little episode *in all its totality,* not just the event itself and the characters who shaped it and were shaped by it, but the room it took place in, what the characters wore, how they stood, who was passing by, and who was under the ever-present clock, what the weather was, who spoke first, what tones he used, what clichés—in other words, "incident" means everything that obtained during the episode.

44. John Frederick (ed.), *Adventures in Fiction,* is organized for such a transition. This useful book opens with five pairs of short stories, continues with a novella, then a short novel, and ends with a long novel.

45. For a different detailed organization for teaching novels, see Margaret Ryan's *Teaching the Novel in Paperback* (New York: The Macmillan Co., 1963), a Literary Heritage Book, which presents not only a sequence for fourteen novels but a teaching plan for each.

46. These plans suggest solutions to the *kinds* of problems that arise when a teacher organizes a large block of work for a class. The plans show how to prepare a calendar, how to prepare and use handouts, how to assign and use assignments, how to evaluate continuously. The plans show when and how to test, how to divide class time approximately and to order activities within a class period—as well as how (once again) to question without telling and to teach so as to give students a chance to achieve the aim. Even if you *never* teach *The Nigger of the Narcissus* or Conrad, you can learn from these plans things that must be known to teach *any* large block of work. And you can learn, furthermore, how to pace work, how to provide for in-class reading, how to word assignments and questions, how to "pitch" a long study for able, average, and less able students. (We realize you may never have a class capable of reading this particular novel and *interested* in doing so. And, to choose this book for a class, students would have to be both.)

As you read these plans, please remember that students doing these assignments and holding these discussions would have previously worked through the kind of first course we have described and the study of two novellas—*at least that.* What would be impossible for rank beginners is quite feasible for the same students once they have had relevant training. Students improve—let us not forget that.

47. Needless to say, the exact same number of study guide questions will not be right for every less able and average class. The teacher would simply adjust the guide to suit each group, as he would adjust the number of questions asked during his in-class oral reading. For suggestions on

"reducing" a guide for certain class, see note 14, "The Teaching of Plays." Notice especially that we would allow more in-class time to do the reading and work on the guides if certain classes could not (or would not) get the work done in the time we suggest—*even* with the kind of "reduction" of questions we outlined in note 14. Allowing such in-class working time (probably on Chapters 3 and 4 of Conrad's novel) would simply mean that the study of the novel would take fifteen days rather than thirteen, say. Nothing need be changed in the teaching plan—just allow one in-class reading period after the fourth day and one after the sixth.

REFERENCES

I. Discussions of The Theory of Fiction: By Writers and Critics

BOOTH, WAYNE C. *The Rhetoric of Fiction*. Chicago: The University of Chicago Press, 1961. This landmark (now in paperback) describes with copious illustration "the rhetorical resources available to the writer of epic, novel, or short story as he tries, consciously or unconsciously, to impose his fictional world upon the reader." Although the book is a unified study, the detailed "Contents" allows the reader to pursue to whatever extent he wishes whichever particular aspects of the subject he is interested in. For instance, if he wants to pursue the whole matter of "Impersonal Narration," he goes to Part 3, pp. 271–398; but if he wishes to concentrate on "The Price of Impersonal Narration: Henry James," he can simply go directly to pp. 339–374.

FORSTER, E. M. *Aspects of the Novel*. New York: Harcourt, Brace and World, Inc., 1927. A Harvest Paperback. Originally the Clark Lectures at Cambridge in 1927, these chapters on people, the plot, fantasy, prophecy, and pattern and rhythm retain all the gusto, vitality, and intimacy of the live speaker communing with the live audience. "You are there!" But don't let the charm of this "ramshackly survey" (as Forster called it) blind you to this novelist's penetrating insights into the craft of fiction. This is a delightful and enlightening introduction to the theory of fiction.

JAMES, HENRY. *The Art of the Novel*. New York: Charles Scribner's Sons, 1937. A Scribner Paperback. The eighteen essays in this book are James' critical prefaces to the New York Edition of his works. An artist's critical rethinking of his creations, the prefaces are filled with discernment that stimulates our discrimination and appreciation and with information that satisfies our curiosity about "where stories come from." Prerequisites to the reading of these essays: a knowledge of the relevant novels and a liking—if not a love—for the Jamesian manner!

LODGE, DAVID. *Language of Fiction*. New York: Columbia University Press, 1966. The thesis of this book is that both interpretive and evaluative criticism of the novel can be "assisted" by detailed reference to the language novelists use. So part one of the book first refutes the arguments offered against the use of such analyses of language in the criticism of prose, and secondly, points out the limitations of some stylistic methods. Part two applies the kind of analysis of language Lodge supports (analysis of diction, figures, syntax, and so on) to the texts of novels by Jane Austen, Charlotte Brontë, Dickens, Hardy, James, and Kingsley Amis.

LUBBOCK, PERCY. *The Craft of Fiction.* New York: The Viking Press, 1957. A Compass Book. Now more than forty years old, this book is still one of the most perceptive studies of "how novels are made." Several great novels that "appear to illustrate most plainly the various elements of the craft" are examined in such a way that the reader can gradually induce the key problems of the novelist's craft and some of the solutions. If you prefer the critic's approach to the writer's, you will prefer this study to Forster's.

O'FAOLAIN, SEAN. *The Short Story.* New York: The Devin-Adair Company, 1951. This well-known discussion of the short story (now in paperback) is divided into two parts: the first, called "The Personal Struggle," describes the personal "voltage" that a writer must invest his story with; the second (and to O'Faolain the secondary) part, called "The Technical Struggle," discusses the role of convention, subject, construction, and language in the creation of stories. For the reader's convenience, the full texts of eight stories used for illustration are reprinted.

RAHV, PHILIP. "Fiction and The Criticism of Fiction," *The Kenyon Review, 18* (Spring 1956), pp. 276–299. This excellent article explores the crucial ways that fiction differs from poetry, and it suggests the need for a criticism—and by implication a teaching—of fiction that is more peculiar to it. If you can read only one short paper on the nature of fiction, read this.

SALE, ROGER (ed.), *Discussions of The Novel.* Boston: D. C. Heath and Co., 1960. Reprinted in this collection are such memorable statements on fiction as: Northrop Frye's "The Four Forms of Fiction," Nathaniel Hawthorne's "Preface to *The House of Seven Gables,*" Henry James' "Preface to *The Portrait of a Lady,*" Mark Schorer's "Technique as Discovery," and Joseph Conrad's "Preface to *The Nigger of the Narcissus.*"

SCHOLES, ROBERT (ed.), *Approaches to the Novel.* San Francisco: Chandler Publishing Co., 1961. This paperbound anthology "presents materials for a Poetics of the Novel." The essays deal, not with specific works, but with the entire genre—with such topics as: mimesis, point of view, plot, narrative structures, the individual and society, art and life. On each topic there is a pair of essays juxtaposing two viewpoints, and these views are of such well-known writers and critics as Northrop Frye, Percy Lubbock, E. M. Forster, Edwin Muir, Virginia Woolf, and Mark Schorer. This is a fine inexpensive introduction to the nature and functions of fiction for the teacher who would like to take such study topic by topic.

SUMMERS, HOLLIS (ed.), *Discussions of The Short Story.* Boston: D. C.

Heath and Co., 1963. Pages vii–60 are particularly relevant; they include Poe's famous "Review of *Twice-Told Tales*," Percy Lubbock's "Point of View," A. L. Bader's "The Structure of the Modern Short Story," and Sean O'Faolain's "On Convention."

WELTY, EUDORA. *Short Stories*. New York: Harcourt, Brace and Company, 1949.

————. *Three Papers on Fiction*. Northampton, Mass.: Smith College Pamphlets, 1962.

Both of these books are collections of short papers that are delightfully written and rich in a writer's insights into the nature of artistic truth, the demands stories make on readers, and the symbolic quality of stories.

Finally, two books that take us "inside fiction" and thereby greatly increase our *understanding* of the nature and the functions of the elements of fiction:

CASSILL, R. V. *Writing Fiction*. New York: Pocket Books, Inc., 1962.

GOODMAN, THEODORE. *The Writing of Fiction*. New York: Collier Books, 1961.

II. Useful "Teachers"

In "Alternative Schemes for the Study of Short Stories," we have described twelve "teachers." All of them, except Edward Bloom's *The Order of Fiction*, are anthologies that reprint the complete texts of many short stories. All of them could, as we said, be used by teachers as references for possible organizations for teaching the short story. All of them could also be used by classes as texts for the study of the short story. But which text for which class? From annotations on each book, the teacher can decide which several books he should review. The teacher's aims and the quality of the readers would determine the final choice.

In note 45 we have mentioned Margaret Ryan's *Teaching the Novel in Paperback* (New York: The Macmillan Company, 1963), A Literary Heritage Paperback. We mention it again here, since notes are not always noticed and this book should be, for it offers both a valid, clearly written discussion of the novelist's craft and skeleton teaching plans for some fourteen novels, including *Shane, The Pearl, The Bridge of San Luis Rey, How Green Was My Valley, Ethan Frome, Cry, the Beloved Country,* and *The Ox-Bow Incident*. This is a fine resource for teachers who, having respect for both students and novels, want valid and feasible suggestions for bringing students to works.

III. Short Story Anthologies

We cite only those collections that would be good texts for almost any teaching scheme you might devise for helping *high school students* learn to read fiction. In other words, in all of these collections the stories are both relevant to the concerns of high school students and various enough in their literary complexity to give you a place to begin and a place to move to. You need only arrange the readings as your scheme dictates.

Collections With Useful Critical Introductions

GARDNER, JOHN, and LENNIS DUNLAP (eds.), *The Forms of Fiction*. New York: Random House, 1965. Includes both short and longer fiction. Good questions, comments, and analyses. Hardbound.

SINGLETON, RALPH (ed.). *Two and Twenty*. New York: St. Martin's Press, 1962. Hardbound.

SHORT, RAYMOND W., and RICHARD B. SEWALL (eds.). *Short Stories for Study*. New York: Henry Holt, and Co., 1941. Hardbound.

THURSTON, JARVIS A. (ed.). *Reading Modern Short Stories*. Chicago: Scott, Foresman & Co., 1955. Critical bibliographies are included. Paperbound.

Collections of Stories

American Short Stories. New York: Globe Book Co., 1967.

CRANE, MILTON (ed.). *Fifty Great American Short Stories*. New York: Bantam Books, Inc., 1965.

————. *Fifty Great Short Stories*. New York: Bantam Books, Inc., 1952.

ERSKINE, ALBERT, and ROBERT PENN WARREN (eds.). *Short Story Masterpieces*. New York: Dell Publishing Co., Inc., 1954.

HARDY, JOHN EDWARD (ed.). *The Modern Talent*. New York: Holt, Rinehart and Winston, Inc., 1964. Paperbound.

JENNINGS, FRANK G., and CHARLES J. CALITRI (eds.). *Stories*. New York: Harcourt, Brace & World, Inc., 1957. Hardbound.

KENNER, HUGH (ed.). *Studies in Change*. Englewood Cliffs, N. J.: Prentice-Hall, Inc., 1965. Paperbound. For good readers.

LYNSKEY, WINIFRED (ed.). *Reading Modern Fiction*. New York: Charles Scribner's Sons, 1962. Paperbound.

PEDEN, WILLIAM (ed.). *Twenty-Nine Stories*. Cambridge, Mass.: Houghton Mifflin Company, 1960. Paperbound.

RIDOUT, ALBERT K., and JESSE STUART (eds.). *Short Stories for Discussion*. New York: Charles Scribner's Sons, 1965. Hardbound.

SOHN, DAVID A. (ed.). *Ten Modern American Short Stories*. New York: Bantam Books, Inc., 1965. A good supplemental anthology for, say, *A Pocket Book* (below).

SPEARE, M. EDMUND (ed.). *A Pocket Book of Short Stories*. New York: Washington Square Press, Inc., 1941.

TAGGARD, ERNESTINE (ed.). *Twenty Grand Short Stories*. New York: Bantam Books, Inc. For less able readers.

Thematic Anthologies

GOLD, HERBERT, and DAVID L. STEVENSON (eds.). *Stories of Modern America*. New York: St. Martin's Press, 1961. Paperbound.

LESSER, M. X., and JOHN N. MORRIS (eds.). *The Fiction of Experience*. New York: McGraw-Hill Book Co., Inc., 1962. Paperbound.

PARKER, DOROTHY, and FREDERICK B. SHROYER (eds.). *Short Story*.

New York: Charles Scribner's Sons, 1965. A fine anthology. Paperbound.

IV. Collections of Novellas

CONRAD, JOSEPH. *Three Short Novels.* New York: Bantam Books, Inc., 1942. Includes *Youth, Typhoon,* and *Heart of Darkness.*

DILLENBECK, MARSDEN V., and JOHN C. SCHWEITZER (eds.). *Seven Novellas.* New York: Charles Scribner's Sons, 1966. Hardbound. Includes John Galsworthy's *The Apple Tree,* Ernest Hemingway's *The Short Happy Life of Francis Macomber,* Henry James' *Daisy Miller,* F. Scott Fitzgerald's *May Day,* Edith Wharton's *The Old Maid,* Joseph Conrad's *Youth,* and Thomas Wolfe's *The Party at Jack's.*

FAULKNER, WILLIAM. *Three Famous Short Novels.* New York: Random House, 1942. Paperbound. Includes *Spotted Horses, Old Man,* and *The Bear.*

Six Great Modern Short Novels. New York: Dell Publishing Co., Inc., 1954. Includes Herman Melville's *Billy Budd* and Katherine Anne Porter's *Noon Wine.*

Afterword

"But what about *'outside reading'*?" It is true that we have no section labeled "outside reading," or "enrichment," or "extensive reading," or "book reports." But we have discussed outside reading. Every time a student writes a critical paper on a new work, every time he reads a poem or a play or a short story that is not discussed in class, he is doing outside reading—but outside reading that is controlled and directly related to what is going on in class, reading that reinforces and tests what he is learning. In "our system" there is, of course, little choice, but there is also little chance that he will be reading what his hand haphazardly falls on—because he must take something. There is little chance of his copying the dust jacket, of his reading half the book and pretending he has read the whole. There is little chance of his covering the impressive outside-reading list by consulting *Masterplots*. In our view, outside reading should be moderate enough to allow students to do it well, and it should be sufficiently related to in-class work to motivate and reward them.

"What about *independent study*?" When in connection with a second or later course, high school students critically read a long play, a pair of novellas, a full-length novel, a group of thematically related works—without benefit of class discussion—and when they prepare a well-written two- to three-page textual or contextual paper on a challenging topic related to their reading, they are doing as much independent study as most good high school students can productively do. And such assignments—requiring as they do precision and imagination in reading and writing and in the use of criticism and sources—are probably the most useful kinds of study that students can engage in. For, these brief, tight studies confront students with the same kinds of problems they will meet in more comprehensive assignments. In small, controlled studies they can learn how to sort, evaluate, and order evidence; they can learn how to avoid making an unpatterned pastiche out of critical opinions; they can learn to distinguish creative scholarship from both pedantry and nonsense.

If, furthermore, the course of study in English is organized so that a teacher has a wide variety of second and later courses to choose from, the needs and interests of able students can be met within the usual class structure. So they will have less need for undertaking comprehensive research studies in lieu of courses or as a major part of them.

"What about *introducing works and units?* You don't just go into the room and hand out novels." Of course, you don't. But what you do before that either is direct preparation—the distribution of vocabulary glosses, study guides, maps, stage plans, and such—or it is direct "selling." We *have* discussed many kinds and degrees of preparation, and we have continually discussed both extrinsic and intrinsic motivation. But we have not discussed "selling." We feel we cannot. Such prologues, when they are effective, are, in every sense, *personal* creative acts. The teacher looks at the work to see what about it would be immediately engaging and significant *to this class* or what about it would at once provoke, puzzle, incite *this class* to want to begin to read. Then, he decides how he can best show this to the class. This decision involves not only what would appeal to the class but what the teacher is capable of doing naturally and effectively. A tour-de-force introduction is one thing; an unintentionally artificial introduction is another. As in anything dramatic, an unintentional false note is fatal. Better no introduction at all than something "rigged," "second-hand," out-of-character for the particular teacher. We are not at all sure that, in "selling," "what worked for me will work for you." So we offer no prescriptions for arresting attention. The piece of literature, the class, the teacher, the moment must suggest what introduction will do that.

"You haven't said a word about *literary history.*" It is true that we have not discussed the much-maligned "survey." But we have outlined—as second and later courses—several kinds of brief, contextual studies. And through our discussion of these, we have implied what a "survey"—which is basically an interrelated series of contextual studies—would entail. When we consider these implications, we know at once why the "survey" so often fails: why it so often becomes names, vital statistics, and titles hung lifelessly on a time line.

A genuine contextual study of *any* period requires a teacher who "knows the period" well, a teacher who "lives in the era" and can "raise that world," can generate a feeling of "how it was" to be a person in it, so that, for the duration of the study of the period, students, accepting the premises of that world, live in it. A "survey" requires a teacher who is "at home" in *many* periods. How many teachers have you known in high school, college, or graduate school who have met this requirement? Generally speaking, our "survey" teachers have been good in one era, mediocre-to-good in another, poor in a third. They have been, as we are, only human.

Think of what knowing any *one* period requires. The teacher must have a factual knowledge of the political, social, religious, and aesthetic beliefs, practices, and values of the period. Furthermore, he must have read, precisely and imaginatively, the major and minor works of the writers of the period. Further still, he must have interrelated his knowledge of the culture and his perceptions of the works so that he sees how works reflect the period, rebel against it, recall the past, herald the future. Finally, though knowing all this is knowing a great deal, knowing a period is *understanding all this feelingly*. Is it any wonder that most teachers know only one period?

Does this mean, then, that a "survey" course is impossible? It probably means, rather, that a "survey" taught by one teacher is. It means that a "survey" course could be carried off splendidly by a *well-organized* team of "specialists." The general lectures on each period should be given by a teacher who has the kind of knowledge of the period that we have been describing, a teacher who has immersed in the period, who can raise its world as a vital culture and can lead high school students to live in it—for a while. Neither a dry rehearsal of data from the mouth of a pedant, nor an exciting drama of misinformation from the department "ham" will do. The lecturer must be a creative scholar. The lectures must be developed so that the classroom discussions of particular works can emerge naturally from them. All this takes planning, and planning takes time. But, for most "survey" teachers, the planning for a "lecture and sections" organization would require only a reallocation of some of the time they are now spending on their own individual preparations. The change would not be more burdensome; psychologically, it would be for most a great relief.

Do high school English faculties have the creative scholars needed for our proposed organization of "survey" courses? *Many* staffs have teachers with special interests in certain periods. *Many* have teachers who, regrettably, are losing or have lost just such interests through disuse. And, if it became widespread practice to have the lectures in literary history given by "specialists" in the various periods, teachers in preparation would have an incentive to develop an "area"—say, the English Renaissance, modern poetry, the Victorians—an "area" that they *really* enjoy studying. If teachers on English faculties have a chance to use their fields, not only the students will benefit. For pursuing a specialty is a stimulating and rewarding experience in itself, and it is a compensation for much in teaching (as in all other jobs) that is merely tolerable.

Given the kind of "team-teaching" arrangement we have described and *given,* of course, *students who are already responsive readers,* we would probably organize the study of literary history to show students how in a series of crucial periods certain continuities—ideas, literary traditions, styles—were gradually modulated. The "survey" in American literature would require approximately seventeen weeks' teaching time, subdivided as follows: The Colonial Period (two lectures); The Federal Period (one week); The American Renaissance, featuring especially *Walden, The Scarlet Letter,* and *Billy Budd* (four weeks); The Genteel Tradition (one week); The End of the Nineteenth Century (three weeks); From 1900 to World War I (three weeks); From 1918 to World War II (four weeks). The "survey" in English literature would require approximately twenty-nine weeks, subdivided as follows: The Anglo-Saxon Period (one lecture); The Middle English Period, featuring Chaucer (two lectures); The Renaissance (five to six weeks); The Early Seventeenth Century and Milton (three weeks); The Eighteenth Century (three weeks); The Romantic Period, including Blake (six weeks); The Victorians (four weeks); From 1890 to World War I (three weeks); From 1918 to World War II (four weeks).

If students do not have a course in literary history in high school, they will not have one—unless they major in English in college. This fact alone should persuade us to give all adequate readers—college-bound and non-academic alike—an opportunity for *at least* one genuine, vital "survey" course.

"You have said little about *what the teacher needs.*" Our critical bibliographies imply what would be valuable in an English department library; our annotated lists of texts and the works listed in our courses suggest what would be worthwhile additions to a bookroom. Our mentions of tapes and of projectors and such in our discussions of lessons assume that that necessary equipment would be available to the teacher.

We hear from all sides about the teacher's need for books and equipment. But we hear less about his need for *a certain kind of school administration*—one that maintains a disciplined school in which teachers may have a chance to teach and students a chance to learn, an administration that knows that the nature of a subject matter cannot be altered to comply with the wishes of this or that pressure group, an administration that recognizes that, as a social institution, the *primary* role of the school is intellectual, an administration that dignifies *all* students by expecting of them nothing less than *their* very best.

In addition to adequate books and equipment and an enlightened administration, the teacher needs *stimulating department meetings*—meetings that are continuing conversations about works of literature and the teaching of works. An individual teacher does not have time to discover for himself several valid interpretations of each play, each poem. He cannot of himself always think of the best way of entering this or that short story. He cannot always decide how to place a particular work most strategically in the unit he is teaching. He cannot himself critically assess all the new texts, the new curricular materials and aids that appear yearly. As anyone who has gone through days in a high school knows, an individual teacher simply does not have time to carry on all these activities. They must be cooperative efforts.

If the agenda of department meetings were cleared of trivia, there would be a half hour available for some teacher to discuss, for instance, a new work he had just taught, to describe his handling of it, to distribute copies of materials he used (including writing topics, tests, exercises, supplementary handouts), and to *honestly* evaluate the plusses and minuses of his effort. This kind of sharing not only helps teachers accumulate materials that are critically assessed, but also stimulates them to innovate in works and methods. Other half-hour periods might be given over to the discussion of the texts of two poems, or to a critical reappraisal of some "standard" work, or to the audition of new tapes. All these activities are some of the most significant kinds of "in-service" education a teacher can have. Let us grant that reading articles in professional journals and attending professional meetings are important sources of materials and methods—especially if the papers presented are valid, concrete proposals. But such occasional articles and such periodic experiences are no substitute for the continuing conversation of the department meeting where teachers discuss how both these extramural proposals and their own can be adapted to solve their own local problems.

Department meetings might also focus occasionally on theoretic questions, questions that will help teachers re-examine both their positions on the nature of works of literature and the implications of their positions for their teaching of literature. Informed discussion of such questions would at least curb those "dead end" arguments between factions who have never examined the assumptions their views are based on; it would at least curb both those "agreements to disagree" on points on which there can be no *basic* disagreement and those forced agreements on issues that admit of several equally valid responses.

When teachers re-examine their positions, they have to give themselves reasons for thinking what they think. As they do this, they will come to recognize that their liking a certain material or method, or their asserting that it is traditional or new or workable does not mean it is "good" or "best to do." What is "good," what is "best to do" is decided on other grounds, and in department meetings, teachers should be discovering or clarifying what those grounds are. Such deliberations would end, for instance, the uncritical, fruitless strife between the ancients and the moderns—between the "opaque projectors—never!" and the "opaque projectors—forever!" Such deliberation would cause both teachers whose only ground for decision is feasibility and those whose sole standard is validity to rethink their positions.

Staff meetings could be wonderfully stimulating, productive events. They *should* be, *must* be, because teachers need them.

Teachers also need, as we mentioned earlier, a *chance to teach something of high interest* to them. If they are to excite and involve students in the reading of works of literature, teachers themselves must continue to be engaged and motivated too. We now hear much about how sensitive a reader a teacher must be, how able a writer. And he *must* be both. But given such a teacher, the high schools must keep him interested and alive.

The usual high school teaching assignment does not do this. And it is not just because the teacher has too many students or too many extracurricular duties, both of which are now generally deplored. It is also because of two other related conditions. One is that the teacher is too often confronted with students whose prior preparation in reading and writing has been so unorganized that they cannot move ahead. And the other is that the teacher is too often condemned to teaching courses that are haphazard, superficial, or unimaginative. These two conditions kill incentive, for they allow no opportunity for depth, no chance for studying what the teacher can present with excitement and satisfaction; indeed, such conditions make useful, interesting exploration of a subject matter virtually an impossibility. The high school teacher's stimulation must come partly from the subject matter he teaches. Consequently, although reduction of class size and curtailment of extra duties are necessities, alone they will not hold good teachers for long. The schools must also have a sequential course of study that provides both a basic reading-writing preparation for all students (in grade 10 or grades 9 and 10) and a series of advanced courses for later years. Both are essential. If schools just add arresting "titles" to their English course of study for grades 11 and 12, nothing will be solved. Advanced courses are not very stimulating for students or teachers if students are not average-to-competent readers. However, if the program of studies did provide sound basic preparation and a variety of second and later courses of increasing difficulty, it would have a good chance of keeping both students *and* teachers engaged and highly motivated.

What does a teacher need? An able administration, a stimulating department, an engaging course of study—and beyond all that? Among other things, he needs to clarify for himself what he considers *the nature of his role* as a teacher of literature. Is he to be the teacher who stands between the work and the reader—always there to "mediate the mystery"? Or is he to be the teacher at the reader's shoulder looking at the page with him? Is he to be the teller who provides several valid interpretations of each work? Or the questioner focusing students on what he knows is of most worth for them, calling their attention to what they have not noticed in works, helping them to see for themselves in a way that teaches *them how* to see for themselves?

If he chooses to "share the book with students," to be the questioning voice over students' shoulders, he assumes all the risks that engaging in a dialogue entails. He will be shown his own "blind spots"; he will be apprised of ambiguities he had not noticed; he will find his interpretations being corrected. As his student-colleagues become the precise and imaginative readers he aims to help them to be, he must be ready to be challenged and to be excelled. And he must be stimulated and delighted by what he has effected.

"But you still have not said anything about . . ." Yes, I know, but as the narrator of Beckett's *Molloy* says, ". . . if I failed to mention this detail . . . it is because you cannot mention everything . . . you must choose between the things worth mentioning and those even less so. For if you set out to mention everything you would never be done, and that's what counts, to be done . . ."

Index